**Second Edition**

# MICROECONOMICS

# Practice, Engage, and Assess

- **Enhanced eText**—The Pearson eText gives students access to their textbook anytime, anywhere. In addition to note-taking, highlighting, and bookmarking, the Pearson eText offers interactive and sharing features. Students actively read and learn through auto-graded practice, real-time data-graphs, figure animations, author videos, and more. Instructors can share comments or highlights, and students can add their own, for a tight community of learners in any class.

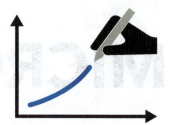

- **Practice**—Algorithmically generated homework and study plan exercises with instant feedback ensure varied and productive practice, helping students improve their understanding and prepare for quizzes and tests. Draw-graph exercises encourage students to practice the language of economics.

- **Learning Resources**—Personalized learning aids such as Help Me Solve This problem walkthroughs and Figure Animations provide on-demand help when students need it most.

- **Personalized Study Plan**—Assists students in monitoring their own progress by offering them a customized study plan based on Homework, Quiz, and Test results. Includes regenerated exercises with unlimited practice, as well as the opportunity to earn mastery points by completing quizzes on recommended learning objectives.

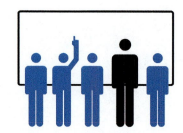

- **Dynamic Study Modules**—With a focus on key topics, these modules work by continuously assessing student performance and activity in real time and, using data and analytics, provide personalized content to reinforce concepts that target each student's particular strengths and weaknesses.

- **Digital Interactives**—Digital Interactives are engaging assessment activities that promote critical thinking and application of key economic principles. Each Digital Interactive has progressive levels where students can explore, apply, compare, and analyze economic principles. Many Digital Interactives include real time data from FRED® that displays, in graph and table form, up-to-the-minute data on key macro variables. Digital Interactives can be assigned and graded within MyEconLab, or used as a lecture tool to encourage engagement, classroom conversation, and group work.

# with MyEconLab®

- **NEW: Math Review Exercises in MyEconLab**—MyEconLab now offers an array of assignable and auto-graded exercises that cover fundamental math concepts. Geared specifically toward principles and intermediate economics students, these exercises aim to increase student confidence and success in these courses. Our new Math Review is accessible from the assignment manager and contains over 150 graphing, algebra, and calculus exercises for homework, quiz, and test use.

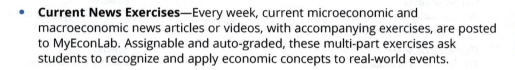

$$P = c + dQ_s$$

  - **Real-Time Data Analysis Exercises**—Using current macro data to help students understand the impact of changes in economic variables, Real-Time Data Analysis Exercises communicate directly with the Federal Reserve Bank of St. Louis's FRED® site and update as new data are available.

- **Current News Exercises**—Every week, current microeconomic and macroeconomic news articles or videos, with accompanying exercises, are posted to MyEconLab. Assignable and auto-graded, these multi-part exercises ask students to recognize and apply economic concepts to real-world events.

  - **Experiments**—Flexible, easy-to-assign, auto-graded, and available in Single Player and Multiplayer versions, Experiments in MyEconLab make learning fun and engaging.

- **Reporting Dashboard**—View, analyze, and report learning outcomes clearly and easily. Available via the Gradebook and fully mobile-ready, the Reporting Dashboard presents student performance data at the class, section, and program levels in an accessible, visual manner.

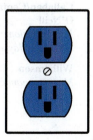

  - **LMS Integration**—Link from any LMS platform to access assignments, rosters, and resources, and synchronize MyLab grades with your LMS gradebook. For students, new direct, single sign-on provides access to all the personalized learning MyLab resources that make studying more efficient and effective.

- **Mobile Ready**—Students and instructors can access multimedia resources and complete assessments right at their fingertips, on any mobile device.

# The Pearson Series in Economics

*denotes MyEconLab titles     Visit www.myeconlab.com to learn more.

**Second Edition**

# MICROECONOMICS

**Daron Acemoglu**
Massachusetts Institute of Technology

**David Laibson**
Harvard University

**John A. List**
University of Chicago

New York, NY

**Vice President, Business Publishing:** Donna Battista
**Director of Portfolio Management:** Adrienne D'Ambrosio
**Senior Portfolio Manager:** Christina Masturzo
**Development Editor:** Cydney Westmoreland
**Editorial Assistant:** Courtney Paganelli
**Vice President, Product Marketing:** Roxanne McCarley
**Strategic Marketing Manager:** Deborah Strickland
**Product Marketer:** Tricia Murphy
**Senior Field Marketing Manager:** Carlie Marvel
**Manager of Field Marketing, Business Publishing:** Adam Goldstein
**Field Marketing Assistant:** Kristen Compton
**Product Marketing Assistant:** Jessica Quazza
**Vice President, Production and Digital Studio, Arts and Business:** Etain O'Dea
**Director of Production, Business:** Jeff Holcomb
**Managing Producer, Business:** Alison Kalil

**Content Producer:** Nancy Freihofer
**Operations Specialist:** Carol Melville
**Creative Director:** Blair Brown
**Manager, Learning Tools:** Brian Surette
**Managing Producer, Digital Studio, Arts and Business:** Diane Lombardo
**Digital Studio Producer:** Melissa Honig
**Digital Studio Producer:** Alana Coles
**Digital Content Team Lead:** Noel Lotz
**Digital Content Project Lead:** Courtney Kamauf
**Full-Service Project Management and Composition:** Cenveo® Publisher Services
**Interior Design:** Cenveo® Publisher Services
**Cover Design:** Cenveo® Publisher Services
**Printer/Binder:** LSC Communications, Inc
**Cover Printer:** LSC Communications, Inc

**Library of Congress Cataloging-in-Publication Data on file**

3  18

ISBN 10:     0-13-449204-8
ISBN 13: 978-0-13-449204-9

# Dedication

*With love for Annika, Aras, Arda, Eli,*
*Greta, Mason, Max, and Noah,*
*who inspire us every day.*

# About the Authors

**Daron Acemoglu** is Elizabeth and James Killian Professor of Economics in the Department of Economics at the Massachusetts Institute of Technology. He has received a B.A. in economics from the University of York, 1989; an M.Sc. in mathematical economics and econometrics from the London School of Economics, 1990; and a Ph.D. in economics from the London School of Economics in 1992.

He is an elected fellow of the National Academy of Sciences, the American Academy of Arts and Sciences, the Econometric Society, the European Economic Association, and the Society of Labor Economists. He has received numerous awards and fellowships, including the inaugural T. W. Schultz Prize from the University of Chicago in 2004, the inaugural Sherwin Rosen Award for outstanding contribution to labor economics in 2004, the Distinguished Science Award from the Turkish Sciences Association in 2006, and the John von Neumann Award, Rajk College, Budapest, in 2007.

He was also the recipient of the John Bates Clark Medal in 2005, awarded every two years to the best economist in the United States under the age of 40 by the American Economic Association, and the Erwin Plein Nemmers Prize, awarded every two years for work of lasting significance in economics. He holds honorary doctorates from the University of Utrecht and Bosporus University.

His research interests include political economy, economic development and growth, human capital theory, growth theory, innovation, search theory, network economics, and learning.

His books include *Economic Origins of Dictatorship and Democracy* (jointly with James A. Robinson), which was awarded the Woodrow Wilson and the William Riker prizes, *Introduction to Modern Economic Growth*, and *Why Nations Fail: The Origins of Power, Prosperity, and Poverty* (jointly with James A. Robinson), which has become a *New York Times* bestseller.

**David Laibson** is the Chair of the Harvard Economics Department and the Robert I. Goldman Professor of Economics at Harvard University. He is also a member of the National Bureau of Economic Research, where he is Research Associate in the Asset Pricing, Economic Fluctuations, and Aging Working Groups. His research focuses on the topics of behavioral economics, intertemopral choice, macroeconomics, and household finance, and he leads Harvard University's Foundations of Human Behavior Initiative. He serves on several editorial boards, as well as the Pension Research Council (Wharton), Harvard's Pension Investment Committee, and the Board of the Russell Sage Foundation. He has previously served on the boards of the Health and Retirement Study (National Institutes of Health) and the Academic Research Council of the Consumer Financial Protection Bureau. He is a recipient of a Marshall Scholarship and a Fellow of the Econometric Society and the American Academy of Arts and Sciences. He is also a recipient of the T. W. Schultz Prize from the University of Chicago and the TIAA-CREF Paul A. Samuelson Award for Outstanding Scholarly Writing on Lifelong Financial Security. Laibson holds degrees from Harvard University (A.B. in economics), the London School of Economics (M.Sc. in econometrics and mathematical economics), and the Massachusetts Institute of Technology (Ph.D. in economics). He received his Ph.D. in 1994 and has taught at Harvard since then. In recognition of his teaching excellence, he has been awarded Harvard's Phi Beta Kappa Prize and a Harvard College Professorship.

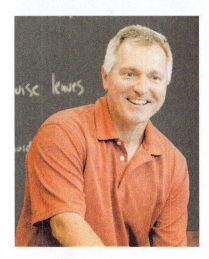

**John A. List** is the Kenneth C. Griffin Distinguished Service Professor in Economics at the University of Chicago, and Chairman of the Department of Economics. He received his B.S. in economics from the University of Wisconsin–Stevens Point and his Ph.D. in economics from the University of Wyoming. Before joining the University of Chicago in 2005, he was a professor at the University of Central Florida, University of Arizona, and University of Maryland. He also served in the White House on the Council of Economic Advisers from 2002–2003, and is a Research Associate at the NBER.

List was elected a Member of the American Academy of Arts and Sciences in 2011, and a Fellow of the Econometric Society in 2015. He also received the Arrow Prize for Senior Economists in 2008, the Kenneth Galbraith Award in 2010, the Yrjo Jahnsson Lecture Prize in 2012, and the Klein Lecture Prize in 2016. He received an honorary doctorate from Tilburg University in 2014, and was named a Top 50 Innovator in the Non-Profit Times for 2015 and 2016 for his work on charitable giving.

His research focuses on questions in microeconomics, with a particular emphasis on using field experiments to address both positive and normative issues. For decades his field experimental research has focused on issues related to the inner workings of markets, the effects of various incentive schemes on market equilibria and allocations, and how behavioral economics can augment the standard economic model. This includes research into why inner city schools fail, why people discriminate, why people give to charity, why firms fail, why women make less money than men in labor markets, and why people generally do what they do.

His research includes over 200 peer-reviewed journal articles and several published books, including the 2013 international best-seller, *The Why Axis: Hidden Motives and the Undiscovered Economics of Everyday Life* (with Uri Gneezy).

# Brief Contents

# Contents

### CHAPTERS ON THE WEB

Web chapters are available on MyEconLab.

**WEB Chapter 1** Financial Decision Making

**WEB Chapter 2** Economics of Life, Health, and the Environment

**WEB Chapter 3** Political Economy

# Preface

We love economics. We marvel at the way economic systems work. When we buy a smartphone, we think about the complex supply chain and the hundreds of thousands of people who played a role in producing an awe-inspiring piece of technology that was assembled from components manufactured across the globe.

The market's ability to do the world's work without anyone being in charge strikes us as a phenomenon no less profound than the existence of consciousness or life itself. We believe that the creation of the market system is one of the greatest achievements of humankind.

We wrote this book to highlight the simplicity of economic ideas and their extraordinary power to explain, predict, and improve what happens in the world. We want students to master the *essential* principles of economic analysis. With that goal in mind, we identify the three key ideas that lie at the heart of the economic approach to understanding human behavior: optimization, equilibrium, and empiricism. These abstract words represent three ideas that are actually highly intuitive.

The breakneck speed of modern technological change has, more than ever, injected economics into the lives—and hands—of our students. The technologies that they use daily illustrate powerful economic forces in action: Uber users observe real-time congestion in the transportation market when they confront surge pricing, and Airbnb travelers explore the relationships among location, convenience, and price by comparing listings near different subway stops in the same city.

As educators, it's our job to transform economic concepts into language, visual representations, and empirical examples that our students understand. Today, markets are much more interactive than they were only a decade ago, and they exemplify that it is not just competitive markets with perfect information that are relevant to our economic lives. Our students routinely take part in auctions, purchase goods and services via organized platforms such as Uber, have to struggle with pervasive informational asymmetries as they participate in online exchanges, and have to guard themselves against a bewildering array of mistakes and traps that are inherent to these new transactions.

In this ever-changing world, students must understand not just well-known economic concepts such as opportunity cost, supply, and demand, but also modern ones such as game theory, auctions, and behavioral mistakes. It is these modern concepts, which are bit parts in most Principles textbooks, that occupy center stage in ours. Today economic analysis has expanded its conceptual and empirical boundaries and, in doing so, has become even more relevant and useful.

This new world provides incredible opportunities for the teaching of economics as well, provided that we adjust our Principles canon to include modern and empirically-based notions of economics. This has been our aim from day one and continues to be our in this second edition.

## New to the Second Edition

In our new edition of *Microeconomics*, evidence-based economics becomes an even more important mainstay of our approach. We have imbued it with new relevance by applying it to many more topics with which our students have first-hand experience. So in addition to updating the existing data and empirical features, we have now added many new empirical examples.

- In Chapter 2 we've added a feature that forces students to wrestle with the question of causality. We discuss a recent research paper that reports a positive correlation between expensive weddings and high rates of divorce. We ask our students to use this finding as a springboard from which to wrestle with the difference between correlation and causality, and to understand the role of omitted variables.
- We've rewritten Chapter 4 to tell the story of the fracking revolution and its remarkable impact on oil and gasoline prices. Supply and demand come alive when students

can see how the recent rightward shift in the oil supply curve, due to the development of fracking technologies, has played a role in halving the equilibrium price of oil.

- The new edition focuses more on the sharing economy—a phenomenon that both permeates our students' lives and provides researchers novel data with which to solve age-old questions. In Chapter 7, we include a new Evidence-Based Economics section on Uber and the invisible hand; drawing from recent papers, we discuss the role of surge pricing in equilibrating driver supply and rider demand. The resulting insights enable our students to more deeply understand the markets that they personally use.
- The revised text also emphasizes the role of microeconomics in examining prominent social issues, from natural disaster management to global inequality. For example, we have added an Evidence-Based Economics box in Chapter 9 titled "What can the government do to lower earthquakes in Oklahoma?", which investigates how to reduce fracking-generated earthquakes by applying the concept of externalities. Elsewhere, we examine inequality through a feature on Scandinavia, a feature on broadband access, and more.
- The revised text also uses the recent election to teach topics like probability. For example, in Chapter 15 we have a new Letting the Data Speak feature that discusses forecasts on the eve of the U. S. Presidential election: a 72% chance of a Clinton victory and a 28% chance of a Trump victory. We give students the analytic tools they need to understand how to interpret such forecasts.

Introductory economics classes draw students with diverse interests and future career paths: with this textbook, we show them how to apply economic thinking creatively to improve their work, their choices, and their daily lives.

One of our main objectives in writing this textbook was to show that the fundamentals of economics are not just exciting, but also alive with myriad personal applications. In the first edition, the themes of optimization, equilibrium, and empiricism were our primary tools for communicating both the surprising power and broad applicability of economics. We believe that the intervening years have confirmed these conceptual priorities; these concepts have become even more relevant for our students.

At a time when competing empirical claims abound and news sources across the political spectrum are denounced as "fake," our students need the skills to systematically question and evaluate what they read. That is why, in our Evidence-Based Economics segments, we examine both the implications *and the limitations* of academic studies. We hope that our textbook will help form a new generation of careful thinkers, smart decision-makers, engaged citizens, and even a few future economists!

# Our Vision: Three Unifying Themes

The first key principle is that people try to choose the best available option: *optimization*. We don't assume that people always successfully optimize, but we do believe that people try to optimize and often do a relatively good job of it. Because most decision makers try to choose the alternative that offers the greatest net benefit, optimization is a useful tool for predicting human behavior. Optimization is also a useful prescriptive tool. By teaching people how to optimize, we improve their decisions and the quality of their lives. By the end of this course, every student should be a skilled optimizer—without using complicated mathematics, simply by using economic intuition.

The second key principle extends the first: economic systems operate in *equilibrium*, a state in which everybody is simultaneously trying to optimize. We want students to see that they're not the only ones maximizing their well-being. An economic system is in equilibrium when each person feels that he or she cannot do any better by picking another course of action. The principle of equilibrium highlights the connections among economic actors. For example, Apple stores stock millions of iPhones because millions of consumers are going to turn up to buy them. In turn, millions of consumers go to Apple stores because those stores are ready to sell those iPhones. In equilibrium, consumers and producers are simultaneously optimizing, and their behaviors are intertwined.

Our first two principles—optimization and equilibrium—are conceptual. The third is methodological: *empiricism*. Economists use *data* to test economic theories, learn about the world, and speak to policymakers. Accordingly, data play a starring role in our book, though we keep the empirical analysis extremely simple. It is this emphasis on matching theories with real data that we think most distinguishes our book from others. We show students how economists use data to answer specific questions, which makes our chapters concrete, interesting, and fun. Modern students demand the evidence behind the theory, and our book supplies it.

For example, we begin every chapter with an empirical question and then answer that question using data. One chapter begins by asking:

*Would a smoker quit the habit for $100 per month?*

Later in that chapter, we describe how smoking rates fell when researchers paid smokers to quit.

In our experience, students taking their first economics class often have the impression that economics is a series of theoretical assertions with little empirical basis. By using data, we explain how economists evaluate and improve our scientific insights. Data also make concepts more memorable. Using evidence helps students build intuition, because data move the conversation from abstract principles to concrete facts. Every chapter sheds light on how economists use data to answer questions that directly interest students. Every chapter demonstrates the key role that evidence plays in advancing the science of economics.

# Features

All of our features showcase intuitive empirical questions.

- In **Evidence-Based Economics (EBE)**, we show how economists use data to answer the question we pose in the opening paragraph of the chapter. The EBE uses actual data from field experiments, lab experiments, or naturally occurring data, while highlighting some of the major concepts discussed within the chapter. This tie-in with the data gives students a substantive look at economics as it plays out in the world around them.

  The questions explored aren't just dry intellectual ideas; they spring to life the minute the student sets foot outside the classroom—*Is Facebook free? Is college worth it? Will free trade cause you to lose your job? Is there value in putting yourself into someone else's shoes? What is the optimal size of government?*

## EVIDENCE-BASED ECONOMICS

### Would a smoker quit the habit for $100 per month?

At the beginning of this chapter, we posed a question concerning whether *a smoker would quit the habit for $100 a month*. The tools of this chapter can help us begin to think about whether such an incentive can work, and why it might work.

In thinking about such a reward, we have learned that the impact of an increase in income leads to changes in the consumer budget constraint and subsequently the demand for goods and services. To see these tools in action, we return to the shopping-spree example. Exhibit 5.5 shows the mechanics behind the effects of an increase in what we have available to spend.

With that foundation laid, we can return to the question of quitting smoking for a month. Given our economic framework, the very same principle that was at work in the shopping-spree problem applies when considering the smoker's problem. By providing $100 for not smoking, we create a trade-off between the current benefits of smoking and the benefits obtained by $100 of increased income. There is also another saving: by not smoking, you save the money otherwise spent on cigarettes or cigars. For simplicity, let's assume that is another $100 per month. Thus the comparison that we need to make is whether, at the margin, $200 of additional monthly income

- **Letting the Data Speak** is another feature that analyzes an economic question by using real data as the foundation of the discussion. Among the many issues we explore are such questions as *Should McDonald's be interested in elasticities? Do wages really go down if labor supply increases? Why do some firms advertise while others don't?*

- In keeping with the optimization theme, in a feature entitled **Choice & Consequence** we ask students to make a real economic decision or evaluate the consequences of past real decisions. We then explain how an economist might analyze the same decision. Among the questions investigated are *Do people really optimize? Should LeBron James paint his own house? Does revenge have an evolutionary logic?*

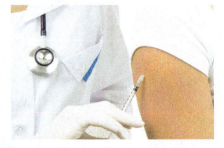
# Organization

**Part I: Introduction to Economics** lays the groundwork for understanding the economic way of thinking about the world. In **Chapter 1**, we show that the principle of *optimization* explains most of our choices. In other words, we make choices based on a consideration of benefits and costs, and to do this we need to consider trade-offs, budget constraints, and opportunity cost. We then explain that *equilibrium* is the situation in which everyone is simultaneously trying to individually optimize. In equilibrium, there isn't any perceived benefit to changing one's own behavior. We introduce the free-rider problem to show that individual optimization and social optimization do not necessarily coincide.

Because data play such a central role in economics, we devote an entire chapter—*Chapter 2*—to economic models, the scientific method, empirical testing, and the critical distinction between correlation and causation. We show how economists use models and data to answer interesting questions about human behavior. For the students who want to explore further, there is an appendix on constructing and interpreting graphs, which is presented in the context of an actual experiment on incentive schemes designed by one of us.

*Chapter 3* digs much more deeply into the concept of optimization, including an intuitive discussion of marginal analysis. We use a single running example of choosing an apartment, which confronts students with a trade-off between the cost of rent and the time spent commuting. We demonstrate two alternative approaches—optimization using total value and optimization using marginal analysis—and show why economists often use the latter technique.

*Chapter 4* introduces the demand and supply framework via a running example of the market for gasoline. We show how the price of gasoline affects the decisions of buyers, like commuters, and sellers, like ExxonMobil. As we develop the model, we explore how individual buyers are added together to produce a market demand curve and how individual sellers are added together to generate a market supply curve. We then show how buyers and sellers jointly determine the equilibrium market price and the equilibrium quantity of goods transacted in a perfectly competitive market. Finally, we show how markets break down when prices aren't allowed to adjust to equate the quantity demanded and the quantity supplied.

**Part II: Foundations of Microeconomics** anchors *Microeconomics* with a deeper exploration of the sources of demand and supply. One important thing that we have learned as teachers is that even after a year of economics, most students really have no idea about the underpinnings of the demand and supply curves—specifically, where the curves actually come from. Most textbooks do not illuminate these issues.

When crafting Chapters 5 and 6, our goal was to provide two stand-alone chapters that would show students that consumption and production are really two sides of the same coin, "glued" together by the idea of incentives. We gather consumer and producer concepts under their own respective umbrellas, and merge material that is spread out over several chapters in other texts. The goal is to show the commonalities and linkages between consumers' and producers' optimization decisions. With this setup, the student is able to view the whole picture in one place and understand how concepts tie together without flipping back and forth between several chapters.

In *Chapter 5*, we look "under the hood" to show where the demand curve actually comes from. We frame the question of how consumers decide what to buy as "the buyer's problem" and discuss the three key ingredients of demand: tastes and preferences, prices, and the budget set. The discussion is intuitive: once these three pieces are in place, the demand curve naturally falls out. This approach leads fluidly to a discussion of consumer surplus, demand elasticities, and how consumers predictably respond to incentives. In this way, the student can readily see holistically why policymakers and business people should concern themselves with the demand side of economics. For the students who want to delve deeper, there is an appendix on income and substitution effects, which is presented as an extension of the text.

In *Chapter 6*, we use the same holistic approach, but here we follow a single company (The Wisconsin Cheeseman, which a coauthor worked at for two high school summers) to showcase "the seller's problem." The seller's problem also has three parts: production, costs, and revenues. In thinking through the seller's problem, it is natural to treat these three components together rather than strew them over separate chapters as in other books. They need to be simultaneously considered by the firm when making optimal choices, so why not present them jointly? The running theme of The Wisconsin Cheeseman makes the chapter quite cohesive, and what was once a difficult puzzle to sort through becomes clear when presented under a single continuous example. For the more inquisitive students there is an appendix showing that for firms with different cost structures, economic profits can exist in long-run equilibrium.

*Chapter 7* takes an aerial view by considering what happens when we put together the buyers of Chapter 5 and the sellers of Chapter 6 in a perfectly competitive market. The chapter begins by asking: can markets composed of only self-interested people maximize the overall well-being of society? The beauty of economics is on full display in this chapter, as it shows that in a perfectly competitive market, the invisible hand creates harmony between the interests of the individual and those of society. Prices guide the invisible hand and incentivize buyers and sellers, who in turn maximize social surplus by allocating resources efficiently within and across sectors of the economy. The chapter uses Vernon Smith's seminal laboratory experiments to provide the evidence that prices and quantities converge to the intersection of supply and demand.

In *Chapter 8* we first walk through a discussion of the production possibilities curve, comparative advantage, and the gains from trade. We move the discussion from individuals trading with each other to trade between states (an innovation in a Principles text) and finally to trade between countries. Students can thus see that the principles motivating them to trade are the same as those motivating states and nations to trade. They develop an understanding that there are sometimes winners and losers in trade, but that overall, the gains from trade are larger than the losses. The key policy issue becomes: can we shift surplus to make trade a win–win for everyone?

If students stopped reading the book at this point, they would be rabid free-market proponents. This is because the beauty of the free market is unparalleled. *Chapter 9* begins a discussion of important cases that frustrate the workings of the invisible hand. When some firms produce, they pollute the air and water. There are some goods that everyone can consume once they are provided, such as national defense. Chapter 9 probes three cases of market failure—externalities, public goods, and common pool resources—and highlights an important link: in all three cases, there is a difference between social and private benefits or social and private costs. The student learns that the invisible hand of Chapter 7 can become "broken" and that government can enact policies in regard to externalities to improve social well-being, provide public goods, and protect common pool resources.

But government intervention can be a two-edged sword, and in *Chapter 10* we ask the question, "How much government intervention is necessary and how much is desirable?" We provide an aerial view of taxation and spending, and study how regulation—the main tool that governments use to deal with the externalities and other market failures of Chapter 10—has its costs and limitations. We see that the trade-off between equity and efficiency represents the nub of the conflict between those who support big government and those who argue for smaller government. The Evidence-Based Economics feature at the end of the chapter tackles the thorny question of the optimal size of government by exploring the deadweight loss of income taxation.

*Chapter 11* motivates the importance of factor markets—the inputs that firms use to make their goods and services—by asking if there is discrimination in the labor market. This question is couched within a general discussion about why people earn different wages in the labor market. This approach allows the student to seamlessly transition from being a demander (as in Chapter 5 as a buyer) to being a supplier (of labor). The economics behind the other major factors of production—physical capital and land—naturally follow from the labor discussion. The chapter concludes by showing several interesting data sets that measure whether discrimination exists in labor markets.

**Part III: Market Structure** introduces the alternatives to the perfectly competitive market: monopolies, oligopolies, and monopolistic competition. This section also provides the tools necessary to understand these market structures.

*Chapter 12* on monopoly connects the student's thinking to Chapter 6, where the seller's problem was introduced, and shows that all of the production and cost concepts learned earlier apply here: production should be expanded until marginal cost equals marginal revenue. To illustrate the "monopolist's problem," we use a running example of the allergy drug Claritin and its 20-year patent to show how a monopoly optimizes. Once again, we use the metaphor of the broken invisible hand to illustrate how a monopoly reallocates resources toward itself and thereby sacrifices social surplus. At this point, the student might wonder why legal market power is ever granted by the government. The opening question, *Can a monopoly ever be good for society?*, discusses the other side of the coin by presenting evidence that a monopoly *can* sometimes be good for society.

At this point in the book, we have covered many of the topics that are treated in existing texts. *Chapter 13* is a point of major departure, as we devote an entire chapter to game theory, which is a source of some of the most powerful economic insights. We emphasize that it helps us better understand the world when we place ourselves in the shoes of someone else. In so doing, the student develops a deeper understanding of how to choose a strategy that is a best response to the strategies of others. We apply game theory to many situations, including pollution, soccer, and advertising, to name a few.

In *Chapter 14*, we present the two market structures that fall between the extremes of perfect competition and monopoly: oligopoly and monopolistic competition. We develop the chapter around the motivating question of how many firms are necessary to make a market competitive. Throughout, we emphasize how oligopolist firms and monopolistically competitive firms set their prices and quantities by considering the choices of their competitors. We connect with previous chapters by framing the discussion in terms of the optimization problem of these firms: the "oligopolist's problem" and the "monopolistic competitor's problem." We show how in the short run it is identical to the monopolist's problem and in the long run to the perfectly competitive model.

**Part IV: Extending the Microeconomic Toolbox** provides a selection of special-topic, optional chapters, depending on the individual instructor's course emphasis. We have included these chapters because we feel that too often the student doesn't get to see the myriad of interesting applications that follow from all those months of learning basic economic principles!

*Chapter 15* studies trade-offs involving time and risk. The chapter begins by asking how the timing of a reward affects its economic value. We show how compound interest causes an investment's value to grow over time. We also show how to discount future financial flows and how to make financial decisions using the net present value framework. The second half of the chapter discusses probability and risk and explains how to calculate expected value. We apply these ideas to the study of gambling, extended warranties, and insurance.

Why does a new car lose considerable value the minute it is driven off the lot? *Chapter 16* examines markets we are all familiar with—ones in which one side of the market has more information than the other. The chapter examines the informational disparities between buyers and sellers in terms of hidden characteristics (for example, a sick person is more likely to apply for health insurance) and hidden actions (for example, an insured person is more likely to drive recklessly). Along the way, we look at many timely topics such as lemons in the used-car market, adverse selection in the health insurance market, and moral hazard in risk and insurance markets.

In *Chapter 17* we explore situations that students sometimes face: auctions and bargaining. Our optimization theme continues as we discuss best strategies and bargaining principles in a variety of settings. We explore the four common types of auctions and provide insights into how economics can help the student bid in auctions—from eBay to estate auctions to charity auctions. We then shift gears and examine bargaining situations that affect our lives daily. To show the power of the bargaining model, we present empirical evidence of who in the household determines how money is spent.

Perhaps the most unusual chapter for a Principles textbook is *Chapter 18*, which is on social economics. Here we introduce new variants of *homo economicus*. We explore two different areas of human behavior: the economics of charity and fairness and the economics of revenge. We then revisit the concept and origin of preferences—do we take satisfaction from contributing to a charity or from exacting revenge on a perceived enemy? This last chapter drives home the fact that economic principles can be extended to every corner of our world. And it teaches us that we can considerably extend our understanding of the world around us by adding insights from our sister sciences—psychology, history, anthropology, sociology, and political science, to name a few.

# MyEconLab®

MyEconLab's powerful assessment and tutorial system works hand-in-hand with the Second Edition of *Microeconomics*. It includes comprehensive homework, quiz, test, interactive, engagement and tutorial options which allow students to test their knowledge and instructors to manage all of their assessment and engagement needs in one program. Students and instructors can register, create and access all of their MyLab courses at www.pearsonmylab.com.

Key Features in the MyEconLab for *Microeconomics*, Second Edition include the following resources for instructors and students:

## Personalized Learning

Not every student learns the same way or at the same rate. With the growing need for acceleration through many courses, it's more important than ever to meet students where they learn. Personalized learning in the MyEconLab gives you the flexibility to incorporate the approach that best suits your course and your students.

## Interactive Graphs

The Interactive Graphs in MyEconLab enhance the student learning experience. Students can manipulate the coordinates and parameters of these graphs and watch the graphs change in real time, thereby deepening their conceptual understanding of the material.

## Study Plan

The Study Plan acts as a tutor, providing personalized recommendations for each of your students based on his or her ability to master the learning objectives in your course. This allows students to focus their study time by pinpointing the precise areas they need to review, and allowing them to use customized practice and learning aids—such as videos, eText, tutorials, and more—to get them back on track. Using the report available in the gradebook, you can then tailor course lectures to prioritize the content for which students need the most support—offering you better insight into classroom and individual performance.

With comprehensive homework, quiz, test, activity, practice, and tutorial options, instructors can manage all their assessment and online activity needs in one program. MyEconLab saves time by automatically grading questions and activities and tracking results in an online gradebook.

Each chapter contains two preloaded homework exercise sets that can be used to build an individualized study plan for each student. These study plan exercises contain tutorial resources, including instant feedback, links to the appropriate chapter section in the eText, pop-up definitions from the text, and step-by-step guided solutions, where appropriate. Within its rich assignment library, instructors will find a vast array of assessments that ask the students to draw graph lines and shifts, plot equilibrium points, and highlight important graph areas, all with the benefit of instant, personalized feedback. This feedback culminates, when needed, with the correct graph output alongside the student's personal answer, creating a powerful learning moment.

After the initial setup of the MyEconLab course for Acemoglu/Laibson/List, there are two primary ways to begin using this rich online environment. The first path requires no further action by the instructor. Students, on their own, can use MyEconLab's Study Plan problems and tutorial resources to enhance their understanding of concepts. The online gradebook records each student's performance and time spent on the assessments, activities, and the study plan and generates reports by student or chapter.

Alternatively, instructors can fully customize MyEconLab to match their course exactly: reading assignments, homework assignments, video assignments, current news assignments, digital activities, experiments, quizzes, and tests. Assignable resources include:

- Preloaded exercise assignment sets for each chapter that include the student tutorial resources mentioned earlier
- Preloaded quizzes for each chapter
- Assignable and gradable exercises that are similar to the end-of-chapter questions and problems and numbered exactly as in the book to make assigning homework easier
- *Real-Time Data Analysis Exercises* allow students and instructors to use the very latest data from the Federal Reserve Bank of St. Louis's FRED site. By completing the exercises, students become familiar with a key data source, learn how to locate data, and develop skills in interpreting data.
- In MyEconLab, select exhibits labeled MyEconLab Real-Time Data display updated graphs with real-time data from FRED.
- *Current News Exercises* provide a turnkey way to assign gradable news-based exercises in MyEconLab. Each week, Pearson scours the news, finds current economics articles, creates exercises around the news articles, and then automatically adds them to MyEconLab. Assigning and grading current news-based exercises that deal with the latest economics events and policy issues have never been more convenient.
- *Econ Exercise Builder* allows you to build customized exercises. Exercises include multiple-choice, graph drawing, and free-response items, many of which are generated algorithmically so that each time a student works them, a different variation is presented.
- Test Item File questions that allow you to assign quizzes or homework that will look just like your exams

MyEconLab grades every problem type (except essays), even problems with graphs. When working homework exercises, students receive immediate feedback, with links to additional learning tools.

- *Experiments in MyEconLab* are a fun and engaging way to promote active learning and mastery of important economic concepts. Pearson's Experiments program is flexible and easy for instructors and students to use.
- Single-player experiments allow your students to play against virtual players from anywhere at any time so long as they have an Internet connection.
- Multiplayer experiments allow you to assign and manage a real-time experiment with your class.

Pre- and post-questions for each experiment are available for assignment in MyEconLab.

## Dynamic Study Modules

Dynamic Study Modules help students study effectively on their own by continuously assessing their activity and performance in real time. Here's how it works: students complete a set of questions with a unique answer format that also asks them to indicate their confidence level. Questions repeat until the student can answer them all correctly and confidently. Once completed, Dynamic Study Modules explain the concept using materials from the text. These are available as graded assignments prior to class, and accessible on smartphones, tablets, and computers. NEW! Instructors can now remove questions from Dynamic Study Modules to better fit their course.

## Enhanced eText

The Enhanced eText keeps students engaged in learning on their own time, while helping them achieve greater conceptual understanding of course material. The concept checks, animations, and interactive graphs bring learning to life, and allow students to apply the very concepts they are reading about. Combining resources that illuminate content with accessible self-assessment, MyEconLab with Enhanced eText provides students with a complete digital learning experience—all in one place.

And with the **Pearson eText 2.0 mobile app** students can now access the Enhanced eText and all of its functionality from their computer, tablet, or mobile phone. Because students' progress is synced across all of their devices, they can stop what they're doing on one device and pick up again later on another one—without breaking their stride.

## Digital Interactives

Economic principles are not static ideas, and learning them shouldn't be a static process. Digital Interactives are dynamic and engaging assessment activities that promote critical thinking and application of key economic principles.

Each Digital Interactive has 3 to 5 progressive levels and requires approximately 20 minutes to explore, apply, compare, and analyze each topic. Many Digital Interactives include real-time data from FRED™ allowing professors and students to display, in graph and table form, up-to-the-minute data on key macro variables.

Digital Interactives can be assigned and graded within MyEconLab or used as a lecture tool to encourage engagement, classroom conversation, and group work.

## Learning Catalytics

Learning Catalytics helps you generate class discussion, customize your lecture, and promote peer-to-peer learning with real-time analytics. As a student response tool, Learning Catalytics uses students' smartphones, tablets, or laptops to engage them in more interactive tasks and thinking.

- Help your students develop critical thinking skills.
- Monitor responses to find out where your students are struggling.
- Rely on real-time data to adjust your teaching strategy.
- Automatically group students for discussion, teamwork, and peer-to-peer learning.

## LMS Integration

You can now link from Blackboard Learn, Brightspace by D2L, Canvas, or Moodle to Pearson MyEconLab. Access assignments, rosters, and resources, and synchronize grades with your LMS gradebook.

For students, single sign-on provides access to all the personalized learning resources that make studying more efficient and effective.

# Instructor Resources

The **Instructor's Manual** for *Microeconomics* was updated by James Hornsten of Northwestern University and includes:

- A chapter-by-chapter outline of the text
- Lecture notes highlighting the big ideas and concepts from each chapter
- Teaching Tips on how to motivate the lecture
- Common Mistakes or Misunderstandings students often make and how to correct them
- Short, real-world Alternative Teaching Examples, different from those in the text

**Active Learning Exercises**, included online and at the end of each Instructor's Manual chapter, were updated by James Hornsten and include:

- 5 to 10 Active Learning Exercises per chapter that are ideal for in-class discussions and group work

The **Solutions Manual**, updated by Scott Ogawa of Northwestern University, includes solutions to all end-of-chapter Questions and Problems in the text. It is available as downloadable Word documents and PDFs.

Three flexible **PowerPoint Presentation** packages make it easy for instructors to design presentation slides that best suit their style and needs:

- Lecture notes with some animated text figures and tables, as well as alternative examples with original static figures
- Figures from the text with step-by-step animation
- Static versions of all text figures and tables

Each presentation maps to the chapter's structure and organization and uses terminology used in the text. Nathan Kemper of University of Arkansas updated the Lecture PowerPoint presentation. Paul Graf of Indiana University, Bloomington, scripted and recorded the animations in MyEconLab.

The **Test Bank** for *Microeconomics* was updated by Daijiro Okada of Rutgers University, Jean-François Mercier of Loyola Marymount University, John Smith of West Point, and Leila Farivar of Ohio State University, and edited and reviewed by Ross vanWassenhove of University of Houston. The Test Bank contains approximately 2,400 multiple-choice, numerical, short-answer, and essay questions. These have been edited and reviewed to ensure accuracy and clarity, and include terminology used in the book. Each question can be sorted by difficulty, book topic, concept covered, and AACSB learning standard to enhance ease of use. The Test Bank is available in Word, PDF, and TestGen formats.

TestGen is a computerized test generation program, available exclusively from Pearson, that allows instructors to easily create and administer tests on paper, electronically, or online. Instructors can select test items from the publisher-supplied test bank, which is organized by chapter and based on the associated textbook material, or create their own questions from scratch. With both quick-and-simple test creation and flexible and robust editing tools, TestGen is a complete test generator system for today's educators.

## Instructor's Resource Center

Instructor resources are available online via our centralized supplements Web site, the Instructor Resource Center (**www.pearsonhighered.com/irc**). For access or more information, contact your local Pearson representative or request access online at the Instructor Resource Center.

# Acknowledgments

As the three of us worked on this project, we taught each other a lot about economics, teaching, and writing. But we learned even more from the hundreds of other people who helped us along the way. For their guidance, we are thankful and deeply humbled. Their contributions turned out to be critical in ways that we never imagined when we started, and our own ideas were greatly improved by their insights and advice.

Our reviewers, focus group participants, and class testers showed us how to better formulate our ideas and helped us sharpen our writing. Through their frequently brilliant feedback, they corrected our economic misconceptions, improved our conceptual vision, and showed us how to write more clearly. Their contributions appear in almost every paragraph of this book. All of their names are listed below.

Our research assistants—Alec Brandon, Justin Holz, Josh Hurwitz, Xavier Jaravel, Angelina Liang, Daniel Norris, Yana Peysakhovich, Maggie Yellen, and Jan Zilinsky—played a critical role at every phase of the project, from analyzing data to editing prose to generating deep insights about pedagogical principles that are woven throughout the book. We learned to trust their instincts on every element of the book, and quickly realized that their contributions were indispensable to the project's success. We are especially indebted to Josh Hurwitz and Maggie Yellen, who have earned our eternal gratitude for many late work nights and for their brilliant editorial and economic insights.

We are also deeply grateful to the many inspiring economists who contributed major components of the project. Scott Ogawa of Northwestern University contributed extensively to the updates of the end-of-chapter questions and problems, which stand out as examples of inspiring pedagogy. James Hornsten of Northwestern University updated the innovative and intuitive Instructor's Manual and Active Learning Exercises. Nathan Kemper and Paul Graf updated the outstanding PowerPoint slides and animations that illuminate and distill the key lessons of the book. Daijiro Okada, Jean-Francois Mercier, John Smith, and Leila Farivar updated the expansive test bank.

Most importantly, we acknowledge the myriad contributions of our editors and all of our amazing colleagues at Pearson. They have marched with us every step of the way. We wouldn't dare count the number of hours that they dedicated to this project, including evenings and weekends. Their commitment, vision, and editorial suggestions touched every sentence of this book. Most of the key decisions about the project were made with the help of our editors, and this collaborative spirit proved to be absolutely essential to our writing. Dozens of people at Pearson played key roles, but the most important contributions were made by Adrienne D'Ambrosio, Director of Portfolio Management; Christina Masturzo, Senior Portfolio Manager; Cydney Westmoreland, Development Editor; Nancy Freihofer, Content Producer; Heidi Allgair, Project Manager; Noel Lotz, Digital Content Team Lead; and Melissa Honig, Digital Studio Producer.

We are particularly grateful to Adrienne, who has been deeply committed to our project from the first day and has tirelessly worked with us on every key decision. We also wish to thank Denise Clinton, who first got us started, and Donna Battista, Vice President, Business Publishing, who championed the project along the way. All of these publishing professionals transformed us as writers, teachers, and communicators. This book is a testimony to their perseverance, their dedication, and their brilliant eye for good (and often bad!) writing. Their commitment to this project has been extraordinary and inspirational. We are profoundly grateful for their guidance and collaboration.

Finally, we wish to thank our many other support networks. Our own professors, who first inspired us as economists and showed, through their example, the power of teaching and the joy that one can take from studying economics. Our parents, who nurtured us in so many ways and gave us the initial human capital that made our entire careers possible. Our kids, who implicitly sacrificed when our long hours on this book ate into family life. And, most profoundly, we thank our spouses, who have been supportive, understanding, and inspirational throughout the project.

This book is the product of many streams that have flowed together and so many people who have contributed their insights and their passion to this project. We are deeply grateful for these myriad collaborations.

# Reviewers

The following reviewers, class test participants, and focus group participants provided invaluable insights.

Adel Abadeer, Calvin College

Ahmed Abou-Zaid, Eastern Illinois University

Temisan Agbeyegbe, City University of New York

Carlos Aguilar, El Paso Community College

Rashid Al-Hmoud, Texas Tech University

Frank Albritton, Seminole Community College

Sam Allgood, University of Nebraska, Lincoln

Neil Alper, Northeastern University

Farhad Ameen, Westchester Community College

Catalina Amuedo-Dorantes, San Diego State University

Lian An, University of North Florida

Samuel Andoh, Southern Connecticut State University

Brad Andrew, Juniata College

Len Anyanwu, Union County College

Robert Archibald, College of William and Mary

Ali Arshad, New Mexico Highlands University

Robert Baden, University of California, Santa Cruz

Mohsen Bahmani-Oskooee, University of Wisconsin, Milwaukee

Scott L. Baier, Clemson University

Rita Balaban, University of North Carolina

Mihajlo Balic, Harrisburg Area Community College

Sheryl Ball, Virginia Polytechnic Institute and State University

Spencer Banzhaf, Georgia State University

Jim Barbour, Elon University

Scott Barkowski, Clemson University

Hamid Bastin, Shippensburg University

Clare Battista, California State Polytechnic University, San Luis Obispo

Jodi Beggs, Northeastern University

Eric Belasco, Montana State University

Susan Bell, Seminole State University

Valerie Bencivenga, University of Texas, Austin

Pedro Bento, West Virginia University

Derek Berry, Calhoun Community College

Prasun Bhattacharjee, East Tennessee State University

Benjamin Blair, Columbus State University

Douglas Blair, Rutgers University

John Bockino, Suffolk County Community College

Andrea Borchard, Hillsborough Community College

Luca Bossi, University of Pennsylvania

Gregory Brock, Georgia Southern University

Bruce Brown, California State Polytechnic University, Pomona

David Brown, Pennsylvania State University

Jaime Brown, Pennsylvania State University

Laura Bucila, Texas Christian University

Don Bumpass, Sam Houston State University

Chris Burkart, University of West Florida

Julianna Butler, University of Delaware

Colleen Callahan, American University

Fred Campano, Fordham University

Douglas Campbell, University of Memphis

Cheryl Carleton, Villanova University

Scott Carrell, University of California, Davis

Kathleen Carroll, University of Maryland, Baltimore

Regina Cassady, Valencia College, East Campus

Shirley Cassing, University of Pittsburgh

Suparna Chakraborty, University of San Francisco

Catherine Chambers, University of Central Missouri

Chiuping Chen, American River College

Susan Christoffersen, Philadelphia University

Benjamin Andrew Chupp, Illinois State University

David L. Cleeton, Illinois State University

Cynthia Clement, University of Maryland

Marcelo Clerici-Arias, Stanford University

Bently Coffey, University of South Carolina, Columbia

Rachel Connelly, Bowdoin College

William Conner, Tidewater Community College

Kathleen Conway, Carnegie Mellon University

Patrick Conway, University of North Carolina

Jay Corrigan, Kenyon College

Antoinette Criss, University of South Florida

Sean Crockett, City University of New York

Patrick Crowley, Texas A&M University, Corpus Christi

Kelley Cullen, Eastern Washington University

Scott Cunningham, Baylor University

Muhammed Dalgin, Kutztown University

David Davenport, McLennan Community College

Stephen Davis, Southwest Minnesota State University

John W. Dawson, Appalachian State University

Pierangelo De Pace, California State University, Pomona

David Denslow, University of Florida

Arthur Diamond, University of Nebraska, Omaha

Timothy Diette, Washington and Lee University

Isaac Dilanni, University of Illinois, Urbana-Champaign

Oguzhan Dincer, Illinois State University

Ethan Doetsch, Ohio State University

Murat Doral, Kennesaw State University

Kirk Doran, University of Notre Dame

Tanya Downing, Cuesta College

Mitchell Dudley, University of Michigan, Ann Arbor

Gary Dymski, University of California, Riverside

Kevin Egan, University of Toledo

Eric Eide, Brigham Young University, Provo

Harold Elder, University of Alabama, Tuscaloosa

Michael Ellerbrock, Virginia Tech

Harry Ellis, University of North Texas

Noha Emara, Columbia University

Lucas Engelhardt, Kent State University, Stark

Erwin Erhardt, University of Cincinnati

Hadi Esfahani, University of Illinois, Urbana-Champaign

Molly Espey, Clemson University

Jose Esteban, Palomar College

Hugo Eyzaguirre, Northern Michigan University

Jamie Falcon, University of Maryland, Baltimore

Liliana Fargo, DePaul University

Leila Farivar, Ohio State University

Sasan Fayazmanesh, California State University, Fresno

Bichaka Fayissa, Middle Tennessee State University

Virginia Fierro-Renoy, Keiser University

Donna Fisher, Georgia Southern University

Paul Fisher, Henry Ford Community College

Todd Fitch, University of California, Berkeley

Mary Flannery, University of Notre Dame

Hisham Foad, San Diego State University

Mathew Forstater, University of Missouri, Kansas City

Irene Foster, George Mason University

Hamilton Fout, Kansas State University

Shelby Frost, Georgia State University

Timothy Fuerst, University of Notre Dame

Ken Gaines, East-West University

John Gallup, Portland State University

William Galose, Lamar University

Karen Gebhardt, Colorado State University

Gerbremeskel Gebremariam, Virginia Polytechnic Institute and State University

Lisa George, City University of New York

Gregory Gilpin, Montana State University

Seth Gitter, Towson University

Brian Goegan, Arizona State University, Tempe

Rajeev Goel, Illinois State University

Bill Goffe, State University of New York, Oswego

Julie Gonzalez, University of California, Santa Cruz

Paul Graf, Indiana University, Bloomington

Philip Graves, University of Colorado, Boulder

Lisa Grobar, California State University, Long Beach

Fatma Gunay Bendas, Washington and Lee University

Michael Hammock, Middle Tennessee State University

Michele Hampton, Cuyahoga Community College

Moonsu Han, North Shore Community College

F. Andrew Hanssen, Clemson University

David Harris, Benedictine College

Robert Harris, Indiana University-Purdue University Indianapolis

Julia Heath, University of Cincinnati

Jolien Helsel, Youngstown State University

Matthew Henry, Cleveland State University

Thomas Henry, Mississippi State University

David Hewitt, Whittier College

Wayne Hickenbottom, University of Texas, Austin

Jannett Highfill, Bradley University

Michael Hilmer, San Diego State University

John Hilston, Brevard College

Naphtali Hoffman, Elmira College and Binghamton University

Kim Holder, University of West Georgia

Robert Holland, Purdue University

Don Holley, Boise State University

Paul Holmes, Ashland University

James A. Hornsten, Northwestern University

Gail Hoyt, University of Kentucky

Jim Hubert, Seattle Central Community College

Scott Hunt, Columbus State Community College

Kyle Hurst, University of Colorado, Denver

Ruben Jacob-Rubio, University of Georgia

Joyce Jacobsen, Wesleyan University

Kenneth Jameson, University of Utah

Kevin Jasek-Rysdahl, California State University, Stanislaus

Andres Jauregui, Columbus State University

Brian Jenkins, University of California, Irvine

Sarah Jenyk, Youngstown State University

Robert Jerome, James Madison University

Deepak Joglekar, University of Connecticut

Paul Johnson, Columbus State University

Ted Joyce, City University of New York

David Kalist, Shippensburg University

Lilian Kamal, University of Hartford*

Leonie Karkoviata, University of Houston, Downtown

Kathy Kelly, University of Texas, Arlington

Nathan Kemper, University Arkansas

Colin Knapp, University of Florida

Yilmaz Kocer, University of Southern California

Ebenezer Kolajo, University of West Georgia

Janet Koscianski, Shippensburg University

Robert Krol, California State University, Northridge

Daniel Kuester, Kansas State University

Patricia Kuzyk, Washington State University

Sumner La Croix, University of Hawaii

Rose LaMont, Modesto Community College

Carsten Lange, California State University, Pomona

Vicky Langston, Columbus State University

Susan Laury, Georgia State University

Myoung Lee, University of Missouri, Columbia

Sang Lee, Southeastern Louisiana University

Phillip K. Letting, Harrisburg Area Community College

John Levendis, Loyola University

Steven Levkoff, University of California, San Diego

Dennis P. Leyden, University of North Carolina, Greensboro

Gregory Lindeblom, Brevard College

Alan Lockard, Binghamton University

Joshua Long, Ivy Technical College

Linda Loubert, Morgan State University

Heather Luea, Kansas State University

Rotua Lumbantobing, Western Connecticut State University

Rita Madarassy, Santa Clara University

James Makokha, Collin County Community College

Liam C. Malloy, University of Rhode Island

Christopher Mann, University of Nebraska, Lincoln

Paula Manns, Atlantic Cape Community College

Vlad Manole, Rutgers University

Hardik Marfatia, Northeastern Illinois University

Lawrence Martin, Michigan State University

Norman Maynard, University of Oklahoma

Katherine McClain, University of Georgia

Scott McGann, Grossmont College

Kim Marie McGoldrick, University of Richmond

Shah Mehrabi, Montgomery Community College

Aaron Meininger, University of California, Santa Cruz

Saul Mekies, Kirkwood Community College

Kimberly Mencken, Baylor University

Diego Mendez-Carbajo, Illinois Wesleyan University

Thomas Menn, United States Military Academy at West Point

Catherine Middleton, University of Tennessee, Chattanooga

Nara Mijid, Central Connecticut State University

Laurie A. Miller, University of Nebraska, Lincoln

Edward Millner, Virginia Commonwealth University

Ida Mirzaie, Ohio State University

David Mitchell, Missouri State University, Springfield

Michael Mogavero, University of Notre Dame

Robert Mohr, University of New Hampshire

Barbara Moore, University of Central Florida

Thaddeaus Mounkurai, Daytona State College

Usha Nair-Reichert, Emory University
Camille Nelson, Oregon State University
Michael Nelson, Oregon State University
John Neri, University of Maryland
Andre Neveu, James Madison University
Jinlan Ni, University of Nebraska, Omaha
Eric Nielsen, St. Louis Community College
Jaminka Ninkovic, Emory University
Chali Nondo, Albany State University
Richard P. Numrich, College of Southern
Nevada
Andrew Nutting, Hamilton College
Grace O, Georgia State University
Norman Obst, Michigan State University
Scott Ogawa, Northwestern University
Lee Ohanian, University of California,
Los Angeles
Paul Okello, Tarrant County College
Ifeakandu Okoye, Florida A&M University
Alan Osman, Ohio State University
Tomi Ovaska, Youngstown State University
Caroline Padgett, Francis Marion University
Zuohong Pan, Western Connecticut State
University
Peter Parcells, Whitman College
Cynthia Parker, Chaffey College
Mohammed Partapurwala, Monroe
Community College
Robert Pennington, University of Central
Florida
David Perkis, Purdue University, West
Lafayette
Colin Phillipps, Illinois State University
Kerk Phillips, Brigham Young University
Goncalo Pina, Santa Clara University
Michael Podgursky, University of Missouri
Greg Pratt, Mesa Community College
Guangjun Qu, Birmingham-Southern
College
Fernando Quijano, Dickinson State
University
Joseph Quinn, Boston College
Reza Ramazani, Saint Michael's College
Ranajoy Ray-Chaudhuri, Ohio State
University
Mitchell Redlo, Monroe Community
College
Javier Reyes, University of Arkansas
Teresa Riley, Youngstown State University
Nancy Roberts, Arizona State University
Malcolm Robinson, Thomas More College
Randall Rojas, University of California, Los
Angeles
Sudipta Roy, Kankakee Community College
Jared Rubin, Chapman University
Jason C. Rudbeck, University of Georgia

Melissa Rueterbusch, Mott Community
College
Mariano Runco, Auburn University at
Montgomery
Nicholas G. Rupp, East Carolina University
Steven Russell, Indiana University-Purdue
University-Indianapolis
Michael Ryan, Western Michigan University
Ravi Samitamana, Daytona State College
David Sanders, University of Missouri,
St. Louis
Michael Sattinger, State University of New
York, Albany
Anya Savikhin Samek, University of
Wisconsin, Madison
Peter Schuhmann, University of North
Carolina, Wilmington
Robert M. Schwab, University of Maryland
Jesse Schwartz, Kennesaw State University
James K. Self, Indiana University,
Bloomington
Katie Shester, Washington and Lee University
Mark Showalter, Brigham Young University,
Provo
Dorothy Siden, Salem State University
Mark V. Siegler, California State University,
Sacramento
Carlos Silva, New Mexico State University
Timothy Simpson, Central New Mexico
Community College
Michael Sinkey, University of West Georgia
John Z. Smith, Jr., United States Military
Academy, West Point
Thomas Snyder, University of Central
Arkansas
Joe Sobieralski, Southwestern Illinois
College
Sara Solnick, University of Vermont
Martha Starr, American University
Rebecca Stein, University of Pennsylvania
Liliana Stern, Auburn University
Adam Stevenson, University of Michigan
Cliff Stone, Ball State University
Mark C. Strazicich, Appalachian State
University
Chetan Subramanian, State University of
New York, Buffalo
AJ Sumell, Youngstown State University
Charles Swanson, Temple University
Tom Sweeney, Des Moines Area
Community College
James Swofford, University of South
Alabama
Kevin Sylwester, Southern Illinois
University
Vera Tabakova, East Carolina University
Emily Tang, University of California, San
Diego

Mark Tendall, Stanford University
Jennifer Thacher, University of New Mexico
Charles Thomas, Clemson University
Rebecca Thornton, University of Houston
Jill Trask, Tarrant County College,
Southeast
Steve Trost, Virginia Polytechnic Institute
and State University
Ty Turley, Brigham Young University
Nora Underwood, University of Central
Florida
Mike Urbancic, University of Oregon
Don Uy-Barreta, De Anza College
John Vahaly, University of Louisville
Ross Van Wassenhove, University of
Houston
Don Vandegrift, College of New Jersey
Nancy Virts, California State University,
Northridge
Cheryl Wachenheim, North Dakota State
College
Jeffrey Waddoups, University of Nevada,
Las Vegas
Parag Waknis, University of Massachusetts,
Dartmouth
Donald Wargo, Temple University
Charles Wassell, Jr., Central Washington
University
Matthew Weinberg, Drexel University
Robert Whaples, Wake Forest University
Elizabeth Wheaton, Southern Methodist
University
Mark Wheeler, Western Michigan University
Anne Williams, Gateway Community
College
Brock Williams, Metropolitan Community
College of Omaha
DeEdgra Williams, Florida A&M University
Brooks Wilson, McLennan Community
College
Mark Witte, Northwestern University
Katherine Wolfe, University of Pittsburgh
William Wood, James Madison University
Jadrian Wooten, Pennsylvania State
University
Steven Yamarik, California State University,
Long Beach
Guy Yamashiro, California State University,
Long Beach
Bill Yang, Georgia Southern University
Young-Ro Yoon, Wayne State University
Madelyn Young, Converse College
Michael Youngblood, Rock Valley College
Jeffrey Zax, University of Colorado, Boulder
Martin Zelder, Northwestern University
Erik Zemljic, Kent State University
Kevin Zhang, Illinois State University

# Microeconomics: Flexibility Chart

| Traditional Approach | Theoretical Approach | Applied Approach |
|---|---|---|
| **Chapter 1:** The Principles and Practice of Economics | **Chapter 1:** The Principles and Practice of Economics | **Chapter 1:** The Principles and Practice of Economics |
| **Chapter 2:** Economic Methods and Economic Questions (optional) | **Chapter 2:** Economic Methods and Economic Questions | **Chapter 2:** Economic Methods and Economic Questions (optional) |
| **Chapter 2 Appendix:** Constructing and Interpreting Graphs | **Chapter 2 Appendix:** Constructing and Interpreting Graphs | **Chapter 2 Appendix:** Constructing and Interpreting Graphs |
| **Chapter 3:** Optimization: Doing the Best You Can (optional) | **Chapter 3:** Optimization: Doing the Best You Can | **Chapter 3:** Optimization: Doing the Best You Can (optional) |
| **Chapter 4:** Demand, Supply, and Equilibrium | **Chapter 4:** Demand, Supply, and Equilibrium | **Chapter 4:** Demand, Supply, and Equilibrium |
| **Chapter 5:** Consumers and Incentives | **Chapter 5:** Consumers and Incentives<br><br>**Chapter 5 Appendix:** Representing Preferences with Indifference Curves | **Section 5.4:** Consumer Surplus (optional)<br><br>**Section 5.6:** Demand Elasticities (optional) |
| **Chapter 6:** Sellers and Incentives | **Chapter 6:** Sellers and Incentives<br><br>**Chapter 6 Appendix:** When Firms Have Different Cost Structures | **Section 6.4:** Producer Surplus (optional) |
| **Chapter 7:** Perfect Competition and the Invisible Hand | **Chapter 7:** Perfect Competition and the Invisible Hand | **Chapter 7:** Perfect Competition and the Invisible Hand |
| **Chapter 8:** Trade | **Chapter 11:** Markets for Factors of Production | **Chapter 8:** Trade |
| **Chapter 9:** Externalities and Public Goods | **Chapter 12:** Monopoly | **Chapter 9:** Externalities and Public Goods |
| **Chapter 10:** The Government in the Economy: Taxation and Regulation | **Chapter 13:** Game Theory and Strategic Play | **Chapter 10:** The Government in the Economy: Taxation and Regulation |
| **Chapter 11:** Markets for Factors of Production | **Chapter 14:** Oligopoly and Monopolistic Competition | **Chapter 11:** Markets for Factors of Production (optional) |
| **Chapter 12:** Monopoly | **Chapter 8:** Trade | **Chapter 12:** Monopoly |
| **Chapter 13:** Game Theory and Strategic Play | **Chapter 9:** Externalities and Public Goods | **Chapter 13:** Game Theory and Strategic Play |
| **Chapter 14:** Oligopoly and Monopolistic Competition | **Chapter 10:** The Government in the Economy: Taxation and Regulation | **Chapter 14:** Oligopoly and Monopolistic Competition |
| **Chapter 15:** Trade-offs Involving Time and Risk (optional) | **Chapter 15:** Trade-offs Involving Time and Risk (optional) | **Chapter 15:** Trade-offs Involving Time and Risk (optional) |
| **Chapter 16:** The Economics of Information (optional) | **Chapter 16:** The Economics of Information (optional) | **Chapter 16:** The Economics of Information (optional) |
| **Chapter 17:** Auctions and Bargaining (optional) | **Chapter 17:** Auctions and Bargaining (optional) | **Chapter 17:** Auctions and Bargaining (optional) |
| **Chapter 18:** Social Economics (optional) | **Chapter 18:** Social Economics (optional) | **Chapter 18:** Social Economics (optional) |

# 1

# The Principles and Practice of Economics

## Is Facebook free?

Facebook doesn't charge you a penny, so it's tempting to say "it's free."

Here's another way to think about it: what do you give up when you use Facebook? Facebook may not take your money, but it does take your time. If you spend an hour each day on Facebook, you are giving up some alternative use of that time. You could spend that time playing soccer, watching Netflix, napping, studying, or listening to music. You could also spend it *making* money. A typical U.S. college student employed 7 hours per week earns almost $4,000 in a year—enough to pay the annual lease on a sports car. A part-time job is just one alternative way to use the time that you spend on Facebook. In your view, what is the best alternative use of *your* Facebook time? That's the economic way of thinking about the cost of Facebook.

In this chapter, we introduce you to the economic way of thinking about the world. Economists study the choices that people make, from big decisions like choosing a career to daily decisions like logging onto Facebook. To understand those choices, they often focus on the costs and benefits involved.

## CHAPTER OUTLINE

| 1.1 | 1.2 | 1.3 | EBE | 1.4 | 1.5 | 1.6 |
|-----|-----|-----|-----|-----|-----|-----|
| The Scope of Economics | Three Principles of Economics | The First Principle of Economics: Optimization | Is Facebook free? | The Second Principle of Economics: Equilibrium | The Third Principle of Economics: Empiricism | Is Economics Good for You? |

- Economics is the study of people's choices.

- The first principle of economics is that people try to *optimize*: they try to choose the best available option.

- The second principle of economics is that economic systems tend to be in *equilibrium*, a situation in which nobody would benefit by changing his or her own behavior.

- The third principle of economics is *empiricism*—analysis that uses data. Economists use data to test theories and to determine what is causing things to happen in the world.

## 1.1   The Scope of Economics

Economics involves far more than money. Economists study *all* human behavior, from a person's decision to lease a new sports car, to the speed the new driver chooses as she rounds a hairpin corner, to her decision not to wear a seat belt. These are all choices, and they are all fair game to economists. Choice—not money—is the unifying feature of all the things that economists study.

In fact, economists think of almost all human behavior as the outcome of choices. For instance, imagine that Dad tells his teenage daughter that she *must* wash the family car. The daughter has several options: she can wash it, she can negotiate for an easier chore, she can refuse to wash it and suffer the consequences, or she can move out (a drastic response, sure, but still an option). Obeying your parents is a choice, though it may not always feel like one.

> Choice—not money—is the unifying feature of all the things that economists study.

### Economic Agents and Economic Resources

Saying that economics is all about choices is an easy way to remember what economics is. To give you a more precise definition, we first need to introduce two important concepts: *economic agents* and *resource allocation*.

An **economic agent** is an individual or a group that makes choices. Let's start with a few types of individual economic agents. For example, a *consumer* chooses to eat bacon cheeseburgers or tofu burgers. A *parent* chooses to enroll her children in public school or private school. A *student* chooses to attend his classes or to skip them. A *citizen* chooses whether or not to vote, and if so, which candidate to support. A *worker* chooses to do her job or pretend to work while texting. A *criminal* chooses to hotwire cars or mug little old ladies. A *business leader* chooses to open a new factory in Chile or in China. A *senator* chooses to vote for or against a bill. Of course, you are also an economic agent, because you make an enormous number of choices every day.

Not all economic agents, however, are individuals. An economic agent can also be a group—a government, an army, a firm, a university, a political party, a labor union, a sports team, or a street gang (Exhibit 1.1). Sometimes economists simplify their analysis by treating these groups as a single decision maker, without worrying about the details of how the different individuals in the group contributed to the decision. For example, an economist might say that Apple prices the iPhone to maximize its profits, glossing over the fact that many employees participated in the analysis—including the arguments and disagreements—that led to the choice of the price.

An **economic agent** is an individual or a group that makes choices.

1.1

1.2

1.3

1.4

1.5

1.6

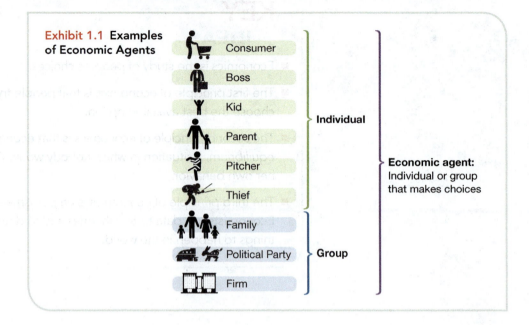

Exhibit 1.1 Examples of Economic Agents

Consumer

Boss

Kid

Parent

Pitcher

Thief

Individual

Family

Political Party

Firm

Group

Economic agent:
Individual or group
that makes choices

**Scarce resources** are things that people want, where the quantity that people want exceeds the quantity that is available.

**Scarcity** is the situation of having unlimited wants in a world of limited resources.

The second important concept to understand is that economics studies the allocation of *scarce resources*. **Scarce resources** are things that people want, where the quantity that people want (if the resources were being given away for free) exceeds the quantity that is available. Gold wedding bands, Shiatsu massages, Coach handbags, California peaches, iPhones, triple-chocolate-fudge ice cream, and rooms with a view are all scarce resources. But a resource doesn't need to be luxurious to be scarce—everyday goods are also scarce, like toilet paper, subway seats, and clean drinking water. **Scarcity** exists because people have unlimited wants in a world of limited resources. The world does not have enough resources to give everyone *everything* they want (for free). Consider sports cars: if sports cars were given away at a zero price, there would not be enough of them to go around. So how does society determine who gets the limited supply of sports cars? In general, how does society allocate all of the scarce resources in the economy?

In a modern economy, consumers like you play a key role in this resource allocation process. You have 24 hours to allocate each day—this is your daily budget of time. You choose how many of those 24 hours you will allocate to Facebook. You choose how many of those 24 hours you will allocate to other activities, including school work and/or a job. If you have a job, you choose whether to spend your hard-earned wages on a sports car. These types of decisions determine how scarce resources are allocated in a modern economy: to the consumers who are able and willing to pay for them.

Economists don't want to impose our tastes for sports cars, hybrids, electric vehicles, SUVs, or public transportation on you. We are interested in teaching you how to use economic reasoning so that *you* can compare the costs and benefits of the alternative options and make the choices that are best for you.

## Definition of Economics

**Economics** is the study of how agents choose to allocate scarce resources and how those choices affect society.

We are now ready to define economics precisely. **Economics** is the study of how agents choose to allocate scarce resources and how those choices affect society.

Our earlier examples all emphasized people's *choices,* and choices play a key role in the formal definition of economics. However, the definition of economics also adds a new element to our discussion: the effects of any individual agent's choices on society. For example, the sale of a new sports car doesn't just affect the person driving off the dealer's lot. The sale generates sales tax, which the government uses to fund projects like highways and hospitals. The purchase of the new car also generates some congestion—that's one more car in rush-hour gridlock. It's another car that might grab the last parking spot on your street. If the new owner drives recklessly, the car may generate risks to other drivers. Economists study the original choice and its multiple consequences for other people in the world.

## Positive Economics and Normative Economics

We now have an idea of what economics is about: people's choices. But why study these choices? Part of the answer is that economists are just curious, but that's only a small piece of the picture. Understanding people's choices is practically useful for two key reasons. Economic analysis

1. Describes what people *actually* do (positive economics)
2. Recommends what people, including society, *ought* to do (normative economics)

The first application is descriptive, and the second is advisory.

Economics is the study of choice.

**Positive economics** is analysis that generates objective descriptions or predictions, which can be verified with data.

**Normative economics** is analysis that recommends what an individual or society ought to do.

**Positive Economics Describes What People Actually Do**   Descriptions of what people actually do are *objective* statements about the world—in other words, statements that can be confirmed or tested with data. For instance, it is a fact that in 2014, 50 percent of U.S. households earned less than $54,462 per year.[1] Of course, these earnings were related to the choices that those households made, including whether to work for pay, which jobs to apply for, and how many hours to work at those jobs. Describing what has happened or predicting what will happen is referred to as **positive economics** or positive economic analysis.

For instance, consider the prediction that in 2025, U.S. households will invest about half of their retirement savings in the stock market. This forecast can be compared to future data and either confirmed or disproven. Because a prediction is eventually testable—after the passage of time—it is part of positive economics.

**Normative Economics Recommends What People Ought to Do**   **Normative economics**, the second of the two types of economic analysis, advises individuals and society on their choices. Normative economics is about what people ought to do. Normative economics is almost always dependent on *subjective* judgments, which means that normative analysis depends at least in part on personal feelings, tastes, or opinions. So whose subjective judgments do we try to use? Economists believe that the people being advised should determine the preferences to be used.

For example, consider an economist who is helping a worker to decide how much risk to take in her investments. The economist might ask the worker about her own preferences regarding investment risk. Suppose the worker said that she wouldn't sleep well at night if her retirement savings were invested in the stock market, which does fall sharply from time to time. The economist would explain that eliminating risk comes at a cost—riskless investments have a lower average rate of return than investments in the stock market. Stocks have had an annual average return that is about 6 percentage points higher per year than the return on riskless investments. If the worker acknowledged this difference and still wanted the riskless investments, the economist would help the worker find such riskless investments. Here the economist plays the role of engineer, finding the investment portfolio that will deliver the level of risk that the worker wants.

And that's the key—*what the worker wants.* In the mind of most economists, it is legitimate for the worker to choose any level of risk, as long as she understands the implications of that risk for her average rate of return—less risk implies a lower average rate of return. When economic analysis is used to help *individual* economic agents choose what is in their personal best interest, this type of normative economics is referred to as *prescriptive economics.*

Sometimes the normative analysis gets more complicated, because there are many economic agents in the picture. We turn to these harder normative analyses next.

**Normative Analysis and Public Policy**   Normative analysis also generates advice to society in general. For example, economists are often asked to evaluate public policies, like taxes or regulations. When public policies create winners and losers, citizens tend to have opposing views about the desirability of the government program. One person's migratory bird sanctuary is another person's mosquito-infested swamp. Protecting a wetland with environmental regulations benefits bird-watchers but harms landowners who would like to develop that land.

Economic agents have divergent views on the future of this swamp. The owner of the property wants to build housing units. An environmentalist wants to preserve the wetland to protect the whooping crane, an endangered species. What should happen?

**Microeconomics** is the study of how individuals, households, firms, and governments make choices, and how those choices affect prices, the allocation of resources, and the well-being of other agents.

**Macroeconomics** is the study of the economy as a whole. Macroeconomists study economy-wide phenomena, like the growth rate of a country's total economic output, the inflation rate, or the unemployment rate.

When a government policy creates winners and losers, economists need to make some ethical judgments to conduct normative analysis. Economists must make ethical judgments when evaluating policies that make one group worse off so another group can be made better off.

Ethical judgments are usually unavoidable when economists think about government policies, because there are few policies that make everyone better off. Deciding whether the costs experienced by the losers are justified by the benefits experienced by the winners is partly an ethical judgment. Is it ethical to create environmental regulations that prevent a real estate developer from draining a swamp so he can build new homes? What if those environmental regulations protect migratory birds that other people value? Are there possible compromises—should the government, for example, try to buy the land from the real estate developer? These public policy questions—which all ask what society *should* do—are normative economic questions.

### Microeconomics and Macroeconomics

There is one other distinction that you need to know to understand the scope of economics. Economics can be divided into two broad fields of study, though many economists do a bit of both.

**Microeconomics** is the study of how individuals, households, firms, and governments make choices, and how those choices affect prices, the allocation of resources, and the well-being of other agents. In general, microeconomists are called on when we want to understand a small piece of the overall economy, like the market for coal-fired electricity generation.

For example, some microeconomists study pollution generated by coal-fired power plants. A microeconomist might predict the level of coal-based pollution over the next decade, basing her forecast on the overall demand for electricity and likely technological developments in the energy industry—including solar- and wind-energy substitutes for coal-fired power plants. Predicting future levels of pollution from coal-fired plants is part of positive economic analysis.

Some microeconomists undertake normative analysis of coal-based pollution. For example, because global warming is largely caused by carbon emissions from coal, oil, and other fossil fuels, microeconomists design new government policies that attempt to reduce the use of these fuels. For example, a "carbon tax" targets carbon emissions. Under a carbon tax, relatively carbon-intensive energy sources—like coal-fired power plants—pay more tax per unit of energy produced than energy sources with lower carbon emissions—like wind farms. Some microeconomists have the job of designing interventions like carbon taxes and determining how such interventions will affect the energy choices of households and firms.

**Macroeconomics** is the study of the economy as a whole. Macroeconomists study economy-wide phenomena, like the growth rate of a country's total economic output, the percentage increase in overall prices (the inflation rate), or the fraction of the labor force that is looking for work but cannot find a job (the unemployment rate). Macroeconomists design government policies that improve overall, or "aggregate," economic performance.

For example, macroeconomists try to identify the best policies for stimulating an economy that is experiencing a sustained period of negative growth—in other words, an economy in recession. During the 2007–2009 financial crisis, when housing prices were plummeting and banks were failing, macroeconomists had their hands full. It was their job to explain why the economy was contracting and to recommend policies that would bring it back to life.

## 1.2 Three Principles of Economics

You now have a sense of what economics is about. But you might be wondering what distinguishes it from the other social sciences, including anthropology, history, political science, psychology, and sociology. All social sciences study human behavior, so what sets economics apart?

**Optimization** means picking the best feasible option, given whatever (limited) information, knowledge, experience, and training the economic agent has. Economists believe that economic agents try to optimize but sometimes make mistakes.

> People make choices that are motivated by calculations of benefits and costs.

**Equilibrium** is the special situation in which everyone is simultaneously optimizing, so nobody would benefit personally by changing his or her own behavior, given the choices of others.

**Empiricism** is analysis that uses data—evidence-based analysis. Economists use data to develop theories, to test theories, to evaluate the success of different government policies, and to determine what is causing things to happen in the world.

Economists emphasize three key concepts.

**1. Optimization:** We have explained economics as the study of people's choices. The study of all human choices may initially seem like an impossibly huge and diverse topic. At first glance, your decision to log on to Facebook tonight does not appear to have much in common with a corporate executive's decision to build a $500 million laptop factory in China. However, economists have identified some powerful concepts that unify the enormous range of choices that economic agents make. One such insight is that most choices are tied together by the concept of *optimization*: picking the best feasible option. Economists do *not* believe that people actually do pick the best feasible option. Rather, economists believe that people *try* to pick the best feasible option. People don't always succeed in optimizing—we are not calculating machines—but people generally try to optimize. There is a great deal of discussion among economists about how well people optimize, a discussion that we will return to in Chapter 2.

Optimization is the first principle of economics. Economists believe that people's goal of optimization—picking the best feasible option—explains most choices that people make, including minor decisions like accepting an invitation to see a movie and major decisions like deciding whom to marry. Of course, these decisions aren't made with a crystal ball. People often make mistakes, but they try to do as well as they can, given the limited information, knowledge, experience, and training that they have.

**2. Equilibrium:** The second principle of economics holds that economic systems tend to be in *equilibrium*, a situation in which no agent would benefit personally by changing his or her own behavior, given the choices of others. The economic system is in equilibrium when each agent cannot do any better by picking another course of action. In other words, equilibrium is a situation in which everyone is simultaneously optimizing.

**3. Empiricism:** The third principle of economics is an emphasis on *empiricism*—evidence-based analysis. In other words, analysis that uses data. Economists use data to develop theories, to test theories, to evaluate the success of different government policies, and to determine what is causing things to happen in the world.

1.1

1.2

1.3

1.4

1.5

1.6

## 1.3 The First Principle of Economics: Optimization

Let's now consider our first principle in more detail. Economics is the study of choices, and economists have a leading theory about how choices are made. Economists believe that people try to optimize, meaning that economic agents try to choose the best feasible option, given whatever (limited) information, knowledge, experience, and training the economic agents have. Feasible options are those that are available and affordable to an economic agent. If you have $10 in your wallet and no credit/debit/ATM cards, then a $5 burrito is a feasible dinner option, while a $50 lobster is not.

The concept of feasibility goes beyond the financial budget of the agent. Many different constraints can determine what is feasible. For instance, it is not feasible to work more than 24 hours in a day. It is not feasible to attend meetings (in person) in New York and Beijing at the same time.

> In the cases where agents make mistakes, normative economic analysis can help them realize their mistakes and make better choices in the future.

Any decision can depend only on the information available at the time of the choice. For example, if you choose to drive from San Diego to Los Angeles and your car is hit by a drunk driver, you are unlucky, but you haven't necessarily failed to optimize. Optimization means that you weigh the information that you have, not that you perfectly foresee the future. When someone chooses the best feasible option *given the information that is available*, economists say that the decision maker is being rational or, equivalently, that he or she is exhibiting rationality. Rational action does not require a crystal ball, just a logical appraisal of the costs, benefits, and risks that are known to the economic agent.

However, if you decide to let a friend drive you from San Diego to Los Angeles and you know that your friend has just had a few beers, this is likely a case in which you are not choosing the best feasible option. Again, evaluating the rationality of a decision means examining the quality of your initial decision, not the outcome. Even if you and your drunk driver arrive at your destination without a crash, your choice to let your friend drive is still a suboptimal choice. Fortunately, you got lucky despite making a bad decision.

We devote much of this book to the analysis of optimization. We explain how to choose the best feasible option, and we discuss some evidence that supports the theory that economic agents often do choose the best feasible option (or something close to it). We also discuss important cases where people fail to choose the best feasible option. In cases where agents make mistakes, prescriptive economic analysis can help them realize their mistakes and make better choices in the future.

Finally, it is important to note that *what* we optimize varies from person to person and group to group. Most firms try to maximize profits, but most individual people are not trying to maximize their personal income. If that were our goal, we'd all work far more than 40 hours per week and we'd keep working well past retirement age. Most households are trying to maximize their overall well-being, which involves a mix of income, leisure, health, and a host of other factors, like social networks and a sense of purpose in life. Most governments, meanwhile, are optimizing a complex mix of policy goals. For most economic agents, then, optimization is about much more than money.

## Trade-offs and Budget Constraints

An economic agent faces a **trade-off** when the agent needs to give up one thing to get something else.

A **budget constraint** shows the bundles of goods or services that a consumer can choose given her limited budget.

All optimization problems involve trade-offs. **Trade-offs** arise when some benefits must be given up in order to gain others. Think about Facebook. If you spend an hour on Facebook, then you cannot spend that hour doing other things. For example, you cannot work at most part-time jobs at the same time you are editing your Facebook profile.

Economists use budget constraints to describe trade-offs. A **budget constraint** is the set of things that a person can choose to do (or buy) without breaking her budget.

Here's an illustration. To keep the analysis simple, suppose that you can do only one of two activities with your free time: surf the Web or work at a part-time job. Suppose that you have 5 free hours in a day (once we take away necessities like sleeping, eating, bathing, attending classes, doing problem sets, and studying for exams). Think of these 5 free hours as your budget of free time. Then your budget constraint would be:

$$5 \text{ hours} = \text{Hours surfing the Web} + \text{Hours working at part-time job}.$$

This budget constraint equation implies that you face a trade-off. If you spend an extra hour surfing the Web, you need to spend one less hour working at a part-time job (unless you secretly use Facebook while you are being paid for a job—in this case, keep your boss off your friend list). Likewise, if you spend an extra hour working at the part-time job, you need to spend one less hour surfing the Web. More of one activity implies less of the other. We can see this in Exhibit 1.2, where we list all the ways that you could allocate your 5 free hours.

**Exhibit 1.2 Possible Allocations of 5 Free Hours (Round Numbers Only)**

Each row reports a different way that a person could allocate 5 free hours, assuming that the time must be divided between surfing the Web and working at a part-time job. To keep things simple, the table only reports allocations in round numbers.

| Budget | Hours Surfing the Web | Hours at Part-Time Job |
|--------|----------------------|------------------------|
| 5 hours | 0 hours | 5 hours |
| 5 hours | 1 hours | 4 hours |
| 5 hours | 2 hours | 3 hours |
| 5 hours | 3 hours | 2 hours |
| 5 hours | 4 hours | 1 hours |
| 5 hours | 5 hours | 0 hours |

Budget constraints are useful economic tools, because they quantify trade-offs. When economists talk about the choices that people make, the economist always takes into account the budget constraint. It's important to identify the feasible options and the trade-offs—the budget constraint gives us that information.

## Opportunity Cost

We are now ready to introduce another critical tool in the optimization toolbox: opportunity cost. Our Web surfing example provides an illustration of the concept. The time that we spend on the Web is time that we could have spent in some other way. In the illustrative example just discussed, the only two alternative activities were surfing the Web and working at a part-time job. But in real life, there are an enormous number of activities that might get squeezed out when you surf the Web—for instance, playing soccer, jogging, daydreaming, sleeping, calling a friend, catching up on e-mail, texting, or working on a problem set. You implicitly sacrifice time on some alternative activities when you spend time surfing the Web.

Generate your own list of alternative activities that are squeezed out when you surf the Web. Think about the best alternative to Web surfing, and put that at the top. Pause here and write that alternative activity down. Calling a friend? Studying for an exam? Going for a jog? What is your best alternative to an hour of Web surfing?

We face trade-offs whenever we allocate our time. When we do one thing, something else gets squeezed out. Joining the fencing team might mean dropping lacrosse. During exam week, an extra hour of sleep means one less hour spent studying or decompressing with friends. You can't write a term paper and update your Facebook page at the same moment. And postponement is not an escape hatch from this economic logic. For example, even if you only postpone writing that term paper, something has got to give when the paper deadline rolls around. (Perhaps studying for your economics final?)

Evaluating trade-offs can be difficult, because so many options are under consideration. Economists tend to focus on the *best* alternative activity. We refer to this best alternative activity as the **opportunity cost**. This is what an optimizer is effectively giving up when she allocates an hour of her time. Recall your own best alternative to surfing the Web. That's your opportunity cost of time online.

Here's another example to drive home the concept. Assume that your family is taking a vacation over spring break. Your choices are a Caribbean cruise, a trip to Miami, or a trip to Los Angeles. (Assume that they all have the same monetary cost and use the same amount of time.) If your first choice is the cruise and your *second* choice is Miami, then your opportunity cost of taking the cruise is the Miami trip.

The concept of opportunity cost applies to all trade-offs, not just your time budget of 24 hours each day. Suppose that a woodworker has a beautiful piece of maple that can be used to make a sculpture, a bowl, or a picture frame. (Assume that they all use the same amount of wood and take the same amount of time.) If the woodworker's first choice is the sculpture and the second choice is the bowl, then the bowl is the opportunity cost of making the sculpture.

**Assigning a Monetary Value to an Opportunity Cost**   Economists often try to put a monetary value on opportunity cost. One way to estimate the monetary value of an hour of your time is to analyze the consequences of taking a part-time job or working additional hours at the part-time job you already have.

The opportunity cost of an hour of your time is at least the value that you would receive from an hour of work at a job, assuming that you can find one that fits your schedule. Here's why. A part-time job is one item in the long list of alternatives to surfing the Web. If the part-time job is at the top of your list, then it's the best alternative, and the part-time job is your opportunity cost of surfing the Web. What if the part-time job is not at the top of your list, so it's not the best alternative? Then the best alternative is even better than the part-time job, so the best alternative is worth more than the part-time job. To sum up, your opportunity cost is either the value of a part-time job or a value that is even greater than that. To turn these insights into something quantitative, it helps to note that the median wage for U.S. workers between 16 and 24 years of age was $11.00 per hour in 2015—this statistic is from the U.S. Bureau of Labor Statistics. A job has many

**Opportunity cost** is the best alternative use of a resource.

attributes other than the wage you are paid: unpleasant tasks (like being nice to obnoxious customers), on-the-job training, friendly or unfriendly coworkers, and resume building, to name just a few.

If we ignore these non-wage attributes, the value of an hour of work is just the wage (minus taxes paid). However, if the positive and negative non-wage attributes don't cancel each other, the calculation is much harder. To keep things simple, we'll focus only on the after-tax wage in the analysis that follows—about $10 per hour for young workers—but we urge you to keep in mind all of the non-wage consequences that flow from a job.

## Cost-Benefit Analysis

Let's use opportunity cost to solve an optimization problem. Specifically, we want to compare a set of feasible alternatives and pick the best one. We call this process *cost-benefit analysis*. **Cost-benefit analysis** is a calculation that identifies the best option by summing benefits and subtracting costs, with both benefits and costs denominated in a common unit of measurement, like dollars. Cost-benefit analysis is used to identify the alternative that has the greatest **net benefit**, which is the sum of the benefits of choosing an alternative minus the sum of the costs of choosing that alternative.

To see these ideas in action, suppose that you and a friend are going to Miami Beach from Boston for spring break. The only question is whether you should drive or fly. Your friend argues that you should drive, because splitting the cost of a rental car and gas "will only cost $200 each." He tries to seal the deal by pointing out "that's much better than a $300 plane ticket."

To analyze this problem using cost-benefit analysis, you need to list all benefits and costs of driving compared to the alternative of flying. Here we'll express these benefits and costs comparatively, which means the benefits of driving compared to flying and the costs of driving compared to flying. We'll need to translate those benefits and costs into a common unit of measurement.

From a benefit perspective, driving saves you $100—the difference between driving expenses of $200 and a plane ticket of $300. We sometimes refer to these direct costs as "out-of-pocket" costs. But out-of-pocket costs aren't the only thing to consider. Driving also costs you an extra 40 hours of time—the difference between 50 hours of round-trip driving time and about 10 hours of round-trip airport/flying time. Spending 40 extra hours traveling is a cost of driving, even if it isn't a direct out-of-pocket cost.

We're now ready to decide whether it is optimal to drive or fly to Florida. We need to express all benefits and costs in common units, which will be dollars for our example. Recall that driving will take an additional 40 hours of travel time. To complete the analysis, we must translate this time cost into dollars. To make this translation, we will use a $10 per hour opportunity cost of time. The net benefit of driving compared to flying is the *benefit* of driving minus the *cost* of driving:

$$(\$100 \text{ Reduction in out-of-pocket costs}) - (40 \text{ Hours of additional travel time}) \times (\$10/\text{hour})$$
$$= \$100 - \$400 = -\$300.$$

Hence, the net benefit of driving is overwhelmingly negative. An optimizer would choose to fly.

Your decision about travel to Miami is a simple example of cost-benefit analysis, which is a great tool for collapsing all sorts of things down to a single number: a dollar-denominated net benefit. This book will guide you in making such calculations. When you are making almost any choice, cost-benefit analysis can help.

To an economist, cost-benefit analysis and optimization are the same thing. When you pick the option with the greatest net benefits, you are optimizing. So cost-benefit analysis is useful for *normative* economic analysis. It enables an economist to determine what an individual or a society should do. Cost-benefit analysis also yields many useful positive economic insights. In many cases, cost-benefit analysis correctly predicts the choices made by actual consumers.

# EVIDENCE-BASED ECONOMICS

1.1

1.2

1.3

1.4

1.5

1.6

## Q: Is Facebook free?

We can now turn to the question posed at the beginning of the chapter. By now you know that Facebook has an opportunity cost—the best alternative use of your time. We now estimate this cost. To do this, we're going to need some data. Whenever you see a section in this textbook titled "Evidence-Based Economics," you'll know that we are using data to analyze an economic question.

In 2016, Web users worldwide spent over 500 million hours on Facebook each day. On a per person basis, each of the over 1.7 billion Facebook users allocated an average of 20 minutes per day to the site.[2] College students used Facebook more intensively; the average college student spends about an hour per day on Facebook.

We estimate that the time spent worldwide on Facebook has an *average* opportunity cost of $5 per hour. We generated this estimate with a back-of-the-envelope—in other words, approximate—calculation that averages together all Facebook users' opportunity costs.

Here's how we did the calculation. First, we assume that users in the developed world—which represents wealthy countries, such as France, Japan, Singapore, and the United States—have an opportunity cost of $9 per hour, which is a typical minimum wage in a developed country. For example, the minimum wages in France and the United States are $12 per hour and $7.25 per hour, respectively. Employers are legally required to pay at least the minimum wage, and most workers in developed countries get paid much more than this. Even people who choose not to work still value their time, since it can be used for lots of good things like napping, texting, dating, studying, playing Angry Birds, and watching movies. It's reasonable to guess that these nonworkers—for instance, students—will also have an opportunity cost of at least the minimum wage.

In the developing world, which represents all countries other than the developed ones, the calculations get a bit trickier. These countries have much lower minimum wages, minimum wages that aren't enforced, or no minimum wage at all. For example, the minimum wage in China varies by region and averages just under $1 per hour. For the purposes of this analysis, we assume that Facebook users in developing countries have an opportunity cost of $1 per hour, reflecting less favorable employment opportunities than those in the developed world.

About half of Facebook users live in developed countries and half live in developing countries, so, given our assumptions, the average opportunity cost is $(1/2) \times \$9 + (1/2) \times \$1 = \$5$ per hour. Accordingly, the *total* opportunity cost of time spent on Facebook is calculated by multiplying the total number of hours spent on Facebook each day by the average opportunity cost of time per hour:

$$\left( \frac{500 \text{ million hours}}{\text{day}} \right) \left( \frac{\$5}{\text{hour}} \right) = \left( \frac{\$2.5 \text{ billion}}{\text{day}} \right).$$

Multiplying this by 365 days per year yields an annualized opportunity cost of over $900 billion. This is an estimate of the cost of Facebook. As you have seen, this is only a crude approximation, since we can't directly observe the opportunity cost of each person's time.

We can also think about this calculation another way. If people had substituted their time on Facebook for work with average pay of $5 per hour, the world economy would have produced about $900 billion more of measured output in 2016. This is more than the annual economic output of Austria.

Finally, we can also estimate the opportunity cost of a typical U.S. college student who spends 1 hour per day on Facebook. Assuming that this student's opportunity cost is equal to $10 per hour, the opportunity cost is $3,650 per year.

$$( \$10/\text{hour}) \times (365 \text{ hours/year}) = \$3,650 \text{ per year.}$$

We chose $10 per hour for the opportunity cost, since the median before-tax wage of 16- to 24-year-old U.S. workers was $11 per hour in 2015, and such low-income workers don't pay much in taxes.

So far, we have gone through a purely positive economic analysis, describing the frequency of Facebook usage and the trade-offs that this usage implies. None of this analysis, however, answers the related question: Are Facebook users optimizing? We've seen that the time spent on sites like Facebook is costly, because it has valuable alternative uses (see Exhibit 1.3). But Facebook users are deriving substantial benefits that may justify this allocation of time. For example, social networking sites keep us up-to-date on the activities of our friends and family. They facilitate the formation of new friendships and new connections. And Facebook and similar sites are entertaining.

Because we cannot easily quantify these benefits, we're going to leave that analysis to you. Economists won't tell you what to do, but we will help you identify the trade-offs that you are making in your decisions. Here is how an economist would summarize the normative issues that are on the table:

Assuming a $10 per hour opportunity cost, the opportunity cost of using Facebook for an hour per day is $3,650 per year. Do you receive benefits from Facebook that exceed this opportunity cost? If the benefits that you receive are less than $3,650, you should scale down your Facebook usage.

Economists don't want to impose their tastes on other people. In the view of an economist, people who get big benefits from intensive use of Facebook should stay the course. However, we do want economic agents to recognize the implicit trade-offs that are being made. Economists are interested in helping people make the best use of scarce

| | Cost per unit | Number of units | Total cost |
|---|---|---|---|
| Starbucks cappuccino | $4 | 52 cups | $208 |
| iPhone | $400 | 1 | $400 |
| Round trip: NYC to Paris | $1,000 | 1 | $1,000 |
| Hotel in Paris | $250 | 4 nights | $1,000 |
| Round trip: NYC to U.S. Virgin Islands | $300 | 1 | $300 |
| Hotel in Virgin Islands | $180 | 4 nights | $720 |
| Eleven iPhone apps | $2 | 11 | $22 |
| **Total** | | | **$3,650** |

**Exhibit 1.3 What Could You Buy with $3,650?**

Everyone would choose to spend $3,650 in their own particular way. This list illustrates one feasible basket of goods and services. Note that this list includes just the monetary costs of these items. A complete economic analysis would also include the opportunity cost of the time that you would need to consume them.

resources like budgets of money and leisure time. In many circumstances, people are already putting their resources to best use. Occasionally, however, economic reasoning can help people make better choices.

|  Question |  Answer |  Data |  Caveat |
|---|---|---|---|
| Is Facebook free? | No. The opportunity cost of Facebook was over $900 billion dollars in 2016. | Facebook usage statistics provided by Facebook. Minimum wage data from around the world. | We can only crudely estimate the opportunity cost for Facebook's 1.7 billion worldwide users. |

# 1.4 The Second Principle of Economics: Equilibrium

In most economic situations, you aren't the only one trying to optimize. Other people's behavior will influence what you decide to do. Economists think of the world as a large number of economic agents who are interacting and influencing one another's efforts at optimization. Recall that *equilibrium* is the special situation in which everyone is optimizing, so nobody would benefit personally by changing his or her own behavior.

An important clarification needs to accompany this definition. When we say that nobody would benefit personally by changing his or her own behavior, we mean that nobody *believes* he or she would benefit from such a change. In equilibrium, all economic agents are making their best feasible choices, taking into account all of the information they have, including their beliefs about the behavior of others. We could rewrite the definition by saying that in equilibrium, nobody perceives that they will benefit from changing their own behavior.

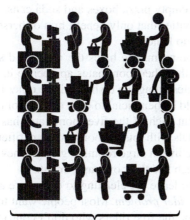 

In equilibrium        Out of equilibrium

In equilibrium, everyone is simultaneously optimizing, so nobody would benefit by changing his or her own behavior.

To build intuition—which means understanding—for the concept of equilibrium, consider the length of the regular checkout lines at your local supermarket (ignore the express lines). If any line has a shorter wait than the others, optimizers will choose that line. If any line has a longer wait than the others, optimizers will avoid that line. So the short lines will attract shoppers, and the long lines will drive them away. And it's not just the length of the lines that matters. You pick your line by estimating which line will move the fastest, an estimate that incorporates everything you can see, including the number of items in each person's shopping cart. Sometimes, you might end up waiting longer because of twists you didn't anticipate: a customer who takes five minutes to find the right change, or someone with a sea of tiny items at the bottom of his cart. Still, economists say that "in equilibrium," all checkout lines will have roughly the same wait time. When the wait times are expected to be the same, no shopper has an incentive to switch lines. In other words, nobody perceives that they will benefit by changing their behavior.

Here's another example. Suppose the market price of gasoline is $2 per gallon and the gasoline market is in equilibrium. Three conditions will need to be satisfied:

1. The amount of gasoline produced by gasoline sellers—oil companies—will equal the amount of gasoline purchased by buyers.
2. Oil companies will only operate wells where they can extract oil and produce gasoline at a cost that is less than the market price of gasoline: $2 per gallon.
3. The buyers of gasoline will only use it for activities that are worth at least $2 per gallon—like driving to their best friend's wedding—and they won't use it for activities that are worth less than $2 per gallon.

In equilibrium, both the sellers and the buyers of gasoline are optimizing, given the market price of gasoline. Nobody would benefit by changing his or her own behavior.

Notice that we've started to think about what happens when many economic agents interact. This could be two chess players, thirty participants in an eBay auction, millions of investors buying and selling shares on the New York Stock Exchange, or billions of households buying gasoline to fuel their tractors, trucks, mopeds, motorcycles, and cars. In all these cases, we assume that everyone is constantly simultaneously optimizing—for instance, at every move in a chess game and during every trade on the New York Stock Exchange. Combined, these choices produce an equilibrium—and economists believe that this kind of equilibrium analysis provides a good description of what actually happens when many people interact.

### The Free-Rider Problem

Let's use the concept of equilibrium to analyze an economic problem that may interest you: roommates. Assume that five roommates live in a rented house. Each roommate can spend some of his or her time contributing to the general well-being of all the roommates by throwing away empty pizza boxes and soda cans. Or each roommate can spend all his or her time on activities that only benefit him or herself—for instance, watching YouTube videos or listening to Pandora.

Imagine that one roommate hates the mess, and starts spending time cleaning up the kitchen. Although the other roommates appreciate it, they have no incentive to chip in! If he spends 30 minutes doing the dishes, all the other roommates benefit without having to lift a finger. It would be beneficial to each of the roommates if everyone chipped in and did a little cleaning. But each of the five roommates has an incentive to leave that to others. Consequently, rentals with lots of roommates are often a mess. The *equilibrium* prediction is that when people live in large rooming groups, they will have messier apartments than if the same people each had their own apartment.

Roommates who leave the cleaning to others are an example of something that economists call the *free-rider problem*. Most people want to let someone else do the dirty work. We would like to be the free riders who don't contribute but still benefit from the investments that others make.

Sometimes free riders get away with it. When there are few free riders and lots of contributors, the free riders might be overlooked. For example, a small number of people sneak onto public transportation without paying. These turnstile jumpers are so rare that they

A free rider in the New York subway system. Are you paying for him to ride the subway?

don't jeopardize the subway system. But if everyone started jumping turnstiles, the subway would soon run out of cash.

In the subway system, free riding is discouraged by security patrols. In rooming groups, free riding is discouraged by social pressure. Even with these "punishment" techniques, free riding is sometimes a problem, because it's not easy to catch the free rider in the act. It's possible to slip over a turnstile in a quiet subway station. It's easy to leave crumbs on the couch when nobody is watching.

People's private benefits are sometimes out of sync with the public interest. Jumping the subway turnstile is cheaper than paying for a subway ticket. Watching YouTube is more fun than sweeping up the remains of last night's party. Equilibrium analysis helps us predict the behavior of interacting economic agents and understand why free riding occurs. People sometimes pursue their own private interests and don't contribute voluntarily to the public interest. Unfortunately, selfless acts—like those of a war hero—are exceptional, and selfish acts are more common. When people interact, each individual might do what's best for himself or herself instead of acting in a way that optimizes the well-being of society.

Equilibrium analysis helps us design special institutions—like financial contracts—that reduce or even eliminate free riding. For example, what would happen in the rooming group if everyone agreed to pay $5 per week so the roommates could hire a cleaning service? It would be easier to enforce $5 weekly payments than to monitor compliance with the rule "clean up after yourself, even when nobody is here to watch you." Pizza crumbs don't have identity tags. So equilibrium analysis explains why individuals sometimes fail to serve the interest of society and how the incentive structure can be redesigned to fix these problems.

# 1.5 The Third Principle of Economics: Empiricism

Economists test their ideas with data. We refer to such evidence-based analysis as empirical analysis or *empiricism*. Economists use data to determine whether our theories about human behavior—like optimization and equilibrium—match up with actual human behavior. Of course, we want to know if our theories fail to explain what is happening in the world. In that case, we need to go back to the drawing board and come up with better theories. That is how economic science, and science in general, progresses.

Economists are also interested in understanding what is *causing* things to happen in the world. We can illustrate what causation is—and is not—via a simple example. Hot days and crowded beaches tend to occur at the same time of the year. What is the cause and what is the effect here? It is, of course, that high temperatures cause people to go swimming. It is not that swimming causes the outside air temperature to rise.

But there are some cases when cause and effect are hard to untangle. Does being relatively smart cause people to go to college, or does going to college cause people to be relatively smart? Perhaps both directions of causation apply. Or perhaps some other factor plays the causal role—for instance, a love for reading might cause people to become smarter *and* cause them to go to college.

We'll come back to the topic of empiricism in general, and causality in particular, in great detail in Chapter 2. Sometimes causes are easy to determine, but sometimes identifying cause and effect requires great ingenuity.

1.1
1.2
1.3
1.4
1.5
1.6

# 1.6 Is Economics Good for You?

Should you take this course? Let's think about this using cost-benefit analysis.

Let's begin by assuming that you've already chosen to go to college. So we can assume that tuition costs and room and board are *sunk costs* (they won't be affected by your decision to take economics). With those costs accounted for, are there any other costs associated with this course? The key opportunity cost of this course is another course that you won't be able to take during your time spent as a student. What other course did economics crowd out? Japanese history? Biochemistry? Russian poetry? If you are taking the two-semester version of this course, then you need to consider the two other courses that economics is crowding out.

> **Learning to make good choices is the biggest benefit you'll realize from learning economics.**

Now consider the benefits of an economics education. The benefits come in a few different forms, but the biggest benefit is the ability to apply economic reasoning in your daily life. Whether you are deciding where to go on vacation or how to keep an apartment with four other roommates clean, economic reasoning will improve the quality of your decisions. These benefits will continue throughout your life as you make important decisions, such as where to invest your retirement savings and how to secure the best mortgage.

Most decisions are guided by the logic of costs and benefits. Accordingly, you can use positive economic analysis to predict other people's behavior. Economics illuminates and clarifies all human behavior.

We also want you to use economic principles when you give other people advice and when you make your own choices. This is normative economics. Learning how to make good choices is the biggest benefit you'll realize from learning economics. That's why we have built our book around the concept of decision making. Looking at the world through the economic lens puts you at an enormous advantage throughout your life.

We also think that economics is a lot of fun. Understanding people's motivations is fascinating, particularly because there are many surprising insights along the way.

To realize these payoffs, you'll need to connect the ideas in this textbook to the economic activities around you. To make those connections, keep a few tips in mind:

- You can apply economic tools, such as trade-offs and cost-benefit analysis, to any economic decision, so learn to use them in your own daily decisions. This will help you master the tools and also appreciate their limitations.
- Even if you are not in the midst of making a decision, you will learn a lot of economics by keeping your eyes open when you walk through any environment in which people are using or exchanging resources. Think like an economist the next time you find yourself in a supermarket or at a used-car dealership, a soccer match, or a poker game.
- The easiest way to encounter economic ideas is to keep up with what's happening in the world. Go online and read a national newspaper like the *New York Times* or *The Wall Street Journal*. News magazines will also do the job. There's even a newsmagazine called *The Economist*, which is required reading for prime ministers and presidents. Almost every page of any magazine—including *People*, *Sports Illustrated*, and *Vogue*—describes events driven by economic factors. Identifying and understanding these forces will be a challenge. Over time, though, you'll find that it gets easy to recognize and interpret the economic story behind every headline.

Once you realize that you are constantly making economic choices, you'll understand that this course is only a first step. You'll discover the most important applications outside class and after the final exam. The tools of economics will improve your performance in all kinds of situations—making you a better businessperson, a better consumer, and a better citizen. Keep your eyes open and remember that every choice is economics in action.

## Summary

- Economics is the study of how agents choose to allocate scarce resources and how those choices affect society. Economics can be divided into two kinds of analysis: positive economic analysis (what people actually do) and normative economic analysis (what people ought to do). There are two key topics in economics: microeconomics (individual decisions and individual markets) and macroeconomics (the total economy).

- Economics is based on three key principles: optimization, equilibrium, and empiricism.

- Choosing the best feasible option, given the available information, is called optimization. To optimize, an economic agent needs to consider many issues, including trade-offs, budget constraints, opportunity costs, and cost-benefit analysis.

- Equilibrium is a situation in which nobody would benefit personally by changing his or her own behavior, given the choices of others.

- Economists test their ideas with data. We call such evidence-based analysis empirical analysis or empiricism. Economists use data to determine whether our theories about human behavior—like optimization and equilibrium—match actual human behavior. Economists also use data to determine what is causing things to happen in the world.

## Key Terms

economic agent *p. 3*
scarce resources *p. 4*
scarcity *p. 4*
economics *p. 4*
positive economics *p. 5*
normative economics *p. 5*

microeconomics *p. 6*
macroeconomics *p. 6*
optimization *p. 7*
equilibrium *p. 7*
empiricism *p. 7*
trade-off *p. 8*

budget constraint *p. 8*
opportunity cost *p. 9*
cost-benefit analysis *p. 10*
net benefit *p. 10*

## Questions

*All questions are available in MyEconLab for practice and instructor assignment.*

1. Why do we have to pay a price for most of the goods we consume?

2. Many people believe that the study of economics is focused on money and financial markets. Based on your reading of the chapter, how would you define economics?

3. Examine the following statements and determine whether they are normative or positive in nature. Explain your answers.

   a. Car sales in Europe rose 9.3 percent from 2014 to 2015.

   b. The U.S. government should increase carbon taxes to reduce carbon emissions that cause global warming.

4. How does microeconomics differ from macroeconomics? Would the supply of iPhones in the United States be studied under microeconomics or macroeconomics? What about the growth rate of total economic output in the national economy?

5. What does a budget constraint represent? How do budget constraints explain the trade-offs that consumers face?

6. This chapter introduced the idea of opportunity cost.

   a. What is meant by opportunity cost?

   b. What is the opportunity cost of taking a year after graduating from high school and backpacking across Europe? Are people who do this being irrational?

7. The costs of many environmental regulations can be calculated in dollars—for instance, the cost of "scrubbers" that reduce the amount of air pollution emitted by a coal factory. The benefits of environmental regulations often are most directly expressed in terms of lives saved (reduced mortality) or decreases in the incidence of a particular disease (reduced morbidity). What does this imply about the cost-benefit analysis of environmental regulations? There is an old saying "You can't put a price on a human life." Do you agree or disagree? Explain.

8. Suppose the market price of corn is $3.50 per bushel. What are the three conditions that will need to be satisfied for the corn market to be in equilibrium at this price?

9. Economists are often concerned with the free-rider problem.

   a. What is meant by free riding? Explain with an example.

   b. Explain why dropping trash on a city street is an example of the free-rider problem.

10. Explain the concept of causation with the help of a simple real-life example.

11. Identify cause and effect in the following examples:

    a. A rise in the worldwide price of peaches and a drought in California;

    b. A surge in cocoa prices and a pest attack on the cocoa crop.

# Problems

*All problems are available in MyEconLab for practice and instructor assignment.*

1. You have already purchased (non-refundable and unsellable) tickets to a concert on Friday night. A friend also invites you to her birthday party on Friday. While you like your friend, you politely decline because you really want to go to the concert.

   a. You learn that your friend is serving flank steak at her party, all-you-can eat and at no charge. Flank steak is your favorite food. Should this affect your decision to go to the concert? Explain by using the term "opportunity cost."

   b. Suppose instead that you notice that the non-refundable concert ticket (that you already purchased) cost you $10; previously you had mistakenly believed the price was $100. Should learning this information affect your decision to go to the concert?

2. You are thinking about buying a house. You find one you like that costs $200,000. You learn that your bank will give you a mortgage for $160,000 and that you will have to use all of your savings to make the down payment of $40,000. You calculate that the mortgage payments, property taxes, insurance, maintenance, and utilities would total $950 per month. Is $950 the cost of owning the house? What important factor(s) have you left out of your calculation of the cost of ownership?

3. You have 40,000 frequent flier miles. You could exchange your miles for a round-trip ticket to Bermuda over spring break. Does that mean your flight to Bermuda would be free? Explain your reasoning.

4. You have decided that you are going to consume 600 calories of beer and snacks at a party Saturday night. A beer has 150 calories and a snack has 75 calories.

   a. Create a table that shows the various combinations of beer and snacks you can consume. To keep things simple, use only round numbers (for example, you could choose 1 or 2 beers but not 1.5 beers).

   b. What is the opportunity cost of a beer?

5. Suppose you are ready to check out and see two lines: Line A has 3 people, while line B has 5 people.

   a. Assume people just chose lines at random and have not yet had a chance to switch lines. Would you consider this situation to be in equilibrium? Why or why not?

   b. Assume that all 8 shoppers are optimizing (i.e., they have had a chance to switch), and that the situation is in equilibrium. What conclusions would you draw?

   c. Of all 8 shoppers, whose behavior is the most informative?

6. Consider the following three statements:

   a. You can either stand during a college football game or you can sit. You believe that you will see the game very well if you stand and others sit but that you will not be able to see at all if you sit and others stand. You therefore decide to stand.

   b. Your friend tells you that he expects many people to stand at football games.

   c. An economist studies photos of many college football games and estimates that 75 percent of all fans stand and 25 percent sit.

   Which of these statements deals with optimization, which deals with equilibrium, and which deals with empiricism? Explain.

7. In 2014, California was in its third year of a major drought. With water supplies dwindling, Governor Brown issued a plea for a voluntary 20 percent reduction in water use. This target was not reached. In early 2015 Governor Brown issued an executive order requiring local water agencies to reduce water use by 25 percent, but no enforcement mechanism was specified. No taxes or fines were in the executive order. State officials hoped that they could achieve compliance without resorting to fines.[3]

   a. From an individual homeowner's perspective, what are the costs and benefits of using water during a drought? Why do you think that the voluntary reduction order in 2014 didn't work?

   **b.** Using concepts from this chapter, explain how you might get individual homeowners to reduce water use during a drought.

   **c.** Eventually, many communities began levying fines on water use. However, while many middle income families dramatically cut water use, wealthy households cut back their water use relatively little.[4] How can you explain this phenomenon from an economic perspective?

**8.** An economist observes that many students spend $100,000 to go to college. This researcher could ask whether such spending is worth it, or she could *assume* that it is worth it. In other words, she could *assume* that students are optimizing and that the education system is in equilibrium. If we assume that students are optimizing, what can the economist conclude about the value of a college education?

**9.** It is the night before your economics final exam and you must decide how many hours to study. The total benefits in the following table shows how many more points you will earn because of increased knowledge. The total cost column shows how many points you will lose because of careless errors due to lack of sleep. (The "marginal" columns show the effect of each additional hour spent studying. These marginal numbers are calculated by taking the difference within a column from one row to the next row.)

| Hours Spent Studying | Total Benefit | Marginal Benefit | Total Cost | Marginal Cost |
|---|---|---|---|---|
| 0 | 0 | – | 0 | – |
| 1 | 10 | 10 | 0 | 0 |
| 2 | 16 | 6 | 3 | 3 |
| 3 | 20 | 4 | 8 | 5 |
| 4 | 20 | 0 | 15 | 7 |

   **a.** If you study in an optimal way, how many points will you earn on the test?

   **b.** Explain how you can find the optimal number of hours for which you should study by using the marginal benefits and marginal costs columns.

# 2 Economic Methods and Economic Questions

## Is college worth it?

If you are reading this book, there is a good chance that you are either in college or thinking about taking the plunge. As you know, college is a big investment. During the 2015–2016 academic year, tuition averaged $3,435 for community colleges, $9,410 for in-state public colleges, $23,893 for out-of-state public colleges, and $32,405 for nonprofit private colleges.[1] And that's not the only cost. Your time, as we have seen, is worth $10 or more per hour—this time value adds at least $15,000 per year to the opportunity cost of a college education.

Why sit in class, then, when you could travel the world or earn money at a job? As with any other investment, you'd like to know how a college education is going to pay you back. What are the "returns to education," and how would you measure them? In this chapter, you'll see that you can answer such questions with models and data.

## CHAPTER OUTLINE

## 2.1 The Scientific Method

In Chapter 1, we explored optimization and equilibrium, the first two principles of economics. Now, to better tie those concepts to the "real world," we turn to the third principle: empiricism.

Empiricism—using data to analyze the world—is at the heart of all scientific analysis. The **scientific method** is the name for the ongoing process that economists, other social scientists, and natural scientists use to:

1. Develop models of the world
2. Evaluate those models by testing them with data

Testing models with data enables economists to separate the good models—those that make predictions that are mostly consistent with the data—from the bad models. When a model is overwhelmingly inconsistent with the data, economists try to fix the model or replace it altogether. By cycling through the two steps—developing models and then testing them—economists can move toward models that better explain the past and even partially predict the future. Given the complexity of the world, we do not expect this process to generate a perfect model—we'll never be able to precisely predict the future! However, economists do expect to identify models that are useful in understanding the world. In this section, we explain what a model is and how it can be tested with data.

### Models and Data

Before the discoveries of the ancient Greek philosophers, everyone believed that the earth was flat. We now know that it is more like a beach ball than a Frisbee. Yet a flat-earth *model* is still actively used. Ask for directions from Google Maps, and you'll be using maps of a flattened planet. For driving directions, nobody keeps a globe in the glove compartment.

Flat maps and spherical globes are both models of the surface of the earth. A **model** is a simplified description of reality. Sometimes economists will refer to a model as a *theory*. These terms are usually used interchangeably.

Because models are simplified, they are not perfect replicas of reality. Obviously, flat maps are not perfectly accurate models of the surface of the earth—they distort the curvature. If you are flying from New York to Tokyo, the curvature matters. But if you are touring around New York City, you don't need to worry about the fact that the earth is shaped like a sphere.

Scientists—and commuters—use the model that is best suited to analyzing the problem at hand. Even if a model/map is based on assumptions that are known to be false, like the flatness of the earth, the model may still help us to make good predictions and good plans for the future. It is more important for a model to be simple and useful than it is for the model to be precisely accurate.

The **scientific method** is the name for the ongoing process that economists and other scientists use to (1) develop models of the world and (2) evaluate those models by testing them with data.

A **model** is a simplified description of reality. Sometimes economists will refer to a model as a *theory*. These terms are usually used interchangeably.

Scientific models are used to make predictions that can be checked with empirical evidence.

**Exhibit 2.1 Flying from New York to Tokyo Requires More Than a Flat Map**

This flat map is a model of part of the earth's surface. It treats the world as perfectly flat, which leads the map maker to exaggerate distances in the northern latitudes. It is useful for certain purposes—for instance, learning geography. But you wouldn't want to use it to find the best air route across the Pacific Ocean. For example, the shortest flight path from New York to Tokyo is not a straight line through San Francisco. Instead, the shortest path goes through Northern Alaska! The flat-earth model is well suited for some tasks (geography lessons) and ill-suited for others (intercontinental flight navigation).

**Exhibit 2.2 New York City Subway Map**

This is a model of the subway system in New York City. It is highly simplified—for example, it treats New York City as a perfectly flat surface, and it also distorts the shape of the city—but it is nevertheless very useful for commuters and tourists.

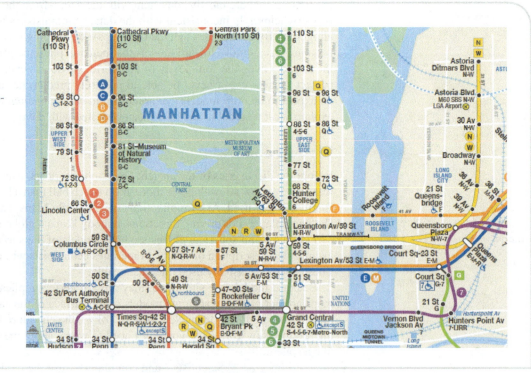

**Empirical evidence** consists of facts that are obtained through observation and measurement. Empirical evidence is also called **data**.

Scientific models are used to make predictions that can be checked with **empirical evidence**—in other words, facts that are obtained through observation and measurement. We also refer to empirical evidence as **data**. Recall from Chapter 1 that economists often describe themselves as empiricists, or say that we practice empiricism, because we use empirical evidence. Empiricists use data to answer questions about the world and to test models. For example, we could test the New York City subway map by actually riding the subway and checking the map's accuracy.

When conducting empirical analyses, economists refer to a model's predictions as **hypotheses**. Whenever such hypotheses are contradicted by the available data, economists return to the drawing board and try to come up with a better model that yields new hypotheses.

**Hypotheses** are predictions (typically generated by a model) that can be tested with data.

## An Economic Model

Let's consider an example of an economic model. We're going to study an extremely simple model to get the ball rolling. But even economic models that are far more complicated than this example are also simplified descriptions of reality.

All models begin with assumptions. Consider the following assumption about the returns to education: *each additional year of education causes your future wages to rise by 10 percent*. Let's put the assumption to work to generate a model that relates a person's level of education to her wages.

Increasing a wage by 10 percent is the same as multiplying the wage by $(1 + 0.10) = 1.10$. Thus, the returns-to-education assumption implies that someone with an extra year of education earns 1.10 times as much as she would have earned without the extra year of education. For example, if someone earns \$15 per hour with 13 years of education, then we predict that a 14th year of education will cause her hourly wage to rise to $1.10 \times \$15$, or \$16.50.

Economists use assumptions to derive other implications. For example, the returns-to-education assumption implies that 2 additional years of education will increase earnings by 10 percent twice over—once for each extra year of education—producing a 21 percent total increase:

$$1.10 \times 1.10 = 1.21.$$

Consider another example. Four additional years of education will increase earnings by 10 percent four times over, implying a 46 percent total increase:

$$1.10 \times 1.10 \times 1.10 \times 1.10 = (1.10)^4 = 1.46.$$

This implies that going to college would increase a college graduate's income by 46 percent compared to what she would have been paid if she had ended her education after finishing high school. In other words, a prediction—or hypothesis—of the model is that college graduates will earn 46 percent more than high school graduates.

In principle, we can apply this analysis to any number of years of education. We therefore have a general model that relates people's educational attainment to their income. The model that we have derived is referred to as the returns-to-education model. It describes the economic payoff of more education—in other words, the return on your educational investment. Most economic models are much, much more complex than this. In most economic models, it takes pages of mathematical analysis to derive the implications of the assumptions. Nevertheless, this simple model is a good starting point for our discussion. It illustrates two important properties of all models.

First, economists know that *a model is only an approximation* and accordingly understand that the model is not exactly correct. Taken literally, the model implies that each person would increase their future wages by exactly 10 percent if they obtained an extra year of education, but this precise prediction is surely false. For example, the final year of college does much more to increase your wages than the second-to-last year of college because that final year earns you the official degree, which is a key line on your resume. Likewise, your college major importantly impacts how much you will earn after college. Those who major in economics, for example, tend to earn more than graduates in most other majors. Our simple model overlooks such distinctions. Just as a flat subway map is only an approximation of the features of a city, the returns-to-education model is only an approximation of the mapping from years of education to wages. The model's predicted relationship between education and wages is a simplification that overlooks lots of special considerations.

Second, *a model makes predictions that can be tested with data*—in this case, data on people's education and earnings. We are now ready to use some data to actually evaluate the predictions of the returns-to-education model.

# EVIDENCE-BASED ECONOMICS

## Q: How much more do workers with a college education earn?

To put the model to the test we need data, which we obtain from the 2014 Current Population Survey, a government data source. This survey collects anonymized data on earnings, education, and many other characteristics of the general population and is available to anyone who wants to use it. When data are available to the general public, they are called "public-use data."

Exhibit 2.3 summarizes the average annual earnings for our test. The returns-to-education model does not match the data perfectly. The exhibit shows that for 30-year-old U.S. workers with 12 years of education, which is equivalent to a high school diploma, average annual earnings are $32,912. For 30-year-old U.S. workers with 16 years of education, which is equivalent to graduation from a 4-year college, average annual earnings are $51,215.

If we simply divide these two average wages—college wage over high school wage—the ratio is 1.56:

$$\frac{\text{Average annual earnings of 30-year-olds with 16 years of education}}{\text{Average annual earnings of 30-year-olds with 12 years of education}} = \frac{\$51,215}{\$32,912} = 1.56.$$

Recall that the returns-to-education model says that each additional year of education raises the wage by 10 percent, so 4 extra years of education should raise the wage by a factor of $(1.10)^4 = 1.46$.

We can see that the model does not exactly match the data. Going from 12 years of education to 16 years is associated with a 56 percent increase in income. However, the model is not far off—the model predicted a 46 percent increase.

**Exhibit 2.3** Average Annual Earnings of 30-Year-Old Americans by Education Level (2014 Data)

People who stop going to school after obtaining their high school diplomas have average annual earnings of $32,912, whereas those who stop going to school after obtaining a 4-year college degree earn $51,215.

Source: 2014 Current Population Survey.

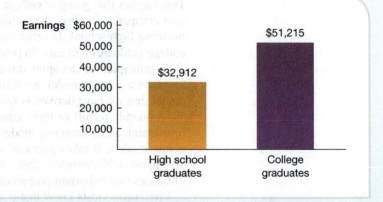

### Question

How much more do workers with a 4-year college education earn compared to workers with a high school degree?

### Answer

Average earnings for a college graduate are 56 percent higher than average earnings for a high school graduate.

### Data

Wages from the Current Population Survey (2014). Compare average wages for 30-year-old workers with different levels of education.

### Caveat

These are averages for a large population of individuals. Each individual's experience will differ.

## Means and Medians

2.1

You may wonder how the data from the Current Population Survey were used to calculate the wages reported above. We used the concept of the *mean*, or *average*. The **mean** (or **average**) is the sum of all the different values divided by the number of values and is a commonly used technique for summarizing data. Statisticians and other scientists use the terms *mean* and *average* interchangeably.

The **mean** (or **average**) is the sum of all the different values divided by the number of values.

We can quickly show how the mean works in a small example. Say that there are five people: Mr. Kwon, Ms. Littleton, Mr. Locke, Ms. Reye, and Ms. Shephard, each with a different hourly wage:

$$Kwon = \$26 \text{ per hour,}$$
$$Littleton = \$24 \text{ per hour,}$$
$$Locke = \$8 \text{ per hour,}$$
$$Reye = \$35 \text{ per hour,}$$
$$Shephard = \$57 \text{ per hour.}$$

If we add the five wages together and divide by 5, we calculate a mean wage of $30 per hour:

$$\frac{\$26 + \$24 + \$8 + \$35 + \$57}{5} = \$30.$$

In addition to calculating the mean value of a group (or "set") of numbers, scientists also frequently calculate the median value of the numbers, which is the "middle" value of the group. Specifically, the **median** value is calculated by ordering the numbers from least to greatest and then finding the value halfway through the list. For example, ordering the data that we just analyzed produces the list: $8, $24, $26, $35, $57. The middle value—the median—is $26. (When there are an even number of items in the list, the median is the midpoint between the two middle values. So the median of the numbers $8, $24, $26, and $35 is the midpoint between $24 and $26: $25.)

The **median** value is calculated by ordering the numbers from least to greatest and then finding the value half-way through the list.

Summing up, the median is the value in the middle of a group of numbers, and the mean is the average value of the group of numbers. When the group of numbers has one or more extreme values, the median and the mean pull apart. For example, suppose that Shephard is extremely highly paid—she might be a corporate lawyer—with an hourly wage of $257 (instead of the original value of $57 per hour). Then the group mean rises to $70 per hour, but the median doesn't change at all: $26 per hour is still the middle wage. Hence, the mean is affected by outliers, which are extreme numbers that are dissimilar to the rest of the numbers in the list, whereas the median is not affected by outliers.

This analysis of a small sample—only five people—illustrates the concepts of means and medians, but convincing data analysis in economics relies on using a large sample. For example, a typical economic research paper uses data gathered from thousands of individuals. So a key strength of economic analysis is the amount of data used. When we showed that education raises earnings, we didn't rely on a handful of *observations*—economists call each piece of data an "observation." Instead, we used data from thousands of surveyed 30-year-olds. Using lots of observations strengthens the force of an empirical argument, because the researcher can make more precise statements.

To show you how to make convincing empirical arguments, this course uses lots of real data from large groups of people. Credible empirical arguments, based on many observations, are a key component of the scientific method.

## Argument by Anecdote

Education is not destiny. There are some people with lots of education who earn very little, and there are some people with little education who earn a lot. When we wrote this book, Bill Gates, a Harvard dropout who founded Microsoft, was the richest person in the world. Mark Zuckerberg, the Facebook CEO, also dropped out of Harvard.

With these two examples in mind, it might be tempting to conclude that dropping out of college is a great path to success. However, it is a mistake to use two anecdotes, or any small sample of people, to try to judge a statistical relationship.

If you study two randomly chosen 30-year-olds, there is almost a one-third chance that the person with only a high school diploma has higher earnings than the one with a 4-year college degree. This fact highlights that there is much more than education that determines your earnings, although getting a college degree will usually help make you money.

When you look at only a small amount of data, it is easy to jump to the wrong conclusion. Keep this warning in mind the next time a newspaper columnist tries to sway you with a few anecdotes. If the columnist backs up her story with data reflecting the experiences of thousands of people, then she has done her job and may deserve to win the argument. But if she rests her case after sharing a handful of anecdotes, remain skeptical. Be doubly skeptical if you suspect that the anecdotes have been carefully selected to prove the columnist's point. Argument by anecdote should not be taken seriously.

There is one exception to this rule. Argument by example is appropriate when you are contradicting a *blanket* statement. For example, if someone asserts that every National Basketball Association (NBA) player has to be tall, just one counterexample is enough to prove this statement wrong. In this case, your proof would be Tyrone "Muggsy" Bogues, a 5-foot 3-inch (133-pound) dynamo who played point guard in the NBA for 15 seasons.

## 2.2 Causation and Correlation

Unfortunately, even reporting that relies on *large* data sets can be misleading. Consider our returns-to-schooling example. Using our large data set on wages and years of education, we've seen that on average, wages rise roughly 10 percent for every year of additional education. Does that mean that staying in school one more year will cause *your* future wages to rise by 10 percent? Not necessarily. Let's think about why this is not always the case with an example.

### The Red Ad Blues

Imagine a department has hired you as a consultant. You have developed a hypothesis about ad campaigns: you believe that campaigns using the color red are good at catching people's attention. To test your hypothesis, you assemble empirical evidence from historical ad campaigns, including the color of the ad campaign and how revenue at the store changed during the campaign.

Your empirical research confirms your hypothesis! Sales go up 25 percent during campaigns with lots of red images and only 5 percent during campaigns with lots of blue images. You race to the chief executive officer (CEO) to report this remarkable result. You are a genius! Unfortunately, the CEO instantly fires you.

What did the CEO notice that you missed?

The red-themed campaigns were mostly concentrated during the Christmas season. The blue-themed campaigns were mostly spread out over the rest of the year. In the CEO's words,

> The red colors in our advertising don't cause an increase in our revenue. Christmas causes an increase in our revenue. Christmas also causes an increase in the use of red in our ads. If we ran blue ads in December, our holiday season revenue would still rise by about 25 percent.

Unfortunately, this is actually a true story, though we've changed the details—including the name of the firm—to protect our friends. We return, in the appendix, to a related story in which the CEO was not as sharp as the CEO in this story.

### Causation versus Correlation

**Causation** occurs when one thing directly affects another.

As in the misguided ad analysis, people often mistake *correlation* for *causation*. **Causation** occurs when one thing directly affects another. You can think of it as the path from cause to effect: turning on the stove *causes* the water in the kettle to boil.

A **variable** is a changing factor or characteristic.

Scientists refer to a changing factor or characteristic, like the temperature of water in a tea kettle, as a **variable**. Scientists say that causation occurs when one variable (for instance, the volume of natural gas burning on a stovetop) causes another variable (the temperature of water in a tea kettle) to change.

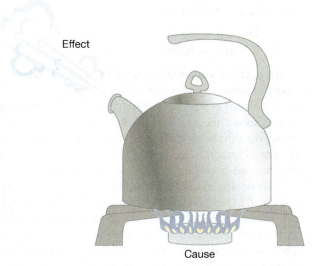

Effect

Cause

From cause to effect.

Does jogging cause people to be healthy? Does good health cause people to jog? In fact, both kinds of causation are simultaneously true.

> **Think of causation as the path from cause to effect.**

**Correlation** means that two variables tend to change at the same time.

**Correlation** means that two variables tend to change at the same time—as one variable changes, the other changes as well. There is some kind of connection. It *might* be cause and effect, but correlation can also arise when causation is not present. For example, students who take music classes score better on their SATs than students who do not take music classes. Some music educators have happily jumped to the conclusion that this relationship is causal: more music causes higher SAT scores.

But don't buy a clarinet for your younger sibling just yet. There is scant evidence of a causal relationship, and there are many alternative explanations for the correlation between music lessons and high SAT scores. Maybe the students who play musical instruments have high levels of general patience, which explains why they thrive in long musical practice sessions *and* why they perform better in school (including studying for the SATs). Maybe students with high levels of general intelligence find musical instruments more appealing, and their intelligence also tends to raise their SAT scores. Maybe the students who play musical instruments tend to have wealthier parents who can pay for tutors that raise their kids' SAT scores.

When two variables are correlated, it suggests that causation may be possible and that further investigation is warranted—it's only the beginning of the story, not the end. Interestingly, when researchers have tried to document a *causal* link from music lessons to higher cognitive ability, they have almost always failed.[2] Accordingly, if a trombone player lost her trombone and dropped out of music class, this would not cause her future SAT scores to fall. Can you think of other situations in which correlation is confused with causality?

Correlations are divided into three categories: *positive correlation*, *negative correlation*, and *zero correlation*. **Positive correlation** implies that two variables tend to move in the same direction—for example, surveys reveal that people who have a relatively high income are more likely to be married than people who have a relatively low income. In this situation, we say that the variables of income and marital status are positively correlated. **Negative correlation** implies that the two variables tend to move in opposite directions—for example, people with a high level of education are less likely to be unemployed. In this situation, we say that the variables of education and unemployment are negatively

**Positive correlation** implies that two variables tend to move in the same direction.

**Negative correlation** implies that two variables tend to move in opposite directions.

When the variables have movements that are not related, we say that the variables have **zero correlation**.

correlated. When two variables are not related, we say that they have a **zero correlation**. The number of friends you have likely has no relation to whether your address is on the odd or even side of the street.

### When Correlation Does Not Imply Causality

There are two main reasons we should not jump to the conclusion that a correlation between two variables implies a particular causal relationship:

1. Omitted variables
2. Reverse causality

An **omitted variable** is something that has been left out of a study that, if included, would explain why two variables that are in the study are correlated.

An **omitted variable** is something that has been left out of a study that, if included, would explain why two variables are correlated. Recall that the amount of red content in the store's ads is positively correlated with the growth rate of their sales. However, the red color does not necessarily cause the store's sales to rise. The arrival of the Christmas season causes both the store's ads to be red and month-over-month sales revenue to rise. Thus, the Christmas season is an omitted variable that explains why red ads tend to occur at around the time that sales tend to rise. (See Exhibit 2.4.)

Is there also an omitted variable that explains why education and income are positively correlated? One possible factor might be an individual's tendency to work hard. What if workaholics tend to thrive in college more than others? Perhaps pulling all-nighters to write term papers allows them to do well in their courses, encouraging them to stay in school. These same tendencies would also allow workaholics to earn more money than others—by staying late on the job, for example, or working on weekends. Does workaholism cause you to earn more and, incidentally, to graduate from college rather than drop out? Or does staying in college cause you to earn those higher wages? What is cause and what is effect?

**Reverse causality** occurs when we mix up the direction of cause and effect.

**Reverse causality** is another problem that plagues our efforts to distinguish correlation and causation. Reverse causality occurs when we mix up the direction of cause and effect. For example, consider the fact that relatively wealthy people tend to be relatively healthy, too. This has led some social scientists to conclude that greater wealth causes better health—because, for instance, wealthy people can afford better healthcare. However, this could be a case of reverse causality: better health may cause greater wealth. For example, healthy people can work harder and have fewer healthcare expenditures than less healthy people. It turns out that both causal channels seem to exist: greater wealth causes better health and better health causes greater wealth!

In our analysis of the returns to education, could it be that reverse causality is at play? That is, could higher wages at age 30 cause you to get more education at age 20? We can logically rule this out. Assuming that you don't have a time machine, it is unlikely that your wage as a 30-year-old causes you to obtain more education in your 20s. So in the returns-to-education example, reverse causality is probably not a problem. But in many other analyses—for example, the wealth-health relationship—reverse causality is a key consideration.

### Exhibit 2.4 An Example of an Omitted Variable

The amount of red content in the store's ads is positively correlated with the growth of the store's revenue. In other words, when ads are red themed, the store's month-over-month sales revenue tends to grow the fastest. However, the redness does not cause the store's revenue to rise. The Christmas season causes the store's ads to be red and the Christmas season also causes the store's sales revenue to rise. The Christmas season is the omitted variable that explains the positive correlation between red ads and revenue growth.

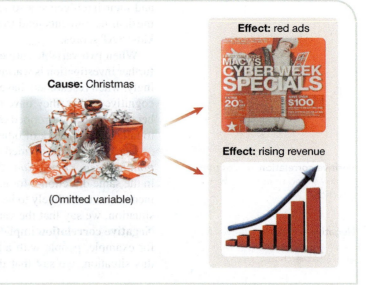

Cause: Christmas

(Omitted variable)

Effect: red ads

Effect: rising revenue

# CHOICE & CONSEQUENCE

## Spend Now and Pay Later?

In a recent paper, two economists, Andrew Francis and Hugo Mialon, used U.S. survey data to calculate the empirical relationship between wedding spending and rates of divorce.[3] They found that more spending on a wedding ceremony or the engagement ring predicts a higher rate of divorce (holding other factors constant). For example, in their sample of women whose weddings cost more than $20,000, the annual likelihood of divorce is 3.5 times higher compared to women whose weddings cost between $5,000 and $10,000.

That's an entertaining piece of empirical evidence. Does this prove that the key to a long marriage is a small wedding, or better yet, an elopement? Does spending more on a wedding actually cause the couple to divorce? Or are there omitted variables at work? What omitted variables might cause people to have fancy weddings and also cause them to end up divorced? Vanity? Pride? Materialism?

Or perhaps expensive weddings create financial strains for the newlyweds, and these strains might cause divorce. So there *might* be a causal path from wedding expenses to divorce rates.

In fact, the authors of this paper aren't claiming to prove that expensive weddings cause divorce. They understand that correlation need not imply causation. With complex examples like this in mind, can we ever determine what is correlation and what is actually causation? Economists have developed a rich set of tools for identifying cause and effect. We turn to some of these tools next.

Do expensive weddings cause divorce? Or is something else going on?

## Experimental Economics and Natural Experiments

An **experiment** is a controlled method of investigating causal relationships among variables.

One method of determining cause and effect is to run an **experiment**—a controlled method of investigating causal relationships among variables. Though you may not read much about economic experiments in the newspaper, headlines for experiments in the field of medicine are common. For example, the Food and Drug Administration requires pharmaceutical companies to run carefully designed experiments to provide evidence that new drugs work before they are approved for use by the general public.

To run an experiment, researchers usually create a treatment (test) group and a control group. Participants are assigned randomly to participate either as a member of the treatment group or as a member of the control group, which is not treated in a special way. **Randomization** is the assignment of subjects by chance, rather than by choice, to a treatment group or to a control group. The treatment group and the control group are treated identically, except along a single dimension that is intentionally varied across the two groups. Ultimately, the purpose of the experiment is to determine the impact of this variation.

**Randomization** is the assignment of subjects by chance, rather than by choice, to a treatment group or a control group.

If we want to know whether a promising new medicine helps patients with diabetes, we could take 1,000 patients with diabetes and randomly place 500 of them into a treatment group—those who receive the new medicine. The other 500 patients would be in the control group and receive the standard diabetes medication that is already widely used. Then we would follow all of the patients and monitor their health changes over the next few years. This experiment would test the causal hypothesis that the new drug is better than the old drug.

Now, consider an economics experiment. Suppose that we want to know what difference a college degree makes. We could take 1,000 high school students who cannot afford college but would like to attend college (if it were free) and randomly place 500 of them into a treatment group, where they had all their college expenses paid. The other 500 students would be placed in the control group. Then we would keep track of all of the original 1,000 students—including the 500 control-group students who weren't able to go to college because they couldn't afford it. We would use periodic surveys during their adult lives to see how the wages in the group that got a college education compare with the wages of the group that did not attend college. This experiment would test the hypothesis that a college education causes wages to rise.

One problem with experimentation is that experiments can sometimes be very costly to conduct. For instance, the college-attendance experiment that we just described would cost tens of millions of dollars, because the researchers would need to pay the college fees for 500 students. Another problem is that experiments do not provide immediate answers to some important questions. For example, learning about how one more year of education affects wages over the entire working life would take many decades. Another problem is that experiments are sometimes run poorly. For example, if medical researchers do not truly randomize the assignment of patients to medical treatments, then the experiment may not teach us anything at all. For instance, if patients who go to cutting-edge research hospitals tend to be the ones who get prescribed the newest kind of diabetes medication, then we cannot identify causation; we don't know whether it was the medication or something else at the fancy hospitals that caused those patients to get better. In a well-designed experiment, randomization alone would determine who got the new medicine and who got the old medicine.

When research is badly designed, economists tend to be very skeptical of its conclusions. We say "garbage in, garbage out" to capture the idea that bad research methods invalidate a study's conclusions.

If we don't have the budget or time to run an experiment, how else can we identify cause and effect? One approach is to study historical data that has been generated by a natural *experiment*. A **natural experiment** is an empirical study in which some process—out of the control of the experimenter—has assigned subjects to control and treatment groups in a random or nearly random way. In many situations, natural experiments are literally the only kind of experiment that we have from which to draw a conclusion. For instance, generals don't randomly choose villages on which to drop bombs—if they did, they would be court martialed. But sometimes, random factors cause some villages to be bombed and other villages to be spared. Melissa Dell, an economist, has explored such a natural experiment to determine the effect of different bombing policies during the Vietnam War. Most natural experiments are far less ethically complex. In a moment, we'll discuss a natural experiment—in this case, a change in mandatory education laws—that led some kids to get an extra year of education.

Economists have found and exploited natural experiments to answer numerous major questions. This methodology can be useful for providing a more definitive answer to our question at hand: What are you getting from your education?

A **natural experiment** is an empirical study in which some process—out of the control of the experimenter—has assigned subjects to control and treatment groups in a random or nearly random way.

## EVIDENCE-BASED ECONOMICS

### Q: How much do wages increase when mandatory schooling laws force people to get an extra year of schooling?

**M**any decades ago, compulsory schooling laws were much more permissive, allowing teenagers to drop out well before they graduated from high school. Philip Oreopoulos studied a natural experiment that was created by a change in these compulsory schooling laws.[4] Oreopoulos looked at an educational reform in the United Kingdom in 1947 that increased the minimum school leaving age from 14 to 15. As a result of this change, the fraction of children dropping out of school by age 14 fell by 50 percentage points between 1946 and 1948.

In this way, those kids reaching age 14 before 1947 are a "control group" for those reaching age 14 after 1947. Oreopoulos found that the students who turned 14 in 1948 and were therefore compelled to stay in school one extra year earned 10 percent more on average than the students who turned 14 in 1946.

Natural experiments are a useful source of data in empirical economics. In many problems, they help us separate correlation from causation. Applied to the returns to education, they suggest that the correlation between years of education and higher income is not due to some omitted variable but reflects the causal influence of education. The returns-to-education model thus obtains strong confirmation from the data. Does a 10 percent return to each additional year of education increase your appetite for more years of schooling?

### Question
How much do wages increase when an individual is compelled by law to get an extra year of schooling?

### Answer
On average, wages rise by 10 percent when kids are compelled to stay in school an extra year.

### Data
United Kingdom General Household Survey. Compare kids in the United Kingdom who were allowed to drop out of school at age 14 with others who were compelled to stay in school an extra year due to changes in compulsory schooling laws.

### Caveat
Factors other than the change in the compulsory schooling laws might explain why the kids who were compelled to stay in school eventually earned more in the workforce (this is an example of an omitted variable).

## 2.3 Economic Questions and Answers

Economists like to think about our research as a process in which we pose and answer questions. We've already seen a couple of these questions. For example, in the current chapter, we asked, "How much do wages increase when mandatory schooling laws force people to get an extra year of schooling?" and in Chapter 1, we asked, "What is the opportunity cost of your time?"

Good questions come in many different forms. But the most exciting economic questions share two properties.

1. *Good economic questions address topics that are important to individual economic agents and/or to our society.* Economists tend to think about economic research as something that contributes to society's welfare. We try to pursue research that has general implications for human behavior or economic performance. For example, understanding the returns to education is important, because individuals invest significant resources to obtain an education. The United States spends nearly a tenth of its economic output on education—$1.5 trillion per year. It is useful to quantify the payoffs from all this investment. If the returns to education are very high, society may want to encourage even more educational investment. If the returns to education are low, we should share this important fact with students who are deciding whether or not to stay in school. Knowing the returns to education will help individuals and governments decide how much of their scarce resources to allocate to educational investment.

2. *Good economic questions can be answered.* In some other disciplines, posing a good question is enough. For example, philosophers believe that some of the most important questions don't have answers. In contrast, economists are primarily interested in questions that can be answered with enough hard work, careful reasoning, and empirical evidence.

Here are some of the economic questions that we discuss in this book. As you look over the set, you will see that these are mostly big questions with significant implications for you and for society as a whole. The rest of this book sets out to discover answers to these questions. We believe the journey will be exhilarating. Let's get started!

| Chapter | Questions |
|---|---|
| 1 | Is Facebook free? |
| 2 | How much more do workers with a college education earn? How much do wages increase when mandatory schooling laws force people to get an extra year of schooling? |
| 3 | How does location affect the rental cost of housing? |
| 4 | How much more gasoline would people buy if its price were lower? |
| 5 | Would a smoker quit the habit for $100 a month? |
| 6 | How would an ethanol subsidy affect ethanol producers? |
| 7 | Can markets composed of only self-interested people maximize the overall well-being of society? Do companies like Uber make use of the invisible hand? |
| 8 | Will free trade cause you to lose your job? What can the government do to lower the number of earthquakes in Oklahoma? |
| 9 | How can the Queen of England lower her commute time to Wembley Stadium? |
| 10 | What is the optimal size of government? |
| 11 | Is there discrimination in the labor market? |
| 12 | Can a monopoly ever be good for society? |
| 13 | Is there value in putting yourself into someone else's shoes? |
| 14 | How many firms are necessary to make a market competitive? |
| 15 | Do people exhibit a preference for immediate gratification? |
| 16 | Why do new cars lose considerable value the minute they are driven off the lot? Why is private health insurance so expensive? |
| 17 | How should you bid in an eBay auction? Who determines how the household spends its money? |
| 18 | Do people care about fairness? |
| Web Chapter 1 | Do investors chase historical returns? |
| Web Chapter 2 | What is the value of a human life? |
| Web Chapter 3 | Do governments and politicians follow their citizens' and constituencies' wishes? |

## Summary

- The scientific method is the name for the ongoing process that economists and other scientists use to (1) develop models of the world and (2) evaluate those models by testing them with data.

- Empirical evidence is facts that are obtained through observation and measurement. Empirical evidence is also called data.

- Economists try to uncover causal relationships among variables.

- One method used to determine causality is to run an experiment—a controlled method of investigating causal relationships among variables. Economists now actively pursue experiments both in the laboratory and in the field. Economists also determine causality by studying historical data that have been generated by a natural experiment.

# Key Terms

scientific method *p. 21*  
model *p. 21*  
empirical evidence (data) *p. 22*  
hypotheses *p. 23*  
mean (average) *p. 25*  
median *p. 25*  

causation *p. 26*  
variable *p. 27*  
correlation *p. 27*  
positive correlation *p. 27*  
negative correlation *p. 27*  
zero correlation *p. 28*  

omitted variable *p. 28*  
reverse causality *p. 28*  
experiment *p. 29*  
randomization *p. 29*  
natural experiment *p. 30*  

# Questions

*All questions are available in* MyEconLab *for practice and instructor assignment.*

1. What does it mean to say that economists use the scientific method? How do economists distinguish between models that work and those that don't?

2. What is meant by empiricism?

3. What are two important properties of economic models? Models are often simplified descriptions of a real-world phenomenon. Does this mean that they are unrealistic?

4. Suppose 5,000 people bought scoops of ice cream on a hot summer day. If the mean number of scoops bought is 2, how many total scoops were sold that day?

5. How does the sample size affect the validity of an empirical argument? When can only one example be enough to prove your point?

6. Explain why correlation does not always imply causation. Does causation always imply *positive* correlation? Explain your answer.

7. Give an example of a pair of variables that have a positive correlation, a pair of variables that have a negative correlation, and a pair of variables that have zero correlation.

8. What is meant by randomization? How does randomization affect the results of an experiment?

9. This chapter discussed natural and randomized experiments. How does a natural experiment differ from a randomized one?

10. Suppose you had to find the effect of seat belt rules on road accident fatalities. Would you choose to run a randomized experiment, or would it make sense to use natural experiments here? Explain.

# Problems

*All problems are available in* MyEconLab *for practice and instructor assignment.*

1. Although the mean and median are closely related, the difference between the mean and the median is sometimes of interest.

   a. Suppose country A has five families. Their incomes are $10,000, $20,000, $30,000, $40,000, and $50,000. What is the median family income in A? What is the mean income?

   b. Country B also has five families. Their incomes are $10,000, $20,000, $30,000, $40,000, and $150,000. What is the median family income in B? What is the mean income?

   c. In which country is income inequality greater, A or B?

   d. Suppose you thought income inequality in the United States had increased over time. Based on your answers to this question, would you expect the ratio of the mean income in the United States to the median income to have risen or fallen? Explain.

2. Consider the following situation: your math professor tells your class (of five students) that the mean score on

the final exam is 80 but the median is 100. How is that possible? Explain.

3. Suppose you come across a study that has discovered a correlation between reading books and life expectancy: People who read more books live longer. Come up with at least one plausible way that this correlation exists even though there is no direct causal link.

4. Some studies have found that people who owned guns were more likely to be killed with a gun. Do you think this study is strong evidence in favor of stricter gun control laws? Explain.

5. As the text explains, it can sometimes be very difficult to sort out the direction of causality.

   a. Why might you think that more police officers would lead to lower crime rates? Why might you think that higher crime rates would lead to more police officers?

   b. In 2012, the *New England Journal of Medicine* published research that showed a strong correlation between the consumption of chocolate in a country and the number of Nobel Prize winners in that country. Do you think countries that want to encourage their citizens to win Nobel Prizes should increase their consumption of chocolate?

c. A recent article in the *Journal of Applied Physiology* found that elderly runners had healthier muscles than a comparison group of the same age. Although the members of the comparison group were all still living independently, they had lower muscle mass and muscle strength than the athletes. The popular press framed the article as proof that exercise causes people to be healthier. Is that the only way to interpret causality in this example?

6. This chapter shows that in general, people with more education earn higher salaries. Economists have offered two explanations of this relationship. The human capital argument says that high schools and colleges teach people valuable skills, and employers are willing to pay higher salaries to attract people with those skills. The signaling argument says that college graduates earn more because a college degree is a signal to employers that a job applicant is diligent, intelligent, and persevering. How might you use data on people with 2, 3, and 4 years of college education to shed light on this controversy?

7. You decide to run an experiment. You invite 50 friends to a party. You randomly select 25 friends and tell them that there will be free food; most of them show up to your party. For the other 25 friends you do not mention the free food; none of these friends show up. Based on the correlation in your data, you conclude that free food causes people to come to parties. A buddy points out "be careful, correlation does not imply causation." How should you respond?

8. Oregon expanded its Medicaid coverage in 2008. Roughly 90,000 people applied, but the state had funds to cover only an additional 30,000 people (who were randomly chosen from the total applicant pool of 90,000). How could you use the Oregon experience to estimate the impact of increased access to healthcare on health outcomes?

9. A simple economic model predicts that a fall in the price of bus tickets means that more people will take the bus. However, you observe that some people still do not take the bus even after the price of a ticket fell.

a. Is the model incorrect?

b. How would you test this model?

# Appendix

# Constructing and Interpreting Charts and Graphs

As you start to learn economics, it's important that you have a good grasp of how to make sense of data and how to present data clearly in visible form. Graphs are everywhere—on TV, on the Web, in newspapers and magazines, in economics textbooks. Why are graphs so popular?

A well-designed graph summarizes a large amount of information—as the saying goes, "a picture is worth a thousand words." In this book, you will find many graphs, and you will see that they provide a way to supplement the verbal description of economic concepts.

> A well-designed graph summarizes a large amount of information—as the saying goes, "a picture is worth a thousand words."

Indeed, visualization can be extremely useful at every stage of economic analysis. As you'll see throughout this book, simple charts and graphs reveal the relationships between variables in a model. Charts and graphs make complicated databases more intuitive by giving the researchers a sense of important underlying properties in the data, like time trends. To demonstrate how data visualizations enhance economic analysis, we will walk you through a recent study that one of us—John List—co-authored, presenting data visualizations along the way.

## A Study about Incentives

Would you study harder for this economics class if we paid you $50 for earning an A? What if we raised the stakes to $500? Your first impulse might be to think "Well, sure . . . why not? That money could buy a new iPhone or maybe a ticket to a Nicki Minaj concert."

As we learned in Chapter 1, though, there are opportunity costs of studying more, such as attending fewer music concerts or spending less time at your favorite coffee house talking with friends. Such opportunity costs must be weighed against the benefits of earning an A in this course. You might conclude that because this question is hypothetical anyway, there's no need to think harder about how you would behave.

But what if the question weren't imaginary?

Over the past few years, thousands of students have actually been confronted with such a financial offer. Sally Sadoff, Steven Levitt, and John List carried out an experiment at two high schools in the suburbs of Chicago over several years in which they used incentives to change students' behavior. Such an experiment allows us to think about the relationship between two *variables*—in this case, how an increase in a financial reward affects student test scores. And it naturally leads to a discussion of cause and effect, which we have just studied in this chapter: we'll examine simple correlations between variables and identify a causal relationship. Both correlation and causation are powerful concepts in gaining an understanding of the world around us—and, as we'll see, data visualizations are crucial tools for this analysis.

## Experimental Design

There are two high schools in Chicago Heights, and both have a problem with student dropout rates. It is not uncommon for more than 50 percent of incoming ninth-graders to drop out before receiving a high school diploma. These problems are not unique to Chicago Heights; many urban school districts face a similar problem.

How can economists help? Some economists have devised incentive schemes to lower the dropout rates and increase academic achievement in schools. In this instance, students were *paid* for improved academic performance.[1]

Let's first consider the experiment to lower the dropout rate. Each student was randomly placed into one of the following three groups:

**Treatment Group with Student Incentives:** Students would receive $50 for each month they met special academic standards (explained below) established by the experimenters.

**Treatment Group with Parent Incentives:** Students' *parents* would receive $50 for each month the special academic standards were met by their child.

**Control Group:** Neither students nor parents received financial compensation linked to academic performance.

A student was deemed to have met the monthly standards if he or she:

1. did not have a D or an F in any classes during that month,
2. had no more than one unexcused absence during that month, and
3. had no suspensions during that month.

## Describing Variables

Before we discover how much money these students actually made, let's consider more carefully the variables that we might be interested in analyzing. As its name suggests, a variable is a factor that is likely to vary or change; that is, it can take different values in different situations. In this section, we show you how to use three different techniques to help graphically describe variables:

1. Pie charts
2. Bar charts
3. Time series graphs

### Pie Charts

> A **pie chart** is a circle split into slices of different sizes. The area of each slice represents the relative importance of non-overlapping parts that add up to the whole.

Understanding pie charts is a piece of cake. A **pie chart** is a circle split into slices of different sizes. The area of each slice represents the relative importance of non-overlapping parts that add up to the whole. Pie charts show how some economic variable can be divided into components that each represent a fraction of the total and that jointly add up to 100 percent.

For example, consider the ethnicity of the students in our experiment. In Exhibit 2A.1, we learn that 59 percent of ninth-graders in the study identify as African American. We therefore differentiate 59 percent of our pie chart with the color blue to represent the proportion of African-American participants in the study. We see that 15 percent of the students identify as non-Hispanic whites, represented by the red piece of the pie. We continue breaking down participation by ethnicity until we have filled in 100 percent of the circle. The circle then describes the ethnic composition of the participants in the study.

**Exhibit 2A.1 Chicago Heights Study Participants by Ethnicity**

The pie segments are a visual way to represent the fractions of all Chicago Heights high school students in the experiment that make up the four different ethnic categories. Just as the numbers add up to 100 percent, so do all of the segments add up to the complete "pie."

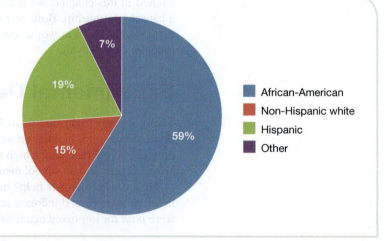

- African-American
- Non-Hispanic white
- Hispanic
- Other

## Bar Charts

A **bar chart** uses bars of different heights or lengths to indicate the properties of different groups.

Another type of graph that can be used to summarize and display a variable is a bar chart. A **bar chart** uses bars (no surprise there) of different heights or lengths to indicate the properties of different groups. Bar charts make it easy to compare a single variable across many groups. To make a bar chart, simply draw rectangles side by side, making each rectangle as high (or as long, in the case of horizontal bars) as the value of the variable it is describing.

For example, Exhibit 2A.2 captures the overall success rates of students in the various experimental groups. In the exhibit we have the **independent variable**—the variable that the experimenter is choosing (the treatment group or control group in the study to which each student is randomly assigned)—on the horizontal or *x*-axis. On the vertical or *y*-axis is the **dependent variable**—the variable that is potentially affected by the experimental treatment. In the exhibit, the dependent variable is the proportion of students meeting the academic standards. Note that 100 percent is a proportion of 1, and 30 percent is a proportion of 0.30.

An **independent variable** is a variable whose value does not depend on another variable; in an experiment it is manipulated by the experimenter.

A **dependent variable** is a variable whose value depends on another variable.

We find some interesting experimental results in Exhibit 2A.2. For instance, we can see from the bar chart that 25.1 percent of students in the Control group (students who received no incentives) met the academic standards. In comparison, 32.5 percent of students in the Parent Incentive group met the standards. This is a meaningful increase in the number of students meeting the standards—evidence that incentives can work.

## Time Series Graphs

A **time series graph** displays data at different points in time.

With pie charts and bar charts, we can summarize how a variable is broken up into different groups, but what if we want to understand how a variable changes over time? For instance, how did the proportion of students meeting the standards change over the school year? A **time series graph** can do the trick. A time series graph displays data at different points in time.

As an example, consider Exhibit 2A.3, which displays the proportion of students meeting the standards in each month in the Control and Parent Incentive groups. Keep in mind that although there are multiple months and groups, we are still measuring only a single variable—in this case, the proportion meeting the standard. As Exhibit 2A.3 makes clear, the number of students meeting the standard is higher in the Parent Incentive treatment group than in the Control group. But notice that the difference within the Parent Incentive and Control groups changes from month to month. Without a time series, we would not be able to appreciate these month-to-month differences and would not be able to get a sense for how the effectiveness of the incentive varies over the school year. As you read this book, keep in mind that the variables we discuss can change over time—and that time series graphs are invaluable in tracking these changes.

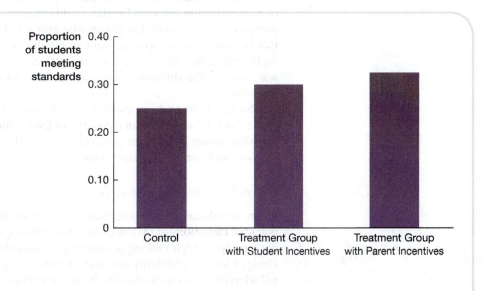

**Exhibit 2A.2 Proportion of Students Meeting Academic Standards by Experimental Group**

The bar chart facilitates comparing numbers across groups in the experiment. In this case, we can compare how different groups perform in terms of meeting academic standards by comparing the height of each bar. For example, the Parent Incentive group's bar is higher than the Control group's bar, meaning that a higher proportion of students in the Parent Incentives group met the standards than in the Control group.

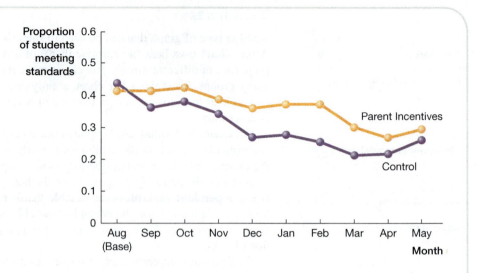

**Exhibit 2A.3 Participants Meeting All Standards by Month**

The time series graph takes some of the information that was in the bar chart and shows how it changes depending on the month of the school year during which the experiment was conducted. The points are connected to more clearly illustrate the month-to-month trend. In addition, by using a different color or line pattern, we can represent two groups (Control and Parent Incentives) on the same graph, giving the opportunity to compare the two groups, just as with the bar chart in the previous exhibit.

# Cause and Effect

We've written about both causation and correlation in this chapter. Economists are much more interested in the former. Causation relates two variables in an active way—*a* causes *b* if, because of *a*, *b* has occurred.

For example, we can conclude in our experimental study that paying money for the students' performance *causes* them to improve their academic performance. This would not necessarily be the case if the experiment were not properly implemented—for example, if students were not randomly placed into control and treatment groups. For instance, imagine that the experimenters had placed all of the students who had achieved poorly in the past in the control group. Then the relatively poor performance of the control group might be due to the composition of students who were assigned to the control group, and not to the lack of financial incentives. Any relationship between academic achievement and payment stemming from such an experiment could be interpreted as a correlation because all other things were not equal at the start of the experiment—the control group would have a higher proportion of low achievers than the other groups.

Fortunately, the Chicago Heights experiment was implemented using the principle of randomization discussed earlier in this chapter. The experimenters split students into groups randomly, so each experimental group had an equal representation of students—that is, attributes like average student intelligence were similar across groups. Accordingly, any difference between the groups' academic performance during the experiment was due to the different experimental conditions, such as differences in financial incentives.

This means that we can claim that the cause of the difference between the performance of the Student Incentive group and that of the Control group is that students in the Student Incentive group were given an incentive of $50, whereas students in the Control group received no incentive for improvement.

## Correlation Does Not Necessarily Imply Causality

Often, correlation is misinterpreted as causation. While correlation can certainly indicate potential causation—a reason to look more closely—it's only a first step. As an example, not long ago, a high-ranking marketing executive showed us Exhibit 2A.4 (the numbers are changed for confidentiality reasons). He was trying to demonstrate that his company's retail advertisements were effective in increasing sales: "It shows a clear positive relationship between ads and sales. When we placed 1,000 ads, sales were roughly $35 million. But see

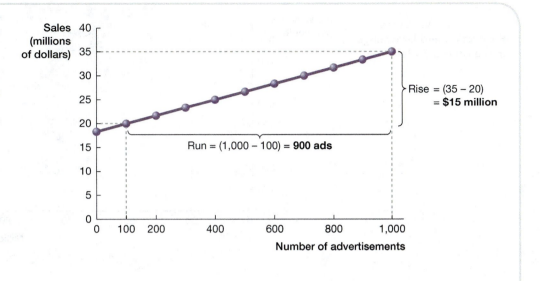

how sales dipped to roughly $20 million when we placed only 100 ads? This proves that more advertisements lead to more sales."

Before discussing whether this exhibit proves causality, let's step back and think about the basic characteristics of Exhibit 2A.4. In such an exhibit we have:

1. The *x*-variable plotted on the horizontal axis, or *x*-axis; in our figure the *x*-variable is the number of advertisements.
2. The *y*-variable plotted on the vertical axis, or *y*-axis; in our figure the *y*-variable is the sales in millions of dollars.
3. The origin, which is the point where the *x*-axis intersects the *y*-axis; both sales and the number of advertisements are equal to zero at the origin.

In the exhibit, the number of advertisements is the independent variable, and the amount of sales is the dependent variable. When the values of both variables increase together in the same direction, they have a positive relationship; when one increases and the other decreases, and they move in opposite directions, they have a negative relationship.

So in Exhibit 2A.4, we find a positive relationship between the two variables. What is the strength of that positive relationship? This is called the slope. The **slope** is the change in the value of the variable plotted on the *y*-axis divided by the change in the value of the variable plotted on the *x*-axis:

> The **slope** is the change in the value of the variable plotted on the *y*-axis divided by the change in the value of the variable plotted on the *x*-axis.

$$\text{Slope} = \frac{\text{Change in } y}{\text{Change in } x} = \frac{\text{Rise}}{\text{Run}}.$$

In this example, the increase in the number of advertisements from 100 to 1,000 was associated with an increase in sales from $20 million to $35 million. Thus, the rise, or the change in sales (*y*), is $15 million and the run, or change in *x*, is 900 ads. Because both are rising (moving in the same direction), the slope is positive:

$$\text{Slope} = \frac{\$35,000,000 \ - \ \$20,000,000}{1000 \text{ ads} \ - \ 100 \text{ ads}} = \frac{\$15,000,000}{900 \text{ ads}} = \$16,667 \text{ per ad.}$$

Thus, our exhibit implies that one more advertisement is associated with $16,667 more in sales. But, does this necessarily mean that if the retailer increases the number of advertisements by one, this will cause sales to increase by $16,667?

Unfortunately, no. While it is tempting to interpret the sales increasing with ads as a causal relationship between the two variables, we cannot be sure that this relationship is causal. In this case, the marketing executive forgot to think about *why* his company so drastically increased its advertisement volume to begin with—after all, the amount of advertising was not determined randomly in an experiment. As it turns out,

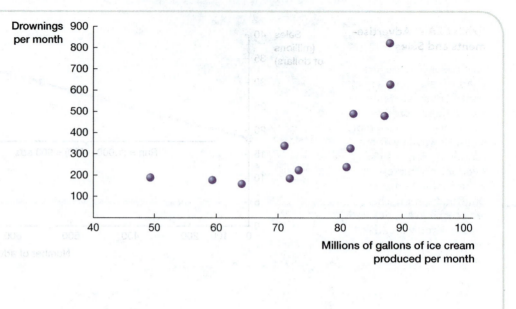

**Exhibit 2A.5** Ice Cream Production and Drownings in the United States

We depict the relationship between monthly ice cream production and monthly drownings. Each of the 12 points represents a single month in 2011. Is this relationship causal or is there an omitted variable that is causing these two variables to move together? Hint: the point in the upper right corner of the exhibit is July and the point in the lower left corner of the exhibit is December!

Sources: Based on Centers for Disease Control and Prevention, and Brian W. Gould, University of Wisconsin Dairy Marketing and Risk Management Program.

the company did so because of the holiday season, a time when sales would presumably have been high anyway.

So, after some further digging (we'll spare you the details), what the data actually say is that the retailer placed more ads during times of busy shopping (around Thanksgiving and in December), but that is exactly when sales would normally be high—because of the holiday shopping season. Similar to what happened in the department store red/blue ad example in this chapter, taking into account seasonal variation wipes out the causal relationship between ads and sales.

This example shows that you should be careful when you connect a few points in a graph. Just because two variables move together (a correlation), they are not necessarily related in a causal way. They could merely be linked by another variable that is causing them both to increase—in this case, the shopping season.

To see the general idea of what is happening more clearly, let's instead graph the quantity of ice cream produced against the number of monthly drownings in the United States. Using data across months in 2011, we constructed Exhibit 2A.5. In Exhibit 2A.5, we see that in months when ice cream production is relatively high, there are a lot of drownings. Likewise, in months when there is relatively little ice cream production, there are far fewer drownings. Does this mean that you should not swim after you eat ice cream?

Indeed, parents persuaded by such a chart might believe that it's causal, and never let their kids eat ice cream near swimming pools or lakes! But luckily for us ice cream lovers, there is an omitted variable lurking in the background. In the summertime, when it is hot, people eat more ice cream *and* swim more. More swimming leads to more drowning. Even though people eat more ice cream cones in the summer, eating ice cream doesn't *cause* people to drown.

Just as a heightened shopping season was the omitted variable in the retailer advertisement example, here the omitted variable is heat—it causes us to swim more *and* to eat more ice cream cones. While the former causes more drownings (as we would all expect), the latter has nothing to do with drowning, even though there is a positive correlation between the two, as shown in Exhibit 2A.5.

Beyond an understanding of how to construct data figures, we hope that this appendix gave you an appreciation for how to interpret visual displays of data. An important lesson is that just because two variables are correlated—and move together in a figure—does not mean that they are causally related. Causality is the gold standard in the social sciences. Without understanding the causal relationship between two variables, we cannot reliably predict how the world will change when the government intervenes to change one of the variables. Experiments help reveal causal relationships; for example, we learned from the Chicago Heights experiment that incentives can affect student performance.

# Appendix Key Terms

pie chart *p. 36*
bar chart *p. 37*

independent variable *p. 37*
dependent variable *p. 37*

time series graph *p. 37*
slope *p. 39*

# Appendix Problems

**A1.** How would you represent the following graphically?

    **a.** Income inequality in the United States has increased over the past 10 years.

    **b.** All the workers in the manufacturing sector in a particular country fit into one (and only one) of the following three categories: 31.5 percent are high school dropouts, 63.5 percent have a regular high school diploma, and the rest have a vocational training certificate.

    **c.** The median income of a household in Alabama was $43,464 in 2012, and the median income of a household in Connecticut was $64,247 in 2012.

**A2.** Consider the following data that show the quantity of coffee produced in Brazil from 2004 to 2012.

| Year | Production (in tons) |
|------|---------------------|
| 2004 | 2,465,710 |
| 2005 | 2,140,169 |
| 2006 | 2,573,368 |
| 2007 | 2,249,011 |
| 2008 | 2,796,927 |
| 2009 | 2,440,056 |
| 2010 | 2,907,265 |
| 2011 | 2,700,440 |
| 2012 | 3,037,534 |

    **a.** Plot the data in a time series graph.

    **b.** What is the mean quantity of coffee that Brazil produced from 2009 to 2011?

    **c.** In percentage terms, how much has the 2012 crop increased over the 2009–2011 mean?

**A3.** Suppose the following table shows the relationship between revenue that the Girl Scouts generate and the number of cookie boxes that they sell.

| Number of Cookie Boxes | Revenue |
|------------------------|---------|
| 50 | $200 |
| 150 | $600 |
| 250 | $1,000 |
| 350 | $1,400 |
| 450 | $1,800 |
| 550 | $2,200 |

    **a.** Present the data in a scatter plot.

    **b.** Do the two variables have a positive relationship or do they have a negative relationship? Explain.

    **c.** What is the slope of the line that you get in the scatter plot? What does the slope imply about the price of a box of Girl Scout cookies?

# 3 Optimization: Doing the Best You Can

## How does location affect the rental cost of housing?

Suppose you have just landed a job near the center of a city and you now need to decide where to live. If you live close to the city center, your round-trip commute will be 15 minutes. If you live in the distant suburbs, your round-trip commute will be 60 minutes. Where will the apartments be relatively less expensive? How will you choose where to live? How should you make the best decision given the trade-offs you face?

In this chapter, we'll dig into the concept of optimization—choosing the best feasible option. You will learn how to optimize by using cost-benefit analysis. And we will apply this knowledge to an example that we revisit throughout the chapter—choosing an apartment.

## CHAPTER OUTLINE

## 3.1 Optimization: Choosing the Best Feasible Option

In Chapter 1, we described economics as the study of choice. Economists usually assume that people make choices by trying to select the best feasible option, given the available information. In other words, people try to optimize. Recall that optimization is the first principle of economics.

Economists use optimization to predict most of the choices that people, households, businesses, and governments make. To an economist, seemingly unrelated decisions—for example, where a college student will travel on spring break, which apartment a worker will rent, or what price Apple charges for an iPhone—are all connected by the unifying principle of optimization. Whatever choices people face, economists believe that they will try to choose optimally. However, economists don't assume that people always *successfully* optimize—an issue that we will return to below.

**Economists use optimization to predict most of the choices that people, households, businesses, and governments make.**

Of course, optimization need not be easy, and optimization is often quite complex. To illustrate the complexity, consider the choice of an apartment. In large cities there are hundreds of thousands of rental apartments, each with different characteristics to consider, such as the number of bedrooms, location, views, and neighborhood amenities.

Making an optimal decision, then, involves juggling multiple trade-offs. For example, how do you compare two apartments, one of which has the benefit of lower rent and one of which has the benefit of a shorter commute? How would you determine which apartment is a better choice for you? In this chapter, we are going to see how to optimally evaluate such trade-offs. We introduce you to the most important optimization tools that economists use.

We have a lot to say about choosing a rental apartment, but remember that the choice of an apartment is just one illustration of the general concept of optimization. We can use the principal of optimization to analyze any decision that an economic agent faces, from the trivial—for instance, the choice of how many miles to jog in a workout—to the profound—how many years of education will you obtain?

Optimization can be implemented using many different techniques. In this chapter, we show you how to optimize using two different techniques, which yield *identical* answers. The first technique simply calculates the total value of each feasible option and then picks the option with the greatest total value. The second technique—*marginal analysis,* which we explain later in the chapter—focuses on differences among the feasible options and finds the best option by analyzing these differences. Because the two optimization techniques yield identical answers, you can decide to use whichever technique you find easier for each particular problem.

## CHOICE & CONSEQUENCE

### Do People Really Optimize?

With all of this talk about optimization, you might be wondering whether people actually do optimize. Do economic agents always pick the best feasible option? Of course not! So why do economists use optimization to predict their choices?

Economists believe that optimization is a useful approximation of some economic behavior, even if people don't *consistently* hit the optimization bull's-eye. Economists are interested in identifying situations in which optimization is a good approximation of behavior and those in which optimization is a bad approximation of behavior.

There is even a branch of economics that specializes in studying this question. **Behavioral economics** explains why people optimize in some situations and fail to optimize in others. Behavioral economists model this range of behavior by combining economic and psychological theories of human decision making.

Several special situations are associated with behavior that is not optimal. For example, when people have self-control problems—like procrastination, or, far worse, addiction—optimization is not a good description of behavior.

People also tend to fail as optimizers when they are new to a task. For instance, the first time individuals play poker, they tend to play poorly—they make rookie mistakes. Consequently, optimization is a better description of behavior when people have lots of experience. For example, as investors gain more years of experience, they tend to make fewer mistakes.

John Campbell, Tarun Ramadorai, and Benjamin Ranish documented this pattern of improving performance in a 2014 research paper. They obtained anonymized data that summarized the activity of 11.6 million investors in India. The researchers found that experienced investors (those with brokerage accounts that have been open a relatively long time) have annual returns that are on average 4.6 percentage points higher than those of their inexperienced peers.[1] The authors named their paper after the Beatles song "Getting Better" and began the paper with this lyric: "It is a little better all the time. (It can't get no worse.)"

Because people aren't born perfect optimizers, optimization is a useful skill to develop. Economists show people how to be better optimizers—such advice amounts to prescriptive economic analysis.

We hope that you use the concept of optimization in two ways: to describe the behavior of knowledgeable decision makers and to identify and improve suboptimal decisions—especially your own!

**Behavioral economics** jointly analyzes the economic and psychological factors that explain human behavior.

## 3.2 Optimization Application: Renting the Optimal Apartment

Let's explore the theory of optimization in more depth. To illustrate ideas, we return to our opening example, in which you are an apartment hunter.

Imagine that you have narrowed your rental choice to four possible apartments—your "short list." Exhibit 3.1 summarizes this short list, including two key pieces of information for each apartment—the monthly rent and the amount of commuting time per month. Exhibit 3.1 assumes that rent decreases the farther you are from work; as rent falls, commuting time increases, generating a trade-off. Later in this chapter, we explain why economic forces predict this inverse relationship between rent and distance from work. We'll also show you empirical evidence that confirms this prediction.

You might wonder about everything that was left out of the summary of information in Exhibit 3.1. What about other differences among these apartments, like how long it takes to walk to the neighborhood laundromat or whether there is a park nearby? We also omitted commuting costs other than time, like the direct dollar cost of public transportation or, if you drive yourself, gasoline and tolls. Shouldn't all these considerations be part of the comparison?

To keep things simple, we will omit other factors for now, even though they *are* important in practice. We omit them to keep the calculations simple and so that the basic economic concepts are easier to understand. As you'll discover in the problems at the end of

## Exhibit 3.1 Apartments on Your Short List, Which Differ Only with Regard to Commuting Time and Rent and Are Otherwise Identical

Many cities have a single central business district—which is often referred to as the city center—where lots of employers are concentrated. In most cities, apartments near the city center cost more to rent than otherwise identical apartments that are far away. Why is this so?

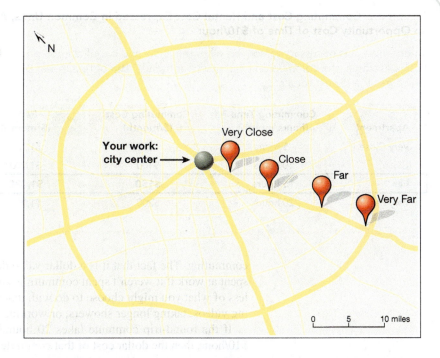

| Apartment | Commuting Time (hours/month) | Rent ($/month) |
|---|---|---|
| Very Close | 5 hours | $1,180 |
| Close | 10 hours | $1,090 |
| Far | 15 hours | $1,030 |
| Very Far | 20 hours | $1,000 |

The proximity of local amenities should also go into a complete optimization analysis, because these amenities change the net benefits of an apartment.

the chapter, once you understand the basic ideas, it is easy to add more details. For now, we will assume that the four apartments—Very Close, Close, Far, and Very Far—are identical except for the differences listed in Exhibit 3.1.

Note, too, that we are focusing only on costs in this example—the cost of commuting time and the cost of rent. We are assuming that the benefits of these apartments are the same—for instance, size or views. If the benefits are the same, then cost-benefit analysis becomes simpler. In normal cost-benefit analysis, the decision maker finds the alternative with the highest value of *net benefit*, which is benefit minus cost. When the benefits are the same across all the alternatives, cost-benefit analysis simplifies to finding the alternative with the lowest cost. That's what we are going to do next.

Exhibit 3.1 contains the information that we need, but, on its own, it does not enable us to choose the best apartment. First, we need to sum the cost of rent and the cost of commuting time to calculate the *total* cost of each apartment. The total cost includes the *direct* cost of rent and the *indirect* cost of commute time.

To sum these two costs, we first need to decide on a common unit of account. Let's pick dollars per month for now. Because rent is already expressed in dollars per month, half of our work has been done for us. All that remains is to translate the indirect cost—commuting time—into the same unit of measurement.

To do this, we use the concept of opportunity cost, which we introduced in Chapter 1. Let's begin by assuming that the opportunity cost of commuting time is $10/hour. This is the hourly value of the alternative activity that is crowded out when you spend more time

**Exhibit 3.2** Commuting Cost and Rental Cost Expressed in Common Units, Assuming an Opportunity Cost of Time of $10/hour

To optimize, it is necessary to convert all of the costs and benefits into common units. In this example, the common unit is dollars per month. The optimum—in bold—is Far, which has the lowest total cost.

| Apartment | Commuting Time (hours/month) | Commuting Cost ($/month) | Rent ($/month) | Total Cost: Rent + Commuting ($/month) |
|---|---|---|---|---|
| Very Close | 5 hours | $50 | $1,180 | $1,230 |
| Close | 10 hours | $100 | $1,090 | $1,190 |
| **Far** | **15 hours** | **$150** | **$1,030** | **$1,180** |
| Very Far | 20 hours | $200 | $1,000 | $1,200 |

commuting. The fact that it is a dollar value doesn't imply that this time would have been spent at work if it weren't spent commuting. An extra hour of time has value to you regardless of what you might choose to do with that time, including napping, socializing, watching videos, taking longer showers, or working.

If the round-trip commute takes 20 hours/month and the opportunity cost of time is $10/hour, then the dollar cost of that commute is

$$\left(\frac{20 \text{ hours}}{\text{month}}\right)\left(\frac{\$10}{\text{hour}}\right) = \left(\frac{\$200}{\text{month}}\right).$$

The first term on the left is commute time per month, which is expressed in hours per month, just as it is in Exhibit 3.1. The term just before the equal sign is the opportunity cost of time, which is expressed as dollars per hour. The "hours" units cancel, leaving a final cost expressed as dollars per month.

Now we are ready to rewrite Exhibit 3.1. Using the calculations that we just illustrated for 20 hours of monthly commuting time, we can calculate costs for a commute of any duration. Exhibit 3.2 reports this commuting cost in dollars per month for all four apartments.

Exhibit 3.2 gives us the answer to our optimization problem. "Far" is the best apartment for a consumer with an opportunity cost of time of $10/hour. This apartment has the lowest total cost—$1,180—taking into account both direct rental costs and indirect time costs of commuting.

We also easily see this result by plotting the total costs. Exhibit 3.3 plots the total cost of each of the four apartments—and, as the dip in the curve clearly shows, Far is the best choice.

**Exhibit 3.3** Total Cost Including Both Rent and Commuting Cost, Assuming an Opportunity Cost of Time of $10/hour

If the consumer chooses optimally, he or she will select Far. This apartment has the lowest total cost, which is the sum of the direct rental cost and the indirect commuting cost (see breakdown in Exhibit 3.2). The commuting cost is calculated by using the consumer's opportunity cost of time, which is $10/hour in this example.

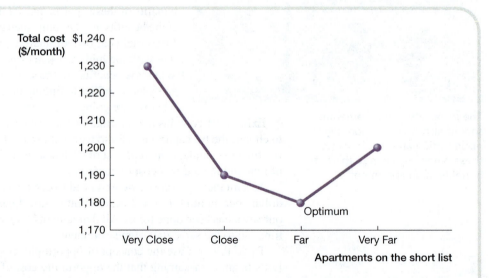

The **optimum** is the best feasible choice. In other words, the optimum is the optimal choice.

Economists call the best feasible choice the **optimum**, which you can see labeled on the total cost curve.

To sum up our discussion so far, *optimization using total value* has three steps:

1. Translate all costs and benefits into common units, like dollars per month.
2. Calculate the *total* net benefit of each alternative.
3. Pick the alternative with the highest net benefit.

## Before and After Comparisons

If apartment hunters make optimal choices, then the choice of an apartment will be affected by a change in the opportunity cost of time. Until now we have assumed that the opportunity cost of time is $10/hour. Let's instead assume that the opportunity cost of time is $15/hour. Why might opportunity cost rise? For example, a freelance worker's opportunity cost of time would rise if his or her hourly wage rose.

How does this increase in the opportunity cost of time change the predicted behavior? Before we take you through it step-by-step, try to use your intuition. How would a change in the value of time affect the optimal decision of where to live? Should commuters with a higher value of time move closer to where they work or farther away?

To answer this question, we again need to translate the indirect cost—commuting time—into the same units as the direct cost of rent, which are dollars per month. Accordingly, we rewrite Exhibit 3.2, assuming instead a $15/hour opportunity cost of time. Exhibit 3.4 reports this commuting cost in dollars per month for all four apartments.

Exhibit 3.4 provides the answer to our new optimization problem. The best apartment for a consumer with an opportunity cost of time of $15/hour now shifts from Far to Close. Close has the lowest total cost—$1,240—taking into account both direct rental costs and indirect time costs of commuting.

Exhibit 3.5 plots the total cost of each of the four apartments assuming a $15/hour opportunity cost of time. Close is the best choice—the optimum.

When the opportunity cost of time increases from $10/hour to $15/hour, it becomes more valuable for the commuter to choose an apartment that reduces the amount of time spent commuting. So the optimal choice switches from a relatively inexpensive apartment with a longer commute—Far—to a relatively expensive apartment with a shorter commute—Close.

Exhibit 3.6 takes the two different cost curves from Exhibits 3.3 and 3.5 and plots them in a single figure. The purple line represents the total cost curve for the commuter with an opportunity cost of $10/hour. The orange line represents the total cost curve for the commuter with an opportunity cost of $15/hour. Two key properties are visible in Exhibit 3.6:

1. The $10/hour cost curve lies below the $15/hour cost curve. The $10/hour curve has lower commuting costs for each apartment, so the total cost, which takes into account both the direct cost of rent and the indirect cost of commuting, is lower for all apartments.

**Exhibit 3.4** Commuting Cost and Rental Cost Expressed in Common Units, Assuming an Opportunity Cost of Time of $15/hour

To optimize, it is necessary to convert all costs and benefits into common units. In this example, the common unit is dollars per month. The optimum—in bold—is Close, which has the lowest total cost.

| Apartment | Commuting Time (hours/month) | Commuting Cost ($/month) | Rent ($/month) | Total Cost: Rent + Commuting ($/month) |
|---|---|---|---|---|
| Very Close | 5 hours | $75 | $1,180 | $1,255 |
| **Close** | **10 hours** | **$150** | **$1,090** | **$1,240** |
| Far | 15 hours | $225 | $1,030 | $1,255 |
| Very Far | 20 hours | $300 | $1,000 | $1,300 |

**Exhibit 3.5 Total Cost Including Both Rent and Commuting Cost, Assuming an Opportunity Cost of Time of $15/hour**

Given the opportunity cost of $15/hour, the optimal choice is Close. This apartment has the lowest total cost, which is the sum of the direct rental cost and the indirect commute cost.

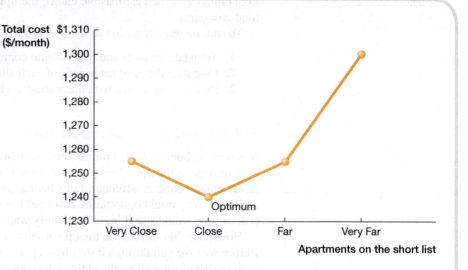

**Exhibit 3.6 Total Cost Curves with the Opportunity Cost of Time Equal to $10/hour and $15/hour**

As the opportunity cost of time rises from $10/hour to $15/hour, the optimal apartment shifts closer to the city center. Employees with a higher opportunity cost of time should choose the apartment with a shorter commute.

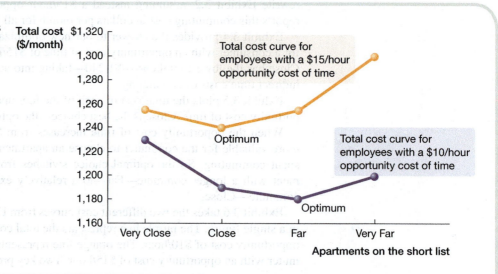

2. The $10/hour curve has a minimum value for Far, while the $15/hour curve has a minimum value for Close. In other words, the optimal apartment switches from Far to Close when the opportunity cost of time rises from $10/hour to $15/hour.

# 3.3 Optimization Using Marginal Analysis

Until now, we have studied the apartment-hunting problem by calculating the total value of each apartment. We are now going to discuss an alternative optimization technique: *optimization using marginal analysis*. Optimization using marginal analysis is often faster to implement than optimization using total value, because optimization using marginal analysis focuses only on the ways that alternatives differ.

Optimization using marginal analysis breaks an optimization problem down by thinking about how costs and benefits *change* as you hypothetically move from one alternative to another. For example, consider two alternative vacations at the same hotel in Miami: a 4-day trip versus a 5-day trip. Suppose that you are choosing between these two options. If you optimize using total value, you evaluate the *total* net benefit of a 4-day trip and compare it to the *total* net benefit of a 5-day trip. Alternatively, you could think only about the *differences* between the two trips. In other words, you could think only about the costs and benefits of the extra day. An optimizer will take the 5-day vacation if the benefit of vacationing for the fifth day exceeds the cost of the fifth day. In choosing between the 4- and 5-day options, the optimizer doesn't necessarily need to worry about the first 4 days, since those 4 days are shared by both the 4-day trip and the 5-day trip. The optimizer can focus on the one thing that differentiates the two vacations: the fifth day.

Economists use the word *marginal* to indicate a difference between alternatives, usually a difference that represents one "step" or "unit" more. The fifth day of vacation is the difference, or margin, between a 4-day vacation and a 5-day vacation.

**Marginal analysis** is a cost-benefit calculation that studies the difference between one feasible alternative and the next feasible alternative.

A cost-benefit calculation that focuses on the difference between one feasible alternative and the next feasible alternative is called **marginal analysis**. Marginal analysis compares the consequences—costs and benefits—of doing one step more of something. Thinking back to our apartment example, marginal analysis can be used to study the costs and benefits of moving one apartment farther away from the city center.

> **Marginal analysis will never change the ultimate answer to the question "what is optimal?" but it will clarify the way that you think about optimization.**

Marginal analysis will never change the ultimate answer to the question "what is optimal?" but it will help clarify the way you think about optimization. Marginal analysis forces us to focus on what is changing when we compare alternatives. Marginal analysis provides another way of finding the optimal choice. Because it gives us insight into the concept of optimization and because we can use it for optimization, marginal analysis is one of the most important concepts in economics.

## Marginal Cost

Let's return to the problem of choosing the best apartment. We go back to this problem to preserve continuity with our earlier analysis; keep in mind, though, that you can use these techniques to optimize in pretty much any situation.

When we studied the problem of choosing a rental apartment, we did not use marginal analysis. Instead, we solved the problem by calculating and comparing the total cost—including direct and indirect costs—of the four apartments. We'll now solve the same apartment-selection problem using marginal analysis. The optimum won't change—we'll confirm that below—but the way that you think about the problem will.

Again consider the commuter with a $10/hour opportunity cost of time. Instead of thinking about each of the apartments in isolation, let's now think about the apartments comparatively. Specifically, let's focus on what changes as we hypothetically "move" from one apartment to the next, stepping farther away from the city center. What is the difference between each pair of apartments?

Exhibit 3.7 helps you think about these changes. The "Commuting Cost" column reports the monthly commuting cost for each apartment, assuming a $10/hour opportunity cost of

**Exhibit 3.7   Cost and Marginal Cost (Assuming a $10/hour Opportunity Cost of Time)**

We can break the problem down by studying the marginal costs of moving farther from the city center. At what point does it make sense to stop moving farther from the city center?

| Apartment | Commuting Cost | Marginal Commuting Cost | Rental Cost | Marginal Rental Cost | Total Cost | Marginal Total Cost |
|---|---|---|---|---|---|---|
| Very Close | $50 | — | $1,180 | — | $1,230 | — |
| Close | $100 | $50 | $1,090 | –$90 | $1,190 | –$40 |
| Far | $150 | $50 | $1,030 | –$60 | $1,180 | –$10 |
| Very Far | $200 | $50 | $1,000 | –$30 | $1,200 | $20 |

time. The "Marginal Commuting Cost" column reports the value of the extra monthly commuting time that is generated by moving one apartment farther from the city center. For example, to move from Close to Far generates additional commuting costs of $50/month. In other words, the "Marginal Commuting Cost" column reports the difference between two commuting costs in adjacent positions on the list. In this particular example, the marginal commuting cost is always the same—the commuting cost rises by the same amount with each move farther away from the city center. This won't generally be the case, but we've set it up this way in this problem to keep things simple. In general, **marginal cost** is the extra cost generated by moving from one feasible alternative to the next feasible alternative.

Now turn to the column labeled "Rental Cost," which reports the monthly rent for each apartment. The "Marginal Rental Cost" column reports the change in the rental cost generated by moving from one apartment to the next apartment—one step farther from the city center. For example, to move from Very Close to Close would save you $90/month, so the marginal rental cost is a negative number, −$90. Likewise, if you moved from Close to Far, you would save an additional $60/month, so the marginal rental cost is −$60.

Finally, we'd like to know the marginal value of total cost. It turns out that we can calculate the marginal value of total cost in two alternative ways. First, we can add up the marginal commuting cost and the marginal rental cost to obtain the marginal total cost. For example, look at the first set of marginal cost numbers and confirm that

$$\$50 + -\$90 = -\$40.$$

In other words, a move from Very Close to Close raises commuting costs by $50 and changes rent by −$90, producing a combined change of −$40.

Alternatively, we could calculate total cost itself. This is done in the column labeled "Total Cost." For instance, for Very Close, the commuting cost is $50 and the rental cost is $1,180, so the total is $1,230. For Close, the commuting cost is $100 and the rental cost is $1,090, so the total cost is $1,190. Total cost *falls* by $40 when we move from Very Close, with total cost $1,230, to Close, with total cost $1,190.

Both methods confirm that the marginal total cost is −$40 when moving from Very Close to Close:

$$\text{Marginal commuting cost} + \text{Marginal rental cost} = \$50 + -\$90 = -\$40$$
$$\text{Total cost of Close} - \text{Total cost of Very Close} = \$1,190 - \$1,230 = -\$40.$$

The fact that we calculated −$40 in both cases is no accident. The match is exact, because it doesn't matter how we decompose costs to calculate marginal total cost. It doesn't matter whether we calculate marginal total cost by summing marginal costs category by category or whether we calculate marginal total cost by subtracting the *total* cost of one apartment from that of the other. Because the answer is the same, you should calculate marginal total cost whichever way is easier for you.

The last column of Exhibit 3.7—marginal total cost—contains all the information that we need to optimize. Start at the top of the column and think about how each "move" away from the city center affects the worker. The first move, from Very Close to Close, has a marginal cost of −$40/month, so it is cost cutting. That move is worth it.

The second move, from Close to Far, has a marginal cost of −$10/month. That move is also cost cutting and thus also worth taking.

The third move, from Far to Very Far, has a marginal cost of $20/month. So that move is not worth taking, because it represents an increase in costs.

To sum up, the first two moves more than paid for themselves and the final move did not. Very Far can't be an optimum, since moving from Far to Very Far made the worker worse off. Very Close can't be an optimum either, since moving from Very Close to Close made the worker better off. Finally, Close can't be an optimum, since moving from Close to Far made the worker better off.

We conclude that Far is the optimum—the best feasible choice. Moving from Close to Far made the worker better off. But moving from Far to Very Far made the worker worse off. Far is the only apartment that satisfies the following property: moving to the apartment makes the worker better off and moving away from the apartment makes the worker worse off. In other words, Far has the virtue that it is a better option than its "neighbors."

**Exhibit 3.8** Total Cost of Each Apartment and the Marginal Cost of Moving Between Apartments (Assuming an Opportunity Cost of $10/hour)

The cost-minimizing choice is Far. We can see this by looking at total cost (in purple) or by looking at marginal cost (in red). Total cost is falling when marginal cost is negative. Total cost is rising when marginal cost is positive. Far is the only apartment that is better than all of its neighbors. Marginal cost is negative when moving to Far and marginal cost is positive when moving away from Far. Thus, Far is the only apartment that satisfies the Principle of Optimization at the Margin.

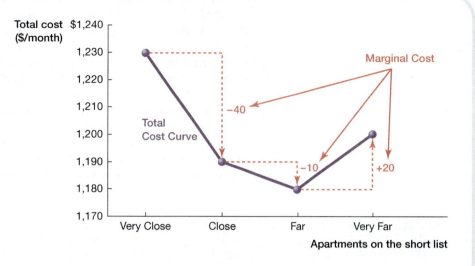

The **Principle of Optimization at the Margin** states that an optimal feasible alternative has the property that moving to it makes you better off and moving away from it makes you worse off.

The optimizer's goal is to make himself as well off as possible—at an optimum, he cannot do any better. In this example—where we are holding all else fixed—the apartment that is better than all its feasible alternatives is also the apartment that minimizes total costs. This is an example of the **Principle of Optimization at the Margin**, which states that an optimal feasible alternative has the property that moving to it makes you better off and moving away from it makes you worse off.

It helps to visualize these ideas. Exhibit 3.8 plots the total cost of each apartment and the marginal cost of moving, one apartment at a time, farther away from the center of town. For instance, moving from Very Close to Close lowers total cost by $40. The vertical portion of the dashed red line shows a change of −$40 between the total cost of Very Close and the total cost of Close.

Optimization using marginal analysis will always pick out a single optimal alternative when the total cost curve has the bowl-like shape in Exhibit 3.8. Where the *total* cost (in purple) is falling, marginal cost (in red) will be negative and marginal analysis will recommend moving farther away from the city center, thereby lowering total cost. After total cost bottoms out, marginal cost will afterward be positive, implying that the renter should move no farther out.

When the total cost curve is not bowl shaped, the calculations get more complicated, but, even in this case, marginal analysis ultimately identifies the same optimum that would emerge if we found the option with the lowest total cost.

Since marginal analysis always picks out the same optimum as minimization of total cost, you can use whichever method is easier for the particular problem that you are analyzing. However, it is important to understand why economists mostly use marginal analysis. Optimization at the margin is simple because you can ignore everything about two alternatives that are being compared except the particular attributes that are different. Marginal analysis reminds you to exclude information that is not relevant to your decision.

To sum up, marginal analysis has three steps:

1. Translate all costs and benefits into common units, like dollars per month.
2. Calculate the marginal consequences of moving between alternatives.
3. Apply the Principle of Optimization at the Margin by choosing the best alternative with the property that moving to it makes you better off and moving away from it makes you worse off.

Marginal analysis—in other words, the three steps outlined above—can be used to solve any optimization problem. Marginal analysis is most commonly used when there is a clear sequence of feasible alternatives. For example, how many hours should you sleep tonight? Six? Seven? Eight? Or Nine? More sleep makes you more rested, but sleep has an opportunity cost—some other activity must be sacrificed if you are going to get more sleep—for instance, breakfast or your 9 a.m. economics lecture. Moving from 6 to 7 to 8 to 9 hours of sleep generates a clear set of steps that can be used for marginal analysis. For example, is it a net benefit to move from 6 to 7 hours of sleep? Is it a net benefit to move from 7 to 8 hours of sleep? Is it a net benefit to move from 8 to 9 hours of sleep? At the optimum, moving up to that number of sleeping hours makes you better off and moving past that number of sleeping hours makes you worse off.

Here are a few more examples in which it is natural use marginal analysis to calculate the optimum. How many hours should you study tomorrow? How many weeks should you be employed this summer? How many miles should you jog in your next workout?

## EVIDENCE-BASED ECONOMICS

### Q: How does location affect the rental cost of housing?

Throughout this chapter, we've been assuming that rental prices are higher near the city center, holding the quality of the apartment fixed. You may have wondered whether we had our facts right.

People often imagine dingy apartments downtown and nice houses out in the country. However, if we want to isolate the effect of location, we need to hold apartment quality constant—for instance, apartment size—and vary *only* location.

Economists Beth Wilson and James Frew assembled a database that contains information on many apartments that were available for rent in Portland, Oregon.[2] They used statistical techniques to effectively compare apartments near the city center to similar apartments that were farther away. Such analysis reveals a strong negative relationship between distance and rent, which is plotted in Exhibit 3.9.

**Exhibit 3.9** **Apartment Rent in Portland, Oregon, Depends on Distance from the City Center**

This plot is drawn for apartments that are identical except for their distance from the city center. The blue line is the approximate location of a ring of highways that encircles most of Portland.

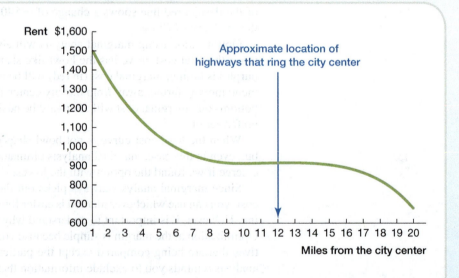

Exhibit 3.9 was calculated for apartments that all have the following features—one bedroom, one bathroom, laundry unit in the apartment, covered parking, cable, and air conditioning—and have none of the following features—a fireplace, access to an exercise room, or access to a pool. The analysis compares the rent of these apartments, holding all their features constant except for the distance to the city center.

Exhibit 3.9 confirms that proximity to the city center raises rents. The closer you get to the city, the higher the rent goes. For example, at a distance of 6 miles from the city center, the typical rent for an apartment with the specified features is nearly $1,000. For an apartment that is 1 mile from the city center, the rent for the "same" apartment is $1,500.

Exhibit 3.9 also displays a noticeable flattening around 12 miles from the city center. Can you guess why rents stop changing in this region? The answer follows from considerations about the opportunity cost of time and the structure of Portland's highway system. Like most large cities, Portland has a ring of fast highways—a "ring road"—about 12 miles from the center of the city. People who live within a few miles of the ring road have the advantage of being near a highway system that speeds up travel time. Because of the ring roads, commute times change relatively little as you go from 9 miles to 14 miles away from the city center.

## Scarcity, Prices, and Incentives

We can now come full circle and return to an important question that we asked previously. Why do rental prices fall as you move farther from the city center? What does this have to do with the topic of this chapter: optimization?

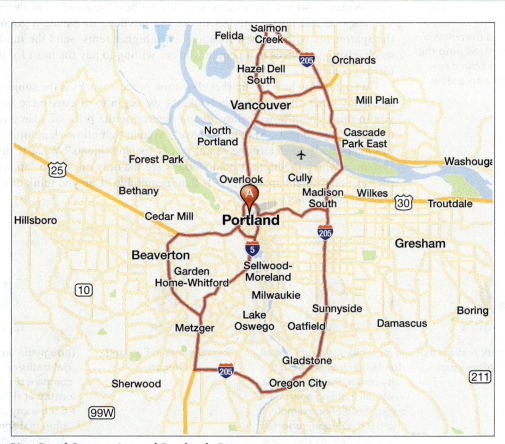

**Ring Road System Around Portland, Oregon**

Like most large cities, Portland has a ring of fast highways—a "ring road"—about 12 miles from the center of the city.

# EVIDENCE-BASED ECONOMICS

*(continued)*

Mt. Hood rises to the east of Portland and presents a beautiful view to apartment dwellers lucky enough to face that way. But not everyone has such spectacular views. Some apartments are on low floors, and some apartments face the less awesome views to the west. Eastern-facing apartments on high floors rent for about 20 percent more than similar apartments that don't have the killer views. To an economist, this price differential is a good way of measuring the dollar value of a scarce resource: a room with a view.

In our analysis, we saw that optimizing commuters would love to live in the city center, but only if the rental prices are the same downtown as they are in distant neighborhoods. But not everyone can live downtown, and not everyone can have a short commute; there just aren't enough downtown apartments to go around. That is an example of economic scarcity—one of the first concepts we studied in Chapter 1.

As we'll see in Chapter 4, the market for apartments determines who gets to have the short commute. Markets allow optimizing landlords and optimizing renters to freely negotiate the rental price of apartments. In the marketplace, the rental price of apartments is determined by market forces rather than by politicians or regulators. The renters with the highest opportunity cost of time bid up the rental price of apartments with the shortest commutes.

As the price of downtown apartments rises, only workers with the highest opportunity cost of time will be willing to rent them. Most other workers will choose to move farther away and accept the consequences of a longer commute. That's a trade-off—more time commuting in exchange for a lower monthly rent.

Market prices have the effect of allocating the downtown apartments to the people who are willing to pay the most for them. This allocation mechanism implies that mostly highly paid workers—and others with a high opportunity cost of time—tend to rent the apartments with the best locations.

Some critics of markets complain that markets are unfair—why should the highest-paid workers also get the apartments with the best locations? The defenders of markets respond that people are paying for the privilege of having a good apartment—the apartments with the best locations have higher rents—and the market allocation mechanism guarantees that people who are willing to pay the most for the best apartments get them.

Understanding how the market allocation process works is the subject of Chapter 4 and many other chapters in this book. As we begin to discuss these issues, we want you to think about how society *should* determine the price of scarce resources, like downtown apartments. Should we have a system that allows landlords and renters to negotiate freely to determine rental prices for apartments? What if this produces a system in which the highest-paid workers are the only ones who can afford to live in the most convenient apartments? Is that inequitable? Can you think of a better way to allocate apartments?

|  |  |  |  |
|:---:|:---:|:---:|:---:|
| **Question** | **Answer** | **Data** | **Caveat** |
| How does location affect the rental cost of housing? | In most cities, though not all, the farther you are from the city center, the more rental costs fall (holding apartment quality fixed). For example, in Portland, Oregon, rents fall by 33 percent as you move from the city center to otherwise identical apartments 6 miles out of town. | Rental prices in Portland, Oregon. | Though the analysis uses special statistical techniques to compare similar apartments located at different distances from the city center, it is possible that some important apartment characteristics were not held fixed in the comparison. This would bias the calculations. |

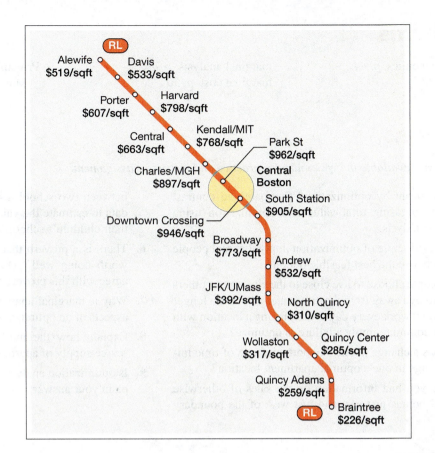

In almost all cities, rent per square foot generally falls with distance to the city center. Here we report the rent per square foot at different stops on Boston's "Red Line," part of the city's subway system. The stop with the highest rent per square foot—Park St—is in the middle of the city. Rent generally falls from there as the line passes out to the suburban subway stops of Alewife (to the north) and Braintree (to the south).

## Summary

- Economists believe that optimization describes, or at least approximates, many of the choices economic agents make. However, economists don't take optimization for granted. A large body of economic research attempts to answer the questions: when do people optimize (or nearly optimize) and when do people fail to optimize? Using optimization to describe and predict behavior is an example of positive economic analysis.

- Optimization also provides an excellent toolbox for improving decision making that is not already optimal. Using optimization to improve decision making is an example of prescriptive economic analysis.

- Optimization using total value has three steps: (1) translate all costs and benefits into common units, like dollars per month; (2) calculate the *total* net benefit of each alternative; and (3) pick the alternative with the highest net benefit.

- Marginal analysis evaluates the change in net benefits when you switch from one alternative to another. Marginal analysis calculates the consequences of doing one step more of something.

- Marginal cost is the extra cost generated by moving from one alternative to the next alternative.

- Optimization using marginal analysis has three steps: (1) translate all costs and benefits into common units, like dollars per month; (2) calculate the marginal consequences of moving between alternatives; and (3) apply the Principle of Optimization at the Margin by choosing the best alternative with the property that moving to it makes you better off and moving away from it makes you worse off.

- Optimization using total value and optimization using marginal analysis yield the same answer. These techniques are two sides of the same coin.

# Key Terms

# Questions

*All questions are available in MyEconLab for practice and instructor assignment.*

1. What is meant by optimization? Compare and contrast optimization using total value and optimization using marginal analysis.

2. Does the principle of optimization imply that real people always choose the best feasible option?

3. Some people choose to live close to the city center; others choose to live away from the city center and take a longer commute to work every day. Does picking a location with a longer commute imply a failure to optimize?

4. Why does a change in one's opportunity cost of time imply a change in one's optimal apartment location?

5. Suppose you had information on the sales of otherwise identical homes just east and just west of the boundary between two school districts. How could you use those data to estimate the value parents place on the quality of their children's schools?

6. There is a proverb that states, "anything worth doing is worth doing well." Do you think an economist would agree with this proverb?

7. Why is marginal analysis helpful for identifying the key aspects of an optimization problem?

8. Explain how the market for apartments allocates the scarce supply of apartments near the city center.

9. Is optimization analysis positive, normative, or both? Explain your answer.

# Problems

*All problems are available in MyEconLab for practice and instructor assignment.*

1. Advances in wireless communication technology reduce the non-financial costs of long commutes: People who ride trains can get work done, and people who drive cars have more entertainment options. If this statement is true, explain the effect on the geographic area of cities. Focus on a person who must decide how close to live to the city center.

2. You are hired as a consultant for a local restaurant. It is considering whether to close at 9:00 p.m., or whether to stay open an extra hour (10:00 p.m.). Based on wages and utility bills, the added cost (the marginal cost) of staying open for each additional hour is $200.

   a. If the additional revenue (the marginal revenue) during the last hour of operation is $250, what would you recommend? By how much will profit change based on your recommendation?

   b. What if the additional revenue were only $100?

   c. What would you need to learn about marginal revenue for you to conclude that 9:00 p.m. is the ideal closing time?

3. Determine whether the following statements better describe optimization using total value or optimization using marginal analysis.

   a. John is attempting to decide on a movie (all movies have the same ticket price). He determines that the new Batman movie provides him with comparatively more of a benefit than the new Spiderman movie and that both the Batman and Spiderman movies have comparatively more of a benefit than the new Superman movie.

   b. Marcia finds that the net benefit of flying from Chicago to Honolulu on a non-stop United Airlines flight is $400, and the net benefit of the same trip flying on a one-stop American Airlines flight is $200.

   c. Nikki decided to jog 3 miles for exercise by reasoning that a 3-mile jog was better than either a 2-mile jog or a 4-mile jog.

   d. At a yard sale, Reagan calculated that she was willing to pay $200 for a queen bed that was being sold for $100 (generating net benefit of $100) and that she was willing to pay $220 for a king bed that was being sold for $300 (generating net benefit of −$80).

4. You are taking two courses this semester, biology and chemistry. You have quizzes coming up in both classes. The following table shows your grade on each quiz for different numbers of hours spent studying for each quiz. (For the purposes of this problem, assume that each hour of study time can't be subdivided.) For instance, the table implies that if you spent 1 hour on chemistry and 2 hours on biology, you would get a 77 on the chemistry quiz and a 74 on the biology quiz.

| Hours of Study | Chemistry | Biology |
|---|---|---|
| 0 | 70 | 60 |
| 1 | 77 | 68 |
| 2 | 82 | 74 |
| 3 | 85 | 78 |

Your goal is to maximize your average grade on the two quizzes. Use the idea of optimization using marginal analysis to decide how much time you should spend studying for each quiz if you have only 1 hour in total to prepare for the two exams (in other words, you will study 1 hour for one exam and 0 hours for the other exam). How would you allocate that single hour of study time across the two subjects? Now repeat the analysis assuming that you have 2 hours in total to prepare for the two exams. How would you allocate those 2 hours across the two subjects? Finally, repeat the analysis assuming that you have 3 hours in total to prepare for the two exams. How would you allocate those 3 hours across the two subjects?

5. Your total benefits from consuming different quantities of gas each week are shown in the following table:

| Gallons/ Week | Total Benefit (dollar equivalent) | Marginal Benefit |
|---|---|---|
| 0 | 0 | — |
| 1 | 4 | |
| 2 | 8 | |
| 3 | 11 | |
| 4 | 14 | |
| 5 | 16 | |
| 6 | 18 | |
| 7 | 19 | |
| 8 | 19 | |

a. Complete the marginal benefit column starting with the step from 0 gallons/week to 1 gallon/week.

b. The price of gasoline is $2.40/gallon. Use the Principle of Optimization at the Margin to find an optimal number of gallons of gas to consume each week.

c. Some policy makers have suggested taxing gasoline to reduce global warming. (Burning fossil fuels such as gasoline releases greenhouse gases, which are a cause of global warming.) Suppose the price of gasoline, including a gasoline tax, rises to $3.60/gallon. Use the Principle of Optimization at the Margin to find an optimal number of gallons of gasoline, given this new tax-inclusive price of gasoline.

6. Scott loves to go to baseball games, especially home games of the Cincinnati Reds. All else being equal, he likes to sit close to the field. He also likes to get to the stadium early to watch batting practice. The closer he parks to the stadium, the more batting practice he is able to watch (the garages all open simultaneously). Find Scott's optimal seat location and parking garage location using the information that follows.

| Seat Location | Price | Value of View |
|---|---|---|
| Diamond Seating | $235 | $200 |
| Club Home | $95 | $130 |
| Club Seating | $85 | $125 |
| Scout Box | $79 | $120 |
| Scout | $69 | $100 |

| Parking Location | Parking Fee (game night) | Missed Batting Practice | Benefit of Arrival Time |
|---|---|---|---|
| Westin Parking Garage | $5 | 60 min | $0 |
| Fountain Square South Garage | $10 | 50 min | $10 |
| West River Parking | $17 | 25 min | $35 |
| East River Parking | $25 | 10 min | $50 |
| Under Stadium Parking | $45 | 0 min | $60 |

7. Suppose the total benefit and total cost to society of various levels of pollution reduction are as follows:

| (1) Pollution Reduction (units) | (2) Total Benefit | (3) Total Cost | (4) Total Net Benefit | (5) Marginal Benefit | (6) Marginal Cost |
|---|---|---|---|---|---|
| 0 | $0 | $0 | — | — | — |
| 1 | $20 | $9 | | | |
| 2 | $38 | $20 | | | |
| 3 | $54 | $33 | | | |
| 4 | $68 | $48 | | | |
| 5 | $80 | $65 | | | |
| 6 | $90 | $84 | | | |

a. Complete column (4).

b. Use total net benefit in column (4) to show that if the U.S. Environmental Protection Agency (EPA) wants to maximize total net benefit, then it should require 3 units of pollution reduction.

c. Complete columns (5) and (6), starting with the step from 0 to 1 unit of pollution reduction.

d. Show that the Principle of Optimization at the Margin also implies that the EPA should require 3 units of pollution reduction.

8. It is possible to use equations to do marginal analysis. Suppose your firm has a marginal revenue given by $MR = 10 - Q$. This means that the seventh unit of output brings in $10 - 7 = \$3$ of additional revenue. The marginal cost for your firm is $MC = 2 + Q$. This means that the seventh unit of output increases cost by $2 + 7 = \$9$.

a. Is it a good idea to produce the seventh unit of output? Why or why not?

b. Find the $Q$ that sets marginal cost equal to marginal revenue $(MC = MR)$. As a preview of upcoming chapters, try to explain why this value maximizes profit.

# 4 Demand, Supply, and Equilibrium

## How much more gasoline would people buy if its price were lower?

In 2016, the retail price of a gallon of gasoline in the United States fluctuated around $2 per gallon. How much gasoline do you buy now? How much would you buy if the price were lower—say, $1 per gallon? How low would it have to go to tempt you to take lots of road trips? What if the price were $0.04 per gallon, so that gasoline was practically free? Amazingly, that's what Venezuelans paid for gas in 2013, due to an extraordinary government subsidy.

In this chapter, we study how buyers and sellers respond to the changing prices of goods and services, and we use the energy market and gasoline as our leading example. How does the price of gas affect the decisions of gas buyers, like households, and gas sellers, like ExxonMobil? How do the decisions of buyers and sellers jointly determine the price of gas when it isn't dictated by government policies?

## CHAPTER OUTLINE

## 4.1 Markets

Every year over 1 billion drivers pull into gas stations around the world. These drivers almost never find that gas stations are "sold out." Most of the time, it takes less than 10 minutes to fill the tank and pull back on the road.

The efficiency of this system is amazing. Nobody tells the companies that run the gas stations how many drivers to expect, and nobody tells the drivers where to fill their tanks. No "fill 'er up" tickets are presold by Ticketmaster or Live Nation. But somehow, there is almost always enough gas for every driver who wants to fill the tank. Drivers get the gas they are willing to pay for, and gasoline companies make enough money to pay their employees and send dividends to their shareholders.

This chapter is about how the gasoline market and other markets like it work. A **market** is a group of economic agents who are trading a good or service plus the rules and arrangements for trading. Agricultural and industrial goods like wheat, soybeans, iron, and coal are all traded on markets. A market may have a specific physical location—like Holland's Aalsmeer Flower Auction—or not. For example, the market for gasoline is dispersed—located on every corner you find a gas station. Likewise, Monster.com (a Web-based job market) operates wherever there's a computer and an Internet connection. To an economist, dating sites/apps like OkCupid, Match, ChristianMingle, Tinder, Hinge, Grindr, and Coffee Meets Bagel are markets, too.

We focus the discussion on markets in which all exchanges occur voluntarily at flexible prices determined by market forces (in contrast to prices fixed by the government). This chapter explains how markets use prices to allocate goods and services. Prices act as a selection device that encourages trade between the sellers who can produce goods at low cost and the buyers who place a high value on the goods.

We illustrate all of this by studying the market for gasoline, which is refined from crude oil, as well as the broader market for energy. You'll see that the price of gasoline is set in a way that implies that gas stations are ready to sell a quantity of gasoline that is equal to the quantity of gasoline that drivers want to buy.

A **market** is a group of economic agents who are trading a good or service plus the rules and arrangements for trading.

Prices act as a selection device that encourages trade between the sellers who can produce goods at low cost and the buyers who place a high value on the goods.

This warehouse in Aalsmeer, Holland, covers an area larger than 100 football fields and hosts thousands of daily auctions for wholesale (bulk) flowers.

If all sellers and all buyers face the same price, it is referred to as the **market price**.

In a **perfectly competitive market**, (1) sellers all sell an identical good or service, and (2) any individual buyer or any individual seller isn't powerful enough on his or her own to affect the market price of that good or service.

A **price-taker** is a buyer or seller who accepts the market price—buyers can't bargain for a lower price, and sellers can't bargain for a higher price.

## Competitive Markets

Think of a city filled with hundreds of gas stations, each of which has an independent owner. The gas station on your block would lose most of its business if the owner started charging $1 more per gallon than all the other stations. Likewise, you wouldn't be able to fill your tank if you insisted on paying $1 less per gallon than the posted price; gas station attendants usually don't cut deals. Drivers of Cadillacs and Kias pay the same price for a gallon of regular unleaded.

To prove that pleading poverty and haggling for a better gas price won't work, try bargaining for a discount the next time you need to fill your tank. Try this only if you have enough gas to reach the next station.

If all sellers and all buyers face the same price, that price is referred to as the **market price**. In a **perfectly competitive market**, (1) sellers all sell an identical good or service, and (2) any individual buyer or any individual seller isn't powerful enough on his or her own to affect the market price. This implies that buyers and sellers are all **price-takers**. In other words, they accept the market price and can't bargain for a better price.

Very few, if any, markets are perfectly competitive. But economists try to understand such markets anyway. At first this sounds kind of nutty. Why would economists study a thing that rarely exists in the world? The answer is that although few, if any, markets are perfectly competitive, many markets come close. Many gas stations do have nearby competitors—often right across the street—that prevent them from charging more than the market price. There are some gas stations that don't have such nearby competitors—think of an isolated station on a country road—but such examples are the exception. If sellers have nearly identical goods and most market participants face lots of competition, then the perfectly competitive model is a good approximation of how actual markets work.

In contrast, there are some markets in which large market participants—like Microsoft in the software market—can single-handedly control market prices; we'll come to markets like that in later chapters.

When two gas stations are located at the same intersection, their prices tend to be very close, and sometimes are exactly the same.

In this chapter, our goal is to understand the properties of markets that are perfectly competitive (identical goods and market participants who can't influence the market price on their own). Along the way, we'll ask three questions.

1. How do buyers behave?
2. How do sellers behave?
3. How does the behavior of buyers and sellers jointly determine the market price and the quantity of goods transacted?

Each of the next three sections addresses one of these fundamental questions.

## 4.2 How Do Buyers Behave?

We start by studying the behavior of buyers. We assume that these buyers are price-takers: they treat the market price as a take-it-or-leave-it offer and don't try to haggle to lower the price. We want to study the relationship between the price of a good and the amount of the good that buyers are willing to purchase. At a given price, the amount of the good or service that buyers are willing to purchase is called the **quantity demanded**.

To illustrate the concept of quantity demanded, think about your own buying behavior. When gas prices rise, do you tend to buy less gas? For example, if gas prices rise, a student who lives off campus might bike to school instead of driving. She might join a carpool or shift to public transportation. If gas prices rise high enough, she might sell her gas guzzler altogether.

Let's quantify these kinds of adjustments. Take Chloe, a typical consumer who responds to increases in gasoline prices by reducing her purchases of gasoline. Chloe may not be able to adjust her gasoline consumption immediately, but in the long run she will use less gas if the price of gas increases—for instance, by switching to public transportation. The relationship between Chloe's purchases of gasoline and the price of gasoline is summarized in the shaded box in the upper-right corner of Exhibit 4.1. This table reports the quantity demanded at different prices and it is called a **demand schedule**. Chloe's demand schedule for gasoline tells us how Chloe's gasoline purchases change as the price of gas changes, **holding all else equal**. The phrase "holding all else equal" implies that everything other than the price of gas is held constant or fixed, including income, rent, and highway tolls. The demand schedule reveals that Chloe increases the quantity of gasoline that she purchases as the price of gasoline falls.

**Quantity demanded** is the amount of a good that buyers are willing to purchase at a given price.

A **demand schedule** is a table that reports the quantity demanded at different prices, holding all else equal.

**Holding all else equal** implies that everything else in the economy is held constant. The Latin phrase *ceteris paribus* means "with other things the same" and is sometimes used in economic writing to mean the same thing as "holding all else equal."

**Exhibit 4.1** Chloe's Demand Schedule and Demand Curve for Gasoline

The lower the price of gasoline becomes, the more gasoline Chloe chooses to buy; in other words, her quantity demanded increases as the price of gasoline decreases. Thus, demand curves are downward-sloping—a high price (on the vertical axis, or y-axis) is associated with a low quantity demanded (on the horizontal axis, or x-axis) and a low price (on the y-axis) is associated with a high quantity demanded (x-axis).

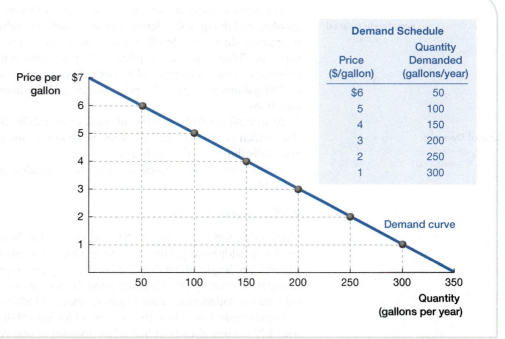

| Demand Schedule | |
| --- | --- |
| Price ($/gallon) | Quantity Demanded (gallons/year) |
| $6 | 50 |
| 5 | 100 |
| 4 | 150 |
| 3 | 200 |
| 2 | 250 |
| 1 | 300 |

The GM Hummer (H2) weighs more than 3 tons and gets about 10 miles per gallon, among a handful of the most fuel *inefficient* personal vehicles in the world. From 2005 to 2008, gasoline prices rose by 30 percent, and Hummer sales fell by 50 percent. At that time, no other car brand experienced sales declines that were this steep. Hummer demand fell so quickly that General Motors shut down the brand in 2010. Gasoline prices plummeted in 2014 and have stayed low since then. As gasoline prices fell, demand for (second-hand) Hummers has risen![1]

## Demand Curves

The **demand curve** plots the quantity demanded at different prices. A demand curve plots the demand schedule.

We'll often want to plot a demand schedule. That is what the demand curve does. The **demand curve** plots the relationship between prices and quantity demanded (again, holding all else equal). In Exhibit 4.1, each dot plots a single point from the demand schedule. For example, the leftmost dot represents the point at which the price is $6 per gallon and the quantity demanded is 50 gallons of gasoline per year. Similarly, the rightmost dot represents the point at which the price is $1 per gallon and the quantity demanded is 300 gallons of gasoline per year. Notice that the *x*-axis represents the quantity demanded. The *y*-axis represents the price per gallon. Economists always adopt this plotting convention—quantity demanded on the *x*-axis and price on the *y*-axis. Economists usually "connect the dots" as we have in Exhibit 4.1, which implies that prices and quantities demanded don't always have to be round numbers.

Two variables are **negatively related** if the variables move in opposite directions.

The demand curve has an important property that we will see many times. The price of gasoline and the quantity demanded are **negatively related**, which means that they move in opposite directions. In other words, when one goes up, the other goes down, and vice versa. In Chloe's case, a gas price of $6 per gallon generates a quantity demanded of 50 gallons per year, and a price of $1 per gallon generates a much greater quantity demanded of 300 gallons per year. The price of gas and the quantity demanded move in opposite directions.

Almost all goods have demand curves that exhibit this fundamental negative relationship, which economists call the **Law of Demand**: the quantity demanded rises when the price falls (holding all else equal).

**Law of Demand:** In almost all cases, the quantity demanded rises when the price falls (holding all else equal).

In this book all demand curves, demand schedules, and graph labels related to demand are in blue.

## Willingness to Pay

Chloe's demand curve can also be used to calculate how much she is willing (and able) to pay for an additional gallon of gasoline. One extra gallon of gasoline is called a "marginal gallon." The height of her demand curve at any given quantity is the amount she is willing to pay for that marginal unit of the good. In other words, the height of her demand curve is the value in dollars that Chloe places on that last gallon of gasoline.

For example, Chloe is willing to pay $4 for her 150th gallon of gasoline. In other words, with 149 gallons already at her at her disposal in one year, Chloe's willingness to pay for

**Willingness to pay** is the highest price that a buyer is willing to pay for an extra unit of a good.

**Diminishing marginal benefit:** as you consume more of a good, your willingness to pay for an additional unit declines.

an additional gallon of gasoline is $4. **Willingness to pay** is the highest price that a buyer is willing to pay for an extra unit of a good.

In contrast, Chloe is willing to pay only $3 for a marginal gallon of gasoline if she already has 199 gallons (for use that year). Chloe's willingness to pay for an additional gallon is negatively related to the quantity that she already has—this is the quantity on the *x*-axis in Exhibit 4.1. The more gasoline that she already has, the less she is willing to pay for an additional gallon. For most goods and services, this negative relationship applies. The more you have of something—for instance, slices of pizza—the less gain there is from acquiring another unit of the same good.

This is an example of a concept called **diminishing marginal benefit**: as you consume more of a good, your willingness to pay for an additional unit declines. An easy way to remember this concept is to think about donuts. My first donut in the morning is worth a lot to me, so I am willing to pay a lot for it. My fourth donut in the same sitting is worth much less to me, so I am willing to pay less for it. In general, the more donuts I eat, the less I am willing to pay for an extra donut.

## From Individual Demand Curves to Aggregated Demand Curves

So far we've talked about a single consumer, Chloe. But we can easily extend the ideas that we have discussed to all buyers of gasoline, including consumers and firms.

Think about the worldwide market for energy. Chloe's demand curve implies that she will increase her use of gasoline when the price of gasoline goes down. Other gasoline users will also increase their consumption of gasoline as its price falls.

Though almost all individual demand curves are downward-sloping, that's about all they have in common. For example, a schoolteacher in Kenya may earn $1,000 per year. For any given price of gasoline, the schoolteacher probably won't consume nearly as much gasoline as a typical worker in the United States (who has about 50 times as much income to spend).

This leaves us with a challenge. How do we account for the gasoline demand of billions of consumers worldwide? Their individual demand curves will obey the Law of Demand, but otherwise they won't look alike. To study the behavior of the worldwide energy market, economists need to study the worldwide demand curve for gasoline, which is equivalent to the sum of all individual demand curves. Economists call this adding-up process the **aggregation** of the individual demand curves.

We begin by showing you how to add up the demand of just two individual buyers. We'll first teach you how to do it with demand schedules. Then we'll show you what that implies for plotted demand curves. Remember that these different ways of thinking about demand are equivalent. Each method reinforces the other.

Exhibit 4.2 contains two individual demand schedules and a total demand schedule. To calculate the total quantity demanded at a particular price, simply add up Sue's and Carlos's quantity demanded at that price. For example, at a price of $4 per gallon, Sue has a quantity demanded of 200 gallons per year. At that same price, Carlos has a quantity demanded of 400 gallons per year. So the aggregate level of quantity demanded at a price of $4 per gallon is 200 + 400 = 600 gallons per year.

Conceptually, aggregating quantity demanded means fixing the price and adding up the quantities that each buyer demands. It is important to remember that quantities are being added together, not prices. Here's an example to help you remember this point. Consider a bakery selling donuts at $1 each. Suppose that two hungry students walk into the bakery and each wants one donut (at the posted price). The total quantity demanded by the two students would be two donuts at a price of $1 per donut (*not* one donut at a price of $2 per donut). Remember this tale of two donuts and you'll avoid getting confused when you calculate total demand schedules.

Exhibit 4.2 also contains plotted demand curves. When a demand curve is a straight line, as in this exhibit, the relationship between price and quantity demanded is said to be linear. Economists often illustrate demand curves with straight lines, because they are easy to explain and easy to express as equations. However, real-world demand curves don't tend to be perfectly straight lines, so the linear model is mostly used as an illustrative case.

The plotted demand curves in Exhibit 4.2 can be aggregated in the same way that the demand schedules are aggregated. Again, look at the quantities demanded at a single price, say $4 per gallon. Sue's demand curve has a quantity demanded of 200 gallons per year.

The process of adding up individual behaviors is referred to as **aggregation**.

## Exhibit 4.2 Aggregation of Demand Schedules and Demand Curves

Demand schedules are aggregated by summing the quantity demanded at each price on the individual demand schedules. Likewise, demand curves are aggregated by summing the quantity demanded at each price on the individual demand curves.

| Sue's Demand Schedule | | Carlos's Demand Schedule | | Total Demand Schedule | |
|---|---|---|---|---|---|
| Price ($/gallon) | Quantity Demanded (gallons/year) | Price ($/gallon) | Quantity Demanded (gallons/year) | Price ($/gallon) | Quantity Demanded (gallons/year) |
| $5 | 100 | $5 | 200 | $5 | 300 |
| 4 | 200 | 4 | 400 | 4 | 600 |
| 3 | 300 | 3 | 600 | 3 | 900 |
| 2 | 400 | 2 | 800 | 2 | 1,200 |
| 1 | 500 | 1 | 1,000 | 1 | 1,500 |

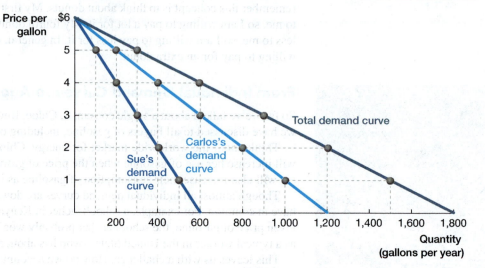

Carlos's demand curve has a quantity demanded of 400 gallons per year. Total quantity demanded at a price of $4 per gallon is the sum of the two individual quantities demanded: $200 + 400 = 600$ gallons per year.

## Building the Market Demand Curve

The **market demand curve** is the sum of the individual demand curves of all potential buyers. It plots the relationship between the total quantity demanded and the market price, holding all else equal.

Exhibit 4.2 shows you how to add up demand curves for just two buyers. We would like to study the demand of all buyers in a market. Economists refer to this as the **market demand curve**. It is the sum of the individual demand curves of all potential buyers. The market demand curve plots the relationship between the total quantity demanded and the market price, holding all else equal.

Billions of economic agents purchase gasoline every year. If we added up the total quantity of gasoline demanded at a particular market price, we could calculate the market demand for gasoline at that price. But economists rarely study the market demand for gasoline. Economists who study energy markets recognize that the gasoline market is very closely tied to all the other markets for products produced from crude oil. Jet fuel, diesel fuel, and automobile gasoline are all produced from oil. Accordingly, when economists study the market for gasoline, we aggregate to the total market for oil. Exhibit 4.3 reports a rough approximation of the worldwide demand curve for billions of barrels of oil (there are 42 gallons per barrel), which is the unit of measurement commonly used in this market.

Finally, note that the demand curve in Exhibit 4.3 is not a straight line, and therefore looks a bit different from the straight demand curves that you saw earlier. This serves as a reminder that the key property of a demand curve is the negative relationship between price and quantity demanded. Demand curves can exhibit this negative relationship without being straight lines.

Exhibit 4.3 also contains a horizontal dashed line that represents the market price of oil in 2016: $50 per barrel. The horizontal price line crosses the demand curve at a point labeled with a dot. At this intersection the buyers' willingness to pay (the height of the demand curve) is equal to the market price of oil. Buyers keep purchasing oil as long as their willingness to pay is greater than the price of oil. At quantities to the left of 35 billion barrels per

**Exhibit 4.3** Market Demand Curve for Oil

The price of a barrel of oil averaged about $50 per barrel in 2016. At that market price, worldwide demand for oil was around 35 billion barrels per year. This demand curve plots the relationship between the price of oil and the quantity demanded.

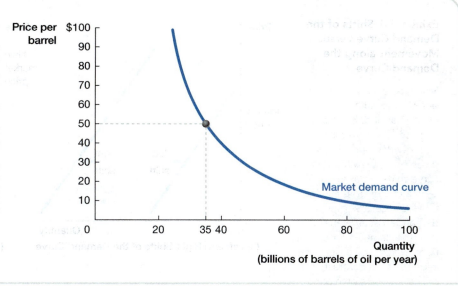

year, willingness to pay (the vertical height of the demand curve) exceeds the market price of $50 per barrel, so buyers gain by purchasing more oil. Oil purchases continue until the buyers reach a quantity demanded of 35 billion barrels per year. At that point, their willingness to pay equals the market price, and they no longer benefit by buying more oil.

## Shifting the Demand Curve

When we introduced the demand curve, we explained that it describes the relationship between price and quantity demanded, holding all else equal. It's now time to more carefully consider the "all else" that is being held fixed.

The demand curve shifts when these five major factors change:

- Tastes and preferences
- Income and wealth
- Availability and prices of related goods
- Number and scale of buyers
- Buyers' beliefs about the future

**Changes in Tastes and Preferences**   A change in tastes or preferences is simply a change in what we personally like, enjoy, or value. For example, your demand for oil products would fall (holding price fixed) if you became convinced that global warming was a significant global problem and it was your ethical duty to use fewer fossil fuels. Because your willingness to buy oil products decreases as a result of your growing environmental worries, your demand curve shifts to the left. We refer to this as a "leftward" shift in the demand curve, because a lower quantity demanded for a given price of oil corresponds to a leftward movement on the *x*-axis. If many people have experiences like this—say the Greenland ice sheet starts to rapidly melt, convincing millions of drivers to buy hybrids—then the market demand curve will experience a shift to the left. See Exhibit 4.4 for an example of a leftward shift in a demand curve.

Naturally, a taste change could also shift a demand curve to the right, corresponding to an increase in the quantity demanded at a given market price. For example, this would happen to your individual demand curve if you started dating someone who lives a few towns away, thereby increasing your transportation needs. Exhibit 4.4 also plots a rightward shift in a demand curve.

This example illustrates two key concepts:

The **demand curve shifts** only when the quantity demanded changes at a given price.

If a good's own price changes and its demand curve hasn't shifted, the own price change produces a **movement along the demand curve**.

- The **demand curve shifts** only when the quantity demanded changes at a given price. Leftward and rightward shifts are illustrated in panel (a) of Exhibit 4.4.
- If a good's own price changes and its demand curve hasn't shifted, the own price change produces a **movement along the demand curve**. Movements along the demand curve are illustrated in panel (b) of Exhibit 4.4.

**Exhibit 4.4 Shifts of the Demand Curve versus Movement along the Demand Curve**

Many factors other than a good's price affect the quantity demanded. If a change in these factors reduces the quantity demanded at a given price, then the demand curve shifts left as in panel (a). If a change in these factors increases the quantity demanded at a given price, then the demand curve shifts right, which is also illustrated in panel (a). In contrast, if only the good's own price changes, then the demand curve does not shift, and we move along the demand curve, as in panel (b).

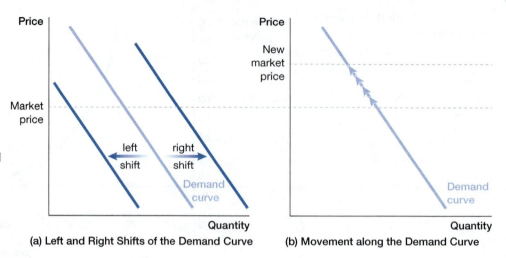

(a) Left and Right Shifts of the Demand Curve

(b) Movement along the Demand Curve

It is important to master these terms, because they will keep coming up. Use Exhibit 4.4 to confirm that you know the difference between a "shift of the demand curve" and a "movement along the demand curve." It helps to remember that if the quantity demanded changes at a given price, then the demand curve has shifted.

We now continue with a discussion of the key factors, other than tastes and preferences, that shift the demand curve.

For a **normal good**, an increase in income shifts the demand curve to the right (holding the good's price fixed), causing buyers to purchase more of the good.

**Changes in Income and Wealth** A change in income or a change in wealth affects your ability to pay for goods and services. Imagine that you recently got your first full-time job and went from a student budget to a $40,000 annual salary. You might buy a car and the gas to go with it. You'd probably also start taking more exotic vacations: for instance, flying to Hawaii rather than taking the bus to visit your friends in Hackensack. Your willingness (directly and indirectly) to buy fuel will now be higher, holding the price of fuel fixed, implying that your demand curve shifts to the right. For a **normal good**, an increase in income shifts the demand curve to the right (holding the good's price fixed), causing buyers to purchase more of the good.

For an inferior good, rising income shifts the demand curve to the left. No insult intended to Spam lovers.

In contrast, consider a good like Spam, which is canned, precooked meat. In the developed world, as people's incomes rise, they are likely to consume fewer canned foods and more fresh foods. If rising income shifts the demand curve for a good to the left (holding the good's price fixed), then the good is called an **inferior good**. This seemingly insulting label is actually only a technical term that describes a relationship between increases in income and leftward shifts in the demand curve.

For an **inferior good**, an increase in income shifts the demand curve to the left (holding the good's price fixed), causing buyers to purchase less of the good.

Two goods are **substitutes** when a rise in the price of one leads to a rightward shift in the demand curve for the other.

**Changes in Availability and Prices of Related Goods** Even if the price of oil hasn't changed, a change in the availability and prices of related goods will also influence demand for oil products, thereby shifting the demand curve for oil. For example, if a city raises the price of public transportation, drivers are likely to increase use of their cars. This produces a rightward shift in the demand curve for gasoline. Two goods are said to be **substitutes** when a rise in the price of one leads to a rightward shift in the demand curve for the other. Public transportation and gas are **substitutes** because a rise in the price of public transportation leads people to use public transportation less and drive their cars more, producing a rightward shift in the demand curve for gasoline.

In contrast, there are some related goods and services that play the opposite role. For example, suppose that a ski resort located 200 miles from where you live decreases its lift ticket prices. The price cut will lead some people to increase their visits to the ski resort, thereby increasing their transportation needs and shifting their demand curve for gasoline to the right. Two goods are said to be **complements** when a fall in the price of one good leads to a rightward shift in the demand curve for the other good.

Two goods are **complements** when a fall in the price of one leads to a rightward shift in the demand curve for the other.

**Changes in Number and Scale of Buyers**   When the number of buyers increases, the demand curve shifts right. When the number of buyers decreases, the demand curve shifts left. The scale of the buyers' purchasing behavior also matters. For example, if the mayor of a small town switches all of the town buses from gasoline to battery power, this will have a much smaller impact on worldwide gasoline demand than a switch by the mayor of the world's largest city, Tokyo.

**Changes in Buyers' Beliefs about the Future**   Changes in buyers' beliefs about the future also influence the demand curve. Suppose that some people begin losing their jobs during the first months of an economy-wide slowdown. Even if you hadn't lost your job, you might still be worried. You could lose your job at some point in the near future, and anticipating this possibility might lead you to build up a rainy-day fund right now. To do this, you might cut your spending by carpooling or eliminating weekend trips to local ski resorts. Such belt-tightening tends to reduce gas usage and shifts the demand curve for oil to the left.

---

### Summary of Shifts in the Demand Curve and Movements along the Demand Curve

**The demand curve shifts when these factors change:**

1. Tastes and preferences
2. Income and wealth
3. Availability and prices of related goods
4. Number and scale of buyers
5. Buyers' beliefs about the future

**The *only* reason for a movement along the demand curve:**

A change in the price of the good itself

---

## EVIDENCE-BASED ECONOMICS

### Q: How much more gasoline would people buy if its price were lower?

**W**e've explained that the quantity of gasoline demanded falls as the price rises. We're now ready to study empirical evidence that backs this up.

Brazil and Venezuela share a border, and they had similar levels of income per person in 2013. Both are also large oil producers—each produced about 3 million barrels per day in 2013. However, they had radically different energy policies. Like most countries, Brazil heavily taxed the sale of gasoline. In contrast, Venezuela aggressively subsidized the sale of gasoline. To compare their policies, we report the U.S. dollar price of gasoline in 2013, when Brazilian drivers paid $5.58 per gallon and Venezuelan drivers paid only $0.04 per gallon. The Venezuelan government provided enough of a subsidy to make gasoline practically free. The Venezuelan government is a major oil producer and supplied enough gasoline to meet consumer demand, even though the price was $0.04 per gallon.

The Law of Demand predicts that a lower price should be associated with a higher quantity demanded, all else held equal. In fact, per person gasoline consumption was almost five times higher in Venezuela than in Brazil in 2013.

Exhibit 4.5 plots the 2013 price of gasoline on the *y*-axis (including taxes and subsidies) and the 2013 quantity of gasoline demanded on the *x*-axis. As you can see, there is a negative relationship between price and quantity demanded. We've also added Mexico to this figure to give you a sense of how another Latin American country (with similar per person income at that time) compares. Mexico provided a small subsidy on gasoline and consequently fell between the other two countries. The Law of Demand predicts a negative relationship between price and quantity demanded, and the data confirm that prediction.

Venezuela's extreme gasoline subsidies were costing the Venezuelan government an enormous amount of forgone revenue (an opportunity cost): they were selling gasoline domestically at a fraction of what they could have received by exporting it. At first, the government reacted by rationing gasoline. Eventually, the authorities realized that the subsidy itself was the real problem. In 2016 the Venezuelan government announced that it would soon reduce or end the subsidy.

But that's not the end of the story. Many other oil-producing countries also aggressively subsidize domestic gasoline consumption—for example, Kuwait and Qatar. As you would expect, these countries have extremely high per capita energy use relative to other wealthy countries.[2]

**Exhibit 4.5** The Quantity of Gasoline Demanded (per person) and the Price of Gasoline in Brazil, Mexico, and Venezuela (2013)

There is a negative relationship between price and quantity demanded in the gasoline market.

*Source:* Data from quantity demanded is from the Organisation for Economic Development and Co-ordination. After-tax, after-subsidy gasoline prices are from AIRINC.

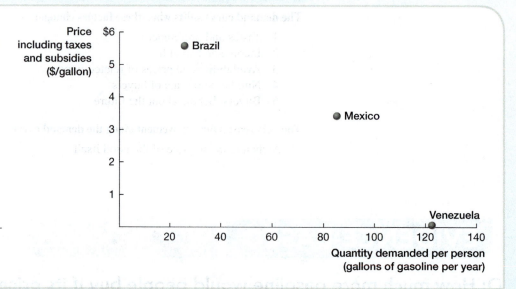

| |  **Question** |  **Answer** |  **Data** |  **Caveat** |
|---|---|---|---|---|
| | How much more gasoline would people buy if its price were lower? | Venezuelans, who paid only $0.04 per gallon of gas in 2013, purchased five times as much per person as Brazilians, who paid $5.58 per gallon. | We compare the quantities of gasoline demanded in Latin American countries with similar levels of income per person and very different gas prices. The variation in gas prices was caused by differences in taxes and subsidies. | Though income levels per person are similar in these countries, the countries have other differences that are not accounted for in this analysis. |

# 4.3 How Do Sellers Behave?

You now understand the behavior of buyers. To understand the complete picture of a market, we also need to study sellers. The interaction of buyers and sellers in a marketplace determines the market price.

We want to analyze the relationship between the price of a good and the amount of the good that sellers are willing to sell or supply. At a given price, the amount of the good or service that sellers are willing to supply is called the **quantity supplied**. Note that in this book, all supply curves, supply schedules, and graph labels relating to supply are in red.

**Quantity supplied** is the amount of a good or service that sellers are willing to sell at a given price.

To build intuition for the concept of quantity supplied, think about a company like ExxonMobil. As the price of oil goes up, ExxonMobil increases its willingness to supply oil that is relatively expensive for the company to discover and extract. Some oil is in deep-water locations where the ocean depth is 2 miles and the oil is another 8 miles below the seafloor. Such wells are drilled by specialized ships two football fields long, which are staffed by hundreds of workers and equipped with robotic, unmanned submarines. Because of the enormous expense, such wells are only drilled when the price of oil is over $60 per barrel.

Drilling for oil from offshore platforms above the Arctic Circle is even more costly. If a single small iceberg could sink the *Titanic*, imagine the challenge of building and protecting stationary oil rigs in areas where tens of thousands of large icebergs pass each year. Offshore oil wells within the Arctic Circle are only drilled when the price of oil is over $70 per barrel. As recently as 2014, oil prices were $100 per barrel, and many of these challenging locations were being developed. The higher the price of oil goes, the greater the number of drilling locations that will be profitable for ExxonMobil. Many observers talk about oil and warn that we are running out of it. In fact, companies like ExxonMobil are only running out of cheap oil. There is more oil under the surface of the earth than we are ever going to use. The problem is that much of that oil is very expensive to extract and deliver to the market.

Drilling from offshore platforms above the Arctic Circle is not profitable unless the price of oil exceeds $70 per barrel. At the other extreme, oil from the deserts of Saudi Arabia costs less than $15 per barrel to extract.

## Supply Curves

ExxonMobil responds to increases in the price of oil by developing new oil fields in ever more challenging locations. Likewise, ExxonMobil responds to decreases in the price of oil by scaling back its exploration program and idling oil rigs. The relationship between ExxonMobil's production of oil and the price of oil is summarized in the boxed supply schedule in Exhibit 4.6. A **supply schedule** is a table that reports the quantity supplied at different prices, holding all else equal. The supply schedule shows that ExxonMobil increases the quantity of oil supplied as the price of oil increases. Exhibit 4.6 also plots ExxonMobil's **supply curve**, which plots the quantity supplied at different prices. In other words, a supply curve plots the supply schedule.

A **supply schedule** is a table that reports the quantity supplied at different prices, holding all else equal.

The **supply curve** plots the quantity supplied at different prices. A supply curve plots the supply schedule.

Two variables are **positively related** if the variables move in the same direction.

The supply curve in Exhibit 4.6 has a key property: the price of oil and the quantity supplied are *positively related*. By **positively related** we mean that the variables move in the same direction—when one variable goes up, the other goes up, too. In the graph, we can easily identify this property, because the curve slopes upward. In almost all cases, quantity supplied and price are positively related (holding all else equal), which economists call the **Law of Supply**.

**Law of Supply**: In almost all cases, the quantity supplied rises when the price rises (holding all else equal).

ExxonMobil starts to produce oil when the price exceeds a level of $10 per barrel. An oil price of $25 per barrel generates a quantity supplied of 0.6 billion barrels per year. A higher oil price of $50 per barrel generates a higher quantity supplied of 1.0 billion barrels per year. At $75 per barrel, the quantity supplied rises to 1.2 billion barrels per year.

## Willingness to Accept

If ExxonMobil is optimizing, the firm should be willing to supply one additional barrel of oil if it is paid at least its marginal cost of production. Recall from the chapter on optimization (Chapter 3) that marginal cost is the extra cost generated by producing an additional

**Exhibit 4.6** ExxonMobil's Supply Schedule for Oil and Supply Curve for Oil

As the price of oil rises (on the y-axis), the quantity of oil supplied increases (on the x-axis), so price and quantity supplied are positively related. Equivalently, we could say that the supply curve is upward-sloping. In this figure, the supply curve is curved, which reflects the fact that ExxonMobil owns only a limited amount of oil reserves and finds it more and more difficult to expand production as the quantity supplied rises.

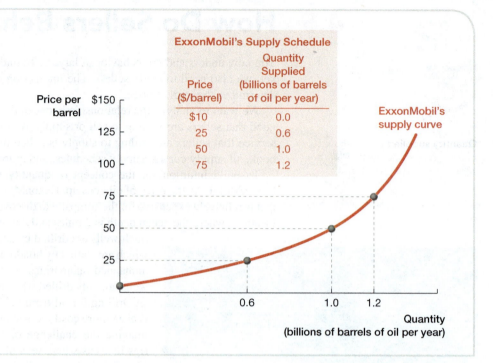

**ExxonMobil's Supply Schedule**

| Price ($/barrel) | Quantity Supplied (billions of barrels of oil per year) |
|---|---|
| $10 | 0.0 |
| 25 | 0.6 |
| 50 | 1.0 |
| 75 | 1.2 |

**Willingness to accept** is the lowest price that a seller is willing to get paid to sell an extra unit of a good. At a particular quantity supplied, willingness to accept is the height of the supply curve. Willingness to accept is the same as the marginal cost of production.

unit. As long as an oil producer is paid at least its marginal cost per barrel, it should be willing to supply an additional barrel of oil.

For an optimizing firm, the height of the supply curve is the firm's marginal cost. For example, ExxonMobil's supply curve implies that if the price of oil is $50, then the quantity supplied is 1.0 billion barrels per year. We can turn this around and say it another way—ExxonMobil is willing to accept $50 to produce its 1 billionth barrel of oil. That's what the supply curve tells us. Economists call this ExxonMobil's **willingness to accept**, which is the lowest price that a seller is willing to get paid to sell an extra unit of a good. For an optimizing firm, willingness to accept is the same as the marginal cost of production. ExxonMobil is willing to accept $50 for an additional barrel because $50 is ExxonMobil's marginal cost when it produces its 1 billionth barrel in a year. If ExxonMobil were to accept less than $50 for its 1 billionth barrel, it would be losing money on that unit of production.

## From the Individual Supply Curve to the Market Supply Curve

The **market supply curve** is the sum of the individual supply curves of all the potential sellers. It plots the relationship between the total quantity supplied and the market price, holding all else equal.

When we studied buyers, we summed up their individual demand curves to obtain a market demand curve. We're now ready to do the same thing for the sellers. Adding up quantity supplied works the same way as adding up quantity demanded. We add up quantities at a particular price. We then repeat this at every possible price to plot the *market supply curve.* The **market supply curve** plots the relationship between the total quantity supplied and the market price, holding all else equal.

Let's start with an aggregation analysis that assumes there are only two oil companies, ExxonMobil and Chevron. Assume that they have the supply schedules listed in Exhibit 4.7. At a price of $50 per barrel, the quantity supplied by Chevron is 0.7 billion barrels of oil per year and the quantity supplied by ExxonMobil is 1.0 billion barrels of oil per year. So the total quantity supplied at the price of $50 per barrel is 0.7 billion + 1.0 billion = 1.7 billion barrels of oil per year. To calculate the total supply curve, we repeat this calculation for each price. The resulting total supply curve is plotted in Exhibit 4.7.

Of course, the market contains thousands of oil producers, not just ExxonMobil and Chevron. The market supply curve is the sum of the individual supply curves of all these thousands of potential sellers, just as the market demand curve is the sum of the individual demand curves of all the potential buyers.

Aggregating the individual supply curves of thousands of oil producers yields a market supply curve like the one plotted in Exhibit 4.8. We've included a dashed line at $50 per barrel, which is the approximate market price that prevailed in the world oil market in 2016. At this price, the total quantity supplied is 35 billion barrels of oil per year.

**Exhibit 4.7**

**Aggregation of Supply Schedules and Supply Curves**

To calculate the total quantity supplied at a particular price, add up the quantity supplied by each supplier at that price. Repeat this for each price to derive the total supply curve.

| Chevron's Supply Schedule | | ExxonMobil's Supply Schedule | | Total Supply Schedule | |
|---|---|---|---|---|---|
| Price ($/barrel) | Quantity Supplied (billions of barrels of oil per year) | Price ($/barrel) | Quantity Supplied (billions of barrels of oil per year) | Price ($/barrel) | Quantity Supplied (billions of barrels of oil per year) |
| $10 | 0.0 | $10 | 0.0 | $10 | 0.0 |
| 25 | 0.4 | 25 | 0.6 | 25 | 1.0 |
| 50 | 0.7 | 50 | 1.0 | 50 | 1.7 |
| 75 | 0.9 | 75 | 1.2 | 75 | 2.1 |

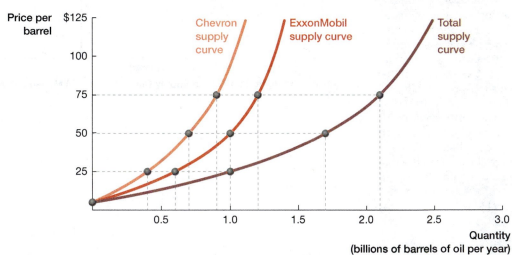

**Exhibit 4.8 Market Supply Curve for Oil**

The market supply curve is upward-sloping, like the supply curves of the individual sellers.

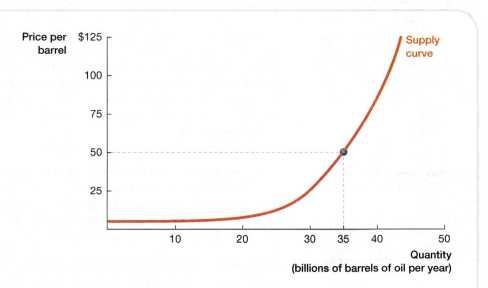

## Shifting the Supply Curve

Recall that the supply curve describes the relationship between price and quantity supplied, holding all else equal. There are four major types of variables that are held fixed when a supply curve is constructed. The supply curve shifts when these variables change:

- Prices of inputs used to produce the good
- Technology used to produce the good
- Number and scale of sellers
- Sellers' beliefs about the future

**Exhibit 4.9** Shifts of the Supply Curve versus Movement along the Supply Curve

Many factors other than a good's price affect the quantity supplied. If a change in these factors decreases the quantity supplied at a given price, then the supply curve shifts left, as illustrated in panel (a). If a change in these factors increases the quantity supplied at a given price, then the supply curve shifts right, which is also illustrated in panel (a). In contrast, if only the good's own price changes, then the supply curve does not shift and we move along the supply curve, which is shown in panel (b).

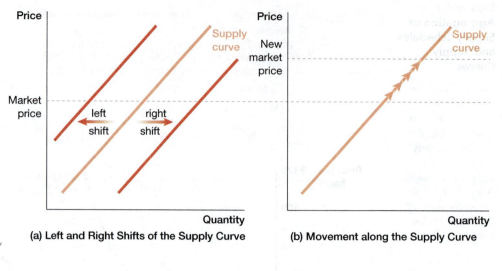

(a) Left and Right Shifts of the Supply Curve

(b) Movement along the Supply Curve

An **input** is a good or service used to produce another good or service.

**Changes in Prices of Inputs Used to Produce the Good**  Changes in the prices of inputs shift the supply curve. An **input** is a good or service used to produce another good or service. For instance, steel is used to construct oil platforms, to create oil drilling machinery, to build pipelines, and to construct oil tankers. Hence, steel is a critical input to oil production. An increase in the price of steel implies that some opportunities to produce oil will no longer be profitable, and therefore optimizing oil producers will choose not to supply as much oil (holding the price of oil fixed). It follows that an increase in the price of steel shifts the supply curve of oil to the left. In other words, holding the price of oil fixed, the quantity of oil supplied falls. In contrast, a fall in the price of steel shifts the supply curve of oil to the right. Panel (a) of Exhibit 4.9 plots these leftward and rightward shifts in the supply curve.

This example illustrates two key concepts:

The **supply curve shifts** only when the quantity supplied changes at a given price.

If a good's own price changes and its supply curve hasn't shifted, the own price change produces a **movement along the supply curve**.

- The **supply curve shifts** only when the quantity supplied changes at a given price. Leftward and rightward shifts are illustrated in panel (a) of Exhibit 4.9.
- If a good's own price changes and its supply curve hasn't shifted, the own price change produces a **movement along the supply curve**. A movement along the supply curve is shown in panel (b) of Exhibit 4.9.

**Changes in Technology Used to Produce the Good**  Changes in technology also shift the supply curve. In recent years, "fracking" (induced hydraulic fracturing) has revolutionized the energy industry. This technology uses pressurized fluids to create fractures in the underground rock formations that surround a drilled well. The fractures enable oil and natural gas to seep out of the rock and be drawn from the well. Fracking has caused a rightward shift in the supply curves for petroleum and natural gas.

**Changes in the Number and Scale of Sellers**  Changes in the number of sellers also shift the supply curve. For example, in 2011 Libyan rebels overthrew Muammar Gaddafi, a dictator who had controlled the country for 42 years. Gaddafi loyalists defended his regime and the fighting dragged on for 6 months. During this period, Libya essentially stopped oil production. Before the war, Libyan wells had been producing about 550 million barrels per year. This is the scale of Libyan production. During the Libyan civil war, the worldwide supply curve shifted to the left by 550 million barrels per year.

A photograph of a Libyan oil refinery burning during the 2011 civil war that overthrew Colonel Muammar Gaddafi. During the war almost all of Libya's oil production was shut down, shifting the world oil supply curve to the left.

**Changes in Sellers' Beliefs about the Future**  Finally, changes in sellers' beliefs about the future shift the supply curve. For example, consider the market for natural gas. Every winter, natural gas usage skyrockets for home heating. This creates a winter spike in natural gas prices. Expecting such price spikes, natural gas producers store vast quantities during the summer (when prices are low by comparison). In other words, natural gas producers use much of their summer natural gas production to build up stockpiles instead of selling all of the summer production to the public. This implies that natural gas suppliers shift the supply curve to the left in the summer. This is an optimization strategy. By pulling supply off the (low-price) summer market and increasing supply in the (high-price) winter market, natural gas suppliers obtain a higher average price. Summarizing this strategy, natural gas producers adjust their supply throughout the year in response to expectations about how the price of natural gas will move in the future.

## Summary of Shifts in the Supply Curve and Movements Along the Supply Curve

**The supply curve shifts when these factors change:**

1. Prices of inputs used to produce the good
2. Technology used to produce the good
3. Number and scale of sellers
4. Sellers' beliefs about the future

**The *only* reason for a movement along the supply curve:**

A change in the price of the good itself

# 4.4 Supply and Demand in Equilibrium

Up to this point, we have provided tools that explain the separate behaviors of buyers and sellers. We haven't explained how to put the two sides of the market together. How do buyers and sellers interact? What determines the market price at which they trade? What determines the quantity of goods bought by buyers and sold by sellers? We will use the market demand curve and the market supply curve to answer these questions. We'll continue to study a perfectly competitive market, which we'll refer to as a "competitive market."

> Competitive markets converge to the price at which quantity supplied and quantity demanded are the same.

Competitive markets converge to the price at which quantity supplied and quantity demanded are the same. To visualize what it means to equate quantity supplied and quantity demanded, we need to plot the demand curve and supply curve on the same figure. Exhibit 4.10 does this.

In Exhibit 4.10, the demand curve (in blue) and the supply curve (in red) for the oil market cross at a price of $50 per barrel and a quantity of 35 billion barrels. Because the demand curve slopes down and the supply curve slopes up, the two curves have only one crossing point. Economists refer to this crossing point as the **competitive equilibrium**. The price at the crossing point is referred to as the **competitive equilibrium price**, which is the price at which quantity supplied and quantity demanded are the same. This is sometimes referred to as the market clearing price, because at this price there is a buyer for every unit that is supplied in the market. The quantity at the crossing point is referred to as the **competitive equilibrium quantity**. This is the quantity that corresponds to the competitive equilibrium price.

At the competitive equilibrium price, the quantity demanded is equal to the quantity supplied. At any other price, the quantity demanded and the quantity supplied will be unequal. To see this, draw a horizontal line at any other price. Only the horizontal line at the competitive equilibrium price equates quantity demanded and quantity supplied.

The **competitive equilibrium** is the crossing point of the supply curve and the demand curve.

The **competitive equilibrium price** equates quantity supplied and quantity demanded.

The **competitive equilibrium quantity** is the quantity that corresponds to the competitive equilibrium price.

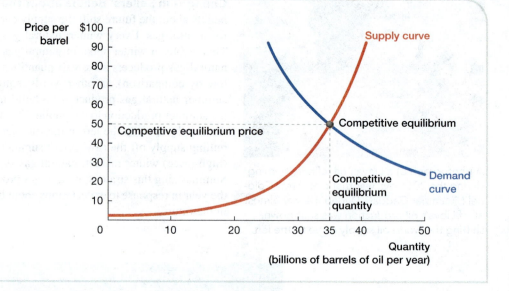

**Exhibit 4.10 Demand Curve and Supply Curve for Oil**

In a competitive market, the market price is the point at which the demand curve intersects the supply curve.

Price per barrel

Competitive equilibrium price

Competitive equilibrium

Supply curve

Competitive equilibrium quantity

Demand curve

Quantity
(billions of barrels of oil per year)

Exhibit 4.11 illustrates a case in which the market is not in competitive equilibrium, because the market price is above the competitive equilibrium price. The higher price makes selling more desirable and buying less desirable, raising the quantity supplied above its competitive equilibrium level and lowering the quantity demanded below its competitive equilibrium level. When the market price is above the competitive equilibrium price, quantity supplied exceeds quantity demanded, creating **excess supply**. For example, Exhibit 4.11 shows that at a market price of $70 per barrel for oil, the quantity supplied of 38 billion barrels of oil per year exceeds the quantity demanded of 29 billion barrels of oil per year.

If the market stayed in this situation, sellers would pump 38 billion barrels of oil per year, but buyers would purchase only 29 billion of those barrels, leaving the difference—9 billion barrels—unsold each year. This would push down oil prices, as enormous stockpiles of oil started to build up around the world. Because existing oil storage tanks are limited in scale and expensive to build, sellers would start undercutting each other's prices to get rid of the rising inventory of unsold oil. Prices would fall. As a result, the situation in Exhibit 4.11 normally wouldn't last for long. Sellers, who are selling nearly identical

*When the market price is above the competitive equilibrium price, quantity supplied exceeds quantity demanded, creating* **excess supply**.

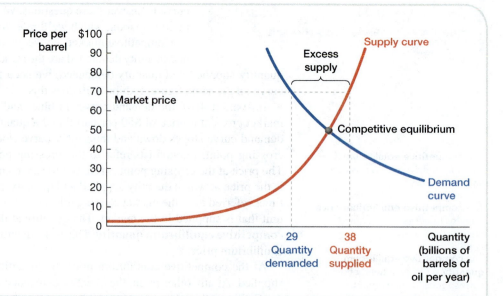

**Exhibit 4.11 Excess Supply**

When the market price is above the competitive equilibrium level, quantity demanded is less than quantity supplied. This is a case of excess supply. In this particular example, the excess supply is 38 − 29 = 9 billion barrels of oil per year.

Price per barrel

Excess supply

Market price

Supply curve

Competitive equilibrium

Demand curve

29
Quantity demanded

38
Quantity supplied

Quantity (billions of barrels of oil per year)

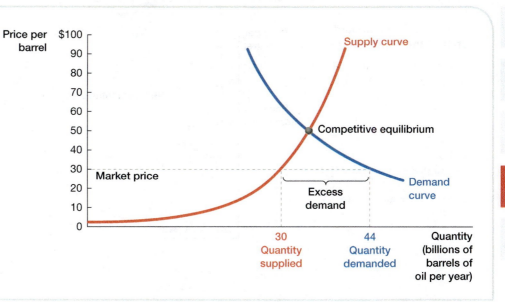

**Exhibit 4.12 Excess Demand**

When the market price is below the competitive equilibrium level, quantity demanded is greater than quantity supplied. This is a case of excess demand. In this case, the excess demand is 44 − 30 = 14 billion barrels of oil per year.

When the market price is below the competitive equilibrium price, quantity demanded exceeds quantity supplied, creating **excess demand**.

barrels of oil, would compete with one another for customers by cutting prices. This would continue until the market price fell back to the competitive equilibrium price. This competitive process plays an important role in pushing the market toward the aptly named competitive equilibrium.

Exhibit 4.12 illustrates the opposite case. When market price is below the competitive equilibrium price, quantity demanded exceeds quantity supplied, creating **excess demand**. In Exhibit 4.12 the quantity demanded of 44 billion barrels of oil per year exceeds the quantity supplied of 30 billion barrels of oil per year. Buyers want 44 billion barrels of oil, but there are only 30 billion barrels available on the market.

The situation in Exhibit 4.12 also normally won't last long. Buyers who aren't getting the goods they want will compete with one another by offering to pay higher prices to get the limited quantity of oil. This will continue until the market price rises to the competitive equilibrium price of $50 per barrel.

## Curve Shifting in Competitive Equilibrium

We are now ready to put this framework into action. We'd like to know how a shock to the world oil market will affect the equilibrium quantity and the equilibrium price of oil.

For example, what would happen if a major oil exporter suddenly stopped production, as Libya did in 2011? This causes a leftward shift of the supply curve, as illustrated in Exhibit 4.13. Since oil has become more scarce, the price of oil needs to rise from its old level to equate quantity supplied and quantity demanded. The rise in the equilibrium oil price is associated with a movement along the demand curve (which hasn't shifted). Because the demand curve is downward-sloping, a rising price causes a reduction in the quantity demanded. In fact, the outbreak of full-scale fighting in Libya and the consequent shutdown of the Libyan oil fields did correspond with an increase in the world price of oil.

Now consider the opposite case. What would happen if a technological breakthrough shifted the supply curve to the right? This causes a rightward shift of the supply curve, as illustrated in Exhibit 4.14. Since oil has become more abundant, the price of oil needs to fall from its old level to equate quantity supplied and quantity demanded. The fall in the equilibrium oil price is associated with a movement along the demand curve (which hasn't shifted). Because the demand curve is downward-sloping, a falling price causes an increase in the quantity demanded.

We can also predict the effect of a shift in the demand curve. For example, what would happen if rising environmental concerns and new energy-saving technologies led consumers to use less oil at any given price? This change in consumer tastes and technology shifts

### Exhibit 4.13 A Leftward Shift of the Supply Curve

A leftward shift of the supply curve raises the equilibrium price and lowers the equilibrium quantity. The original equilibrium is located at the grey dot. The new equilibrium is marked by the black dot, where the original demand curve and the new supply curve intersect.

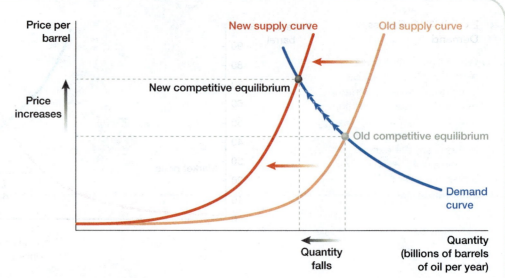

### Exhibit 4.14 A Rightward Shift of the Supply Curve

A rightward shift in the supply curve lowers the equilibrium price and raises the equilibrium quantity. The original equilibrium is located at the grey dot. The new equilibrium is marked by the black dot, where the original demand curve and the new supply curve intersect.

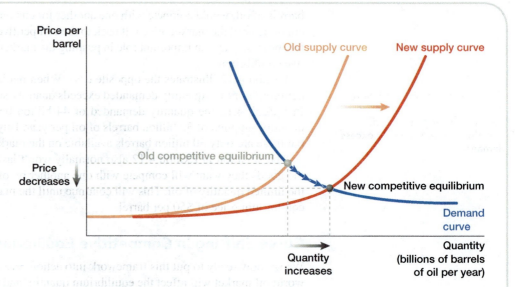

## LETTING THE
# DATA SPEAK

## Technological Breakthroughs Drive Down the Equilibrium Price of Oil

In fact, from 2011 to 2016 the supply-curve shift in Exhibit 4.14 actually occurred, due in part to a boom in fracking-based oil extraction. Recall that "fracking" uses pressurized fluids to create fractures in underground rock. To illustrate this technology, consider a single 1.5-mile-deep fracking well that BP drilled in Texas during the summer of 2016. At six different depths, BP turned the vertical drill bit 90 degrees to create three *horizontal* mile-long pipes at each depth. This system of underground hori-

zontal drilling generated over 18 miles of deep horizontal pipes, which are now being used to fracture the energy-rich rock and capture released oil and natural gas.

Fracking enabled the United States to increase oil production by 70 percent from 2011 to 2016 (from 2.1 to 3.4 billion barrels per year).[3] The fracking boom contributed to a rightward shift in the worldwide supply curve for oil. This shift played an important role in driving oil prices down from $100 per barrel in 2011 to $50 in 2016.

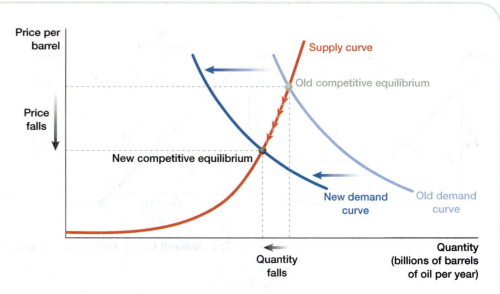

**Exhibit 4.15** A Leftward Shift of the Demand Curve

A leftward shift in the demand curve lowers the equilibrium price and lowers the equilibrium quantity. The original equilibrium is located at the grey dot. The new equilibrium is marked by the black dot, where the original supply curve and the new demand curve intersect.

Price per barrel

Supply curve

Old competitive equilibrium

Price falls

New competitive equilibrium

New demand curve

Old demand curve

Quantity (billions of barrels of oil per year)

Quantity falls

the demand curve for oil to the left, which is plotted in Exhibit 4.15. Accordingly, the price of oil needs to fall from its old level to equate quantity supplied and quantity demanded. The decrease in the equilibrium oil price is associated with a movement along the supply curve (which hasn't shifted). Because the supply curve is upward-sloping, a falling price causes a reduction in the quantity supplied.

Using demand and supply curves to study markets enables economists to resolve puzzles. For example, in Exhibit 4.14, the market price of oil drops and people buy less oil! Hearing those two facts might sound perplexing. Shouldn't a drop in the price of oil lead to an increase in oil buying? In Exhibit 4.15, you can see that the drop in the price of oil is caused by a shift of the market demand curve to the left. This leftward shift causes the price to fall and the fall in price causes the quantity supplied to fall. So the fall in price and the fall in the equilibrium quantity are both consequences of the leftward shift in the demand curve.

So far we have studied examples in which only one curve—either the demand or supply curve—shifts at a time. But life isn't always this simple. Sometimes both curves shift at the same time. For example, the fracking revolution has shifted the supply curve for oil to the right at the same time that rising environmental consciousness and energy-saving technology have shifted the demand curve for oil to the left.

We want to know what happens in such mixed cases. Exhibit 4.16 shows how simultaneous shifts in the supply and the demand curves translate into changes in the market price and the quantity of transactions. As you can imagine, there are many possible combinations of shifts. This exhibit takes you through one group of cases. The problems at the end of the chapter take you through other cases.

In all three panels of Exhibit 4.16, the demand curve shifts left and the supply curve shifts right. The three panels graph three different special cases. We represent the old demand curve in light blue (labeled $D_1$) and the new demand curve in dark blue (labeled $D_2$). Likewise, the old supply curve is light red (labeled $S_1$) and the new supply curve is dark red (labeled $S_2$). The grey dot marks the old competitive equilibrium, where the old demand curve and the old supply curve intersect. The black dot marks the new competitive equilibrium, where the new demand curve and the new supply curve intersect. The old competitive equilibrium price is $P_1$ and the new competitive equilibrium price is $P_2$. The old competitive equilibrium quantity is $Q_1$ and the new competitive equilibrium quantity is $Q_2$.

In all three panels, the equilibrium price falls: $P_2$ is less than $P_1$. However, the direction of adjustment of the equilibrium quantity depends on the relative size of the shifts in the demand and supply curves. In the panel (a), the leftward shift in demand dominates

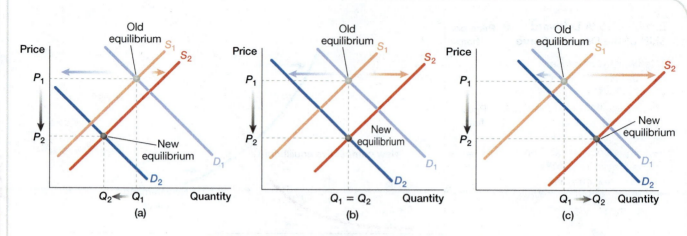

**Exhibit 4.16 The Demand Curve Shifts Left and the Supply Curve Shifts Right**

When the demand curve shifts left and the supply curve shifts right, the competitive equilibrium price will always decrease ($P_2$ is always less than $P_1$). However, the competitive equilibrium quantity may decrease ($Q_2$ less than $Q_1$ in panel (a)), stay the same ($Q_2$ equal to $Q_1$ in panel (b)), or increase ($Q_2$ greater than $Q_1$ in panel (c)).

and the equilibrium quantity falls from $Q_1$ to $Q_2$. In panel (b), the equilibrium quantity stays exactly the same: $Q_1 = Q_2$. In panel (c), the rightward shift in supply dominates and the equilibrium quantity rises from $Q_1$ to $Q_2$. Summing up, when the demand curve shifts left and the supply curve shifts right, the competitive equilibrium price will always decrease, but the competitive equilibrium quantity may move in either direction or stay the same.

# 4.5 What Would Happen If the Government Tried to Dictate the Price of Gasoline?

Our analysis has concluded that competitive markets will end up at the competitive equilibrium—the point where the supply and the demand curves cross. But this can happen only if prices are allowed to respond to market pressures.

However, some markets have prices that are set by laws, regulations, or social norms. Economists are interested in the way that all markets work, even markets that are not allowed to reach a competitive equilibrium. We illustrate these issues by considering markets without a flexible price.

Take another look at Exhibit 4.12. When the market price of gasoline is artificially held below the level of the competitive equilibrium price, the quantity of gasoline demanded exceeds the quantity supplied. Accordingly, many drivers who would like to buy gas at the market price won't be able to do so.

In a situation like this, the allocation of gasoline is determined by something other than who is willing to pay for it. During the U.S. oil crisis of 1973–1974, the U.S. government effectively capped the price of gasoline, causing quantity demanded to exceed quantity supplied. This is referred to as a price ceiling. Drivers soon realized that there was excess

At the end of 1973, the U.S. government effectively capped the price of gasoline, creating a situation of excess demand.

This photograph was taken in 1974. Why did price caps on gasoline lead to these results?

demand at the capped price, leading them to show up early to get whatever gas was available. Lines began to form earlier and earlier in the day.

A *New York Times* reporter wrote, "Everywhere lines seemed to be the order of the day. In Montclair, N.J., Mrs. Catherine Lee got up at 4:20 one morning and drove to her filling station to be first on line. She had to settle for second place—No. 1 had gotten there at 3:15. Mrs. Lee fluffed up the pillow she had brought, threw two comforters over herself, and slept for three hours until the station opened." Some drivers devised ingenious means of getting around the system. "In Bedford, Massachusetts, a businessman drove his auto into a Hertz car rental lot, ordered a car, received it complete with a full tank of gas, siphoned the gas into his own car, paid Hertz their daily rental fee—no mileage charge, of course—and drove home in his car to enjoy his full tank of gas."[4]

The lines were an optimal response by buyers who understood that there was excess demand. Because quantity demanded exceeded quantity supplied, gas stations frequently ran out of gas. During the peak of the crisis, 20 percent of stations ran out of fuel. Getting in line early—very early—was an optimal way of assuring that you'd be able to fill your own tank.

Some folks didn't like waiting in long lines, particularly when they suspected that the station was going to run out of fuel before they got their turn at the pump. "They're out of their minds, they're turning sick. They'll kill you. They're fighting amongst themselves. They'll shoot you with a gun. They're all sick." Does this sound like a scene from the latest zombie movie? It's actually a gas station attendant describing his customers during the gasoline crisis of 1973–1974. An owner of another station put it this way: "It was mayhem. They were fighting in the streets and one customer pulled a knife on another one. And that was *before* we opened."

Economic history is filled with stories of governments that try to fix the price of goods instead of letting the market generate an equilibrium price. Price controls often do not work out well and governments keep forgetting this lesson.

The following Choice & Consequence feature details one more example of a failed effort to fix a price. As you read it, ask yourself how the goods in question could have been allocated differently.

# CHOICE
## &CONSEQUENCE

## The Unintended Consequences of Fixing Market Prices

What would happen if your town announced a first-come, first-served sale of 1,000 Apple laptops for $50 each? Would the residents form an orderly line and patiently wait their turn?

In Henrico County, Virginia, such a laptop sale was actually conducted. County residents began lining up at 1:30 A.M. on the day of the sale. When the gates opened at 7 A.M., more than 5,000 people surged into the sale site, pushing and shoving their way to get to the computers. Elderly people were trampled underneath the human tidal wave, and a baby's stroller was crushed. Eventually, about 70 police officers were called in to restore order. Seventeen people were injured and four landed up in the hospital. And after the uproar died down, more than 4,000 people were left with nothing to show for all the trouble. Of those who did manage to obtain one of the computers, many later sold them.[5]

The Henrico County computer sale resulted in a situation of excess demand. At the fixed price set by the county, $50 per laptop, the quantity demanded of 5,000 exceeded the quantity supplied of 1,000. Exhibit 4.17 illustrates the fact that there were not enough laptops to go around. The people who got laptops were not necessarily

the ones who were willing to pay the most. Instead, the consumers who got the laptops were the ones who were able and willing to fight their way through the crowd. Even if we assume that the laptops were subsequently resold to other people who valued the laptops more, the stampede itself caused many injuries. A stampede is a bad way to allocate society's resources.

Economists are often asked to provide advice on how to design markets that will work well. Naturally, a flexible price would have made this market work better, and it would have raised far more revenue for Henrico County.

Alternatively, the market could have been organized as an auction with bids received by phone or e-mail. The county could have auctioned off the 1,000 laptops to the 1,000 highest local bidders.

Even a random lottery would have worked much better than the stampede. The stampede allocated the laptops to the people who were the most physically aggressive and led to numerous injuries. A random lottery would have allocated the laptops to the people who got lucky. And these lucky winners would have been free to sell their laptops to anyone who valued them more than they did.

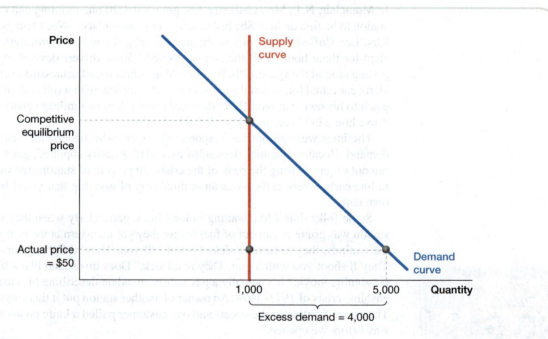

**Exhibit 4.17 Excess Demand for Henrico County's Laptops**

By fixing the price at $50 per laptop, Henrico County created a situation of excess demand. At this price, the quantity demanded (5,000 laptops) exceeded the quantity supplied (1,000 laptops). To equate the quantity demanded and the quantity supplied, a much higher price was needed: the competitive equilibrium price. The vertical supply curve reflects the fact that the supply of laptops at the $50 sale was fixed at 1,000 units.

# Summary

■ A market is a group of economic agents who are trading a good or service plus the rules and arrangements for trading. In a perfectly competitive market, (1) sellers all sell an identical good or service, and (2) individual buyers or individual sellers aren't powerful enough on their own to affect the market price of that good or service.

■ Quantity demanded is the amount of a good that buyers are willing to purchase at a given price. A demand schedule is a table that reports the quantity demanded at different prices, holding all else equal. A demand curve plots the demand schedule. The Law of Demand states that in almost all cases, the quantity demanded rises when the price falls (holding all else equal).

■ The market demand curve is the sum of the individual demand curves of all potential buyers: the quantity demanded is summed at each price. It plots the relationship between the total quantity demanded and the market price, holding all else equal.

■ The demand curve shifts only when the quantity demanded changes at a given price. If a good's own price changes and its demand curve hasn't shifted, the own price change produces a movement along the demand curve.

■ Quantity supplied is the amount of a good or service that sellers are willing to sell at a given price. A supply schedule is a table that reports the quantity supplied at different prices, holding all else equal. A supply curve plots the supply schedule. The Law of Supply states that in almost all cases, the quantity supplied rises when the price rises (holding all else equal).

■ The market supply curve is the sum of the individual supply curves of all potential sellers: the quantity supplied is summed at each price. It plots the relationship between the total quantity supplied and the market price, holding all else equal.

■ The supply curve shifts only when the quantity supplied changes at a given price. If a good's own price changes and its supply curve hasn't shifted, the own price change produces a movement along the supply curve.

■ The competitive equilibrium is the crossing point of the supply curve and the demand curve. The competitive equilibrium price equates quantity supplied and quantity demanded. The competitive equilibrium quantity is the quantity that corresponds to the competitive equilibrium price.

■ When prices are not free to fluctuate, markets fail to equate quantity demanded and quantity supplied.

# Key Terms

market *p. 59*
market price *p. 60*
perfectly competitive market *p. 60*
price-taker *p. 60*
quantity demanded *p. 61*
demand schedule *p. 61*
holding all else equal *p. 61*
demand curve *p. 62*
negatively related *p. 62*
Law of Demand *p. 62*
willingness to pay *p. 63*
diminishing marginal benefit *p. 63*

aggregation *p. 63*
market demand curve *p. 64*
demand curve shifts *p. 65*
movement along the demand curve *p. 65*
normal good *p. 66*
inferior good *p. 66*
substitutes *p. 66*
complements *p. 67*
quantity supplied *p. 69*
supply schedule *p. 69*
supply curve *p. 69*

positively related *p. 69*
Law of Supply *p. 69*
willingness to accept *p. 70*
market supply curve *p. 70*
input *p. 72*
supply curve shifts *p. 72*
movement along the supply curve *p. 72*
competitive equilibrium *p. 73*
competitive equilibrium price *p. 73*
competitive equilibrium quantity *p. 73*
excess supply *p. 74*
excess demand *p. 75*

# Questions

*All questions are available in MyEconLab for practice and instructor assignment.*

1. What is meant by holding all else equal? How is this concept used when discussing movements along the demand curve? How is this concept used when discussing movements along the supply curve?

2. What is meant by diminishing marginal benefits? Are you likely to experience diminishing marginal benefits for goods that you like a lot? Are there exceptions to the general rule of diminishing marginal benefits? (*Hint*: Think about batteries that you would use in a flashlight that requires two batteries.) Explain your answer.

3. How is the market demand schedule derived from individual demand schedules? How does the market demand curve differ from an individual demand curve?

4. Explain how the following factors will shift the demand curve for Gillette shaving cream.

   a. The price of a competitor's shaving cream increases.

   b. With an increase in unemployment, the average level of income in the economy falls.

   c. Shaving gels and foams, marketed as being better than shaving creams, are introduced in the market.

5. What does it mean to say that we are running out of "cheap oil"? What does this imply for the price of oil in the future?

6. What does the Law of Supply state? What is the key feature of a typical supply curve?

7. What is the difference between willingness to accept and willingness to pay? For a trade to take place, does the willingness to accept have to be lower, higher, or equal to the willingness to pay?

8. Explain how the following factors will shift the supply curve for sparkling wine.

   a. New irrigation technology increases the output of grapes in a vineyard.

   b. Following an increase in the immigration of unskilled labor, the wages of wine-grape pickers fall.

   c. The government sets a minimum wage for seasonal employment.

9. How do the following affect the equilibrium price in a market?

   a. A leftward shift in demand

   b. A rightward shift in supply

   c. A large rightward shift in demand and a small rightward shift in supply

   d. A large leftward shift in supply and a small leftward shift in demand

10. Why was a fixed price of $50 not the best way of allocating used laptops? Suggest other possible ways of distributing the laptops that would be efficient.

# Problems

*All problems are available in MyEconLab for practice and instructor assignment.*

1. Suppose the following table shows the quantity of laundry detergent that is demanded and supplied at various prices in Country 1.

| Price ($) | Quantity Demanded (million oz.) | Quantity Supplied (million oz.) |
|---|---|---|
| 2 | 65 | 35 |
| 4 | 60 | 40 |
| 6 | 55 | 45 |
| 8 | 50 | 50 |
| 10 | 45 | 55 |
| 12 | 40 | 60 |
| 14 | 35 | 65 |

   a. Use the data in the table to draw the demand and supply curves in the market for laundry detergent.

   b. What is the equilibrium price and quantity in the market?

   c. The following tables give the demand and supply schedules for two of Country 1's neighboring countries, Country 2 and Country 3. Suppose these three countries decide to form an economic union and integrate their markets. Use the data in the table to plot the market demand and supply curves in the newly formed economic union. What is the equilibrium price and quantity in the market?

**Country 2**

| Price ($) | Quantity Demanded (million oz.) | Quantity Supplied (million oz.) |
|---|---|---|
| 2 | 35 | 5 |
| 4 | 30 | 10 |
| 6 | 25 | 15 |
| 8 | 20 | 20 |
| 10 | 15 | 25 |
| 12 | 10 | 30 |
| 14 | 5 | 35 |

**Country 3**

| Price ($) | Quantity Demanded (million oz.) | Quantity Supplied (million oz.) |
|---|---|---|
| 2 | 40 | 10 |
| 4 | 35 | 15 |
| 6 | 30 | 20 |
| 8 | 25 | 25 |
| 10 | 20 | 30 |
| 12 | 15 | 35 |
| 14 | 10 | 40 |

2. Demand for books is given by the following table.

| Price ($) | Quantity of Books Demanded |
|---|---|
| 0 | 1,000 |
| 20 | 600 |
| 40 | 200 |
| 60 | 0 |

   a. Plot each point on a well-labeled diagram, with quantity on the *x*-axis and price on the *y*-axis.

   b. Assume that the demand curve is linear between each of the points in the demand schedule above. Using this assumption, connect the dots with straight lines. What is the quantity demanded when the price is $10?

   c. Assume the Law of Demand is true. Also assume the information provided by the demand schedule is correct. However, make no other assumptions. In particular, you should no longer assume that the demand curve is linear between the points in the demand schedule. What can you say about the quantity demanded when the price is $25?

3. Explain how simultaneous shifts in demand and supply curves could explain these situations:

   a. The price of insulin injection kits, used by diabetic patients, increases from $45 to $52, but the equilibrium quantity remains the same.

**b.** A pest attack on the tomato crop increases the cost of producing ketchup. A mild winter causes cattle herds to be unusually large, causing the price of hamburgers to fall. The equilibrium quantity of ketchup is unchanged.

4. Sketch generic supply and demand curves for the housing market and label the equilibrium price and quantity.

   **a.** A booming economy increases the demand for housing. Show the shift in the demand curve on your graph. What does this do to the price and quantity in the market?

   **b.** You and a friend both notice that more houses are built in response to this change. Your friend says, "this is a sign that the supply curve is shifting as well." You respond, "no, this is actually just a shift *along* the supply curve." To help your friend understand, demonstrate what you mean on your graph.

   **c.** As it turns out, there actually is a shift in the supply curve due to an unrelated breakthrough in construction that lowers the cost of building houses. In what direction does the supply curve shift? Show this on your graph.

   **d.** Relative to the original price and quantity, what is the overall effect of both shifts on price and quantity?

5. Brazil is the world's largest coffee producer. There was a severe drought in Brazil in 2013–2014 that damaged Brazil's coffee crop. The price of coffee beans doubled during the first 3 months of 2014.

   **a.** Draw and discuss a supply-and-demand diagram to explain the increase in coffee prices.

   **b.** Are coffee and tea substitutes or complements? Explain.

   **c.** What do you think the impact of this drought has been on the equilibrium price and quantity of tea? Draw a supply-and-demand diagram for the tea market to explain your answer.

6. There is a sharp freeze in Florida that damages the orange harvest and as a result, the price of oranges rises. Will the equilibrium price of orange juice rise, fall, or remain constant? Will the equilibrium quantity of orange juice rise, fall, or remain constant? Present a supply-and-demand diagram to explain your answers.

7. For each of the following situations, sketch the demand curve as accurately as possible.

   **a.** Appendectomy is a life-saving operation that some people need. Regardless of the price, the quantity demand is 300,000 every year.

   **b.** For any price above $5 absolutely nobody will buy your lemonade, but for any price below $5 you find that you are able to sell as much lemonade as you like.

   **c.** There is only one buyer. For any price above $100 this buyer wants nothing. For any price at or below $100 this buyer wants exactly 20 units.

8. Land in Sonoma, California, can be used either to grow grapes for pinot noir wine or to grow Gravenstein apples. The demand for pinot noir shifts sharply and permanently to the right. What will be the effect of the rightward shift in demand for pinot noir on the equilibrium price and quantity of Gravenstein apples?

9. Suppose one of your friends offered the following argument: a rightward shift in demand will cause an increase in price. The increase in price will cause a rightward shift of the supply curve, which will lead to an offsetting decrease in price. Therefore, it is impossible to tell what effect an increase in demand will have on price. Do you agree with your friend? If not, what is the flaw in your friend's reasoning?

10. New York decides to reduce the consumption of sugary soda by imposing a minimum price of $2.50 per soda. The current equilibrium price is $1.50. Sketch the supply and demand for soda and show the effect of this policy. Clearly label the excess supply in your diagram.

11. Lobsters are plentiful and easy to catch in August but scarce and difficult to catch in November. In addition, vacationers shift the demand for lobsters further to the right in August than in any other month. Compare the equilibrium price and quantity of lobsters in August to the equilibrium price and quantity of lobsters in November. Present and discuss a supply-and-demand diagram to explain your answers.

12. As part of U.S. sugar policy (in 2013), the government offered to buy raw sugar from domestic sugarcane mills at an average price of 18.75 cents per pound. This gov-

ernment offer was made for as much raw sugar as the sugarcane mills produced. Any raw sugar purchased by the government was not sold in the domestic market, as this might have caused raw sugar prices to fall.

a. Under this policy, what do you think the government's demand curve for sugar looks like?

b. What impact does this policy likely have on domestic sugar prices? Explain your reasoning with a supply-and-demand diagram.

13. Suppose demand in a market is described by the equation $Q_D = 6 - P$.

a. Sketch demand.

b. Write out the demand schedule for each integer price up to $6 ($0, $1, $2, . . . , $6).

c. What if another buyer shows up who is "willing to pay any amount" for one unit. If we take her word at face value, what does the new demand look like?

14. *Note: This problem requires some basic algebra.* The demand for computers is $Q_D = 15 - 2P$, where $P$ is the price of computers. Initially, the supply of computers is $Q_S = P$.

a. Find the original equilibrium price and quantity.

b. Suppose the prices of memory chips and motherboards (two important components in computers) rise and as a consequence, the supply curve for computers becomes $Q_S = -3 + P$. Find the new equilibrium price and quantity.

# Consumers and Incentives

## Would a smoker quit the habit for $100 a month?

At first thought, you might believe that convincing people to quit smoking really has nothing to do with economics. In fact, you might think that smoking isn't even an economic decision. This chapter shows you how economics touches every aspect of our lives by focusing on incentives—rewards or penalties that motivate a person to behave in a particular way. For instance, you may want to earn an "A" in this course to make your parents proud. Or, maybe you want to do well in this course because you think it will help you gain admission to a premier graduate program or land a high-paying job upon graduation. Or maybe you want to succeed just to prove to yourself that you can do it.

Incentives are as numerous as the behaviors they're designed to change. Some are financial in nature, as when a salesperson earns a commission on a sale. Others are moral or ethical in nature, like that impulse to make your parents proud. Others are coercive: if you don't use your hockey stick properly in a game of ice hockey—say you trip your opponent with it—you'll find yourself sitting in the penalty box.

Incentives shape the choices we make—which makes them critical to the study of economics. One of the main tasks of an economist is recognizing these various motives and using them to shape behavior through designing incentive schemes. Economists have been designing incentive schemes for decades—whether to get people back to work after a spell of unemployment, to promote safe sex, or to stimulate charitable contributions—nothing is off limits to an economist.

So, does a financial incentive like paying people to stop smoking work? We'll find out the answer to that question in this chapter. This chapter also explains why human behavior is often so predictable. In short, the chapter provides you with the economic tools to design incentive schemes to promote your own goals as well as better understand the world we live in.

## CHAPTER OUTLINE

## 5.1 The Buyer's Problem

The first question that we explore is "How do consumers decide what to buy?" We can frame this question as a problem—the buyer's problem. You've probably experienced this problem when walking into a mall or browsing on Amazon.com—the options seem endless, but your money isn't. Economists identify three essential ingredients of the buyer's problem:

1. What you like
2. Prices of goods and services
3. How much money you have to spend

Together, these ingredients provide the foundations for the demand curves introduced in Chapter 4. In the next chapter, we study the other side of the market—the elements that make up the "seller's problem," which provide the foundation for the supply curves introduced in Chapter 4.

First, as a buyer, you want to buy goods and services that you like, because you prefer to buy what tastes good, sounds good, or looks good. You must also consider prices of the various goods and services that interest you. Prices are important because that extra dollar spent on an iPhone means one less dollar spent on a latte at Starbucks. And that trade-off, of course, stems from a third consideration: you only have a limited amount of money to spend. We wish our wallets were bottomless, but all of us have limited money to spend; this budget constraint forces you, as a consumer, to make important trade-offs.

Under certain assumptions, simply knowing these three ingredients— what you like, prices, and how much money you have to spend—leads to a set of powerful implications and rules that govern the buyer's problem. What emerges from this straightforward economic model are answers to simple questions, such as whether to buy a new pair of shoes at Zappos. com or to spend your money on a skateboard. We now look in more detail at these three key ingredients.

> Simply knowing these three ingredients—what you like, prices, and how much money you have to spend—leads to a set of powerful implications.

### What You Like

The benefits that you receive from consuming goods and services are a direct result of your tastes and preferences. If you like the taste of Diet Coke, for example, you will receive benefits from drinking a can. When it comes to the buyer's problem, economists assume that the consumer attempts to maximize the benefits from consumption. This makes sense: when you buy something, you choose what you think will give you the most satisfaction.

As part of the buying decision, consumers must figure out how to make the most of every dollar and, in the process, must consider the trade-offs that they face. For example, the dollar used to help buy a PS4 could have helped buy a Kindle or a new laptop instead. These are the opportunities that you forgo when purchasing a PS4.

What do our buying decisions signal about us as consumers? Consider a common situation: spending your birthday money at the mall. If you purchase a pair of Lucky jeans for $50, we know that you like Lucky jeans, but what else do we know? In fact, we know that you wouldn't trade your new pair of jeans for a $50 pair of shoes at the mall. Indeed, we know that of all the things that you could have purchased for $50, at the moment you bought the jeans you thought *nothing* in the mall was better to purchase.

Your own tastes and preferences might not seem obvious to you. They might depend on your current mood or change as you grow older. Your buying decisions, however, will reveal a great deal about your tastes and preferences. They will show that from the set of all the things that you are *able* to buy, you most prefer the things that you *choose* to buy.

## Prices of Goods and Services

Prices are the most important incentives that economists study; they allow us to formally define the relative cost of goods. Say that a pair of jeans has a price of $50 and a sweater has a price of $25. So if you purchase a pair of jeans, we know that you like those jeans more than you like two sweaters. We can also say that the opportunity cost of buying a pair of jeans is two sweaters. In this chapter, we assume that each good has a price that is fixed—a non-negotiable sticker price—and that consumers can buy as much of any good as they want at the fixed price if they have sufficient money to pay for it. In this way, our consumer is a price-taker. As we discussed in Chapter 4, this is an assumption typically made to describe perfectly competitive markets.

The rationale behind this assumption is that an individual consumer tends to buy only a tiny fraction of the total amount of a produced good. Because each buyer is only a small part of the market, an individual purchase will not have an effect on the market as a whole. For example, when you go to the mall, you might purchase only one of millions of pairs of jeans sold annually, so your decision to buy does not meaningfully affect the price of jeans.

When considering prices, you must take into account not only the price of the good you wish to purchase but also the prices of all other available goods. The relative prices of goods determine what you give up when you purchase something, so they are important when making the purchase decision.

## CHOICE & CONSEQUENCE

### Absolutes Versus Percentages

You are planning on purchasing a flat-screen television for your dorm room. After doing some research you find that the local Walmart is selling your preferred brand for $500. The Best Buy located across town is selling the same television for $490. Do you drive across town to buy it?

You figure $10 is just not enough of a savings from $500, so you choose to buy from the local Walmart.

Now consider another purchase decision: buying a calculator. In this case, Walmart has your preferred calculator for $20. The Best Buy located across town is selling the same calculator for $10. Do you drive across town to buy it? Makes sense to drive across town, right? You are saving 50 percent!

You have just committed a common decision-making error. When making optimal decisions, you should focus on the *absolute* marginal benefits and marginal costs, not the *proportional* ones. Had you focused on absolute marginal benefits, you would have noticed that these decision problems are identical: in each case you would have saved $10 by driving across town.

If it pays to drive across town to purchase the calculator, it certainly pays to do the same for the flat-screen television.

$10 is $10!

## How Much Money You Have to Spend

The final ingredient of the buyer's problem is what you can buy. The **budget set** is the set of all possible bundles of goods and services that a consumer can purchase with her income. Economists usually describe the budget set in the context of another concept—the *budget constraint*. The budget constraint represents the goods or activities that a consumer can choose that exactly exhaust her entire budget. We will make two assumptions about the budget constraint. First, we'll assume that consumers do not save or borrow. We know, of course, that many consumers do save and borrow, but for now we want to keep our model simple by focusing exclusively on buying decisions. This assumption allows us to focus more sharply on how we can use the budget constraint to learn about important economic concepts. Second, we plot the budget constraint as a smooth line, even though our examples will be using whole units. We do this as a matter of convenience, and it does not affect the analysis.

Let's continue with the example of your birthday money. Assume that your parents decide to surprise you on your 21st birthday with a $300 shopping spree. For simplicity, assume that this money is to be spent on only two goods—jeans or sweaters. In reality, of course, you could buy any number of other goods, but focusing on two goods draws out the most important insights from the economic model. And, once you understand the two-good case, it is straightforward to extend the analysis to more goods. Remember that you have exactly $300 to spend, and the price of jeans is $50 per pair and the price of each sweater is $25. Exhibit 5.1 provides the budget constraint and budget set for your shopping spree problem.

A first aspect of Exhibit 5.1 that might be confusing is the axis labels. Note that the quantities of pairs of jeans and sweaters are plotted on the x- and y-axes, respectively. In Chapter 4, we focused on demand and supply curves, which have quantity and price on the x- and y-axes. When plotting the budget constraint, however, the quantity of each good is on the x- and y-axes. That means the intercepts of the budget constraint represent the maximum quantity of each good that can be purchased if you buy only that good. So, the intercept values are the total dollars available divided by the price of the good measured on that axis. For example, the x-intercept is calculated as $300 divided by $50, or 6 pairs of jeans.

A second feature of Exhibit 5.1 is the triangular area. This area represents the budget set—all possible combinations of goods (often called "bundles" in economics) that you can purchase. The solid blue line represents the budget constraint—the various quantities that you can purchase using all of your birthday money. The budget constraint is a straight line, because you face a fixed price for jeans and sweaters that does not change with the number of goods that you buy. What else is the figure telling us?

1. We can see important trade-offs at work. For example, if you choose Bundle B, you are buying 2 pairs of jeans and 8 sweaters. Compared to Bundle A, you have

---

**Exhibit 5.1 The Budget Set and the Budget Constraint for Your Shopping Spree**

With $300 to spend on sweaters and jeans, the budget set summarizes the bundles of sweaters and jeans that could be purchased. The budget constraint shows the bundles that exactly exhaust the entire budget. The table shows a few possible bundles on the budget constraint, while the figure plots the quantity of jeans on the x-axis and the quantity of sweaters on the y-axis.

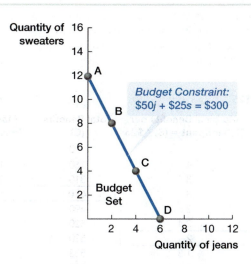

Budget Constraint: $50j + $25s = $300

**Four Bundles on the Budget Constraint**

| Bundle | Quantity of Sweaters | Quantity of Jeans |
|--------|----------------------|-------------------|
| A | 12 | 0 |
| B | 8 | 2 |
| C | 4 | 4 |
| D | 0 | 6 |

2 more pairs of jeans but at the expense of 4 sweaters. If you look at the table accompanying the graph, you can see the trade-offs between the amounts of pairs of jeans and sweaters.

2. Because your budget constraint is a straight line, its slope is constant. This means that your opportunity cost is constant.

And how, exactly, do we define that opportunity cost? We can think of it, very simply, as the number of sweaters you have to give up when you buy an additional pair of jeans. Mathematically, we can express this idea as a simple formula:

$$\text{Opportunity cost}_{\text{jeans}} = \frac{\text{Loss in sweaters}}{\text{Gain in jeans}},$$

where the loss in sweaters measures the number of sweaters that you must give up for one additional pair of jeans. Remember that the price of jeans is double that of sweaters, so opportunity cost$_{\text{jeans}}$ = 2 sweaters—this represents the opportunity cost of buying one pair of jeans. Another way to compute the opportunity cost of buying jeans is to consider the budget constraint. Because in this case it is a straight line, you can divide the $y$-intercept (12) by the $x$-intercept (6) to compute your opportunity cost of buying jeans.

A similar formula provides the opportunity cost of buying sweaters:

$$\text{Opportunity cost}_{\text{sweaters}} = \frac{\text{Loss in jeans}}{\text{Gain in sweaters}}.$$

Opportunity cost$_{\text{sweaters}}$ = ½ pair of jeans. This simply means that for every 2 sweaters that you decide to purchase, you have to give up 1 pair of jeans. This follows from the fact that the price of jeans is twice the price of sweaters ($50 versus $25). Again, you can also compute this opportunity cost from the $x$- and $y$-axes of the budget constraint (6 divided by 12 = ½ pair of jeans).

## 5.2 Putting It All Together

Now that we have the three ingredients of the buyer's problem in place, we can begin to construct how we use these elements to optimize—to do the best we can given our preferences, prices, and budget. As an example, consider Exhibit 5.2, which lists the ingredients to solve the shopping-spree problem. In Exhibit 5.2 we have assumed that you have certain

### Exhibit 5.2 Your Buyer's Problem ($300 available)

The total benefits from consuming a given number of sweaters or jeans are presented, as are the marginal benefits from consuming each additional unit. Finally, the marginal benefit per dollar spent is included. The bolded rows are the quantities of sweaters and jeans that maximize total benefits when you have $300 to spend.

| | Sweaters $25 | | | Jeans $50 | | |
|---|---|---|---|---|---|---|
| Quantity | Total Benefits (A) | Marginal Benefits (B) | Marginal Benefits per Dollar Spent = (B) / $25 | Total Benefits (C) | Marginal Benefits (D) | Marginal Benefits per Dollar Spent = (D) / $50 |
| 0 | 0 | | | 0 | | |
| 1 | 100 | 100 | 4 | 160 | 160 | 3.2 |
| 2 | 185 | 85 | 3.4 | 310 | 150 | 3 |
| 3 | 260 | 75 | 3 | 410 | 100 | 2 |
| 4 | 325 | 65 | 2.6 | 490 | 80 | 1.6 |
| 5 | 385 | 60 | 2.4 | 520 | 30 | 0.6 |
| 6 | 435 | 50 | 2 | 530 | 10 | 0.2 |
| 7 | 480 | 45 | 1.8 | 533 | 3 | 0.06 |
| 8 | 520 | 40 | 1.6 | 535 | 2 | 0.04 |

preferences, as indicated by the marginal benefits you receive from jeans and sweaters. Note that in the benefits columns, we do not specify what units of measurement we are working with—for example, dollars or some other measure of value. But it is helpful to use similar units when comparing benefits and costs. For illustrative purposes, therefore, let's assume that the benefits are measured in dollars, because working with common units enables us to combine, and therefore *compare*, costs and benefits using operations like addition and subtraction.

Although the benefit numbers in Exhibit 5.2 are fictitious, they do follow patterns that we observe from people's true preferences. For example, as we learned in Chapter 4, marginal benefits are larger for the first units than the later units. You can see this pattern for sweaters, which have $100 of marginal benefits for the first sweater but only $60 for the fifth sweater. The same pattern holds for jeans. Do you have similar preferences? Does the first Snickers bar typically taste better than the fourth?

So, how should you spend your $300? The problem calls for an approach based on marginal thinking. Using such an approach, you purchase the available good that yields the highest marginal benefits per dollar spent. Therefore, you should ask yourself: on which good should my first dollars be spent? Let's see how this approach works:

> An optimizing buyer makes decisions at the margin.

**(1)** The first sweater yields $100 in marginal benefits, whereas the first pair of jeans yields $160 in marginal benefits. Even though the first sweater has a lower marginal benefit than jeans, its price is half that of jeans, so you find that buying the sweater still yields the highest marginal benefits per dollar spent (the sweater yields 4 ($100/$25) in benefits per dollar spent, whereas the jeans yield 3.2 ($160/$50)). So you should purchase the sweater.

**(2)** Still thinking at the margin, you realize that your next choice should be to buy another sweater: buying the first pair of jeans yields $160 in marginal benefits, whereas buying another sweater yields $85 in marginal benefits. The marginal benefits per dollar spent favor buying the sweater.

**(3)** If you continue to reason in this way, you will find the quantities at which you optimize your total benefits—buying 6 sweaters and 3 pairs of jeans, exactly exhausting your budget of $300 and yielding $845 in total benefits. This optimal choice, which is bolded in Exhibit 5.2, maximizes your total benefits because there is no other spending pattern that yields a greater level of total benefits.

This solution highlights two important features of the buying problem. First, you should make your purchase decisions based on marginal benefits per dollar spent. Second, in doing so, an important conclusion results: when optimizing, the marginal benefit that you gain from the last dollar spent on each good is equal.

This decision rule can be summarized via a simple equation:

$$\frac{MB_s}{P_s} = \frac{MB_j}{P_j},$$

where $MB_s$ is the marginal benefit from sweaters, $MB_j$ is the marginal benefit from jeans, and $P_s$ and $P_j$ are the respective prices of sweaters and jeans.

Economists sometimes call this the "equal bang for your buck" rule. In our shopping-spree example, you received $50 of marginal benefits from buying the sixth sweater and $100 of marginal benefits from buying the third pair of jeans. Therefore, we have:

$$\frac{\$50}{\$25} = \frac{\$100}{\$50}.$$

Why does this rule hold? Because if marginal benefits are not equal, then you can do better—be happier—by shifting consumption toward the good that has higher marginal benefits per dollar spent.

This rule can easily be extended to the case with a large number of goods. It teaches us that in equilibrium, the ratio of marginal benefits to price must be identical across goods. If this is not the case, then you can purchase a different basket of goods and be better off. You will notice that this rule of making decisions at the margin follows directly from the cost-benefit principle discussed in Chapter 1.

At this point, it might be useful for you to prove to yourself that 6 sweaters and 3 pairs of jeans is indeed optimal, or doing the best you can. Consider two examples. First, what if you purchased 3 sweaters and 2 pairs of jeans? This would satisfy the equal bang for your buck rule. But, it does not maximize your satisfaction because you are not spending all of your money, which means you are inside of your budget constraint. Second, what if you purchased 8 sweaters and 4 pairs of jeans? This would also satisfy the equal bang for your buck rule. But, it is not affordable. These two examples highlight that the optimal bundle is achieved when (1) it satisfies the optimization equal bang for your buck rule, and (2) it's a purchase on the budget constraint.

While considering these examples, you might be thinking that while the sweaters and jeans numbers work well, the world might not always fit so neatly together algebraically. For example, there are some goods that are indivisible and have a high price—large-ticket items such as big-screen televisions, automobiles, houses, and yachts—which are typically consumed only infrequently.

This point is valid and very thoughtful. In these instances, buying the first house might provide higher marginal benefits per dollar spent than you gain from consuming other goods, but buying the second house yields fewer marginal benefits per dollar spent than other goods. In cases where goods are not easily divisible and our decision rule cannot be met exactly, the general intuition still holds: you should always spend each additional dollar on the good for which your marginal benefits per dollar spent are the largest.

What factors might change how many jeans and sweaters you purchase in equilibrium? There are two important ones that we now consider: changes in price and changes in income.

## Price Changes

Consider what happens to our buyer's problem if the price of sweaters doubles to $50. Jeans and sweaters now have the same price. What must happen to the budget constraint with this change in price? Exhibit 5.3 gives us the answer. If you now buy all sweaters on your shopping spree, you can buy only 6 sweaters, so the y-intercept must change to 6. Does the x-intercept change? No, because the price of jeans has not changed.

What Exhibit 5.3 shows is that when the price of one good relative to the price of the other good changes, the slope of the budget constraint must also change. Now if you buy an additional sweater, you can purchase 1 less pair of jeans, so the opportunity cost$_{sweaters}$ = 1 pair of jeans. This stands to reason because the prices are now equal.

A *decrease* in the price of either good will cause the budget constraint to pivot outward. For example, let's return to our original set of prices, but now assume that the price of jeans is cut in half—to $25 per pair. In this case, the budget constraint pivots outward and the x-intercept moves to 12. Exhibit 5.4 shows how the budget constraint pivots with a decrease in the price of jeans. Again, the prices for both goods are identical after this price change, and therefore the opportunity cost$_{jeans}$ = 1 sweater.

**Exhibit 5.3 An Inward Pivot in the Budget Constraint from a Price Increase**

Reproducing the figure in Exhibit 5.1 with an increase in the price of sweaters, we see that the budget constraint pivots inward. (Note that the term "pivot" signifies that one of the intercepts does not change.) This is because the consumer's income can buy fewer units of a good if the price goes up. The slope also changes, because the opportunity cost changes when the price of one good changes.

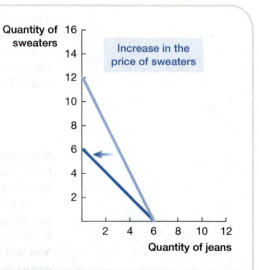

**Exhibit 5.4** An Outward Pivot in the Budget Constraint from a Price Decrease

A decrease in the price of one good causes the budget constraint to pivot outward. This is because the consumer's income can buy more units of a good if the price goes down. The slope also changes, because the opportunity cost changes when the price changes.

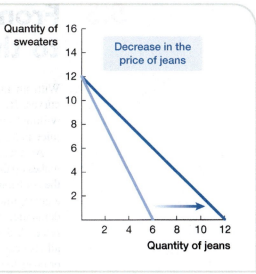

How do price changes affect the buyer's problem? When a price changes, the opportunity cost changes. This will cause the buyer to change the optimal quantities consumed. Below we show how such price changes influence how many jeans and sweaters you purchase.

## Income Changes

Another important factor that influences how many jeans and sweaters you purchase is how much money you have to spend—such cases revolve around changes in an individual's income, or budget. One example is if your shopping-spree gift turned out to be $600 instead of $300. Exhibit 5.5 shows the new budget constraint and how this change in income causes the budget constraint to shift outward. When income is doubled, the y-intercept and x-intercept of the budget constraint also must double, because you have twice as much income. You can now buy more.

Even with the expansion of income, however, the relative prices stay the same. In Exhibit 5.5, the identical slopes of the two budget constraints reflect that the opportunity cost remains the same: buying 1 additional pair of jeans still precludes the purchase of 2 sweaters.

**Exhibit 5.5** An Outward Shift in the Budget Constraint from an Increase in Income

An increase in income shifts the budget constraint outward. To see this, consider what happens to the number of jeans and sweaters you can buy if your budget increases—the quantities go up. Furthermore, the slope will not change, because the opportunity cost of purchasing either sweaters or jeans does not change with an increase in income.

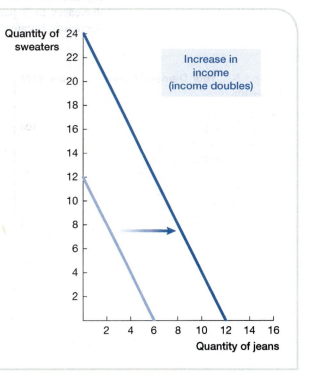

## 5.3 From the Buyer's Problem to the Demand Curve

With an understanding of how to spend optimally, we can begin to construct demand curves. Recall from Chapter 4 that willingness to pay is the highest price that a buyer is willing to pay for a unit of a good. Hence, if your willingness to pay for 1 gallon of orange juice is $10.00, it means that's the *highest* price that you are willing to pay for it.

An individual's willingness to pay measured over different quantities of the same good makes up the individual's *demand curve*. As we learned in Chapter 4, the demand curve isolates the contribution that a good's own price makes toward determining the *quantity demanded* in a given time period, keeping everything else the same. We also saw in Chapter 4 that quantity demanded refers to the amount of a good that buyers are willing to purchase at a particular price. A demand curve maps how quantity demanded responds to price changes, holding all else equal. We all have demand curves for many goods—from dinner dates to movies to oranges to cars to the *Twilight* series.

Let's look at a demand curve by continuing with the shopping-spree example. With the three pieces of the buyer's problem in place, we can derive your demand curve. We saw from our marginal analysis above that when the price of jeans is $50, you purchase 3 pairs of jeans. Thus, one point on your demand curve for jeans is price = $50, quantity demanded = 3.

What about if the price of jeans rises to $75? Using marginal analysis similar to what we used above, from Exhibit 5.2 we can compute that you now purchase 2 pairs of jeans. And, when the price of jeans rises to $100, your quantity demanded is 1 pair. Similarly, if the price decreases to $25, then your quantity demanded is 4 pairs of jeans. You can verify all of these optimal bundles through marginal analysis. These combinations represent the demand curve and are displayed in Exhibit 5.6.

We produce Exhibit 5.6 by making optimal decisions based on the buyer's problem. Every point on your demand curve represents a unique price and quantity level. Therefore, the demand curve provides an indication of how many pairs of jeans you would like to buy at each price level. In Exhibit 5.6 we plot the demand curve as smooth, even though you would be unable to buy 3.5 pairs of jeans. We do this merely for convenience. As we move from the individual to the entire market of buyers, the units of quantity demanded will be so large that the demand curve will be smooth.

We can see that your demand curve slopes downward: at a price of $25 your quantity demanded is 4 pairs of jeans, but at a price of $50 per pair your quantity demanded decreases to 3 pairs. It only makes sense that as price increases, quantity demanded decreases, because the opportunity cost of buying a pair of jeans increases.

**Exhibit 5.6 Your Demand Curve for Jeans**

The demand curve shows how the quantity demanded depends on the price of the good. The table summarizes the quantity demanded of pairs of jeans at different prices. The figure plots those numbers with quantity demanded on the x-axis and price on the y-axis.

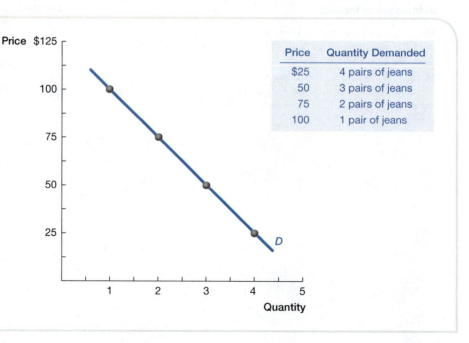

| Price | Quantity Demanded |
|-------|-------------------|
| $25   | 4 pairs of jeans  |
| 50    | 3 pairs of jeans  |
| 75    | 2 pairs of jeans  |
| 100   | 1 pair of jeans   |

What factors other than your tastes and preferences and the price of jeans might affect how many pairs you buy? Our earlier examination of the buyer's problem provides hints. The key to the answer involves prices of related goods and the budget set. Changes in the prices of related goods and the amount of money available both cause the demand curve to shift. In addition, as mentioned in Chapter 4, if your expectations of what is going to happen in the future change, then that also will shift the demand curve.

# 5.4 Consumer Surplus

**Consumer surplus** is the difference between the willingness to pay and the price paid for the good.

So far we've learned that in an effort to do the best we can, we should recognize the incentives that we face and make decisions based on marginal analysis. That is, we should consider the marginal benefits and marginal costs in our decision making. In markets, the process of optimal decision making by consumers often yields total benefits well above the price that we pay for goods. Economists give these market-created benefits a name—*consumer surplus*. **Consumer surplus** is the difference between the willingness to pay and the price paid for the good.

To illustrate how to calculate consumer surplus, let's continue with the shopping-spree example and consider the purchase of jeans more closely. Exhibit 5.7 provides the relevant points from your demand curve in Exhibit 5.6. Exhibit 5.7 shows that your willingness to pay for the first pair of jeans is $100. Because the market price is $50, you have gained $50 ($100 − $50) in consumer surplus from purchasing this first pair of jeans. Your willingness to pay for the second pair of jeans is $75; thus you gain $25 in consumer surplus from purchasing the second pair of jeans. How much consumer surplus do you gain from the third pair of jeans? The answer is zero, because your willingness to pay ($50) is exactly equal to the price ($50) that you pay for this pair of jeans.

Putting all of the numbers together, you might be wondering why your consumer surplus ($75) is considerably lower than the total benefits that you received from buying the three pairs of jeans (from Exhibit 5.2, the total benefits from purchasing three pairs of jeans is $410, and you pay $150 for the jeans, yielding net benefits of $260). This is because the two measures are importantly different: consumer surplus measures the difference between your willingness to pay (your demand curve) and what you actually pay for the good. The total benefits displayed in Exhibit 5.2 provide how much overall *satisfaction* you gain from consuming the good.

> Consumer surplus is the difference between what a buyer is willing to pay for a good and what the buyer actually pays.

**Exhibit 5.7 Computing Consumer Surplus**

Consumer surplus is the vertical distance between your maximum willingness to pay and the market price, which we represent with blue lines.

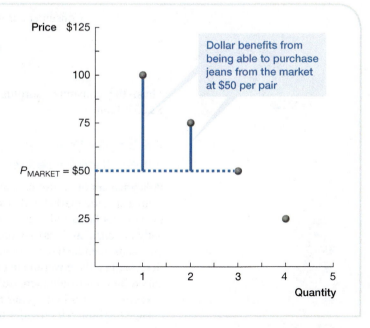

Dollar benefits from being able to purchase jeans from the market at $50 per pair

### Exhibit 5.8  Market-Wide Consumer Surplus

Here we plot a market demand curve for jeans—notice that the quantity sold has increased considerably. Visually, you can think of the market-wide consumer surplus as the area of the triangle below the market demand curve and above the market price.

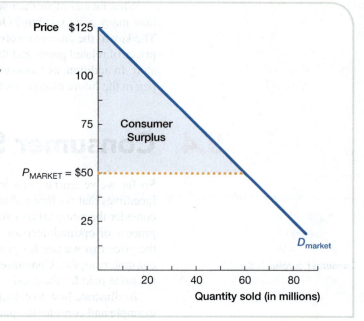

To develop intuition into this relationship at a bit deeper level, consider a different everyday purchase: gasoline for your car. You might typically purchase gasoline at the local 7-Eleven for $2.25 per gallon but be willing to pay $3 per gallon. This means that for each gallon purchased, you receive $0.75 in consumer surplus. Now let's say that a new RaceTrac gas station opens directly across the street from 7-Eleven and sells gasoline for $2.50 per gallon. You might now be willing to pay only $2.50 per gallon of gasoline at 7-Eleven. As such, even though the overall *satisfaction* you gain from gasoline has not changed, your consumer surplus has decreased to $0.25 per gallon. Market forces cause changes in consumer surplus but do not typically change satisfaction from actual consumption.

Computing consumer surplus for the market as a whole is calculated similarly. As we learned in Chapter 4, we can horizontally sum individual demand curves to obtain a market demand curve. Assume that upon doing so, we find that the market demand curve for jeans is given by Exhibit 5.8.

In Exhibit 5.8, "consumer surplus" represents the total market consumer surplus. Because the demand curve is linear, the area of the consumer surplus triangle can be computed as the base of the triangle multiplied by the height of the triangle multiplied by ½:

$$\text{Consumer surplus} = \frac{\text{Base of triangle} \times \text{Height of triangle}}{2}$$

$$= \frac{60 \text{ million} \times \$75}{2} = \$2.25 \text{ billion.}$$

Thus, the consumer surplus that all consumers receive from the jeans market is $2.25 billion.

### An Empty Feeling: Loss in Consumer Surplus When Price Increases

Policymakers often use consumer surplus to measure the dollar value of consumer gains from a specific market and how those gains change with proposed legislation. How might the concept be useful in a practical sense? When working in the White House, one of the authors considered various policies to clean up groundwater. One potential solution was that jeans manufacturers would have to stop using certain chemical treatments on their fabrics. Say that the government concluded that if this policy took effect, the treatment chemical prohibition would increase the market price of jeans from $50 to $75. What happens to consumer surplus in the jeans market if everything else stays the same except for this price change? Exhibit 5.9 provides the answer.

## Exhibit 5.9 Market-Wide Consumer Surplus When Prices Change

When price increases, consumer surplus decreases. This graph visually summarizes why—the higher the price, the smaller the difference between the willingness to pay and the market price. Furthermore, the higher the price, the lower the quantity demanded.

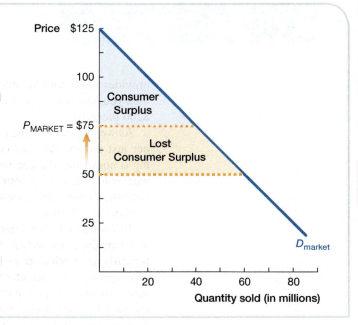

Exhibit 5.9 shows the new consumer surplus, shaded in light blue. We find that market consumer surplus is now equal to 40 million × $50/2 = $1 billion. As a consumer, this development gives you an empty feeling, as many price increases do, because you have lost consumer surplus. In this situation, the market has lost $1.25 billion ($2.25 billion − $1 billion) in consumer surplus, which is shaded in orange. You, personally, have just lost $50 in consumer surplus from the jeans market (your surplus is now $25). When determining whether to enact the new prohibition, policymakers compare such losses in consumer surplus to the benefits gained in cleaner groundwater to make a final policy decision (they also consider changes in *producer surplus*, which we discuss in the next chapter).

## EVIDENCE-BASED ECONOMICS

## Would a smoker quit the habit for $100 per month?

At the beginning of this chapter, we posed a question concerning whether *a smoker would quit the habit for $100 a month*. The tools of this chapter can help us begin to think about whether such an incentive can work, and why it might work.

In thinking about such a reward, we have learned that the impact of an increase in income leads to changes in the consumer budget constraint and subsequently the demand for goods and services. To see these tools in action, we return to the shopping-spree example. Exhibit 5.5 shows the mechanics behind the effects of an increase in what we have available to spend.

With that foundation laid, we can return to the question of quitting smoking for a month. Given our economic framework, the very same principle that was at work in the shopping-spree problem applies when considering the smoker's problem. By providing $100 for not smoking, we create a trade-off between the current benefits of smoking and the benefits obtained by $100 of increased income. There is also another saving: by not smoking, you save the money otherwise spent on cigarettes or cigars. For simplicity, let's assume that is another $100 per month. Thus the comparison that we need to make is whether, at the margin, $200 of additional monthly income provides more benefits than the current benefits you gain from smoking. If they do, then you quit smoking. If they do not, then you continue smoking and miss out on the $200 incentive.

As we discussed in the chapter opening, incentives come in many different forms—not just money. Another complementary approach that is often used to curb smoking is nonfinancial incentives. Such an approach includes advertisements highlighting what smoking does to your teeth and gums, warnings prominently placed on packs of cigarettes, counseling, social pressure, and banning smoking in public places, forcing smokers to go outside.

To explore whether financial and nonfinancial incentives can encourage smokers to quit smoking, researchers have designed randomized experiments. The experiments typically are carried out as follows. The researcher recruits smokers who are voluntary participants in a research experiment to help them quit smoking. The researcher then randomly assigns these participants to control and treatment groups. Those in the control group receive no financial incentive but are monitored to test whether they quit. To measure compliance, biochemical tests are used to confirm that the participants have not smoked during the experimental period. In this way, those in the incentive treatment group receive the reward if the biochemical test reveals that they are smoke-free. If they are found to have smoked, then no financial incentive is awarded.

One such study enrolled 179 subjects at Philadelphia Veterans Affairs Medical Center in a 10-week program to stop smoking. Subjects were randomly assigned to either a control group that received only the standard program or to a treatment group that received incentives in addition to the standard program.[1] The standard program comprised informational meetings every 2 weeks, where 2 weeks' worth of nicotine patches were distributed to the participants. In addition to the informational meetings and nicotine patches, the participants in the treatment group received $20 for each meeting attended, and $100 if they were smoke-free 30 days after the program was completed.

The main results of the experiment are displayed in Exhibit 5.10, which shows the percentage of people in the treatment and control groups who were smoke-free 30 days after the program was completed. The results highlight the power of incentives: 16.3 percent of the incentivized participants were found to have quit smoking. This rate is nearly four times greater than the 4.6 percent quitting rate of the non-incentivized group. This short-term effect of incentives is supported by several other studies.[2]

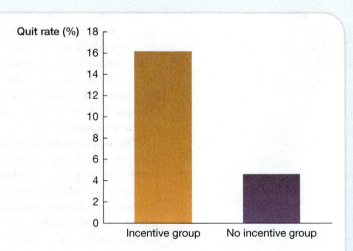

**Exhibit 5.10  Experimental Results from Smoking Study**

This figure summarizes the results from the smoking study. Each bar depicts the percentage of participants that quit smoking. As you can see, the percentage of smokers that quit in the incentive group is a great deal higher than in the no-incentive group.

Equally as important, however, is whether these people remained smoke-free after the incentive program was over. The Philadelphia Veterans Affairs experiment followed up with the experimental subjects 6 months after the program, again using biochemical tests. What do you think the researchers found?

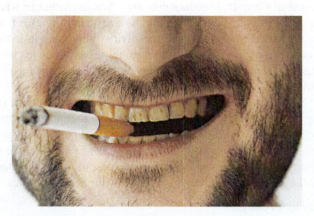 

Which would make you quit smoking?

The results are enlightening. The researchers report that the 16.3 percent quit rate observed among the incentivized group had dropped to 6.5 percent. This was only slightly larger than the percentage of quitters in the control group, which remained at 4.6 percent. A clear conclusion from this literature is that financial incentives are quite powerful: when incentives are in place, many people quit smoking, because the benefits of quitting exceed the benefits of smoking. But when the financial incentives end, people tend to return to their old habit of smoking.

Can you think of other behaviors that financial incentives might change? Upon reading this chapter, you will likely not be surprised to learn that economists have. For example, as we learned in the appendix to Chapter 2, economists have used financial incentives to improve student performance. As those data suggest, receiving a financial reward of $50 per month caused high school students to improve their academic performance considerably—their grades and attendance levels improved. In another study, economists measured the effects of paying students to go to the gym. Again, the results confirm the power of financial incentives—students in the incentivized group were much more frequently in the gym working out than those not receiving financial rewards. With these results in hand, several normative questions arise: should the government use taxpayer dollars to pay people to quit smoking, to go to the gym, or to finish high school? We leave this for you to decide.

|  Question |  Answer |  Data |  Caveat |
| --- | --- | --- | --- |
| Would a smoker quit the habit for $100 a month? | Yes, some will! | Field experimental data. | One should take care to understand that after the incentives are removed, many people who quit to earn the cash begin smoking again. |

# 5.5  Demand Elasticities

So far, we've learned the nuts and bolts about where the demand curve comes from and whether quantity demanded increases or decreases when price changes. But suppose we want more precise answers as to exactly how responsive quantity demanded is to a change in price. As we discussed in Chapter 3, economists are often interested in what happens after a certain variable changes; here, we'll talk about how to quantify these effects using a concept called *elasticity*. **Elasticity** measures the sensitivity of one economic variable to a change in another. In other words, it tells us how much one variable changes when another changes. More precisely, elasticity is a ratio of percentage changes in variables.

**Elasticity** is the measure of sensitivity of one variable to a change in another.

> Elasticity measures the sensitivity of one economic variable to a change in another.

Note that elasticity is not the same as the slope of a line. By measuring changes in percentage terms, elasticity goes a step deeper than the slope relationship. Elasticity is an important concept because it takes into account not only the direction of change but also the size of the change. Elasticities come in many forms, but in this chapter we focus on the most important ones associated with demand curves:

1.  The price elasticity of demand
2.  The cross-price elasticity of demand
3.  The income elasticity of demand

## The Price Elasticity of Demand

We know from the Law of Demand that when the price of a good increases, the quantity demanded generally falls. But what we do not know from this law is *by how much* quantity demanded falls. The **price elasticity of demand** measures the percentage change in quantity demanded of a good resulting from a percentage change in the good's price. Formally, the price elasticity of demand is calculated as

The **price elasticity of demand** measures the percentage change in quantity demanded of a good due to a percentage change in its price.

$$\text{Price elasticity of demand } (\varepsilon_D) = \frac{\text{Percentage change in quantity demanded}}{\text{Percentage change in price}}.$$

To show how to calculate this elasticity, let's consider your demand schedule for jeans in Exhibit 5.6. When the price is $25 per pair you buy 4 pairs, but when the price increases to $50 per pair you buy only 3 pairs. This means that when the price increases by 100 percent (from $25 to $50), your quantity demanded decreases by 25 percent (from 4 to 3 pairs), yielding an elasticity of demand equal to

$$\frac{-25\%}{100\%} = -0.25.$$

Two features of this computation are important. First, because of the Law of Demand, the price elasticity of demand will generally be negative. Because this is the case, economists often drop the minus sign when reporting elasticities (mathematicians denote this as an absolute value), so we would state here that our price elasticity of demand is 0.25. We follow that convention here. Note that higher price elasticities mean that consumers are more responsive to a change in price.

Second, the distinction between whether a good has a price elasticity of demand greater than or less than 1 is of great import. Why? Suppose that you are working at your university bookstore and the manager wants to increase *revenues* from mug sales. Currently your store sells 20 mugs per week for $5 each, yielding revenues of $100 (20 mugs × $5). To increase revenues, your manager's first instinct might be to raise the price of mugs from $5 to $6.

We know from the Law of Demand that this 20 percent price increase will lower the *quantity* of mugs purchased, but we need to understand the elasticity of demand before we can make predictions about how revenues change. Assume that after the price increase, your store sells 12 mugs per week, yielding revenues of $72 (12 mugs × $6). Even though you raised the price of mugs, your revenues decreased. What is happening here?

The price elasticity of demand provides the answer. In this case, when price increased by 20 percent, the percentage change in quantity demanded decreased by 40 percent (8/20). This means that the price elasticity of demand is 2 (40 percent/20 percent). When the price elasticity of demand is greater than 1, the percentage change in quantity demanded is greater than the percentage change in price. This means that any price increase will lead to lower revenues.

Alternatively, if the price elasticity of demand had been less than 1, the percentage change in quantity demanded would be lower than the percentage change in price. Consider the case where the same 20 percent price increase lowers quantity demanded by only 10 percent. The price elasticity is now 0.5 (10 percent/20 percent). In this case, mug revenues would increase to $108 (18 mugs × $6) if you raised the price from $5 to $6.

Finally, had the price elasticity of demand been exactly equal to 1, a 20 percent price increase would lower the quantity demanded by exactly 20 percent. In this situation, any price increase would leave revenues unchanged. In sum, the revenues that your store brings in critically depend on the price elasticity of demand.

**Moving Up and Down the Demand Curve**   At this point, you might be wondering whether elasticity varies over the demand curve. Let's consider an example to find out.

Exhibit 5.11 uses data from a recent survey to explore how much people are willing to pay for a Mike Trout baseball card. The demand curve is for Jacob, and shows how much he would pay for various quantities of Mike Trout's baseball card. Point A on the demand curve informs us that at a price of $5, Jacob's quantity demanded is 1 card; point B tells us that at a price of $1, Jacob's quantity demanded is 5 cards. What is the price elasticity at these two points?

First, let's calculate the price elasticity beginning at the higher price point on the demand curve, point A ($P = \$5, Q = 1$). Say that price drops to $1, effectively moving along the demand curve until point B. In this case, price decreases by 80 percent ($4/$5) and quantity demanded increases by 400 percent (4/1). Therefore, the price elasticity of demand is equal to 5 (400/80 = 5). So Jacob is very responsive to price changes at point A.

Second, let's calculate the price elasticity of demand beginning at point B ($P = \$1, Q = 5$), for a price increase to $5. This moves along the demand curve from point B to point A. Now the price elasticity is 0.20 (the percentage change in quantity demanded is 80 percent, and the percentage change in the good's price is 400 percent).

This analysis reveals three important insights about elasticities. First, elasticity is a much different concept than the slope of the line. Even though the slope is the same over the entire demand curve (because demand is linear), the elasticity varies. This is because the ratio of price to quantity changes as we move along the demand curve. For example, at point A, the ratio is 5/1 whereas at point B it is 1/5. As this ratio grows, demand becomes more elastic.

---

**Exhibit 5.11  Jacob's Demand Curve for Mike Trout Baseball Cards**

On this linear demand curve for Mike Trout baseball cards, we highlight the way that price elasticity varies along a linear demand curve. The figure shows that demand becomes more inelastic as we move down the demand curve: at point A demand is elastic, whereas at point B demand is inelastic.

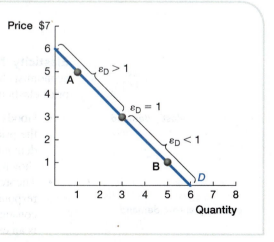

This leads to the second insight: elasticities tend to vary over ranges of the demand curve. You can see this in Exhibit 5.11. On the upper half of a linear demand curve, the elasticity is greater than 1, and on the lower half, the elasticity is less than 1. What this means is that the elasticity from point A to point B is different than the elasticity from point B to point A. Finally, in the exact middle of a linear demand curve, the elasticity is equal 1.

## Moving Up and Down the Demand Curve

### Arc Elasticities

One thing that you might be puzzled by is the fact that the elasticity is different depending on what you use as the starting and ending points. This is one reason why economists use the approach described in the Mike Trout example for small price changes.

Another measure that economists often calculate is *arc elasticity*. The **arc elasticity** achieves a stable elasticity regardless of the starting point by using the average price and quantity in the calculation:

$$\text{arc } \varepsilon_D = \frac{(Q_2 - Q_1)/[(Q_2 + Q_1)/2]}{(P_2 - P_1)/[(P_2 + P_1)/2]}.$$

The upside of this formula for calculating elasticities is that regardless of where you start, the elasticity will be the same if you are examining changes over the same range of the demand curve. This is because the arc elasticity is a method of computing elasticities that measures at the midpoint of the range.

To see this fact, let's return to our example of Mike Trout baseball cards. First, let's calculate the price elasticity of demand beginning at $P = \$5$, $Q = 1$, and explore what happens when price drops to $1. Plugging the numbers into the formula, we have

$$\text{arc } \varepsilon_D = \frac{(5 - 1)/[(5 + 1)/2]}{(1 - 5)/[(1 + 5)/2]}$$

which equals 1. If we begin instead at the point $P = \$1$, $Q = 5$, and consider a price increase to $5, we estimate the arc elasticity as

$$\text{arc } \varepsilon_D = \frac{(1 - 5)/[(1 + 5)/2]}{(5 - 1)/[(5 + 1)/2]}.$$

Again, this equals 1. With this approach, moving from point A to point B provides an elasticity identical to moving from point B to point A.

When doing economic analysis we recommend that you compute the arc elasticity because this will provide you with a more accurate description of consumer responsiveness.

**Elasticity Measures** Because of the importance of the price elasticity of demand, economists have developed a terminology to classify goods based on the magnitude of the price elasticity:

- Goods with a price elasticity of demand greater than 1 have **elastic demand**. When the price elasticity of demand is greater than 1, the percentage change in quantity demanded is greater than the percentage change in price. Economic research has shown that peanut butter and olive oil tend to have elastic demand.
- Theoretically, demand may be **perfectly elastic**, which means that demand is highly responsive to price changes—the smallest increase in price causes consumers to stop consuming the good altogether. The blue (horizontal) line in panel (a) of Exhibit 5.12 is an example of a perfectly elastic demand curve.

The **arc elasticity** is a method of calculating elasticities that measures at the midpoint of the demand range.

Goods that have **elastic demand** have a price elasticity of demand greater than 1.

A very small increase in price causes consumers to stop using goods that have **perfectly elastic demand**.

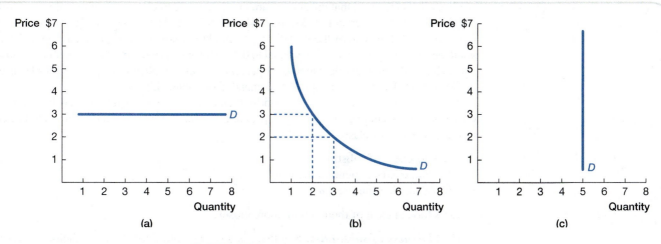

**Exhibit 5.12 Examples of Various Demand Curves**

From left to right, three demand curves are plotted to visually summarize a perfectly elastic, a unitary, and a perfectly inelastic demand curve. Although we will mainly deal with simple linear demand curves, extreme cases like these can be useful to consider for intuition.

5.1
5.2
5.3
5.4
5.5

Goods that have **unit elastic demand** have a price elasticity of demand equal to 1.

- Goods with a price elasticity of demand equal to 1 have **unit elastic demand**. For such goods, a 1 percent price change affects quantity demanded by exactly 1 percent. In this case, a price increase does not affect total expenditures on the good. Economists have found that wine has unitary elastic demand. The blue line in panel (b) of Exhibit 5.12 is an example of a unit elastic demand curve, where elasticity is measured using the arc elasticity.

Goods that have **inelastic demand** have a price elasticity of demand less than 1.

- Goods with a price elasticity of demand less than 1 have **inelastic demand**. When the price elasticity of demand is less than 1, the percentage change in quantity demanded is less than the percentage change in price. Research within economics has taught us that goods such as cigarettes and potato chips are not very responsive to price changes and thus have inelastic demand.

Quantity demanded is unaffected by prices of goods with **perfectly inelastic demand**.

- Demand can also be **perfectly inelastic**, which means that quantity demanded is completely unaffected by price. The blue (vertical) line in panel (c) of Exhibit 5.12 is an example of perfectly inelastic demand. The phrase "gotta have it" describes such goods, which include insulin for diabetics.

**Determinants of the Price Elasticity of Demand** Exhibit 5.13 lists a handful of elasticity estimates that economists have generated with consumption and price data over the past several decades. One way to think about these numbers is to consider the types of goods that you might purchase when shopping at a supermarket. For example, as you walk in, you might see a display of olive oil. Economists have found that olive oil has an elastic demand: a 1 percent increase in the price of olive oil yields a 1.92 percent decrease in quantity demanded

**Exhibit 5.13 Examples of Various Price Elasticities**

Price elasticities are presented for a number of goods that are commonly consumed. The higher the price elasticity of demand, the more elastic is the demand for that good. For example, demand for shampoo is inelastic, whereas demand for olive oil is elastic.

| Goods Category | Price Elasticity[3] |
|---|---|
| Olive Oil | 1.92 |
| Peanut Butter | 1.73 |
| Ketchup | 1.36 |
| Wine | 1.00 |
| Laundry Detergent | 0.81 |
| Shampoo | 0.79 |
| Potato Chips | 0.45 |
| Cigarettes | 0.40 |

of olive oil. This means that consumers are quite sensitive to changes in olive oil prices. You might walk an aisle over and see ketchup, which also is an elastic good, with a price elasticity equal to 1.36. At the end of the next aisle, you might see potato chips, which are an inelastic good, because the price elasticity is equal to 0.45. This means that changes in their price cause small changes in quantity demanded: a 1 percent increase in the price of potato chips leads to a 0.45 percent decrease in the quantity demanded of potato chips.

What do you think makes some goods, such as olive oil and ketchup, elastic, whereas others, such as shampoo and potato chips, are inelastic? Economists have pinpointed three primary reasons for elasticity differences:

1. Closeness of substitutes
2. Budget share spent on the good
3. Available time to adjust

Let's look at each of them a little more closely.

**(1) *Closeness of substitutes*.** Say there is a strike among local cheese factory workers and the price of pizza skyrockets. You should ask yourself, "Is there another good, a *substitute good*, available that I like nearly as much as pizza?" If the answer is yes, then you will be more likely to switch to that good—perhaps hamburgers—rather than continue to purchase pizza at the higher price. In this way, the number of available substitutes affects how responsive consumers are to price changes: *as the number of available substitutes grows, the price elasticity of demand increases.*

**(2) *Budget share spent on the good*.** The budget share relates to how important the good is in your consumption bundle. People should give more weight to "important" goods and less weight to unimportant ones. If the good represents a small fraction of your overall purchases—say, a $0.50 key chain that you replace every five years—you likely will not be overly concerned if the local factory workers strike and the price of key chains doubles. It is just not important to your overall budget and so you are not sensitive to price changes, even large ones. Alternatively, if the good represents a large fraction of your budget—say, a house or furniture purchase—then you are likely to be more responsive to price changes. In general, *as you spend more of your budget on a good, the price elasticity of demand increases.*

**The hummer**

As we discussed in Chapter 4, skyrocketing gas prices in 2008 led some people to stop buying Hummers.

**(3)** *Available time to adjust.* Time is an important element in that people are more responsive to price changes in the long run than in the short run. When the price of oil jumped to $150 per barrel in the summer of 2008 and a gallon of gasoline nationwide was $4, did everyone immediately stop driving? No. But people might have skipped that extra trip to the grocery store or passed on an extra visit to Grandma's house to save on gasoline.

The key is that it is difficult to make major changes in the short run, because you are constrained with what can be done over a short period of time. For example, the Hummer owner may have wanted to trade in her Hummer for a hybrid, but there may have been significant switching costs that prevented a reasonable trade. Her options would have been much more flexible in the long run; for example, she could arrange to carpool to work or move to an apartment near where she works. Such instances highlight the fact that *consumers, in general, respond much less to price changes in the short run than in the long run.*

## The Cross-Price Elasticity of Demand

The **cross-price elasticity of demand** measures the percentage change in quantity demanded of a good due to a percentage change in another good's price.

Economists are interested in much more than merely how changes in a good's price affect consumers. Another type of elasticity that economists consider is how quantity demanded for one good changes when the price of a substitute or complement good changes. This is called the **cross-price elasticity of demand** and is a measurement of the percentage change in quantity demanded of a good due to a percentage change in another good's price. Formally, the cross-price elasticity is written as:

$$\text{Cross-price elasticity} = \frac{\text{Percentage change in quantity demanded of good x}}{\text{Percentage change in price of good y}}.$$

This measure provides the elasticity of demand for good x with respect to the price of good y.

If a cross-price elasticity is negative, then the two goods are complements. As discussed in Chapter 4, two goods are complements when the fall in the price of one leads to a right shift in the demand curve for another. For example, if the price of iPods falls, you want more of them, but also your demand for headphones is likely to increase. The size of the cross-price elasticity determines the strength of the positive shift in your demand for headphones.

If a cross-price elasticity is positive, then the two goods are substitutes. Two goods are substitutes when the rise in the price of one leads to a right shift in the demand curve for the other. For example, an iPad would be a substitute for a Microsoft Surface. Thus, if the price of an iPad increases substantially, instead of spending your money on the iPad, you might buy a Microsoft Surface instead.

Exhibit 5.14 summarizes a handful of cross-price elasticities that economists have generated with consumption and price data over the past several decades. A first insight from these examples is that goods such as meat and fish, clothing and entertainment, and whole and low-fat milk are substitutes for one another. At the other end of the spectrum, meat and potatoes are complements, as are food and entertainment. A second insight from Exhibit 5.14 is the magnitudes of the cross-price elasticities. For example, when considering whole milk and low-fat milk, a cross-price elasticity of 0.5 tells us

**Exhibit 5.14 Examples of Various Cross-Price Elasticities**

This table of cross-price elasticities for a variety of goods shows that meat and fish are substitutes, whereas food and entertainment are complements.

| Goods | Cross-Price Elasticity[4] |
|---|---|
| Meat and Fish | 1.6 |
| Clothing and Entertainment | 0.6 |
| Whole Milk and Low-Fat Milk | 0.5 |
| Meat and Potatoes | −0.2 |
| Food and Entertainment | −0.7 |

that a 10 percent increase in the price of whole milk leads to a 5 percent increase in demand for low-fat milk. Economists have found such estimates useful for predicting how changes in one part of the economy will influence demand in another. Policymakers use such estimates to gain an understanding of how taxation of one good affects the demand for another.

## The Income Elasticity of Demand

The **income elasticity of demand** measures the percentage change in quantity demanded due to a percentage change in income.

A third type of elasticity measurement has to do with how changes in income affect consumption patterns. The **income elasticity of demand** informs us of the percentage change in quantity demanded of a good due to a percentage change in the consumer's income. The income elasticity is calculated as

$$\text{Income elasticity} = \frac{\text{Percentage change in quantity demanded}}{\text{Percentage change in income}}$$

and reveals how a change in income affects the quantity demanded of a good. The sign and magnitude of income elasticities are of particular interest to economists. Goods are usually classified into two categories:

When income rises and consumers buy more of a good, it is a **normal good**.

When income rises and consumers buy less of a good, it is an **inferior good**.

- **Normal goods**: A good is normal if the quantity demanded is directly related to income; when income rises, consumers buy more of a normal good.
- **Inferior goods**: A good is inferior if the quantity demanded is inversely related to income; when income rises, consumers buy less of an inferior good.

Exhibit 5.15 summarizes a handful of income elasticity estimates that economists have generated. These data show that goods such as foreign vacations, healthcare, and electricity are normal goods. At the other end of the spectrum, goods such as rice and public transit are inferior: the more we earn, the less we consume.

Exhibit 5.15 shows that the *magnitude* of the income elasticity for normal goods can vary significantly. For example, if your income increases by 10 percent, your consumption of electricity increases by only 2.3 percent. The same 10 percent change in income, however, leads to a large change in foreign vacations—a 10 percent rise in income is associated with a 21 percent increase in foreign vacation expenditures. Goods with an income elasticity above 1 are called *luxury goods*.

Economists have found income elasticities useful for forecasting how income changes will affect the overall economy. These numbers are important for policymakers, because they help inform how proposed rules concerning income taxes might influence consumption of various goods and services.

**Exhibit 5.15 Examples of Various Income Elasticities**

At the top of the table are luxury goods, such as vacation homes, followed by other normal goods, such as gasoline, and finally by inferior goods, such as rice and public transit.

| Goods | Income Elasticity[5] |
|---|---|
| Foreign Vacation | 2.10 |
| Domestic Vacation | 1.70 |
| Vacation Home | 1.20 |
| Healthcare | 1.18 |
| Meats | 1.15 |
| Housing | 1.00 |
| Fruits and Vegetables | 0.61 |
| Gasoline | 0.48 |
| Cereal | 0.32 |
| Environment | 0.25 |
| Electricity | 0.23 |
| Rice | −0.44 |
| Public Transit | −0.75 |

### Should McDonald's Be Interested in Elasticities?

Businesses are interested in the bottom line—profits. But before any profit target can be reached, businesses must bring in revenues. Revenues are simply the amount of money a business brings in from selling its goods and services. For example, a back-of-the-envelope calculation suggests that in 2011, McDonald's sold 15.6 billion hamburgers at a price of about $2.50 each. Therefore, McDonald's brought in $39 billion dollars of revenues through hamburger sales.

How hamburger revenues respond to price and income changes is a question of particular interest to McDonald's. As we discussed in this chapter, the secret to determining how revenues change when prices change is elasticity.

As we showed, when demand is inelastic, an increase in McDonald's hamburger prices will lead to an increase in revenues. On the other hand, when demand is elastic, an increase in the price of burgers will cause a decrease in revenues. This is the case because when demand is inelastic, an increase in price causes a relatively small decrease in quantity demanded, so revenues will increase. When demand is elastic, an increase in price causes a relatively large decrease in quantity demanded—so large that revenues actually decrease.

Because of this interesting property, price elasticities are important to businesses and policymakers. Studies of the elasticity of demand for fast-food restaurants suggest an *industry* elasticity of 0.8.[6]

So why doesn't McDonald's raise the price of its hamburgers? (*Hint*: Think about whether McDonald's faces the industry elasticity. If not, will the elasticity McDonald's faces be greater or less than the industry elasticity? Another consideration is how hamburger prices affect sales of other products at McDonald's.)

We have just learned that other elasticities are important, too. For example, food and entertainment have a negative cross-price elasticity (–0.7), meaning that they are complements.

If McDonald's hamburgers have a similar relationship with entertainment, then when the price of entertainment goes up by 10 percent, McDonald's can expect the demand for its product to decrease by 7 percent—an important insight for pricing and inventory purposes.

Likewise, upon understanding how income changes affect demand for its products, McDonald's can use advertising, pricing, or other means to maintain a healthy bottom line.

## Summary

- As a consumer, you optimize by solving the buyer's problem, which dictates that you make decisions at the margin, recognizing both financial and nonfinancial incentives.

- Individual demand curves are derived from the three components of the buyer's problem: what we like, prices, and how much money we have to spend.

- Consumer surplus measures the difference between an individual's willingness to pay and what the consumer actually pays for a good or service. Policymakers often use consumer surplus to measure how proposed legislation impacts consumer surplus.

- An elasticity measures the sensitivity of one economic variable to a change in another. Important elasticity measures include the price elasticity of demand, the income elasticity of demand, and the cross-price elasticity of demand. Elasticity measurement is especially important for businesses and policymakers who want to understand how consumer behavior changes in response to a price or policy change.

- Combining knowledge of the decision-making rules that result from the buyer's problem with an understanding of elasticities, we can more reliably understand how we ourselves will respond to incentives, and we can more effectively create the proper incentives to change the behavior of others in a predictable way.

# Key Terms

# Questions

*All questions are available in* MyEconLab *for practice and instructor assignment.*

1. Why are consumers in a competitive market considered to be price-takers?

2. How does a consumer's budget set differ from his budget constraint? For a consumer with a given level of income, will the budget set have more combinations of goods or will the number of combinations be higher for the budget constraint?

3. Consider the following figures in which the light blue line is the original budget constraint for a consumer and the dark blue line is the new one. Examine each case and explain what could have caused the change.

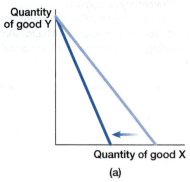

(a)

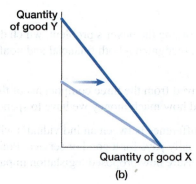

(b)

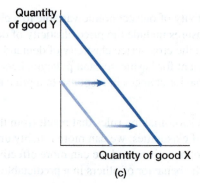

(c)

4. Why is a consumer's satisfaction maximized when the marginal benefit from the last dollar she spent on one good is equal to the marginal benefit from the last dollar she spent on another good?

5. What is meant by consumer surplus? How is it calculated?

6. Consider the following supply and demand diagram:

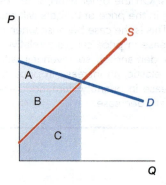

Identify which of the three areas labeled A, B, and C represents consumer surplus in this market.

7. Do all consumers receive the same level of consumer surplus? Explain with an example.

8. Consider a good that you do not like at all, perhaps turnips. Given the market price for turnips, what would be your consumer surplus?

9. Why does a demand curve with a constant slope not have a constant elasticity?

10. What does the price elasticity of demand show? In the market for sweaters, suppose Green's price elasticity of demand is 0.2, Smith's price elasticity is 1.2, and the price elasticity of all the other consumers is greater than 0.2 but less than 1.2. Could the market price elasticity be less than 0.2 or greater than 1.2?

11. How is the price elasticity of demand calculated using the arc elasticity method?

12. How is cross-price elasticity of demand used to determine whether two goods are substitutes or complements?

13. What can income elasticity of demand tell us about the nature of a good?

**14.** Examine the accuracy of the following statement: "Given that burgers and fries are complementary goods, if the price of fries increases, the quantity demanded of both goods will fall."

**15.** If a good is considered to be a luxury good, does it mean that the Law of Demand does not hold?

**16.** During an economic slump, such as the 2008 recession, what pricing strategies could a fast-food chain such as McDonald's use to maintain its sales? Use some of the concepts discussed in this chapter in your answer.

# Problems

*All problems are available in MyEconLab for practice and instructor assignment.*

**1.** Each school-week night you can play video games, talk on the phone, or watch a movie. You have a total of five nights to spend doing one of these three things.

    **a.** Fill out the marginal benefit columns.

    **b.** Your friend tells you to play video games for two nights and talk on the phone for the other three nights. What will be your total benefit from this plan?

    **c.** Use the marginal benefit columns to argue why your total benefit will increase if you play video games less often and watch one movie instead.

    **d.** What is the best way to use your five nights? What is the total benefit? Use the marginal benefits columns to find the answer more easily.

| Quantity (nights): | Play Video Games | | Talk on Phone | | Watch a Movie | |
|---|---|---|---|---|---|---|
| | Total Benefit | Marginal Benefit | Total Benefit | Marginal Benefit | Total Benefit | Marginal Benefit |
| 0 | 0 | — | 0 | — | 0 | — |
| 1 | 20 | | 5 | | 3 | |
| 2 | 22 | | 10 | | 6 | |
| 3 | 23 | | 12 | | 9 | |
| 4 | 23 | | 14 | | 12 | |
| 5 | 23 | | 15 | | 15 | |

**2.** Maya earns $1,000 per month and spends her income on clothing and books. Suppose the price of books is $40 and the price of clothing is $25.

    **a.** Show Maya's budget constraint in a diagram. Identify the slope and intercepts of this budget constraint.

    **b.** Suppose the price of books rises to $50, Maya's income remains $1,000, and the price of clothing remains $25. Draw a new diagram that shows Maya's new budget constraint. Identify the slope and intercepts of this budget constraint.

    **c.** Now suppose the book price remains at $40, but the price of clothing has fallen to $20 and Maya's income has fallen to $800. Draw a new diagram that shows Maya's new budget constraint. Identify the slope and intercepts of this budget constraint.

    **d.** Compare the budget constraints you drew to answer parts (b) and (c) of this question.

**3.** Suppose the price of X is $40, the price of Y is $50, and a consumer has income of $400.

    **a.** Draw the budget constraint for this consumer. What is the opportunity cost of buying one unit of good X?

    **b.** Which of the following combinations of X and Y will be represented by a point on the consumer's budget constraint? Plot the three bundles in your budget constraint diagram.

        **i.** 10 units of X and 1 unit of Y

        **ii.** 5 units of X and 4 units of Y

        **iii.** 1 unit of X and 2 units of Y

**4.** Akio consumes two goods, books and sweaters. His income is $24, the price of a sweater is $4, and the price of a book is $2.

    **a.** Suppose Akio's parents give him $8 for his birthday. Draw Akio's budget set.

    **b.** Now suppose Akio's parents had given him two sweaters for his birthday instead of giving him $8. Akio is a very polite young man and would never return a gift that his parents had given him. Draw Akio's budget set.

**5.** Hanna has $100 to spend on movies and concerts. Suppose the price of a movie ticket is $10 and the price of a concert ticket is $50.

    **a.** Create the budget constraint for movie tickets and concert tickets for Hanna.

    **b.** Show the change in the budget constraint that would occur if the price of concert tickets dropped to $40.

c. Show the change in the budget constraint that would occur if the price of movie tickets doubled.

d. Show the change in the budget constraint that would occur if Hanna had $200 rather than $100.

e. Explain why we are not able to determine where on the budget constraint Hanna would choose to consume.

6. You get a new job in a tropical climate and so you need to buy shorts (s) and T-shirts (t). Your budget constraint is given by $20s + $5t = $60.

a. Based on this formula, what must be the price of a T-shirt? In other words, how much does one T-shirt cost?

b. Complete the following table, which shows several options that fall on your budget constraint.

c. Plot the budget constraint, with shorts (s) on the x-axis and T-shirts (t) on the y-axis.

d. What is the opportunity cost of shorts in terms of T-shirts?

### Bundles on the Budget Constraint

| Bundle | Quantity of Shorts (s) | Quantity of T-shirts (t) |
|--------|------------------------|--------------------------|
| A | 0 | |
| B | 1 | |
| C | 2 | |
| D | 3 | |

7. The total benefit for burgers and beers is given below. Burgers cost $10 and beers cost $20.

| | Total Benefit (Burgers) | Total Benefit (Beers) |
|---|-------------------------|------------------------|
| 1 | 15 | 30 |
| 2 | 30 | 50 |
| 3 | 45 | 60 |
| 4 | 60 | 65 |

a. What is the marginal benefit of a third beer?

b. What is the "bang for the buck" of a second burger?

c. Using the "bang for the buck" principle, explain why it would never be optimal to purchase two burgers and two beers.

8. Consider the following demand schedule:

| Price | Quantity |
|-------|----------|
| $9 | 52 |
| $11 | 48 |
| $13 | 40 |

a. Use the midpoint formula to calculate the elasticity of demand (i) when the price rises from $9 to $11 and (ii) when the price rises from $11 to $13.

b. When the price rises from $9 to $11, does expenditure rise, fall, or remain constant? What about when the price rises from $11 to $13?

c. Why should you have anticipated your answers to (b) once you had answered part (a)?

9. You work at a convenience store and make note of changes to sales after the price of liquid soap unexpectedly increases by 10 percent. You notice that sale of shampoo goes *up* by 5 percent and sale of lotion goes *down* by 2 percent. Calculate the cross-price elasticities, and comment on whether each product is a substitute for liquid soap or a complement for liquid soap.

10. Three years after graduating from college you get a promotion and a 20 percent raise. Your consumption habits change accordingly. Use the following information to determine your income elasticity of demand, and state whether the good is a normal good, an inferior good, or a luxury good.

a. You consume 10 percent fewer frozen hot dogs.

b. You consume 5 percent more pork chops.

c. You consume 30 percent more sockeye salmon.

11. Walmart and Target are both discount retailers. However, during the recession of 2007–2009, Target's same-store sales fell while sales at Walmart actually increased. Examine the following statements and identify the ones that could explain this outcome.

i. Walmart stocks more goods like food and health items than Target.

ii. Target positions itself in the market as a low-cost retailer of home accessories and clothing.

iii. Walmart's annual revenues have, on average, been higher than Target's annual revenues.

iv. Both Target and Walmart attract a lot of price-sensitive customers.

v. The unemployment level in the United States increased substantially during the recession of 2009.

12. Nadia consumes two goods: food and clothing. The price of food is $2, the price of clothing is $5, and her income is $1,000. Nadia always spends 40 percent of her income on food regardless of the price of food, the price of clothing, or her income.

a. What is her price elasticity of demand for food?

b. What is her cross-price elasticity of demand for food with respect to the price of clothing?

c. What is her income elasticity of demand for food?

13. Suppose demand is given by $Q_D = 6 - P$.

a. Graph the demand curve.

b. If the price is $2, what is the consumer surplus?

c. If the price goes up to $4, what is the new consumer surplus? This new surplus should be *lower*; explain why.

# Appendix

## Representing Preferences with Indifference Curves: Another Use of the Budget Constraint

Our goal in this chapter was to learn how consumers make choices. Through the lens of the buyer's problem, we learned about the importance of preferences, prices, and the budget constraint. Although we focused mainly on prices and the budget constraint, preferences are also very important. While we presented benefit figures in the examples, we did not explain where those benefit numbers were coming from. In this Appendix, we provide a "behind the scenes" look at how economists think about preferences.

Let's continue with the jeans and sweaters example. Exhibit 5.2 shows the benefits of each pair of jeans and each sweater. Recall that you have $300 to spend on sweaters and jeans. In the chapter, we plotted this budget constraint—but we can also plot your preferences. To do so, economists commonly use a concept called the **indifference curve**. An indifference curve is the set of bundles that provide an equal level of satisfaction for the consumer. Economists often call this level of satisfaction **utility**, which is simply an abstract measure of satisfaction.

Exhibit 5A.1 uses the data from Exhibit 5.2 and displays two such indifference curves alongside your $300 budget constraint. The intuition of an indifference curve is that regardless of where you are on that curve, you are equally happy, or have the same level of utility. Consider the first indifference curve ($U = U_1$). If we choose point A (6 sweaters and 3 pairs of jeans), we know that it gives you the same level of satisfaction as point B (4 sweaters and 5 pairs of jeans). In fact, from Exhibit 5.2 we know that each bundle gives you $845 in total benefits.

What's convenient about indifference curves is that they summarize every possible bundle of sweaters and jeans that gives you the same level of utility. Importantly, as indifference curves move away from the origin, the level of utility increases. So, as a consumer you want to be on the indifference curve that is the farthest from the origin. When this curve is plotted with the budget constraint, all of the elements of the buyer's problem are summarized: the budget constraint summarizes what you can afford and the indifference curve summarizes what you like.

The combination of the budget constraint and the indifference curve shows the point at which you maximize your utility, or satisfaction, subject to your budget constraint. To see this idea graphically, we focus on the budget constraint and the indifference curve $U = U_1$ in Exhibit 5A.1. Along this indifference curve your utility is constant, and along the budget constraint is every bundle of sweaters and jeans that you can afford. The point of tangency of the two, at point A, is the bundle that you can afford and that maximizes

> An **indifference curve** is the set of bundles that provide an equal level of satisfaction for the consumer.
>
> **Utility** in economics is a measure of the satisfaction or happiness that comes from consuming a good or service.

---

**Exhibit 5A.1 Introducing Indifference Curves**

Plotting the budget line from Exhibit 5.1, this graph introduces two indifference curves, which are derived from the benefit data in Exhibit 5.2. At any point on a given indifference curve, the total benefits are constant, so that it makes no difference to the consumer which point on the curve is chosen—hence the term "indifference curve." Take $U = U_1$; at points A and B total benefits are equal.

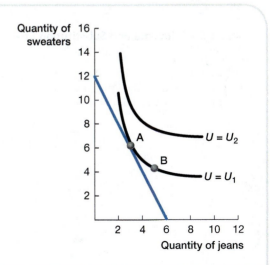

your satisfaction. You'll notice that the tangency of the indifference curve in Exhibit 5A.1 and the budget constraint from earlier is at 6 sweaters and 3 jeans, just as we found in our marginal analysis before.

Indifference curves can also help us think about how choices change in response to changes in prices or income. In Exhibit 5A.1 we plot only two indifference curves, but for any given level of utility, there is an indifference curve. As we learned in this chapter, as income increases, the budget constraint shifts to the right; likewise, the budget constraint pivots in response to a price change. Combining an understanding of indifference curves with knowledge of the budget constraint informs us about how consumption changes when income or prices change. We avoid discussing the exact mechanics of this here, but just about every intermediate microeconomics textbook includes a discussion of these building blocks.

Instead, we briefly discuss one of the most important conceptual issues associated with price changes. Consider if the price of jeans is cut in half: instead of $50 per pair, they are now $25 per pair. You might react in one of two ways: this is super news: "I feel 'wealthier' now, so I am going to buy more jeans *and* sweaters." Economists call this an **income effect**, because this change in consumption moves you to a higher (or "better") indifference curve. A second way in which you might react is to say: "jeans are now relatively cheap compared to sweaters, so I will buy more jeans and fewer sweaters." Economists call this a **substitution effect**, because this change in consumption moves you along a given indifference curve.

So, what do you think is the end result of these two effects? We know that you will certainly buy more jeans—our marginal analysis and demand curve told us that at a price of $25, you will purchase 4 pairs of jeans relative to the 3 pairs you were purchasing when the price was $50. And by the same marginal analysis, we know you will also buy more sweaters (8 instead of 6). However, how we get to this final optimum is a far more subtle point. On the one hand, jeans are relatively more affordable, meaning the substitution effect should increase your quantity demanded of jeans. On the other hand, looking back to Exhibit 5.2, we can see that the marginal benefit of jeans drops very quickly after the fourth pair, whereas the marginal benefit for sweaters does not decrease rapidly, meaning the income effect may favor sweaters.

In this case, we find that with this price change, the number of jeans purchased increases to 4, and the number of sweaters increases to 8. Exhibit 5A.2 shows both effects graphically. Point A is the original optimum from the shopping spree where you buy 6 sweaters and 3 pairs of jeans. When the price of jeans drops to $25, the budget constraint pivots outward. Point C is the new optimum after the price of jeans drops to $25. The price drop causes you to buy 4 pairs of jeans and 8 sweaters. How do you get there? Through a combination of income and substitution effects.

To graphically visualize the two effects, we start at point A and ask: in theory, how many sweaters and pairs of jeans would you buy at our original indifference curve ($U_1 = \$845$) with jeans at this new, lower price? The answer is found at the tangency of our original indifference curve and the dashed budget constraint with the same slope as our new, pivoted-out red budget constraint. This dashed-line curve has a slope of $-1$ (since the ratio of the price of jeans to the price of sweaters is now $\$25/\$25 = 1$) and intersects both the

An **income effect** is a consumption change that results when a price change moves the consumer to a lower or higher indifference curve.

A **substitution effect** is a consumption change that results when a price change moves the consumer along a given indifference curve.

**Exhibit 5A.2 Income and Substitution Effects**

A change in price has two effects on consumption—an income effect and a substitution effect. If the price of jeans is halved, then the budget line pivots outward from the original blue line to the new red line. Point A is the original optimum, and point C is the new optimum.

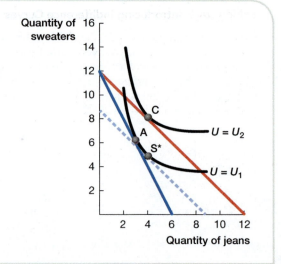

### Exhibit 5A.3 Your Buyer's Problem ($300 available; price of jeans dropped to $25)

As in Exhibit 5.2, each row summarizes the benefits from consuming a given quantity of sweaters or jeans. The total benefits from consuming a given number of sweaters or jeans are presented, as are the marginal benefits from each additional unit. Finally, the marginal benefit per dollar spent is included. Note the significant drop-off in marginal benefits per dollar spent after the fourth pair of jeans.

| Quantity | Sweaters $25 | | | Jeans $25 | | |
|---|---|---|---|---|---|---|
| | Total Benefits (A) | Marginal Benefits (B) | Marginal Benefits per Dollar Spent = (B) / $25 | Total Benefits (C) | Marginal Benefits (D) | Marginal Benefits per Dollar Spent = (D) / $25 |
| 0 | 0 | | | 0 | | |
| 1 | 100 | 100 | 4 | 160 | 160 | 6.4 |
| 2 | 185 | 85 | 3.4 | 310 | 150 | 6 |
| 3 | 260 | 75 | 3 | 410 | 100 | 4 |
| 4 | 325 | 65 | 2.6 | 490 | 80 | 3.2 |
| 5 | 385 | 60 | 2.4 | 520 | 30 | 1.2 |
| 6 | 435 | 50 | 2 | 530 | 10 | 0.4 |
| 7 | 480 | 45 | 1.8 | 533 | 3 | 0.12 |
| 8 | 520 | 40 | 1.6 | 535 | 2 | 0.08 |

x- and y-axes at 8.5 units. This tells us that the substitution effect due to cheaper jeans has given us the chance to achieve the same utility as before ($845) while spending less money ($25 × 8.5 = $212.50 < $300), a feat that would be impossible at the former $50 price point for jeans. The new tangency occurs at point S*, and it tells us that the substitution effect moves your consumption of jeans from 3 to 4 and your consumption of sweaters from 6 to 4.5 (for convenience, we assume that you can purchase half units).

But stopping there would mean neglecting the $87.50 "extra" you now have to spend—the new lower price of jeans has made you relatively wealthier. Moving from point S* to point C summarizes the income effect of the new lower price. You can see that the income effect has a large impact, moving consumption of sweaters from 4.5 to 8 while keeping consumption of jeans unchanged at 4. For jeans, this might seem like a counterintuitive result—having *more* income left the quantity of jeans that you buy unchanged after the substitution effect. But let's not forget our discussion of marginal analysis and income elasticity in Section 5.5.

Consider Exhibit 5A.3, which updates the marginal benefits per dollar spent to account for the decrease in the price of jeans. Notice that when buying the fifth pair of jeans, the marginal benefit per dollar spent is 1.2 ($30/$25), whereas purchasing a fifth sweater has a marginal benefit per dollar spent of 2.4 ($60/$25). In fact, after the fourth pair of jeans, you really have little interest in buying more jeans because the marginal benefit of an extra sweater is always higher. What does this suggest about the income elasticity for jeans over this range? Importantly, it shows that whether jeans are a normal good depends on how many pairs of jeans you already own.

## Appendix Questions

**A1.** What is an indifference curve? Can two indifference curves intersect? Explain your answer.

**A2.** Explain the income and substitution effects of an increase in the price of one good on an individual's consumption choice.

**A3.** Consider indifference curves for goods X and Y. Suppose we plot the quantity of good Y on the y-axis and the quantity of good X on the x-axis.

a. Why are indifference curves downward-sloping?

b. What is the economic interpretation of the slope of an indifference curve?

c. Following what we learned in this Appendix, indifference curves would flatten out as someone consumes more of good X and less of good Y. What are we assuming when we draw indifference curves that become flatter?

## Appendix Key Terms

indifference curve *p. 111*
utility *p. 111*

income effect *p. 112*

substitution effect *p. 112*

# 6 Sellers and Incentives

## How would an ethanol subsidy affect ethanol producers?

In every market, there are buyers and sellers. Taco Bell sells tacos, Apple sells iPhones, Old Navy sells casual clothing, and Amazon.com sells nearly everything. Service markets also feature buyers and sellers: you purchase tune-ups from mechanics, guitar lessons from music instructors, and rides from Uber. In the previous chapter, you learned a set of decision rules that lead to optimal outcomes for the buyer; in this chapter, you'll learn a set of decision rules that optimize outcomes for the seller.

We begin with the seller's problem, which has many of the same basic ingredients as the buyer's problem discussed in Chapter 5. In much the same way that consumers choose the optimal bundle of goods and services to maximize their net benefits, sellers choose what to produce and how much to produce to maximize *their* net benefits: profits.

Our discussion in this chapter continues to focus on perfectly competitive markets. We show that, like optimizing consumers, optimizing sellers rely on marginal thinking. To understand the rules that govern this thinking—that govern the seller's problem—all we'll need is information about market prices and the costs of production. The insights in this chapter will help you understand and predict how proposed public policies influence behavior and outcomes of firms. They also provide general guidance on how you should run your own business interests should your entrepreneurial spirit inspire you to launch a start-up, open a Subway sandwich shop, or build an ethanol plant.

## CHAPTER OUTLINE

## 6.1 Sellers in a Perfectly Competitive Market

We begin our study of how firms make decisions by assuming that they do so in *perfectly competitive markets*. Three conditions characterize perfectly competitive markets:

- No buyer or seller is big enough to influence the market price.
- Sellers in the market produce identical goods.
- There is free entry and exit in the market.

The first two assumptions are important because they ensure that agents in this type of market are price-takers—a term we've already discussed in Chapters 4 and 5. Just as a consumer can buy as much as she wants at the market price, sellers are price-takers in that they can sell as much as they want at the market price. The rationale behind this assumption is that an individual seller tends to sell only a tiny fraction of the total amount of a good produced. Because the seller's output is small relative to that of the market, the individual choice of how much to produce isn't going to be important for market outcomes. But the *combined* effect of many sellers' decisions *will* affect the market price.

We can see this by considering the decisions of a local farmer. If the farmer decides to rotate crops and grow corn this year rather than soybeans, this choice does not cause price fluctuations throughout the world. However, if every farmer in the world decided to grow corn this year instead of soybeans, the price of corn would decrease dramatically and the price of soybeans would increase.

The third assumption—that firms can enter and exit industries as they please—has important consequences for the market as a whole. One example of a market where sellers can enter and exit as they please is selling on eBay. At any time you can decide to enter the DVD market by auctioning off your DVD collection on eBay. Sellers can pretty much enter and exit freely in many other familiar markets, including lawn care, automobile repair, retail shops, and farming.

## 6.2 The Seller's Problem

The overarching goal of the seller is to maximize net benefits, or profits. The seller's problem therefore revolves around an optimization problem: "How do I decide what and how much to produce?" We can frame this question as a problem—the seller's problem—just as

6.1

6.2

6.3

6.4

6.5

6.6

when we looked at the buyer's problem in Chapter 5 and discussed how consumers make buying decisions.

Think of your local pizzeria. After buying ingredients, the owner creates a masterpiece with dough, sauce, and toppings; when the steaming pizza exits the oven, he sells it to buyers. In this analogy, the seller's problem has three main components. First, the seller must know how the inputs combine to make the outputs: what tomato-to-garlic ratio, for example, will make just the right sauce? Second, the seller must know how much it costs to produce a pizza. For instance, how much does the brick oven cost, and what about the cost of ingredients and workers' wages? Does it matter that new ingredients need to be purchased each time he produces a pizza, while the oven sits ready for use? Finally, the seller must know how much he can sell the pizza for once it is produced. So we can say that the three elements of the seller's problem are:

1. Making the goods
2. The cost of doing business
3. The rewards of doing business

We'll now look at each of these elements in more detail.

## Making the Goods: How Inputs Are Turned into Outputs

A **firm** is any business entity that produces and sells goods or services.

**Production** is the process by which the transformation of inputs to outputs occurs.

A **firm** is a business entity that produces and sells goods or services; it can consist of thousands of people, a few people, or a single person. Every firm faces the decision of how to combine inputs to create outputs. **Production** is the process by which the transformation of inputs (such as labor and machines) to outputs (such as goods and services) occurs. The relationship between the quantity of inputs used and the quantity of outputs produced is called the *production function*.

To begin to understand the production function, let's consider a real-life company in Sun Prairie, Wisconsin: The Wisconsin Cheeseman. The firm is a mail-order gift company that packs and mails food and floral products and ships them all over the world. Let's focus exclusively on one of the services that it provides: packing cheese into cheese boxes. The Cheeseman relies on two main inputs: labor to pack the cheese into boxes—a task that one of the co-authors of this book spent two teenage summers doing—and **physical capital** (equipment and structures). Physical capital is any good, including machines and buildings, used for production.

**Physical capital** is any good, including machines and buildings, used for production.

The **short run** is a period of time when only some of a firm's inputs can be varied.

The **long run** is a period of time when all of a firm's inputs can be varied.

A **fixed factor of production** is an input that cannot be changed in the short run.

A **variable factor of production** is an input that can be changed in the short run.

**Marginal product** is the change in total output associated with using one more unit of input.

While hiring and firing workers can be done in a short period of time, altering physical capital takes much longer. Economists refer to the **short run** as a period of time when only some of a firm's inputs can be varied—for The Cheeseman, labor. Alternatively, the **long run** is defined as a period of time wherein a firm can change any input. This means that physical capital is a **fixed factor of production**—an input that cannot change in the short run—and that labor is a **variable factor of production**—an input that can change in the short run.

Exhibit 6.1 provides information on The Wisconsin Cheeseman's short-run production function. It shows how the output varies with the number of workers employed (we've changed the actual numbers because those are proprietary information). Columns 1 and 2 show how The Cheeseman's daily production of cheese boxes varies with the number of employees it hires. The first worker can complete 100 cheese boxes per day. Two workers can pack 207 cheese boxes per day. Therefore, the *marginal product* of adding the second worker is 107 cheese boxes per day—the amount by which total output changes with the addition of the second worker (207 − 100). So we can define **marginal product** as the additional amount of output obtained from adding one more unit of input (in this case, workers).

For The Cheeseman, the only way to change production in the short run is to change the number of workers. Exhibit 6.2 provides a graphical summary of the relationship between the number of workers and the number of cheese boxes packed: the short-run production function. Exhibits 6.1 and 6.2 reveal three important characteristics of production for The Cheeseman.

(**1**) The marginal product increases with the addition of the first few workers. This feature suggests that, for example, two laborers working together can produce more than the sum of their production in isolation. This might happen because the first two workers *specialize* in a particular portion of the cheese-packing task that they are good at completing.

**Exhibit 6.1  Production Data for The Wisconsin Cheeseman**

The Wisconsin Cheeseman is tasked with choosing how much output to generate per day, and the table summarizes the number of workers the firm will need for any given level of output. The first column is the number of cheese boxes produced per day, the second column is the number of workers employed, and the third column is marginal product: the additional output produced by each additional input (in this case, workers).

| Details of Production | | |
|---|---|---|
| **(1)**<br>Output per Day | **(2)**<br>Number of Workers | **(3)**<br>Marginal Product |
| 0 | 0 | |
| 100 | 1 | 100 |
| 207 | 2 | 107 |
| 321 | 3 | 114 |
| 444 | 4 | 123 |
| 558 | 5 | 114 |
| 664 | 6 | 106 |
| 762 | 7 | 98 |
| 854 | 8 | 92 |
| 939 | 9 | 85 |
| 1,019 | 10 | 80 |
| 1,092 | 11 | 73 |
| 1,161 | 12 | 69 |
| 1,225 | 13 | 64 |
| 1,284 | 14 | 59 |
| 1,339 | 15 | 55 |
| 1,390 | 16 | 51 |
| 1,438 | 17 | 48 |
| . . . | . . . | . . . |
| 1,934 | 38 | 10 |
| 1,834 | 39 | −100 |

**Exhibit 6.2  The Short-Run Production Function for The Cheeseman**

Plotted here is the number of workers on the x-axis and the number of cheese boxes produced on the y-axis. As the number of workers goes up, the number of cheese boxes that can be produced tends to increase, but notice that the first 10–15 workers lead to much steeper increases in production than the 25th–35th additional worker. Also notice that the last worker actually reduces productivity.

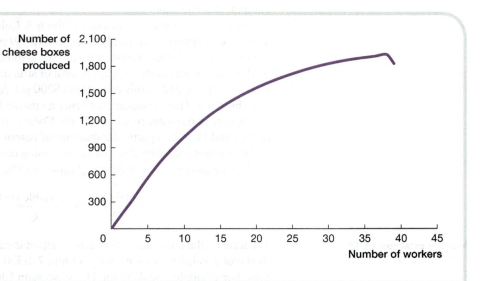

**Specialization** is the result of workers developing a certain skill set in order to increase total productivity.

In **specialization**, workers develop specific skill sets so as to increase total productivity. To see specialization in action, simply pay attention during your next visit to Subway. Watch your sandwich move down a well-coordinated line: the first worker prepares the bread and arranges the meats; then the second worker layers on the veggies, sprinkles oils, and cuts the sandwich. Finally, the third worker packages the sandwich and tallies the bill. A true assembly line of beauty, something that specialization has created naturally.

**(2)** The marginal product eventually decreases with successive additions of workers. That is, as more and more workers are added, they begin to add less and less to total production. For example, the marginal product of the fourth worker is 123 boxes, whereas it is only 114 boxes for the fifth worker. Economists call this decreasing production pattern the **Law of Diminishing Returns**. This law states that at a certain point of successive increases in inputs, marginal product begins to decrease. This law might apply for a number of reasons. For example, with a set amount of physical capital, successive increases in labor eventually lead to lower output per worker because there is idle time—workers cannot use the machines as often as they would like.

**(3)** Adding too many workers can actually decrease overall production. This point refers to the fact that adding too many workers can be counterproductive. Indeed, this is exactly the situation with the last worker that The Cheeseman hires: Exhibit 6.1 shows that adding the thirty-ninth worker has a negative marginal product of 100 boxes! You can see this situation vividly in Exhibit 6.2, where the production curve begins to slope downward at that point. Management should send this worker home, dispatch him to a different task, or even have him wash the owner's dog, because he is lowering production of cheese boxes. This might happen because congestion causes workers to get in the way of one another.

## The Cost of Doing Business: Introducing Cost Curves

We now look at the second component of the seller's problem: what the firm must pay for its inputs, or the **cost of production**. Similar to the two factors of production discussed above, there is a natural division in the total cost of production:

$$\text{Total cost} = \text{Variable cost} + \text{Fixed cost}.$$

This equation has three parts. **Total cost** is the sum of variable and fixed costs. **Variable costs (VCs)** are those costs associated with variable factors of production. In The Cheeseman's case, these are costs associated with workers and therefore change with the level of production in the short run. In contrast to VCs, a **fixed cost (FC)** is a cost associated with a fixed factor of production, such as structures or equipment, and therefore does not change with production in the short run. Indeed, in the short run, The Wisconsin Cheeseman has to pay for these factors even if it produces nothing, because the firm cannot sell its plant and equipment in the short run.

These costs are summarized in Exhibit 6.3. Column 4 shows VCs—because workers at The Cheeseman are paid a daily wage of $72 ($9 per hour, 8 hours per day), the daily VCs increase by $72 for each worker hired. We assume that The Cheeseman can hire as many workers as it wants at this wage. The cost of structures and machinery represents the cost of physical capital, and in this example is $200 per day. These are the FCs given in column 5 of Exhibit 6.3. These costs are the same no matter how many workers are hired. Thus, FCs do not vary in the short run, but VCs do. Column 6 shows total cost (TC), which is the sum of VCs and FCs for a particular quantity of output.

We are provided with three more interesting cost concepts if we divide both sides of our total cost equation by total output $Q$ (quantity The Cheeseman produces):

$$\frac{\text{Total cost}}{Q} = \frac{\text{Variable cost}}{Q} + \frac{\text{Fixed cost}}{Q}.$$

The term on the left-hand side of this equation is called **average total cost (ATC)**, which is total cost divided by total output. Column 7 in Exhibit 6.3 shows the ATC for The Cheeseman. For example, the ATC for The Wisconsin Cheeseman with an output of 321 units is computed by taking the total cost of $416 and dividing it by the total output of 321, which yields $1.29, as shown in Exhibit 6.3. This means that when The Cheeseman produces 321 units, the average cost per cheese box packed is $1.29.

The first term on the right-hand side of this equation is called the **average variable cost (AVC)**, which is the total variable cost divided by total output. For The Cheeseman, when it produces 321 units, its AVC is $0.67, which means that it pays its variable factor of production (labor) an average of $0.67 per cheese box packed.

6.1
6.2
6.3
6.4
6.5
6.6

The **Law of Diminishing Returns** states that successive increases in inputs eventually lead to less additional output.

The **cost of production** is what a firm must pay for its inputs.

**Total cost** is the sum of variable and fixed costs.

A **variable cost (VC)** is the cost of variable factors of production, which change along with a firm's output.

A **fixed cost (FC)** is the cost of fixed factors of production, which a firm must pay even if it produces zero output.

**Average total cost (ATC)** is the total cost divided by the total output.

**Average variable cost (AVC)** is the total variable cost divided by the total output.

**Exhibit 6.3 Costs of Production with Additional Cost Concepts for The Wisconsin Cheeseman**

The Wisconsin Cheeseman produces cheese boxes; this exhibit summarizes the cost of various levels of production. The total cost is the sum of fixed and variable costs. The average total cost is the sum of average fixed and average variable costs. The marginal cost is the change in total cost associated with producing one more unit of output. For convenience, the numbers are rounded.

| | | | | | | | | | |
|---|---|---|---|---|---|---|---|---|---|
| Cost of Production | | | | | | | | | |
| (1) Output per Day (Q) | (2) Number of Workers | (3) Marginal Product = Change in (1) | (4) Variable Cost (VC) = $72 × (2) | (5) Fixed Cost (FC) | (6) Total Cost (TC) = (4) + (5) | (7) Average Total Cost (ATC) = (6)/(1) | (8) Average Variable Cost (AVC) = (4)/(1) | (9) Average Fixed Cost (AFC) = (5)/(1) | (10) Marginal Cost (MC) = Change in (6)/Change in (1) |
| 0 | 0 | | $0 | $200 | $200 | | | | |
| 100 | 1 | 100 | $72 | $200 | $272 | $2.72 | $0.72 | $2.00 | $0.72 |
| 207 | 2 | 107 | $144 | $200 | $344 | $1.66 | $0.70 | $0.97 | $0.67 |
| 321 | 3 | 114 | $216 | $200 | $416 | $1.29 | $0.67 | $0.62 | $0.63 |
| 444 | 4 | 123 | $288 | $200 | $488 | $1.10 | $0.65 | $0.45 | $0.59 |
| 558 | 5 | 114 | $360 | $200 | $560 | $1.00 | $0.65 | $0.36 | $0.63 |
| 664 | 6 | 106 | $432 | $200 | $632 | $0.95 | $0.65 | $0.30 | $0.68 |
| 762 | 7 | 99 | $504 | $200 | $704 | $0.92 | $0.66 | $0.26 | $0.73 |
| 854 | 8 | 92 | $576 | $200 | $776 | $0.91 | $0.67 | $0.23 | $0.78 |
| 939 | 9 | 85 | $648 | $200 | $848 | $0.90 | $0.69 | $0.21 | $0.85 |
| 1,019 | 10 | 80 | $720 | $200 | $920 | $0.90 | $0.71 | $0.20 | $0.90 |
| 1,092 | 11 | 73 | $792 | $200 | $992 | $0.91 | $0.73 | $0.18 | $0.99 |
| 1,161 | 12 | 69 | $864 | $200 | $1,064 | $0.92 | $0.74 | $0.17 | $1.04 |
| 1,225 | 13 | 64 | $936 | $200 | $1,136 | $0.93 | $0.76 | $0.16 | $1.13 |
| 1,284 | 14 | 59 | $1,008 | $200 | $1,208 | $0.94 | $0.79 | $0.16 | $1.22 |
| 1,339 | 15 | 55 | $1,080 | $200 | $1,280 | $0.96 | $0.81 | $0.15 | $1.31 |
| 1,390 | 16 | 51 | $1,152 | $200 | $1,352 | $0.97 | $0.83 | $0.14 | $1.41 |
| 1,438 | 17 | 48 | $1,224 | $200 | $1,424 | $0.99 | $0.85 | $0.14 | $1.50 |

**Average fixed cost (AFC)** is the total fixed cost divided by the total output.

Finally, **average fixed cost (AFC)** is the total fixed cost divided by the total output. For The Cheeseman, when it produces 321 units, its AFC is $0.62, which means that it pays its fixed factor of production (physical capital) an average of $0.62 per cheese box packed. What this all means is that of the $1.29 ATC when The Cheeseman produces 321 units, $0.67 goes to VCs (labor) and $0.62 goes to FCs (physical capital).

Our last cost concept is *marginal cost*, which is presented in column 10 of Exhibit 6.3. **Marginal cost (MC)** is the change in total cost associated with producing one more unit of output. Marginal cost can be written as:

**Marginal cost (MC)** is the change in total cost associated with producing one more unit of output.

$$\text{Marginal cost} = \frac{\text{Change in total cost}}{\text{Change in output}}.$$

When The Wisconsin Cheeseman produces 321 units, a MC of $0.63 means that it costs The Cheeseman $0.63 to produce the 321st cheese box. Exhibit 6.3 also reveals another interesting relationship: MC and marginal product are inversely related to one another. As one increases, the other automatically decreases. To see why, consider The Cheeseman's production and cost relationships. When The Cheeseman adds its first few workers (up to four), the marginal product increases, decreasing MC. Yet, as more workers are hired, marginal product decreases, which increases MC. For example, hiring the fifth worker decreases marginal product to 114 units and increases the MC to $0.63.

6.1

6.2

6.3

6.4

6.5

6.6

**Exhibit 6.4** MC, ATC, and AVC Curves for The Wisconsin Cheeseman

This figure plots several cost measures with the output (or quantity) on the x-axis and the cost (or price) on the y-axis. Each cost measure is plotted across various output levels. Notice that the MC curve intersects the ATC and AVC curves at their respective minimums.

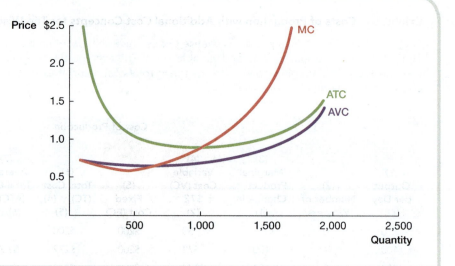

Using the data from Exhibit 6.3, Exhibit 6.4 shows a graphical representation of the important relationships between costs and quantity produced: the MC curve, ATC curve, and AVC curve for The Cheeseman. Output quantity is plotted on the x-axis and costs (in dollars) on the y-axis. One interesting feature about these cost curves is that when the MC curve is below the average cost curves (both ATC and AVC), they must be falling or sloping downward, and when the MC curve is above the average cost curves, they must be rising or upward-sloping.

Why? This is by itself the very nature of the definition of MC. To capture this intuition, think of your overall grade point average (GPA) as ATC and your semester GPA as MC. Say that in your freshman year you earn all Bs, a 3.0 GPA. Now let's say that in your sophomore year you earn straight As, a 4.0 GPA. What will happen to your overall GPA? It will rise; in fact, if you take the same number of credits in each of your freshman and sophomore years, your cumulative GPA will now be 3.5. Now what happens to your overall GPA if in your junior year you earn all Cs, a GPA of 2.0? It decreases. This is because your new grades are below the average that you established in your first 2 years.

This also provides the intuition for why MC intersects AVC and ATC at their minimums: when MC is below ATC and AVC, they must be falling; and when MC is above ATC and AVC, they must be rising, as in Exhibit 6.4. An understanding of these curves leads to powerful implications, as we discuss next.

## The Rewards of Doing Business: Introducing Revenue Curves

We are now ready to look at the third component of the seller's problem: the price at which a firm can sell its goods. A firm makes money from selling goods, and The Wisconsin Cheeseman is no different. The **revenue** of a firm is the amount of money it brings in from the sale of its outputs. Revenue is determined by the price of goods sold times the number of units sold:

**Revenue** is the amount of money the firm brings in from the sale of its outputs.

$$\text{Total revenue} = \text{Price} \times \text{Quantity sold.}$$

Recall that in perfectly competitive markets, sellers can sell all they want at the market price. Thus, they are price-takers.

But what determines the price of cheese boxes? Chapter 4 can lend insights to this question: the price comes from the intersection of the market demand curve and the market supply curve. This is just like any other market equilibrium you learned about in Chapter 4: the intersection of market supply and market demand gives the equilibrium price.

Exhibit 6.5 reveals this intuition. Panel (a) of Exhibit 6.5 shows the market supply and market demand curves. Recall that we can construct the market demand curve as described in Chapters 4 and 5. We can construct the market supply curve in exactly the same manner as the market demand curve—through horizontally summing the individual supply curves. To see

6.1

6.2

6.3

6.4

6.5

6.6

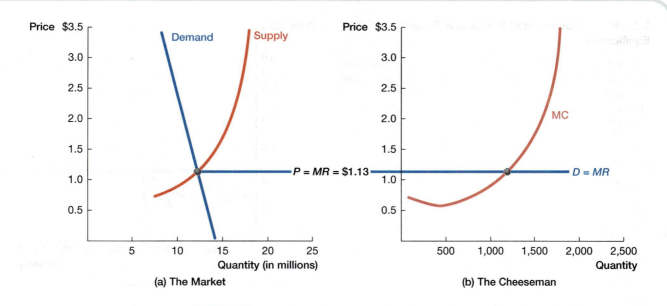

**Exhibit 6.5** Supply and Demand: The Market Versus The Wisconsin Cheeseman

Panel (a) summarizes the market supply and market demand curves for cheese boxes. The price determined by the market equilibrium is the price The Cheeseman faces, which is shown in panel (b). We think of that price as representing the demand curve The Cheeseman faces, which is the flat blue line. This demand curve is equal to MR because it represents the change in revenues from selling one more cheese box.

how this works, let's assume that in equilibrium, the cheese box packing industry has 10,000 identical firms, which each produce 1,225 cheese boxes per day. Thus, a total of 12,250,000 cheese boxes are packed daily in this market. As shown in panel (b) of Exhibit 6.5, this equilibrium quantity occurs at an equilibrium price of $1.13 per cheese box packed.

At this point, it is important to recognize the difference between the demand curve facing The Cheeseman and the demand curve in a perfectly competitive market. As panel (b) of Exhibit 6.5 reveals, a perfectly competitive firm, such as The Wisconsin Cheeseman, faces a horizontal demand curve, or a demand curve that is perfectly elastic. What this means is that The Cheeseman can pack as many cheese boxes as it desires and be paid the market equilibrium price ($1.13) for every cheese box packed. If The Cheeseman attempts to charge a little bit more than $1.13 per box, it will have no customers because buyers can go to a different packer and pay $1.13 per box. In addition, there is no reason for The Cheeseman to lower its price below $1.13 to attract buyers because it can sell all it wants at $1.13 per box.

**Marginal revenue (MR)** is the change in total revenue associated with producing one more unit of output.

Besides showing the demand curve facing The Cheeseman, panel (b) of Exhibit 6.5 shows the *marginal revenue* curve. **Marginal revenue (MR)** is the change in total revenue associated with producing one more unit of output. In a perfectly competitive market, MR is equal to the market price. Therefore, the MR curve is equivalent to the demand curve facing sellers. Because the price that The Cheeseman faces is $1.13, the MR is $1.13 for every cheese box packed. We are now in a position to learn about the good stuff—making money!

## Putting It All Together: Using the Three Components to Do the Best You Can

The **profits** of a firm are equal to its revenues minus its costs.

Now that we have the three components of the seller's problem in place, we can use them to show how a firm maximizes its profits, since that is the goal of the seller. The **profits** of a firm are the difference between total revenues and total costs:

$$\text{Profits} = \text{Total revenues} - \text{Total costs.}$$

For The Wisconsin Cheeseman to determine its profits, there is only one more question to answer: how much to produce? To figure out what quantity maximizes profits, we need to think about a production level and conduct a thought experiment as to how producing a bit

6.1

6.2

6.3

6.4

6.5

6.6

**Exhibit 6.6 Movement of Production Toward Equilibrium**

The red curve is The Cheeseman's MC curve, and the blue line is The Cheeseman's MR curve. At point A, The Cheeseman should produce more to increase profits. At point B, The Cheeseman should produce less. To maximize profits, Cheeseman produces where MC equals MR.

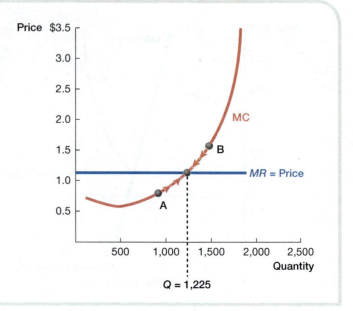

more or a bit less affects both revenues and costs. That is, the key behind maximizing profits is to think about the firm's MRs and MCs. This is an application of optimizing from Chapter 3.

To see how this works, consider Exhibit 6.6, which recreates panel (b) of Exhibit 6.5. Let's first think about point A in the exhibit. At this point, The Cheeseman hires 9 workers and it produces 939 cheese boxes (see Exhibit 6.1). At this production level, it costs $0.85 to pack the last cheese box, as given by the MC in Exhibit 6.3. We know that The Cheeseman is paid $1.13 for each packed box.

Can The Cheeseman earn higher profits? Yes. If it produces one more cheese box, it increases revenues by $1.13, which is greater than the $0.85 it costs to produce. Profit could be increased by $0.28 just by selling one more cheese box! This provides a general rule: if a firm can produce another unit of output at a MC that is less than the market price (that is, MC < price), it should do so, because it can make a profit on producing that unit.

Consider the other side of the coin: if The Cheeseman produced at point B—hiring 17 workers and producing 1,438 units—its MC of producing the last unit is greater than the market price ($1.50 versus $1.13). Thus, it loses money by producing that last unit. The company therefore shouldn't produce it and should hire fewer workers.

In fact, with this marginal decision making in mind, it's straightforward to see how a firm maximizes its profits. It should expand production until:

$$\text{Marginal revenue} = MC.$$

> **The goal of the seller is to maximize net benefits, or profits.**

This is the same as producing where price equals MC, because MR equals price in a perfectly competitive market.

How can we compute the level of profits at this point? One aid is to overlay the ATC curve on Exhibit 6.6, which we do in Exhibit 6.7. Because total revenues = Price × $Q$ and total costs = $ATC \times Q$, we can write total profits as:

$$\text{Price} \times Q - ATC \times Q = (\text{Price} - ATC) \times Q.$$

In other words, we can compute total profits by taking the difference between price and ATC at the point of production and multiplying that difference by the total quantity produced. In the case of producing at $MR = MC$, this provides the shaded area in Exhibit 6.7. We can compute this area as follows:

$$(P - ATC) \times Q = (\$1.13 - \$0.93) \times 1,225 = \$245.$$

This follows because The Cheeseman is paid $1.13 per box at a production level of 1,225 boxes. At this level of production, the ATC cost is $0.93 (see Exhibit 6.3). So, taking the

6.1

6.2

6.3

6.4

6.5

6.6

**Exhibit 6.7** Visualizing The Wisconsin Cheeseman's Profits with MC, MR, and ATC

Adding The Cheeseman's ATC to Exhibit 6.6 allows us to visualize profits graphically. The shaded box represents The Cheeseman's profits. To see why, remember that profits are the difference between total revenue and total costs. Because MR represents price and ATC represents the cost per unit produced, their difference at the quantity where MC equals MR multiplied by quantity produced yields total profits: ($1.13 − $0.93) × 1,225 = $245.

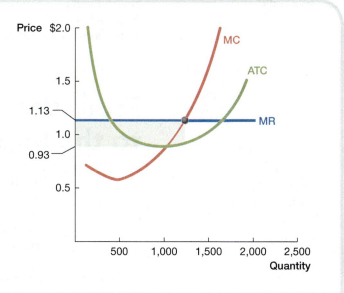

price of $1.13 and subtracting the ATC of $0.93, we get $0.20, which is per-unit profit. We then multiply this per-unit profit by quantity sold, or 1,225, to find the daily profit figure of $245. This profit level is equal to the base times the height of the shaded rectangle in Exhibit 6.7. Because $MR = MC$ at this level of production, we know that this choice optimizes profits and represents the equilibrium for The Cheeseman: once producing at this point, The Cheeseman will not change its production activities unless something else in the market changes.

Profits of only $245 a day might seem trivial, but note that when economists discuss profits we are expressing something much different from what you're used to reading about in the newspapers. For example, when a major corporation reports "record profits," it is reporting what economists call *accounting profits*. **Accounting profits** are equal to revenues minus explicit costs. Explicit costs are the sorts of line-item expenditures that accountants carefully tally and report, like wages for workers or equipment expenditures. But firms also face implicit costs. For example, the owner of The Wisconsin Cheeseman may have a high opportunity cost of time that he is sacrificing in order to run The Cheeseman (to see where an implicit cost like this would play out in Exhibit 6.3, the cost of the owner's time would be included in the Fixed Cost column). Much like the cost of labor and machines, this implicit cost is subtracted from revenues to produce our conception of profits: *economic*

**Accounting profits** are equal to total revenue minus explicit costs.

# CHOICE
## &CONSEQUENCE

## Maximizing Total Profit, Not Per-Unit Profit

When thinking about Exhibit 6.6, you might have asked yourself: "once at point A, increased production serves to make MC closer to MR; why would a firm do that?" This is a common way of thinking if you are trying to maximize *profit per unit*. The flaw in this reasoning is that it only takes half of the optimal solution into consideration. That is, from the total profit equation it takes only (Price − ATC) into consideration.

Recall that total profit comprises not only how different price is from ATC, but also *how many* units you actually sell. The data in Exhibit 6.3 show this intuition for

The Wisconsin Cheeseman. Because MR is a horizontal line, the per-unit profit is maximized when the ATC is at its lowest point. This happens to be point A in Exhibit 6.6. But it's not difficult to compute that The Cheeseman's profit at this point is lower than when production is expanded until $MR = MC$. In fact, at point A, daily profit is $215.97. This is much smaller than the daily profit of $245 when profits are optimized. This might seem like a trivial difference, but if you translate these numbers across several plants and over several years, you're talking about big money.

**Economic profits** are equal to total revenue minus both explicit and implicit costs.

*profits*. **Economic profits** are equal to total revenue minus both explicit and implicit costs. As a result, it is still feasible to run a business that is earning small (or even zero) economic profits, as we demonstrate later in this chapter.

## 6.3 From the Seller's Problem to the Supply Curve

**The firm's supply curve relates output to prices.**

The $MR = MC$ rule is powerful because, by linking the market price to the MC curve, we can determine in the short run how a competitive firm changes its output when the market price changes. That is, it permits us to describe the firm's supply curve, which relates output to prices. To see why, think about how the market price determines the firm's output choice.

For instance, how would The Cheeseman change its behavior if the price for packing cheese increased to $1.41 per box, as shown in Exhibit 6.8? We would expect The Cheeseman to increase its quantity supplied, but by how much? Using the intuition discussed earlier, we expect The Cheeseman to expand production until $MC = MR_3$, which occurs at 1,390 units.

If, however, the market price for cheese boxes decreased to $0.78 per box (also shown in Exhibit 6.8), The Cheeseman would decrease production until $MC = MR_2$, which occurs at 854 units. Importantly, we can trace out The Cheeseman's supply curve by completing this exercise for various price levels.

### Price Elasticity of Supply

**Price elasticity of supply** is the measure of how responsive quantity supplied is to price changes.

When considering how responsive the firm is to price changes, we can use elasticity measures—much as we did in Chapter 5 for buyers. For sellers, the most important measure that economists use is called the **price elasticity of supply**: the measure of how responsive quantity supplied is to price changes. It is computed as:

$$\text{Price elasticity of supply } (\varepsilon_s) = \frac{\text{Percentage change in quantity supplied}}{\text{Percentage change in price}}.$$

The price elasticity of supply will tend to be positive, because as price increases, firms tend to increase their quantity supplied.

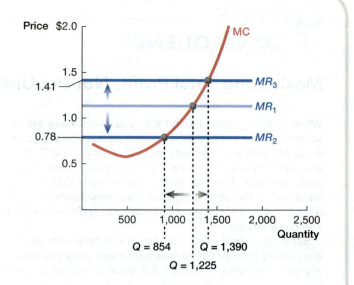

**Exhibit 6.8** Impact of Price Changes on The Wisconsin Cheeseman

If the market price changes, the MR curve that The Cheeseman faces will also change. Here, when The Cheeseman faces an upward shift of the MR curve to $MR_3$, production will increase. In contrast, if The Cheeseman faces a downward shift of the MR curve to $MR_2$, production will decrease.

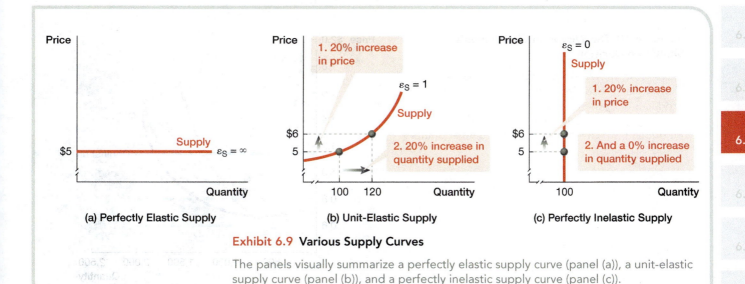

**Exhibit 6.9 Various Supply Curves**

The panels visually summarize a perfectly elastic supply curve (panel (a)), a unit-elastic supply curve (panel (b)), and a perfectly inelastic supply curve (panel (c)).

Characterizing supply curves is quite similar to the descriptions we used to describe demand curves in Chapter 5. For example, an *elastic supply* means that quantity supplied is quite responsive to price changes: any given percentage change in price leads to a larger percentage change in quantity supplied (elasticity greater than 1). Panel (a) in Exhibit 6.9 shows the extreme case: a perfectly elastic supply curve. In this case, even a very small change in price leads to an infinite change in quantity supplied.

Alternatively, an *inelastic supply* means that any given percentage change in price causes a smaller percentage change in quantity supplied (elasticity less than 1). An extreme case is depicted in panel (c) of Exhibit 6.9. Here the supply curve is perfectly inelastic: at every price level, the same quantity is supplied. An example of such a case is an oil refinery that is operating at full capacity: even if gasoline prices increase, it cannot increase production in the short run. Similarly, if corn prices suddenly jump in July, it is difficult for Iowan farmers to produce more corn in the short run. They can plant more corn next year, but not this year.

In between these two extremes are typical supply curves—those that are upward-sloping. One example is presented in panel (b) of Exhibit 6.9. In these cases, the steeper the supply curve is, the less sensitive quantity supplied will be to price changes. Panel (b) of Exhibit 6.9 shows a special type of supply curve, one that is *unit-elastic*. A price increase from $5 to $6 (a 20 percent increase) leads to a 20 percent increase in quantity supplied; likewise, a price decrease from $6 to $5 (a 17 percent decrease) leads to a 17 percent decrease in quantity supplied. For unit-elastic supply curves, the elasticity is equal to 1: a 1 percent change in price leads to a 1 percent change in quantity supplied.

Much like demand elasticities, the size of supply elasticities is determined by several factors. Key determinants include whether the firm has excess inventories—if The Cheeseman has several tons of cheese on hand, it can more easily increase production quantities. Likewise, how long the firm has to respond to price changes is important—the longer the time to respond is, the more elastic the supply will be. Finally, if workers are readily available, then supply will be more elastic because the firm can respond to price increases by quickly hiring workers.

## Shutdown

**Shutdown** is a short-run decision to not produce anything during a specific period.

With an understanding of how quantity supplied responds to price changes, we can consider extreme market situations, such as when the firm should shut down, or suspend, operations. A **shutdown** is a short-run decision to not produce anything during a specific time period. Think about the case when the market price drops to $0.59 per cheese box. Now, the $MR = MC$ rule directs The Cheeseman to produce at point S in Exhibit 6.10 (444 units). Is this a profit-maximizing point of production?

6.1

6.2

6.3

6.4

6.5

6.6

**Exhibit 6.10** The Wisconsin Cheeseman's Shutdown Decision

This exhibit shows several different MR curves, allowing us to visualize when The Cheeseman produces and when it shuts down. The original MR curve is well above the other two MR curves introduced, which intersect the MC curve at points C and S.

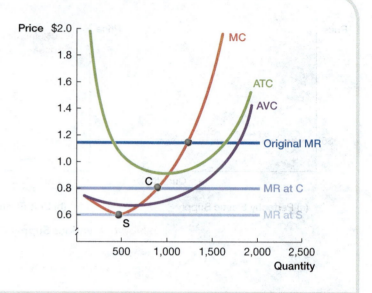

The answer is no. This is because at this particular price, the firm does not even bring in enough money to cover its AVC of $0.65 per unit. Why? Note that the price is below AVC at this point ($0.59 < $0.65); thus if The Cheeseman continues operations, it is paying the variable input—workers—more to produce cheese boxes than the firm is bringing in per cheese box.

The Cheeseman should shut down because by doing so, it would lose only the FCs of production ($200) rather than the FCs ($200) plus the uncovered VCs ($0.06 per unit, or 444 × $0.06 = $26.64). This is so because by shutting down the plant, it employs no workers, and hence has zero VC.

You might think, "Wait a second! Why shut down and absorb the FCs? By producing, The Cheeseman can at least earn some revenues." That is true. The Cheeseman would bring in money by remaining in operation, but for every unit it produces it is paying labor $0.06 more than it is receiving in MR. The optimization rule that follows is that if revenues do not cover all of the VCs, then shutdown is optimal in the short run:

The firm should shut down if price is less than AVC.

So, should The Cheeseman ever produce in the short run if total costs exceed total revenues? The answer is yes. Consider point C in Exhibit 6.10. This is a point of production where price is greater than AVC, but price is less than ATC. In this case, the price is greater than AVC; thus all of the VCs are covered by revenues. This is an instance when The Cheeseman should continue operations even though it is losing money, because besides covering all VCs, it is also covering a fraction of the FCs.

You might think that it does not make sense for The Cheeseman to continue production at point C; after all, the firm is losing money! Why not shut down? The key is that we assume FCs are **sunk costs**, which are a special type of cost that, once they have been committed, can never be recovered (think of a 5-year building lease—The Cheeseman is by law required to pay rent over the entire 5-year period). That is, The Cheeseman can't retrieve sunk costs in the short run. One of the important things to remember about sunk costs is that once they are committed, *they shouldn't affect current or future production decisions.* The reason for this is simple: these costs are sunk. That is, lost, regardless of what action is chosen next—they can't affect the relative costs and benefits of current and future production decisions. By continuing operations at point C, The Cheeseman is at least covering some of the FC.

These examples lead to construction of the short-run supply curve for The Cheeseman: *it is the portion of its MC curve that lies above AVC.* If the market price puts The Cheeseman at a point on its MC curve that lies below the minimum of the AVC curve, then the firm should shut down. Otherwise, it should produce. Exhibit 6.11 shows The Cheeseman's short-run supply curve as the MC curve above the AVC curve.

**Sunk costs** are costs that, once committed, can never be recovered and should not affect current and future production decisions.

6.1

6.2

6.3

6.4

6.5

6.6

**Exhibit 6.11** Short-Run Supply Curve: Portion of the MC Above AVC

Here we reproduce Exhibit 6.4, but we've done two things to the original MC curve. First, we're now referring to it as the short-run supply curve and second, the portion below the AVC curve is cut off because at prices below the minimum AVC the firm shuts down.

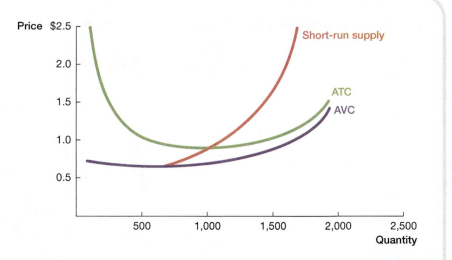

---

# CHOICE
## &CONSEQUENCE

### Marginal Decision Makers Ignore Sunk Costs

Imagine that you are asked to help in a fund-raising effort for your college.[1] You learn that your college has an old call center that it doesn't use. You ask why, and the reply is "Even though we raise more money with phone calls, the cost of making a call is $1, while the cost of mailing a letter is only $0.50." You are shocked—how could each call be that expensive?

After a little prodding, your college lets you know how their experts calculated these cost figures. They had simply summed the cost of the computer-networked phone-banking system your school had purchased years before and the cost of paying students to make calls, then divided that amount by the total number of calls to obtain the ATC of a call. Of

course, they didn't take into account the fact that the school had already bought the computers and therefore that cost was sunk. That sunk cost should not affect the decision of whether to call or mail.

Through the correct calculations, you learn that the MC of every call is very, very low—equal only to the amount you would have to pay a caller for a few minutes of time! Given that you raise more money through calls, and the MC of a phone call is less than the MC of sending a letter, after reading this chapter, you will know to immediately advise your college to pick up the phones and start dialing! This is because to optimize, you should make decisions using marginal thinking, which means ignoring sunk costs.

---

## 6.4 **Producer Surplus**

**Producer surplus** is the difference between the market price and the marginal cost curve.

Similar to the concept of consumer surplus, economists also have a means of measuring surplus for sellers. This is called *producer surplus*. **Producer surplus** is computed by taking the difference between the market price and the MC curve.

Thus, graphically, producer surplus is the area above the MC curve and below the equilibrium price line. In this way, it is distinct from economic profits, as we measured in Exhibit 6.7, because economic profits include a consideration of total cost, not just MC.

> **Producer surplus is the area above the MC curve and below the equilibrium price line.**

Let's consider producer surplus for The Cheeseman. Assume that The Cheeseman is facing a market price of $2, as depicted in Exhibit 6.12.

As it turns out, The Cheeseman can produce many units at a MC below the market price. In Exhibit 6.12, we depict this surplus as the

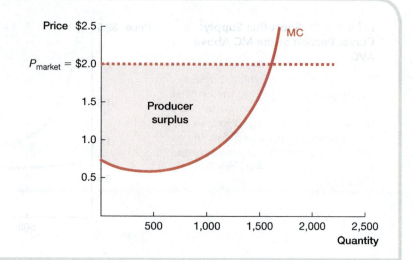

**Exhibit 6.12 Measuring Producer Surplus**

The vertical distance between the market price and the MC to produce each unit represents producer surplus.

pink-shaded region that is below the market price and above The Cheeseman's MC curve. Notice the similarity between this and consumer surplus—whereas a consumer's surplus arises from being willing to pay above the market price, a producer's surplus arises from selling units at a price that is above MC.

Similar to consumer surplus, we can add up sellers' producer surplus to obtain the total producer surplus in the market. We do this by measuring the area above the MC curve that is below the equilibrium price line to compute producer surplus for the entire market.

When we have linear supply curves, we can use a mathematical formula to compute the producer surplus. Consider panel (a) of Exhibit 6.13, which shows a supply curve for daily trucking services to ship cheese from Madison, Wisconsin, to Milwaukee, Wisconsin. If the equilibrium market price is $100 per trip, then we compute the producer surplus as the base of the triangle multiplied by the height of the triangle multiplied by ½:

$$\text{Producer surplus} = \tfrac{1}{2} \times (\text{Base of triangle} \times \text{Height of triangle})$$
$$= \tfrac{1}{2} \times (4 \times \$80) = \$160.$$

This means that total producer surplus per day is $160 in this market.

There are several ways in which producer surplus can increase or decrease. For example, if a shift in the market demand curve causes a higher equilibrium market price, then producer surplus increases, because the area above the supply curve and below the equilibrium price line gets larger. This is shown in panel (b) of Exhibit 6.13. Now producer surplus is $\tfrac{1}{2} \times (5 \times \$100) = \$250$.

**Exhibit 6.13 Producer Surplus for Trucking Services**

The two panels show the supply curve for trucking, with dotted red lines representing the MR curve faced by the producer. Panel (a) shows that producer surplus is the triangle below MR and above the supply (MC) curve. Panel (b) shows what happens to producer surplus when the price increases.

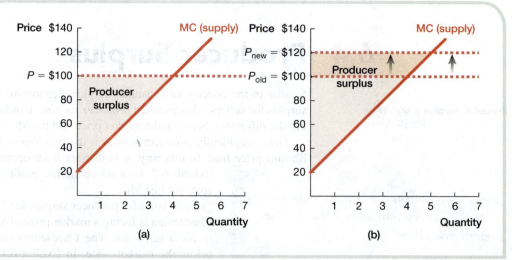

## 6.5 From the Short Run to the Long Run

Thus far we have only considered The Cheeseman's daily production decision, and in doing so, we've treated the facilities and machinery (or physical capital) that The Cheeseman uses as fixed. But firms often think about more than just each day's production. For example, many businesses issue quarterly or annual reports that discuss the firm's long-term outlook. In this section, we move from the daily supply decision to the long run, where The Cheeseman can combine any quantity of labor and physical capital to maximize profits.

What exactly is the long run, though? As we have already noted, the long run is defined as a period of time in which all factors of production are variable. That is, in the long run, there are no fixed factors of production, because even machines and buildings can be retrofitted, purchased, expanded, or sold. Because of this fact, there are important differences between a firm's short- and long-run supply curves.

These differences can be understood by considering The Cheeseman's production decisions. In the short run, if it wants to change production, it can only do so by hiring or laying off workers. This is because only labor is variable in the short run. In the long run, however, The Cheeseman searches for the optimal combination of workers *and* building size (physical capital). That is, in the long run, The Cheeseman is able to combine workers and physical capital to achieve the minimal ATC for each output level. This difference causes the short-run cost curves to be above the long-run cost curve.

To see the relationship between the short- and long-run cost curves, consider short-run ATCs for three different plant sizes: one small, one medium, and one large. These are each shown in panel (a) of Exhibit 6.14. Because in the long run The Cheeseman is able to choose the plant size that minimizes costs, its long-run ATC lies below the three short-run ATCs. One way to think about it is that the average cost rises more in the short run with increased production because The Cheeseman can only hire more labor; in the long run, it can hire more labor and purchase more physical capital.

As panel (a) of Exhibit 6.14 shows, the long-run ATC curve has a pronounced U-shape. On the downward portion of the U, ATC decreases as output increases. Over this range, **economies of scale** exist. For The Wisconsin Cheeseman, we find that economies of scale occur over the daily output range until it reaches about 444 units. Such an effect might

> **Economies of scale** occur when ATC falls as the quantity produced increases.

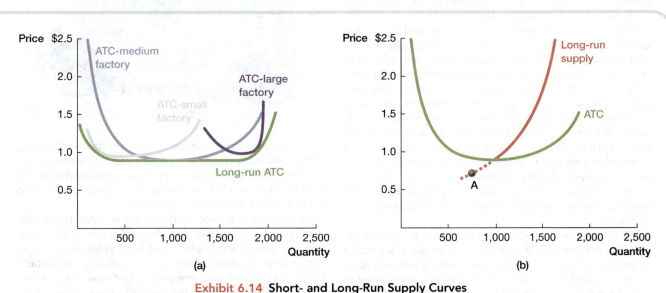

**Exhibit 6.14** Short- and Long-Run Supply Curves

In the long run, The Cheeseman is not constrained by its facilities. The dark green curve in panel (a) shows the long-run ATC curve of The Cheeseman with several examples of ATCs that The Cheeseman would face in the short run for a given factory size. Panel (b) shows the long-run supply curve.

occur because as the scale of the plant gets bigger, workers have more opportunities to specialize. When ATC does not change with the level of output, the plant experiences **constant returns to scale**. This occurs over the output range of 444 to 1,690. **Diseconomies of scale** occur when ATC increases as output rises. For The Cheeseman, this occurs at output levels exceeding 1,690. It might happen because management teams begin to get spread too thin or duplication of tasks occurs.

**Constant returns to scale** exist when ATC does not change as the quantity produced changes.

**Diseconomies of scale** occur when ATC rises as the quantity produced increases.

**Exit** is a long-run decision to leave the market.

### Long-Run Supply Curve

Panel (b) of Exhibit 6.14 shows the long-run supply curve (MC curve) alongside the long-run ATC curve. We can use this MC curve to construct The Cheeseman's long-run supply curve in a way similar to how we derived the short-run supply curve from the MC curve.

Consider point A. Should The Cheeseman produce at this price? The answer is no, because this price is lower than ATC, and therefore The Cheeseman is spending more money to produce cheese boxes than it is paid for them. So total revenue is less than total costs, leading to a negative economic profit.

There is really no choice for Cheeseman but to *exit* the industry, because it cannot profitably exist at the equilibrium price. Note that **exit** is a long-run decision to leave the market. We can therefore state a long-run decision rule:

Exit if price is less than ATC or, likewise, if total revenue is less than total cost.

## CHOICE & CONSEQUENCE

### Visiting a Car Manufacturing Plant

Recently, we visited Chrysler's car manufacturing plant in Sterling Heights, Michigan, where thousands of cars are produced annually by thousands of workers. The assembly plant houses highly skilled workers and plenty of robotics to put together the various pieces to create a final product—combining sheet metal with hundreds of loose parts to make a shiny-rimmed automobile.

In one part of the plant, we saw a welded frame (the chassis) moving along a large conveyor belt. The conveyor belt swerved through many teams of workers, who were responsible for adding to this initial baseline component.

One team carefully set the engine in place. The next put in front and rear suspension, a different team later installed the transmission, then another team was responsible for the steering box, and yet another for the brake system. Before the car was painted with three coats of glossy paint, inspectors made sure no defects were apparent. Finally, before leaving the lot, even more inspectors made sure that the brakes, windshield wipers, windows, and other parts were operating up to standard.

What is noteworthy about this process is the *specialization* that occurred. Each worker had a single job: install a specific part, inspect, or paint. Each specific job involved a complex set of tasks that must be precisely completed to provide the quality and quantity necessary to ensure the plant was optimizing profits.

We can imagine that if workers instead were dispatched to build these cars separately, they would not be able to produce one per day in total. But, with specialization, this

plant can produce hundreds of cars per day. In this way, a large assembly plant can produce more cars per worker than a small assembly plant can. This is exactly what Henry Ford realized in 1908, when he introduced the world to the first affordable car—the Model T.

Although at the time Ford had many advantages—for example, the success of the Model T arose in part from using vanadium steel, which put Ford years ahead of its competition—specialization was especially important. Ford's plants then and every car plant now reaps economies of scale. Much as for The Wisconsin Cheeseman, economies of scale are achieved when ATC declines as output increases. One of the key features of production in prosperous modern economies is that specialization leads to more output per worker.

This reasoning naturally leads to the construction of a long-run supply curve for The Cheeseman that is different from its short-run supply curve: *the long-run supply curve is the portion of its MC curve that lies above ATC.* This is shown in panel (b) of Exhibit 6.14 with the solid red line depicting the long-run supply curve. The dotted line below ATC is the portion of the supply curve that exists in the short run but not in the long run, because it is between the AVC and ATC curves, as shown in Exhibit 6.11.

The Cheeseman's total profit in the long run is computed exactly like its short-run profit: total revenue minus total cost. Thus, profit equals the difference between price and ATC multiplied by the quantity sold: $(P - ATC) \times Q$. Accordingly, when computing producer surplus in the long run, we take the difference between market price and the seller's long-run MC curve.

From knowing how to derive the short- and long-run supply curves, a natural question arises: what factors determine where the firm's supply curve is located on the graph? Because the supply curve is the MC curve above the AVC curve (in the short run) or above the ATC curve (in the long run), the answer to this question revolves around cost considerations. As with the individual demand curve, there are factors that cause the firm's supply curve to shift leftward or rightward. These factors are more fully discussed in Chapter 4, but they include input prices (such as labor costs) and technological innovations.

# 6.6 From the Firm to the Market: Long-Run Competitive Equilibrium

Much like the short- and long-run analyses for the individual firm, at the industry level there are critical distinctions between the short run and the long run. The primary difference is that even though the number of firms in the industry is fixed in the short run, in the long run, firms can enter or exit the industry in response to changes in profitability. This is because in the long run, they have the ability to change both labor *and* physical capital.

> **Even though the number of firms in the industry is fixed in the short run, in the long run, firms can enter or exit the industry in response to changes in profitability.**

## Firm Entry

When would a firm decide to enter a market? Steve's Wholesale Cheese (an actual firm in Sun Prairie, Wisconsin, located near The Wisconsin Cheeseman) is considering entering the cheese-packing industry, which currently has 10,000 identical firms. Suppose Steve's Wholesale is identical to The Cheeseman and to the other firms. Further, assume that the current market price is above Steve's minimum long-run ATC, as at point E of Exhibit 6.15.

**Exhibit 6.15  Steve's Wholesale Cheese Entry Decision**

Considering a new firm, Steve's Wholesale (which is identical to The Cheeseman), we see that there are potential profits to earn by entering the industry. We can see this by noting that the area of the shaded box representing economic profits is greater than zero when the market price is $1.13.

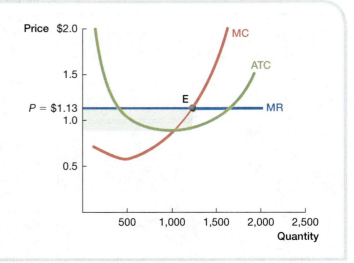

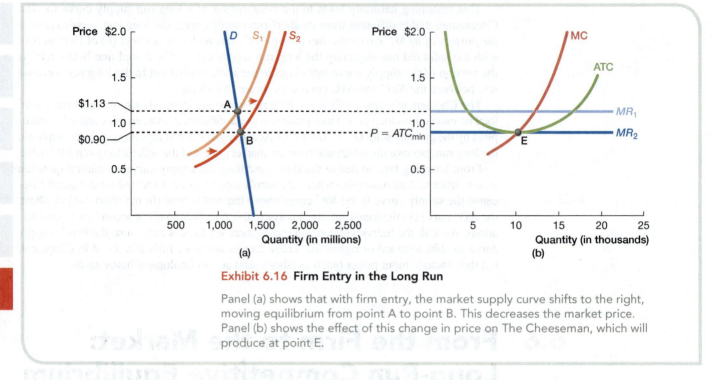

**Exhibit 6.16 Firm Entry in the Long Run**

Panel (a) shows that with firm entry, the market supply curve shifts to the right, moving equilibrium from point A to point B. This decreases the market price. Panel (b) shows the effect of this change in price on The Cheeseman, which will produce at point E.

There is **free entry** into an industry when entry is unfettered by any special legal or technical barriers.

Should Steve enter? The answer is yes. Notice that because the price is $1.13, which is greater than Steve's ATC of $0.93, Steve can enter the industry and make a profit of $(P - ATC)$ on each unit produced. In this case, Steve would earn profits given by the area of the shaded rectangle $(P - ATC) \times Q$. Therefore, Steve's Wholesale Cheese should take advantage of this opportunity and enter the cheese-packing business.

It's not hard to imagine that many firms would make this calculation, realize they can be profitable in the industry, and decide to enter. What would happen then? If there is **free entry** into the industry—which means entry is unfettered by any special legal or technical barriers—the entry process continues until the last entrant drives the market price down to the minimum ATC. Let's walk through why this is the case.

First, think about what entry of new firms does to the market supply curve. Because the market supply curve is the summation of individual firms' supply curves, adding new firms causes the industry to provide higher quantity at any given price. After all, the entrants must be added to the existing industry total. In other words, entry shifts the market supply curve to the right.

This shift will cause the market price to fall. Why? Panel (a) of Exhibit 6.16 provides the intuition. We know that the market price in a perfectly competitive industry is determined by the intersection of the market demand and market supply curves (point A in the exhibit). A shift to the right of the market supply curve from $S_1$ to $S_2$ lowers the market price from $1.13 to $0.90 (point B in panel (a) of Exhibit 6.16).

Will another firm decide to enter? No, because the market price drops to the minimum of the ATC curve (point E in panel (b) of Exhibit 6.16). At this point, the market reaches an equilibrium, because no more firms will enter. For this example, Steve's Wholesale entering the market moved the price down to the minimum ATC of the industry, resulting in zero economic profits. There is now no longer a profit incentive for other suppliers to enter.

If, after Steve's Wholesale enters, the new price remains above the minimum ATC, then another firm will enter. After all, an incentive remains to enter this market—positive profits! This entry further shifts the market supply curve to the right, lowering the market price even more. This process continues until the market price is driven to the minimum ATC of the industry. At that point, entry stops.

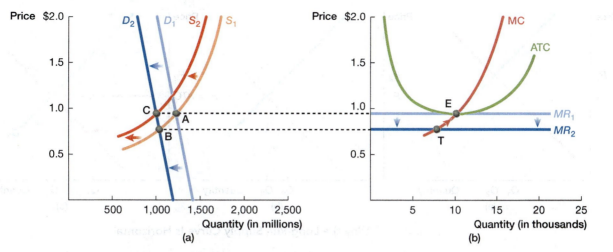

**Exhibit 6.17 Firm Exit After Demand Shifts Leftward**

Panel (a) shows that if market demand shifts to the left, price will decrease from point A to B. At this new price, firms will exit, which will cause the market supply curve to shift to the left, moving the market equilibrium to point C and putting The Cheeseman at point E in panel (b).

## Firm Exit

Now suppose that once we reach that equilibrium, a group of researchers issues a report claiming that touching cheese can cause skin irritation in toddlers. This announcement causes the market demand curve for cheese boxes to shift leftward. Assume that this shift of the market demand curve for cheese boxes causes the equilibrium price to change from $0.90 to $0.71, as in panel (a) of Exhibit 6.17, where the price drops from point A to B. The price is now below the minimum ATC of the firms, as shown in panel (b) of Exhibit 6.17 at point T. This causes firms in the industry to make negative profits. Therefore, if there is **free exit** from the market—in which a firm's exit is unfettered by any special legal or technical barriers—in the long run, some cheese packers will close shop and leave the industry. Because we've assumed that all firms are identical, all firms in the market are equally unprofitable and would prefer to exit. You might wonder which firms will exit first. There are a couple of ways to think about this. One is that a lucky few may figure out that they're losing money before the others do, and they leave first. The other, probably more realistic, possibility is that cost differences exist across firms, and the highest-cost firms exit first. We examine an example of this in the appendix to this chapter, but for now let's continue with the example of all firms being identical.

> There is **free exit** from an industry when exit is unfettered by any special legal or technical barriers.

This exit from the industry causes the market supply curve to shift leftward, raising the market price from point B to point C in panel (a) of Exhibit 6.17. Just as entry continued until the price was driven down to the minimum ATC, exit continues until the market price rises to the minimum ATC. Once this point is reached, we are in a long-run equilibrium. This occurs at point E in panel (b) of Exhibit 6.17.

Notice that regardless of initial demand or supply shifts and accompanying price changes in the market, entry or exit causes the market to reach the minimum of the long-run ATC curve. That is, the equilibrium quantity in the market might change due to market demand and supply shifts, but the equilibrium price *always* returns to the minimum of the long-run ATC.

## Zero Profits in the Long Run

We can see that free entry and free exit are forces that push the market price in a perfectly competitive industry toward the long-run minimum ATC. This leads to two important outcomes under our perfectly competitive market assumption.

First, even though the industry's short-run supply curve is upward-sloping for the reasons we discussed above, the industry's *long-run* supply curve is horizontal at the long-run

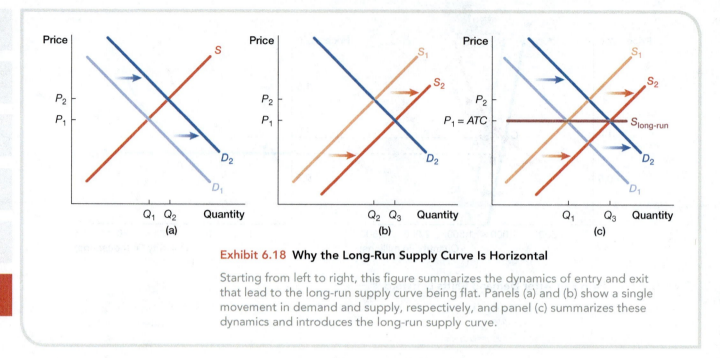

**Exhibit 6.18 Why the Long-Run Supply Curve Is Horizontal**

Starting from left to right, this figure summarizes the dynamics of entry and exit that lead to the long-run supply curve being flat. Panels (a) and (b) show a single movement in demand and supply, respectively, and panel (c) summarizes these dynamics and introduces the long-run supply curve.

minimum ATC level. Why? Price always returns to the minimum ATC, and because ATC does not change, price always remains the same in the long run. This is because variations in long-run industry output are absorbed by firm entry and exit, causing long-run quantity to change while equilibrium price remains the same.

Let's walk through an example to illustrate this intuition. Consider panel (a) in Exhibit 6.18, which shows an initial market demand of $D_1$ and supply of $S$. The initial equilibrium quantity is $Q_1$ and price is $P_1$, which we know is equal to the minimum ATC.

Suppose market demand shifts rightward to $D_2$. While prices might temporarily rise, entry of new firms in the long run shifts the supply curve to the right, as in panel (b) of Exhibit 6.18. As entry continues, supply eventually reaches $S_2$, and price falls back to the long-run minimum ATC, or a price of $P_1$. If we connect the two long-run equilibria, we have the market's long-run supply curve $S_{\text{long-run}}$, which is horizontal at $P_1$, shown in panel (c) of Exhibit 6.18.

So we see that in the long run, price equals the minimum of ATC because of entry and exit. Because identical firms stand ready to enter or exit the industry, in the long run, as much quantity as necessary can be produced at the minimum ATC.

The second long-run outcome achieved with free entry and exit is that firms in a perfectly competitive market earn zero economic profits in equilibrium. Economic profits serve as an important signal as to whether firms are better off in this industry or in some other industry: if economic profits are positive, then entry occurs until economic profits fall to zero. If economic profits are negative, exit occurs until these profits rise to zero. Free entry and exit forces price to the minimum ATC, and therefore economic profits are zero in the long-run equilibrium.

An important assumption that we make in this analysis is that firms are identical and can hire inputs (labor and physical capital) at a constant cost (in this case, the industry can hire as many workers as it desires at $72 per day). When firms are not identical in terms of their cost structure, we find results that diverge from this zero economic profit conclusion. In such cases, low-cost firms can earn positive economic profits in long-run equilibrium. We leave this case to be discussed further in the appendix.

## Economic Profit Versus Accounting Profit

If you're thinking from an entrepreneur's perspective, maybe the zero-profit implication of firm entry and exit makes you despair. After all, why even try to start a business if the end result will be profitless? As we discussed earlier, there is one important reason why you shouldn't think this way: economic profits are not the same as accounting profits. As a business owner, when economic profits are zero, it simply means that you cannot earn more money if you take your talents to a different industry—you are being paid at least your opportunity cost of time.

Let's think through the difference between accounting and economic profits with an example. On January 20, 2011, newspaper clippings in Sun Prairie, Wisconsin, announced that the Wisconsin Cheeseman was closing. Wisconsin Cheeseman President and CEO Dave Mack noted that the restructuring would lead to 80 employees losing their jobs.

To some, this came as a surprise, because they believed that The Wisconsin Cheeseman had been earning a profit. Why would a company earning a profit go out of business? The answer lies in the definition of profit—even though The Cheeseman might have been earning positive accounting profits, economic profits might have been negative. For instance, assume that if The Cheeseman were not in its current line of business, its next best use for its management team and physical capital would be to set itself up as a warehouse for fast-food storage for nearby Madison.

In fact, let's go further and assume that The Cheeseman could increase its profits considerably if it decided to shift from the cheese-packing industry to the fast-food storage business. In such a case, accounting profits of cheese packing might indeed be positive, whereas economic profits are negative. This is because the implicit costs of cheese packing—the opportunity cost of management time and plant—must be considered. Much like the cost of labor, this implicit cost is subtracted from revenues to produce the economist's conception of profits.[2]

# EVIDENCE-BASED ECONOMICS

## Q: How would an ethanol subsidy affect ethanol producers?

A **subsidy** is a payment or tax break used as an incentive for an agent to complete an activity.

At the beginning of this chapter, we asked how an ethanol **subsidy** would affect ethanol producers. The ethanol production industry is approximately perfectly competitive, so the tools of this chapter can help us understand this question. In Chapter 10, we discuss taxes and subsidies more fully.

We can begin to shed light on this issue by exploring whether economic profits for the industry increase when subsidies are given. We have learned in this chapter that one sign of positive economic profits is firm entry. Thus, we can ask, how did the number of ethanol plants change when the U.S. government subsidized the ethanol industry? Exhibit 6.19 plots the total number of ethanol plants in orange and the number of plants under construction or being expanded in blue. In 2006, every gallon of ethanol-based fuel was effectively subsidized by $0.51 with a refundable tax credit, and when President Bush announced in his 2006 State of the Union address that ethanol plants would remain in favor, the number of ethanol plants under construction skyrocketed, as displayed in Exhibit 6.19. In 2009, the subsidy dropped to $0.45 per gallon and construction of new firms fell back considerably, to levels observed before 2006 (though the construction rates had been falling from 2007 to 2009).

Ultimately, the increase and decrease in ethanol plants in response to subsidies suggests that economic profits were driving entry and exit, but the ethanol industry was affected by many factors during this time, making it difficult to determine whether the subsidies themselves caused the number of plant openings to change. For example, prices of corn—an important input to ethanol production—dipped to record lows in 2005. This by itself could lead to expansion of ethanol plants if investors believed corn prices would stay low. And macroeconomic conditions changed dramatically during 2008, so these impacts could influence plant construction and expansion.

One approach to provide further evidence relevant to our question of interest is to construct an artificial market where everything is identical except the presence of the

**Exhibit 6.19 Number of Ethanol Plants and Number of Plants under Construction**

We plotted the total number of ethanol plants and the number under construction or being expanded in this exhibit. Note the vertical dashed line. It denotes the day that President Bush promoted ethanol in his State of the Union address.

*Source:* Data from Renewable Fuels Association.

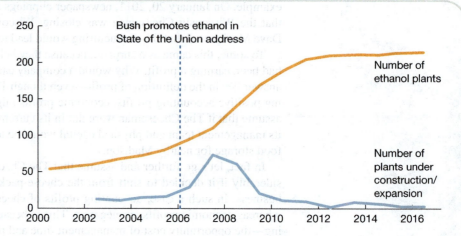

subsidy and then compare it to the market that receives the subsidy. We did just that, by setting up a lab experiment where students act as potential ethanol producers.[3]

Put yourself in the shoes of a subject who participated in this laboratory experiment. The experiment was set up to examine cases that included government subsidies for ethanol production and cases where ethanol subsidies were not available. In this experiment, each of 12 producers received the same cost curves and each producer made the entry decision in each of six periods (that is, they made the entry choice six times). If they enter, then their plant capacity is to produce 2 million gallons of ethanol and they are paid the difference between their revenues and their costs as their earnings. Panel (a) of Exhibit 6.20 plots the MC and ATC curves for sellers in the no-subsidy treatment. The cost curves in the subsidy treatment are shown in panel (b) of Exhibit 6.20. Each firm in the subsidy treatment has a $0.25 lower cost of production for every gallon.

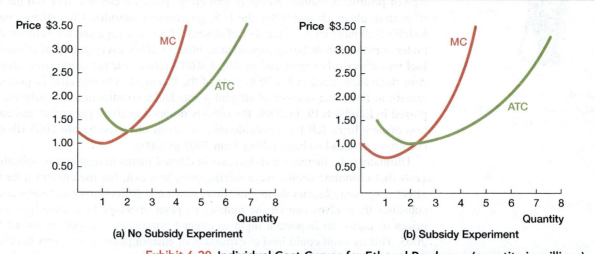

**Exhibit 6.20 Individual Cost Curves for Ethanol Producers (quantity in millions)**

The exhibit plots the MC and ATC curve for ethanol producers under two different scenarios. Panel (a) illustrates when ethanol producers have no subsidy, and panel (b) shows when ethanol producers have a $0.25 per gallon subsidy.

6.1

6.2

6.3

6.4

6.5

6.6

## Exhibit 6.21 Price and Quantities in Lab Experiment

The table summarizes the price and quantity of ethanol for experimental subjects. The left-hand column shows the price in increments of $0.05. The right-hand column shows the corresponding quantity, in millions of gallons, in the market.

| Price per Gallon | Total Number of Gallons on the Market (in millions) |
| --- | --- |
| $1.40 | 2 |
| $1.35 | 4 |
| $1.30 | 6 |
| $1.25 | 8 |
| $1.20 | 10 |
| $1.15 | 12 |
| $1.10 | 14 |
| $1.05 | 16 |
| $1.00 | 18 |
| $0.95 | 20 |
| $0.90 | 22 |
| $0.85 | 24 |

The experimental subjects are told that supply-and-demand conditions dictate that prices will be as displayed in Exhibit 6.21, which shows that if one seller enters the market, then there will be 2 million gallons produced and the price per gallon will be $1.40. In this case, for the subsidized seller, the profits are $(P - ATC) \times$ quantity, or ($1.40 - $1.00) $\times$ 2 million, which is $800,000. For the nonsubsidized seller, the profits are $(P - ATC) \times$ quantity, or ($1.40 - $1.25) $\times$ 2 million, which is $300,000.

What do you think happened in each round of the no-subsidy and subsidy treatments? How would you choose if you were an experimental participant? Exhibit 6.22 provides a summary of the experimental results. Panel (a) in Exhibit 6.22 shows that in round 1 of the no-subsidy treatment, 11 of the 12 sellers entered the market. Thus, 22 million gallons of ethanol were produced, and the equilibrium price was $0.90 per gallon. Therefore, every seller lost $0.35 per gallon $(P - ATC$, or $0.90 - $1.25). These losses caused 3 sellers to drop out of the market for round 2, leaving 8 sellers and a price of $1.05 per gallon. Still, in round 2, sellers were still losing money. This cannot continue in equilibrium. Exhibit 6.22 shows that it does not: by the fourth round, the equilibrium number of sellers prevails—4 sellers enter, yielding a market price of $1.25 per gallon. This number continues for the remainder of the experiment. Ethanol prices converged to the point where price equaled the minimum ATC, yielding economic profits of zero for every subject.

Panel (b) of Exhibit 6.22 reveals the data for the subsidy treatment. In this case, too few sellers (5) enter the market in round 1. With only 5 sellers, a price of $1.20 prevails. This means that every seller earns $0.20 per gallon produced $(P - ATC$, or $1.20 - $1.00). Profits cause other firms to enter, as can be seen in panel (b) of Exhibit 6.22. By the 6th round, the equilibrium number of 9 sellers enters the market, leading to a price of $1 per gallon. Again, price ends up equaling the minimum ATC. In this case, even though there is a subsidy, quantity increases to drive economic profits to zero, just as theory would predict.

This experiment confirms what we would expect from a competitive industry: entry and exit stabilize to a zero-profit equilibrium in each case. That is, regardless of the presence of a subsidy, economic profits are driven to zero in the long run. As for our opening question, what we have learned is that producers in perfectly competitive industries are influenced in the short run by subsidies, but firms in a competitive industry—like the ethanol industry—should not pin their hopes on reaping positive economic profits in the long run, because entry will drive long-run economic profits to zero.

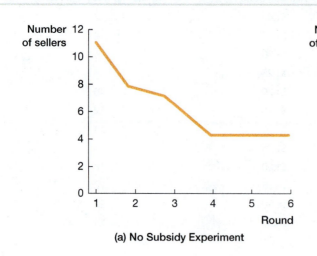

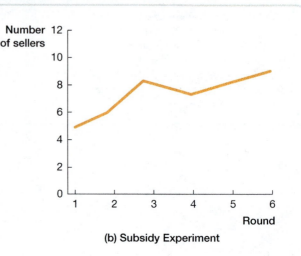

(a) No Subsidy Experiment

(b) Subsidy Experiment

**Exhibit 6.22 Results from Experimental Study**

The panels summarize the number of sellers in the experimental market over rounds of trading. Panel (a) is for the no-subsidy condition. Panel (b) is for the $0.25 per gallon subsidy.

### Question

How would an ethanol subsidy affect ethanol producers?

### Answer

It depends on whether we are considering the short run or the long run. The ethanol producer should understand that long-run economic profits will be zero in equilibrium.

### Data

Market data combined with a lab experiment.

### Caveat

It might be difficult to generalize results from the lab experiment. Also, during the time we examined data from the ethanol industry, many factors were changing at once, making it difficult to establish cause and effect.

## Summary

- Sellers optimize by solving the seller's problem, which dictates that decisions are made on the margin: expand production until MC equals MR.

- Short- and long-run supply curves provide an indication of sellers' willingness to sell at various price levels.

- The difference between price and the MC curve is producer surplus.

- Free entry and exit cause long-run economic profits to equal zero in a perfectly competitive market.

- With an understanding of decision-making rules from the seller's problem and the forces of free entry and exit, we can not only better understand how to run our own business but also better predict how sellers will respond to incentives.

# Key Terms

# Questions

*All questions are available in MyEconLab for practice and instructor assignment.*

1. Suppose one firm accounts for 55 percent of the global market share for a product, while 147 other firms account for the remaining 45 percent of the market. With such a large number of buyers and sellers, is this market likely to be competitive? Explain your answer.

2. Do you think sellers in a perfectly competitive market can price their goods differently? Explain your answer.

3. How would the introduction of legal or technical barriers to entry affect the long-run equilibrium in a perfectly competitive market?

4. Use a graph to show the relationship between the MC curve and the ATC curve for a competitive firm. What can you conclude about ATC when MC is less than ATC?

5. Why is it that the industry demand curve slopes downward when the demand curves faced by individual firms in perfectly competitive markets are horizontal?

6. How does a firm in a competitive market decide what level of output to produce in order to maximize its profit?

7. Is it possible for accounting profit to be positive but economic profit to be negative? Explain with an example.

8. The following graph shows three supply curves with varying degrees of price elasticity:

Identify the perfectly elastic, perfectly inelastic, and unit-elastic supply curves.

9. Would a profit-maximizing firm continue to operate if the price in the market fell below its average cost of production in the short run?

10. What is meant by producer surplus? How is producer surplus in a competitive market calculated?

11. In each of the following cases, identify whether a competitive firm's producer surplus will increase, decrease, or remain unchanged.

   **i.** The demand for the product increases.

   **ii.** The firm's MC of production increases.

   **iii.** The market price of the product falls.

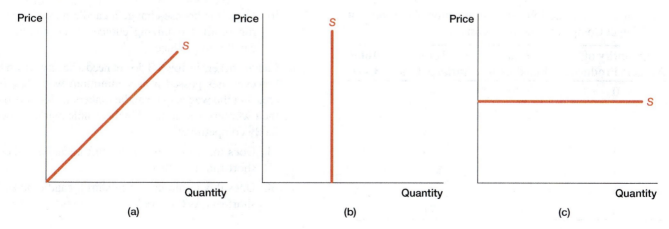

(a)          (b)          (c)

**12.** The following graph shows the long-run ATC cost curve for a perfectly competitive firm:

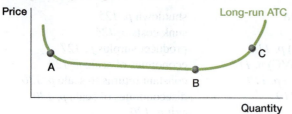

Refer to points A, B, and C on the graph, and identify where the firm would experience economies of scale, constant returns to scale, and diseconomies of scale.

**13.** How does the long-run supply curve differ from the short-run supply curve for a perfectly competitive firm? Explain your answer.

**14.** If some sellers exit a competitive market, how will this affect equilibrium?

# Problems

*All problems are available in MyEconLab for practice and instructor assignment.*

**1.** Fixing up old houses requires plumbing and carpentry work. Jack (who is a jack of all trades but is a master of none) is a decent carpenter and a decent plumber but is not particularly good at either. He can fix up two houses in a year if he does all the carpentry and plumbing himself. His wage is $50,000 per year.

 **a.** What is Jack's ATC of fixing up two old houses?

 **b.** George is an excellent plumber, and Harriet is an excellent carpenter. George can do all the plumbing, and Harriet can do all the carpentry to fix up five houses per year. Each earns a wage of $50,000 per year. If George and Harriet work together and fix up five old houses each year, what is their average cost?

 **c.** What does this problem tell you about one of the sources of economies of scale?

**2.** Salmon fishing in Alaska is a seasonal business; May through September is the best time to bait salmon and halibut. Toland Fisheries, a small commercial fishery, recorded its highest ever catch last year. It started this year's fishing season with the same number of workers and equipment. With the new season also starting well, Toland has increased hiring substantially. However, the fishery did not make any additional investment in trawlers and other fishing equipment.

 **a.** Other things remaining unchanged, what is likely to happen to the marginal product of each new worker in the short run?

 **b.** Is the outcome likely to be different in the long run? Explain your answer.

**3.** You are given the following information about the ABC Widget Company's short-run costs:

| Quantity of Widgets Produced | Total Fixed Cost | Total Variable Cost | Total Cost |
|---|---|---|---|
| 0 | $10 | — | — |
| 1 | — | $1 | — |
| 2 | — | $3 | $13 |
| 3 | — | $6 | $16 |
| 4 | — | $10 | — |
| 5 | — | — | $25 |
| 6 | $10 | $21 | — |

 **a.** Find the AFC of producing 5 widgets.

 **b.** Is the MC of the third widget greater than the ATC of producing 2 widgets? Does the production of the third widget lead to an increase in ATC or does it decrease ATC?

 **c.** Find the ATC of producing 4 widgets.

 **d.** Find the MC of producing the sixth widget.

**4.** Fill in the ATC and MC columns in the following table:

| Output | Total Cost | Average Total Cost | Marginal Cost |
|---|---|---|---|
| 0 | $14 | | |
| 1 | 15 | | |
| 2 | 18 | | |
| 3 | 24 | | |
| 4 | 36 | | |

 **a.** Use the MC curve to determine how many units this firm would supply if the market price were $10.

 **b.** Assuming free entry and exit of other firms, based on the ATC curve, what will the price be in the long run?

**5.** Every candle maker in Town A must have a license. The cost of a license is the same regardless of the number of candles a business produces.

 **a.** Assuming that the candle market is perfectly competitive:

  **i.** Does this license shift a candle maker's short-run AFC curve?

  **ii.** Does this license shift a candle maker's short-run AVC curve?

  **iii.** Does this license change a candle maker's short-run profit-maximizing choice of the number of candles to produce?

 **b.** Candle makers in Town B do not need a license. Town B, however, has passed a new minimum wage law increasing the wages that candle makers in Town B pay their workers. Assuming that the candle market is perfectly competitive:

  **i.** Does this minimum wage shift a candle maker's short-run AFC curve?

  **ii.** Does this minimum wage shift a candle maker's short-run AVC curve?

**iii.** Does this minimum wage change a candle maker's short-run profit-maximizing choice of the number of candles to produce?

6. You are one of five identical firms (i.e., you all have the same costs) that sell widgets. Each day you have a fixed cost of $9 to operate. The marginal costs of your first through fifth widgets are $1, $2, $3, $7, and $8, respectively. You have a capacity constraint of 5, and you can only produce a whole number of widgets.

   a. What is the average variable cost (AVC) for a firm that produces 2 widgets?

   b. What is the market-level quantity supplied given a price of $2.50?

   c. Suppose the market-level demand is fixed at 18. In other words, there is perfectly inelastic demand. What is the equilibrium price in the short run?

   d. Given perfect competition, what will be the price in the long run?

7. There are many identical firms with a simple cost structure: Total cost for $Q = 0$ is $6 and total cost for $Q = 1$ is $8. Each firm is incapable of producing anything more; in other words, total cost is infinite for any $Q$ larger than 1.

   a. What is the fixed cost? What is the marginal cost of the first unit?

   b. In the short run, above what price will firms supply one unit each?

   c. If firms are free to enter and exit this market, what will be the long-run price?

8. Some cities have much stricter zoning laws and regulatory controls than other cities. A recent study found that increases in the demand for housing in cities with strict zoning laws led to large increases in the price of housing. It also claimed that in cities with lax zoning laws, increases in the demand for housing led to much smaller increases in the price of housing. What, in your opinion, could explain these results? (*Hint:* Zoning laws regulate the uses of land in a city.)

9. You read a story in the newspaper about a car company that has recently been fined $5 billion by government regulators. The fine is for past infractions that are no longer relevant to how the firm produces cars going forward. The article contains the statement "clearly the company will now need to raise prices in order to recover this loss." Evaluate this claim based on the ideas described in this chapter.

10. This problem asks you to think carefully about sunk costs.

    a. The International Space Station (ISS) is a habitable satellite that was launched by NASA and space agencies of other countries. In 2009, NASA was considering shutting down the ISS within the next 5 to 6 years. Among those who were opposed to this idea of de-orbiting the ISS was Senator Bill Nelson, who was quoted as saying, "If we've spent a hundred billion dollars, I don't think we want to shut it down in 2015." Identify the flaw in the senator's reasoning.

    b. You are planning to build an apartment building. Your market research department estimates that your revenues will be $9.0 million. Your engineering department estimates the cost will be $6.0 million. You have started construction and spent $1.5 million to build the foundation when the recession begins. This causes the market research department to revise its revenue estimates downward to $4.0 million. Should you complete the apartment building?

11. Larry Krovitz is a salesman who works at a used-car showroom in Sydney, Australia. It's the last week of July, but he has not yet met his sales target for the month. A customer, Harold Kumar, who wants to buy a Ford Fiesta, walks into the showroom. After taking one of the cars for a test drive, Harold decides to buy it. While $11,000 was the least that Larry would have been willing to accept for that car, he quotes a price of $15,000. After some bargaining, the car is sold for $12,000.

    a. What is the producer surplus in this case?

    b. If Larry bought the car for $8,000, what is his profit?

    c. Is producer surplus always equal to profit? Explain your answer.

12. The following table shows the long-run total costs of three different firms:

    | Output | Firm I | Firm II | Firm III |
    |--------|--------|---------|----------|
    | 1 | $8 | $5 | $7 |
    | 2 | $14 | $12 | $12 |
    | 3 | $18 | $21 | $15 |
    | 4 | $20 | $32 | $24 |

    a. Do firms I and II experience economies of scale? Or do they experience diseconomies of scale?

    b. Minimum efficient scale is the lowest level of output at which long-run average cost is minimized. Find firm III's minimum efficient scale.

13. Suppose TC is given by $TC = 16 + Q^2$. This implies that MC is $MC = 2Q$.

    a. Give the formula for ATC.

    b. If the market price were $5, how many units of output would this firm want to supply?

    c. What will the price be in the long run?

# Appendix

# When Firms Have Different Cost Structures

We have thus far considered cases with many identical firms. Many of the industries you've encountered, though, likely don't satisfy this assumption. Some firms have better technologies than others. Some firms have more experienced or savvy entrepreneurs than others. Some might have access to critical inputs, such as natural resources. For example, some farmers might have land more suitable for growing certain crops than others. All these factors might lead firms to have different costs of production. What do supply curves look like in such industries? How does the equilibrium change?

It is important to note that our main lesson from the body of the chapter also holds in this case: *every firm expands production until MC = MR = P, unless shutdown or exit is optimal.* And we continue to construct the market supply curve from the summation of individual firm supply curves. The main difference between the case of identical firms and the one where firms are different is that the equilibrium price in the latter equals the long-run ATC of the last entrant. This has important implications, because in this case, some firms earn positive economic profits, even in the long-run equilibrium.

To see why, suppose that a new seed is developed that produces a wonderful new fruit. Market demand is enormous for this fruit, which can be grown across pasturelands in the United States. But the best growing conditions are gently rolling plots of land, where laborers can more easily pick the fruit. Thus, costs will vary by land type. Using this information, we are able to rank farmers by their ATC to produce a bushel of this new fruit.

In this scenario, we would expect that farmers with the lowest ATC would enter the market first and earn the greatest economic profits. After they enter, the next farmers to enter the market have land that is not as well suited for growing the fruit. Therefore, those farmers will have a higher ATC than the first set of market entrants. If we continue with this thought experiment, we find that the last farmer to enter the market will be the farmer with zero economic profits. This farmer is indifferent between entering the industry at the market price and not entering. Indeed, if the market price were to fall even a little, she would not wish to enter the industry.

To show how this works, consider Exhibit 6A.1. A rightward shift in the market demand curve leads to an increase in price, as shown in panel (a) of Exhibit 6A.1. This increase in price causes firms to enter the industry, thereby shifting the supply curve rightward, as in panel (b) of the exhibit. These new entrants have higher costs than the existing firms, causing the equilibrium price to settle at the point where the last entrant has zero economic profits: price equals the minimum of his long-run ATC. In this case, an upward-sloping long-run supply curve results, as in panel (b) of the exhibit. With an upward-sloping long-run supply curve, the equilibrium price is above the ATC for the farmers with the best plots of land (those with the lowest ATC). This allows these low-cost farmers to enjoy profits in the long run compared to the case of a horizontal long-run supply curve. This result shows that in equilibrium, economic profits can be positive in the long run if sellers have different costs.

Exhibit 6A.2 recaps the basic results we obtain when we consider the implication of free entry and exit in a competitive market.

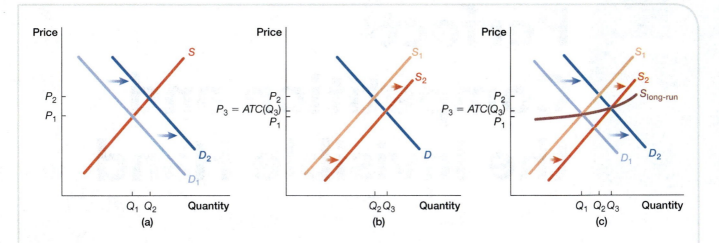

**Exhibit 6A.1 Equilibrium When Firms Have Different Cost Structures**

Panel (a) shows an increase in industry demand, so demand shifts right (increases) from $D_1$ to $D_2$. The resulting increase in price from $P_1$ to $P_2$ means that firms are now realizing positive economic profits in this industry ($P > ATC$). In response to this increase in economic profits, there is entry into the industry, which causes the industry supply to shift right (increase), as shown in panel (b). In response to entry, industry output increases, and the price in the market begins to fall from $P_2$. Entry will continue until the marginal firm (the last firm to enter the industry) earns zero economic profits, which occurs at the new price. But, since there is heterogeneity in firm costs, with the lowest-cost producers being first in the market, entry subsides before price returns to its initial level, $P_1$. Note that in panel (b), the final equilibrium price, $P_3$, is greater than the initial equilibrium price in the market, $P_1$. Panel (c) combines the initial increase in market demand with the subsequent market entry to illustrate both the initial equilibrium in the market ($Q_1$, $P_1$) and the final market equilibrium ($Q_3$, $P_3$). Again, since firms have different cost structures, the zero-profit condition holds when the marginal firm faces a price equal to its ATC. The long-run supply curve for the market is simply the locus of long-run market equilibria and is upward-sloping.

**Exhibit 6A.2 Economic Outcomes in Models of Identical and Nonidentical Firms**

Short- and long-run profits and supply curves are summarized for two different types of markets. The first set of rows is for a market with identical firms. The second set of rows is for nonidentical firms.

| Firm Cost Structures | Profits and Industry Supply | |
| --- | --- | --- |
| | **Short Run** | **Long Run** |
| **All firms have identical cost structures** | Positive economic profits possible | All firms earn zero economic profits |
| | Upward-sloping industry supply curve | Horizontal industry supply curve |
| **Firms' cost structures vary** | Positive economic profits possible | All firms except the marginal firm earn positive economic profits |
| | Upward-sloping industry supply curve | Upward-sloping industry supply curve |

# 7 Perfect Competition and the Invisible Hand

## Can markets composed of only self-interested people maximize the overall well-being of society?

In the previous two chapters we provided descriptions of the decision problems facing the main actors in any market: buyers and sellers. We found that when each of them follows certain rules of behavior, each will maximize his or her *own* well-being—a good thing, because we all want to do the best we can. But when all of these self-interested people are put together in a competitive market, can anything but chaos result?

At first glance it does seem as if pandemonium reigns in many markets—bidding wars on eBay, stockbrokers frantically waving their arms as they try to buy or sell, buyers and sellers haggling over prices at flea markets. Obvious disarray. All of this chaos, it seems, is driven by market participants simply looking out for #1—themselves.

Adam Smith, the father of economics, viewed the chaos quite differently. He conjectured that self-interest was a necessary ingredient for an economy to function efficiently. This view is put forth most elegantly in his treatise *The Wealth of Nations* (1776):

> It is not from the benevolence of the butcher, the brewer, or the baker, that we expect our dinner, but from their regard to their own interest.[1]

## CHAPTER OUTLINE

# KEY IDEAS

- The invisible hand efficiently allocates goods and services to buyers and sellers.

- The invisible hand leads to efficient production within an industry.

- The invisible hand allocates resources efficiently across industries.

- Prices direct the invisible hand.

- There are trade-offs between making the economic pie as big as possible and dividing the pieces equally.

This insight has become known as the power of the "invisible hand." It is a forceful idea in economics because it suggests that when all of the assumptions of a perfectly competitive market are in place, the pursuit of individual self-interest promotes the well-being of society as a whole, almost as if the individual is led by an invisible hand to do so.

In this chapter, we discuss the important implications of the invisible hand. We will show that when we impose the assumptions of perfect competition, the market system creates harmony between the interests of the individual and those of society. We will find that in such cases the free market is almost magical in that it allocates the production and final consumption of goods and services in a perfectly efficient manner. We will learn that the secret to how the market efficiently allocates scarce resources is by allowing prices to influence buyers and sellers—regardless of whether we are discussing traders at the New York Stock Exchange, buyers and sellers in flea markets in Atlanta, or people frequenting garage sales in Los Angeles. In this way, once we grasp the workings of the invisible hand, we better understand the world around us.

## 7.1 Perfect Competition and Efficiency

To begin, let's consider more carefully the perfectly competitive markets discussed in Chapters 4–6. For simplicity, let's assume that our market is composed of only seven buyers and seven sellers who are price-takers. Each wants to buy or sell a used iPhone 6 in good condition. Because the iPhones are all in similar condition, we can assume that they are identical. Madeline, Katie, Sean, Dave, Ian, Kim, and Ty are buyers in the market, and each of their *reservation values* (willingness-to-pay values) is listed in Exhibit 7.1. A **reservation value** is the price at which a person is indifferent between making the trade and not doing so. We learn from Exhibit 7.1 that Madeline is willing to pay $70 for an iPhone, Katie $60, on down to Ty, who is willing to pay $10 for an iPhone. Together, these data can be combined to form the market demand curve displayed in Exhibit 7.2.

Tom, Mary, Jeff, Phil, Adam, Matt, and Fiona are all sellers in the market, and each of their reservation values (willingness-to-sell values, or marginal costs) is also contained in Exhibit 7.1. From the exhibit, we learn that Tom is willing to sell his iPhone for $10, Mary for $20, on up to Fiona, who will sell her iPhone for no less than $70. Together, these values can be combined to make up the market supply curve displayed in Exhibit 7.2.

What is the equilibrium price in this case? The equilibrium price is determined by the intersection of the market demand and market supply curves. Exhibit 7.2 shows that this intersection yields a price of $40—which happens to be the price at which Dave is willing to buy an iPhone and Phil is willing to sell his iPhone.

**Reservation value** is the price at which a trading partner is indifferent between making the trade and not doing so.

**Exhibit 7.1 Reservation Values of Buyers and Sellers in the iPhone Market**

In the iPhone market, we have seven buyers and seven sellers, each with their own reservation values for an iPhone. Together, the seven buyers make up the market demand for iPhones and the seven sellers compose the market supply for iPhones.

| Buyer | Reservation Value ($) | Seller | Reservation Value ($) |
|---|---|---|---|
| Madeline | 70 | Tom | 10 |
| Katie | 60 | Mary | 20 |
| Sean | 50 | Jeff | 30 |
| Dave | 40 | Phil | 40 |
| Ian | 30 | Adam | 50 |
| Kim | 20 | Matt | 60 |
| Ty | 10 | Fiona | 70 |

**Social surplus** is the sum of consumer surplus and producer surplus.

What is the quantity traded at this equilibrium price of $40? Similar to equilibrium price determination, we compute the equilibrium quantity level by again looking at the intersection of the market demand and market supply curves. On so doing, we find that the equilibrium quantity is four iPhones. This follows because four people (Madeline, Katie, Sean, and Dave) are willing to pay *at least* $40 for an iPhone, while four sellers (Tom, Mary, Jeff, and Phil) have reservation values less than or equal to $40. In this example, we assume that if a person is indifferent to trading, as Dave and Phil are at $40, he or she trades.

## Social Surplus

An important outcome from buyers and sellers optimizing in perfectly competitive markets is that *social surplus* is maximized. **Social surplus** is the sum of *consumer surplus* and *producer surplus*, which we studied in Chapters 5 and 6. As we discussed in those two chapters, consumer surplus is the difference between the buyers' reservation values and what the buyers actually pay, and producer surplus is the difference between the price and the sellers' reservation values (marginal cost). So, social surplus represents the total value from trade in the market. For social surplus to be maximized, the highest-value buyers are making a purchase and the lowest-cost sellers are selling. In this way, buyers and sellers as distinct groups are doing as well as they possibly can—they're optimizing.

To see why social surplus is maximized at the competitive market equilibrium, look at panels (a), (b), and (c) of Exhibit 7.3, which breaks down Exhibit 7.2 into simpler chunks. Notice that social surplus—the sum of the areas shaded blue and red—is graphically given in all three panels by the area between the market demand and market supply curves from the origin to the quantity traded. Panel (b) shows the social surplus at the competitive market equilibrium. We compute this surplus by summing the consumer and producer surplus of each market participant. For example, because Madeline is willing to pay $70 for an iPhone, but actually pays only $40, her consumer surplus is $30. Likewise, because Tom is willing to sell his iPhone for $10, but receives $40, his producer surplus is $30. By

**Exhibit 7.2 Demand and Supply Curves in the iPhone Market**

When we plot the demand and supply schedules from Exhibit 7.1, we end up with stepwise curves because each individual only demands or supplies one unit. The curves intersect at the equilibrium price of $40, and at that price, four iPhones will be sold, identifying the equilibrium quantity of iPhones.

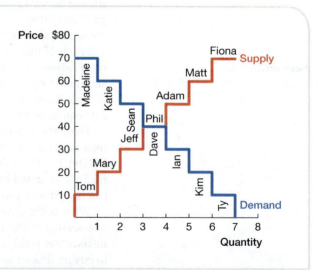

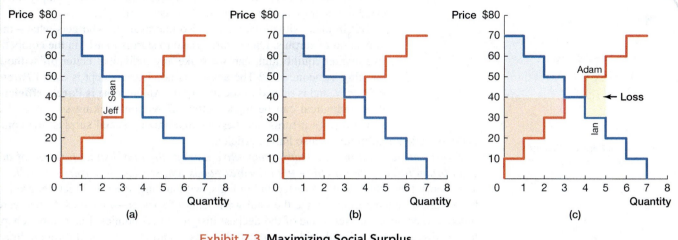

**Exhibit 7.3 Maximizing Social Surplus**

When a cap of two iPhones is imposed, the situation is as depicted in panel (a). Social surplus is not maximized, because Sean and Jeff do not make profitable trades. On the flip side, when a minimum of five iPhones traded is imposed, as in panel (c), Adam and Ian now trade, even though the cost to the seller (Adam) is higher than the benefit to the buyer (Ian), leaving us worse off compared to the social optimum. Leaving the iPhone market to act without outside direction, as in panel (b), generates the maximum amount of social surplus, precisely because it does not leave out profitable trades (as in (a)) or force unprofitable trades (as in (c)).

performing this computation for each of the people who trade, we learn that the social surplus adds up to $120, composed of $60 in consumer surplus and $60 in producer surplus.

To understand a little better why the competitive equilibrium maximizes social surplus, consider what would happen if we restricted the quantity sold in the market to be below the equilibrium quantity. Say we restrict the number of trades to two: that is, the two highest-value consumers buy from the two lowest-cost sellers. That means Madeline and Katie buy and Tom and Mary sell. Regardless of the price at which the trade occurs, the result will be as depicted in panel (a) of Exhibit 7.3. In this situation, we find a lower total surplus compared to the competitive market equilibrium outcome: the market now achieves $100 in total surplus (this can be found by taking the difference between the reservation values of Madeline and Katie ($130) and those of Tom and Mary ($30)). This figure is lower than the $120 of surplus achieved in the competitive equilibrium of panel (b).

What would happen if, instead, we expanded the trading opportunities and enforced trade of five iPhones? That is, we have the five highest-value buyers purchasing from the five lowest-cost sellers. Panel (c) of Exhibit 7.3 illustrates this case. With five sellers, we need to go all the way up the supply curve and include Adam, the fifth-lowest-cost seller. Likewise, we need to go all the way down the demand curve to Ian, the fifth-highest-value buyer. We now not only obtain the surplus in the competitive market equilibrium (when four trades are made, as in panel (b) of Exhibit 7.3) but we also obtain the yellow-shaded region in panel (c).

The yellow-shaded region in panel (c) represents losses from forcing a fifth trade. This is because the seller values the fifth item more than the buyer does. The loss in this case is equal to $20: $50 – $30, or Adam's cost minus Ian's benefit. This loss occurs because the marginal benefit of having Ian receive an iPhone ($30) is less than the marginal cost of having Adam give up his iPhone ($50). Because marginal benefits are lower than marginal costs, our decision rules developed in earlier chapters suggest that this is not an optimal action to take. In this case, total surplus decreases from $120 in the competitive equilibrium to $100 ($120 − $20).

## Pareto Efficiency

We now know that the competitive market equilibrium is efficient in the sense that all mutually advantageous trades take place: no more, no less. In this way, there are no unexploited gains to trade. Accordingly, the competitive market equilibrium maximizes social surplus: this is the best that society as a whole can do if it is simply interested in maximizing the total size of the economic pie.

But in many situations we are also interested in who gets what—the allocation of surplus. One natural place to start is to ask: in the competitive market equilibrium, can we make any individual better off without harming someone else? The answer is no. This concept is called *Pareto efficiency*, and is related to social surplus. An outcome is **Pareto efficient** if no individual can be made better off without making someone else worse off. As it turns out, besides maximizing social surplus, the competitive market equilibrium is also Pareto efficient.

*So we can say that in a perfectly competitive market, the first distinct function of the equilibrium price is that it efficiently allocates goods and services to buyers and sellers.* The theory that purely self-interested individuals, without any specific direction, are led by the invisible hand to maximize the total well-being of society—almost as if they were ordered to do so—represents one of the deepest insights in economics. Later in the chapter, we discuss the empirical evidence (recall that this is knowledge gained through direct observation and measurement) of whether this theoretical prediction has empirical support.

An outcome is **Pareto efficient** if no individual can be made better off without making someone else worse off.

## 7.2 Extending the Reach of the Invisible Hand: From the Individual to the Firm

While the invisible hand holds sharp results for individuals, it also has a considerably broader scope when applied to the concepts of Chapter 6. Consider a firm that owns two manufacturing plants, each of which produces microchips to sell in a perfectly competitive market. The two plants are quite different, with one being built in the late 1970s and the other in 2010. The older plant therefore has less advanced production technologies and higher production costs than the newer plant, as depicted in Exhibit 7.4. The exhibit shows that at each production level, the newer plant can produce microchips at a lower marginal cost than the older plant.

The firm has historically allowed each plant to operate independently, with both plant managers tasked with maximizing their own plant's profits. If the price of microchips is $10, what quantity of microchips should each of the plant managers choose to maximize profits? An application of the seller's decision rule that we learned in Chapter 6 is appropriate: in the short run, if price is greater than average variable cost ($P > AVC$), then each plant should expand production until marginal cost equals price. Let's assume that $P > AVC$.

**Exhibit 7.4 Marginal Costs for Two Manufacturing Plants**

The old manufacturing plant, with its less productive capital, faces a higher marginal cost to produce than the new plant. Represented graphically, this means that the old manufacturing plant's marginal cost curve (pink) is higher than the new plant's marginal cost curve (red) for any given quantity of production.

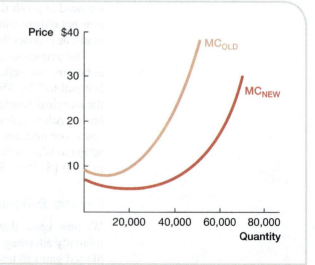

## Exhibit 7.5 Optimal Production Quantity at the Old Manufacturing Plant

The old manufacturing plant will maximize profits by producing at the point where the benefit from selling an additional unit ($10) is equal to the cost of producing that additional unit. The old plant achieves this goal at a quantity of 20,000 units. The total costs that the old plant faces are represented by the shaded region. Recall that economic profits = $Q \times (P - ATC) = 20,000 \times (\$10 - \$10) = \$0$.

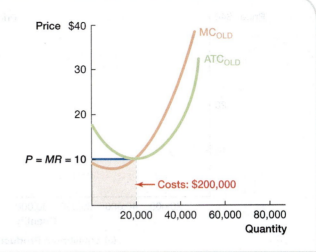

Therefore, the manager of the older plant will expand production until the marginal cost equals price (or, $MC = P = MR$), because marginal revenue equals price in a perfectly competitive market, as we learned in Chapter 6. This occurs at a quantity level of 20,000, as shown in Exhibit 7.5. The manager of the new plant will make her optimization decision similarly and have her plant produce 50,000 units, as shown in Exhibit 7.6.

The total cost of production can be computed by multiplying the average total cost times the quantity ($ATC \times Q$), as shown in the shaded region under the average total cost (ATC) curve in Exhibits 7.5 and 7.6. For the old plant, we see that this total cost is $\$10 \times 20,000 = \$200,000$. For the new plant, the total cost is $\$7.50 \times 50,000 = \$375,000$. While the old plant is earning zero economic profits (because $P = ATC$), the new plant is earning an economic profit of $50,000 \times (\$10 - \$7.50) = \$125,000$.

At the annual shareholders' meeting, both plant managers report important statistics to the new CEO, including production and cost figures. The CEO is devastated by these figures, exclaiming: "given the differences in technologies and costs, I am astounded that the older plant is producing at all!" He assumes that it must be due to the "old boys" network, further noting that "we cannot continue to keep old and inefficient plants open just because our friends work there."

As his first edict, the new CEO announces that "it is time to move to the twenty-first century; we must immediately move all production to the new plant. This new plant will produce the entire 70,000 microchips (20,000 + 50,000) itself because of its better technologies; in this way, we will demonstrate to the world how our firm is moving progressively forward to make our shareholders better off."

The plant managers try to explain to the CEO the errors in his economic reasoning—that he should be thinking on the margin—but the CEO is sure of his intuition on this one. The

## Exhibit 7.6 Optimal Production Quantity at the New Manufacturing Plant

Just as in the case of the old manufacturing plant in Exhibit 7.5, the new plant takes the market price ($10) and produces at the point where marginal cost equals the market price. Given that the new plant faces a lower marginal cost than the old plant, we would expect that at the price of $10, the new plant would have a higher level of production, and this is precisely the case, as the new plant produces 50,000 units. Note also that the new plant is earning economic profits because $P > ATC$. In this case, profits = $50,000 \times (\$10 - \$7.50) = \$125,000$.

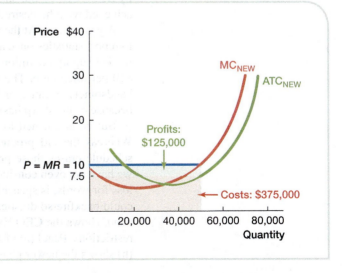

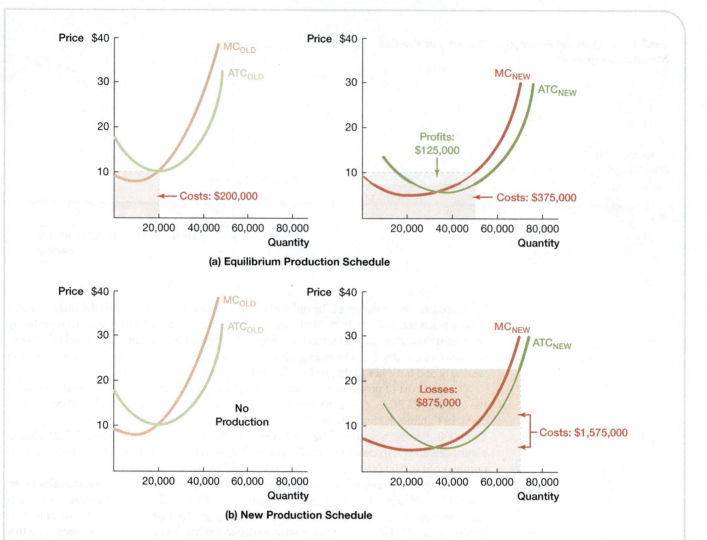

**(a) Equilibrium Production Schedule**

**(b) New Production Schedule**

**Exhibit 7.7 The Impact of Enforced Production Schedules**

The CEO is dealt a crushing defeat—by imposing conditions on the two plants according to his intuitions, he has increased costs, wiped out economic profits, and introduced economic losses of $875,000 (Profit = $Q \times (P - ATC)$) = 70,000 × ($10 − $22.50) = −$875,000).

CEO's directive is enforced and leads to the plants' annual production changes, as shown in Exhibit 7.7. At the enforced levels of production, the total cost of production is given by $ATC \times Q$, or the shaded regions under the ATC curves in the exhibit. The CEO has achieved what he desired: the new plant is now producing all 70,000 microchips.

A year passes. At the next annual shareholders' meeting, the new plant manager returns to report statistics once again to the CEO. The manager discloses that market demand and market supply conditions have yielded the same pricing environment as that of last year: $10 per microchip. The CEO views this as great news—he suspects that profits will rise handsomely because of his edict; he envisions people comparing him to Warren Buffet because of his sharp business acumen.

But he is crushed to learn that overall profits are down considerably from last year. Whereas the old production schedule brought $125,000 in economic profits, the new schedule erases those profits and replaces them with economic losses of $875,000 (and we have not even considered the fixed costs of the old plant!). The CEO, almost never at a loss for words, is speechless, only able to mutter words of amazement about how his plan could backfire so drastically. The plant manager, understanding the power of the invisible hand, shows the CEO Exhibit 7.8, which includes marginal costs and the CEO's quantity restrictions. Panel (a) of Exhibit 7.8 shows the older plant's marginal cost curve, and panel (b) shows the newer plant's marginal cost curve.

**Exhibit 7.8** Marginal Cost Curves for the Old Plant and the New Plant

Under the CEO's imposition, the old plant (pink) produces zero (panel (a)), while the new plant (red) produces 70,000 units (panel (b)). The exhibit shows that the CEO could have shifted production from the new plant to the old plant and saved money.

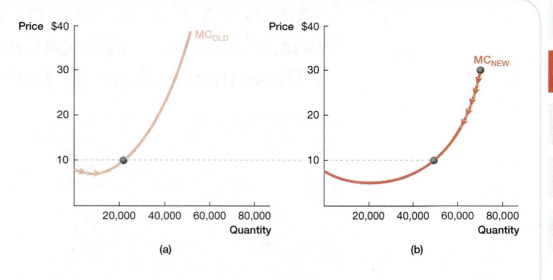

(a)

(b)

The plant manager explains that under the CEO's plan, the new plant produced the last microchip at a marginal cost of $30, as shown in panel (b) of the exhibit. This marginal cost is much greater than the $10 that it would have cost the older plant to make its first microchip, as displayed in panel (a) of the exhibit. In this way, if production of that one unit could have been shifted from the new plant to the older plant, overall costs would have been lowered by $20 = $30 − $10, enhancing overall profits by $20!

The CEO wonders just how far one can push this marginal reasoning. The plant manager shows him the arrows in Exhibit 7.8, which indicate that the same logic can be used until the marginal costs are equalized across plants, or at a point where $MC_{OLD} = MC_{NEW}$. The manager stresses that at this point, the overall production costs across the two plants will be minimized, because they cannot profitably shift production any further.

In an inspired moment, the CEO notes that these optimal production numbers are exactly the levels reached by the plants a year earlier, before the CEO intervened ($MC_{OLD} = MC_{NEW} = $ Price $= $10). He openly wonders how, in the pursuit of their own self-interest, the plant managers could organize production to minimize total costs, in turn optimizing profits for the firm. In his own roundabout way, the CEO has just stumbled across one of the most important insights described by Adam Smith in *The Wealth of Nations*, when noting that the entrepreneur "intends only his own gain," but he is "led by an invisible hand to promote an end which was no part of his intention."

The moral of the fable? Under the assumptions of a perfectly competitive market, allowing the market to operate freely not only permits each plant manager to maximize his or her own plant's profits by producing where $MR = MC$ but in so doing the plants also achieve something that neither plant manager set out to do: minimize total costs of production. This is true because $MC_{OLD} = MC_{NEW}$, which is a necessary condition to minimize total costs across the producers.

Importantly, in so doing, the plant managers also maximize the total profits of the two plants combined. In this sense, it is remarkable that market forces dictate that production across the two plants is allocated in a manner that is optimal for the social good: producing goods using the least amount of scarce resources. This is exactly what the CEO aimed to do, but failed. Yet when the competitive market is allowed to operate efficiently, we do not need a central planner (or a CEO) dictating goals for the betterment of society. Plant managers are willing to do that chore on their own, without even knowing it. So we can say that *in a competitive market, the second distinct function of the equilibrium price is that it efficiently allocates the production of goods in an industry.* Why? Because an optimizer expands production until $MC = P$; thus marginal costs are equalized across firms, because all firms face the same market price.

*Where's his hand?*

# 7.3 Extending the Reach of the Invisible Hand: Allocation of Resources Across Industries

We just learned that the invisible hand optimally allocates scarce resources and arranges production patterns in an industry. But the economy is much more complicated than two plants in a small town. How can we determine whether any specific industry is producing too much or too little? Let's turn to a new example to explore whether the invisible hand has power in allocating scarce resources *across* industries. To do so, we need to dig a level deeper into the lessons learned in Chapter 6.

As an illustration, consider a different perfectly competitive market—the delivery of paper products for publishing houses—with identical sellers making positive economic profits in the short run. This market situation is depicted in Exhibit 7.9. As you can see in the exhibit, at a price of $25 per ton, there are economic profits. But with economic profits, what happens?

Chapter 6 taught us that positive economic profits are a powerful force that attracts entrants. Other delivery companies want to enter because they, too, would like to earn economic profits. We illustrate the effect of entry in panels (a) and (b) of Exhibit 7.10. Panel (a) shows that firm entry causes the market supply curve to shift rightward (from $S_1$ to $S_2$). This shift causes the equilibrium price to decrease (from $25 to $12) and the equilibrium quantity to increase (from 500 million to 620 million).

When does entry stop? As we learned in Chapter 6, entry stops when the market price decreases all the way down to where the marginal cost curve intersects the average total cost curve. In this example, the equilibrium price is $12 per ton, as shown in panel (b) of Exhibit 7.10. This is because at any price higher than $12 per ton, other delivery firms would still like to enter because they can earn positive economic profits. Once the price reaches the minimum of the ATC curve, we are in equilibrium because $P = MC = ATC$, which means that there is zero economic profit and therefore no reason for more firms to enter.

This example shows what happens when positive economic profits exist in an industry: resources flow to that industry because of the profits available. This behavior causes resources to flow from less productive uses to more productive uses. That is, businesses seek to improve their profits, and in so doing, they move resources into the production of goods and services that society values the highest.

What happens if the equilibrium price lies below the ATC curve? Consider a related delivery business: the trucking market in the corn belt, where truckers haul corn from farmers' fields to grain mills for $10 per ton of corn. This market is currently in a situation where price is less than average total cost ($P < ATC$), as depicted in Exhibit 7.11. This means that truckers should exit because they are earning negative economic profits, or losses.

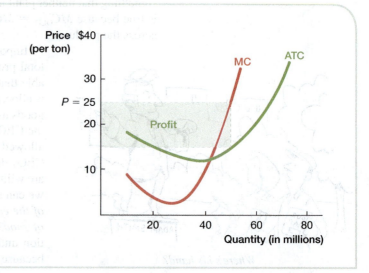

**Exhibit 7.9 Economic Profits in the Paper Delivery Business**

The paper delivery business faces a market price of $25 per ton. Average total costs are well below $25 at the chosen quantity, generating economic profits (represented by the green rectangle). With free entry into this industry, others will enter the paper delivery business.

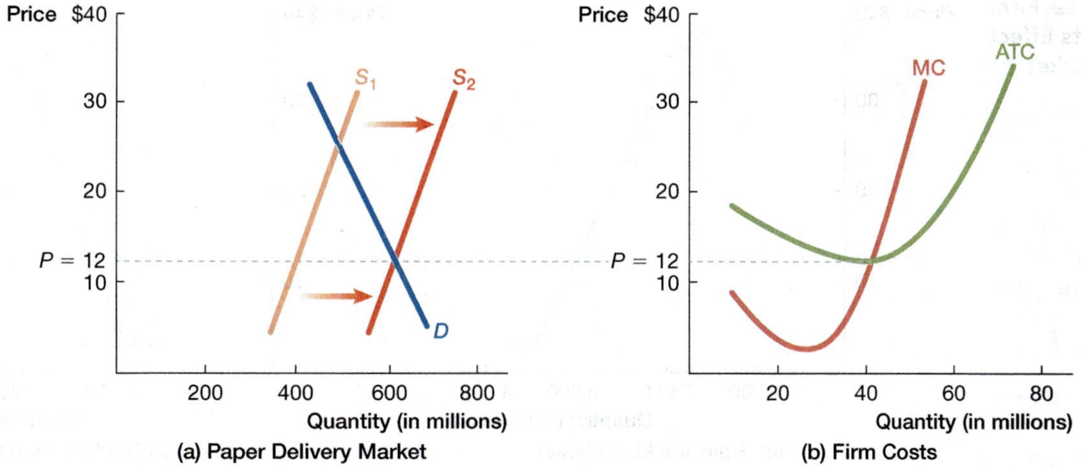

**(a) Paper Delivery Market**

**(b) Firm Costs**

**Exhibit 7.10 Firm Entry and Its Effect on the Market**

As additional firms enter the paper delivery market, the supply curve shifts rightward, reducing the market price. Entry continues as long as economic profits exist ($P > ATC$). However, as soon as the economic profits go to zero, firms will no longer have an incentive to enter the paper delivery business, and firm entry will cease.

Where will these truckers go? One possibility is that the truckers will begin to deliver paper products for publishing houses. This, of course, is not necessary, as there are thousands of other jobs for truckers, but it is one distinct possibility. We demonstrate the effect of such a shift of truckers out of the grain trucking market in panel (a) of Exhibit 7.12: the supply curve shifts leftward, increasing the equilibrium price (from $10 to $12) and decreasing the equilibrium quantity (from 3,200 to 3,000 million tons of corn transported).

When does exit from hauling corn stop? Much as in the case of entry, truckers exit until the price rises to the minimum of the ATC curve, as shown in panel (b) of Exhibit 7.12. Again, once the market price reaches the minimum of the ATC, we are at the point of equilibrium because $P = MC = ATC$, so there is no reason for further firm exit.

This simple example illustrates that the power of the invisible hand extends well beyond individuals trading in markets and managers at microchip plants. What we have just learned is that competitive markets provide strong incentives for profit-seeking entrepreneurs to shift their resources from unprofitable industries to profitable ones. This shifting of resources continues until exactly the right amount of production occurs in each industry.

**Exhibit 7.11 Economic Losses in the Trucking Market**

The trucking market faces a market price of $10 per ton of corn delivered. At this price, average total costs are higher, generating economic losses (represented by the pink rectangle). With free entry and exit, truckers will exit this industry.

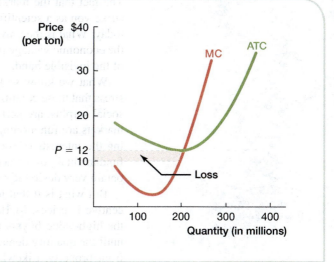

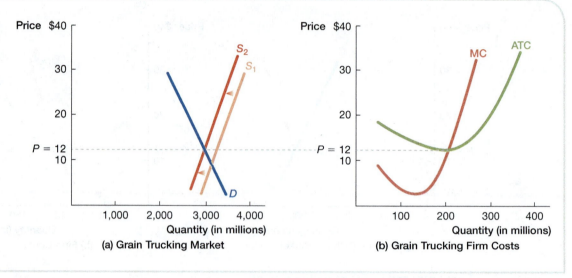

**Exhibit 7.12** Firm Exit and Its Effect on the Market

The grain trucking market currently faces economic losses, so firms will exit, reducing supply until the point where there are zero economic losses, which occurs where $P = MC = ATC$.

(a) Grain Trucking Market

(b) Grain Trucking Firm Costs

Such shifting of resources leads to a very important outcome: in a perfectly competitive market equilibrium, production occurs at the point of minimum ATC, as shown in Exhibits 7.10 and 7.12. Because resources leave those industries in which price cannot cover their costs of production and enter those industries where price can cover their costs of production, the total value of production is maximized in equilibrium. In this way, the market price is acting as an incentive for sellers to promote the greatest good for society—move scarce resources to their highest possible use—even though sellers are solely attempting to maximize their own profits.

This reasoning leads to a third distinct function of equilibrium prices in a competitive market: *they allocate scarce resources across industries in an optimal manner.* This is because the industry equilibrium is where $P = ATC = MC$, and this happens only at the minimum point of the ATC curve. Viewed through this lens, entry and exit of firms is a good sign that the market is working, not a sign that something has run afoul.

> Entry and exit of firms is a good sign that the market is working, not a sign that something has run afoul.

Indeed, if we observe no entry and no exit, we should be worried that the free market is not functioning well: the carrot of economic profit and the stick of economic losses might not be serving their allocative purposes in this case.

## 7.4 Prices Guide the Invisible Hand

The fact that the market can do the world's work without anyone being in charge might strike you as a scientific mystery as fascinating as the great challenges facing humankind today: What is the universe made of? What is the biological basis of consciousness? From the economic vantage point, you might wonder just how far open we can crack the mystery of the invisible hand.

What we know so far is that when the right conditions are in place—and we should stress that these conditions are quite strict—self-interest and social interest, as measured by social surplus, are perfectly aligned. This is what led Adam Smith to comment that when markets are functioning well, those who are promoting their self-interest are also promoting the interests of society more broadly, as if led by an "invisible hand" to do so. This fundamental point teaches us that when markets align self-interest with social interest, we obtain very desirable results.

But what is it that leads agents to act in this manner? The short answer is that the incentive is prices. Market prices act as the most important piece of information, leading the high-value buyers to buy and the low-cost sellers to sell. For example, prices adjust until the quantity demanded of oceanfront property equals the quantity supplied of oceanfront property. Likewise, prices force entrepreneurs to allocate the production of goods efficiently, whether across firms in the same industry or across industries in the global economy. The flow of labor and physical capital to sectors with the highest rewards causes the production to be at just the right level in a competitive market equilibrium.

It seems almost unrealistic to believe that prices can be the sole organizer of thousands of markets that are linked in ways that we still do not begin to understand. No one has knowledge of all the links among timber markets in Canada, corn markets in Iowa, fishing markets on Cape Cod, tea markets in China, and the tourism market in Costa Rica, but the fact that the pricing system can order behavior across such a vast array of markets, individuals, and groups highlights the power of incentives in the market system.

Nobel Laureate Vernon Smith, a pioneer in the use of laboratory experimentation in economics, had this to say about prices:

> How is it that the pricing system accomplishes the world's work without anyone being in charge . . . . Smash it in the command economy and it rises as a Phoenix with a thousand heads . . . . No law and no police force can stop it, for the police become as large a part of the problem as of the solution . . . . The pricing system . . . is a scientific mystery . . . to understand it is to understand something about how the human species got from hunter-gathering through the agricultural and industrial revolutions to a state of affluence.[2]

We can understand some of the workings of how price guides the invisible hand when considering a stark anecdotal example that one of the authors experienced when he lived in central Florida in the late 1990s. During that time, there was a flurry of hurricane warnings and activity. In each instance, such goods as sheets of plywood to board windows, bottled water, bags of ice, and generators in case of power outages were in strong demand. As you now know, such a surge in demand shifts the demand curve rightward, increasing price.

To illustrate, consider the market for bottled water. What would happen if the demand for bottled water in central Florida suddenly increased? This situation is depicted in Exhibit 7.13. At any given price level, more units are desired under the new demand curve ($D_2$) than under the old demand curve ($D_1$).

How would the invisible hand operate in this case? The increase in price would reverberate through the economy, incentivizing water distributors to make special trips to central Florida to fill the increased demand. Indeed, seeing trucks with out-of-state license plates unloading bottled water was a common occurrence during such periods. The invisible hand guided these out-of-state truckers to meet demand by trucking water to Floridian consumers, because these truckers could make more profits than they otherwise would have earned in their other activities.

Local officials understandably complained of price gouging during this time. In some cases, officials tried to force the price to remain unchanged during times of hurricanes. A government restriction on the price a firm can charge for a good or service is called a **price control**. As we discussed in Chapter 4, if price controls are binding (that is, price is held below the equilibrium price), a shortage results: quantity demanded exceeds quantity supplied, as shown in Exhibit 7.14.

A **price control** is a government restriction on the price of a good or service.

It is interesting to note that during hurricane seasons when price gouging was especially criticized and sellers were more forcefully told to keep prices low, fewer truckers with

---

**Exhibit 7.13  A Right Shift of the Demand for Bottled Water**

With a hurricane looming, demand for bottled water shifts right from $D_1$ to $D_2$. In response, sellers increase their quantity supplied until the market achieves a new equilibrium, where $D_2$ intersects $S$.

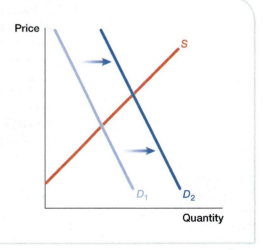

## Exhibit 7.14 Shortages: Quantity Demanded Exceeds Quantity Supplied

If we hold the price at the old equilibrium price, suppliers have no extra incentive to meet the increased demand for bottled water, creating a shortage.

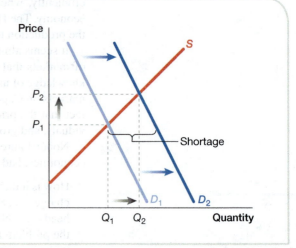

out-of-state license plates would arrive with fresh bottled water. This response makes sense within the model of the market system: if prices are not allowed to rise and reward market participants, suppliers' response will not be as swift, if at all. This is because restricting the price to its old level does not give entrepreneurs an incentive to supply their product—in this case, water. If truckers did not service the market before the hurricane under the old prices, why would they now if they were interested solely in maximizing profits? The price control that the officials enforced eliminated the price incentive, ensuring that residents would have *less* drinking water than they otherwise would have had without such price controls.

By artificially limiting quantity, the price control creates another problem: how do we allocate the bottled water that is available ($Q_1$ in Exhibit 7.14)? Free markets ration goods with prices—anyone who desires a bottle of water at the market price simply pays it and receives the water. The market is efficient, because those who are willing to pay the most receive the good. But when price controls are imposed, the market is no longer free to operate efficiently. In cases like this, people typically form long lines to purchase the water. This is not only frustrating but also inefficient: our time is valuable, and the water does not always go to those who value it the most.

### Deadweight Loss

**Deadweight loss** is the decrease in social surplus from a market distortion.

Economists call the decrease in social surplus that results from a market distortion a **deadweight loss**. The deadweight loss from a price control can be seen in Exhibit 7.15. Panel (a) of Exhibit 7.15 shows the social surplus if the market is allowed to operate freely: quantity traded is $Q_2$ at an equilibrium price of $P_2$. Consumer surplus is Triangle A and producer surplus is Triangle B. Thus, social surplus is Triangle A + Triangle B.

Panel (b) shows how restricting the price to $P_1$ affects the market. The price control prevents buyers and sellers from realizing all the gains to trade. With the price control in place, consumers pay a price of $P_1$ per bottle of water and they consume $Q_1$ bottles. Consumer surplus is now area C, and producer surplus is triangle E. By keeping the price artificially low, the government helps consumers (area C in panel (b) is larger than triangle A in panel (a)) but hurts producers (the area of triangle B in panel (a) is larger than the area of triangle E in panel (b)). Overall, there is lost surplus because of this imposition. The loss in surplus is triangle D in panel (b). This area is called the "deadweight loss" from the price control. Whether you are comfortable with this trade-off is a question for normative economics.

In sum, binding price controls have three effects: (1) they lower social surplus, because the number of trades decreases compared to the number in a free market; (2) they redistribute surplus from one side of the market to the other. In the case of a price ceiling, as shown here and discussed in Chapter 4, the surplus is transferred from producers to consumers; and (3) for the people who benefit, there is a reallocation of surplus, which occurs

> The decrease in social surplus that results from a market distortion is a deadweight loss.

### Exhibit 7.15 Deadweight Loss from Price Controls

Panel (a) shows a free market. Equilibrium price ($P_2$) and quantity ($Q_2$) lead to consumers receiving triangle A (consumer surplus) and producers receiving triangle B (producer surplus). Social surplus is maximized. In panel (b), a price control has been imposed: price is restricted to be below the equilibrium price. A deadweight loss equal to area D results. Now consumer surplus is area C and producer surplus is area E. Social surplus has decreased by the amount of the deadweight loss because of the price control.

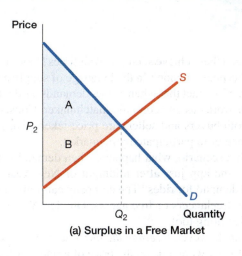

(a) Surplus in a Free Market

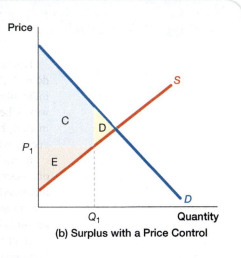

(b) Surplus with a Price Control

through non-price mechanisms. In our example of price controls, those consumers who are willing to wait the longest, are the most connected, or simply those who are the strongest, receive the good. As a result, some consumers benefit, while others are made worse off.

You will note that this situation is very similar to what occurred in the iPhone example in Section 7.1. When we restricted the quantity traded to two iPhones, we found a lower total surplus compared to the competitive market equilibrium outcome. Going back to Exhibit 7.3, we can see that the deadweight loss of restricting trade in the iPhone example was $20: the surplus of the trade between Sean and Jeff. In Chapter 10 we discuss at much greater length how taxes lead to deadweight loss.

# EVIDENCE-BASED ECONOMICS

## Q: Do companies like Uber make use of the invisible hand?

### Ubernomics at work

It's a minute past midnight on New Year's Day, and New York City streets are packed with revelers. Now that the ball has dropped, they are starting to make their way home—which, for many of them, means "Ubering." By using a car service app like Uber, people returning home don't need to track down a taxi or hop on a train—they can request a car with the touch of a finger.

Since emerging in 2010, Uber has disrupted the taxi industry in cities around the world. The transportation company's success has been attributed in part to fast response times: pull up the app, click on a few buttons, begin your ride within minutes. This advantage has been documented in several cities. In Portland, Oregon, for example, a government study found average wait times for ride-sharing services like Uber and Lyft of around 6 minutes, compared to an average wait time for taxis of 10 minutes.[3] In New York City, meanwhile, the average wait time for an Uber in September 2015 was a mere 3.4 minutes.[4] More impressively, these wait times remain consistently low even during times of high demand, like late on a Saturday night.

EVIDENCE-BASED ECONOMICS *(continued)*

7.1

7.2

7.3

7.4

7.5

How can Uber achieve such low wait times? Does the invisible hand have anything to do with this phenomenon? In the language of supply and demand, low wait times are an indication of the fact that when a rider demands a ride, Uber quickly supplies one. In this way, Uber works as an economic matchmaker. Consistent with a perfectly competitive market, both buyers and sellers are price-takers. They see a price from Uber, and they decide whether to participate in the market.

In such a scenario, what happens when demand surges—when, for example, everyone opens the app just after midnight of New Year's Eve? How can Uber meet the increased demand for rides? The company can't just dispatch more drivers—remember, drivers are freelancers or free agents. On New Year's Eve, they would probably rather be out celebrating too!

Uber can, however, *leverage the invisible hand* and control a crucial incentive: prices. Imagine if Uber were to keep the price of a ride constant following a spike in demand—this would be like a price control for bottled water after a hurricane. In this case, the quantity demanded would exceed the quantity supplied: there would be a shortage of rides.

Panel (a) in Exhibit 7.16 depicts this scenario: if price is held at $10, many people will have long waits and some will never even find a ride within a reasonable time period. By allowing the price to rise—say, to $20—Uber entices more drivers to get on the road and existing drivers to move into the area (or work longer shifts) to pick up the passengers who agree to pay. In panel (b) of Exhibit 7.16, this corresponds to a movement *along the supply curve*, to reach the new equilibrium point.

Does this simple supply and demand analysis really correspond to the real world that we live in or is it just theoretically convenient? Can the invisible hand actually be so powerful in clearing the market and matching riders to drivers? Economists Jonathan Hall, Cory Kendrick, and Chris Nosko report that it can. In their study, they explore Uber's use of surge pricing.[5] They present data from a natural experiment—an episode where, because of a technical glitch that occurred just after midnight on New Years Eve, prices were not allowed to rise during a demand spike.

What do you think happened because of this 20-minute surge price outage? Well, the "vital signs" of the market around the outage time of 1 A.M. first show the ballooning level of

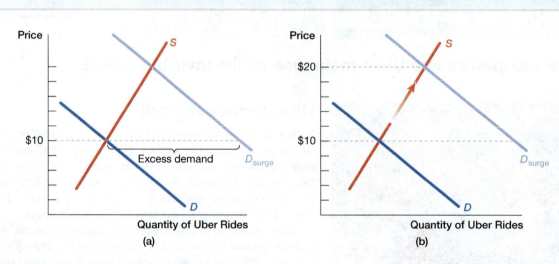

**Exhibit 7.16** **Price Increase from Demand Surge**

This exhibit shows the effects of an increase in demand for Uber rides—and how surge pricing can help move the market to equilibrium. Panel (a) shows a scenario without surge pricing: even after an increase in demand, the price remains at $10. Without a price incentive drawing more drivers to the road, many riders are left without a ride. In panel (b), meanwhile, using a surge price of $20 brings the market to equilibrium; as quantity supplied increases, we move upward along the supply curve.

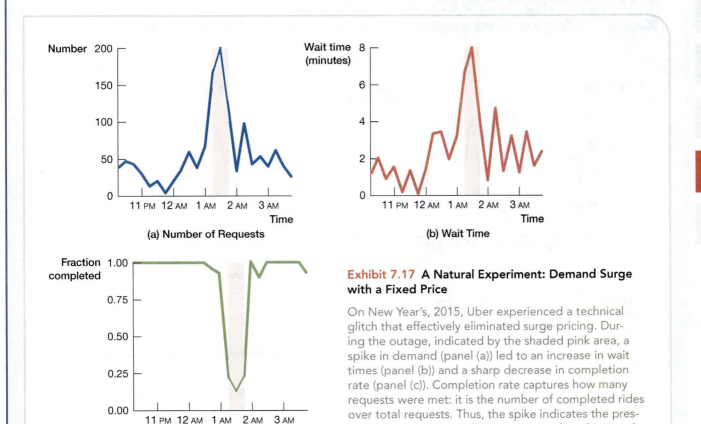

**(a) Number of Requests**

**(b) Wait Time**

**(c) Completion Rate**

**Exhibit 7.17 A Natural Experiment: Demand Surge with a Fixed Price**

On New Year's, 2015, Uber experienced a technical glitch that effectively eliminated surge pricing. During the outage, indicated by the shaded pink area, a spike in demand (panel (a)) led to an increase in wait times (panel (b)) and a sharp decrease in completion rate (panel (c)). Completion rate captures how many requests were met: it is the number of completed rides over total requests. Thus, the spike indicates the presence of excess demand, just as we predicted in panel (a) of Exhibit 7.16.

requests during the outage—panel (a) of Exhibit 7.17. Because prices were not allowed to rise due to the outage, wait times increased dramatically, as can be seen in panel (b). Importantly, because prices were not allowed to rise to clear the market, the completion rate of trips (i.e., the fraction of rides requested that were completed) plummeted. This is shown in panel (c) of Exhibit 7.17. Those people who were able to get rides at the usual price during a moment of peak demand must have been quite pleased, given the shortage of cars. Plenty of would-be riders, however, were unable to complete a trip in a timely fashion, even though they were willing to pay higher prices. Market efficiency was frustrated as prices were not able to attract drivers. This inefficiency is similar to the effects of a price control, shown in Exhibit 7.15.

If the technical outage had not happened, how would the market have operated? Consider a second example of a demand spike, but in this case prices are allowed to rise. Exhibit 7.18 depicts Uber wait times and requests directly after a sold-out Ariana Grande concert. During the shaded surge period, you can see that the number of users requesting an Uber rises only slightly (panel (a)). That is, the increase in price caused those low-value buyers to find alternate forms of transportation. You can also see that wait times go up only slightly as well, from 2 to 3.5 minutes (panel (b)). Importantly, the completion rate remains close to 100 percent throughout the entire time period—before, during, and after surge pricing, as shown in panel (c) of Exhibit 7.18.

Even though Uber price surges act as an invisible hand to clear the market, they have stirred up controversy. On New Year's 2015, users faced surge prices as high as 9.9 times the normal fare. Some users reported rides costing over $100, even $200. In Los Angeles, it is reported that one 3.86-mile ride cost $117. These dramatic price hikes might remind you of the "price gouging" discussed in the context of water bottles during a hurricane. Indeed, after accusations of price gouging from users and the New York State attorney general, Uber agreed to cap surge prices during emergencies across the United States.

# EVIDENCE-BASED ECONOMICS

*(continued)*

7.1
7.2
7.3
7.4
7.5

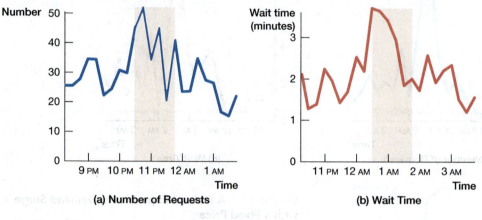

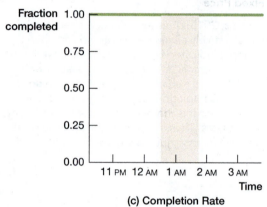

**Exhibit 7.18** Demand Surge with Flexible Pricing

This exhibit shows Uber requests (panel (a)), wait times (panel (b)), and completion rates (panel (c)) directly after an Ariana Grande concert on March 21, 2015. During the shaded surge period, both requests and wait times increase only slightly, while completion rate remains near 100 percent. As in panel (b) of Exhibit 7.16, then, the increase in price helps equilibrate supply and demand, allowing for almost every request to be completed.

While those consumers who actually secure a timely ride like this price cap, it may also prevent the market from operating properly—as with the price control on bottled water, this policy may lead to transportation shortages when people need rides most. Ultimately, picking the right policy is a problem for normative economics. Can you think of a policy that would keep supply adequately high without dramatically increasing the price for individual riders?

|  |  |  |  |
| --- | --- | --- | --- |
| **Question** | **Answer** | **Data** | **Caveat** |
| Do companies like Uber make use of the invisible hand? | Yes. | Natural experiments. | Data are drawn from two particular episodes. One shows how a technical glitch caused the market to fail to operate efficiently. The other illustrates what happened when prices were allowed to change and clear the market. Both episodes took place during times of predictable demand increases. |

### The Command Economy

To understand the difficulty of what the invisible hand accomplishes, it is instructive to consider cases where countries have attempted to place strong controls on the economy, in effect trying to do the job of the invisible hand. One example of the dramatic differences that can result is the case of Korea. After World War II in 1945, the Soviet Union and the United States agreed on the surrender and disarming of Japanese troops in Korea. The Soviet Union accepted the surrender of Japanese weaponry north of the 38th parallel, and the United States accepted the surrender south of the 38th parallel. Both countries established governments and market systems sympathetic to their own ideologies, leading to Korea's current division into two political entities: North Korea and South Korea.

Today the economic system implemented by the Soviet Union in North Korea is one of the few remaining command economies, where a centralized authority determines the goods and services produced. With the aid of the United States, South Korea established a market economy based on price signals and strong economic incentives. The market economy in South Korea remains vibrant today. This situation is, in effect, a unique natural experiment that permits an exploration of what happens to two similar areas when we impose a command economy in one and a market economy in the other.

Let's look at the two economies a little more closely. One place to start is the market value of final goods and services produced in each country in a given period of time, or what economists call the **gross domestic product** (GDP). Exhibit 7.19 shows the real per capita GDP in North Korea and South Korea from 1950 to 2008. The differences are

**Gross domestic product** (GDP) is the market value of final goods and services produced in a country in a given period of time.

---

## CHOICE & CONSEQUENCE

### FEMA and Walmart After Katrina

In the wake of Hurricane Katrina in the summer of 2005, much of the Gulf Coast had been pummeled by wind and inches upon inches of rain. Water was everywhere, but often undrinkable. Basic provisions we take for granted, like drinking water, weren't easy to come by, and the Federal Emergency Management Agency (FEMA) was caught flat-footed.

In response to catastrophic events like a hurricane or an earthquake, the caricature of private industry is that firms will gouge customers. Sometimes this is true, but in response to Katrina, there was one unlikely hero: Walmart. In fact, the Mayor of Kenner, a suburb of New Orleans, had this to say about Walmart's response: "the only lifeline in Kenner was the Walmart stores. We didn't have looting on a mass scale because Walmart showed up with food and water so our people could survive."

Indeed, in the three weeks after Katrina, Walmart shipped almost 2,500 truckloads of supplies to storm-damaged areas. These truckloads reached affected areas before FEMA, whose troubles responding to the storm were so great that it shipped 30,000 pounds of ice to Maine instead of Mississippi. These stories and more are described in an article by Steven Horwitz that summarizes the divergent responses to Katrina by private industry and FEMA.[6]

How was Walmart able to be so effective in its response? Well, it maintains a hurricane response center of its own that rivals FEMA's, and prior to the storm's landfall, it anticipated a need for generators, water, and food, so it effectively diverted supplies to the area. Walmart's emergency response center was in full swing as the storm approached, with fifty employees managing the response from headquarters.

This sounds like FEMA's job, though—why did Walmart respond so heroically? Simple economics. Walmart understood that there would be an important shift of the demand curve for water, generators, and ice in response to the storm, and the textbook response to such shifts is an increase in quantity supplied. Lucky for us, few are better at shipping provisions around the country than Walmart.

Walmart enjoys one other advantage over FEMA: the company knows the market for provisions. Every day, Walmart must consider the demands of its millions of consumers and supply products that maximize its profits. In contrast, FEMA has no such incentives, so when it is suddenly tasked with responding to a devastating storm like Katrina, FEMA will be forced to intuit what people need. As in 2005, by the time they're ready to act, a private firm like Walmart will have already solved the shortage problem.

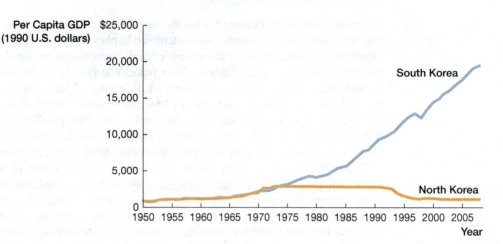

**Exhibit 7.19 Per Capita GDP of North Korea and South Korea, 1950–2008**

Starting in the mid-1970s, South Korea began pulling away from North Korea in terms of per capita GDP. Beginning around the mid-1980s, South Korea has exhibited tremendous growth, whereas North Korea has been stagnant.

*Source:* Data from Statistics on World Population, GDP and GDP Per Capita, 1–2008 AD (Horizontal file, © Angus Maddison). Available at http://www.ggdc.net/maddison/.

dramatic. For North Korea, per capita GDP grew from $850 to only $1,133 over this time period. In contrast, for South Korea, per capita GDP grew from roughly $850 to $18,356. To put these differences into perspective, consider that very poor countries such as Sudan and Nicaragua have per capita GDP of approximately $1,015, very close to North Korea's level. In fact, today the wealth of Bill Gates exceeds the annual GDP of North Korea.

Exhibit 7.20 highlights other differences between North and South Korea measured in recent years. The exhibit shows the dramatic differences in imports, exports, outputs in agricultural and manufacturing areas, and the level of services available. Interestingly, the statistics point to the fact that under a command system, North Korea has had a very difficult time developing beyond an agricultural economy.

Perhaps the most vivid image of the differences between North and South Korea is Exhibit 7.21. This amazing image was made in December of 2000 by a U.S. satellite taking shots of regions of the world at night. In a news briefing on December 23, 2002, Defense Secretary Donald Rumsfield commented, "if you look at a picture from the sky of the Korean Peninsula at night, South Korea is filled with lights and energy and vitality and a booming economy; North Korea is dark." While the most vibrant area is the capital city of South Korea, Seoul, even outside of Seoul several locations within South Korea dwarf the lighted developments of the sharpest blip in North Korea, which occurs in the capital city, Pyongyang.

**Exhibit 7.20 North Korea and South Korea Compared along a Variety of Dimensions**

Here, the picture from the previous exhibit is examined more deeply, showing the vibrancy of trade in South Korea and the reliance on agriculture in North Korea.

| Indicator | South Korea | North Korea |
| --- | --- | --- |
| 2008 GDP | $1,344 billion | $40 billion |
| 2008 GDP rank | 13th | 95th |
| 2008 exports value | $355,100 million | $2,062 million |
| 2008 imports value | $313,400 million | $3,574 million |
| Percentage of GDP—industrial | 39.5% | 43.1% |
| Percentage of GDP—services | 57.6% | 33.6% |
| Percentage of GDP—agricultural | 3% | 23.3% |

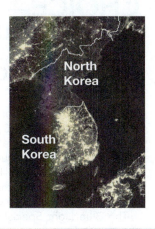

**Exhibit 7.21** The Story of Two Different Economies

The night sky paints a stark picture of the economic differences between North and South Korea.

North Korea

South Korea

## The Central Planner

Why is it difficult for command economies to operate effectively and experience significant, sustained GDP growth? Let's take an extreme case by putting yourself in the shoes of a central planner. Pretend that you are in charge of the U.S. economy with the goal of maximizing the well-being of your citizens and that you have a command economy, not a free-market economy, on your hands. What would you do? How would you coordinate the millions of individual consumers, businesses, resource suppliers, and sellers? How would you make sure that the tractor manufacturing plant in Racine, Wisconsin, had the necessary steel, rubber, glass, and other critical inputs to produce tractors? How many cars should the Chrysler plant in Belvidere, Illinois, produce? Should the last bit of copper from mines in Utah be used to produce electrical wires or pots and pans? What about the natural gas that flows from the fields of Texas; should those cubic meters be used to warm homes in Boston or in Denver? Or should they be used to power the chemical plants in Biloxi, Mississippi?

After considering these queries, you likely have begun to more fully appreciate the linkages between industries. If the silica sand mines do not produce enough silica, glass manufacturing plants will be unable to meet their production goals. This shortage of glass will result in a lower quantity of glass for such goods as lights, mirrors, countertops, LCDs, and windshields for cars. If windshields are not provided to the Chrysler plant in Belvidere, Illinois, in a timely manner, workers will experience significant down time, and Chrysler will not reach its production goals. The chain reaction will continue to propagate through the economy: as fewer cars move off the line and fewer cars are shipped via rail and over the road, shipping companies will not meet their shipping goals. Automobile dealerships subsequently will receive fewer cars to sell, thereby lowering the number of new cars sold and the commissions of car dealers. This lowering of income will in turn cause car dealers to take fewer vacations to sandy beaches, which sets off its own chain reaction in the tourism industry. And on and on in a great game of dominoes!

When the interests of economic agents coincide, a **coordination problem** of bringing the agents together to trade arises.

As you can see, the **coordination problem** of bringing agents together to trade is a difficult one for central planners. And after you have solved the coordination problem, you need to think about how to tackle the **incentive problem**: that is, aligning the interests of the agents. In market economies, prices—not central planners—incentivize producers, and the bottom line of profits is what determines success for entrepreneurs.

When the optimizing actions of two economic agents are not aligned, these agents face an **incentive problem**.

But in planned economies, rewards are based on meeting quantity targets. Consider the plant manager who is dispatched to produce wood boards for backyard decks. If he is told the target is based on weight, he produces only very long, wide, bulky boards, because he wants to maximize weight and is unresponsive to shipping costs or consumer desires. If he is told the target is based on quantity, he produces only very short, narrow, and thin boards. He doesn't much care if they fall apart when a consumer stands on them while barbequing, because the manager is not rewarded for quality. Stories such as these abound from planned economies.

Difficulties like these suggest that the reason for the fall of most planned systems (Cuba and North Korea represent the last bastions of command economies) is that the central planner does not fully understand consumer wants and needs and the production capabilities

## CHOICE
## &CONSEQUENCE

### Command and Control at Kmart

"Attention, Kmart Shoppers! Attention, Kmart Shoppers! Handbag sale on aisle 3, 50 percent off; handbag sale on aisle 3, 50 percent off. Get there fast before they are all gone."

If you have ever frequented Kmart, you surely have heard an announcement like this. You likely remember the flashing blue light, and the accompanying flock of shoppers rushing to the celebrated aisle to fight over the swag.

The Blue Light Special began in 1965 in a local Indiana Kmart. The clever store manager made good use of a police car light to draw attention to items that were languishing in the store. Sam Walton, founder of Walmart, has lauded the idea as one of the greatest sales promotion ideas ever.

What few people know is that behind this brilliance is a command system that surely limits its profitability. In the early days of the Blue Light Specials, Kmarts were allowed to choose goods to be discounted, taking advantage of local knowledge and weather-related conditions.

Nowadays, rather than permitting each store to choose the goods to be discounted, all goods sold on Blue Light Specials are dictated from the corporate office in Hoffman Estates, Illinois, months in advance. Moreover, every day exactly the same goods are sold on Blue Light Specials, regardless of whether the store is located in Laramie, Wyoming, or Washington, D.C.

Much as the central planner loses the benefits of observing unfettered market prices when she directs production decisions, Kmart has lost the ability over the years

to take advantage of the decentralized knowledge of its store managers.

Clearly, when a December winter storm hits Laramie, the local Kmart should not be bound to decisions made thousands of miles away the previous July. Local market conditions dictate a different mix of products to be offered.

Likewise, when a torrid summer dry spell hits Washington, D.C., and a rainy spell hits Seattle, Washington, why should the Blue Light Specials at D.C. Kmarts be exactly the same as those at Kmarts in Seattle?

It is important to remember that the beauty of the invisible hand does not merely lie in the operation of traditional markets that we frequent. It manifests itself everywhere—within friendships, families, communities, firms, and countries. In the case of Kmart, it would be better if the decision maker were not a central planner but the invisible hand itself, which is an allocation device difficult to replicate.[8]

of every sector of the economy, and it is difficult to incentivize workers if prices are not utilized. Because any individual knows only a small fraction of all that is known collectively, it is impossible to replicate the work of the invisible hand. This truth is captured in Nobel Laureate Friedrich Hayek's words:

> The marvel is that in a case like that of a scarcity of one raw material, without an order being issued, without more than perhaps a handful of people knowing the cause, tens of thousands of people whose identity could not be ascertained by months of investigation are made to use the material or its products more sparingly; that is, they move in the right direction.[7]

## 7.5 Equity and Efficiency

A market economy has features that are remarkable at providing price signals that guide resources in a way that maximizes social surplus and makes the economy efficient. Market forces act to eliminate waste—guiding resources to their correct destinations—and provide incentives for all market participants to promote their own interests, which in turn promote the broader interests of society. In this way, maximizing efficiency directs us toward making the societal pie as large as possible.

But it is important to recognize that the standard of maximizing social surplus is just one way to measure the progress of an economy. Another consideration is how the pie is allocated. For example, many citizens might believe that every person should have proper

**Equity** is concerned with the distribution of resources across society.

access to food, housing, and basic healthcare. Pushing this notion even further, a social planner might also be concerned with *equity*. **Equity** is concerned with how the pie is allocated to the various economic agents. To some, equity means an even distribution of goods across society. Several important questions arise concerning equity and efficiency.

Should we help the homeless man on the corner, or assist an unemployed worker? What about starving children in Africa? They have virtually no income, implying that they are excluded from almost every market, because their willingness to pay is not high enough to buy many goods. In fact, they cannot afford even the most basic necessities at the market price. Just because the competitive market equilibrium maximizes social surplus, and is efficient, does not mean that the resulting distribution is morally satisfactory.

Several important questions arise concerning equity and efficiency. These are questions in the domain of normative economics, and they are often debated by policymakers and economists. In a perfectly competitive equilibrium, we know that Pareto efficiency holds. This means that it is not possible to make a starving African child better off without making someone else worse off. Thus, it is possible that in order to increase the well-being of a starving child, it will be necessary to take a few hundred dollars from other people.

Of course, such redistribution of wealth is important to modern societies, and we'll see in later chapters that governments and private charities intervene in the functions of the market for this very reason. We will find that this kind of intervention presents an important trade-off between efficiency and equity, and that as a society we continually have choices over efficiency and equity. This is one major purpose of taxation. We will learn in later chapters that a host of interesting questions arise when we consider taxation and government's role in the economy.

If you stopped reading this book at this point, you would be a rabid free-market proponent. This is because the beauty of the economic

"Now that we've hired you we would like to restructure the position."

---

# EVIDENCE-BASED ECONOMICS

## Q: Can markets composed of only self-interested people maximize the overall well-being of society?

The discussion in this chapter may have piqued your interest about the workings of the invisible hand. But, it may have left you longing for more concrete demonstrations of whether the theory is actually descriptive of reality. In particular, you may be thinking that although we conceptually showed various features of the competitive market equilibrium, we never presented any empirical evidence suggesting that any of it is actually true in practice—or at least approximately true.

To do so is difficult, however, because much like the central planner in planned economies, we do not observe market demand and market supply curves, so we cannot test whether prices and quantities are tending toward their equilibrium values. How could we ever go beyond the conceptual arguments of this chapter and show some real empirical evidence that the invisible hand does, in fact, operate as economists believe?

To show how economists have tackled this thorny question, let's narrow it down and put you in the shoes of a trader on the New York Stock Exchange via a small experiment. Say you walk into your economics classroom and find on the desk in front of you a note card that tells you two things: whether you are a buyer or a seller, and your reservation value. That is, for buyers, the value on the card represents the highest price that they will pay (reservation value), and for sellers, the value on the card represents the lowest price that they will accept (again a reservation value, but from the opposite point of view). So, for example, referring back to the scenario at the beginning of this chapter, we would see that Madeline's card would specify "$70: Buyer" and Adam's card would specify "$50: Seller."

You are then informed that if you are a buyer, you can buy one unit per period, and if you are a seller, you can sell one unit per period. There will be five periods in the experiment. Your earnings will be determined as follows: for both buyers and sellers, the difference between the trade price and the reservation price will determine market earnings. Thus, for instance, if you are a buyer with a reservation value of $25 and you manage to buy a unit at $20, your market earnings are $5. You might recall that we call this *consumer surplus*. Likewise, if you are a seller with a reservation value of $5 and you manage to sell a unit at $20, then you've earned $15 of producer surplus. After completion of each trade, the exchange price is announced, so that all buyers and sellers are made aware of the most recent transaction.

Each market period lasts 10 minutes. During the market period, buyers should raise their hand to make public offers, which the monitor for the experiment will write on the board. Sellers should do the same. The prices that the buyers submit are called *bid prices* in Wall Street lingo, and the prices that sellers submit are called *ask prices*. The basic idea is that buyers want to buy from the sellers with the lowest ask prices, and sellers want to sell to the buyers with the highest bid prices. Once a sale has been cleared, the bids and asks are removed, and a new set of bids and asks can be submitted. This simple arrangement has similarities to how trading actually works on the New York Stock Exchange—bids and asks are yelled out and if they match, a trade is executed.

We are now ready to begin the experiment.

The bell rings to start Trading Period 1, and very quickly bid prices and ask prices come in. A buyer to your right yells out "bid $10!" The experimenter writes down this bid on a whiteboard. Other buyers behind you follow suit, raising the $10 bid successfully. At the same time, sellers submit their asks, each narrowly beating the last so they can have the business of the highest buyer. You yell out "buy $20!" and a seller takes your offer. Having a reservation price of $25, you feel good, because you just netted $5 in Trading Period 1. You can now rest on your laurels until Trading Period 2 begins.

## Double Oral Auction

A **double oral auction** is a market where sellers orally state asks and buyers orally state offers.

This type of experiment has come to be known as a *double oral auction* and was first experimentally studied by Vernon Smith. In a **double oral auction**, both bids and asks are orally stated, just as we have done in this experiment. In his study of such auctions, Smith found reassuring results. He tested many different market variants, varying the elasticity of supply and demand and the numbers of buyers and sellers. In spite of all of these changes, the markets still approached equilibrium price and quantity with great accuracy.

Exhibit 7.22 shows one example. Panel (a) of the exhibit shows the supply and demand curves for participants in Smith's double oral auction experiments with quantity on the *x*-axis and price on the *y*-axis. The supply and demand curves are just the summation of each buyer's or seller's reservation values, which have been given to them at the beginning of the experiment—just like in the example in Exhibit 7.2. Panel (b) of Exhibit 7.22 shows the price of each completed transaction in each period plotted in the order in which the transactions occurred. That is, the *x*-axis is the transaction number, and the *y*-axis is the price paid, with the horizontal dotted line representing the equilibrium price predicted by the supply and demand curves in panel (a). Initially, the market price is below the market equilibrium, but by the third trading period, the price is very close to the equilibrium prediction.

From the perspective of markets like the New York Stock Exchange, Smith's double oral auction results are a triumph for the incredible workings of the invisible hand. Smith's results show the power of our theory, in that the equilibrium price is very close to where the supply and demand curves intersect. Digging deeper into these and related data, we find that the high-value buyers buy, the low-cost sellers sell, and no one else executes a trade.

You might be thinking that yes, this is a swift example, but it's a far cry from the markets that you typically frequent. That is, how often do you encounter markets that

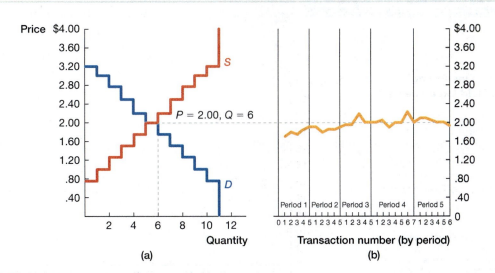

**Exhibit 7.22  One Example from Smith's (1962) Experiments**

Panel (a) shows the supply and demand curves that describe the double-oral-auction market. The intersection of the supply and demand curves identifies the equilibrium price and quantity. Although these equilibrium values are theoretical predictions, they are borne out in the real-life activities of Smith's buyers and sellers, as the equilibrium price approaches the predicted value in panel (b).

*Source:* Based on Vernon L. Smith, "An Experimental Study of Competitive Market Behavior," *Journal of Political Economy* 70(2): 1962, 111–135.

resemble the conditions of a double oral auction? Unless you have worked as a trader on Wall Street, your answer is probably "never." If you consider the sorts of markets in which you have participated, you are probably much more likely to have frequented the local grocery store where prices are on price tags, or even a market where you can haggle with sellers, such as a used-car lot or an open-air market.

### Bilateral Negotiations

If we allowed buyers and sellers to mingle with one another and negotiate privately to buy and sell goods, would the results be as promising as what Smith found in his double oral auctions? This is exactly the question that one of the authors (List) addressed when he completed several field experiments across many different types of open-air markets: from sports card conventions where experts traded sports cards, to Disney World where kids and adults traded pins. Like Smith, List gave buyers and sellers reservation values and recorded prices publicly after transactions. Unlike Smith, List had actual buyers and sellers engaging in **bilateral negotiations**—in which a single buyer and a single seller confront each other with bids and asks—rather than yelling out the offers to the group.

A **bilateral negotiation** is a market mechanism in which a single seller and a single buyer privately negotiate with bids and asks.

Across a myriad of settings—using a range of different trader types, market demand and market supply curves, and different numbers of buyers and sellers—List found a strong tendency for prices to approach the competitive equilibrium. The result even held for young children! One example from List's study is given in Exhibit 7.23. The exhibit shows the price of each transaction on the y-axis, and each transaction is represented sequentially on the x-axis. These data indicate that the market converges to the intersection of supply and demand (which is represented here as a price between the two dotted lines, one at $13 and one at $14).

An implication of this research is that even in decentralized real-world markets, prices and quantities converge to where demand meets supply. In fact, even with a small number of buyers and sellers—as few as six of each—List found that price and quantity converged to the intersection of demand and supply. In this way,

> The invisible hand is much stronger than many first assumed.

## EVIDENCE-BASED ECONOMICS *(continued)*

**Exhibit 7.23 One Example from List's Field Experiments**

Although the participants in List's experiment did not have the benefit of a central auctioneer to help announce bids and asks, List found that the prices of the negotiated trades approached the theoretical equilibrium price.

*Source:* From John A. List, "Testing Neoclassical Competitive Theory in Multilateral Decentralized Markets," *Journal of Political Economy,* 112, no. 5 (2004): 1131–56. University of Chicago Press.

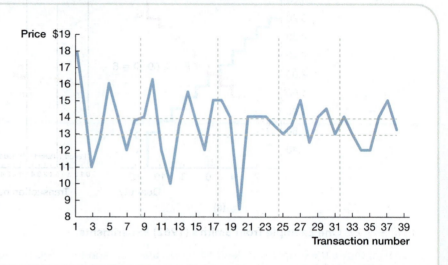

the invisible hand is much stronger than many first assumed, as these markets often come close to full efficiency: social surplus is nearly maximized in many of the markets. And the question that we posed at the beginning of this chapter—can markets composed of only self-interested people maximize the overall well-being of society?—is answered in the affirmative.

| **Question** | **Answer** | **Data** | **Caveat** |
|---|---|---|---|
| Can markets composed of only self-interested people maximize the overall well-being of society? | Yes. | Lab and field experiments. | Experiments explore whether the high-value buyers buy, whether the low-cost sellers sell, and whether the correct number of trades occurs. Data are not gathered across firms in an industry or across industries. Therefore, we show only the first of the three basic results of a perfectly competitive equilibrium. |

system is unparalleled. Yet, there are important instances that frustrate the workings of the invisible hand. For example, when a firm produces, it might pollute the air or water, causing harm to people. Likewise, if a firm is not a price-taker, but has the power to set prices, the firm might be able to cause a reallocation of resources toward itself, and social surplus might not be maximized.

We explore how these and other realistic situations frustrate the invisible hand's workings in the coming chapters. Such examples lead us to consider the appropriate mix between free markets and government intervention. We will learn that all successful modern economies have a mix of government and free markets.

## Summary

■ When the strong assumptions of a perfectly competitive market are in place, markets align the interests of self-interested agents and society as a whole. In this way, the market harmonizes individuals and society so that in their pursuit of individual gain, self-interested people promote the well-being of society as a whole.

■ The remarkable tendency of individual self-interest to promote the well-being of society as a whole is orchestrated by the invisible hand.

■ The invisible hand efficiently allocates goods and services to buyers and sellers, leads to efficient production within an industry, and allocates resources efficiently across industries.

■ The invisible hand is guided by prices. Prices incentivize buyers and sellers, who in turn maximize social surplus—the sum of consumer surplus and producer surplus—by simply looking out for themselves.

■ We can measure the progress of an economy by measuring social surplus—how big the societal pie is. But we can also measure progress by considering questions of equity—how the pie is distributed among agents.

## Key Terms

reservation value *p. 145*
social surplus *p. 146*
Pareto efficient *p. 148*
price control *p. 155*

deadweight loss *p. 156*
gross domestic product *p. 161*
coordination problem *p. 163*
incentive problem *p. 163*

equity *p. 165*
double oral auction *p. 166*
bilateral negotiation *p. 167*

## Questions

*All questions are available in MyEconLab for practice and instructor assignment.*

1. All else being equal, does an elastic or inelastic demand curve result in higher social surplus? How does elasticity of supply affect social surplus?

2. How do economic profits and losses allocate resources in an economy?

3. How will the invisible hand move corn prices in response to:

   a. a flood that destroys a great deal of the corn crop?

   b. a rise in the price of wheat (a substitute for corn)?

   c. a change in consumer tastes away from corn dogs toward hot dogs?

   d. an increase in the number of demanders in the corn market?

4. Hardware stores charge higher prices for snow shovels after a big snow storm. What role do prices play in the snow shovel market? Should the government step in and keep the prices low? Show your reasoning with a supply and demand exhibit. Be sure to discuss deadweight loss.

5. The market for economics textbooks is in equilibrium. The government decides to relax export restrictions on paper, leading to an increase in the demand for paper. How does social surplus in the market for textbooks change? Why? Present a diagram as part of your explanation.

6. What could explain why South Korea's GDP per capita increased so much faster since the 1970s than North Korea's GDP per capita?

7. In a command economy, a planning agency sets prices for various inputs and final goods. In a market economy, supply and demand determine the prices of various goods. In both cases, there is a set of prices operating in the economy. Then why are market economies considered more efficient than planned economies?

8. If your professor decided to give all students the highest grade in the class, would that affect your classmates' incentives to study?

9. Sofia, a political science student, thinks that the government should intervene to revive declining industries like video stores and print newspapers. The government, she reasons, can resolve the coordination problem of getting the agents in these markets to trade. Do you agree with her? Explain your answer.

10. Are all efficient outcomes also equitable? Explain.

11. Are there real-world markets that resemble double oral auctions? Suppose you had to organize a double oral auction for a good that has perfectly elastic demand. Do you expect prices to approach the competitive equilibrium?

**12.** Imagine you are a buyer in a double oral auction with a reservation value of $10, and there is a seller asking for $8.

    **a.** How much will you gain from accepting this offer?

**b.** If you are the only buyer, and you know that the lowest ask price is $2, should you accept this offer?

# Problems

*All problems are available in MyEconLab for practice and instructor assignment.*

**1.** The following diagram shows the market demand and market supply for sweaters. Calculate consumer surplus, producer surplus, and social surplus in this market.

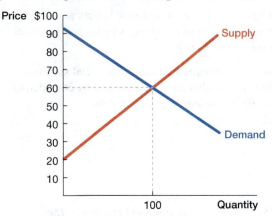

**2.** Consider the supply and demand curves shown in Section 7.1 (graphed in Exhibit 7.2). Suppose the price is limited to $55 at minimum (a "price floor").

    **a.** At the price of $55, which people buy? What is the consumer surplus?

    **b.** At the price of $55, two iPhones will be purchased, but there are five willing sellers. What is the highest possible producer surplus? What is the lowest possible producer surplus?

**3.** There are four consumers willing to pay the following amounts for an electric car:

| Consumer 1: | Consumer 2: | Consumer 3: | Consumer 4: |
|---|---|---|---|
| $70,000 | $20,000 | $80,000 | $40,000 |

There are four firms that can produce electric cars. Each can produce one car at the following costs:

| Firm A: | Firm B: | Firm C: | Firm D: |
|---|---|---|---|
| $30,000 | $60,000 | $40,000 | $20,000 |

Each firm can produce at most one car. Suppose we want to maximize the difference between consumers' willingness to pay for electric cars and the cost of producing those cars; that is, we want to maximize social surplus.

    **a.** How many electric cars should we produce?

    **b.** Which firms should produce those cars?

    **c.** Which consumers should purchase those cars?

    **d.** Find the maximum social surplus in the electric car market.

**4.** Let us continue with the electric car example from Problem 3. Suppose the market for electric cars is competitive.

    **a.** Show that the equilibrium price in this market is $40,000.

**b.** Which firms will produce an electric car if the price is $40,000?

**c.** Which consumers will buy an electric car when the price is $40,000?

**d.** Calculate consumer surplus, producer surplus, and social surplus when the price is $40,000.

**e.** Compare your answers to those for Problem 3.

**5.** Sara and Jim are going to lunch together and rank the restaurant options in the following way. Which restaurant choices would be Pareto efficient?

| | Sara's Preferences | Jim's Preferences |
|---|---|---|
| Chipotle | 4th | 3rd |
| Naf Naf | 1st | 4th |
| Panera | 2nd | 5th |
| Potbelly | 3rd | 2nd |
| Blaze | 5th | 1st |

**6.** The market for electric drills in a certain country is characterized by a large number of buyers and sellers, and every buyer who wants a drill and can afford one has bought one. In other words, the market for drills is in equilibrium.

    **a.** Does this also mean that the market is Pareto efficient? Explain your answer.

    **b.** If some of the buyers in this market are now willing to pay more than they did earlier, would your answer change?

**7.** Compared to the market for cars, the market for vintage buttons has fewer buyers and sellers. Social surplus is likely to be higher in the market for cars than in the vintage button market. Is it then correct to assume that the outcome in the car market is Pareto efficient while in the vintage button market it is not? Explain.

**8.** The following tables show a small firm's long-run average cost of manufacturing a good at two different plants:

| Plant 1 | | | |
|---|---|---|---|
| Quantity | Total Cost | Average Cost | Marginal Cost |
| 1 | $50 | | |
| 2 | $106 | | |
| 3 | $164 | | |
| 4 | $224 | | |
| 5 | $287 | | |
| 6 | $355 | | |
| 7 | $430 | | |
| 8 | $520 | | |
| 9 | $618 | | |

| Plant 2 | | | |
|---|---|---|---|
| Quantity | Total Cost | Average Cost | Marginal Cost |
| 1 | $20 | | |
| 2 | $52 | | |
| 3 | $90 | | |
| 4 | $130 | | |
| 5 | $175 | | |
| 6 | $227 | | |
| 7 | $285 | | |
| 8 | $345 | | |
| 9 | $407 | | |

a. Complete the third and fourth columns of each table.

b. Suppose the price of the good is $60. How much should the firm produce in each plant in order to maximize the firm's profit? Find the firm's profit.

c. A new manager is assigned to the production department. He thinks that the firm can profitably move all production to Plant 2 since the average cost of production is lower in Plant 2 than in Plant 1. If the firm uses only Plant 2, how much should it produce to maximize profits? Find the firm's profit. Assume zero fixed cost.

9. You run a small classroom market experiment with only three buyers and three sellers. The willingness to pay (reservation value) for buyer A is $7; for buyer B it is $5; and for buyer C it is $3. The willingness to accept (reservation value) for seller X is $2; for seller Y it is $4; and for seller Z it is $6.

a. Sketch the supply and demand curves in this market.

b. What is the equilibrium quantity?

c. What is the social surplus given this outcome?

d. What if in your experiment, seller X and buyer C agree to a price of $2.50, seller Y and buyer B agree to a price of $4.50, and seller Z and buyer A agree to a price of $6.50. All participants have managed to find a trade that benefits them individually, and yet this is not an efficient outcome. In terms of social surplus, why not?

10. Suppose a market for cheap sunglasses is in a long-run competitive equilibrium and that the price is $10. Every producer of sunglasses sells 5,000 pairs. A cloudy summer decreases the demand for sunglasses, which causes the market price to change. As a consequence, in the short run, will each firm sell more sunglasses, fewer sunglasses, or the same number of sunglasses? Also, describe what will happen in the long run.

11. The equilibrium rent in a town is $500 per month, and the equilibrium number of apartments is 100. The city now passes a rent control law that sets the maximum rent at $400. The diagram that follows summarizes the supply and demand for apartments in this city.

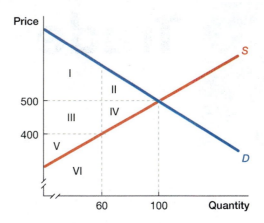

a. Use the figure to complete the following table.

| Surplus | Before Rent Control | After Rent Control | Change |
|---|---|---|---|
| Consumer surplus | | | |
| Producer surplus | | | |
| Social surplus | | | |

b. Use your answers to part (a) of this problem to answer the following questions.

i. Did consumer surplus definitely rise, definitely remain constant, or definitely fall, or is the direction of the change in consumer surplus unclear?

ii. Did producer surplus definitely rise, definitely remain constant, or definitely fall, or is the direction of the change in producer surplus unclear?

iii. Did social surplus definitely rise, definitely remain constant, or definitely fall, or is the direction of the change in social surplus unclear?

12. According to reports in the Chinese media, commuters in Beijing are facing a somewhat paradoxical situation: they find it difficult to get a cab while hundreds of cabs lie idle during rush hour. The demand for taxis in Beijing has increased as average incomes have risen. Government-determined gasoline prices have also increased. But the government, worried about rising prices for cab rides, has left the cabs' base fare unchanged.

a. Use supply and demand curves to explain what has happened in the market for cabs in Beijing.

b. Based on your understanding of how the invisible hand works, what do you think should be done to correct this problem?

13. Ashley is willing to pay $7, Bill is willing to pay $5, and Carrie is willing to pay $1.

a. Sketch the demand curve.

b. Write out the demand schedule for each integer price up to $8 ($0, $1, $2, . . . , $8).

c. Find the consumer surplus if the price is $2.

d. What if another buyer shows up who is "willing to pay any amount" for one unit. If we take her word at face value, what does the new demand curve look like?

# 8 Trade

## Will free trade cause you to lose your job?

As protesters cover their faces for protection from the fumes of the fire and tear gas released by Seattle police, hundreds of World Trade Organization (WTO) delegates are stranded, unable to pass through the blockade of 40,000 people at the WTO Ministerial Conference of 1999. This free trade protest, sometimes called "the Battle of Seattle," was not an uncommon event, as its predecessor—the worldwide "Carnival Against Capitalism"—garnered a similar number of demonstrators.

Faced with such passionate opposition to free trade, you may be surprised to learn the major lesson of this chapter: *free trade always benefits both trading partners*. This is a key reason we observe so much interdependence in the world today. If free trade is always beneficial, what has upset these protesters? Are they being irrational? Would a brief course in economics have prevented 40,000 people from blockading the streets of Seattle?

In fact, we will see that there is nothing irrational in the protesters' stance and that they likely will not be comforted by even the best course in economics. This follows from the second lesson of the chapter: *within any trading country, some individuals may be made worse off by trade*. The losses potentially arise from reduced consumer or producer surplus, lost jobs, or lower wages. Importantly, however, we will learn that the gains from trade reaped by the winners more than compensate for the losses of the losers. The key is to develop policies so that everyone can realize the gains from trade.

## CHAPTER OUTLINE

| 8.1 | 8.2 | 8.3 | 8.4 | 8.5 | EBE |
|---|---|---|---|---|---|
| The Production Possibilities Curve | The Basis for Trade: Comparative Advantage | Trade Between States | Trade Between Countries | Arguments Against Free Trade | Will free trade cause you to lose your job? |

# KEY IDEAS

- The production possibilities curve tells us how much we can produce from existing resources and technology.

- The basis for trade is comparative advantage.

- Specialization is based on comparative, not absolute, advantage.

- There are winners and losers in trading states and countries.

- The winners from trade can more than compensate the losers.

- Important arguments against free trade exist.

## 8.1 The Production Possibilities Curve

Take a look at your tennis shoes. Where were they made? We'd guess in China, the world's largest shoe exporter. Do you own a Wii? It's manufactured in Japan, one of the major exporters of consumer electronics. What about your haircut? We suspect that you did not trim those bangs yourself. Why do so many people and countries rely on others for goods and services? What are the gains to such interdependence?

The underlying motivation for trade, whether it occurs between a barber and a butcher or between the United States and China, relies on one simple principle: *we can all be better off by trading with one another, because trade allows total production to be maximized.* To see how, we begin with an example that might hit close to home.

In an effort to make some spare cash, you take on a freelance weekend job creating Web sites and computer programs to run on each Web site. Your first job is to create 240 Web sites and produce 240 specific computer programs to run applications on each Web site. Because each Web site and computer program is unique, you must start from scratch to produce each one. You now have to figure out how to complete these tasks. Taking an economic approach, you recognize that your new job resembles, in a sense, a two-good economy (Web sites and programs), and you want to figure out how much you can accomplish—your production possibilities—in an 8-hour day.

After some experimentation, you gather enough data to create Exhibit 8.1. The exhibit shows output levels based on the number of hours spent on each of the two tasks. For instance, if you work an entire 8-hour day creating computer programs, you are able to

**Exhibit 8.1 Your Production Schedule**

The exhibit shows how the time you spend maps into the number of Web sites and computer programs you create. For example, you could spend 6 hours producing Web sites and 2 hours producing computer programs. In this case you would produce 6 Web sites and 4 computer programs.

| Hours Spent on Web Sites | Number of Web Sites Produced | Hours Spent on Computer Programs | Number of Computer Programs Produced |
|---|---|---|---|
| 8 | 8 | 0 | 0 |
| 7 | 7 | 1 | 2 |
| 6 | 6 | 2 | 4 |
| 5 | 5 | 3 | 6 |
| 4 | 4 | 4 | 8 |
| 3 | 3 | 5 | 10 |
| 2 | 2 | 6 | 12 |
| 1 | 1 | 7 | 14 |
| 0 | 0 | 8 | 16 |

### Exhibit 8.2 The Production Possibilities Curve

The PPC is a graphical representation of the production schedule. Much like the budget constraint from Chapter 5, the slope represents the number of computer programs that you forgo when you produce an additional Web site. Points on the PPC (such as point B and point D) are attainable and efficient, points inside the PPC (such as point A) are attainable and inefficient, and points outside the PPC (such as point C) are unattainable.

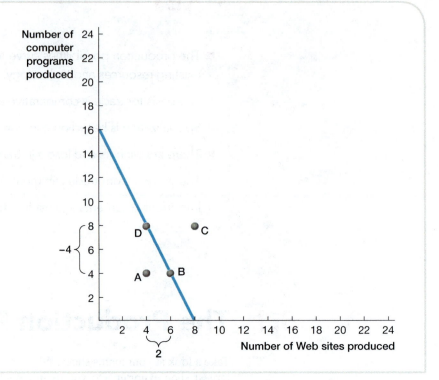

A **production possibilities curve (PPC)** shows the relationship between the maximum production of one good for a given level of production of another good.

produce 16. Alternatively, if you focus your entire work day on designing Web sites, you can create 8. Spending a little time on each task yields intermediate production levels.

A simple way to plot these data is with a **production possibilities curve (PPC)**, which shows the relationship between the maximum production of one good for a given level of production of another good. Exhibit 8.2 takes the data from Exhibit 8.1 to show your "economy's" PPC by indicating the combinations of Web sites and computer programs that you can produce in an 8-hour period. The PPC is quite similar to the budget constraint that we discussed in Chapter 5: it tells us how much we can produce from existing resources and technology.

In Exhibit 8.2, the *x*-axis represents the number of individual Web sites that you complete, and the *y*-axis represents the number of computer programs that you complete. The exhibit highlights the trade-offs that you make when deciding what to produce. If you committed all your effort to making Web sites, you could prepare 8 of them per day. Alternatively, if you spent all your time programming, you could complete 16 computer programs per day. These are the most extreme trade-offs that can be made. As such, they form the endpoints of the PPC for your economy, which is represented by the blue line.

But there are choices that you can make between these extremes. When considering a PPC, it is useful to remember the following rules:

- Points on the PPC, such as point B in Exhibit 8.2—6 Web sites produced and 4 computer programs produced—are attainable and efficient.
- Points inside the PPC, such as point A—4 Web sites produced and 4 computer programs produced—are attainable but inefficient.
- Points beyond the PPC, like point C—8 Web sites produced and 8 computer programs produced—are unattainable.

Therefore, any point on or below the PPC represents possible production levels in an 8-hour day. Production combinations on the PPC are both attainable and efficient; that is, they can be achieved, and they make full use of your resources (your time, in this case). Any combination outside the line, like point C, is unattainable. This is because in an 8-hour day you cannot produce this number of Web sites (8) and programs (8)—it is technically not feasible, given your skills and available resources.

Why do we say that any point inside the PPC is attainable but not efficient? The reason is that you could produce more with your time. Consider point A. In this case, you could, for example, use your time more efficiently and produce 2 more Web sites (moving rightward

I will always choose a lazy person to do a difficult job . . . because he will find an easy way to do it. —Bill Gates

from point A to point B), or 4 more computer programs (moving upward from point A to point D), or a combination of some number of additional Web sites and computer programs (moving up and right from point A to your PPC). People and firms are inside their PPC when they do not efficiently produce. For example, a car manufacturer, such as Chrysler, might not have the optimal mix of workers and machines, leading it to produce inside its PPC. In general, it is optimal to find a point on the PPC where production combinations are both attainable and efficient, such as points B or D of the exhibit.

## Calculating Opportunity Cost

Exhibit 8.2 shows that when you produce more Web sites, you produce fewer computer programs. This makes sense—if you are spending your time producing Web sites, then you cannot produce computer programs. This is the opportunity cost, or what you give up to produce one additional Web site. Just like the trade-off you faced in Chapter 5 on your buying spree, you can compute the opportunity cost of Web sites by using a formula:

$$\text{Opportunity cost}_{\text{Web sites}} = \frac{\text{Loss in computer programs}}{\text{Gain in Web sites}},$$

where the loss in computer programs measures the number of computer programs that must be given up for the gain in Web sites. How do we get these numbers?

We get them by taking the absolute value of the slope of the PPC in Exhibit 8.2. To find the slope, we take the "rise" between two points on the $y$-axis and divide it by the "run" on the $x$-axis. The rise is the amount by which the number of computer programs changes, and the run is the amount by which the number of Web sites changes. In Exhibit 8.2, we see that from point D to point B, the value on the $y$-axis changes from 8 to 4. On the $x$-axis, the value changes from 4 to 6. So, we have

$$\text{Opportunity cost}_{\text{Web sites}} = -\frac{4}{2} = -2.$$

The absolute value of $-2$ is 2. The opportunity cost of creating one more Web site, then, is 2 computer programs. A similar formula provides the opportunity cost of producing computer programs:

$$\text{Opportunity cost}_{\text{programs}} = \frac{\text{Loss in Web sites}}{\text{Gain in computer programs}}.$$

So we have

$$\text{Opportunity cost}_{\text{programs}} = -\frac{2}{4} = -\frac{1}{2}.$$

The absolute value is $1/2$. Thus, the opportunity cost of creating one more computer program is $1/2$ a Web site, which means that for every computer program you produce, you give up being able to produce $1/2$ of a Web site (you will notice that the opportunity costs are reciprocals; this is always the case for a linear PPC).

On making these calculations, you become rather nervous about completing the tasks of your new job while trying to maintain your grades and an active social life—you will need to spend 45 days just to finish the first task! This is because it will take you 15 full days to complete the computer programs ($240 = 16$ per day for 15 days), and an additional 30 full days to complete the Web sites ($240 = 8$ per day for 30 days).

Your friend, another economics major, calmly advises you not to worry, because she knows a student named Olivia who has taken on a similar freelance job. At first, you do not really understand how this helps you, because anyone saddled with a similarly horrific job would have no time to assist a complete stranger!

Nevertheless, you are desperate, so you approach Olivia. After a discussion, you learn that Olivia faces the same Mount Everest that you do—completing 240 computer programs and 240 Web sites while trying to maintain her grades and an active social life.

But there's an interesting wrinkle to the situation: Olivia has talents different from yours. She is relatively more proficient at Web site production. Exhibit 8.3 overlays Olivia's PPC on your PPC; you can see that Olivia's opportunity cost is different from yours. You also

**Exhibit 8.3** **Two Production Possibilities Curves**

Olivia's PPC is represented together with your PPC. While you must sacrifice 2 computer programs to produce an additional Web site, Olivia needs to sacrifice only $\frac{1}{2}$ of a computer program for an additional Web site. Can you trade to lower the number of workdays?

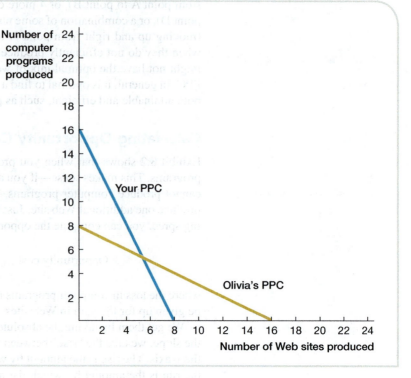

realize that Olivia is in exactly the same boat as you—like you, it will take her 45 days to complete her first job (30 days for the computer programs and 15 days for the Web sites).

How can you and Olivia minimize your work time? Should you rely on each other, or go it alone? And if you believe that joining forces is the correct path forward, how should the work be allocated between the two of you?

# 8.2 The Basis for Trade: Comparative Advantage

One place to start when answering such questions is to recognize the principle of *comparative advantage*, which revolves around the notion of figuring out what you are relatively good at doing. More formally, **comparative advantage** is the ability of an individual, firm, or country to produce a certain good at a lower opportunity cost than other producers. Do you have a comparative advantage at producing either of the goods? What about Olivia—does she have a comparative advantage? The answer to both questions is yes.

**Comparative advantage** is the ability of an individual, firm, or country to produce a certain good at a lower opportunity cost than other producers.

The key to determining who has a comparative advantage is to compare individual opportunity costs. You have a comparative advantage in producing computer programs, because you forgo only $\frac{1}{2}$ of a Web site to produce 1 computer program. Olivia forgoes 2 Web sites to produce one computer program. Because $\frac{1}{2}$ is less than 2, your opportunity cost of producing computer programs is the lower one in this two-person economy.

> The key to determining who has a comparative advantage is to compare individual opportunity costs.

Performing similar calculations, we find that Olivia has a comparative advantage in producing Web sites because she forgoes only $\frac{1}{2}$ of a computer program to produce each Web site, whereas you forgo 2 computer programs to produce each Web site. The following table summarizes the opportunity costs for Web sites and computer programs:

| Individual | Web Site Opportunity Cost | Computer Program Opportunity Cost |
|---|---|---|
| You | 2 computer programs | $\frac{1}{2}$ Web site |
| Olivia | $\frac{1}{2}$ computer program | 2 Web sites |

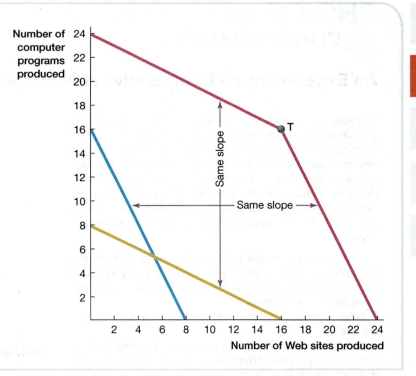

**Exhibit 8.4 The Gains from Specialization**

With complete specialization, each day you produce 16 computer programs and Olivia produces 16 Web sites (point T on the graph). The change in the output of both computer programs and Web sites to the left of point T is determined entirely by the slope of Olivia's PPC. Similarly, it is your PPC that determines the change in total production to the right of point T.

## Specialization

So what does all of this mean? It means that if you agree to trade with each other, if you *specialize* in producing what you are relatively good at, and Olivia specializes in producing what she is relatively good at, then you will both be better off. Complete specialization occurs when each individual, firm, or country produces only what it has a comparative advantage in and relies on trade for the other goods and services it needs.

The gains from trade in this case are tremendous, as revealed in Exhibit 8.4. To understand how to construct Exhibit 8.4, consider if both you and Olivia committed all of your time to producing computer programs. Twenty-four computer programs would be produced. Now if we were to take 1 hour away from computer program writing and allocate it to Web site construction, whose hour (which worker's time) would we switch to Web site production? Since the opportunity cost of Olivia producing a Web site is lower than yours ($^1/_2$ a computer program forgone versus 2 computer programs forgone), we would shift an hour from Olivia. If we wanted even more Web sites, we would continue to shift Olivia's hours until she is completely specializing in Web site production (Point T in Exhibit 8.4). If we wanted to produce even more than 16 Web sites, the trade-off/opportunity cost will now increase to 2 computer programs forgone for each additional Web site, because we begin to have you produce Web sites.

A key insight from Exhibit 8.4 is that at point T, you and Olivia can produce a daily output of 16 Web sites *and* 16 computer programs. This works because you specialize in what you are good at—writing programs—and Olivia specializes in what she is good at—creating Web sites.

So for complete specialization, you produce all 480 computer programs and Olivia produces all 480 Web sites. Of these 480 computer programs, you use 240 of them for your freelance job and give the remaining 240 to Olivia. In turn, she gives you 240 Web sites. The mere ability to trade with one another leads both of you to completely specialize, decreasing your work time from 45 days to 30 days!

## Absolute Advantage

At this point you might be thinking that the example above is "cooked." The key, you might argue, is that you and Olivia have different talents and, indeed, symmetrical ones at that: your opportunity cost is the inverse of Olivia's opportunity cost. To see that the power of comparative advantage is more general than this simple scenario, let's continue with the

# CHOICE & CONSEQUENCE

## An Experiment on Comparative Advantage

Suppose that you walk into an economics lab experiment to make a little money. When you arrive, the experimenters pair you with another student and let you know that you can produce combinations of keys and locks at the rate specified by the blue line in the chart to the right, and that your partner can do so at the rate specified by the tan line. Your task is to select a production point along your PPC. At the same time, your partner makes her choice.

After you have made your selection, your choice will be combined with that of your partner. Every key and lock *pair* entitles each partner to $10. Spare keys and locks are worth nothing.

What key/lock production combination should you choose?

A key consideration is, what do you and your partner have a comparative advantage in producing? The production possibilities and opportunity costs are summarized in the table below the chart.

In this type of experiment, many subjects either maximize the pairs that they alone can produce or simply choose the largest number they can. For example, subjects like you typically choose 8 keys, and your partner typically maximizes what he or she can produce, choosing 6 keys. In this case, you both wind up earning nothing!

Why? Though you can produce more keys than locks, you should choose to make only locks because you have a comparative advantage in producing locks. Likewise, your partner should choose to make only keys. In this way, you each can produce 6, allowing you to walk away with earnings of $60 each. Following your comparative advantage leads you and your partner to coordinate production.

Each individual should specialize in the production of the item in which they have a comparative advantage

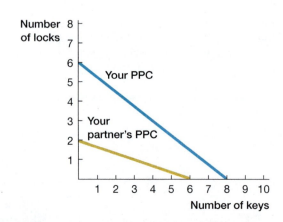

| Individual | Production Possibility | |
| --- | --- | --- |
| | Keys | Locks |
| You | 8 | 6 |
| Experiment partner | 6 | 2 |

| Individual | Opportunity Cost | |
| --- | --- | --- |
| | Opportunity Cost of Keys (locks forgone to gain a key) | Opportunity Cost of Locks (keys forgone to gain a lock) |
| You | 3/4 lock | 4/3 key |
| Experiment partner | 1/3 lock | 3 keys |

(e.g., lower opportunity cost), so your experiment partner should specialize in producing keys, producing a total of 6 keys, and you should specialize in producing locks, manufacturing a total of 6 locks.

---

example and assume that you take an intensive 1-week course on Web site production and design. The new knowledge that you gain causes your Web site productivity to triple, causing your PPC to pivot about the *y*-axis. Your new PPC is shown in Exhibit 8.5, alongside Olivia's PPC.

You can now produce 24 Web sites in 1 day, compared with 8 before the training. Therefore, if you now go it alone, you can produce a daily output of 16 computer programs or 24 Web sites. So you will need to work only 25 days—15 days on computer programs and 10 days on Web sites. This is much less than the 45 days when you were working on your own before the training, and it is even less than the 30 days you needed to work when you traded with Olivia. But does it mean that trade cannot help in this case?

No, but the gains from trade are now less obvious. You might be thinking that you are now better than Olivia at both tasks, so why do you need her help? Being better at both tasks means that you have an *absolute advantage* at producing both Web sites and computer programs. In general terms, an **absolute advantage** is the ability of an individual, firm, or country to produce more of a certain good than other competing producers, given the same amount of resources (in this case, production in an 8-hour day).

**Absolute advantage** is the ability of an individual, firm, or country to produce more of a certain good than other competing producers, given the same amount of resources.

**Exhibit 8.5** **An Illustration of Absolute Advantage**

After taking a course in Web site design, you can produce more computer programs (16 versus 8) and more Web sites (24 versus 16) than Olivia. This gives you an absolute advantage in both types of production.

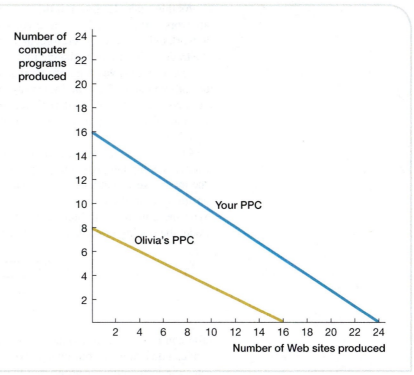

Despite your newfound superior skill, you might be surprised to learn that gains to trade still remain. This is so because even though you can produce more Web sites and computer programs in a given day than Olivia can produce, you do not have a comparative advantage in producing both goods. With linear PPCs, unless two people have exactly the same opportunity cost, one will always have a comparative advantage in producing one good and the other person in producing the other good. Why? Because one person is relatively better at one task than the other, and vice versa.

So what are the gains to specialization and trade in this case? To answer this question, we must first compute who has a comparative advantage in production of each of the goods. The following table summarizes the new opportunity costs:

| Individual | Opportunity Cost of Web Sites | Opportunity Cost of Computer Programs |
|---|---|---|
| You | $2/3$ computer program | $3/2$ Web sites |
| Olivia | $1/2$ computer program | 2 Web sites |

Even though you have taken classes in Web site production, Olivia still has a comparative advantage in producing Web sites. At $1/2$ of a computer program, her opportunity cost remains lower than your opportunity cost of producing a Web site, $2/3$ of a computer program. Likewise, you maintain your comparative advantage in producing computer programs because your opportunity cost is $3/2$ Web sites, whereas Olivia's is 2 Web sites.

Accordingly, we can follow the example above and have each of you completely specialize: you produce 480 programs, and Olivia produces 480 Web sites. And you can get the jobs done by both working 30 days.

Does this make sense? How can it be that even after receiving Web site training, you are no better off? Do you really need Olivia's help? Without her, you need to work only 25 days—15 days on computer programs and 10 days on Web sites. What should you do?

## The Price of the Trade

The terms of trade is the negotiated exchange rate of goods for goods.

The reason this example does not lead to a more advantageous outcome for you is because we held the *terms of trade* constant from the first example: 1 Web site for 1 computer program. The **terms of trade** is the negotiated exchange rate of goods for goods. The principle of comparative advantage, while powerful, does not provide an exact terms of trade, but it does provide a range in which trade will occur. In this way, it prescribes how the gains to trade are split between the two parties.

As this example shows, if the exchange rate is 1 computer program for 1 Web site, you are worse off from trade because you are working 30 days, whereas with no trade you need to work only 25 days. Therefore, at a one-for-one trading rate, you would not participate in the trade. Is there any exchange rate for which you would trade?

The answer is yes. There is a range of terms of trade that would be mutually beneficial to both you and Olivia, and this range can be found by considering opportunity cost. You both consider your own internal trade-off between Web sites and computer programs and compare that to the terms of trade. If the trade makes you better off, you do it. Otherwise you do not.

Consider each person's computer program opportunity cost. You give up $^3/_2$ Web sites for every computer program you produce. So for you to give Olivia one computer program, she must give you at least $^3/_2$ Web sites. Now put yourself in Olivia's shoes. Given her opportunity cost, the most she is willing to give up for 1 computer program is 2 Web sites. With these numbers in hand, the rule is straightforward: for both people to engage in the trade, the trading price must lie between their opportunity costs. For this example:

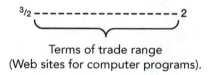

Terms of trade range
(Web sites for computer programs).

You can now see why a one-for-one trade does not work: it is outside of this range, and you can do better on your own. Likewise, if you insisted that you receive more than 2 Web sites for each computer program, Olivia would not agree to trade, because she is better off on her own.

Understanding the terms of trade reveals which of the trading partners reaps the gains of trade. Prices closer to $^3/_2$ Web sites per program favor Olivia, while prices closer to 2 Web sites per program favor you. Why? This is so because Olivia is producing Web sites, and the fewer she gives up per program, the better off she will be. Likewise, you are producing programs, and the more Web sites you receive in return for each program, the better off you will be. A price right in the middle—1.75 Web sites per program—provides you and Olivia with the same gains from trade.

This example also highlights that the gains to trade shrink as the trading partners become more alike. Before you took the intensive 1-week course on Web site production and design, trading with Olivia showed great gains, because you were each good at different tasks: you were proficient at writing computer programs and Olivia at producing Web sites. This led to a substantial gain due to trade. As you became more similar to Olivia, the gains to trade shrank.

> The gains to trade shrink as the trading partners become more alike.

## 8.3 Trade Between States

Just as you and Olivia have different talents, individual states in the United States have quite distinct advantages. Consider the undergraduate student living in Minnesota. On any given day, she wakes up to a chilled glass of orange juice, slips on her leather boots, and drives her Chrysler Jeep to class. Just in these three simple tasks, she has taken advantage of goods produced in Florida, California, and Michigan. Although you might not realize it, many of the everyday products you consume are produced in states other than where you live. Why is that the case?

Think of it this way. Alaska would have a difficult time producing pineapples just as Hawaii would provide a relatively poor environment for growing corn. If trade were not allowed to occur between states—say, by law or because transportation costs were too high (think of life for your great-great grandparents)—some people might lack even the most basic modern necessities. Cotton clothing would be an unknown in the northern states, while technologies that make our life easier, like iPads, would be everywhere in California but might not yet have arrived in the eastern part of the country. Many states would have

# CHOICE & CONSEQUENCE

## Should LeBron James Paint His Own House?

Having won four National Basketball Association MVPs and three championships in the past 6 years, LeBron James is known as the best basketball player on the planet. But his talents extend well beyond dunking a basketball. In fact, with a wingspan of over 7 feet, LeBron is proficient at many tasks.

Think about interior painting. Coupling his wingspan with his 6-foot-8-inch height, LeBron can paint entire interior walls of homes without ever using a ladder! In this way, LeBron is much more efficient than many professional painters—he has an absolute advantage in not only basketball but also painting.

With such talents, does it make sense for him to paint the interior walls of his own house when he wants a color change?

As you've learned, it does not. Everyone (including LeBron) will be better off if LeBron sticks to the task for which he has a comparative advantage—playing basketball—everyone except the opposition, that is.

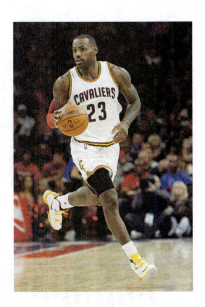

An **export** is any good that is produced domestically but sold abroad.

An **import** is any good that is produced abroad but sold domestically.

no access to salmon, while states like New York and Nebraska would be without grapefruit juice. Citizens of Wyoming might still be riding horseback, and people living in many northern states might suffer vitamin C deficiencies.

Of course, states do not exist in isolation; just as for you and Olivia, differences in comparative advantage permit trading partners to gain from trade. Producers in every state in the United States ship goods to other states, and every state has citizens who consume goods made in other states. A good that is made in California and shipped to Wisconsin is called an **export** for California and an **import** for Wisconsin. In the next section we discuss trade between countries. In this case, an export is any good that is produced domestically but sold abroad. An import is any good that is produced abroad but sold domestically. Exports and imports are a useful way to measure trading activity.

Exhibit 8.6 reveals just how important interstate trade is today. The Bureau of Transportation Statistics keeps track of all interstate commodity shipments by state of origin and state of destination. In addition, the Bureau of Transportation Statistics tracks commodity shipments from U.S. states to other countries. Exhibit 8.6 captures all this information in a way that provides an indication of how vibrant trade is between U.S. states. In the exhibit, for each state, the total value of interstate trade (state to state) is divided by the total value of international trade. This exhibit tells us just how large a role interstate trade plays in the grand scheme of U.S. global trade.

We find that this ratio is the highest in Tennessee, which means that of all the states, Tennessee trades the most with other states compared to its trade with other countries. This is partly because Tennessee sends a lot of agricultural, chemical, and transport products to other states. States such as Arkansas, Oklahoma, Rhode Island, and Wyoming also engage in substantial interstate trade compared to trading with other countries. Overall, the average ratio of interstate to international trade is 7.86 across the United States, meaning that trade between states is almost 8 times more valuable than international trade!

An interesting pattern in Exhibit 8.6 is that states with lower ratios of interstate-to-international trade are typically coastal/border states, while states with high ratios of interstate-to-international trade are typically in the interior of the United States. This tendency highlights the importance of transportation costs in determining trade patterns.

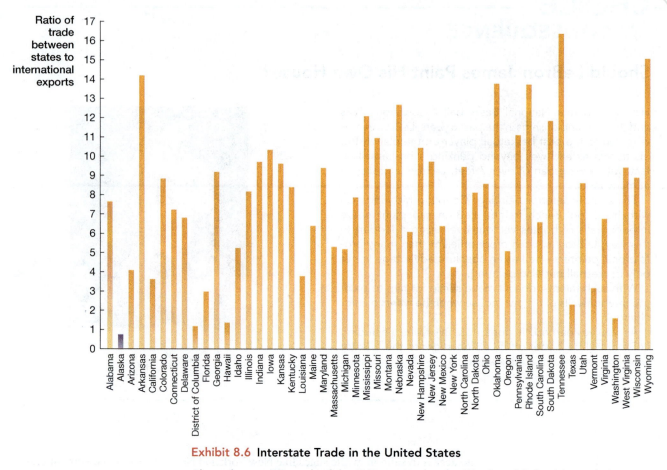

**Exhibit 8.6** Interstate Trade in the United States

Along the x-axis is each of the U.S. states plus the District of Columbia, and along the y-axis is the corresponding ratio: value of goods flowing to other states divided by the value of goods flowing to other countries. Values above 1 represent states that export more goods to other states than they export to other countries, whereas values below 1 (only Alaska in the exhibit) represent states that export fewer goods to other states than they export to other countries.

*Sources:* Based on Bureau of Trade Statistics Commodity Flow Survey 2007, U.S. Census Bureau.

## Economy-Wide PPC

Trade between you and Olivia revolved around comparative advantage and was shown in your joint PPC. Imagine adding together the production possibilities of hundreds of thousands or millions of people—you quickly get a smoothly curved line pointing away from the origin, as in Exhibit 8.7. The exhibit shows a PPC for farmers growing apples (on the y-axis) and oranges (on the x-axis). Point A corresponds to production that is attainable but inefficient. Point B is attainable and efficient. Point C is unattainable with current resources and technology.

The curvature represents the general principle of increasing opportunity cost mentioned in Chapter 1. We see increasing opportunity costs in the economy-wide PPC because moving to production extremes is difficult, as some inputs are quite well suited for producing apples, whereas other inputs are better suited for producing oranges. Thus, as you move resources increasingly into production of one good, the opportunity cost of doing so increases at an increasing rate.

What determines the location of a state's PPC? In the short run, the PPC is fixed. But in the long run, resources are not fixed, so increases in natural resources or changes in productivity due to population growth, changes in technology, and increases in worker education shift the PPC outward. Among U.S. states, the factors that contribute most

## Exhibit 8.7 A PPC with Increasing Opportunity Cost

When we encountered PPCs before, the opportunity cost of one good in terms of the other was constant—the slope of the PPC. However, with a curved PPC, we see that whereas going from producing 0 oranges to producing 1 orange reduces apple production by a small fraction, moving from 6 oranges to 7 oranges reduces apple production by more than 2, demonstrating an increase in opportunity costs.

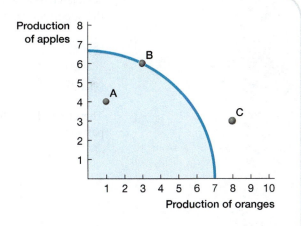

to the location of the PPC are the natural resources and the stock of human-made resources (technology) available to the state, as well as the education, work habits, and experience of the labor force, the relative abundance of labor and physical capital, and the climate.

Exhibit 8.8 shows an example of how one of these productivity catalysts—improved technology—makes producers better off and shifts the PPC outward. Suppose that a new fertilizer is invented that increases maximum orange production by 3 units and maximum apple production by 1 unit. These increases will cause the PPC shown in Exhibit 8.8 to shift from PPC A to PPC B, where farmers can produce more apples and more oranges with their current set of resources.

## Comparative Advantage and Specialization Among States

In our earlier example, we learned that the ability to trade allowed you and Olivia to specialize in production of the goods that you were best at producing. As a result, both of you were better off. Exactly the same forces that operate on the individual level to form the basis for trade also operate on the state level.

Consider another example. Suppose that the states of California and Florida are both producers and consumers of apricots and bananas but that California has a comparative advantage in producing apricots and Florida has a comparative advantage in producing bananas. What do you think should happen?

Similar to the situation between you and Olivia, California should focus its production on apricots, whereas Florida should focus on producing bananas. Such comparative

## Exhibit 8.8 How Improved Technology Shifts the PPC

With the advent of new fertilizer technology, the PPC shifts outward, representing the ability to produce more apples for every choice of orange production, and vice versa.

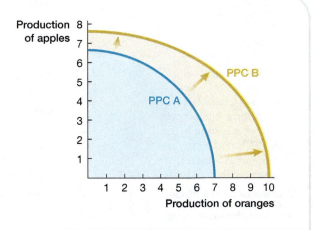

advantage represents a basis for trade. In addition, the trading price will be determined by the opportunity costs. For instance, assume that the opportunity costs are as follows:

| State | Opportunity Cost of Apricots | Opportunity Cost of Bananas |
|---|---|---|
| California | $\frac{1}{5}$ banana | 5 apricots |
| Florida | 8 bananas | $\frac{1}{8}$ apricot |

Therefore, the trading price must be within the following range to be acceptable to both parties:

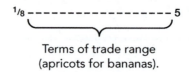

Terms of trade range
(apricots for bananas).

This is the same logic at work for the price of the trade that we saw in the previous section with you and Olivia. The terms of trade, or the exchange rate of apricots for bananas, allows both states to be better off through specialization and trade.

# 8.4 Trade Between Countries

We suspect that if you sneak into your grandparents' closet and check the tag on your grandma's 1970 dress, it will say that the dress was manufactured in the United States. Do the same for your grandpa's 1963 suit that he wore for his wedding—perhaps it was made in Chicago or Philadelphia? Conduct the same investigation in your parents' closets, and you will find a mix of goods that were much more likely produced abroad. Now take a peek at the tags on your own clothes—they were likely manufactured in another country that might not even have been manufacturing clothes in the 1960s and 1970s.

Such differences in sources for apparel are due to international trade. As Exhibit 8.9 shows, since 1960 the volume of U.S. trade has grown dramatically. In 2015 alone, the value of goods and services imported into the United States was more than $2,600,000,000,000. That is a whopping $2.6 *trillion* of imports annually! This number is over 21 times greater than the value of imports in 1960. Moreover, these increases in trade are not due purely to an increased level of production over time: in 1980, imports were only 10.3 percent of overall U.S. production, whereas now imports are more than 15 percent of overall U.S. production. The world is most definitely becoming more interdependent.

Our exports have also grown dramatically: they are now more than 20 times greater than our level of exports in 1960. Yet they lag our current level of imports, making the U.S. a

**Exhibit 8.9 U.S. Exports and Imports since 1960**

The graph shows the total value of U.S. exports and imports from 1960 to 2015 in real dollars. While the values of imports and exports are nearly identical in the earlier years, the gap between U.S. imports and exports becomes apparent in the mid-1970s and continues to expand as imports grow faster than exports.

*Source:* Based on U.S. Bureau of Economic Analysis, National Income and Product Accounts.

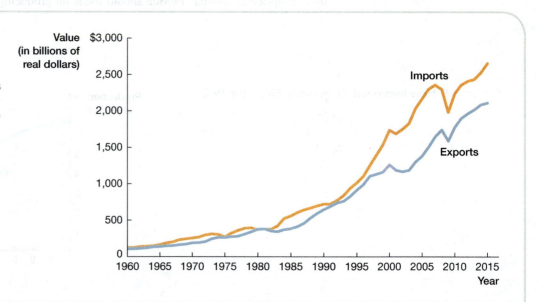

**Exhibit 8.10 U.S. Imports and Exports of Crude Oil since 1960**

Contrast the relative difference between the (real) dollar values of total U.S. imports and exports (Exhibit 8.9) and the relative difference in imports and exports of crude oil. This is just one example of the diversity in trade behavior that is missed if we consider only aggregate data.

*Source:* Based on U.S. Energy Information Administration.

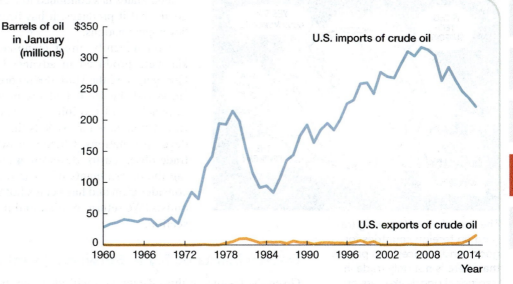

A **net importer** means that imports are worth more than exports over a given time period.

**net importer**—that is, a country for which imports are worth more than exports over a given time period. In fact, as Exhibit 8.9 shows, the United States has been a net importer since the mid-1970s. In later chapters, we return to this pattern of trade and discuss whether U.S. citizens should be concerned about the high levels of net importation in recent years.

This aggregate trading pattern, however, does not hold true for all types of goods. For example, the United States has historically exported very little crude oil, but it has imported millions of barrels of crude oil monthly. In fact, the level of imports has substantially increased since 1960, as shown in Exhibit 8.10.

So what types of goods are causing this major shift in the balance of imports and exports for the United States that we observe in Exhibit 8.9? As Exhibit 8.11 shows, manufactured goods have played an important role. The exhibit shows that although the

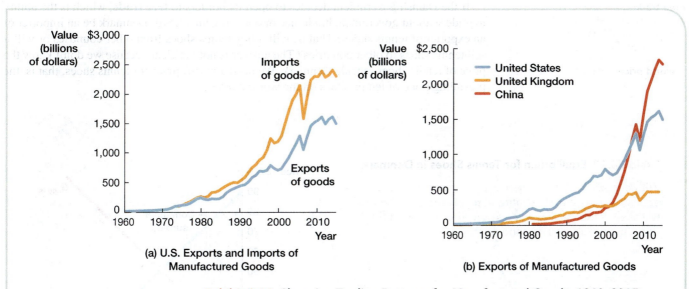

(a) U.S. Exports and Imports of Manufactured Goods

(b) Exports of Manufactured Goods

**Exhibit 8.11 Changing Trading Patterns for Manufactured Goods, 1960–2015**

This exhibit presents a deeper dive into the aggregate U.S. export and import data depicted in Exhibit 8.9 by excluding the contribution of services (consulting, medical care, etc.). Taken together, the panels suggest that a large part of the changing global trading patterns coincides with developing countries, such as China, exporting much more.

*Sources:* Based on U.S. Bureau of Economic Analysis, U.S. National Income and Product Accounts, and the International Monetary Fund.

*Note:* Disaggregated tracking of China's manufacturing exports only began in 1984 as part of a general policy of internal economic liberalization and reform.

The growth in outsourcing (relying on foreign countries for goods and services) has proven that there is not only trade in traditional goods like cars or clothing, but there is also trade in services. For example, more and more customer service hotlines are managed overseas. So when you call an airline company late at night, you might be talking to someone in the daytime in India!

United States has continued to increase the number of manufactured goods that it produces, it has been importing more and more from developing nations.

Until recently, most manufactured goods on the world market were produced in advanced economies—the United States, Germany, and the United Kingdom. Recently, however, China has surpassed the United States in manufactured exports, as shown in panel (b) of Exhibit 8.11. The value of manufactured exports from China now far exceeds that from the United States and other developed nations. China's growth is indicative of the pattern of trade observed for developing countries as a whole. Understanding the determinants of these trade patterns merits more serious consideration and has been a hot topic of recent research for economists. We return to this trend in the Evidence-Based Economics section.

## Determinants of Trade Between Countries

Given the lessons of this chapter, you will likely not be surprised to learn that comparative advantage underlies the trading patterns observed in Exhibits 8.9–8.11. To illustrate this key idea more succinctly and to reveal its economic underpinnings, let's consider the market for tennis shoes in Denmark.

To make the point most clearly, we assume that all tennis shoes are identical and that Danish buyers and sellers are price-takers. Furthermore, we assume that Denmark currently does not trade with other countries. From Denmark's perspective, therefore, the market for tennis shoes consists solely of Danish buyers and sellers.

As Exhibit 8.12 shows, under these assumptions, the domestic price is given by the intersection of the Danish demand and the Danish supply curves. In this case, the equilibrium price for a pair of tennis shoes is $50, and the equilibrium quantity of tennis shoes is 2 million pairs. As we learned in Chapter 5, consumer surplus is the triangle below the demand curve and above the market price. Likewise, as Chapter 6 showed, producer surplus is the triangle above the supply curve and below the market price.

If the Danish government decides to open its borders to **free trade**, which is the ability to trade without government hindrance or encouragement, will Denmark be an importer or an exporter of tennis shoes? That is, will it buy tennis shoes from other countries or will it sell tennis shoes to other countries? The answer is not yet clear because we don't know the price of tennis shoes outside Denmark. We need a **world price** for tennis shoes, that is, the prevailing price of tennis shoes on the world market.

**Free trade** is the ability to trade without hindrance or encouragement from the government.

A **world price** is the prevailing price of a good on the world market.

**Exhibit 8.12 Equilibrium for Tennis Shoes in Denmark**

With our assumption of a perfectly competitive market, the equilibrium price and quantity of tennis shoes in Denmark will arise in the familiar way—at the intersection of the domestic supply and demand curves.

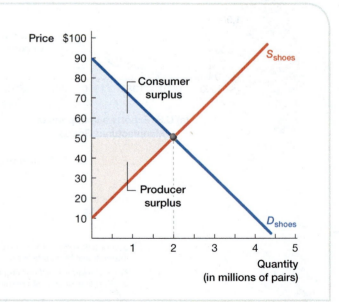

## Fair Trade Products

### What's Behind the Boom?

In response to the feeling that the growth of free trade has led to the exploitation of developing countries, a new market has opened up for the consumer concerned with a broad variety of production-related issues, including the environment, fair labor practices, and child labor in the developing world. Goods imported from the developing world that meet certain criteria are certified by third-party organizations as "fair trade" products.

To receive a fair trade label, the production of a good has to meet certain standards. For example, if the producer doesn't allow unionization, uses child or slave labor, or doesn't adhere to the U.N. Charter on Human Rights, then the product can't be classified as fair trade.

Consumers can't seem to get enough fair trade products. Sales growth for fair trade goods has reached double-digit proportions over the past decade. Surprisingly, sales continued to expand even after the 2008 recession, growing 15 percent in 2009.[1]

In spite of the recent surge in demand for fair trade products, not everyone is a fan. Overseeing billions of dollars of production isn't easy, and the capacity for certifying organizations to enforce labor standards sometimes can't keep up with the increasing demand for fair trade products.[2]

So the answer to whether Denmark will import or export comes down to a simple comparison: is the Danish domestic price for tennis shoes above or below the world price for tennis shoes?

- If Denmark's domestic price is below the world price, then it will become an exporter of tennis shoes.
- If Denmark's domestic price is above the world price, then it will become an importer of tennis shoes.

We turn to both scenarios now and explore who wins and who loses when Denmark begins to trade.

### Exporting Nations: Winners and Losers

Let's delve a little more deeply into the scenario in which Denmark's domestic price for tennis shoes is below the world price, and it becomes an exporter. We'll assume that the world price for a pair of tennis shoes is $75—well above the equilibrium domestic price of $50. Will Danish suppliers continue to supply Danes with tennis shoes for $50? The answer is no, because they can sell as many pairs of tennis shoes on the world market as they can produce for a price of $75 and make more money.

As Exhibit 8.13 shows, in this case Danish suppliers will increase their production from 2 million pairs of tennis shoes to 3.25 million pairs and receive the world price of $75 per pair. At that price, Danish consumers no longer demand as many pairs of tennis shoes: the price has gone up, so they decrease their quantity demanded by moving along their demand curve until the price of $75 is reached. This movement stops when the quantity demanded reaches 0.75 million pairs, at a price of $75 per pair.

This situation leads to an excess supply of production in Denmark. This excess supply of 2.5 million pairs of tennis shoes $(3.25 - 0.75 = 2.50)$ is subsequently sold on the

### Exhibit 8.13 Winners and Losers in an Exporting Nation

Once Denmark is open to free trade, its suppliers make their decisions based on a market price that is higher than the domestic equilibrium price of $50, increasing their quantity supplied to 3.25 million shoes. However, at this higher price, domestic quantity demanded is reduced, and the surplus shoes are sold to the world market. In this case, producers win by being able to charge a price above $50 per pair, thus capturing areas B and C in addition to A (which they already had prior to free trade). In contrast, Danish consumers see a reduction in surplus due to the higher price they must pay for tennis shoes, losing area B to producers.

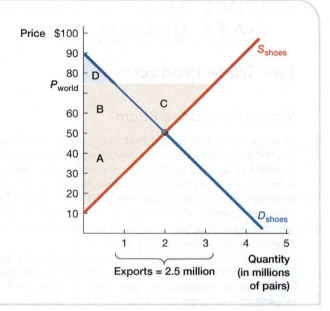

Will his shoes be sold domestically or abroad?

world market. Because Denmark is a small producer of tennis shoes, this added supply does not change the world price.

So who wins and who loses when Denmark opens its borders to trade and becomes an exporter? A comparison of producer and consumer surplus measures provides the answer. A first consideration is that Danish sellers are clearly better off. They are now selling more tennis shoes, and the price is higher for each pair. The sellers' gain can be computed from the change in producer surplus. In Exhibit 8.13, we see that before trade was allowed, Danish producer surplus was equal to area A. This is the area above the supply curve and below the market price. After permitting trade, the new producer surplus is equal to areas A + B + C. Thus, Danish sellers experience an increased producer surplus of B + C because of trade.

For Danish consumers, though, the story is much different. Without trade, they purchased 2 million pairs of shoes per year at $50 per pair, receiving a consumer surplus of areas B + D in Exhibit 8.13. After opening to trade, they purchase only 0.75 million pairs of shoes and pay $75 per pair. Now consumer surplus is only area D. Thus, Danish buyers experience a decreased consumer surplus equal to area B because the country opened to trade.

We can therefore draw two conclusions about what happens when a country opens itself to trade and becomes an exporter of goods and services:

1. Sellers win.
2. Buyers lose.

However, we also need to look at the big picture—there are gains to trade for Denmark as a whole. In Exhibit 8.13, area C represents what Danes as a whole gained from opening to trade. In principle, this area highlights that Denmark is better off because of trade and that the winners' gains are greater than the losses of the losers, opening up the possibility that the winners can compensate the losers. If the Danes were so inclined, one way for this to happen would be to tax shoe producers and transfer the revenues to shoe consumers (though the situation of winners fully compensating losers rarely happens, as we discuss below).

## Importing Nations: Winners and Losers

Now let's consider the flip side. If Denmark's domestic price is above the world price, then it will be an importer of tennis shoes. Let's assume that the world price for a pair of tennis shoes is now $25, well below the equilibrium domestic price of $50. We depict this scenario in Exhibit 8.14, which shows that in this case Danish suppliers will curb their production to

## Exhibit 8.14 Winners and Losers in an Importing Nation

Once Denmark is open to trade, its buyers will only pay the world price, which is lower than the domestic equilibrium price without trade of $50. This decreases quantity supplied to 0.75 million shoes. However, at this lower price, domestic quantity demanded is increased and the excess demand is covered by shoes from the world market. In this case, consumers are better off, because they pay a price below $50 per pair, thus capturing areas C and D in addition to B (which they already had prior to trade). In contrast, producers in Denmark see a reduction in surplus due to the lower price, losing area C to consumers.

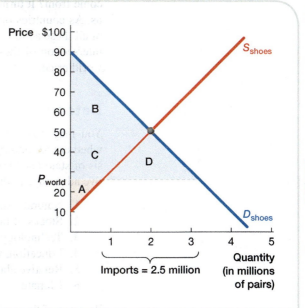

0.75 million pairs of shoes by changing quantity supplied, or sliding down the market supply curve until $25 is reached. At that price, Danish consumers demand 3.25 million pairs of shoes: the price has gone down, so they move along their demand curve until the price of $25 is reached (shown on the lower dotted line). This movement stops when the quantity demanded reaches 3.25 million pairs at a price of $25.

These movements lead to excess demand in Denmark. This excess demand of 2.5 million pairs of tennis shoes $(3.25 - 0.75 = 2.50)$ is subsequently purchased on the world market, making Denmark an importer of tennis shoes. Because Denmark is a small buyer of tennis shoes, this added demand does not change the world price.

So who wins and who loses when Denmark opens its borders to trade and becomes an importer? Again, a comparison of producer and consumer surplus measures allows us to answer this question. For sellers, producer surplus is lowered because they are now selling fewer pairs of tennis shoes and the price of each pair sold is lower. Their loss can be seen from the decreased level of producer surplus in Exhibit 8.14: before trade, producer surplus was areas A + C; after trade, it is only area A. Thus, Danish sellers experience a decreased producer surplus of area C.

For consumers, the story is the opposite. They are now purchasing more shoes at a lower price, so they must be better off. Exhibit 8.14 shows by how much: before trade, consumer surplus was area B; after trade, it is areas B + C + D. Thus, Danish buyers experience an increased consumer surplus equal to areas C and D because the country has opened to trade.

We can therefore draw two conclusions about what happens when a country opens itself to trade and becomes an importer of goods and services:

1. Sellers lose.
2. Buyers win.

And once again, the overall gains to trade for Denmark are positive, represented by area D in Exhibit 8.14. This area highlights the fact that even when countries are net importers, they are net gainers. As a whole, Denmark is much better off, allowing the winners to potentially compensate the losers. Taxing consumers and sending the revenues to shoe producers is one way in which such compensation can take place. (We discuss further the pros and cons of such taxation in Chapter 10.)

## Where Do World Prices Come From?

In the cases above, when we illustrate the impact that free trade has on Denmark's tennis shoe market, we fix the world price for tennis shoes to make a point about the winners and losers of free trade. But where do world prices for tennis shoes, or any good for that matter, come from? It turns out that our supply and demand framework does a good job of telling us. As countries open up their borders and act on their comparative advantages, the sum of all these actions lets us consider a world supply and a world demand for a product. The intersection of these two (world supply curve and world demand curve) determines the world price.

### Determinants of a Country's Comparative Advantage

You may now be wondering what determines a country's comparative advantage and whether the country can predict trade flows before opening itself to trade. As in our analysis of state-level trading in the United States, the factors that contribute most to comparative advantage at the country level are:

1. Natural resources (to a large degree, beyond the countries' control, unless squandered)
2. Stocks of human-made resources (more controllable; depend on the PPC)
3. Technology
4. Education, work habits, and experience of the labor force
5. Relative abundance of labor and physical capital
6. Climate

Because of the wide array of these determinants and their changing nature, it is clear that comparative advantage can change over time—just as when you took the computer programming course (see Section 8.1)! A country-level example is Japan's investment in human capital, which helped nurture skills and technology to generate a winning formula for becoming a leading car manufacturing nation. Likewise, technological advances that permit a more cost-effective means of exploiting a country's stock of natural resources can change the nature of comparative advantage.

## 8.5 Arguments Against Free Trade

We've seen the significant gains associated with free trade between countries, so why would any country ever want to hinder trade? Why were the protestors cited in the opening to this chapter so passionate in their opposition to free trade? Why did both President Trump and Democratic nominee Hilary Clinton create platforms that challenged free trade during the 2016 Presidential campaign? Several arguments are typically set forth:

1. National security concerns
2. Fear of the effects of globalization on a nation's culture
3. Environmental and resource concerns
4. Infant industry arguments
5. Potential negative effects on local wages and jobs

We briefly discuss the first four arguments in turn, reserving the fifth argument concerning wages and jobs for the section on Evidence-Based Economics near the end of the chapter.

*We drive Japanese cars, drink French wine, eat Mexican food, use American computers, buy Canadian lumber and take vacations in Italy. How can you OPPOSE free trade?*

### National Security Concerns

As we learned in Chapter 7, allowing resources to flow freely has the effect of allocating resources in and across industries efficiently. But that may mean the creation of "banana republics"—nations that specialize in the production of one good. Though this might be efficient economically, it may not be optimal in a defense-oriented world, where national security is an important consideration. A country will not produce just oranges if it fears military attack from other nations. Rather, it will invest in steel production and defense technology and will maintain a variety of agricultural industries to preserve its integrity in times of war. Likewise, even in times of peace, a country might be hesitant to completely specialize, because it might find itself too reliant on other countries. For example, because many modern economies depend on oil imports, many cite such reliance as a national security concern.

## Fear of Globalization

**Globalization** is the shift toward more open, integrated economies that participate in foreign trade and investment. Some nations, however, want to maintain their culture's uniqueness and therefore view globalization as a serious concern. That is to say, as the world becomes increasingly interdependent, it also becomes increasingly homogeneous—decades ago China had no McDonald's; now in large cities there is one on every corner. In addition, Starbucks now serves coffee in more than sixty countries—some people fear the loss of their cultural identity through such globalization. Such preferences are an important consideration for leaders around the world.

**Globalization** is the shift toward more open, integrated economies that participate in foreign trade and investment.

Does free trade lead to more e-waste going from the United States to developing countries, such as India?

## Environmental and Resource Concerns

Tangible goods, such as clothing and food, are not the only things traded by countries; such abstract goods as environmental quality may be traded as well. Countries with lax environmental policies allow for relatively more pollution from firms than do countries with strong environmental policies. Opponents of free trade often cite these policy differences as creating "pollution havens" in poor countries. These countries, in an effort to promote economic growth and jobs, use lax pollution regulations to attract industry. A similar argument exists for natural resources, such as ivory. The argument is that free trade endangers the stock of animals that provide ivory (for example, elephant, walrus, and narwhal), because openness to trade leads to higher demand for ivory, threatening species extinction. In Chapter 9, we discuss more broadly how governments protect such resources.

## Infant Industry Arguments

Opponents of free trade also cite the "infant industries" argument, in which governments protect their fledgling domestic industries against more advanced competitors. For example, to help Toyota grow, the Japanese government forced General Motors and Ford out of the country in 1939. Generally, infant industry arguments rely on the idea that in industries with economies of scale or substantial learning by doing, it is important for policymakers to protect local firms early in their development. In addition, starting a company in isolation may deprive it of "technological spillovers" that its competitors, all located near one another, may enjoy—the isolated company will be the last to learn of trade secrets.

Ultimately, the basis of any infant industry argument is that a company is currently too weak to withstand competition from other firms. To survive, the company requires government protection. **Protectionism** is the idea that free trade can be harmful, and government intervention is necessary to control trade.

Protectionism takes many forms, and has been used as a means to block the growing interdependence in the world. We now turn to one such example—*tariffs*.

**Protectionism** is the idea that free trade can be harmful, and government intervention is necessary to control trade.

## The Effects of Tariffs

As we discussed in the chapter opener, many individuals worry about their own jobs when trade increases between countries. Historically, one of the most popular forms of government protectionism is to impose **tariffs**, which are taxes levied on goods and services transported across political boundaries. Protectionism via an imposed tariff is not free, however. Indeed, by their very nature, tariffs interfere with equilibrium prices and quantities, artificially reducing social surplus in a country.

**Tariffs** are taxes levied on goods and services transported across political boundaries.

## Exhibit 8.15 The Effect of a Tariff

Here we revisit the example of Denmark as an importing country, but now the government of Denmark enacts a tariff. By raising the price using the tariff, the government earns revenues from the tariff (area I), and producer surplus rises by area E. But consumers are worse off (they lose areas E, G, I, and J), and there is a deadweight loss of areas G and J because of the tariff.

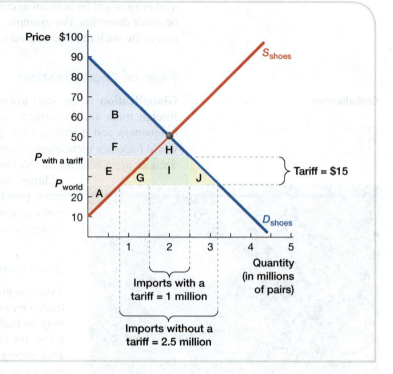

> By their very nature, tariffs interfere with equilibrium prices and quantities, artificially reducing social surplus in a country.

To show how, let's reconsider the example of Denmark as an importing nation of tennis shoes. Assume that for infant industry reasons, the Danish government decides to invoke a $15 tariff on every pair of imported tennis shoes to protect Danish suppliers. That is, the government collects $15 from the foreign producer for every pair of tennis shoes that crosses Danish borders. Exhibit 8.15 shows the effect of such a tariff.

Notice that before the tariff is imposed, consumer surplus is given by the sum of the colored regions labeled B, F, E, and G, H, I, and J. This is the area under the demand curve but above the world price line. The pink triangle labeled area A is domestic producer surplus. This is the area above the supply curve but below the world price line.

After Denmark imposes a $15 tariff on shoes, the local market price rises from $25 to $40. The imposition of the tariff reduces consumer surplus to the area above the new price line and below the domestic demand curve—areas B, F, and H. Therefore, the loss in consumer surplus from the tariff is areas E, G, I, and J. Where does this lost surplus go?

Area E goes to producers, so their new surplus is areas A + E. They are better off because they can now sell shoes to the local market at $40 rather than $25. The government is also better off since area I goes to the government. The government receives the number of import goods times the tariff price in revenue. This revenue equals $15 × 1 million = $15 million, or the area of rectangle I.

What about areas G and J? This is the deadweight loss of the tariff. As we discussed in Chapter 7, market distortions often lead to deadweight loss. In this case, the Danish economy loses the two triangles labeled G and J. This is the cost that the Danes pay to protect the tennis shoe industry by imposing a tariff.

From this analysis, we can see one reason economists in general do not favor such protectionism—it raises prices for consumers and lowers social surplus. This might be one reason why some countries have been moving away from using tariffs. Exhibit 8.16 shows the dutiable imports ratio from 1891 to 2015. This is a measure of the ratio of tariff revenues (duties) collected to the value of dutiable imports. The orange line marks a series of tariff increases, called the Smoot-Hawley tariffs, in the United States during the Great Depression. After the imposition of these peak tariffs, the United States quickly

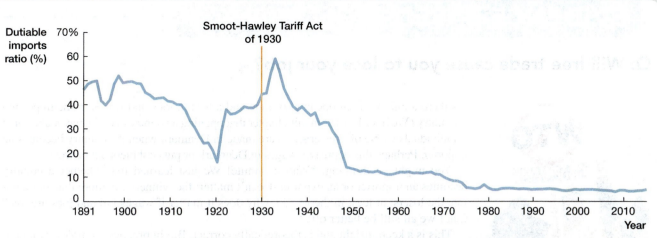

Exhibit 8.16 **Changes in Import Tariffs in the United States, 1891–2015**

The x-axis is time and the y-axis is the dutiable imports ratio. This is the ratio of tariff revenues (duties) collected to the value of dutiable imports. It is usually reported as a percentage. The 1920s and 1930s saw a dramatic increase in this ratio. Over time, however, the ratio has been steadily decreasing.

*Source:* Based on U.S. International Trade Commission.

# CHOICE
# &CONSEQUENCE

## Tariffs Affect Trade Between Firms

So far we have considered how tariffs affect consumers and producers of a particular good, such as shoes. But producers of shoes themselves often rely on inputs that are imported, such as string for the laces, leather for the uppers, or rubber for the soles.

A 2013 episode of the podcast Planet Money highlights the interconnectedness of world trade by following a plain cotton T-shirt on its journey of production, from a farm on the Mississippi Delta where the cotton is grown, to a spinning factory in Colombia, to a plant in Bangladesh where the shirts are sewn together.

The fact of the matter is that most U.S. imports are intermediate goods. That is, they are parts and materials imported to make a final product that we buy, like tennis shoes or iPhones. The proportion of U.S. imports that are intermediate goods was 64.6 percent in 1993. The fact that U.S. firms import so much of their inputs used for production suggests that reducing tariffs will increase trade among firms and reduce their costs of production.

An analysis by economists Lorenzo Caliendo and Fernando Parro studies the importance of tariffs on trade of intermediate goods among member countries of the **North American Free Trade Agreement (NAFTA)**: the United States, Canada, and Mexico.[3] They find that NAFTA's tariff reductions increased the total size of the U.S. economy by 0.08 percent, a seemingly small amount. The NAFTA tariff reductions, however, increased trade between firms by 41 percent, demonstrating the importance of tariffs for firms interested in trade.

The **North American Free Trade Agreement (NAFTA)** is an agreement signed by Canada, Mexico, and the United States to create a trilateral trade bloc and reduce trade barriers among the three countries.

learned about one effect of limiting free trade—other countries will respond in kind! Other nations began charging American companies new duties. America consequently reduced its tariffs, likely saving millions of dollars through increased consumer and producer surplus.

## Q: Will free trade cause you to lose your job?

Is there a link between opening to trade and a loss in jobs and wages in the importing country? We have learned in this chapter that opening a country to trade may make some individuals worse off: fewer shoes are made in Denmark when the country becomes an importer. Perhaps this depresses wages in Denmark or puts cobblers out of work.

You might be thinking: "Wait a minute! We just learned that whether a country becomes an importer or an exporter doesn't matter; the winners can more than compensate the losers, at least in theory. So, why does it matter if wages fall and jobs are lost? Can't we all still be better off?"

This is a keen insight and is theoretically correct. But in practice, complete compensation of losers from opening an economy to international trade is difficult. First, as we discuss in Chapter 10, the government might not be able to effectively carry out such policies. Second, it is often difficult to pinpoint exactly who the winners are and how much they each gained, and who the losers are and how much they each lost. It is often the case that the losers are spread throughout the economy and sometimes are touched in very small ways. Thus we can conclude that opening an economy up to trade clearly expands the pie, but some people might end up with a smaller piece than they used to have.

In trying to answer the question of whether opening an economy to trade adversely affects jobs and wages, it is instructive to consider the experience of the United States when it began to trade with countries that held a comparative advantage in certain industries. Over the past half-century, new producers of textiles and other manufactured goods have emerged (for instance, Exhibit 8.11 shows the emergence of China).

We've also seen in this chapter that when a country is a net importer—as is the United States for manufactured goods—domestic consumers gain and domestic producers lose. For example, New England was a key producer of textiles and manufactured goods during the first half of the twentieth century, but with the importation of manufactured goods from abroad, thousands of textile workers lost their jobs. So jobs are lost because of the effects of international trade. Nevertheless, with the expansion of other sectors, such as the high-tech and Internet-based industries, the unemployment rate in the New England states has been among the lowest in the United States. This example highlights the fact that people whose skills become obsolete because of the effects of international trade can invest time and resources in more education and training. On doing so, they have a good chance to find work. Consistent with this evidence, the data also suggest that many workers displaced because of NAFTA's passage soon found gainful employment.

Even though the U.S. experience suggests that workers have an opportunity to land on their feet, another key empirical question related to lost jobs remains: how important has opening to trade been in affecting wages? Economists have spent a fair amount of time and effort in addressing this question. The typical approach is to draw on large data sets, which span several years and include information on hundreds of thousands of workers' wages across several different sectors of the economy. These data sets are then examined to determine whether wages of workers change as an economy opens to trade.

The first wave of economic studies published in the 1990s reports very small, or inconsequential, effects of trade on wages of workers in those parts of the labor force that produce goods competing with those coming in from abroad.[4] These studies suggest that there is no strong evidence from the data to back the major claim of trade critics.

Yet before concluding that wages are not negatively influenced when a country opens to trade and becomes a net importer, Exhibit 8.11 of this chapter points to an important phenomenon that has occurred in recent years. Led by China, which has a comparative advantage in labor with its large workforce, manufacturing imports from developing countries have risen dramatically since 1990. Overall, imports from developing countries have grown from roughly 2.5 percent of U.S. GDP in 1990 to 6 percent of U.S. GDP in 2006. This trend is important because developing countries have a large pool of workers who are paid considerably lower wages than the manufacturing workers of our historical trading partners.

This could mean that in more recent years, trade has had a much more important effect on wages in the states than we observed in the past. Scholars are just beginning to address this issue, using more recent data. The evidence gathered thus far does not point to anything conclusive. For example, economist Robert Lawrence reports that using more recent data does not change the overall picture of the studies published in the 1990s—there remains little empirical evidence that trade negatively influences wages.[5] Yet, very recent evidence from economists Peter Schott and Justin Pierce suggests real impacts.[6] Their paper focuses on the effect of low tariffs on certain Chinese imports. They find that goods with low tariffs led to a decrease in U.S. employment in these industries, along with an increase in Chinese imports. Thus their paper suggests that trade with China has indeed led to a decrease in U.S. manufacturing employment. Meanwhile, economist Paul Krugman, the 2008 Nobel Laureate, has argued that the data are far too murky to yield reliable empirical results.[7] In the end, we believe that at this point there is not enough evidence to conclude definitely whether opening to trade leads to lost jobs and lower wages. But empirical work should continue. Do you have any ideas about how to proceed?

### Question

Will free trade cause you to lose your job?

### Answer

Some workers might lose their jobs, but there is no systematic evidence that shows opening up to trade harms workers broadly.

### Data

Import and export data combined with local wage and job data.

### Caveat

U.S. trading partners have changed over recent years to include countries with a comparative advantage in labor, opening up the possibility that trade with our new partners is actually harming U.S. workers more than previous data suggest.

## Summary

- People and countries are dependent on one another for goods and services. Although there are potential costs to this interdependency, the gains associated with taking advantage of specialization in the production of goods and services can be considerable.

- Specialization and trade, which are driven by comparative advantage, not only allow us to consume beyond our individual PPC but also lead to a wider variety of goods and services.

- Whereas comparative advantage revolves around measuring production relative to the opportunity costs that you and the other person incur, absolute advantage relates to production per unit of inputs.

- When a country opens up to trade, there are winners and losers. The gains from trade are larger than the losses. One key to avoiding protests about free trade, like the one we saw in Seattle in 1999, is to develop policies so that everyone can reap the gains from trade.

- Empirically, the data do not reveal the sweeping job losses for U.S. workers that trade critics cite. There is certainly a displacement of workers due to trade, but many workers soon find other jobs. Likewise, the supposed negative effect of trade on wages is difficult to find in the data. Beyond lost jobs, however, those against free trade often cite national security concerns, loss of cultural identity, environmental and resource concerns, and infant industry arguments.

## Key Terms

production possibilities curve (PPC) *p. 174*

comparative advantage *p. 176*

absolute advantage *p. 178*

terms of trade *p. 179*

export *p. 181*

import *p. 181*

net importer *p. 185*

free trade *p. 186*

world price *p. 186*

globalization *p. 191*

protectionism *p. 191*

tariffs *p. 191*

North American Free Trade Agreement (NAFTA) *p. 193*

## Questions

*All questions are available in MyEconLab for practice and instructor assignment.*

1. Consider the figure at the right. The blue line shows how many units of goods A and B a worker in Taiwan can produce, and the tan line shows the number of units of goods A and B that a worker in Korea can produce. Does this figure indicate anything about either worker having a comparative or absolute advantage in either good?

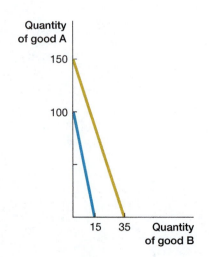

2. Is it true that a country needs to have an absolute advantage in the production of a good to benefit from trade in that good? Explain.

3. What is meant by terms of trade? How is it determined?

4. What does a production possibilities curve (PPC) show? What is the difference between a PPC that is linear and one that curves away from the origin?

5. Explain the impact, if any, of each of the following on the PPC.

   a. Europe's population fell by 30–60 percent following an outbreak of bubonic plague, also known as the Black Death, in the fourteenth century.

   b. In the next 20 years, a sizable proportion of the U.S. labor force is expected to be comprised of people who are older than 65.

   c. Canada recently discovered large reserves of shale gas (shale gas is natural gas that is trapped in fine-grained sedimentary rock).

6. How has the pattern of trade changed in the United States since 1960? What are the types of goods that are causing the shift in the balance of imports and exports in the United States?

7. Many service-sector jobs in the United States have moved to foreign countries where these jobs are done at a fraction of the cost they incur domestically. The outsourcing of jobs overseas is heavily debated by politicians, policymakers, and economists in the United States. Based on your understanding of trade and the benefits and losses from trade, how do you think outsourcing affects social surplus in the domestic economy?

8. What are the sources of a country's comparative advantage?

9. What are some of the common arguments against free trade?

10. What is the problem with the argument that infant industries need to be protected from foreign competition?

11. If opening an economy up to trade always benefits both trading partners, why is free trade controversial?

12. The mercantilist economic doctrine was widely followed from the sixteenth to the eighteenth centuries in Europe. Mercantilists advocated the use of tariffs to restrict trade, as they believed that countries that export more than they import will enjoy increased wealth. What could be the problem with such an economic policy?

13. Since the "winners" from free trade can more than compensate the "losers," why does it matter if wages and employment fall when a country engages in free trade?

14. Consider the following diagram. The discussion in the text implies that if this country imposes a tariff, social surplus will fall by the sum of area A and area B. Intuitively, why is A part of the deadweight loss from this tariff? Intuitively, why is B part of the deadweight loss from this tariff?

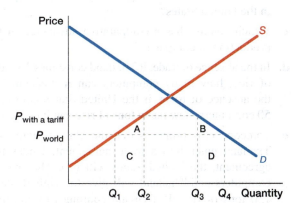

# Problems

*All problems are available in MyEconLab for practice and instructor assignment.*

1. Justin has 5 days in a work week; each day he can create either 2 Android apps or 1 Apple app. Pallas also has 5 days to work; each day she can produce either 2 Android apps or 3 Apple apps.

   a. Sketch the production possibilities curve (PPC) for Justin. Place Android apps on the horizontal axis.

   b. Sketch the PPC for Pallas.

   c. Sketch the single PPC for both Justin and Pallas.

   d. What does Justin have a comparative advantage at producing? Why?

   e. What does Pallas have a comparative advantage at producing? Why?

2. A country has two types of workers, skilled and unskilled. Workers can produce either computers or steel. Output per worker is as follows.

|  | Output per Worker | |
| --- | --- | --- |
| Type of Worker | Computers | Steel |
| Unskilled | 3 | 2 |
| Skilled | 5 | 3 |

Do skilled workers have an absolute advantage in the production of computers? Do unskilled workers have a comparative advantage in the production of steel? Explain your answers carefully.

3. Suppose a country has 100 westerners and 100 easterners. A westerner can produce either 6 units of food or 2 units of national defense; an easterner can produce either 2 units of food or 1 unit of national defense.

   a. Show that easterners have a comparative advantage in the production of defense.

**b.** Suppose this country has decided it wants to produce 60 units of defense. Would the country have more food to consume if the westerners produced these 60 units of defense or if the easterners produced this defense?

**c.** Why should you have anticipated your answer to part (b) of this question?

**d.** Now suppose this country institutes a draft and chooses people for the military randomly. Suppose further that it drafts 20 westerners and 20 easterners (who together will produce 60 units of defense). How much food will the country produce if it chooses to have a military draft?

4. There are 10 workers in Thailand, and each can produce either 2 computers or 30 tons of rice. There are 20 workers in the United States, and each can produce either 5 computers or 40 tons of rice.

**a.** Draw the PPC for each country. In each case, identify the intercepts and the slopes of the PPC.

**b.** What is the opportunity cost of computers in Thailand? What is the opportunity cost of computers in the United States?

**c.** Which country has a comparative advantage in the production of computers?

**d.** In the absence of trade, if Thailand consumes 150 tons of rice, how many computers can it consume? In the absence of trade, if the United States consumes 50 computers, how many tons of rice can it consume?

**e.** Someone now proposes that the United States and Thailand enter into a trade agreement. Under this agreement, the United States will give Thailand 10 computers and Thailand will give the United States 120 tons of rice. If Thailand continues to consume 150 tons of rice, how many computers will it be able to consume under this proposal? If the United States continues to consume 50 computers, how many tons of rice will it be able to consume under this proposal?

**f.** Should Thailand accept this proposal? Should the United States accept this proposal?

5. Amanda is a student working part-time at an insurance company. Amanda can work only 5 hours a day. Her manager informs her that she needs to review 250 documents and process 250 insurance claims in the next 10 days. The following table shows how many documents and claims Amanda can work on in a given number of hours:

| Hours Spent on Documents | Documents | Hours Spent on Insurance Claims | Claims |
|---|---|---|---|
| 1 | 10 | 1 | 5 |
| 2 | 20 | 2 | 10 |
| 3 | 30 | 3 | 15 |
| 4 | 40 | 4 | 20 |
| 5 | 50 | 5 | 25 |

**a.** Create a PPC for Amanda.

**b.** What is the slope of the curve?

**c.** What is her opportunity cost of reviewing one document?

6. Consider the following three countries. Each can produce wheat, sheep, ore, brick, or wood. Production per worker is shown in the table. Each country has an equal number of workers.

| | Redistan | Whiteny | Blueland |
|---|---|---|---|
| Wheat | 1 | 1 | 2 |
| Sheep | 1 | 2 | 2 |
| Ore | 1 | 2 | 0 |
| Brick | 2 | 1 | 3 |
| Wood | 2 | 1 | 1 |

**a.** Which country has an absolute advantage in producing wheat?

**b.** In terms of the opportunity cost of sheep, which country has a comparative advantage in producing brick?

**c.** A fourth country (Yellowlia) offers to give a unit of ore in exchange for one of wood. Which countries would probably want to trade with Yellowlia?

7. The remote island nations of Nearway and Farway produce fish and coconuts and have recently decided to engage in trade with one another. Use the table to answer the following questions.

| Characteristic | Coconuts Nearway | Coconuts Farway | Fish Nearway | Fish Farway |
|---|---|---|---|---|
| Optimal production without trade | 200 | 300 | 100 | 200 |
| Specialization: Optimal production with trade | | 600 | 500 | |
| Imported goods | 250 | | | 250 |
| Post-trade allocation | | | | |
| Gains from trade | | | | |

**a.** Calculate the opportunity costs of producing fish and coconuts in Nearway and Farway, and then determine who has the comparative advantage in the production of each good.

**b.** Using what you learned in part (a), fill in the blanks in the table.

**c.** Which nation received the better deal in this trade? Explain using the terms of trade range.

**d.** Would Nearway and Farway ever trade 60 coconuts for 20 fish? Why or why not?

8. The world price can be higher than the domestic price; this generates exports rather than imports. Copy the following supply and demand curves for pounds of cheese

in Wisconsin. Notice that the world price is *above* the domestic equilibrium price.

**Cheese in Wisconsin**

**a.** Highlight the pounds of cheese exported from Wisconsin (a length, not an area).

**b.** Shade in the area that represents the consumer surplus with free trade. Relative to the domestic market alone, has consumer surplus increased or decreased?

**c.** Shade in the area that represents the producer surplus with free trade. Relative to the domestic market alone, has producer surplus increased or decreased?

**d.** Within Wisconsin, who wins and who loses from free trade in cheese?

9. Suppose your country imports wheat. The price of wheat rises from $P_1$ to $P_2$ and your country continues to import wheat. Present and discuss a diagram to answer the following questions. Did imports rise or fall? Did consumer surplus rise or fall? Did producer surplus rise or fall? Did social surplus rise or fall?

10. Dominic is willing to pay $12 for a single pizza; Stephany is willing to pay $7; and Tyler is willing to pay $5. There are no other potential consumers of pizza. Cheezbuzz, the supplier of pizza, has a cost of $1 for the first pizza, $2 for the second pizza, $3 for the third, $4 for the fourth, and so on.

**a.** In a closed market equilibrium, what is the social surplus?

**b.** Suppose pizza has a world price of $10.50. How many pizzas will be exported?

**c.** Now suppose pizza has a world price of $2.50. What will be the social surplus?

11. Suppose domestic demand is $Q_D = 16 - P$ and domestic supply is $Q_s = P$. The world price is $2 and the import tariff is $3 per unit. First make a sketch, and then find the following values. Each value will be represented by an area in your sketch.

**a.** Consumer surplus

**b.** Producer surplus

**c.** Government revenue

**d.** Deadweight loss of the tariff

# 9 Externalities and Public Goods

## How can the Queen of England lower her commute time to Wembley Stadium?

Imagine yourself sitting in your economics classroom waiting for the start of class. You are chatting with your neighbors about how free trade might not be so bad after all, and other students are buzzing about the power of the invisible hand as they search for their preferred seats. Your professor strolls in with her usual materials in tow, but something unusual is clutched in her right hand. After setting down her bag, she takes out a match from a matchbox. Confidently, she strikes the match and lights up the cigar in her right hand. One student gasps; another shrieks in delight. Your economics professor is smoking a cigar in class! "Students, welcome to the world of externalities," your professor says boldly.[1]

You might ask yourself, how do externalities fit in with the markets we have studied thus far? In short, they don't. So far in our study of markets, we have focused solely on buyers and sellers, who are the only ones affected by the market transaction. But we know that many times, the actions of one party affect the well-being of countless other parties—like people smoking cigars or factories belching out smoke. In situations like these, the invisible hand may fail to allocate resources efficiently. For instance, many people may suffer from a polluting factory's emissions without ever benefiting from the production that caused the pollution.

## CHAPTER OUTLINE

Economists call such examples *externalities*. An externality occurs when there is a spillover from one person's actions to a bystander. If left alone, people will generally not account for how their actions affect others—whether positive or negative. For instance, think about automobiles for a minute. They not only contribute to the global warming problem but also create traffic congestion. But have you ever chosen *not* to drive a car because of the extra congestion that your vehicle will cause? Neither have we. And that is the crux of why such externalities are called market failures.

In this chapter, we will see that in the case of externalities, governments can enact policies to push market outcomes toward a greater level of social well-being. For example, one possible policy to alleviate traffic jams is to impose a fee on automobile drivers using particular roads. It's precisely that proposal that we'll examine in our Evidence-Based Economics feature at the end of the chapter, which will help us answer the opening question about lowering the queen's commute time.

A related example of when the free market fails to arrive at a socially efficient outcome if left alone is in the provision of *public goods* (such as national defense) or in the protection of *common pool resources* (such as an open-access lake). The link among all three of these market failures is that there is a difference between social and private benefits or social and private costs, causing the individual to face different incentives than society faces. Accordingly, much like the case with externalities, we will find that government can play a critical role in providing public goods and protecting common pool resources.

# 9.1 Externalities

It's morning, and you wake up to an alarm clock buzzing. You roll out of bed, walk to the bathroom, flip on the light, and turn on the shower. Hot water bursts out, and the exhaust fan ensures that the shower area remains fog-free. You have been awake for only 15 minutes on this day, but you already have made use of electricity four times—by using the alarm clock, the bathroom light, the water heater, and the ceiling fan.

Electricity obviously benefits all of us in many ways, but the power company incurs production costs to provide electricity. As we learned earlier, the market arrives at a price for electricity that reflects both these factors—marginal benefits and marginal costs. In Exhibit 9.1 we make the assumption that the electricity industry is a perfectly competitive market. The market demand curve in the exhibit shows consumers' willingness and ability to pay for electricity, and the market supply curve reflects producers' marginal costs of generating it. As we learned in Chapter 7, it is at the equilibrium point where these two

### Exhibit 9.1 The Market for Electricity

The downward-sloping market demand curve (D) intersects the upward-sloping market supply curve (S) to determine the equilibrium price ($P_{market}$) and equilibrium quantity ($Q_{market}$) of electricity.

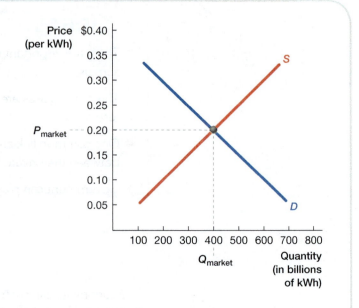

lines intersect that the invisible hand most efficiently allocates resources: the point at which social surplus is maximized.

But what Exhibit 9.1 does *not* show is that when producing electricity, plants typically emit nasty pollutants, including sulfur dioxide and nitrogen oxides, which can cause lung irritation, bronchitis, and pneumonia. You also cannot see in a graph like this that at high dosage levels, the mercury released from coal-burning power plants has been linked to birth defects. Global warming has also been linked to pollutants emitted from power plants.

In economic terms, the power plant imposes an externality on the public as a by-product of producing electricity. An **externality** occurs when an economic activity has either a spillover cost to or a spillover benefit for a bystander. In this case, the plant is imposing a negative externality, because by producing electricity, it creates a spillover cost that it does not consider when making production decisions. Because the owners of the plant do not have to pay for the costs that the plant imposes on society, they do not take into account the health or discomfort of the citizenry in their production decisions. That is, free markets allocate resources in a way that ignores these negative externalities.

> An **externality** occurs when an economic activity has either a spillover cost to or a spillover benefit for a bystander.

## A "Broken" Invisible Hand: Negative Externalities

Let's return to Exhibit 9.1, where we show the market demand and market supply curves for electricity. We can first ask ourselves, why is this outcome efficient? The answer is that it is efficient because at that point social surplus is maximized: every buyer who is willing and able to pay the equilibrium price for electricity ends up, in fact, consuming electricity. And, because plants expand production until $MC = MR = P$, social surplus is maximized: both consumers and producers do as well as they can in equilibrium.

When there are negative externalities present, however, this market outcome is no longer efficient. This is because negative externalities impose an additional cost on society that is not explicitly recognized by the buyers and sellers in the market. For electricity generation, this additional cost comes from pollution, a by-product of electricity production. In computing the efficient outcome, we must adjust the supply curve to take account of the negative externalities or external costs. That is, as we discussed in Chapter 6, the supply curve is the marginal cost curve for the firm and includes a plant's expenditures for inputs, such as labor. The external costs that society bears as a result of the plant's pollution are ignored. However, to arrive at the efficient production level, we need to recognize both the firm's marginal

Many firms pollute when they produce goods for us to consume.

**Exhibit 9.2 The Socially Optimal Quantity and Price of Electricity**

Negative externalities lead to external costs of production that the private firm will not account for when making decisions. The marginal external cost is the vertical distance between supply and marginal social cost (MSC). If we take the marginal external cost into account, a higher equilibrium price and a lower equilibrium quantity result.

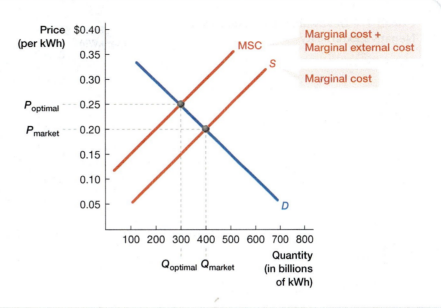

cost and the marginal external costs of production. Together, they sum to the *marginal social cost* of production.

So what does this mean for the efficient level of output? Exhibit 9.2 shows the answer graphically. Exhibit 9.2 reveals that at each level of production we must include both the marginal cost of the plant to produce plus the marginal external cost of the pollution. This new curve is called the *marginal social cost (MSC)* curve, because it includes both the marginal cost of the firm and the marginal external cost imposed on society (*MSC* = *Marginal cost* + *Marginal external cost*). Recall that the original supply curve is the marginal cost curve of the electricity producer—the MSC is therefore the marginal cost of the externality plus this marginal cost.

> Negative externalities impose an additional cost on society that is not explicitly recognized by the buyers and sellers in the market.

Taking into account the extra costs imposed on society by the plant's pollution, we can see that $Q_{optimal}$ is less than $Q_{market}$, because when a negative externality must be accounted for, a smaller quantity of electricity should be generated since it is now more costly to produce each unit. Thus, in cases where there are negative externalities, markets (if left alone) will produce too much, resulting in too much pollution.

You might wonder just how much this negative externality costs society. We can explore this question graphically by considering Exhibit 9.3. Let's begin with the equilibrium quantity level, $Q_{market}$ = 400 billion kWh (kilowatt hours). In the free market, this is the unit of production that equates marginal willingness to pay with the marginal cost of producing that unit of electricity ($0.20 = $0.20). But with the negative externality, we see that the marginal social cost is $0.30 for the last unit, not $0.20. This means that by producing that last unit, we actually caused social well-being to go down by $0.10 = $0.30 − $0.20 (the marginal social cost from producing the last unit minus the marginal benefit from producing the last unit). So if we do not produce that last unit, we will save $0.10. Recall from Chapter 7 that *deadweight loss* is a decrease in social surplus that results from a market distortion. If producing that last unit caused a deadweight loss of $0.10, what is the total deadweight loss associated with the externality?

Extending the reasoning from the last unit produced to all units produced between $Q_{optimal}$ and $Q_{market}$, we arrive at the yellow-shaded region in Exhibit 9.3. This is the area between the marginal social cost curve and the market demand curve between units $Q_{optimal}$ and $Q_{market}$. The triangle represents the sum of the losses for each unit—the difference between the total marginal cost and total marginal benefits to society as a whole. Thus, the yellow-shaded triangle represents the deadweight loss of the negative externality. As a way to check your work, the deadweight loss is usually in the form of an arrow-like triangle with the arrow pointing in the direction that society would prefer. In the case

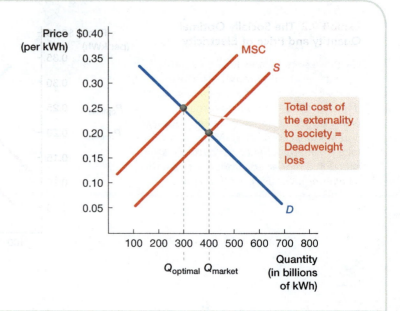

**Exhibit 9.3 Deadweight Loss Due to a Negative Externality**

In producing the last unit of production, a deadweight loss of $0.10 resulted. Doing a similar exercise for all units produced to the right of the social optimal production level ($Q_{optimal}$), we can graphically represent the deadweight loss as the yellow triangle.

depicted in Exhibit 9.3, the arrow points leftward, meaning society prefers less production than the free market provides.

One important feature of this discussion is that pollution is not driven to zero—that is not the goal. Rather, the optimal solution calls for us to recognize the marginal cost of the pollution externality to society. On recognizing the marginal external cost, as in this example, it is often the case that we are left with some pollution. This is for two main reasons: pollutants in moderate dosages are in many cases not very damaging, and it is very costly to produce some goods without releasing any pollution.

## A "Broken" Invisible Hand: Positive Externalities

There are important situations that are a mirror image of negative externalities—positive externalities, which occur when an economic activity has a spillover *benefit* that is not considered when people make their own decisions. As with negative externalities, positive externalities are all around us. For instance, a resident of Sarasota who landscapes her property will probably enhance the value of her neighbors' property, even though they had nothing to do with the decision to landscape.

Another important example of a positive externality is educational attainment, which not only helps a student through better employment opportunities and higher wages but also confers significant benefits on others. These benefits can come in many forms, but the ones most often cited are the following:

1. Education often increases civic engagement, thereby contributing to a more informed democratic society.
2. An educated workforce is vital for innovation and adoption of new technologies.
3. An educated citizenry will be less likely to commit crime.

Among economists and policymakers, the positive externality argument is a commonly cited justification for government involvement in education. To show why, let's begin with Exhibit 9.4, which illustrates the market demand and market supply curves for education. For clarity, let's continue with the assumption that education is a perfectly competitive market. Therefore, $Q_{market}$ is an efficient outcome: with no externalities, the invisible hand is driving the market to an efficient equilibrium.

In the case of positive externalities, however, the invisible hand does not yield socially efficient results. This is because positive externalities create external social benefits that are reaped by others. Exhibit 9.5 reveals an example of positive externalities, which can be thought of as the difference between the demand curve (which is marginal benefit) and the

> **Positive externalities create external social benefits that are reaped by others.**

## Exhibit 9.4 The Market Equilibrium for Education

As in Exhibit 9.1, we depict a market without externalities. The optimal production is reached where the market demand curve for education intersects the market supply curve for education.

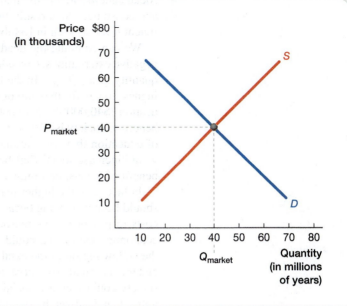

*marginal social benefit (MSB) curve*. Therefore, the MSB curve is the marginal (private) benefit plus the marginal external benefit: $MSB$ = Marginal benefit + Marginal external benefit.

Consider Exhibit 9.5 more closely. The efficient amount of education from the viewpoint of society is given by $Q_{optimal}$. This is where society's marginal benefit from another unit of education equals the marginal cost of producing that unit of education. But this won't be the same as the equilibrium quantity in a free market. The education industry will only produce until its marginal cost equals the private demand for education, not the social demand. This is because the industry can only sell its output to education buyers. For practical reasons, it cannot charge people who enjoy the external benefit of education production—those people who benefit from a more informed citizenry or less crime, for example.

We can now see the inefficiency created by not recognizing the positive externality. Even though there are years of education (between $Q_{market}$ and $Q_{optimal}$) from which marginal

## Exhibit 9.5 Deadweight Loss of a Positive Externality

Features of an educated populace, such as better informed policymaking, mean that private benefits of education will understate total benefits. Graphically, this means that the marginal social benefit curve will be higher than the demand curve for any amount of production. This leads to an underproduction of education, leading to a deadweight loss to society that is equal to the yellow triangle.

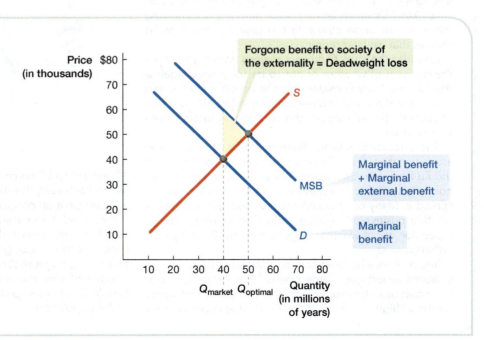

social benefits are greater than the marginal cost to produce, these years are never produced and consumed. As a result, the market quantity will be too low relative to the socially efficient level, as seen in Exhibit 9.5, resulting in a deadweight loss.

We can compute the deadweight loss in much the same way as we did in the case of negative externalities. Consider Exhibit 9.5 once again, and let's begin with the equilibrium quantity level, $Q_{market}$. In the free market, this was the unit of production that equated willingness to pay for that unit of education with the marginal cost of producing that unit of education ($40,000 = $40,000). But with the positive externality, we see that the marginal benefit to society is $60,000 ($40,000 private + $20,000 external benefit) for the last unit of education that was purchased. This means that if we would produce that last unit, we would increase social well-being by $20,000 = $60,000 − $40,000 (the marginal social benefit of the last unit minus the marginal social cost of the last unit).

In fact, with the higher marginal benefit due to the positive externalities, we see that we should keep producing because the marginal gains to society are greater than the marginal costs to produce. This reasoning continues until we reach point $Q_{optimal}$. The amount of economic benefit that could be gained if we produced the optimal quantity is shown in the yellow region of the exhibit. This is the area between the marginal social benefit curve and the marginal cost curve between units $Q_{market}$ and $Q_{optimal}$. This area reflects how much society could increase social surplus if it produced at the efficient level. Again, you will notice that deadweight loss takes the form of an arrow-like triangle pointing in the direction that society would prefer.

### Pecuniary Externalities

You might be thinking as you read this chapter that every market action has an externality. For example, if millions of new consumers enter the market and decide to buy iPhones,

## CHOICE
## &CONSEQUENCE

### Positive Externalities in Spots You Never Imagined

Externalities are the result of agents trying to do the best they can and ignoring how their actions affect others. In this sense, it would be wrong to think of externalities as "mistakes." Externalities may result from just *not knowing* the harm we cause others. In this case, we might make choices that we later regret.

Consider the case of flu vaccinations. When you make the decision of whether or not to be vaccinated against the flu, you likely consider only the private benefits and costs from the vaccination—namely, the benefits or costs to yourself. But you are not the only person to incur benefits or costs.

If you decide to take the flu shot, others gain: once you are vaccinated, they are now protected against catching the flu from you. But people can also lose if you choose not to get the shot, because you could catch the flu and spread it. Many of us would not take such externalities—whether positive or negative—into account when making a decision about whether to get a flu shot. But they nevertheless exist.

Researchers who have studied the externalities of vaccinations report quite large effects.[2] For instance, in certain situations, the external effect of you getting a flu shot can be as high as 1.5 infections. Given that approximately

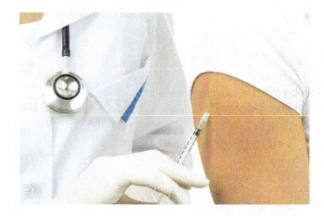

10 percent to 20 percent of the U.S. population contracts the flu each year, this estimate reveals the potential value in flu vaccination programs.

If you find it important to take account of your own externalities, the next time you are weighing your private benefits and costs of getting a flu vaccination, remember that not getting a shot could result in as many as 1.5 more infections for everyone else. In this sense, by avoiding the needle you have imposed a great externality on the rest of the population.

market demand will shift rightward, increasing price. If you were planning on buying an iPhone, these consumers have just imposed a negative externality on you!

This is good intuition. Every market does have this type of externality, at least in the short run. Economists think of this kind of externality as a different species compared to the externality examples above. The two types of externalities we have just studied have much different implications—they create market inefficiencies.

The example of more people buying a good and thereby causing a negative market impact for others is called a *pecuniary externality*. **Pecuniary externalities** exist when market transactions affect other people, but only through the market price. This defining attribute of pecuniary externalities—that they act only through prices—is critically important. It means that pecuniary externalities do not create market inefficiencies. Here's why.

Remember that negative and positive externalities lead to "wrong" equilibrium quantities. They do so because they create an external cost or external benefit that is not reflected in the market price. Pecuniary externalities don't create these effects. Precisely because their impact is completely embodied in prices, the market price *correctly* reflects the society-wide impact of market transactions. You could say that pecuniary externalities are necessary for efficient markets because as goods become more or less scarce, their price should change. Negative and positive externalities, such as pollution and education, cause market inefficiencies, because goods are either over- or under-produced and consumed.

A **pecuniary externality** occurs when a market transaction affects other people only through market prices.

## 9.2 Private Solutions to Externalities

When externalities are present, the market outcome is inefficient. Exhibits 9.3 and 9.5 in the previous section reveal the inefficiencies of not taking externalities into account. Conceptually, the exhibits show the following two important points:

1. When there are negative externalities present, free markets produce and consume too much.
2. When there are positive externalities present, free markets produce and consume too little.

If, in the presence of negative externalities, too much of a good is being produced, and in the presence of positive externalities, too little of a good is being produced, then how does society achieve a more efficient outcome? Several possibilities have emerged—some involve private citizens working it out themselves, while others include government intervention. In this section we consider a number of private solutions.

One fundamental theme unites the multiple solutions to externalities, whether public or private: *internalizing the externality*. When individuals or companies take into account the full costs and benefits of their actions because of some public or private incentive, economists say that they are **internalizing the externality**. When the external effects of their actions are internalized, the general result is that the market equilibrium moves toward higher social well-being.

When agents account for the full costs and benefits of their actions, they are **internalizing the externality**.

To understand how internalizing the externality works in the area of private solutions, we'll consider the scenario of a power plant that is currently emitting tons of toxins in waterways, which adversely affects local fishermen. Place yourself in the seat of a city mayor, and think about what you would do if the fishermen came clamoring to you for help in curbing the plant's emissions.

Your first thought might be to read the city pollution ordinances to check whether there is a law against polluting the waterways. Suppose you find that there is no such regulation—the power plant has the right to pollute for free. Thus, in actuality, the power plant has the right to pollute. Amazing!

Your next thought might be to impose laws that establish new regulations on the power plant. This is most people's first instinct, because a common misperception is that government is the *only* source of change when, in fact, private organizations have affected change for years. Such private solutions to externality problems usually require parties to negotiate with one another or a social enforcement mechanism to be in place. Let's see how bargaining can work.

## Private Solution: Bargaining

To gain a sense of how bargaining can work, let us continue with the power plant and fishermen example. Say you discover the power plant can eliminate the toxins that it emits by purchasing and installing scrubbers (a technology that cleans water and air before they are released into the ecosystem). But scrubbers are expensive to purchase and maintain. The best cost estimate is that over the next decade, the cost of the necessary scrubbers will be $5 million. However, because the power plant holds the right to pollute by law, it does not have to install expensive equipment.

On the other side of the equation are the fishermen. Their scientists tell them the pollution has gotten to such dangerous levels that there is a chance the entire fishing industry could be shut down within a matter of years. Their analysis further tells them that the power plant is, in fact, the main culprit, emitting tons of toxins into the waterways weekly. The fishermen conclude that if they can convince the power plant to install the scrubbers, they will receive benefits over the next decade of approximately $7 million.

In this case, what is the outcome if the fishermen and power plant do not communicate? Left to itself, the power plant is clearly not interested in spending $5 million on scrubbers because it does not gain from such a purchase. As you can see, this market outcome is not socially efficient because total well-being could be increased. In fact, the amount of money left on the table is $2 million ($7 million − $5 million). You might recall from Chapter 8 that you can think of this as the gains to trade.

So does this mean that pollution will continue at the current rate because the power plant has the legal right to do what it desires? Can economics help solve this impasse? As it turns out, economics *does* play a critical role. The legal rights do not have to be the deciding factor; a private deal can be struck.

How can we be so sure? You know that fishermen are willing to pay up to $7 million to rid the waterways of the power plant's pollution, whereas it costs the power plant only $5 million to abate pollution. Therefore, a deal will be brokered in which the fishermen give an amount of money between $5 million and $7 million to the power plant, and the power plant installs and maintains the scrubbers. What is not clear is where exactly in the $5-million to $7-million price range the deal will be struck (as was observed in Chapter 8 about the range of possible terms of trade).

Now let's consider when the opposite case is at work: upon looking into the local ordinances, say that you had found a law against the power plant polluting the waterways. You would have then informed the power plant that it was out of compliance. If it chose at that point not to shut down, it would then have installed the scrubbers, thereby eliminating the water pollution.

The remarkable bottom line is that regardless of whether the law permits the power plant to pollute or not, the economically efficient outcome is achieved either way—the plant installs and maintains the scrubbers, because abating pollution provides the highest social value.

## The Coase Theorem

A **property right** gives someone ownership of a property or resources.

The **Coase Theorem** states that private bargaining will result in an efficient allocation of resources.

This insight—that negotiation leads to the socially efficient outcome regardless of who has the legal **property right** (ownership of property or resources)—is called the **Coase Theorem**, after the Nobel Laureate economist who proposed it, Ronald Coase. The theorem's implication is powerful: private bargaining will lead to an efficient allocation of resources. This means that the person who values ownership the most will end up owning the property right; in other words, the outcome will match his preferences. In this example, since the value of clean water is higher than the cost of scrubbers, private bargaining will lead to an outcome of clean water.

The end result of the Coase Theorem, then, is that government intervention is not necessary to solve externality problems—private bargaining can do the job. Although we reach the efficient outcome regardless of initial property rights, who holds the initial property rights is not irrelevant. This is because the initial property right allocation is an important determinant of the final distribution of surplus.

> **The end result of the Coase Theorem . . . is that government intervention is not necessary to solve externality problems—private bargaining can do the job.**

That said, we should be cautious about relying too much on private solutions to externalities for the following reasons:

1. The assumption that the parties involved—those creating the externality and those suffering from it—can negotiate economically is critically important. This means that as long as the *transaction costs* associated with negotiating aren't too high, the efficient economic outcome can be achieved.

2. Whether the property right is clearly defined is important; in many cases, the law is not clear on who holds it.

3. The number of agents on each side of the bargaining table matters. It's easy enough to imagine that bargaining can lead to an efficient solution with a small number of affected people. But it is more difficult to see how such bargaining could work between, say, a power plant and 100,000 affected fishermen.

The Coase Theorem applied to this situation would say that whether the plant has the right to pollute or the 100,000 fishermen have the right to clean water, the end result will be the efficient amount of water quality. If the plant does have the right to pollute, then 100,000 fishermen must coordinate on how to pay the plant to cut back its emissions. If the fishermen have the right to clean water, then the power plant will have to pay them to be able to emit pollution if that is the efficient solution. But as a practical matter, it is difficult for 100,000 fishermen to somehow negotiate their own agreements with a plant about the allowable level of emissions and who gets compensated. In this case, a governmental rule might be the most efficient means to address the externality. This is because the *transaction costs* associated with bargaining might be too high.

**Transaction costs** are the costs of making an economic exchange.

Hence, even when property rights are perfectly established, the cost of bargaining itself—the **transaction costs** associated with making an economic exchange—might be too high to permit this sort of arrangement from happening. This transaction cost includes not only direct expenditures, such as legal fees and your time, but also the cost of an awkward situation: it might be difficult to walk next door and bargain with your neighbor about the amount of dog droppings his pet can leave on your front yard. With this in mind, we turn to a second popular private means to address the market failure of externalities: social enforcement mechanisms.

## Private Solution: Doing the Right Thing

Does the logo to the left look familiar? If you've seen it on your kitchen appliances, your computer, or your windows, you have approved-energy-efficient products. The ENERGY STAR program is a joint program introduced in 1992 by the U.S. Environmental Protection Agency (EPA) and the U.S. Department of Energy to promote energy-efficient products. ENERGY STAR is a voluntary labeling program designed to identify and promote energy-efficient products to reduce greenhouse-gas emissions. The first kinds of products to be labeled ENERGY STAR were computers and monitors. The program now includes over sixty product categories, including major appliances, office equipment, lighting, and home electronics. Today, you can hardly miss the stickers when entering a workplace.

The ENERGY STAR program has worked both because there are financial incentives associated with such products (reduced electricity cost and potential tax savings) and because it involves a social enforcement mechanism: it gives us information about "green products" and invokes a moral code that you should "do the right thing" and purchase them. No official government regulations tell people that they have to buy ENERGY STAR products, but the substantial growth in the program since 1992 is a testament to the power of motivating people to try to do their part for the environment. In economic language, the moral code of doing one's part is internalizing externalities.

Once you give it some thought, you realize that social enforcement mechanisms are operating all around us and help us take externalities

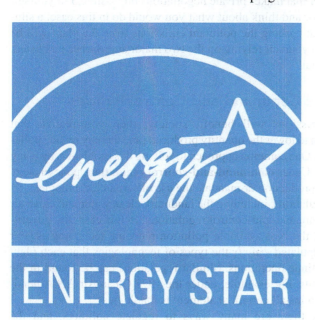

Do you buy ENERGY STAR goods?

into account. For instance, later in this chapter we learn that private organizations, such as the Sierra Club, are quite successful at protecting the environment. The charity Smile Train does incredible work with overseas children who have cleft palates. Closer to home, when waiting in line for a ride at *Disney World* or in a supermarket checkout line, we rarely observe people "line jumping." People generally refrain from that practice not because there is a stiff financial penalty for doing so, but because their actions will likely be frowned on by the people who bear the costs of their rudeness. Such socially imposed costs lead to a reduction in the quantity of line jumping to the net benefit of society. Shame, guilt, and the risk that we will be publicly decried are all effective social enforcement mechanisms. In particular, all these social controls help internalize the negative externality imposed on others, leading to less of such behavior.

Although private solutions can prove quite effective, direct government intervention might be necessary when private interventions fail. Such solutions usually take the form of rules that restrict production in some form, taxation, or requiring permits for production. We now consider several examples of government solutions to externalities.

# 9.3 Government Solutions to Externalities

There are many ways in which markets fail, or at least fall short of the ideal competitive market outcomes described in Exhibits 9.1 and 9.4. Whenever markets fail, policymakers need to consider the following question: can the government bring about a particular outcome more efficiently than the market? We have learned that there are potentially important private solutions to externalities, including bargaining over outcomes and relying on social enforcement mechanisms. Yet these also are apt to fall short in certain situations.

Governments respond to externalities in two main ways:

1. *Command-and-control policies*, in which the government directly regulates the allocation of resources
2. *Market-based policies*, in which the government provides incentives for private organizations to internalize the externality

Let's return to the case of the power plant's release of pollutants. Suppose the plant also emits air pollutants that affect millions of households in neighboring states. In such a case, the costs are dispersed in a manner that makes private negotiations impossible. Put yourself in the shoes of the federal regulator and think about what you would do in this case: a situation in which you are certain that curbing the pollutant emissions from the plant will be beneficial to society. You will find yourself relying on the two major approaches just listed, to which we now turn in more detail.

## Government Regulation: Command-and-Control Policies

If you know that curbing emissions will benefit society, then you realize that $Q_{market} > Q_{optimal}$, and an approach to lower the quantity produced (and thereby reduce pollution) is a step in the right direction. One common approach to solving this problem is by using *command-and-control regulation*. Under **command-and-control regulation**, policymakers either directly restrict the level of production or mandate the use of certain technologies.

Many early environmental regulations, including the landmark clean water and clean air legislation of the 1970s, were command-and-control regulations. In this case, the government required polluters to adopt the best available pollution-reducing technologies. For example, the Clean Water Act stipulated *exactly* the types of technologies that each plant had to install if they were to continue operations. Similar regulations can be found in the various Clean Air Act Amendments. For example, under the 1977 Clean Air Act Amendments, new polluting plants had to install certain abatement technologies.

As you might have guessed, there are many ways to regulate polluters, and the command-and-control technique might not be the most efficient course of regulatory action

**Command-and-control regulation** either directly restricts the level of production or mandates the use of certain technologies.

to curb pollution. For one thing, this type of regulatory action typically provides few incentives for producers to search for more cost-effective ways to reduce pollution. This happens because regulators have directed attention to the wrong target—they mandate the technology that the producer must use. This pushes the producer to develop efficient methods with which to use the mandated technology. Rather than focusing producer efforts on developing cheaper ways to use the mandated technology, the regulator should incentivize producers to find or develop the most cost-effective technologies.

## EVIDENCE-BASED ECONOMICS

## Q: What can the government do to lower the number of earthquakes in Oklahoma?

After reading this question, two things may have come to mind. First, this is ludicrous—the government might be powerful, but it cannot control the number of earthquakes. Second, maybe someone in Alaska or California would care about this problem, but why would Oklahomans? Indeed, until the past decade, Alaska and California dominated the earthquake scene: they each had hundreds more earthquakes that you could feel (magnitude 3 or greater on the Richter scale) than all of the other forty-eight states combined.

Yet recently something extraordinary has happened. Oklahoma, traditionally a seismic-free state, has witnessed an incredible surge of earthquakes. In 2015, Oklahoma had more than 300 times the number of earthquakes than its annual average from 1973 to 2008. Exhibit 9.6 shows the time series for 2000–2015. The average before 2009 was about 2 quakes per year of magnitude 3 or higher, but by 2015 this number had reached 680. This means that in 2015, Oklahoma had more earthquakes than the rest of the continental states combined! Indeed, California had fewer than one-third the number of earthquakes of magnitude 3 or higher in 2015 compared to Oklahoma.

What is behind this earthquake trend? According to scientists F. Rall Walsh and Mark Zoback, the answer lies with the activities of oil and gas companies—specifically, their wastewater disposal.[3] When an oil rig hydraulically fractures rock layers for oil (typically referred to as "fracking"), it produces saltwater as a by-product. This wastewater

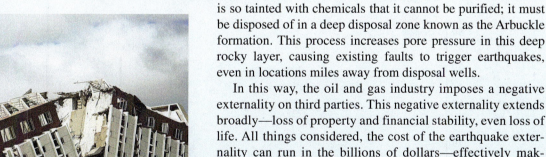

is so tainted with chemicals that it cannot be purified; it must be disposed of in a deep disposal zone known as the Arbuckle formation. This process increases pore pressure in this deep rocky layer, causing existing faults to trigger earthquakes, even in locations miles away from disposal wells.

In this way, the oil and gas industry imposes a negative externality on third parties. This negative externality extends broadly—loss of property and financial stability, even loss of life. All things considered, the cost of the earthquake externality can run in the billions of dollars—effectively making the marginal social cost much higher than the marginal cost that firms face. As we have learned in this chapter, one way to tackle externalities of this sort is via command-and-control regulation.

What would be the shape of such regulation in this case? To answer this question, it is instructive to explore the solutions that the state of Kansas used to tackle its own earthquake problem. Much like Oklahoma, Kansas experienced a sudden increase in seismic activity, as shown in Exhibit 9.7, which plots monthly earthquake activity for earthquake magnitudes of 2–4. Before 2014 seismic activity was virtually nonexistent, but the number of earthquakes exploded in 2014 and 2015.

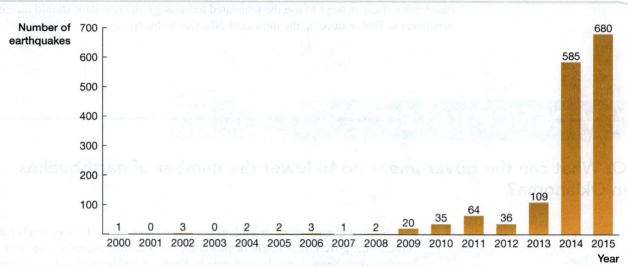

**Exhibit 9.6** The Number of Earthquakes in Oklahoma

Since 2008 the number of earthquakes of magnitude 3 or higher in Oklahoma has grown from an annual average of about 2 to 680.

To tackle its problem, in March 2015 the State of Kansas issued an official order reducing saltwater injection rates. The order implemented a system of graduated mandated limits. The mandated cap was 16,000 barrels of saltwater per day, which was to decrease to 8,000 barrels of saltwater per day within 100 days after the issuance of the order. If the goals were not met, each failure would result in a penalty of up to $10,000 per day of continuing violation.

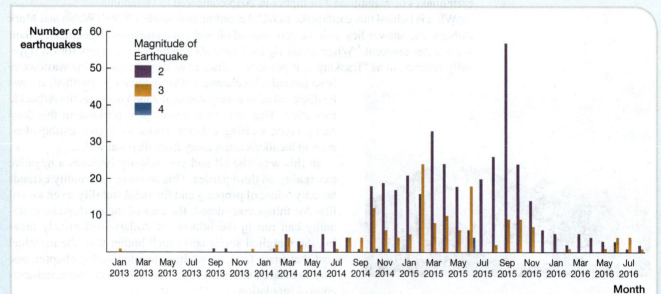

**Exhibit 9.7** Results of the March 2015 Command-and-Control Regulation in Kansas

Comparing the number of earthquakes after the March 2015 policy took effect to the number of pre-policy quakes, we find a significant decrease in earthquakes of magnitudes 2–4. These trends suggest that the Kansas command-and-control regulation helped achieve its goal.

How did this policy work out? Exhibit 9.7 provides some summary details. The exhibit shows that by December 2015, earthquake activity had considerably decreased from the levels of late 2014 and 2015. Indeed, across all magnitude levels—2, 3, and 4—the policy seems to be working quite well. We suspect that if Oklahoma wants to lessen the rumblings felt underground, this is one option that should be considered carefully.

|  |  |  |  |
|---|---|---|---|
| **Question** | **Answer** | **Data** | **Caveat** |
| What can the government do to lower the number of earthquakes in Oklahoma? | It can enact command-and-control regulation to regulate the problem. | Actual policy enacted in Kansas in March 2015 to lower its earthquake frequency. | This is only one of several approaches. Others include private bargaining and market-based solutions. |

## Government Regulation: Market-Based Approaches

A **market-based regulatory approach** internalizes externalities by harnessing the power of market forces.

Given that you are interested in efficient regulation, you decide not to make use of the command-and-control approach and instead turn to a **market-based regulatory approach**. A market-based approach internalizes externalities by harnessing the power of market forces. What does this mean in terms of the power plant scenario? With the market-based approach, the method for reducing pollution is essentially left to the emitter—the power plant itself. Thus, there is a greater incentive to develop new ways to reduce pollution than in the command-and-control approach. The most prominent market-based approaches to dealing with externalities are *corrective taxes* and *subsidies*.

## Corrective Taxes

A **Pigouvian tax**, or a **corrective tax**, is a tax designed to induce agents who produce negative externalities to reduce quantity toward the socially optimal level.

Let's return to the case of the local power plant. Because its production is creating a negative externality, it is producing too much. So you want the power plant to cut back on production, because doing so moves the quantity produced toward the efficient level. You can do this through taxes on the production from the plant. Such government taxes are called **corrective taxes** or **Pigouvian taxes**, named after economist Arthur Pigou, a pioneer in describing how such taxes would work. A corrective tax is a tax designed to induce agents who produce negative externalities to reduce quantity toward the socially optimal level.

Given that you understand there is an externality, what should you do? Your first step is to estimate the marginal external cost. Economists have developed tools to help policymakers calculate such costs, and in the Letting the Data Speak box on page 215 we discuss one example. In this case, let's assume that policymakers estimate the marginal external cost as given in Exhibit 9.8. The next step is to levy a corrective tax in this amount to reduce the equilibrium quantity to the social optimum.

That is, you levy a per-unit tax equal to the marginal external cost of the externality—which is $0.10 per unit, as shown in Exhibit 9.8. Because the level of the tax is equal to the difference between $S$ and MSC, plants now choose a profit-maximizing output that is equal to $Q_{optimal}$. Looked at in another way, the Pigouvian tax creates a virtual market supply curve that is identical to the MSC curve by having each plant consider the externality when making production choices. They consider the externality because they account for the corrective tax when making their production decisions. Thus, the tax exactly aligns private and society's incentives. In effect, the corrective tax internalizes the pollution externality. This results in the efficient market outcome.

## Exhibit 9.8 Effect of a Pigouvian Tax

As a social planner, you understand that you must internalize externalities. One solution is to tax each unit of production by the amount of the negative externality. Such a tax allows the externality to be internalized, resulting in a more efficient outcome.

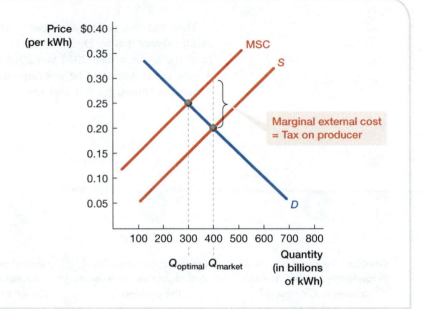

## Corrective Subsidies

**Corrective subsidies**, or **Pigouvian subsidies**, are designed to induce agents who produce positive externalities to increase quantity toward the socially optimal level.

The same reasoning that holds for negative externalities also applies to positive externalities: the government can use **corrective subsidies**, or **Pigouvian subsidies,** to internalize the externality. A **corrective subsidy** is designed to induce agents who produce positive externalities to increase quantity toward the socially optimal level. In the case of positive externalities, a subsidy is used to correct the externality.

Let's return to the case of education, which is shown in Exhibit 9.9. In this case, what should you do? Much like when there is a negative externality, you need to first estimate the marginal social benefit of education. After doing so, the next step is to levy a corrective subsidy in this amount to increase the equilibrium quantity to the social optimum.

That is, you levy a per-unit subsidy equal to the marginal social benefit of the externality—which is $20,000 per year, as shown in Exhibit 9.9. This is the difference between D and MSB. Again, because the level of the subsidy is equal to this difference,

## Exhibit 9.9 Effect of a Pigouvian Subsidy on the Education Market

By introducing Pigouvian subsidies, the government can increase the equilibrium quantity. This subsidy moves us toward a more efficient outcome.

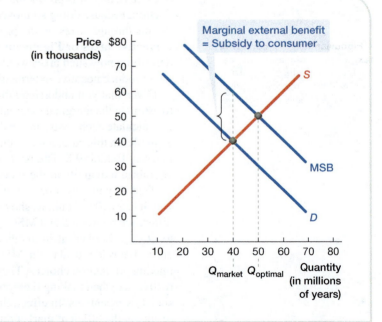

# LETTING THE
## DATA SPEAK

### How to Value Externalities

A key challenge to policymakers is estimating the external costs or benefits of an activity. For instance, in the case of air pollution from the local power plant, how do policymakers know the costs of lower air quality? One approach is to examine how prices of goods that trade in markets are affected by air quality. This is exactly what economists Kenneth Chay and Michael Greenstone did to evaluate the value of cleaning up various types of air pollution after implementation of the Clean Air Act of 1970.[4] Before 1970, there was little federal regulation of air pollution, and the issue was not high on the agendas of state legislators. As a result, many counties allowed factories to operate without any regulation on their pollution, and in several heavily industrialized counties, pollution had reached very high levels. In particular, in many urban counties, air pollution, as measured by the total amount of suspended particles, had reached dangerous levels.

The Clean Air Act established guidelines for what constituted excessively high levels of five particularly dangerous pollutants. According to these guidelines, the Environmental Protection Agency and the states would enforce reductions of total suspended particle quantities in noncompliant counties. Following the Act in 1970 and the 1977 amendment that strengthened the implementation of the Act, requiring any increasing emissions coming from new investments to be offset by reductions in emissions from other sources in the same county, there were improvements in air quality (again gauged by total suspended particle measure).

Chay and Greenstone investigated how housing prices changed in the counties where, because of the Clear Air Act, air quality improved significantly. They found significant improvements in house prices (and no appreciable change in average county incomes). As a result, they estimate that there was approximately $45 billion aggregate increase in housing values because of the Clean Air Act. Policymakers make use of such estimates to help guide their choices of corrective taxes and subsidies.

individuals now have an incentive to choose the socially efficient level of education, or $Q_{optimal}$. In this manner, the Pigouvian subsidy creates a virtual demand curve that is identical to the MSB curve by having individuals consider the externality when making their education choices. You consider the externality because when deciding whether to obtain more years of schooling, you take account of the corrective subsidy. Thus, the subsidy exactly aligns your and society's incentives. In effect, the corrective subsidy internalizes the positive externality. This results in the efficient market outcome.

As you likely know firsthand, such incentives are often used as policy tools. The federal government subsidizes education tremendously, beginning in pre-kindergarten classes and up through PhD programs. The creative ways in which such government subsidies are structured range from funding public education to special government college scholarships to highly subsidized school loans. All of this occurs because the government is trying to encourage education in an attempt to correct the market failure that occurs when you make your education choices.

In sum, externalities potentially drive a wedge between social benefits and costs and private benefits and costs. This wedge creates a distortion (deadweight loss) if the quantity levels of the free market equilibrium diverge from those of the social optimum. Corrective taxes and subsidies can cause agents to internalize their externalities. In using such taxes, the government raises tax revenues, but that is not its main goal. Rather, it is attempting to align private and social incentives. To do so, it critically relies on estimates of externalities. A vibrant area of research in economics continues to develop to estimate the costs and benefits of externalities. How would you estimate the dollar value of externalities?

An informed citizenry can lead to better political outcomes.

# DATA SPEAK

## Pay as You Throw: Consumers Create Negative Externalities Too!

If you have any roommates, you're probably well aware of a perfect setting for a Pigouvian tax: trash. With a trash can stuffed full by multiple roommates, it's often a lot of work to carry the bag of trash out to the dumpster or trash can. Sometimes roommates anticipate this cost and just let the trash in the can pile higher and higher.

Ultimately someone has to take it out, though, and there is often no great mechanism to incentivize this behavior. Cities have a similar problem, but on a much more massive scale. Namely, people buy and throw out tons of stuff, and disposing of all that trash isn't free. In an attempt to reduce this waste and the cost it imposes, cities have adopted Pigouvian taxes that have been called "Pay-As-You-Throw." These programs charge people a small price for each bag of trash that they produce. That price, of course, is the cost to the city for disposing of each bag, and in theory, this sort of tax should move people to internalize the cost of their negative externality.

Pay-As-You-Throw programs have been run in 4,032 communities in 43 states, covering about 10 percent of the population of the United States, and the overwhelming conclusion is that these programs reduce the amount of trash people throw out. One survey of communities suggested that moving to a Pay-As-You-Throw program reduced household trash by more than a ton per year![5]

This reduction comes in part from a reduction in waste creation but also from an increase in recycling. All told, the Pigouvian tax on trash does seem to accomplish what Pigou theorized so long ago—that with a corrective tax, consumer decisions will start to move toward the social optimum.

# 9.4 Public Goods

Many people from the Midwest are familiar with the blare of a tornado siren signaling that a funnel cloud is swirling toward their city. Once the siren sounds, no one can exclude others from hearing it, and one person hearing the siren does not affect the ability of others to hear it. These two properties—that no one can prevent others from consumption and that one person's consumption doesn't prevent another person's consumption—distinguish *public goods*. They are different from the goods we've studied so far—*private goods*—which are traded in markets where buyers and sellers meet and, if they agree on price, ownership is transferred.

To understand the nature of a public good, it is useful to compare and contrast public goods and private goods in more detail. There are two characteristics that differentiate them:

**Once a non-excludable good is produced, it is not possible to exclude people from using the good.**

1. **Excludability.** Private goods are excludable, meaning that people can be kept from consuming them if they have not paid for them. Public goods are **non-excludable**, meaning that once such goods are produced, it is not possible to exclude people from using them.

**A non-rival good is a good whose consumption by one person does not prevent consumption by others.**

2. **Rivalry in consumption.** Private goods are rival in consumption, meaning that they cannot be consumed by more than one person at a time. Public goods are **non-rival in consumption**, meaning that one person's consumption does not preclude consumption by others.

**A public good is both non-rival and non-excludable.**

To summarize, we can say that private goods are excludable and rival in consumption and **public goods** are non-excludable and non-rival in consumption.

Exhibit 9.10 aids us in thinking about different types of goods in the economy based on their degree of excludability and rivalry. Let's look at the four categories of goods in the exhibit in more detail.

1. Ordinary private goods, shown in the upper-left corner of Exhibit 9.10, are both highly excludable and highly rival in consumption. Think about a Snickers candy bar that

## Exhibit 9.10 Four Types of Goods

Goods can be classified along two features: excludability and rivalry. Excludability decreases from left to right, whereas rivalry in consumption decreases from top to bottom.

| | | Excludability | |
|---|---|---|---|
| | | High | Low |
| Rivalry | High | Ordinary private goods (e.g., clothes, food, furniture) | Common pool resource goods (e.g., fish, water, natural forests, food at a picnic) |
| | Low | Club goods (e.g., cable TV, pay-per-view TV, Wi-Fi, music downloads) | Public goods (e.g., national defense, early warning systems, earth protection programs) |

you have just purchased at the book store: once you purchase and eat that specific candy bar, no one else can; you have perfectly excluded others from buying that particular Snickers bar. Thus, your consumption has reduced the ability of another person to consume the candy bar; in fact, your consumption has created a one-to-one reduction in Snickers bars available to others. A large fraction of the goods and services that we buy and sell in the market economy have these same properties, and that is why we have implicitly assumed this to be the case when modeling demand and supply in previous chapters.

**2.** In the lower-left corner of the exhibit, we find another category of goods—those that are highly excludable but non-rival in consumption. We call such excludable, non-rival goods **club goods**—economists also commonly refer to them as "artificially scarce" goods. For instance, perhaps after you read this chapter, you will turn on the television to watch your favorite cable television show. In so doing, you will not affect the ability of others to watch that same show. Therefore, cable TV is a non-rival good, because many people can watch at the same time without disrupting the ability of others to watch. However, individuals can be excluded from watching cable TV if they do not pay for the service. Thus, it is a good that is excludable. Club goods present a bit of a conundrum when sold as a private good. They are non-rival, so the marginal cost of providing one extra unit is small (perhaps even zero), but they tend to require large fixed costs, like wiring cable all around the world for cable TV. If sold at marginal cost, firms would never cover the large fixed costs they bear. Consumers often have a positive willingness-to-pay for such goods, though. As a result, club goods typically are not sold in perfectly competitive markets.

> A **club good** is non-rival but excludable.

**3.** The upper-right corner shows a category of goods called **common pool resource goods**, which are non-excludable but rival in consumption. For instance, an open-access lake is available to all fishermen, but the fish they catch cannot be caught by another fisherman and are thus rival. Likewise, if you are at a picnic, what happens when the hamburgers run out? You must settle for your second choice, a hot dog. We discuss this type of good in further detail later in the chapter.

> **Common pool resource goods** are a class of goods that are rival and non-excludable.

**4.** A much different class of goods appears in the lower-right corner of the exhibit—public goods. Recall that they are goods that are non-rival in consumption and are non-excludable. Consider protecting the earth from climate change. Governments around the world spend billions of dollars annually to curb harmful greenhouse gases. Even if people failed to pay their taxes to support such environmental programs, governments cannot exclude them from enjoying the benefits. That is, while cable television is an excludable good, enjoying earth's comfortable climate is not. National defense and local warning systems are other examples of public goods that we enjoy daily.

Public goods present particular problems for markets to provide because consumers do not see the value proposition in buying them. When purchasing a Nintendo DS, it is clear what you get for your $100. What are you getting if you send in $100 to the U.S. government for national defense? You will be protected by the Defense Department regardless of whether you sent in the cash. And because your $100 makes no appreciable difference between a successful and unsuccessful national defense system, you likely will not send in $100 in the first place. Why send $100 to the U.S. government and receive little in return when you can send the same $100 to Amazon.com and get a Nintendo DS game system?

A **free-rider problem** occurs when an individual who has no incentive to pay for a good does not pay for that good because nonpayment does not prevent consumption.

This example represents a key problem with efficiently providing public goods: we want them, but we aren't willing to pay for them because we can't be excluded from consuming them once they are provided. And the same is true for everyone. Thus, public goods suffer from what economists call a **free-rider problem**, in which a person has no incentive to pay for a good because failure to pay doesn't prevent consumption. Free riders either consume more than their fair share or pay less than their fair share of the good's cost.

Such cases represent situations in which government intervention can potentially raise social surplus. But how much of the public good should the government provide if it wants to maximize social surplus? Are there other ways to provide it? We turn to these questions now.

### Government Provision of Public Goods

What makes public goods different from private goods is precisely their non-rival and non-excludable nature. Their non-excludability represents a distinct opportunity for government to step in and provide them because it can levy taxes for their provision. Standard cost-benefit logic applies to the case of providing public goods: the government should expand production until marginal benefits equal marginal costs. That is, if the marginal benefits exceed the marginal costs of providing the next unit, it should be provided.

Conceptually we can calculate the optimal level of public good provision once we know the market demand curve and the marginal costs associated with providing various levels of a public good. To construct the market demand curve, we must first know the individual demand curves. Before doing so, let's revisit how we constructed the market demand curve for private goods.

Recall that in that case we added horizontally. That is, we summed the total quantity demanded of all consumers at a given price to compute the market demand at that price.

---

## CHOICE & CONSEQUENCE

### The Free-Rider's Dilemma

Imagine that you and nine other students walk into an economics lab experiment with the hope of earning some cash. The moderator gives each of you $10 and explains that you can anonymously, and simultaneously, contribute any portion of it back to a public goods (or group) account. The contributions collected will be doubled and then redistributed equally among you and the nine other students.[6]

For example, if you each contribute half of your endowment, or $5, to the group account, it then contains $50 = 10 × $5. After the doubling, that would mean that $100 is to be split equally among all 10 players. In the end, you walk away with $15: $10 from the group account and the $5 you opted not to put into the group account.

How much of your $10 would you contribute?

It is clear that to maximize the group's take-home earnings, everyone should contribute the full $10 to the group fund. This would increase the total money earned in the experiment from $100 to $200, or $20 per person. Why, then, do experiments show that contributions average less than $2, with around half the participants contributing nothing?

For the group, the marginal benefit of contributing outweighs the marginal cost of contributing. But for the individual, that isn't the case. If you give $1 to the group account, then the group as a whole receives $2 (a marginal benefit of $1), but you yourself are only guaranteed 20 cents of that dollar back. That is, by contributing that $1 to the group account, you cost yourself 80 cents!

Armed with this knowledge, you can see that you can maximize your take-home earnings by contributing *nothing* to the group account.

Let's walk through a simple illustration. Let's just assume that everyone else contributes everything to the group account. What are your payoffs if you contribute nothing versus if you contribute everything?

Contribute zero payoff:

$$\$10 + \frac{\$90 \times 2}{10} = \$28.$$

Contribute everything payoff:

$$\$0 + \frac{\$100 \times 2}{10} = \$20.$$

As you can see, by free riding and contributing nothing to the public good, you are $8 better off versus when you contribute everything.

Because the same incentives are alive in the real world when it comes to public goods, it is not surprising that many of us are free riders!

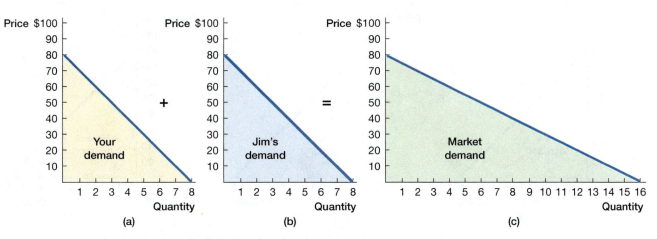

**Exhibit 9.11 Constructing a Market Demand Curve for a Private Good**

To derive the market demand curve, we find how much quantity you and Jim demand at a given price and then sum horizontally to depict the market demand curve.

Exhibit 9.11 provides a summary example of a two-person market. Panel (a) contains your demand curve for pairs of jeans, and panel (b) contains Jim's demand curve for pairs of jeans. For simplicity, both curves are drawn smoothly even though it would be hard for you to buy 2.5 pairs of jeans. At a price of $50, you demand 3 pairs and Jim demands 3 pairs. This leads to a total market demand of 6 pairs at $50, as depicted in panel (c) of the exhibit. After summing all quantities demanded horizontally, we are left with the market demand curve in panel (c).

Construction of the market demand curve for public goods follows similar logic. However, the nature of public goods' non-rivalry and non-excludability matters a great deal when moving from the individual to the market demand curve for public goods. Instead of summing horizontally, as is the case for private goods, the market demand for public goods is found by *vertically* summing the individual demand curves. This is necessary because the public good is non-rival, so you and Jim can each consume every unit of the good at the same time. Therefore, to arrive at a market demand curve, we add the individual demand curves vertically because this gives us a measure of the amount of money consumers are willing to pay for each unit of the public good.

Let's put this intuition into action. Assume that we are again talking about you and Jim, but now we are considering the demand for space missions, a public good that potentially leads to new insights, which are non-excludable and non-rival, that will benefit all humankind (by unlocking the mysteries of space). For comparison purposes, assume that you and Jim have exactly the same demand curve for space missions as you had for jeans, again made smooth for simplicity.

Exhibit 9.12 shows your demand curve for space missions in panel (a), Jim's in panel (b), and the market demand curve for the public good in panel (c). At each level of public good provision, the market demand curve tells us how much the market would be willing to pay for an additional unit of the public good.

As you can see, because you value the first space mission at $80, and Jim also values it at $80, the total marginal benefit for this first space mission trip is $160, as shown in panel (c). This is called the market demand for one unit because it is the total amount of money consumers are willing to pay for the first unit of the public good. Likewise, you value the third space mission at $50, and Jim values it at $50. Therefore, the marginal benefit to society of this third space mission is $100, as shown in panel (c). In other words, prices are summed at each quantity level on the individual demand curves to derive the market demand curve for public goods.

To compute exactly how much of the public good the government should provide, the supply (marginal cost curve) of space missions must be plotted alongside the market demand curve for space missions. We do this in Exhibit 9.13. To compute the equilibrium level of space missions, we follow our decision principles discussed earlier: we should expand

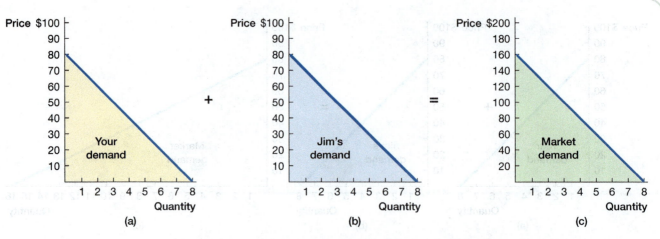

Exhibit 9.12 Constructing a Market Demand Curve for a Public Good

Public goods need to be valued based on the marginal benefit that a single unit of the good provides to society. For this reason, market demand curves for public goods are added along the vertical axis, producing a total willingness to pay for each unit of the public good.

the number of space missions until the marginal benefit equals the marginal cost, which occurs at $Q_{optimal}$ in Exhibit 9.13. At this point, total surplus is maximized, because all the gains in the market are reaped. This is because quantity demanded equals quantity supplied, or marginal benefits equal marginal costs. In Chapter 10 we explore the different ways in which the government can raise funds to pay for public goods such as space missions.

## Private Provision of Public Goods

Over breakfast, you might listen to National Public Radio (NPR). If so, you likely have learned about the rain forests of Borneo, Indonesia, or the Amazon, which are being purchased by private organizations in an attempt to preserve them from being clear-cut. Or perhaps you have heard about recent breakthroughs of researchers working to cure cancer. Each of these activities, and many more that provide private goods with positive externalities or provide public goods, are funded by private sources.

Although governments importantly provide public goods, they are not the sole providers. Many public goods are routinely provided through other channels, such as private

Exhibit 9.13 The Equilibrium Point for Providing a Public Good

Once the market demand and supply (marginal cost) curves for space missions are set, we can rely on the decision rules that we've learned so far to find the optimal amount of space missions for society. This quantity will be at the intersection of the market demand and market supply curves, where the marginal benefit of the last space mission equals the marginal cost.

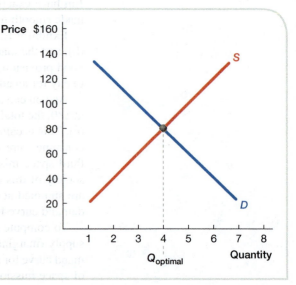

**Private provision of public goods** takes place when private citizens make contributions to the production or maintenance of a public good.

donations, which are indeed an effective way to provide public goods. **Private provision of public goods** refers to any situation in which private citizens make contributions to the production or maintenance of a public good. Many avenues exist for such provision, but the most important is through private donations of time and money. For example, through private donations NPR is made available throughout the United States. Globally, rain forests are being saved through private cash donations to the World Wildlife Fund. Cures for ailments ranging from carpal tunnel syndrome to heart disease have been financed in part by individuals donating dollars to research funds. Likewise, Wikipedia is maintained by the masses donating their time and knowledge.

So what is the scope of private donations of money? Exhibit 9.14 shows the tremendous growth in charitable giving in the United States over a 44-year period. Since 1971, individual contributions to charitable causes have increased from roughly $125 billion annually to approximately $375 billion per year by 2015. Even though the recent giving levels already represent an important fraction of our economy, experts predict that the combination of increased wealth and an aging population will lead to an even higher level of giving in the coming years.

But there is more to the world than just the United States. How does giving in the United States compare to giving rates in other countries around the world? We must be careful when making such comparisons; differences could arise because some countries use taxes to fund more public goods than others. In this case, all else being equal, we should expect low-tax countries to have fewer public goods provided by the government and more public goods provided by charitable giving. Likewise, many people volunteer time to a charitable cause rather than give money. With such considerations in mind, we consider one of the most comparable data sets across countries. In 2010, the polling company Gallup asked people all over the world one simple question: "have you donated money to a charity in the past month?" Exhibit 9.15 shows that a majority of people answered "yes" in developed regions. Even in underdeveloped regions, the proportion of people giving is above 10 percent, suggesting that donations to charity are an important phenomenon all over the world.

You might be thinking that, considering the voluntary nature of giving, this form of public good provision might be preferable to governments providing public goods. But we should be careful with this line of reasoning, because certain important public goods, such as national defense or local weather alerts, might be considerably underprovided if left to private sources.

An example can help us understand the danger of leaving public good provision entirely in the hands of the private market. Many scientists believe that species are currently going extinct at a faster rate than at any time in the history of our planet, with the exception of cataclysmic encounters, such as collisions with extraterrestrial objects or massive volcanic eruptions. To deal with this problem, hundreds of conservation groups have been

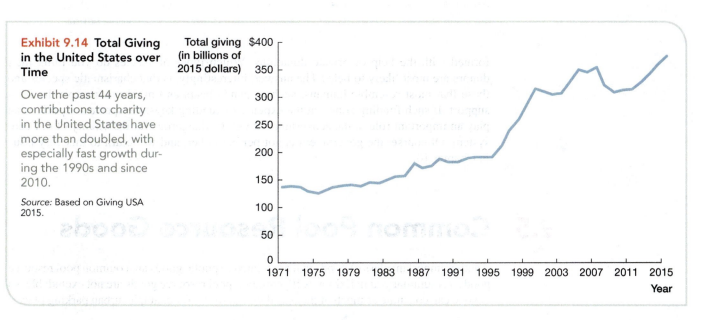

**Exhibit 9.14** Total Giving in the United States over Time

Over the past 44 years, contributions to charity in the United States have more than doubled, with especially fast growth during the 1990s and since 2010.

*Source:* Based on Giving USA 2015.

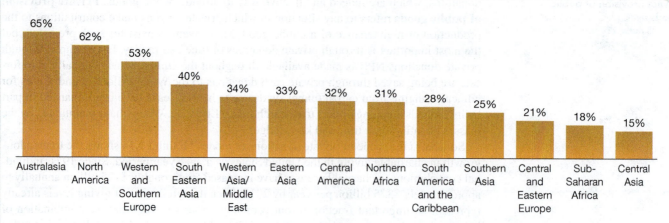

Australasia 65% · North America 62% · Western and Southern Europe 53% · South Eastern Asia 40% · Western Asia/Middle East 34% · Eastern Asia 33% · Central America 32% · Northern Africa 31% · South America and the Caribbean 28% · Southern Asia 25% · Central and Eastern Europe 21% · Sub-Saharan Africa 18% · Central Asia 15%

**Exhibit 9.15 Giving Money by Region of the World in 2010**

The percentage of people answering "yes" to the question, "have you donated money to a charity in the past month?" is depicted here by world region. For example, 65 percent of people surveyed in Australasia (Australia, New Zealand, New Guinea, and neighboring islands) answered "yes."

**Which Species Would You Rather Preserve?**

Potential donors tend to support charismatic species, such as panda bears, rather than keystone species, such as ochre sea stars, that do not have as much visual appeal.

formed with the help of private donations. Which types of species do you think their donors are most likely to help? The answer, interestingly, is that charismatic species and those that most resemble humans, such as panda bears and monkeys, receive the most support. If such funding comes at the expense of funding keystone species—species that play an important role in the ecosystem—it will be dangerous for the vitality of our ecosystem. Of course, the government is not perfect either, and we return to this very issue in Chapter 10.

## 9.5 Common Pool Resource Goods

Another important class of goods that are related to public goods are common pool resource goods. As summarized in Exhibit 9.10, common pool resource goods are not excludable, so anyone can consume as much of them as they can find—for example, urban parking places, coral reefs, and hamburgers at a student picnic. Unfortunately, common pool resources *are* rival goods, meaning that every Diet Coke that Jack drinks at the student party results in one less Diet Coke for others to drink. This leads to an important negative externality that Jack imposes on all others.

The externality involved with a common pool resource arises because of the combination of open access and depletion through use. When deciding how much to fish in a lake, for example, people using the lake consider only their own private marginal costs of use—even though this use depletes the resource for everyone. This is a classic negative externality: individuals use too much of the resource, because they do not consider how others are affected. This result is analogous to the free-market equilibrium quantity being higher than the optimal equilibrium quantity in our earlier examples of negative externalities. Because each person who accesses the lake creates this same externality, the total use of the lake is above what is socially optimal.

Other examples abound in the world around us: too much water is extracted from aquifers, too many trees are cut on public lands, too many communications devices jam airwaves, too many donuts are eaten by one individual from the office donut box, and so on. Such overuse can result in the **tragedy of the commons**, which occurs when a common resource is used too intensely. In some cases, the consequences of this overuse can be severe: instead of preserving a sustainable fishery, for example, overfishing can destroy entire populations and even whole species. It's not that fishermen prefer to drive their prey to extinction; in fact, they obviously would prefer a viable population. But depletion like this can result because of the presence of a negative externality—in this case, too many users of the resource.

Solutions to the tragedy of the commons are similar to those discussed earlier in the chapter for some types of externalities. These interventions can be used by governments or other organized public or private regulatory bodies. For example, a Pigouvian tax can be applied to every fish that is taken out of Lake Michigan. Or, because users of common pool resources have incentives to join together to self-regulate use of the resource, it might be possible for people to organize a system that implements a maximum catch in any given year.

When feasible, outright privatization of the resource—turning its control over to a single owner—can also work. Ownership eliminates the externality problem, because any depletion from use is borne by the owner, who controls access to the resource. It gives the owner

The **tragedy of the commons** results when common pool resources are dramatically overused.

# CHOICE
## &CONSEQUENCE

### Tragedy of the Commons

In medieval times property rights were poorly defined. Typically, royalty controlled all the property and used arcane mechanisms to divvy up land for use. The fact that the market was not allowed to act led to some bizarre practices, perhaps none as famous among social scientists as the management of feeding livestock.

Livestock were the lifeblood of any community, offering dairy and meat, but this came at a cost: livestock had to be fed, typically by grazing the land. And those who owned livestock were frequently required to feed them in a common patch of land.

This reliance on common land led to perverse incentives. In particular, owners of livestock could purchase an extra goat or cow and reap all the rewards privately. That extra livestock had to graze somewhere, though, and the cost of lost grazing land was borne equally by all in the community. Thus, the common grazing area would slowly but surely be overused.

This phenomenon became known as the *tragedy of the commons*, a term popularized by an ecologist, Garrett Hardin, but the example of livestock overgrazing common land comes from a nineteenth-century essay by the early British economist William Forster Lloyd.[7]

What makes the tragedy of the commons so tragic isn't just economic inefficiencies. It's that, in the worst case, the owners of livestock could one day find themselves with nowhere to feed their animals because of overgrazing. The same perverse incentive structure is at work in many real-world situations.

Can you name some? What economic tools can we use to solve the tragedy of the commons?

incentives to regulate access in a way that maximizes the resource's value to the owner. Because efficient use of the resource creates the biggest "pie" for the owner—that is, maximizes what users are collectively willing to pay to access it—the owner has the incentive to encourage an efficient level of use.

# CHOICE
## &CONSEQUENCE

### The Race to Fish

Imagine that you are a fisherman who owns a private pond fully stocked with 100 bluegill fish. Because you own the property rights to the pond, you are the only one who can fish at the pond. Therefore, you can catch as many bluegill as you want. But you know that in the late spring in 70°F water, the female deposits around 40,000 eggs in a shallow nest near the sandy shore. Two to six days later, the eggs hatch, and the male guards the young fry during their first days.

Knowing this, how many fish will you catch?

You will likely decide not to catch all the bluegill, instead leaving many in the pond to restock your supply for the next season.

Now imagine that this pond is a common pool resource—anyone and everyone can fish from it, and one more fish on another angler's line means one less fish on yours. Would you still be careful to leave a lot of fish in the pond for next season?

Both real-world situations and lab experiments conducted by Nobel Laureate Elinor Ostrom have shown us that you probably wouldn't.[8] After all, if you decide to leave, say, fifty fish in the pond, who is to stop another fisherman from catching those fish?

This line of thinking may lead everyone to keep fishing until there is absolutely nothing left. As you just learned,

this type of situation is referred to as the tragedy of the commons; a dilemma in which multiple individuals acting in their own self-interest deplete a shared limited resource, when in the long run it isn't in anyone's best interest to do so.

How might the fishermen in our example prevent this from happening?

EVIDENCE-BASED ECONOMICS

9.1

9.2

9.3

9.4

9.5

## Q: How can the Queen of England lower her commute time to Wembley Stadium?

In the late 1990s, traffic became so congested in central London that travel times spiked above the nineteenth-century average—before the introduction of the car![9] Elected on a reformist platform, London's mayor vowed to make a strong play for fixing London's traffic woes once and for all.

As we have learned in this chapter, the basic theory behind externalities is straightforward: if there is a negative externality that you wish to solve, a Pigouvian tax can internalize the externality. In this case, the negative externality is that drivers enter the road without regard to how their presence is affecting others. Thus, a Pigouvian tax can help lesson the congestion problem.

This may sound simple, but translating economic theory to the real world can sometimes be challenging. One problem to be solved in London was how to charge for use of the roads. Simple tollbooths can often create just as many traffic jams as they are tasked to prevent.

Another question to answer was what the size of the tax should be. London settled for a daily flat charge of 5 pounds per day (although this was later increased to 10 pounds per day with hybrid vehicles paying no tax).[10] This fee was called a "congestion charge." Although one might argue that instead of a daily usage tax the government should have charged a mileage-based tax, policymakers decided that for the sake of simplicity, they would charge a daily usage tax. And to avoid creating unnecessary congestion, the daily charge would be enforced with the use of video cameras at roads on the outside of the city. Drivers would have to buy a daily pass at retail outlets, online, or with their cell phones, and drivers caught without having a daily pass were charged heavy fines.

How did it all turn out? Exhibit 9.16 provides some summary details. Comparing traffic patterns the year before the congestion charge was implemented to the year after, total traffic had been reduced by 12 percent, and this gain was mostly due to lower automobile traffic. All in all, economists estimated that the congestion charges had reduced traffic

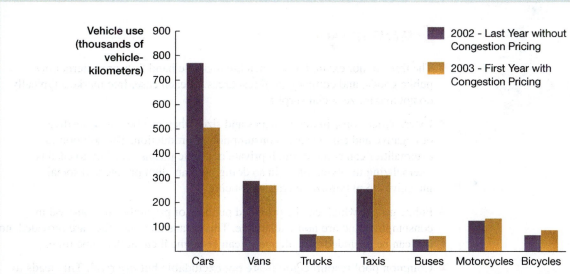

**Exhibit 9.16 Results of the Congestion Charge**

Comparing total kilometers traveled by different types of vehicles just before and just after the introduction of congestion pricing shows that drivers of private vehicles (cars, vans, and trucks) all reduced their vehicle use, whereas drivers of taxis, low-emission vehicles (motorcycles and bicycles), and high-occupancy vehicles (buses) all increased their use. Taken together, these trends suggest that London's congestion charge helped achieve the mayor's goal.

circulating in the city center by 15 percent and traffic entering the zone by 18 percent. Also important in analyzing the benefits of the policy was its impact on the reliability of travel (or the variability of travel time), which improved by an average of 30 percent.

As Exhibit 9.16 shows, the introduction of the congestion tax had the effect of increasing the use of public transportation. As drivers became discouraged from driving into the city because of the congestion charge, they began relying on buses. In addition, more people chose to travel by bicycle. All in all, the program has been a huge success; the Queen of England can now get to Wembley Stadium to watch a Rolling Stones concert in a more timely fashion!

If mayors of American cities would like to achieve similar success, they might wish to take London as an example. However, they should be aware of the political landmines they will face along the way. A similar plan was put forward by New York City Mayor Michael Bloomberg, who proposed the introduction of congestion pricing in Manhattan. The plan was greeted with much resistance; it was blocked by the New York State legislature, and with Mayor Bloomberg's retirement, the congestion tax is no longer being considered. In Chapter 10, we dive deeper into government taxation and learn why taxes have their critics.

| **Question** | **Answer** | **Data** | **Caveat** |
|---|---|---|---|
| How can the Queen of England lower her commute time to Wembley Stadium? | She can convince the mayor of London to enact a tax on automobiles in and around London. | Actual policy enacted in London in the late 1990s and still in place today serves as a model. | This is only one of several approaches. Others include private solutions, such as social mechanisms and voluntary compliance. |

## Summary

- The three major examples of when the invisible hand fails are externalities, public goods, and common pool resources. In each case, free markets typically do not maximize social surplus.

- Externalities come in many shapes and sizes: they can be either positive or negative and can occur in consumption or production. The solution to externalities can come through private or public means. The key to each is internalizing the externality; in so doing, we can align private and social incentives to maximize overall well-being.

- Public goods, which can be provided publicly or privately, are non-rival in consumption and are non-excludable. This means that once they are provided, no one can be excluded, and all agents can consume them at the same time.

- Common pool resource goods are not excludable but *are* rival. This leads to an important negative externality that one person imposes on all others: once the bluegill is taken out of the stream, no one else can catch it. Therefore, solutions to common pool resource problems mirror solutions to externalities.

- A key link between externalities, public goods, and common pool resources is that there is a difference between the private benefits and costs and the social benefits and costs.

# Key Terms

externality *p. 202*
pecuniary externality *p. 207*
internalizing the externality *p. 207*
property right *p. 208*
Coase Theorem *p. 208*
transaction costs *p. 209*
command-and-control regulation *p. 210*

market-based regulatory approach
   *p. 213*
corrective taxes or Pigouvian taxes
   *p. 213*
corrective subsidies or Pigouvian
   subsidies *p. 214*
non-excludable goods *p. 216*

non-rival goods *p. 216*
public goods *p. 216*
club goods *p. 217*
common pool resource goods *p. 217*
free-rider problem *p. 218*
private provision of public goods *p. 221*
tragedy of the commons *p. 223*

# Questions

*All questions are available in* MyEconLab *for practice and instructor assignment.*

1. Why are externalities called market failures? Are pecuniary externalities also an example of market failure?

2. Explain whether the following are examples of externalities.

   a. Alisha did not sleep well, because her neighbor was playing loud music.

   b. Rochelle was late for a job interview, because her alarm did not go off.

   c. José, who is allergic to pollen, is sick from the flowers that grow in his garden.

3. If the production of a particular good causes a negative externality, would the equilibrium quantity in a competitive market be less than the efficient quantity or would it be greater than the efficient quantity?

4. What does it mean to say that an individual or firm has internalized an externality?

5. What is the Coase Theorem? Under what conditions will the Coase Theorem break down?

6. How does a command-and-control policy differ from a market-based policy?

7. What are Pigouvian taxes and subsidies? How do governments decide when to levy a tax or provide a subsidy?

8. Classify the following goods as private goods, common pool resources, club goods, or public goods.

   a. Health insurance

   b. Radio spectrum

   c. A video on YouTube

   d. A mosquito control program in a city

   e. A library's collection of e-books

9. How do public goods differ from common pool resources? Explain.

10. Why is it difficult for the market to deliver socially efficient quantities of goods like clean air or street lighting?

11. When does the free-rider problem arise?

12. Why is the market demand curve for public goods calculated as a vertical summation of individual demand curves?

13. What is meant by the tragedy of the commons? Use an example to explain your answer.

# Problems

*All problems are available in* MyEconLab *for practice and instructor assignment.*

1. The European Union banned certain pesticides for 2 years after studies found links between the use of these insecticides and a decline in the bee population. In particular, research has shown that the use of imidacloprid, clothianidin, and thiamethoxam on flowering crops has adversely affected the honeybee population in North America and Europe.

   a. Consider the private market for these pesticides. Use supply and demand curves to show the equilibrium level of pesticides that will be produced and consumed.

   b. How might the impact of the insecticide on honeybees be modeled as a marginal external cost? Show

   the deadweight loss from this externality in the graph you drew for part (a) of this question.

   c. Is the private market outcome socially efficient?

2. A friend in your environmental economics study group suggests that taxes on pollution are ineffective because they do not eliminate *all* pollution. Based on the ideas from this chapter, explain what is wrong with this argument. Should the goal of any policy be to eliminate all pollution? If not, what should be the goal?

3. Jones and Smith live in the same apartment building. Jones loves to play his opera recordings so loudly that

Smith can hear them. Smith hates opera. Jones receives $100 worth of benefits from his music, and Smith suffers $60 worth of damages.

  **a.** From an efficiency perspective, should Jones be allowed to play his opera music?

  **b.** Suppose the apartment building does not have any rules about noise. Jones and Smith can bargain at zero cost. Will they reach an agreement where Jones gives up his beloved operas?

  **c.** Now suppose the apartment building passes a rule that says residents are not allowed to play music their neighbors can hear if any of the neighbors object. As before, Jones and Smith can bargain at zero cost. Will Jones be allowed to play his music?

4. Suppose you are willing to pay $15 for one framed painting in your dorm room and $5 more for a second painting. Your roommate is willing to pay $10 for one painting and has no interest in a second painting.

  **a.** Sketch your individual demand curve for paintings (a step function with maximum quantity of 2). Also sketch your roommate's demand curve for paintings.

  **b.** Assume you have a divided room such that the paintings are private goods. Sketch the overall demand curve for paintings by both you and your roommate.

  **c.** Instead assume the room is quite open such that each painting is a public good that both you and your roommate can enjoy. Sketch the new social benefit curve (the "market demand") for paintings.

5. There are 20 fish in a lake and 10 fishers who catch fish. There are two days allowed for fishing, and after the first day, whatever fish remain will double in number. The options are 1 (fish lightly) or 2 (fish intensely). On the first day each fisher gets 1 or 2 fish, based on this choice. On the second day the available fish are split evenly among all fishers. For example, if 4 fishers choose to fish lightly and 6 choose to fish heavily, then the 4 remaining fish will double to 8 and these are split evenly on the second day. In this example, fishers who fish lightly end up with $1 + 8/10 = 1.8$ fish, while fishers who fish heavily end up with $2 + 8/10 = 2.8$ fish.

  **a.** Collectively, what should the fishers do to maximize total number of fish caught over the span of the two days? How many fish will each fisher get?

  **b.** Josh is one of the fishers. What should he do if he knows all the other 9 fishers are fishing lightly on the first day? How many fish will he end up with?

  **c.** What will Josh do if he knows all the other 9 fishers are fishing intensely on the first day? How many fish will he end up with? What is the new total for all fishers combined?

  **d.** Is there ever a situation in which it is better for an individual fisher to fish lightly on the first day?

6. Malaria is spread by mosquitoes. That is, a mosquito spreads malaria by biting an infected person and later infusing malaria into a different person. A study by Jeffrey Sachs and others shows a strong correlation between the incidence of malaria in a country and poverty. Malaria

is known to exist in poor countries; it has also been found that the incidence of malaria exacerbates poverty. One of the simplest and most effective ways of preventing the occurrence of malaria is by using insecticide-treated nets.

  **a.** Consider the private market for insecticide-treated nets. Use supply and demand curves to show the equilibrium level of nets that will be produced. Is this outcome socially efficient?

  **b.** In the graph, how would you account for the insecticide-treated nets' effect on poverty? What happens to the level of output in the market?

  **c.** How could the government encourage the production of the efficient number of nets?

7. Many cities tax or ban plastic grocery bags. The rationale for these taxes and bans is an externalities argument: plastic bags are an eyesore; take up space in landfills; and damage fish, birds, and other wildlife.

  **a.** In a diagram, show the efficient number of plastic bags and the equilibrium number of plastic bags in the absence of any government policies.

  **b.** Show the efficiency loss from plastic bags in your diagram.

  **c.** Show the tax on plastic bags that would lead to the efficient outcome.

8. A college campus must decide whether to spend $40,000 to clear sidewalks of snow during the winter. There are 4,000 students. One thousand of these students are willing to pay up to $30 each to walk on a snowless sidewalk. The other 3,000 are willing to pay $8 each.

  **a.** In terms of efficiency, should the university pay $40,000 to keep snow off of the sidewalks?

  **b.** Suppose the university imposed a $10 fee on each student to cover the cost. This would raise the $40,000 necessary but might make many students upset. What would happen if the decision to clear snow were put up for a university-wide vote?

  **c.** A university administrator proposes the following: the 3,000 students willing to pay $8 must in fact pay $8 each. This raises $24,000. The students willing to pay $40 have to pay only $16 each (for $16,000 more, for a total of $40,000). Why might this policy not work in practice?

9. There is a road between the suburbs and downtown. The road is congested at rush hour. If 100 people use the road at rush hour, the trip takes 30 minutes. If the 101st person enters the road, everyone has to slow down, and the trip now takes 31 minutes. People value their time at $6 per hour (that is, $0.10 per minute). For simplicity, ignore all costs of using the road other than the cost of time.

  **a.** What is the total social cost of 100 people using the road at rush hour?

  **b.** What is the marginal social cost of the 101st person?

  **c.** The governor of this state (who has taken a Principles of Economics course) would like to institute a toll that would equal the costs the last driver who uses the road imposes on the other drivers. How high should the toll be on this road during rush hour?

d. Suppose that at noon 50 people are using the road. The road is not congested, and the trip takes just 20 minutes. If the 51st driver enters the road, no one has to slow down, and the trip continues to take 20 minutes. How high should the toll be at noon?

10. A three-person city is considering a fireworks display. Anne is willing to pay $50 to see the fireworks, Bob is willing to pay $15, and Charlie is willing to pay $15. The cost of the fireworks is $60.

   a. In terms of efficiency, should the fireworks display be offered?

   b. Will any single citizen provide the display on his or her own?

   c. Suppose the town decides to put the matter to a vote. If at least two people vote in favor of the fireworks display, each person will be taxed $20 and the fireworks display will be held. How many people will vote in favor of the display?

11. Three roommates—Tinker, Evers, and Chance—share an apartment. It is really cold outside, and they are considering turning up the thermostat in the apartment by 1, 2, 3, or 4 degrees. They know that each time they raise the temperature in the apartment by 1 degree, their heating bill will rise by $8. Their individual marginal benefits from making it warmer in the apartment are as follows:

| | Marginal Benefit | | |
|---|---|---|---|
| Increase in Temperature | Tinker | Evers | Chance |
| 1 degree | $5 | $4 | $3 |
| 2 degrees | $4 | $3 | $2 |
| 3 degrees | $3 | $2 | $1 |
| 4 degrees | $2 | $1 | $0 |

   a. Find the marginal social benefit from making it 1, 2, 3, or 4 degrees warmer.

   b. By how many degrees should they raise the temperature?

12. Suppose demand is $Q_D = 16 - P$ and supply is $Q_S = P$. There is a constant positive externality of $4 per unit (Marginal external benefit = $4). Find the maximum possible social surplus.

# 10

# The Government in the Economy: Taxation and Regulation

## What is the optimal size of government?

It's early November, and the presidential race is at fever pitch, growing more intense every day. You are beginning to grasp the major issues but are still in need of a bit more information before casting your vote next week. As you eat breakfast, you decide to flip on the TV to learn more about the candidates. You listen to a persuasive argument from the Democratic candidate, who is urging businesses to reduce their carbon emissions. She states that if elected, she will propose new taxes on polluters to address the inherent dangers of climate change: polluters must pay for their pollution! This makes sense to you: why not levy a tax on polluters to more closely align their interests with those of society? She closes by confidently stating that "now is the time to improve our lives, with the helping hand of a government working for you."

Later that day, you return home from economics class and decide to veg out on the couch for a few hours. After this morning's viewing, you are now firmly in the Democratic camp. But when you turn on the TV, this time you see the Republican candidate, who is complaining about the inefficiencies created

## CHAPTER OUTLINE

## KEY IDEAS

- In the United States, governments (federal, state, and local) tax citizens and corporations to correct market failures and externalities, raise revenues, redistribute funds, and finance operations.

- Through direct regulation and price controls, governments can intervene to influence market outcomes.

- Although government intervention sometimes creates inefficiencies, it often results in improved social well-being.

- Weighing the trade-offs between equity and efficiency is one task of an economist.

- It is up to each individual to decide when and where government intervention makes the most sense.

by taxes and the oversized, incompetent government bureaucracy. New pollution taxes will harm *all* consumers, he claims. He suggests that corruption has become commonplace in government: even seemingly honest officials are bamboozling the taxpayer. What we need, he says, is less government intrusion in our lives. He ends with a persuasive line: "The beginning of massive government intervention is the end of any great society."

Uh-oh. Now you are torn. The Republican candidate was quite convincing. But so was the Democratic one. Which story is correct? Whom should you believe? Do we need more or less government intervention in the economy?

In this chapter we will learn that by its very nature, government intervention can be a double-edged sword. Well-designed regulation can improve societal outcomes, but poorly designed regulation stifles economic efficiency. We'll also look at where the government's money comes from and where it goes, how government intervenes in the economy, and what that intervention costs. Along the way, you will pick up tools that will help you answer the complex question of the optimal role of government in our economy—how much government intervention is necessary? How much is desirable?

## 10.1 Taxation and Government Spending in the United States

The federal government is the central government established by the U.S. Constitution. It is the largest governing body in the United States, holding jurisdiction over all fifty states. Yet when we refer to "the government," we do not necessarily mean just the federal government. In fact, the federal government collects only about two-thirds of total taxes in the U.S. economy.

There are also state and local governments that impose and collect taxes and spend the revenues they generate. State governments, as the name implies, hold jurisdiction over particular states. Local governments exist at the county and city levels; they, too, collect taxes from, and spend them in the interest of, their respective residents. A single citizen can fall under the jurisdiction of a city government, county government, state government, and federal government simultaneously and thus owe taxes to each.

**Exhibit 10.1 Total Government Spending and Total Government Tax Revenue as a Percentage of National Income (1929–2015)**

Total government spending and tax revenues have been increasing over the past several decades. When government spending exceeds tax revenues, the government is running a budget deficit. Conversely, when government tax revenues exceed spending, the result is a budget surplus.

*Source:* Bureau of Economic Analysis, National Income and Product Accounts. U.S. Department of Commerce.

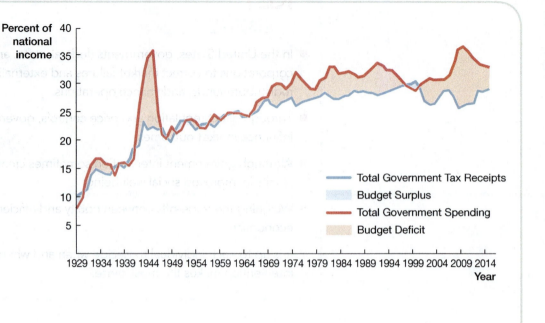

Legend:
— Total Government Tax Receipts
  Budget Surplus
— Total Government Spending
  Budget Deficit

To appreciate the reach of government in the United States, consider Exhibit 10.1, which plots total government spending and tax revenues. This exhibit shows that government spending has grown over time and now accounts for more than 30 percent of U.S. national income. Notice also the spike in the mid-1940s, which shows a substantial increase in government spending due to World War II. Tax revenues have grown in tandem as well. For example, in 2015, total government tax revenues stood at $5,224.3 billion. It may be hard to believe that such massive tax revenues fall short of spending, but Exhibit 10.1 shows that this is often the case. When government tax revenues fall below spending, the government runs a **budget deficit**. When the converse happens and tax revenues exceed spending, the government is running a **budget surplus**.

A **budget deficit** occurs when tax revenues do not cover government spending.

A **budget surplus** occurs when tax revenues exceed government spending.

**Tax revenues**, or **receipts**, are the money a government collects through a tax.

A **payroll tax** (also known as **social insurance tax**) is a tax on the wages of workers.

## Where Does the Money Come From?

Exhibit 10.2 provides a summary of how the federal government raises revenues. In 2013, for example, the federal government collected over $2,775 billion in **tax revenues,** or **receipts**, which is equivalent to about $19,347 per person in the civilian labor force. These receipts are collected via various types of taxes, as shown in the exhibit.

1. *Individual income taxes* represent the largest portion—roughly 47 percent in 2013.
2. *Payroll taxes* represent about a third of the federal government's receipts. A **payroll tax**, also known as a **social insurance tax**, is a tax on wages that employers are

**Exhibit 10.2 Federal Receipts by Category in 2013**

The largest component of federal government revenues comes from the individual (federal) income tax, followed by social insurance tax receipts. Corporate income tax, excise taxes, and other sources of income make up a much smaller percentage of federal receipts.

*Source:* White House Office of Management and Budget, FY 2015 Historical Tables. The White House.

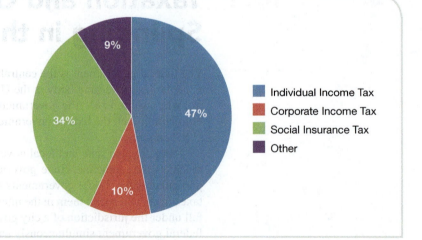

Legend:
■ Individual Income Tax
■ Corporate Income Tax
■ Social Insurance Tax
■ Other

**Corporate income taxes** are taxes paid by firms to the government from their profits.

**Excise taxes** are taxes paid when purchasing a specific good.

required to withhold from employees' pay. On your paystub, these are often listed as Federal Insurance Contribution Act taxes, or FICA taxes.

3. *Corporate income tax* provides 10 percent of the overall pie. **Corporate income tax** is generated from taxing profits earned by corporations.

4. *All other taxes* make up the remaining 9 percent. This includes **excise taxes**, which are taxes paid when purchasing specific goods such as alcohol, tobacco, and gasoline.

The sources of revenue for state and local governments are quite different from those for the federal government. Exhibit 10.3 displays the types of taxes levied by these governments and the receipts brought in by each. The pie chart of revenue in the exhibit is split into five pieces.

**(1)** The largest slice of the pie at 30 percent is the *All Other* category, which encompasses miscellaneous taxes and fees that state and local governments collect. These include, among others, tolls on roads and sales from public transportation tickets, vehicle licenses, and hunting and fishing licenses.

**(2)** The next biggest portion at 22 percent is *Revenue from the Federal Government*, which are taxes collected at the federal level and then redistributed to the states (often used to redistribute resources toward poorer states with otherwise relatively low tax receipts).

**Sales taxes** are paid by a buyer, as a percentage of the sale price of an item.

**(3) Sales taxes** account for the next largest portion at 18 percent. Unless you live in one of the few states that does not have a sales tax, you are likely quite familiar with sales taxes, which are calculated as a percentage of the sale price of an item and are usually collected from a buyer by a seller at the time of sale. The seller then passes the tax on to the proper government agencies. Some items, such as basic necessities, are exempt from sales taxes; these exemptions are determined independently by each state and local government. The value-added tax (VAT) is similar to the sales tax, except that it is imposed at each stage of the production process leading up to the final sale rather than being entirely collected at the time of sale of the final good.

**(4)** At 17 percent of tax revenues, *property taxes* also constitute a robust slice of the revenues. These are taxes on land and structures on which local governments rely to fund schools, libraries, and public services such as police and fire protection.

**(5)** Similar to the federal government, forty-three state governments and many local governments collect *individual income taxes*. These amounted to 13 percent of total receipts in 2013. Though the type of tax is the same, each state's rates vary and are generally less than federal individual income tax rates. The seven states that do *not* collect any income taxes are Alaska, Florida, Nevada, South Dakota, Texas, Washington, and Wyoming (in addition, New Hampshire and Tennessee only tax dividend and interest income). Before you plan your next big move, however, keep in mind that these states tend to make up for not taxing income with higher tax rates in other categories or lower provision of public goods.

**Exhibit 10.3 State and Local Receipts by Category in 2013**

State and local governments receive a much smaller fraction of their tax revenues from individual income taxes than does the federal government. Instead, property taxes, income taxes, and transfers from the federal government account for the bulk of their revenues.

*Source:* U.S. Census Bureau, 2013 State and Local Finances Survey. U.S. Census Bureau.

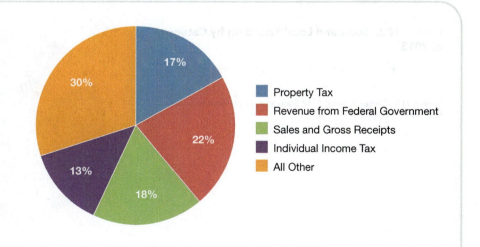

- Property Tax
- Revenue from Federal Government
- Sales and Gross Receipts
- Individual Income Tax
- All Other

Some state and local governments also collect *corporate income taxes,* though this category accounts for a much smaller share of receipts—2 percent in 2013.

## Why Does the Government Tax and Spend?

Four main factors influence government taxation and spending decisions:

- Raising revenues
- Redistributing funds via transfer payments
- Financing operations
- Correcting market failures and externalities

**Raising Revenues** Most taxation in our economy is intended to raise revenues for the funding of public goods such as national defense, public education, police protection, and infrastructure projects. We saw in Chapter 9 that markets will, in general, fail to provide optimal amounts of public goods. This failure, in turn, motivates governments to levy taxes and use the returns for the provision of public goods, which benefit a large number of citizens.

Exhibit 10.4 provides a summary of how federal government revenue is spent. National defense and Social Security comprise the two largest categories of federal spending. The federal government does not spend a large fraction of its budget on education, policing, and infrastructure, which are all included in the "Other" category. But state and local governments do, as we see in Exhibit 10.5.

**Exhibit 10.4** **Federal Government Spending by Category in 2013**

The federal government spends most of its money on national defense and Social Security, followed by other transfer programs—in particular, income security, Medicare, and health.

*Source:* White House Office of Management and Budget, FY 2015 Historical Tables. The White House.

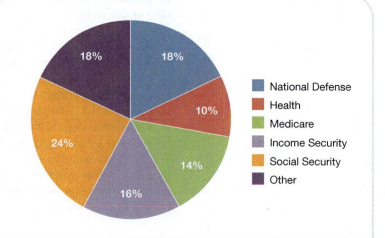

**Exhibit 10.5** **State and Local Spending by Category in 2013**

The two biggest items of spending for state governments are education and public welfare.

*Source:* U.S. Census Bureau, 2013 State and Local Finances Survey. U.S. Census Bureau.

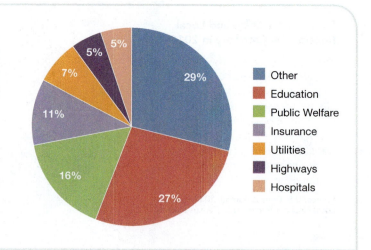

Exhibit 10.5 indicates that 27 percent of state and local government spending went toward public education, which includes schools from pre-kindergarten all the way up to state universities. Large fractions of these state and local receipts were also spent on highways, one type of infrastructure spending. Policing, together with firefighting, libraries, transportation, parks, and sewage, are included in the "Other" category.

**Redistributing Funds** The second major objective of government taxation and spending is redistribution. As we discuss in the next chapter, market outcomes can be quite inequitable, with high levels of inequality and poverty coexisting alongside huge fortunes for a few. Governments in all advanced economies in general, and the U.S. government in particular, use transfer payments and the tax system to limit the extent of such inequality and the economic hardships that poorer households in the society suffer.

**Transfer payments** refer to payments from the government (which are not made as a payment for the provision of a good or service) to certain groups, such as the elderly or the unemployed. In Exhibit 10.4, you can see that, aside from national defense spending, the bulk of federal government spending is made up of payments under the umbrella of Social Security, Medicare, and health. *Social Security*, also known as the Old-Age, Survivors, and Disability Insurance program, is the largest transfer program and was introduced by President Franklin D. Roosevelt in 1935 to provide economic security to the elderly, the disabled, widows, and fatherless children. *Medicare*, introduced by President Lyndon Johnson in 1965, provides health insurance to Americans aged 65 and older and makes up another large part of federal spending.

*Income security* includes unemployment compensation, Supplemental Security Income, the refundable portion of the Earned Income and Child Tax Credits, food stamps

**Transfer payments** occur when the government gives part of its tax revenue to some individual or group.

# CHOICE
## &CONSEQUENCE

### The Government Budget Constraint

Governments tax because they need revenues to spend. This is just a simple restatement of the *government budget constraint*, which is no different than the budget constraint facing a household. If you would like to spend more, you would need to generate more income, either by earning more or by borrowing more. The same applies to governments.

Though simple, the government budget constraint has major implications. The first one is that there are no "fiscal free lunches"—every good and useful program costing money will have to be financed one way or another. This important implication is often ignored or purposefully hidden by policymakers and politicians, because they like to emphasize the services they will deliver but not how they will finance them. So presidential campaigns are full of big promises of new programs and even tax cuts, and when economists look at the numbers, they just don't add up.

One consequence of this tendency of politicians (or, some would say, of our political system) is a bias toward government debt: the shortfall of spending promises relative to tax revenues can be made up by government borrowing.

Another trick that politicians can sometimes play is to increase what some call "unfunded liabilities," which refers to spending that creates future debt or liabilities for the government, but is not viewed as current borrowing by our accounting standards. The leading example of this is our Social Security system, which pays out to the current retirees and is financed, primarily, by Social Security taxes on those who work today (and those workers will receive their benefits in the future when they retire, and their benefits will be financed by taxes imposed on workers in the future). Though this type of social security system is common around the world and has certain efficiency and distributional advantages, it also implies that current benefits do not show up as government spending financed by debt, even though they are essentially the same as government debt: if the government were to borrow today to spend more on, say, food stamps, it would then have to impose taxes to pay back this amount in the future. This would generally show up as government debt. But in the case of Social Security, it does not show up as debt. For this reason, some economists have proposed constructing more comprehensive accounts of the fiscal balance of the government, including liabilities created by Social Security. This has motivated some economists, such as Laurence Kotlikoff, to favor more comprehensive measures of the government's obligations. Kotlikoff, in particular, favors a measure he calls the "infinite-horizon fiscal gap," which takes the difference between government receipts and expenditures and extends them into the future to include liabilities like Social Security. In 2015, he estimated this fiscal gap to be about $210 trillion, which is sixteen times greater than the official U.S. debt at the time.[1]

Market outcomes can be quite inequitable, with high levels of inequality
and poverty coexisting alongside huge
fortunes for a few. Governments in all
advanced economies in general, and
the U.S. government in particular, use
transfer payments and the tax system
to limit the extent of such inequality and the economic hardships that
poorer households in the society suffer.

A **progressive tax system** involves
higher tax rates on those earning
higher incomes.

The **average tax rate** for a
household is given by total taxes
paid divided by total income.

The **marginal tax rate** refers to how
much of the last dollar earned is
paid out in tax.

(also known as the Supplemental Nutrition Assistance Program), family
support, child nutrition, and foster care. Health comprises such major
mandatory programs as Medicaid, the State Children's Health Insurance
Program, federal employees' and retirees' health benefits, and healthcare
for Medicare-eligible military retirees.

Exhibit 10.5 shows that public welfare also makes up a significant part
of state and local budgets. This item consists of transfer payments to persons in need, including direct cash assistance (under the Old Age Assistance and Temporary Assistance for Needy Families programs), vendor
payments made to private purveyors for medical care, burials, and other
services provided under welfare programs.

But governments do not rely just on spending to limit inequality. The
tax system itself is *progressive,* meaning highly redistributive in many
economies, including that of the United States.

A **progressive tax system** is one in which tax rates increase with taxable base incomes, so that the rich pay higher tax rates than the less well-
to-do. To understand this system more precisely, we need to distinguish between *average*
and *marginal tax rates.* The **average tax rate** faced by a household is the total tax paid
divided by total income earned. The **marginal tax rate**, on the other hand, refers to how
much of the last dollar earned the household pays in taxes. The United States has a progressive federal income tax system in that high-income individuals pay higher average taxes
and higher marginal taxes. The "Letting the Data Speak" box illustrates the relationship
between marginal and average tax rates in a progressive system, using federal tax information from 2015.

Exhibit 10.7 shows an important consequence of a progressive tax system: the rich earn
a high share of the national income but pay an even higher share of total taxes. For example, the richest 1 percent earns 17.8 percent of national income but also pays 29.7 percent

## LETTING THE
# DATA SPEAK

## Understanding Federal Income Tax Brackets

Your tax bracket corresponds to your marginal tax rate
(which is higher than your average tax rate because the
federal tax system is progressive). Exhibit 10.6 gives the
marginal tax rate single individuals had to pay in 2015.

Using the information provided in this exhibit, you can
compute the amount you have to pay in taxes. Suppose
that your taxable income (after deductions and exemptions)
is equal to $100,000. Then your tax would be calculated
as follows:

$$(9,225 - 0) \times 10 \text{ percent} = \$922.50$$
$$+ (37,450 - 9,226) \times 15 \text{ percent} = \$4,233.60$$

$$+ (90,750 - 37,451) \times 25 \text{ percent} = \$13,324.75$$
$$+ (100,000 - 90,751) \times 28 \text{ percent} = \$2,589.72$$
$$\text{Total} = \$21,070.57$$

This puts you in the 28 percent tax bracket, because your
*marginal tax rate*—the tax rate applied to the last dollar added to your taxable income—is 28 percent. But your
*average tax rate* is lower. In particular, it is given by the total
amount of taxes you pay, $21,070.57, divided by your total
income, $100,000, and is thus $\frac{21,070.57}{100,000} = 21.07$ percent.

**Exhibit 10.6** Federal
**Taxes in 2015 for a Single**
**Individual**

| If your taxable income is between ... | Your tax bracket is ... |
| --- | --- |
| $0 and $9,225 | 10 percent |
| $9,226 and $37,450 | 15 percent |
| $37,451 and $90,750 | 25 percent |
| $90,751 and $189,300 | 28 percent |
| $189,301 and $411,500 | 33 percent |
| $411,501 and $413,200 | 35 percent |
| $413,201 and above | 39.6 percent |

Source: Tax Rate Schedule X, Internal Revenue Code section 1c. U.S. Internal Revenue Service.

**Exhibit 10.7** The Distribution of Income and Federal Taxes in 2015

To interpret the exhibit, match colors across columns. For example, the purple boxes show that those in the 60th to 80th percentiles of income earn 19.36 percent of national income and pay 16.14 percent of the federal taxes.

*Source:* United States Department of the Treasury. U S. Department of the Treasury.

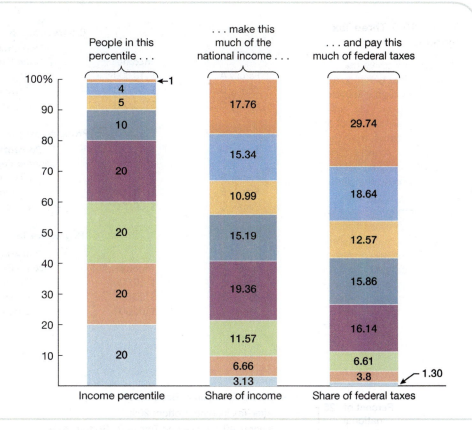

People in this percentile . . .  . . . make this much of the national income . . .  . . . and pay this much of federal taxes

The United States has a progressive federal income tax system in that high-income individuals pay higher average taxes and higher marginal taxes.

In a **proportional tax system**, households pay the same percentage of their incomes in taxes regardless of their income level.

A **regressive tax system** involves lower tax rates on those earning higher incomes.

of total federal taxes. People between the 60th and 80th percentiles of the income distribution, in contrast, pay about the same percentage in taxes as they earn, while those in the bottom 60 percent of the earnings distribution pay less in taxes than their percentage of the national income.

The alternatives to the progressive tax system are the *proportional* and *regressive tax systems.* In a **proportional tax system**, households pay the same percentage of their incomes in taxes regardless of their income level; in other words, the marginal and average tax rates do not vary with income. In a **regressive tax system**, the marginal tax and average tax rates decline with income so that low-income households pay a greater percentage of income in taxes than do high-income households. Exhibit 10.8 provides examples of progressive, proportional, and regressive taxes. In the United States, income taxes are progressive, and Social Security and property taxes tend to be regressive.

As a result of transfer programs and progressive taxation, the post-tax income distribution in the United States is more equal than the pre-tax income distribution. We depict this in Exhibit 10.9, which plots the pre-tax and the post-tax income shares of the top (richest) 1 percent and the lowest (poorest) 20 percent of households in the United States. Even though these figures do not include the transfer payments related to healthcare, they already indicate that government redistribution reduces inequality substantially. For example, in 2011 the pre-tax income share of the lowest 20 percent of U.S. households was 3.9 percent, while their post-tax income share was 4.7 percent; after transfers, the share is even higher, at 6.3 percent. Conversely, the effect of tax and transfer programs is to reduce the income share of the top 1 percent from 16.2 percent pre-tax to 12.1 percent including taxes and transfers.

**Financing Operations**   Governments also tax to pay for their own operations, including the salaries of presidents, members of Congress, and other politicians, and for the sizable bureaucracy in charge of the day-to-day running of government operations and services. Some economists, such as William Niskanen,[2] argue that politicians and government bureaucrats have a tendency to increase the government budget and the reach of the government—independent of the useful roles of government listed above. Though most

**Exhibit 10.8 Three Tax Systems**

With a progressive tax system, those earning more, like family C in this exhibit, pay a higher tax rate, and thus a higher fraction of their incomes in taxes, than the rest (families A and B). In a proportional tax system, everybody pays the same tax rate. In a regressive tax system, family C pays a lower tax rate than those households earning less, such as families A and B (but we can also see that the total amount of taxes paid by family C is still higher than those paid by families A and B).

| Progressive Tax | | | |
|---|---|---|---|
| | Income | Percentage of Income Paid in Tax | Amount of Tax |
| Family A | $ 10,000 | 10 percent | $ 1,000 |
| Family B | $ 50,000 | 20 percent | $10,000 |
| Family C | $100,000 | 30 percent | $30,000 |

| Proportional Tax | | | |
|---|---|---|---|
| | Income | Percentage of Income Paid in Tax | Amount of Tax |
| Family A | $ 10,000 | 20 percent | $ 2,000 |
| Family B | $ 50,000 | 20 percent | $10,000 |
| Family C | $100,000 | 20 percent | $20,000 |

| Regressive Tax | | | |
|---|---|---|---|
| | Income | Percentage of Income Paid in Tax | Amount of Tax |
| Family A | $ 10,000 | 20 percent | $2,000 |
| Family B | $ 50,000 | 4 percent | $2,000 |
| Family C | $100,000 | 2 percent | $2,000 |

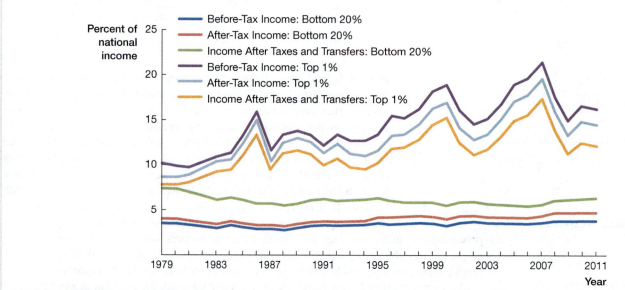

**Exhibit 10.9 The Pre- and Post-Tax Income Share of the Top 1 Percent and Bottom 20 Percent (as a Percentage of National Income) from 1979 to 2011**

Because of the progressivity of the federal tax system, the post-tax income share of the top 1 percent is less than their pre-tax income share, while the post-tax income share of the bottom 20 percent is more than their pre-tax income share.

*Source:* White House Office of Management and Budget, FY 2015 Historical Tables. The White House.

economists and social scientists would not agree that this is the major driver of government size, many would agree that certain parts of the government bureaucracy are inefficiently large. We return to this issue later in this chapter.

**Correcting Market Failures and Externalities**   In Chapter 9 we saw how the government sometimes imposes taxes to correct market failures or externalities. Though important in principle, this use of taxation is far less prevalent, in practice, than the three discussed above.

# LETTING THE
## DATA SPEAK

### Reducing Inequality the Scandinavian Way

So what does a more equal society look like—and what might it take to get there? The Scandinavian countries—Denmark, Norway, Sweden, Finland, and Iceland—offer one potential model. You may have heard politicians talk about Scandinavia as a guide for forging a more equitable society. During the 2016 Democratic primary, for example, candidate Bernie Sanders used Scandinavian social policies as an examplar in support of his proposal to increase the progressivity of the U.S. tax system.

A recent book, edited by Finnish economists Tarmo Valkonen and Vesa Vihriälä, confirms that Scandinavian countries have lower inequality and much more generous social welfare systems. These authors also give us clues about how these countries achieve these outcomes. Surprisingly, tax progressivity is not a particularly important factor. Scandinavian countries tax labor income progressively, while applying a proportional tax on capital income. But more important than the progressivity of labor income taxes is the higher rate of taxation. In Scandinavia, tax revenues make up between 38 percent and 50 percent of GDP (in 2015) compared to 26 percent in the United States. Moreover, tax revenues are used for funding generous social welfare programs, further reducing inequality. Exhibit 10.10 shows how taxes and transfers affect two measures of inequality: the Gini coefficient and the poverty rate. The Gini coefficient is a measure of overall income inequality. If the society had perfect equality (everybody having the same income), the Gini coefficient would be 0, while in a society with the highest possible inequality (where all income is in the hands of a single individual or household), it would take the value 1. In contrast, the poverty rate is defined as the percentage of the population that earns less than 50 percent of the median income in the country.

The exhibit shows that the United States is more unequal than Scandinavian countries according to the Gini coefficient and has a higher poverty rate. However, interestingly, the U.S. pre-tax inequality and poverty rates do not look very different from those of Scandinavian countries. The big differences are in the post-tax and transfer numbers, and especially in poverty rates after taxes and transfers. Scandinavian countries' success in limiting inequality and poverty thus appears to be related not so much to lower levels of market inequality before taxes, but to their generous transfer (social welfare) programs.

Still, Scandinavia is no utopia—since the Great Recession, unemployment and inequality have started to creep up. Differences in taxes and transfers among Scandinavian countries, too, have challenged the very idea of a uniform "Scandinavian model."

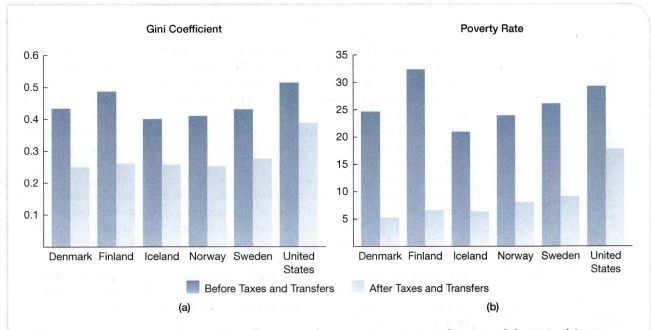

(a)        (b)

**Exhibit 10.10 Pre- and Post-Tax Gini Coefficients and Poverty Rates in Scandinavia and the United States**

This exhibit shows pre-tax and post-tax Gini coefficients (which measure overall income inequality) and poverty rates for Denmark, Finland, Iceland, Norway, Sweden, and the United States. The poverty rate is defined as the percentage of people who earn less than 50 percent of the median income in the country. This exhibit thus indicates that the big difference between Scandinavia and the United States lies not in pre-tax inequality and poverty rates, but in post-tax numbers.

*Source:* Data from Organisation for Economic Co-operation and Development.

# Taxation: Tax Incidence and Deadweight Losses

Who bears the *burden of taxes*—meaning, who actually pays the tax?

At first glance, the answer to the question of who bears the tax burden seems obvious: whoever is taxed bears the burden. If a tax is imposed on a consumer, then the consumer bears it. If it's imposed on sellers (producers), they bear it. But we will learn in this section that interestingly enough, things that are not simple: the tax burden can be shared between a buyer and a seller even if it seems to fall on just one of them. The term **tax incidence** refers to how the burden of the tax is distributed across various agents in the economy.

**Tax incidence** refers to how the burden of taxation is distributed.

To illustrate, let's consider city government officials in New Orleans who want to raise money to build a park next to Bourbon Street. Understanding that the local restaurants are doing well, they decide to levy a tax of $2 on every plate of jambalaya being sold per day. Every time a restaurant sells a plate of jambalaya, it must send $2 to the city government. Let's see how this tax on sellers affects market outcomes.

Panel (a) of Exhibit 10.11 shows the market demand and market supply of jambalaya plates and the pre-tax equilibrium, which involves a daily quantity of 4,000 plates of jambalaya being sold at the equilibrium price of $6.50 a plate. Panel (b) in Exhibit 10.11 shows what happens when a tax of $2 per plate is imposed on the sellers. We also plot the post-tax supply curve ($S_{tax}$). We see that at every quantity level, the post-tax supply curve ($S_{tax}$) is $2 higher than the old (pre-tax) supply curve $S$. To understand why, note that with $2 from the sale of every plate going to the government, the sellers are receiving $2 less than the sale price. For example, if the plates are sold at $6.50, the sellers get only $4.50. But then, after the tax, at $6.50, they will be willing to supply only what they would have supplied at $4.50 on the original supply curve. Panel (b) shows that the tax reduces the quantity of jambalaya plates purchased per day from 4,000 to 2,500 and raises the equilibrium price to $7.50 a plate. (So after allowing for the $2 in tax, a seller now receives $5.50 = $7.50 − $2, and market supply is 2,500 plates.)

Can you see what is happening here? First, there is a gap of $2 between what the consumer pays and what the supplier receives, resulting from the $2 tax on jambalaya plates. Second, not all of this falls on the restaurants: the consumer is paying $1 more per plate— half the $2 tax burden—and the supplier is receiving $1 less per plate (thus also bearing half of the tax burden).

This change in market equilibrium affects consumer and producer surpluses, as shown in panel (b) of Exhibit 10.11. Consumer surplus is now given by the blue-shaded area labeled CS, and producer surplus is given by the pink-shaded area PS. The green area represents the portion of revenues that producers pass on to the government. This is the tax revenue, and it is equal to the size of the tax multiplied by the number of plates sold. In this case, with a $2 tax, 2,500 plates are served per day at a price of $7.50 (the intersection point of $D$ and $S_{tax}$). So, daily tax revenues are given by $2,500 \times \$2 = \$5,000$.

This decomposition in panel (b) also shows that the yellow triangle, which was part of consumer and producer surplus before the tax, is now part of neither. Nor does it accrue to the government as revenue. It therefore represents the *deadweight loss of taxation*. The deadweight loss of taxation is the loss in total surplus—or, put differently, the decline in consumer and producer surpluses not made up by the increase in tax revenues—due to the gap that the tax has created between the price received by sellers and the price paid by consumers. In this example, this gap is exactly equal to the $2 tax. The deadweight loss can be computed easily using the formula for the area of a triangle: ½ base (change in quantity) × height (tax). In our case, this is equal to $\frac{1}{2} \times \$2 \times 1,500 = \$1,500$.

To understand tax incidence, we turn to panel (c) of Exhibit 10.11. Here we see that the government has taken the portion of pre-tax consumer surplus labeled "Incidence on consumers." We calculate this by finding the portion of tax revenue that lies above the pre-tax equilibrium price of $6.50. This portion of tax revenue used to be part of consumer surplus but is no longer part of it. Thus it represents the incidence of taxes on consumers. Similarly, the portion of tax revenue that lies below the pre-tax equilibrium is the incidence of the tax on producers—the portion of tax revenue that is lost producer surplus. This result shows that although the tax is placed on sellers of jambalaya, both

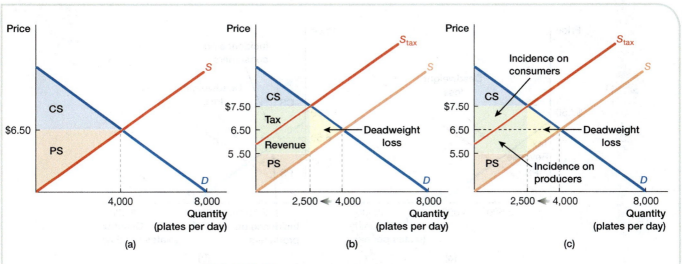

**Exhibit 10.11  A $2 Tax on Producers**

In panel (a) the pre-tax equilibrium is 4,000 plates at $6.50 per plate. In this panel, we can also see the consumer surplus (CS), the area underneath the demand curve and above the price of $6.50, shaded blue, and the producer surplus (PS), the area above the supply curve and below the price of $6.50, shaded pink.

In panel (b), we see the implications of a tax of $2 on a plate of jambalaya. Because for every plate of jambalaya they sell, restaurants have to pay $2 to the government, the post-tax supply curve is shifted to the left by $2. Intuitively, if the producers charge a price of $7.50, they will take home only $5.50 (and pay the remaining $2 to the government as tax per plate). But then they will only be willing to supply at $7.50 after the tax what they would have supplied at $5.50 before the tax—since $5.50 is what they will receive in this case.

Once we have the post-tax supply curve, the equilibrium is straightforward to find; it is given by the intersection of this post-tax curve and the demand curve. We can also see that the post-tax equilibrium price of a plate of jambalaya is $7.50, and 2,500 plates are consumed. This panel also shows how consumer surplus and producer surplus have shrunk. In between the two, shaded in green, is the tax revenue, given by $2 times 2,500 = $5,000. The yellow triangle represents the deadweight loss of taxation, the loss in total surplus due to the tax.

Panel (c) shows tax incidence. Consumers are now paying $7.50 per plate of jambalaya, $1 more than in the pre-tax equilibrium; and sellers are taking home $5.50 per plate, $1 less than in the pre-tax equilibrium, so that in this example the tax incidence is 50 percent on consumers and 50 percent on sellers.

buyers and sellers bear its burden. In fact, in the example we have shown in Exhibit 10.10, the incidence on consumers is equivalent to 50 percent of the tax, even though the tax was placed on sellers!

Let's return to the government officials in New Orleans, who now face another challenge. After the tax is in place for only a few months, the local merchants begin to clamor. They are unhappy with paying the $2 tax. In a town hall meeting, the merchants hatch a seemingly clever plan: "Because most of our patrons are from out of town, let's tax *buyers* $2 for every plate of jambalaya that they purchase. This way, they—not us—will pay for our new park." The town officials, anxious to placate the restaurant owners, think this is a great idea. They immediately repeal the tax on restaurants and impose it on consumers. They conclude that since buyers are now responsible for paying the tax, sellers should be much better off. Is this true?

Exhibit 10.12 helps us answer this question. In panel (a) of the exhibit, we see that the $2 tax on every plate of jambalaya creates a new (post-tax) demand curve for jambalaya, labeled $D_{tax}$. We construct this post-tax demand curve by subtracting $2 from the price associated with every quantity on the pre-tax demand curve $D$—or by shifting the demand

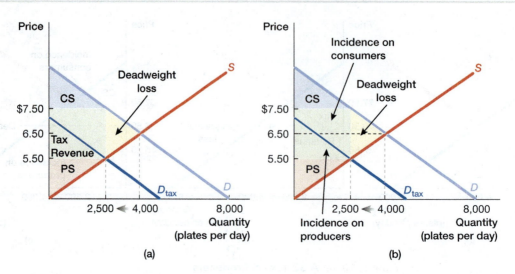

**Exhibit 10.12  A $2 Tax on Consumers**

When the $2 tax is imposed on consumers, we see that the post-tax equilibrium is the same quantity as in the case where the $2 tax rate was imposed on sellers. The sizes of the consumer and producer surpluses, tax revenue, and deadweight loss are also the same as in Exhibit 10.11. Panel (b) shows that, perhaps even more strikingly, 50 percent of the incidence is on consumers and 50 percent is on sellers, just as in Exhibit 10.11. This illustrates a more general phenomenon: in competitive markets, tax incidence, as well as the equilibrium, is independent of whether the tax is imposed on consumers or sellers.

curve to the left such that the gap between the post-tax curve and the pre-tax tax curve is everywhere $2. This procedure is intuitive. Take a consumer contemplating the purchase of a plate of jambalaya before the tax. If the market price is $5.50, this is exactly what the consumer would pay. Next take the same consumer after the tax of $2 is imposed. Now, when the market price is $5.50, she has to pay $7.50 (= $5.50 + $2). This implies that the number of plates that consumers will be willing to consume at $5.50 when there is a $2 tax is exactly equal to their demand at $7.50 (in the absence of the tax). Repeating this argument for any price, we can see that the entire post-tax demand curve is the same as the pre-tax demand curve shifted to the left by $2.

But once you shift the demand curve to the left by $2, you will see that the equilibrium quantity is the same as in panel (b) of Exhibit 10.10: 2,500 plates are sold per day (consumers pay $7.50, and suppliers get $5.50 per plate). And here is the important point: the deadweight loss, again represented by the yellow triangle, is also identical— equal to $1,500. Let's again compute tax incidence: the incidence on consumers— the portion of tax revenue that lies above the pre-tax equilibrium price (in this case, $6.50)—is given by the same green rectangle. The incidence on producers—the portion of the tax revenue that lies below the pre-tax equilibrium price—is also the same green rectangle. Remarkably, the outcome is identical to the case in which the tax was imposed on producers!

We seem to have stumbled across a conundrum. Notice that the incidence of the tax on producers doesn't change even though under the original tax system jambalaya producers had to pay the government, whereas, in the new tax system, consumers have to pay the government. Why doesn't it change? It's because in the first case, when producers of jambalaya were taxed, menu prices rose from $6.50 to $7.50. Thus, consumers paid $7.50 per plate and producers' net revenue was $5.50 ($7.50 − $2 tax) per plate. In the second case, when consumers are directly taxed, the equilibrium menu price decreases to $5.50 because of the consequences of the tax. Thus, again, producers receive

> In competitive markets, tax incidence and equilibrium prices and quantities are independent of whether the tax is imposed on consumers or producers.

$5.50 per plate in net revenues, but, because of the tax, consumers pay a total of $7.50 for every dish of jambalaya they consume.

# CHOICE
## &CONSEQUENCE

## The Deadweight Loss Depends on the Tax

Prime Minister Margaret Thatcher and President Ronald Reagan shared views on many taxation policies.

The deadweight losses of taxation imply that for every dollar of tax raised, the cost is greater than a dollar. This is what the economist Arthur Okun called the "leaky bucket"—the government finds that it must pour in more than one gallon of revenue to finance one gallon of services.[3]

But some types of taxes might create fewer leakages than others. *Lump-sum taxes*, which are taxes that require every citizen to pay the same amount, regardless of his or her circumstances, typically create fewer leakages than taxes on income or transactions. This is because they do not introduce the gap that leads to

the deadweight loss of taxation shown in Exhibits 10.11 and 10.12. Imagine that the government imposed a lump-sum tax on all residents of New Orleans rather than the tax on plates of jambalaya; then the equilibrium in the jambalaya market would not be subject to the tax distortions we saw there. With lump-sum taxes, all citizens in an economy would pay the government the same fee—say, $5,000—regardless of their earnings or market demand. Such taxes do not distort behavior, and therefore there is no deadweight loss associated with imposition of such taxes. Although such taxes are rare, there are examples in practice. For example, in 1989 during the third administration of Prime Minister Margaret Thatcher, the government in Great Britain enacted a law requiring local authorities to replace their system of local property taxes with a lump-sum head or poll tax. Every adult would now pay the same amount of tax, called the Community Charge, to the local government, with the amount determined by each locality. In practice, these types of taxes are rarely used, because they go against one of the major objectives of governments: redistribution. (And Thatcher's poll tax was not a huge success. Its unpopularity propelled a challenge to her leadership of the Conservative Party and ended her political career.)

As we have seen, governments often tax so as to redistribute away from the rich and toward the poor, the disabled, or the elderly. But lump-sum taxes force rich and poor people to pay the same amount—and thus incur a higher tax rate on the poor. They are thus regressive taxes.

We are encountering a general phenomenon here: in competitive markets, tax incidence and equilibrium prices and quantities are independent of whether the tax is imposed on consumers or producers.

**The Effects of Demand and Supply Elasticities on the Tax Burden**   The fact that the incidence of the tax is identical for buyers and sellers in the examples above is due to how we drew the market demand and market supply curves. That is, buyers and sellers were equally sensitive to price changes at the original equilibrium. However, in general, the elasticity of market demand will *not* be identical to the elasticity of market supply.

Exhibit 10.13 provides an illustrative example. Panel (a) of the exhibit shows the market for jambalaya using the same figures as in the example above (Exhibit 10.11). In panel (b) of Exhibit 10.13, we make the market supply curve more elastic than the market demand curve. This means that sellers are more responsive to price changes than buyers are. Thus, when we shift up the supply curve to reflect the $2 tax, quantity decreases by more than before—all the way down to 2,000. The demand curve is the same, so, given the lower quantity, we also end up with a higher equilibrium price: $8.

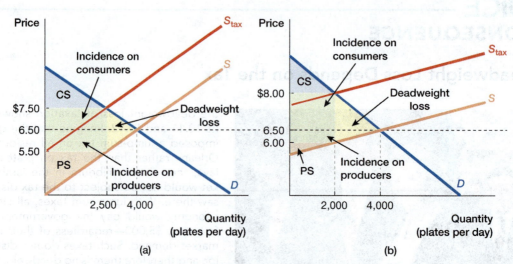

**Exhibit 10.13 Tax Incidence When Supply Is More Elastic Than Demand**

Tax incidence falls more on the inelastic part of the market. In panel (a), tax incidence falls equally on consumers and sellers. In panel (b), we keep the demand curve the same, but consider a more elastic (flatter) supply curve. With the increase in elasticity, the post-tax supply curve (drawn as the dotted line in this figure) meets demand at a lower equilibrium quantity and higher post-tax price. Now tax incidence falls much more on consumers.

More importantly for our purposes, this change in elasticity affects tax incidence. Panel (b) reveals that when the supply curve becomes more elastic, a smaller portion of tax revenue lies below the pre-tax market price. So buyers bear more of the tax burden because the market supply curve is more elastic than the market demand curve.

What happens if we reverse the situation and make the demand curve more elastic than the supply curve? Exhibit 10.14 provides the answer: now it is the producers who bear more of the burden of the tax.

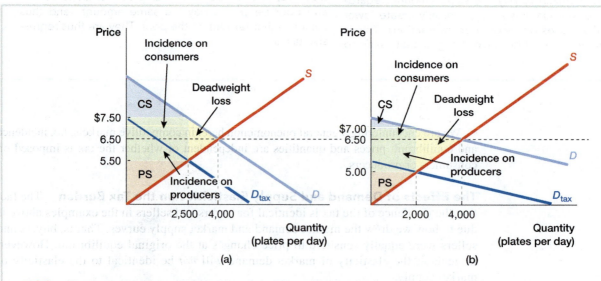

**Exhibit 10.14 Tax Incidence When Demand Is More Elastic Than Supply**

Tax incidence falls more on the inelastic part of the market (again). In panel (a), tax incidence falls equally on consumers and sellers. In panel (b), we keep the supply curve the same but consider a more elastic (flatter) demand curve. The dotted, post-tax demand curve shows how the increased elasticity of demand leads to lower equilibrium quantity (2,000 units) and lower equilibrium prices ($7). More importantly for our focus, now that demand is more elastic, tax incidence falls more on the sellers.

This leads us to a general rule:

The tax burden falls less heavily on the side of the market that is more elastic—that is, more responsive to price changes. When supply is more elastic than demand, the tax burden falls more heavily on buyers. When demand is more elastic than supply, the tax burden falls more heavily on sellers.

The intuition behind why this is true revolves around what an elasticity measures. Recall that when buyers are more price-elastic, they have more alternatives to turn to. Thus, when the price rises, they can easily switch to purchasing another good. If buyers are price inelastic (i.e., not sensitive to price changes), they have few good alternatives. Thus, they must "swallow" the higher price and continue to purchase the taxed good despite the higher price. This means that the more elastic buyer will bear less of the price increase than the less elastic buyer. The same logic applies to the producer side.

There is another impact of elasticities on the tax burden, which can also be seen from Exhibits 10.13 and 10.14: as supply or demand becomes more price-elastic, the deadweight loss of taxation increases. This means that the greater the price elasticity of either supply or demand, the greater the deadweight loss will be, all other things being equal.

Recapping what we have learned from Exhibits 10.13 and 10.14, we see that whenever one side of the market becomes more elastic, its share of the burden of taxation declines and the overall tax burden also declines.

## 10.2 Regulation

As we saw in Chapter 9, externalities and various market failures can have significant societal costs. The main tool that governments use to deal with externalities and other sources of market failures is *regulation* (including direct regulation and price controls). **Regulation** refers to actions by the federal or local government directed at influencing market outcomes, such as the quantity traded of a good or service, its price, or its quality or safety. This also may involve antitrust activities that prevent some firms from exercising excessive monopoly power, as well as activities that are useful for enforcing laws and property rights and resolving disputes to improve the market allocation of resources. We saw in Chapter 9 how the government can use Pigouvian taxes and subsidies to correct externalities. In many instances, however, the government often directly regulates the activity that creates negative externalities. For example, governments typically prevent firms from dumping hazardous waste into rivers rather than simply taxing them. Governments also often use regulation to limit the market power of certain firms, which, by creating a departure from competitive markets, constitutes another major source of market failures, as we discuss in Chapter 12. In this section, we look at direct regulation and price controls as used by the government to affect market outcomes.

**Regulation** refers to actions by the federal or local government directed at influencing market outcomes, such as the quantity traded of a good or service, its price, or its quality and safety.

### Direct Regulation

**Direct regulation (command-and-control regulation)** refers to direct actions by the government to control the amount of a certain activity.

A common form of government intervention in markets is **direct regulation (command-and-control regulation**, which we already discussed in the context of pollution in Chapter 9). Direct regulation (or command-and-control regulation) refers to direct actions by the government to control the amount of a certain activity. Direct regulations affect just about every walk of life, from the safety of foods and drugs to the miles per gallon our automobiles achieve to when we can drop out of school. In many cases, such regulations serve important purposes. For example, consider a prominent regulator of the quality of goods: the Food and Drug Administration (FDA). The FDA represents one of the most complex bureaucracies in the United States, employing 9,000 people and operating on a budget of approximately $2 billion per year. It is not a perfect organization. Far from it—it is often blamed, sometimes deservedly, for being slow to allow new drugs to reach the market. Nevertheless, the FDA does play an important role. It makes sure that drugs that are marketed do, in fact, have the functions that they are supposed to have. The FDA is also charged with preventing fly-by-night companies from selling snake oil, so to speak, to unsuspecting consumers.

This type of regulation, aimed at ensuring that complex products meet certain quality and disclosure requirements, would be difficult to leave to the market itself, as it would be costly for each consumer to obtain such information. If each consumer had to individually verify that a drug was safe to take, it would lead to a massive duplication of effort.

Though regulation plays an indispensable role in modern society, it has costs and limitations. Consider a quick thought experiment on quantity regulations. Quantity regulations, which include fishing quotas, zoning restrictions, antismoking laws, and blue laws (laws that restrict liquor sales on Sundays), can be found throughout any market economy. Let's assume now that the government determines that there is a shortage of physicists. In fact, it pronounces that because of the positive externalities that physicists bestow on society, we should have 5,000 more of them. It proceeds to use quantity regulation to choose 5,000 people to become physicists, without any market mechanism to guide those choices. Would this approach yield an efficient result?

Likely not. Unlike market forces that guide resources to their best use, this type of command system would probably fail miserably: a gifted artist or a dedicated bond trader might be forced into a career solving complicated mathematical equations for which he or she has no particular talent. As we learned in Chapter 9, a Pigouvian subsidy is a viable alternative, because it uses market forces to encourage people at the margin to internalize the externality. If there is an appropriately chosen subsidy to becoming a physicist, then it won't be random people who choose to enter physics, but those who had the talent to become a physicist and yet were previously indifferent between, say, a career as a bond trader and one as a physicist, thus attracting the right people into this profession.

**Price Controls: Price Ceilings and Price Floors**   As we discussed in Chapter 7, sometimes the government intervenes in a market directly by setting a maximum or minimum price for which goods and services sell. Such intervention to regulate prices is called price controls. Here we examine two types of price controls—price ceilings and price floors.

*Price Ceilings*   A **price ceiling** is a cap on the price of a market good or service. One important example is rent control—referring to the maximum amount that landlords can charge renters or the maximum amount by which they can increase rent. Rent controls are often introduced partly as a redistributive tool—because renters are typically poorer than landlords and end up spending a large portion of their incomes on rent.

In the United States, rent controls began during World War I and remain in many cities today, including New York City, San Francisco, Los Angeles, and Washington, D.C. The idea of rent control is noble. However, economic analysis shows that rent control does create important inefficiencies; some of these may help potential renters and others may not. Thus a careful economic analysis is necessary for evaluating the benefits and costs of rent control.

Suppose that in an effort to help renters in San Francisco, the local government places a price control on apartments in the form of a price ceiling. You can see in Exhibit 10.15 that

> A **price ceiling** is a cap or maximum price on a market good.

---

**Exhibit 10.15 The Effect of a Price Ceiling**

Without rent control, the intersection of the market supply and market demand curves for apartments leads to an equilibrium at the price of $1,200 per month and 4,000 units are rented. A rent control imposing a price ceiling of $750 reduces the rent per unit to $750 but also creates a shortage of 3,000 apartments: at this lower price, the quantity demanded increases to 5,500 units, while landlords, moving down the supply curve, reduce the quantity supplied to 2,500.

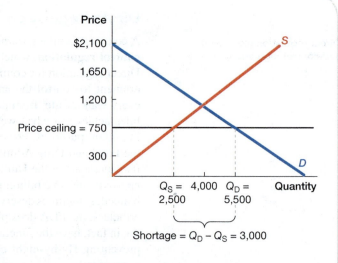

**Exhibit 10.16 Consumer and Producer Surplus with Rent Controls**

Without rent control, the equilibrium is at a rent of $1,200 per month, and panel (a) shows that the consumer surplus is given by the area shaded blue and the producer surplus by the area shaded pink. Panel (b) depicts the situation after rent control is imposed at $750 per month. Producer surplus falls because landlords receive only $750 rent for each of 2,500 units (this can be seen with a smaller shaded pink triangle). Consumer surplus depends on which of the 5,500 potential renters get the 2,500 units on the market at the rent of $750 per month. Panel (b) draws the consumer surplus under the assumption that those with the highest willingness to pay are the first in line for apartments. Even in that best case scenario, the sum of consumer and producer surpluses is less than in panel (a), and the difference is the deadweight loss created by rent control shown as the yellow triangle.

without rent control, the equilibrium is a rent of $1,200 per month and 4,000 apartments are rented. Now consider a rent control imposing a price ceiling of $750 per month. What are the implications of this regulation?

Exhibit 10.15 helps us answer this question. At $750 per month, shown by the black line, the quantity supplied ($Q_S$) decreases to 2,500 units. At this lower rent, quantity demanded ($Q_D$) has increased to 5,500 units. In consequence, there is now a *shortage* of 3,000 apartment units at the price of $750 (5,500 − 2,500 = 3,000). Landlords won't supply as many apartments at the lower rate of $750 as they would at the price of $1,200. For instance, at $750, rather than rent, they might use some apartments as a secondary residence for themselves. At the same time, more renters will want to rent at the lower price, but there won't be as many apartments available. There is excess demand: the price ceiling has caused an inefficiently low quantity of apartments to be available.

As we discussed in Chapter 7, this shortage caused by the government-imposed rent control carries a cost—a deadweight loss. Panel (a) of Exhibit 10.16 shows consumer and producer surplus (areas labeled CS and PS, respectively) before the government imposes a price ceiling. Panel (b) shows the situation after government-imposed regulation, assuming that among the renters, those with a greater willingness to pay are first in line to get an apartment. Under this assumption, the 2,500 units go to the 2,500 consumers with the highest willingness to pay. The resulting deadweight loss is shown by the yellow triangle in the exhibit.

You might ask yourself: if rent control is so clearly welfare-reducing, why do we have it in practice? One reason is that it does not reduce everybody's welfare. As you can see by comparing panels (a) and (b) in Exhibit 10.16, consumer surplus is higher under the rent control (panel (b)) than without the rent control (panel (a)). In addition, rent control can serve a distributive purpose: if the renters who manage to snag an apartment are poor, the policy has effectively redistributed money from the generally better-off landlords to their typically poorer tenants. But, of course, some renters are hurt by the rent control: fewer of them are now able to find an apartment. Moreover, rent control may discourage landlords from maintaining apartments, since even a poorly maintained apartment will find takers in the market with a shortage of apartments.

**Exhibit 10.17  A Leftward Shift of the Demand Curve**

If the demand curve for apartments shifts to the left, so that without rent control the intersection between the market supply and market demand curves would now be at a rent of $600 per month, then the rent control regulation at $750 a month would have no bite, because the price ceiling is now above the price that would prevail in the absence of the rent control.

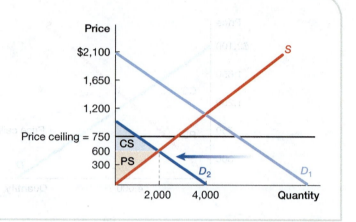

**When Price Ceilings Have No Bite**  Consider what would happen if a large manufacturing plant in Oakland expanded and hired thousands of people from San Francisco. Now many people want to live in Oakland rather than San Francisco. The demand curve for rental units in San Francisco shifts leftward, as shown in Exhibit 10.17. This shift of the demand curve to $D_2$ leads to an equilibrium market price of $600, corresponding to the intersection of the new demand curve and the original supply curve. Now the government regulation has no bite because this price is below the price ceiling of $750. As you can see in Exhibit 10.17, the only time price ceilings have an effect on the market is when they are *below* the market clearing price.

**Price Floors**  Sometimes the government steps in to impose a minimum price on a product or service. The result is a **price floor**, which represents a lower limit on the price of the product or service. A prominent example of price floors is that of minimum wage requirements. Minimum wage laws were first enacted in New Zealand in 1894, and now more than 90 percent of all countries have them. In the United States, the federal government has set a minimum wage of $7.25 per hour, meaning that it is the lowest wage an employer may pay a worker (workers receiving tip income can be paid $2.13 per hour). Several states have minimum wage laws prescribing that within their boundaries, employers have to pay even more. For example, in the state of Illinois, employers must pay workers at least $8 per hour.

A price floor has similar implications to those of a price ceiling, except that instead of a shortage, a price floor causes a surplus—quantity supplied at a price floor would typically be greater than quantity demanded. Because price floors tend to keep the price artificially high, surplus is shifted from consumers to producers, or in the context of the labor market, where it takes the form of a minimum wage, it shifts surplus from employers to workers. Thus, a price floor not only has deadweight loss but also reallocates surplus to sellers (or workers in the context of the minimum wage).

A **price floor** is a lower limit (below which the price cannot fall) on the price of a market good.

## 10.3  Government Failures

We have now seen several ways in which governments may intervene in the economic system. Though many of these interventions have well-defined, worthy objectives and some of them are essential for the proper functioning of markets, we have seen that they also create a range of inefficiencies that need to be taken into account. These include deadweight losses of taxation or inefficiencies from price controls or direct regulations. Those who hold that the role of the government in the economy should be minimized emphasize not only these costs but also a broader set of inefficiencies associated with government interventions, sometimes called **government failures**. In this section, we outline some of these costs.

**Government failures** refer to inefficiencies caused by a government's interventions.

## The Direct Costs of Bureaucracies

Every government program needs bureaucrats and bureaucracies to monitor its implementation. Bureaucrats have to be paid. They are also taken out of the productive sectors of the economy. That is, instead of working at a manufacturing plant or as a manager at Amazon.com, the bureaucrats are engaged in regulation or tax collection. This observation does not suggest that bureaucrats are unproductive at what they do—they implement regulation. However, in the absence of regulation, these workers would have been productive in other jobs, and this lost production represents the opportunity cost of government work.

In this way, the allocation of time and talent of individuals to bureaucracy is an important cost of government. This cost is increased by the fact that bureaucracies sometimes don't function efficiently. Though the various government agencies employ many well-intentioned and efficient individuals, there are long lines, arbitrary decisions, and always a few not-so-helpful employees. These are the kinds of inefficiencies we have come to expect from big bureaucracies. Government intervention in the form of direct regulation may also entail similar costs as firms and their employees work to meet certain government-set objectives rather than creating goods and services.

## Corruption

**Corruption** refers to the misuse of public funds or the distortion of the allocation of resources for personal gain.

Equally as important as the deadweight losses associated with government intervention and the inefficiencies of bureaucracies is the corruption that large governments engender. **Corruption** refers to the misuse of public funds or the distortion of the allocation of resources for personal gain. Consider one example—the billions of dollars that go annually to African governments as foreign aid. In the past 60 years, more than $1 trillion has been transferred from developed countries to Africa, and foreign aid to all countries in 2014 exceeded $130 billion. Much of it comes from governments of developed nations and a significant portion from charities.

But only a small fraction of this money ever reaches its target audience. Economists have estimated that the amount of money that actually reaches its intended destination may be as little as from 5 percent to 15 percent—that means as little as a nickel of every dollar that you send reaches the recipient! Some of the lost aid is eaten up by the inefficiencies of the bureaucracies that operate the foreign aid machine, and even more is appropriated by corrupt politicians and bureaucrats. For example, a recent study found that only 13 percent of education grants reached schools (and most schools received no aid) in Uganda.[4] This type of corruption is extreme but not unusual.

You might be thinking that corruption is not an issue in developed countries, where there is a good system of checks and balances and watchdog agencies waiting for a public official to misstep are everywhere. The evidence suggests otherwise. For instance, in the United States, corruption is not difficult to find. In 2008, fifteen sitting members of Congress were under criminal investigation, mostly for inappropriately using public funds or gifts from businesses that constituted conflicts of interest.

If we consider the number of convictions of public officials across states, similar insights are gained. For instance, from 1977 to 1987 there were roughly 800 corruption convictions per year.[5] The most corrupt state, New York, had roughly 50 times more corruption convictions than the average state during that time period. Such corruption levels continue unabated across states today. In 2014, the Department of Justice reported that 989 federal, state, and local employees had been convicted on corruption charges. In spite of recent drama, New York is no longer the heavyweight champion of corruption—Texas actually leads all states in convictions from 2005 to 2014.

All in all, we cannot expect the government to function as seamlessly as the exhibits in this chapter indicate. The government will often make mistakes, the bureaucracy will be inefficient and slow, and politicians can be corrupt, seeking to capture the process of decision making and exploit it for their own benefit or ideological ends. When evaluating government policies, both the benefits and the costs of government intervention have to be considered. At one extreme, if the benefits are high and the costs are unimportant, a range of direct regulations and government interventions are justified. At the other extreme, if the benefits are limited and the costs are very large, the optimal arrangement might be one of a "night watchman" type government, which shoulders some basic functions such as providing policing and law enforcement, but does not intervene in most economic activities.

## Underground Economy

You have likely seen lawn care workers, snow shovelers, and babysitters handed cash for their work. Or you may have a waiter friend who makes killer tips but does not report them on his taxes. The *underground economy*, sometimes also referred to as the *black market*, includes activities, such as those above, where income taxes are not paid, as well as illegal activities, such as drug dealing and prostitution.

In modern economies, black markets cover an array of activities and are generally found in areas where the benefits of such activities are the highest—either because of high tax rates or because the activity is illegal and therefore the good is not provided in the formal market.

One prime example of an underground economy created because of an illegal product was the result of Prohibition in the 1920s. After the United States outlawed alcohol in 1919, smugglers arranged deliveries to speakeasies and private bars. The result was an era of big organized crime—think of Al Capone—and an estimated $500 million in lost tax revenues annually. Such an example illustrates some of the problems that an underground economy generates:

1. When it involves goods and services that have been legally banned, the underground economy undermines the ban.
2. When underground transactions occur in markets for legal goods and services in order to avoid taxes or regulations, they put legitimate businesses at a disadvantage.
3. To compensate for the lost revenue, governments must levy higher taxes.
4. Criminals spend vast resources trying to evade the law (and authorities spend resources to catch criminals), which are not effective uses of society's resources.

*"Now THAT is a thin line. Let's ignore it."*

# 10.4 Equity Versus Efficiency

In this chapter and the previous one, we have traced two faces of government. One provides valuable services ranging from public goods to efficiency-enhancing regulations and redistribution. The other introduces deadweight losses via taxation or worse, unnecessary regulations and even corruption. How do we balance out those two different facets of government intervention in the economy? This question is perhaps nowhere as central as in deciding the extent of government redistribution, which revolves around the issue of *equity-efficiency trade-off*. The **equity-efficiency trade-off** refers to the balance between ensuring an equitable allocation of resources (equity) and increasing social surplus or total output (efficiency). Most would agree that equity and efficiency are the two most important goals for government policy.

Exhibit 10.18 depicts the typical trade-off society faces. What it shows is that the two goals—equity and efficiency—are often, but not always, in conflict. When social inequality is high, above the point marked A in the exhibit, further increases in inequality reduce social surplus: as we move up the vertical axis, further increasing social inequality, we also move down the horizontal axis, reducing social surplus. This could be for several reasons: for example, greater social inequality could create distortions by preventing some people from competing with others on a level playing field or by increasing conflict in society. However, for levels of social inequality below point A, further declines in inequality also come at the cost of lower social surplus—due to, for example, the deadweight losses involved in redistributive taxation. Now as we limit social inequality moving down the vertical axis, we also move down the horizontal axis, reducing social surplus. This trade-off between equity and efficiency represents the nub of the conflict between those who support big government and those who call for smaller government.

The **equity-efficiency trade-off** refers to the balance between ensuring an equitable allocation of resources (equity) and increasing social surplus or total output (efficiency).

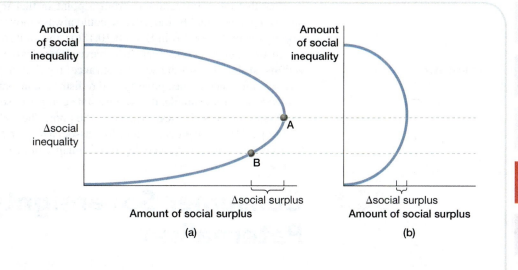

**Exhibit 10.18 The Equity-Efficiency Trade-off**

The government can often achieve greater social equality but only at the expense of greater inefficiencies, thus introducing a trade-off between equity and efficiency over a certain range. When social inequality is very high, there may be no conflict between equity and efficiency. We see this trade-off in both panels, but the steeper upward sloping portion in panel (a) indicates that there is a greater cost of reducing inequality in terms of social surplus than in panel (b).

> The trade-off between equity and efficiency represents the nub of the conflict between those who support big government and those who call for smaller government.

Where do you want to be along this curve? The answer to this question depends on your (normative) value judgments—for instance, is equity more important to you than efficiency? You may, for example, prefer to live in a fairly efficient society, even if this comes at the cost of considerable social inequality (corresponding to a point like B in Exhibit 10.18 panel (a)). In contrast, some of your classmates might be willing to put up with greater inefficiencies and lower social surplus in order to achieve greater equality (approaching the origin). In a broad sense, the portion of the curve between the origin and point A in this exhibit represents the dividing line between Democrats and Republicans: on one hand, Presidents Clinton and Obama have emphasized the importance of reducing social inequality, arguing that the rich need to pay more in taxes. Presidents Reagan and George W. Bush, on the other hand, have argued that high tax rates distort decisions and have opted for tax reforms based on efficiency grounds.

Though economic analysis does not tell us what those value judgments should be, such analysis is crucial both because it determines the shape of the curve, thus providing us the menu from which we have to make our choices between equity and efficiency, and because it also highlights some of the choices that are "dominated" (meaning that they are always worse than some other available options). Let's start with the first useful role of economic analysis, which we can understand by comparing Exhibit 10.18 panels (a) and (b). The first has a curve that is much flatter (in the upward-sloping region) than the latter. This implies that the economy modeled in Exhibit 10.18 panel (a) has a much greater cost of reducing social inequality in terms of social surplus than the economy in Exhibit 10.18 panel (b). You can see this by observing that the same reduction in social inequality (Δsocial inequality, indicated by the vertical distance between the two dashed lines in the exhibit) shown on the vertical axis of the two exhibits corresponds to a much greater change in the amount of social surplus (Δsocial surplus) in panel (a) than in panel (b) in Exhibit 10.18.

The second useful role of economic analysis can also be seen from these two exhibits. There's an entire downward-sloping portion to the relationship between inequality and social surplus (i.e., the upper half of the curve between the y-axis and point A). This corresponds to the region in which there is no trade-off between reducing social inequality and increasing surplus, because in this range, inequality is so high that it starts interfering with the proper functioning of the economy (for example, high inequality leads to crime or lack of efficient allocation of individual talent, because those who are much poorer than the rest cannot attend the best schools). Economic analysis, by highlighting the possibility of this downward-sloping range, is useful for societal decision making, because the individual or policymaker who values both equity and efficiency would always strive to establish policies that move an economy from a point in that region of the curve to somewhere between points A and B. Indeed, one could always move from any point in this downward-sloping region to point A in Exhibit 10.18(a), thus improving both equity and efficiency.

All developed nations seek to achieve some degree of equality in their society. The **welfare state** refers to the set of insurance, regulation, and transfer programs utilized to create a safety net, reduce poverty, and redistribute income from the rich to the poor. In the United States, for example, the welfare state comprises several programs, such as Medicaid and food stamps, which are targeted to the poor. The welfare state is even more expansive in Europe. Despite the deadweight loss associated with such systems, many European nations choose to promote some degree of equality in income.

The **welfare state** refers to the set of insurance, regulation, and transfer programs operated by the government, including unemployment benefits, pensions, and government-run and -financed healthcare.

## 10.5 Consumer Sovereignty and Paternalism

Beyond promoting equality, some economists have argued that government intervention is necessary because individuals may suffer from decision errors or may find it difficult to evaluate certain choices. For example, many people do not have the finance background necessary to navigate the world of retirement savings account options. In such situations, they can make mistakes that are costly to themselves. Should the government try to prevent them from making such mistakes?

One answer to whether the government should engage in these types of actions relates to the concept of *consumer sovereignty*. **Consumer sovereignty** is the view that choices made by a consumer reflect his or her true preferences, and outsiders, including the government, should not interfere with these choices. Some economists argue that we should evaluate all resource allocations according to the preferences of consumers at the time they make a decision. If those preferences are wrong or turn out to be wrong after the fact, so be it.

At the other end of the spectrum is *paternalism*. **Paternalism** is the view that consumers do not always know what is best for them, and the government should encourage or induce them to change their actions. Many crucial reformers who played important roles in the founding of the welfare state, from William Beveridge in the United Kingdom to Franklin Delano Roosevelt and Lyndon Johnson in the United States, held this view. This approach gives the government an active hand in designing choices to help individuals make the right decisions—decisions they might not have made by themselves.

The Social Security system in the United States, which forces individuals to save for old age, was born out of paternalism. Laws that ban substance abuse are also motivated, in part, by paternalism. In contrast, in a world with no externalities, consumer sovereignty would allow individuals to consume as many drugs as desired, even if the drugs were addictive and potentially harmful.

In fact, the big difference between paternalism and consumer sovereignty is a normative one. How much do we value consumer sovereignty in and of itself? And how much do we want to allow the government to interfere in individual decision making? It's a murky area. Nevertheless, economists find their voices on both sides of the debate. We briefly review both sides now.

**Consumer sovereignty** is the view that choices made by a consumer reflect his or her true preferences, and outsiders, including the government, should not interfere with these choices.

**Paternalism** is the view that consumers do not always know what is best for them, and the government should encourage or induce them to change their actions.

### The Debate

Those economists toward the paternalistic end of the spectrum would probably say that some mistakes simply result from the fact that individuals are not used to making decisions of a certain type. For example, most people, when first confronted with investing in the stock market, may not understand the implications of their decisions. Advocates for government intervention believe that the government can help—by providing information. In their view, this is not a violation of consumer sovereignty; in fact, it corresponds to a strengthening of it, because better information drives better decisions.

Some economists go somewhat further and suggest that the government should also play the role of "nudging" individuals in the right direction. If the government is convinced, for example, that individuals are not saving enough for retirement or are making investment choices that are too risky, then it can design savings schemes to encourage people to save more or to invest in less risky assets.

The pure consumer sovereignty view would be that the government's business is not to "nudge" people into choices they can make on their own. Economists favoring this view would suggest that any kind of paternalism requires that some group of people (the government, the elite, intellectuals) knows what's good for consumers. Although this may sometimes be true, it generally raises several philosophical and practical problems. How can the government make extremely complicated decisions for us? How can we trust the government to really have our interests in mind? How can we distinguish between differences in opinions and preferences and those cases in which people really are making mistakes?

Beyond these questions, it is important to note that every government intervention is costly and paid for by tax revenues. Thus, every activity relinquished to the government increases the deadweight loss that society faces. In the end, we urge you to be the judge of how acceptable you find government intervention in individual choices. It is a normative question.

## EVIDENCE-BASED ECONOMICS

### What is the optimal size of government?

As you have probably concluded by now, this question is difficult to answer, because it will depend on your value judgments. We can probably state with some certainty, however, that a minimal amount of government intervention in the economy is necessary. An economy needs some amount of law and order, some national defense, some regulation, some redistribution, and so on. So, most people would agree that government needs to be in the picture in some way.

But that still leaves a broad range, and you have to use your own value judgments to decide where you want to be in that range. You're not completely alone, though—economics can serve as a useful guide. Rather than answering the question "Is more government good or bad?," economics can help you weigh the costs and benefits of specific government interventions. And, in a case that calls for intervention, economics can help improve the design of policies.

Let's consider two specific areas to make our general point about how the tools of economics can help you think about the optimal size of government.

**1.** As we have shown, a major efficiency loss of taxation is deadweight loss. Thus, the debate on the reach of government should hinge on the effect of its actions: the larger the deadweight loss, the worse the policy, all else being equal. In those cases with large deadweight losses, one can make the argument that it is a bad place for the government to intervene.

**2.** The government typically operates in a slow-moving manner. A significant drag on the economy can result if regulators cannot move swiftly in response to changing market conditions.

We now focus on the first of these and then discuss the second in the box at the end of this section.

A first consideration with this approach is that a heavy reliance on income taxation may result in more deadweight loss than would a broader spectrum of taxes (federal sales tax, estate taxes, etc.). This is because when the tax rate increases, the deadweight loss of taxation increases by even more (you can see this point by revisiting Exhibit 10.11 and increasing the tax from $2 to $4, and you will see that the deadweight loss triangle is now much larger). This implies that, all else being equal, it is better to have many small tax sources rather than one large one. In this sense, when formulating policies, we should always compare the marginal deadweight loss of the last dollar raised from different sources of taxation to the marginal benefit of an additional dollar of tax revenue. For a tax that distorts behavior, the marginal benefit may not be worth the deadweight loss, which suggests the need to decrease this tax.

In the United States, the bulk of tax revenue is raised from income taxes. At the extremes, economists have a pretty good idea of the impact of income taxes on a worker's decision to supply labor. If there is a 100 percent tax on income, then there is really no reason to work—your take-home pay would always be $0! A tax that large is likely to be labeled absolutely inefficient by economists, because the cost to society of no one working would be much larger than the tax revenue generated.

But what if the tax rate were closer to present levels of the marginal federal tax rate (25 percent for someone earning $40,000 a year; see Exhibit 10.6)? If Americans get to keep 75 cents of every dollar that they earn, will everyone stop working or will they just carry on as if there were no tax on their income at all? The elasticity of labor supply gives us a convenient number with which to assess this question. Remember that elasticities are just a percentage change in quantity divided by a percentage change in price. In the case of labor supply, the tax rate changes the price of working—how much you get paid—and the quantity is the number of hours worked.

If the supply of labor is elastic, then the number of hours someone works is very sensitive to the wage rate. Thus, an increase in income taxes will have a large impact on labor supply. This lost work will create a lot of deadweight loss. But if labor supply is inelastic, then a tax increase won't cause a big change in the number of hours a worker supplies, which means that the increase in deadweight loss won't be large.

To estimate the elasticity of labor supply, economists have used data taken from workers' responses to large changes in income tax rates. Early empirical studies found that the Reagan tax cuts of the 1980s led to around a 6 percent increase in the number of hours worked—resulting in a relatively large elasticity estimate.[6] However, when economists used richer data sets to estimate the same elasticity, they obtained very small elasticity values, ranging between 0 and 0.1.[7]

As research progressed, economists began to focus on the impact of tax rates on a worker's reported taxable income. Initial analysis found very high elasticities of between 1.3 and 1.5,[8] but much of the early research on this topic looked only at the *short-run* response to higher marginal tax rates. However, this can differ from the *long-run* elasticity, because individuals may respond more strongly to a temporary change in taxes (that is, you may want to work more for a year if taxes are very low during that year, but if taxes are very low permanently, you may end up not working as hard). In fact, subsequent research focusing on long-run elasticities yielded much smaller estimates.

In general, these estimates suggest that the labor supply results have been decidedly mixed. This is probably why the two views of labor taxation persist today, and why this topic represents an important area for future research. As soon as the estimates begin to point to a smaller elasticity range, economists will be able to provide more precise estimates of the deadweight loss of income taxation.

Still, the size of government affects much more than inefficiencies associated with taxes. Even if there is very little deadweight loss associated with raising taxes, the sorts of government failures discussed above might also tip the scale against government intervention. Quantitative analysis of such government failures is another active area of current research.

**Question**

What is the optimal size of government?

**Answer**

It depends, but the deadweight loss of taxation and other costs of government intervention play a key role.

**Data**

Various data sources, including measures of the elasticity of labor supply.

**Caveat**

A range of empirical estimates of labor supply elasticities has surfaced.

# LETTING THE
## DATA SPEAK

### The Efficiency of Government Versus Privately Run Expeditions

A glimpse into the possibility that the government may respond to situations more slowly than private, profit-seeking enterprises is provided by a study comparing the success rates of government-funded expeditions to the North Pole and Northwest Passage versus privately funded voyages.[9] The research, conducted by economist Jonathan Karpoff, found that privately funded expeditions were smaller, cheaper, less likely to lose personnel, less likely to lose their ships, and more likely to achieve their objectives. Plus, the difference in outcomes between private and public expeditions was large. For example, publicly funded expeditions had an average of 5.9 deaths per expedition versus 0.9 deaths per privately funded expedition.

Karpoff was able to go a step further and see *why* privately funded expeditions were so much more successful than public expeditions. He found that their chief advantage was an ability to adapt to new technology quickly.

Many publicly funded expeditions were so slow to adapt to new technology that they didn't even supplement their crew's diets with vitamin C, even though knowledge of the relationship between scurvy and vitamin C deficiency had been known for centuries. Privately funded expeditions also developed innovations of their own. Chief among these was their ability to learn from the native population about shelter, clothing systems, and overland travel.

This research provides one example of the nimbleness of private voyages compared to that of public voyages. Although not definitive, it provides an example of how the tools of economics can help you think about the optimal extent of government intervention. How general this result is remains a question, but it does illustrate a common criticism of big government: its slow response can be a drag on economic efficiency.

# CHOICE
## &CONSEQUENCE

### Taxation and Innovation

We have seen that choosing high taxes has a range of consequences (including deadweight losses and inefficiencies) in addition to the redistributive aims that the government is trying to achieve. An additional adverse consequence of high taxes for a government might be to encourage the high earners to emigrate to other countries. Recent work by economists Ufuk Akcigit, Salmone Baslandze, and Stefanie Stantcheva shows that high-income innovators become much more likely to move to other countries in response to high taxes, and this tendency has fairly major consequences on a socially very useful activity—innovation.[10] They estimate that higher top tax rates would increase the total number of high-income ("superstar") domestic innovators emigrating from the United States and reduce the number of foreign innovators immigrating to the United States. In total, a 10 percentage point increase in the top tax rate would reduce the total number of domestic superstar innovators in the United States by 0.1 percent and foreign superstar innovators residing in the United States by 18.4 percent. These effects are quite consequential. For example, even ignoring the broader benefits of innovation on others, these authors estimate that the additional loss from a 10 percentage point increase in the top tax rate could be as large as $2.5 trillion. (Because there is considerable uncertainty about

how much income and innovation generates, the actual loss could be much larger than this, or if one takes into account the broader benefits from innovation, the loss might be even smaller).

These numbers suggest potentially significant additional costs to increased taxation of high earners beyond those captured by labor supply elasticities and deadweight losses. Not only would a country unilaterally increasing top tax rates lose revenues because of the flight of high-income innovators, but it would also miss out on the new technologies that these individuals would have otherwise created domestically. Think, for example, what would have happened to the U.S. economy if innovators and entrepreneurs such as Larry Page and Sergey Brin (who founded Google) or Steve Jobs (who founded Apple) located their companies in another country.

But for those wishing to increase top tax rates, the glass is only half empty. Imagine what would happen if all advanced economies increased their top tax rates in tandem. Then no country would become relatively more attractive for these high-income innovators and entrepreneurs, and tax authorities would not have to worry about their flight. This reasoning points to a more general conclusion: when undertaking major changes in tax structure, international policy coordination on taxes is central.

## Summary

■ Government can play an important role in ensuring that markets are competitive, efficient, and equitable.

■ Key roles of the government include: taxation to raise funds to provide public goods, such as national defense, policing, and infrastructure investments that would not be provided adequately by the market; the use of tax and transfer programs to achieve a more equitable distribution of resources in society; and the use of taxes and subsidies as well as regulation to correct market failures.

■ The costs of government interventions must be compared carefully with their benefits.

■ Economics is most useful not as a value judgment on whether government is good or bad, but for understanding what sorts of activities require government intervention.

## Key Terms

budget deficit *p. 232*
budget surplus *p. 232*
tax revenues (or receipts) *p. 232*
payroll tax (or social insurance tax) *p. 232*
corporate income taxes *p. 233*
excise taxes *p. 233*
sales taxes *p. 233*
transfer payments *p. 235*

progressive tax system *p. 236*
average tax rate *p. 236*
marginal tax rate *p. 236*
proportional tax system *p. 237*
regressive tax system *p. 237*
tax incidence *p. 240*
regulation *p. 245*
direct regulation (or command-and-control regulation) *p. 245*

price ceiling *p. 246*
price floor *p. 248*
government failures *p. 248*
corruption *p. 249*
equity-efficiency trade-off *p. 250*
welfare state *p. 252*
consumer sovereignty *p. 252*
paternalism *p. 252*

## Questions

*All questions are available in MyEconLab for practice and instructor assignment.*

1. When does a government run a budget surplus?

2. Government spending in the United States has grown over time and now accounts for more than 40 percent of U.S. national income. Does this mean that the government has been consistently running a budget deficit?

3. How does the federal government raise revenue? What is the largest source of revenue for the federal government? Do state governments raise revenue from the same sources as the federal government?

4. What are the factors underlying government taxation and spending decisions?

5. How do governments use spending and taxation to reduce inequality and poverty in an economy?

6. What are the different types of tax systems? Give one example of each type of tax system.

7. What is meant by tax incidence? Is the entire burden of the tax always borne by those on whom it is imposed?

8. Are lump-sum taxes regressive or progressive? Is the deadweight loss of taxation the same for different types of taxes?

9. What is meant by direct regulation? Give a few examples of direct regulation.

10. What are the costs associated with government intervention in an economic system? Given that there are costs involved with government intervention in an economy, why do governments choose to intervene in markets?

11. What is a black market? What types of goods are likely to be traded in a black market? What problems do black markets pose in an economy?

12. How would you depict the trade-off between equity and efficiency on a graph? How would a government decide where it wants to be on this curve?

13. Explain the terms "paternalism" and "consumer sovereignty."

14. Why are there two different views on the effect of taxation on labor supply in the United States?

15. If your goal is to minimize the deadweight loss from a tax, would you tax goods for which demand is elastic or goods for which demand is inelastic, everything else being equal? Explain using a diagram.

# Problems

*All problems are available in MyEconLab for practice and instructor assignment.*

1. The following table gives the 2013 federal income tax rates for a single individual.

| Income | Rate |
|---|---|
| $0 to $8,925 | 10% |
| $8,925 to $36,250 | 15% |
| $36,250 to $87,850 | 25% |
| $87,850 to $183,250 | 28% |
| $183,250 to $398,350 | 33% |
| $398,350 to $400,000 | 35% |
| $400,000 and above | 39.60% |

   a. Calculate the total tax payable for an individual who earns $250,000 a year.

   b. What is the marginal tax rate?

   c. Calculate the average tax rate.

2. Britain taxed windows from 1696 until 1851. Under the 1747–1757 tax rates, you would pay no tax if your home had 0–9 windows, but if your home had 10–14 windows you would pay a tax of 6 pence per window *for every window in your home.*

   a. In what way is the window tax similar to the U.S. income tax?

   b. In what way is the window tax different from the U.S. income tax?

   c. Do you think that from 1747 to 1757, the number of new homes with 9 or fewer windows increased from the pre-1747 days? Explain.

3. Many people have argued that an income tax should be "marriage neutral," that is, two people should pay the same total tax whether they are married or they are single. Suppose Amanda earns nothing, Ben earns $60,000, and Cathy and Dylan each earn $30,000. They are all single.

   a. Amanda pays no tax because she has no income. If they all live in a country that has a progressive income tax, which will be higher: the tax that Ben pays or the sum of the taxes Cathy and Dylan pay?

   b. Amanda marries Ben and Cathy marries Dylan. This country taxes married couples based on a family's total income. Show that the newlyweds Amanda and Ben will pay the same tax as Cathy and Dylan's family.

   c. Is the income tax in this country marriage neutral?

4. Consider a simple opportunity for trade: You are renting a new condo and the previous tenant offers to sell her old couch. You are the sole buyer and you have a willingness to pay of $200. The previous tenant is the sole seller and has a willingness to accept of $120.

   a. Regardless of what price you and the previous tenant agree to, what is the social surplus, assuming you are able to come to some sort of mutually beneficial agreement?

   b. Suppose the condo association imposes a $50 fee (i.e., a tax) for each item left in the condo during the move-in/move-out. Will you still be able to reach an agreement? What is the effect on social surplus?

   c. Suppose the fee were raised to $100. What would be the effect on social surplus? In other words, what is the deadweight loss of this new policy?

5. Consider the following supply and demand for hats. Suppose there is a $3 tax per hat. This exercise will demonstrate that the effect of the tax does not depend on who is required to actually pay the tax.

| Price (price paid for b; price received for c) | Supply | Demand | Supply with $3 tax on sellers (part b) | Demand with $3 tax on buyers (part c) |
|---|---|---|---|---|
| $0 | 0 | 120 | | |
| $1 | 10 | 100 | | |
| $2 | 20 | 80 | | |
| $3 | 30 | 60 | | |
| $4 | 40 | 40 | | |
| $5 | 50 | 20 | | |
| $6 | 60 | 0 | | |

   a. Sketch the supply and demand curves. What would the equilibrium quantity and price be if there were no tax?

   b. Now, assume the $3 tax is levied on sellers; for example, when the price paid is $4, the sellers will receive $1 per unit and supply 10 hats. Complete the new column and add the new supply curve to your graph.

   c. Repeat, but with tax instead levied on the buyers. What is the equilibrium price paid and price received?

   d. Regardless of how the tax is levied, what fraction of the $3 tax (tax incidence) is paid by the buyers?

6. The following diagram shows the effect of a $4 tax.

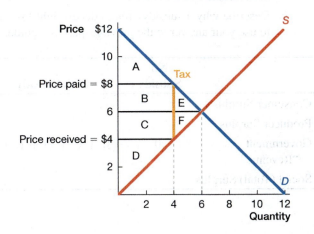

**a.** Complete the table using the letters from the diagram on the preceding page.

**b.** Based on this calculation, what is the deadweight loss of the tax? This is the difference in social surplus between the two columns.

**c.** Redraw a similar diagram, except with a perfectly inelastic (vertical) supply curve. Explain why the deadweight loss is zero in this case.

| | No Tax | With Tax |
|---|---|---|
| Consumer Surplus | | |
| Producer Surplus | | |
| Government Tax Revenue | 0 | B + C |
| Social (Total) Surplus | | |

**7.** This chapter has focused on the effect of taxes. Let's consider the effect of subsidies, which also generate deadweight loss. A subsidy creates a gap between the price received by sellers and the price paid by buyers.

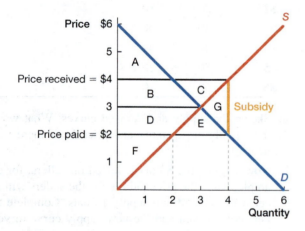

**a.** Complete the table using the letters from the above diagram. The government "revenue" is negative, because a subsidy requires a payment by the government.

**b.** Based on this table, what is the deadweight loss of the subsidy? (Hint: this is the difference in social surplus between the two columns.)

**c.** Describe why a subsidy creates deadweight loss. Try to use your answer to the previous part as a guide.

| | No Subsidy | With Subsidy |
|---|---|---|
| Consumer Surplus | | |
| Producer Surplus | | |
| Government "Revenue" | 0 | −(B + C + D + E + G) |
| Social (Total) Surplus | | |

**8.** Suppose the supply and demand schedules for cell phones are as follows:

| Price | Demand | Supply |
|---|---|---|
| $2 | 10 | 0 |
| $3 | 9 | 0 |
| $4 | 8 | 0 |
| $5 | 7 | 1 |
| $6 | 6 | 2 |
| $7 | 5 | 3 |
| $8 | 4 | 4 |
| $9 | 3 | 5 |
| $10 | 2 | 6 |
| $11 | 1 | 7 |
| $12 | 0 | 8 |

**a.** Make a sketch of supply and demand.

**b.** Find the equilibrium price and quantity in the cell phone market.

**c.** Suppose the government sets a maximum price (a price ceiling) of $6. How many cell phones are traded? Add the price ceiling to your sketch.

**d.** Suppose the government instead sets a minimum price (a price floor) of $10. How many cell phones are traded? Add the price floor to your sketch.

**9.** Some government agricultural policies involve price controls. Other agricultural policies, however, involve quantity controls.

**a.** The equilibrium price of wheat is $5 and the equilibrium quantity is 100. Draw a supply and demand diagram that shows the equilibrium in the wheat market.

**b.** Suppose the government institutes a policy that prohibits wheat farmers from growing more than 80 bushels of wheat in total. How would this policy change the supply curve for wheat?

**c.** Use your supply and demand diagram to show that the government policy in part (b) would raise the equilibrium price and lower the equilibrium quantity of wheat.

**d.** Show that the policy in part (b) will lead to a deadweight loss in the wheat market.

**10.** Create a sketch that shows the trade-off between equity and efficiency. Highlight the portion of the curve where there is a fundamental trade-off between equity and efficiency. In this region, what is the cost of moving up the curve? What is the cost of moving down the curve?

**11.** Consider the following reservation values for buyers and sellers of soccer balls.

| Buyers | Willingness to pay | Sellers | Willingness to accept |
|---|---|---|---|
| Alex | $70 | Clint | $10 |
| Hope | $50 | Tim | $30 |
| Carli | $30 | Michael | $40 |
| Abby | $10 | Landon | $60 |

a. Sketch the supply and demand. (It will be a step function; see Exhibit 7.2 for an example.)

b. What are the producer surplus, consumer surplus, and social surplus given the market-clearing price of $40?

c. With the goal of making soccer more accessible, the government imposes a $20 price ceiling on soccer balls. What is the new producer surplus? What is the new consumer surplus, assuming Alex is able to buy a soccer ball? What is the social surplus? Based on this, what is the deadweight loss? Highlight deadweight loss on your graph.

d. It is possible that Carli buys a soccer ball given the price floor of $20. If she is able to, what is the deadweight loss of the price ceiling? Is it higher or lower than before? Why?

12. The following graph shows the supply $(Q_S = 2P)$ and demand $(Q_D = 12 = P)$ for cigarettes. The government decides to impose $6 tax on each cigarette.

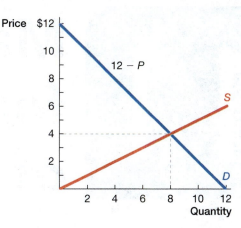

a. What is the producer surplus, consumer surplus, and social surplus when there is no tax on cigarettes?

b. With the tax, verify that the price paid increases to $8.

c. What are the tax revenue, producer surplus, and consumer surplus? What is the social surplus? What is the deadweight loss?

d. It appears that a tax on cigarettes lowers surplus. What argument can be made in support this tax? In other words, what have we failed to consider in our analysis?

# 11 Markets for Factors of Production

## Is there discrimination in the labor market?

In her acceptance speech to become the Democratic Party's presidential candidate in the 2016 election, Secretary Hillary Rodham Clinton noted "we just put the biggest crack in the glass ceiling." The "glass ceiling" that she referred to implies that there is a limit to how far certain individuals—in this case, women—can climb in the workforce. Does a glass ceiling really exist in the U.S. labor market?

As always, data help us answer the question. One interesting fact is that over the past several decades, women have represented *at most 3 percent* of U.S. CEOs. Why do women appear to be so underrepresented in the upper echelons of companies? Is the discrepancy because of discrimination against women? Is it because they tend to take time away from paid work to raise their children?

The lack of women at the top of companies is only the tip of the iceberg when it comes to differences across people in labor markets. For example, in the past several decades, for every dollar men earned, women earned roughly 80 cents. Similar differences are found when comparing people of different race, age, and even physical attractiveness!

Can economics explain such differences?

So far, we have focused our attention on goods that we as consumers buy: cell phones, cheese boxes, cakes, and electricity. In this chapter we examine what producers buy: *inputs to produce those goods*. The major inputs that we will consider are labor, machines (physical capital), and land. In so doing, we explore the reasons people earn different wages in the labor market, and why some rise to the top while others remain at mid-level. Our discussion of the labor market will bring us to a general understanding of the determinants of wages. When thinking about how well our model represents the real world, we will return to our opening question.

## CHAPTER OUTLINE

## 11.1  The Competitive Labor Market

The market for labor is of particular importance in the economy because it affects all of us. You are directly influenced by the labor market when you are looking for a job or are employed and earning money. In this chapter, instead of firms acting as suppliers, as we have viewed them so far, firms are the buyers (demanders) of labor. And, individuals, like you, are the suppliers of labor.

The market for labor, then, is composed of suppliers (workers) and demanders (firms). Workers produce goods and services and therefore are known as factors of production—a term we've met before in Chapter 6. Remember that a factor of production is used in the production of other goods.

Markets for factors of production are somewhat different from markets for goods and services that we consume, because the demand for factors of production is derived from the demand for final goods and services. A firm first makes the decision to produce a good or service and then decides which factors are necessary to produce that good or service.

Although firms tend to use many factors of production, the main factors that we will focus on are labor, machines (physical capital), and land. For instance, consider the iPad. To produce it, Apple uses labor (in the form of computer hardware and software engineers), physical capital (in the form of machinery to build the good), and land (from Cupertino, California to Chengdu, China to house its various production sites).

In the market for labor, the roles of demander and supplier are reversed: Businesses are buyers (demanders) of labor and individual workers are suppliers.

> All firms rely on labor as a major factor of production.

### The Demand for Labor

A typical firm in modern economies uses dozens, likely hundreds, of different machines, ranging from computers to lasers to old-fashioned assembly lines. Nevertheless, all firms rely on labor as a major factor of production. Workers operate machines and often perform tasks more efficiently than machines, because human beings have judgment skills that machines still lack. In this sense, a firm's desire to achieve its production objectives causes it to demand labor.

Let us return to The Wisconsin Cheeseman, the cheese-packing firm we discussed in Chapter 6. We'll begin by holding fixed the other factors of production that this company uses—physical capital and land—and focus exclusively on labor. That is, we will focus on the short-run decisions facing The Cheeseman. We'll also assume that this company is a price-taker in the product market.

## Exhibit 11.1 The Wisconsin Cheeseman's Production Function

The production function describes the number of cheese boxes that The Cheeseman can produce by hiring additional workers. Crucially, eventually each additional worker that The Cheeseman hires has a smaller incremental effect on the number of cheese boxes produced, demonstrating the Law of Diminishing Returns.

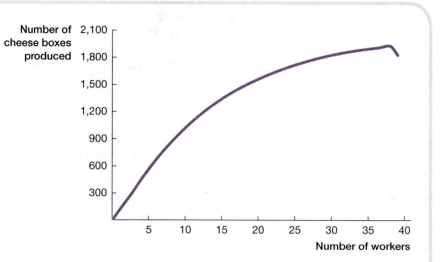

We saw in Chapter 6 that The Wisconsin Cheeseman can increase the production of cheese boxes by employing more people. Exhibit 11.1 shows the relationship between the number of cheese boxes produced and the number of workers employed. The numbers that underlie the figure are shown in Exhibit 11.2. Exhibits 11.1 and 11.2 make clear the Law of Diminishing Returns, which we studied in Chapter 6. Recall that this law states that the marginal productivity of an additional unit of labor eventually decreases as we increase the number of workers.

From Chapter 6, we are familiar with the first three columns in Exhibit 11.2. For example, column (3) gives the marginal product of labor. This informs us of how many more cheese boxes will be produced when The Cheeseman hires another worker. When we

## Exhibit 11.2 Production Data for The Wisconsin Cheeseman

The Cheeseman is tasked with choosing how much output to generate per day and how many employees to hire to produce that level of output. The table summarizes the number of workers the firm will need for any given level of output and how much value each additional worker adds. Column (1) shows cheese boxes produced per day, column (2) shows the number of workers employed, column (3) shows the marginal output produced by each additional worker, and column (4) shows the VMPL, which denotes the value of marginal product of labor and is equal to the price of a cheese box multiplied by the marginal product of labor (MPL). This represents the dollar value of this additional output.

| (1) Output per Day | (2) Number of Workers Employed | (3) Marginal Product of Labor | (4) VMPL = MPL × P = Column (3) × $2 |
|---|---|---|---|
| 0 | 0 | | |
| 100 | 1 | 100 | $200 |
| 207 | 2 | 107 | $214 |
| 321 | 3 | 114 | $228 |
| ... | ... | ... | ... |
| 1,019 | 10 | 80 | $160 |
| 1,092 | 11 | 73 | $146 |
| 1,161 | 12 | 69 | $138 |
| 1,225 | 13 | 64 | $128 |
| 1,284 | 14 | 59 | $118 |
| 1,339 | 15 | 55 | $110 |
| 1,390 | 16 | 51 | $102 |
| 1,438 | 17 | 48 | $96 |
| ... | ... | ... | ... |
| 1,934 | 38 | 10 | $20 |
| 1,834 | 39 | −100 | −$200 |

**Exhibit 11.3 Demand for Labor**

We can depict the quantity of labor demanded at each wage rate. We assume that the marginal cost of an additional worker is $110 (orange line). This allows us to identify the equilibrium quantity as 15 employees, where VMPL = daily wage of a worker.

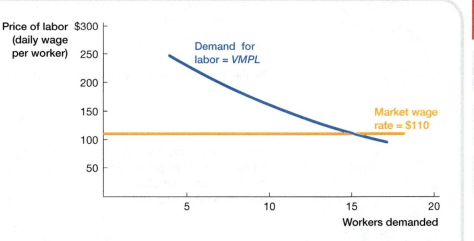

The **value of marginal product of labor** is the contribution of an additional worker to a firm's revenues.

multiply this number by the price of cheese boxes, we obtain the **value of marginal product of labor** (VMPL). The VMPL is the contribution of an additional worker to a firm's revenues; it is equal to the marginal product of labor times the price of a cheese box. For mathematical clarity, we assume the price of a cheese box is $2, so column (4) obtains the value of marginal product of labor by multiplying by 2 the number in column (3).

Now assume that The Wisconsin Cheeseman currently employs 14 workers and is considering expanding its workforce. Exhibit 11.2 shows that the value of the marginal product of the fifteenth worker is $110 per day (additional revenue = VMPL = 55 additional boxes of cheese × $2 per box = $110). If The Cheeseman is maximizing its profits, should it hire the fifteenth worker?

Let's start with a daily wage of $118. Should The Cheeseman expand to the fifteenth worker? No. We know this because the value of adding the last worker is his VMPL—$110 for the fifteenth worker. It is not profitable to pay a worker $118 who brings in only an additional $110 in revenues.

What about at a daily wage of $105? Now the story changes. Hiring the fifteenth worker increases profits because the daily wage is less than the additional revenue of $110. The implication is that for The Cheeseman to be optimally purchasing labor—not paying more than it's worth—it expands its workforce until the VMPL is equal to the daily wage of the worker.

This optimizing action enables us to translate the value of marginal product of the firm into its labor demand. Exhibit 11.3 illustrates the labor demand of The Wisconsin Cheeseman, which traces the value of marginal product shown in Exhibit 11.2. The labor demand curve of a firm is downward-sloping because its value of marginal product is decreasing—a consequence of the Law of Diminishing Returns. In Exhibit 11.3, we assume that the market wage rate is $110 per day. At this wage, the optimal number of workers for The Cheeseman to hire is 15, where the demand for labor intersects the market wage.

Two ideas are implicit in this derivation, and it is useful to spell them out. First, The Wisconsin Cheeseman sells its cheese boxes in a competitive market, and therefore from Chapter 6 we know that it can sell as many cheese boxes as it wants at the market price. Second, we assume that the labor market is also perfectly competitive, so The Cheeseman can hire as many workers as it wishes at the market wage.

We have now seen two ways in which a firm like The Wisconsin Cheeseman maximizes its profits:

1. In Chapter 6, it chose the total quantity of production in order to maximize profits, and we saw that this led to the condition: expand production until marginal cost = price.
2. In this chapter, we see that the firm maximizes profits by optimally choosing its labor by expanding its workforce until the marginal product of labor × price = VMPL = wage.

How do these two conditions relate to each other? Do they conflict? That is, does a competitive firm struggle to optimize the number of employees it hires while simultaneously optimizing its output?

Reassuringly, these two conditions are *identical*: once one is in place, the other follows. To see this, divide both sides of

$$\text{Marginal product of labor} \times \text{Price} = \text{Wage}$$

by the marginal product of labor (MPL), which leads to

$$\text{Price} = \frac{\text{Wage}}{\text{MPL}}.$$

This is simply the wage divided by the marginal product of labor. Say that an additional worker costs $110 per day and has a marginal product of 55 boxes of cheese. In this case, producing 55 more cheese boxes costs $110. Thus, the marginal cost is $110/55, or $2. This shows that wage/MPL equals marginal cost. Therefore,

$$\text{Marginal cost} = \frac{\text{Wage}}{\text{MPL}} = \text{Price}.$$

This derivation shows that when The Wisconsin Cheeseman expands its workforce until VMPL = wage, it is also producing where price = marginal cost.

## 11.2  The Supply of Labor: Your Labor-Leisure Trade-off

> **You must decide how much to work and how much to "play" or simply "not work."**

When considering whether you should take a summer job at a firm like The Cheeseman, what trade-offs are you facing? On the one hand, you can more easily afford a new laptop if you decide to work, but it comes at an expense—missing out on fun with your friends over the summer. Economists denote nonpaying activities, such as having fun with your friends, as "leisure."

In Chapter 5, we focused on the buyer's problem, in which your choice between various goods and services determined your level of satisfaction. When considering the choice between labor and leisure, you must decide how much to work and how much to "play" or simply "not work."

There would seem to be one major difference between the two scenarios, however. You decide whether or not to buy goods and services based on their prices—an iPad might cost $600, whereas a MacBook Pro might cost $1,200. But what's the price of hanging out with your friends? Isn't it free? Well, just as we learned in Chapter 1 that Facebook isn't free, the same is true for leisure. This is because the "price" of leisure is the *opportunity cost of leisure*, and that opportunity cost is the lost wages from not working.

So, how do you make an optimizing decision when deciding how much to work or hang out with your friends? By now, you likely anticipate the answer: you should set marginal benefits equal to marginal costs. In this case, that means you should consume leisure up to the point at which the marginal benefit equals the marginal cost, where the marginal cost is the wage rate. We can write this condition simply as

$$\text{Marginal benefit of leisure} = \text{Wage}.$$

Would you rather work over the summer or master Call of Duty?

Let's put these observations into action by considering an example. Exhibit 11.4 shows the total days of labor supplied per year for Alice and Tom at various wage rates. For example, at a wage rate of $100 per day, Alice would work 205 days per year and Tom would work 125 days per year. One first consideration is how the number of days worked changes with increases in the wage rate. Both Alice and Tom work more at higher wage rates. This is intuitive: if the campus bookstore offered you $64 per day (for working 8 hours) you might not accept, but if it raised the daily wage to $200 per day, you might wait in line for a chance to work. Exhibit 11.5 translates Alice's and Tom's labor supply choices in Exhibit 11.4 to individual labor supply

**Exhibit 11.4** Total Days of Labor Supplied per Year for Alice and Tom

Here we can see how the labor-leisure trade-off plays out for Alice and Tom. For example, if the going rate for an 8-hour day is $25, Alice will work 25 days that year, but Tom won't work at all. However, at a daily rate of $125, Alice works 260 days and Tom works 155 days.

| Wage Rate (per 8-hour day) | Alice | Tom |
|---|---|---|
| $ 25 | 25 | 0 |
| $ 50 | 95 | 50 |
| $ 75 | 150 | 90 |
| $100 | 205 | 125 |
| $125 | 260 | 155 |
| $175 | 310 | 190 |
| $225 | 350 | 230 |
| $275 | 365 | 280 |
| $375 | 365 | 340 |
| $500 | 365 | 365 |
| $600 | 365 | 365 |

curves. One important property of both labor supply curves is that as we get closer and closer to 365, which would mean working every day, it takes bigger and bigger wage increases to induce the same increase in the days worked per year. In fact, once we reach the maximum supply of 365 days a year, both Alice's and Tom's labor supply curve becomes vertical, indicating that they can no longer increase their labor supplies no matter what the wage.

To construct the *market* supply curve, we need to aggregate the individual labor supply curves. To do this, we horizontally sum the individual labor supply curves (meaning that we sum the amounts that each individual supplies to the market at each value of the wage). Suppose the market consists of only Alice and Tom. In this case, at a daily wage rate of $50, they combine to provide 145 days of work (Alice works 95 days; Tom works 50 days). At a daily wage rate of $100, they combine to provide 330 days of work (Alice works 205 days; Tom works 125 days). Summing at each wage level produces the market supply curve, which is depicted in panel (c) of Exhibit 11.5.

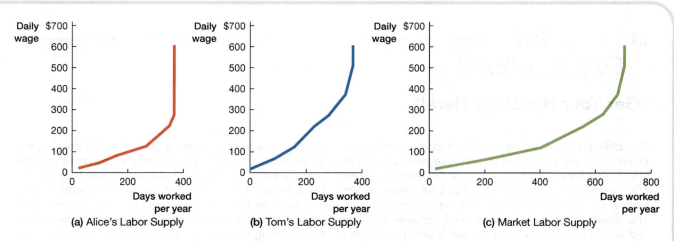

(a) Alice's Labor Supply    (b) Tom's Labor Supply    (c) Market Labor Supply

**Exhibit 11.5** Individual Labor Supply Curves

Panel (a) depicts Alice's annual work days at each daily wage, and panel (b) does the same for Tom. By summing the hours that Alice and Tom are willing to work at a given daily wage, we construct the labor market supply curve. Thus, at a daily wage of $175, Alice works for 310 days and Tom works for 190 days. Together they work 500 days at a daily wage of $175. We construct the market supply curve by similarly summing Alice and Tom's labor supplies at each value of the daily wage. Diagrammatically, this is equivalent to summing their labor supply curves horizontally.

## CHOICE & CONSEQUENCE

### Producing Web Sites and Computer Programs

You might recall that in Chapter 8, you accepted a free-lance job producing Web sites and computer programs. Let's say that your wage was $10 per hour. If your employer raised your wage to $10,000 per hour, would that lure you to work more hours? For many, the answer may not be completely obvious. On the one hand, you can maintain a nice lifestyle by working very few hours if you are paid $10,000 per hour. On the other hand, the cost of leisure—your forgone wages—just increased by a great deal.

An economic analysis of the problem does not imply that along the entire wage range, labor supply slopes up when wages go up. Over the wage range that most people think about, it does make sense that on average, people work more for more money, just like Alice and Tom. This is

called the *substitution effect*, a term that we introduced in the appendix to Chapter 5. The substitution effect implies that when the price of leisure increases, people will substitute working for relaxing.

However, another term we discussed in Chapter 5 is the *income effect*, which implies that when wages increase, your total income increases and you can afford more expensive things, such as more leisure time. The relative strength of these opposing forces on each individual's decision making determines the slope of his or her labor supply curve.

Economists have explored many situations to determine whether the slope of the labor supply curve is positive or negative. What do you think they found? One example is in the next "Letting the Data Speak."

### Labor Market Equilibrium: Supply Meets Demand

Let us now put labor demand and labor supply together and explore the equilibrium implications in the cheese-packing industry. Consider Exhibit 11.6, where we aggregate over several hundred laborers and several dozen firms competing in the labor market for cheese packers. As usual, the intersection of the supply and demand curves gives the market equilibrium, which determines both the equilibrium wage rate and the amount of labor supplied and demanded in the market. The market supply and demand curves allow us to further our understanding of how different factors affect the market demand and market supply of labor.

## LETTING THE DATA SPEAK

### "Get Your Hot Dogs Here!"

One difficulty of measuring the labor supply curve in practice is that many employees do not have perfect flexibility in choosing how many hours to work. For example, many office workers must agree to work 9 to 5, and they may not have a lot of flexibility in deciding their overtime hours. This does not mean that the trade-off between earnings and leisure that we have emphasized is unimportant. But it does mean that estimating labor supply will be difficult.

An interesting study by economist Gerald Oettinger overcomes this difficulty by looking at the labor supply of stadium vendors in a major league baseball stadium during the season.[1] These vendors, who sell hot dogs, beer, cotton candy, lemon ice, peanuts, popcorn, and soda at major-league games, are subcontractors who decide their own working hours. They do not receive a fixed wage;

instead, their effective wage is determined by the demand for products they sell. More people at the games means more sales for the vendors, and people attend games at predictable times—particularly on the weekends and on nice weather days. The advantage of this set-up to test economic theory is that individual vendors are free to set their working hours, thus approximating the situation we have modeled.

Oettinger found that the vendors, who determine whether or not to work on a given day simply by looking at a calendar and the weather forecast, worked 55 percent to 65 percent more often when they expected their earnings to double. In essence, these vendors display the sort of behavior that economic theory would predict. Namely, when presented with a higher potential salary, they work more.

**Exhibit 11.6** Labor Market Equilibrium

By putting together what we have learned about diminishing marginal returns to labor and a positive relationship between wages and labor provided, we can now fully describe the labor market with a downward-sloping demand curve and upward-sloping supply curve, the intersection of which deter-mines the equilibrium wage rate and quantity of labor.

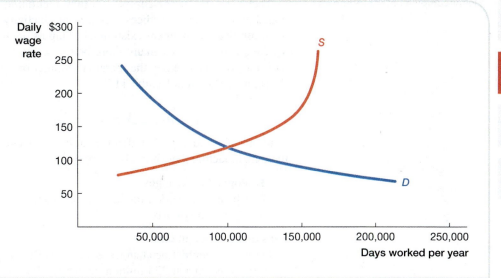

## Labor Demand Shifters

There are several key determinants of where the labor demand curve will be situated. Two important factors are:

1. Price of the good that the firm is producing
2. Technology of the firm

Concerning the price of the good that the firm is producing, let's again consider The Wisconsin Cheeseman. Assume that the popularity of cheese increases, which causes a rightward shift in the market demand curve for cheese boxes. This shift increases the equi-librium price of cheese boxes. The higher price increases the VMPL—the value of mar-ginal product of laborers who pack cheese. This in turn will cause The Cheeseman and other firms in the industry to demand more workers, leading to a rightward shift of the labor demand curve (to $D_2$), as shown in Exhibit 11.7. This shift will cause the equilibrium wage and employment level to increase, as shown in the exhibit.

A second factor that shifts the labor demand curve is the technology of the firm. For example, assume that robots take over part of the cheese-packing process, lowering the marginal product of labor. This could happen if the robots were a substitute for labor and leaves workers doing menial tasks that are not as productive as cheese packing. How would that affect the labor de-mand curve? This would cause the labor demand curve to shift to the left, lowering equilibrium wages and employment levels. This type of technology is a **labor-saving technology**. It is a type of technology that substitutes for existing labor inputs, reducing the marginal product of labor.

A **labor-saving technology** is a type of technology that substitutes for existing labor inputs, reducing the marginal product of labor.

**Exhibit 11.7** A Rightward Shift in the Labor Demand Curve

The labor demand curve shifts rightward if the price of the good that the firm is producing increases. It also shifts rightward if a labor-complementary technology is introduced.

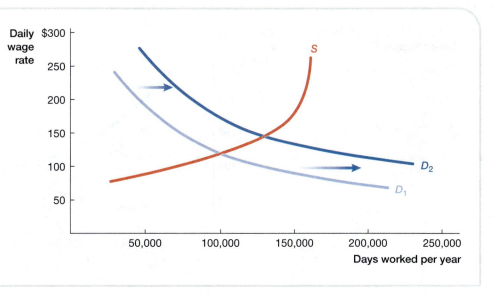

A **labor-complementary technology** is a technology that complements existing labor inputs, increasing the marginal product of labor.

There are also **labor-complementary technologies**, such as the case when an automated process increases cheese packers' productivity. Labor-complementary technologies are those that complement existing labor inputs, increasing the marginal product of labor. Workers can now pack many more boxes because of the technology. Such a change in technology that increases the marginal product of labor shifts the labor demand curve to the right, as shown in Exhibit 11.7.

## Factors That Shift Labor Supply

Shifts in labor supply also affect equilibrium wage and employment levels. We discuss three main factors that shift labor supply:

1. Population changes
2. Changes in worker preferences and tastes
3. Opportunity costs

Let's discuss each in turn.

In terms of population changes, the Census Bureau projects that the U.S. population will grow from its current 324 million people to 398 million people by 2050—an increase of roughly 75 million people. This is because of both a greater number of births and immigration. The immigration projections tell an interesting story—the Census Bureau estimates that 64 percent of the population increase will be attributable to immigration. In the simplest scenario, when immigrants move into an area, the supply of workers increases. This increase causes the labor supply curve to shift rightward, as in Exhibit 11.8. Such a shift causes lower wages and higher employment levels.

Changes in preferences and taste also affect the labor supply. In 1975, 46.3 percent of women were working. By 2014, this number had increased to about 57 percent (compared to 69.2 percent for men in 2014). One explanation for this phenomenon is that women might have more of a "taste" for work than they did decades ago. This could have occurred because many women began entering the labor force during the mobilization for World War II and continued to do so, especially over the past three decades. Over time, preferences may have evolved such that women now are both more willing to, and are socially expected to, participate in the labor market than they were before World War II. As more and more women enter the labor market, the labor supply curve shifts rightward, as in Exhibit 11.8. Because women have higher college enrollment rates than men have (71.3 percent compared with 61.3 percent for 2012 high school graduates according to the Bureau of Labor Statistics), this change in preference might be here to stay, because more women will likely want to reap the returns from their education by entering the labor market.

Finally, opportunity costs play a role in shifting the labor supply curve. Focusing, for example, in the labor market for cheese packers, if other job opportunities diminish, the workforce of potential cheese packers grows. More specifically, if the local steel mill shuts

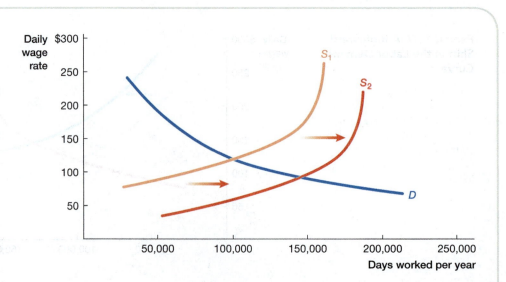

**Exhibit 11.8  A Shift in the Labor Supply Curve**

Through an increase in the labor force population, a shift in tastes, or a reduction in outside opportunities, more workers are willing to work at any given wage rate, shifting the labor supply curve rightward from $S_1$ to $S_2$.

# LETTING THE
## DATA SPEAK

### Do Wages Really Go Down If Labor Supply Increases?

To test whether an increase in labor supply leads to lower wages, economist Joshua Angrist turned to the Palestinian occupied territories in the West Bank of the Jordan River and the Gaza Strip.[2] These territories were captured by Israel from Jordan and Egypt in 1967. Though their economies flourished due to the integration with Israel, no institutions of higher education existed in the area for another 5 years. Accordingly, anyone pursuing a university degree had to leave to do so, and similarly, anyone in these territories with a university degree had earned it elsewhere.

In 1972, to increase employment opportunities for Palestinians in occupied territories, Israel spearheaded the creation of twenty institutions of higher education in the West Bank and the Gaza Strip. As you might expect, these new institutions dramatically and rapidly increased the local supply of workers with a higher education.

Using data gathered from the Territories Labor Force Survey between 1981 and 1991, Angrist found that the average schooling level of men aged 18 to 64 increased from 7.7 years in 1981 to 8.65 years in 1991. The fraction of the labor force with at least 13 years of schooling increased by 5

percentage points, and the fraction with less than 12 years of schooling fell by 14 percentage points. Between 1981 and 1986 alone, over 6,600 students graduated from a university in the West Bank or the Gaza Strip. In this same span of time, wages earned by highly educated workers—those with 13 or more years of schooling—dropped significantly. Before the increase in educated labor supply, highly educated workers earned up to 40 percent more than high school graduates. However, after the increase they earned less than 20 percent more.

Does this prove that an increase in labor supply lowers wages? It is certainly consistent with that notion, but it is important to recognize that there may be other explanations for what we see in the data. For example, neighboring Jordan funded a portion of public-sector employment in the territories, but the growth of its economy slowed around 1982. This likely staunched the flow of resources into the territories, pulling wages and employment down, while strikes, curfews, and civil disorder during the Palestinian uprising could also have been partly responsible for the lower earnings of highly educated workers in the Palestinian territories.

down, many workers will be unemployed and looking for work. Some of them will turn to cheese packing, and this increase in the number of workers willing to pack cheese will shift the labor supply curve rightward, as in Exhibit 11.8. This shift, in turn, will lead to lower wages for cheese packers.

When might opportunity costs lead to a lower number of cheese packers? Think of the case where a new Toyota plant opens in the city. Now cheese packers have better job opportunities, and therefore some of them begin working at the new Toyota plant. This will cause the labor supply curve for cheese packers to shift leftward, raising equilibrium wages.

## 11.3 Wage Inequality

The model of the labor market we developed in the previous section determines a single equilibrium wage for a single industry. In practice, there is considerable inequality in wages and earnings among workers within a given industry and across industries. Exhibit 11.9 shows the distribution of average wages for hourly workers in the United States in 2015.

The exhibit puts workers into one of ten groups. People in the first group represent workers in the lowest 10 percent of earners. People in the tenth group represent the top 10 percent of earners. Groups between these two extremes represent earners from 10 percent to 20 percent (Group 2), 20 percent to 30 percent (Group 3), and so on. What we readily observe from Exhibit 11.9 is that the top-earning workers earn much more than other workers. In fact, these workers earn more than 6 times what the lowest-earning workers are paid.

Why do these differences in wages arise? How can we extend our model of labor market equilibrium to incorporate them? We turn to a discussion of three important features of the labor market that may give rise to differences in wages across workers:

1. Differences in human capital
2. Differences in compensating wages
3. Discrimination in the job market

**Exhibit 11.9** U.S. Hourly Wage Distribution (2015)

If there were no wage inequality, we would expect all the bars to be the same height. However, it is evident from the graph that this is not the case, indicating considerable inequality in wages.

*Source:* Data from Bureau of Labor Statistics, U.S. Department of Labor, *Current Population Survey.*

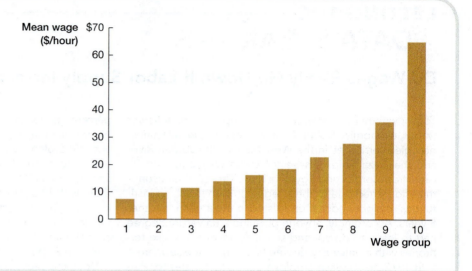

Mean wage ($/hour)

Wage group

## Differences in Human Capital

One explanation for the wage differences observed in Exhibit 11.9 is that people have very different levels of skills and therefore different levels of productivity. Economists refer to each person's stock of skills for producing output or economic value as **human capital**. Differences in human capital result in differences in wages.

**Human capital** is each person's stock of skills for producing output or economic value.

One major source of differences in human capital is education attainment. You and everyone in your class are working to increase the knowledge that you can use in your working life. Mathematics will help you solve problems and train your reasoning skills, economics will help you develop an ability to evaluate the consequences of your actions, and English will help you better express your ideas. All of these skills, and many more, are necessary to produce many goods and services.

Another way to improve your human capital is through experience. The empirical evidence shows that the more time you spend at a particular job, the more productive you will become. This type of productivity increase tends to be either job specific or industry specific. Job-specific (or firm-specific) human capital is accrued when a worker learns how best to complete a task at her specific job, but that experience does not make her more productive when working for other firms. For example, learning how to operate a unique inventory system gives a worker a skill that translates to more productivity in her firm, but not necessarily to more productivity in other firms.

In contrast, industry-specific training may be accrued when a mechanic learns how to change tires and thus becomes more productive not only in his own firm, but also in competing firms. One often-cited factor explaining why men earn more money than women is because women tend to spend more time working part time or out of the labor force. According to the Bureau of Labor Statistics, 24.4 percent of women in the labor force worked

Why does Peyton Manning earn more than a physical education teacher?

# CHOICE & CONSEQUENCE

## Paying for Worker Training

Many union advocates argue that firms should pay for all training sessions. After all, a good training program makes workers better at their job—that is, training makes them more productive.

We must remember that in a competitive market, any worker who has improved basic ("general") skills will also be more productive in general … at *any* firm. So, firms will compete for this worker until they push wages up to the value of marginal product of labor. But this means that the worker collects all of the gains from his training (by receiving a higher wage). This means that the firm providing the training does not gain anything from its training expenditure, but the worker does gain from having the general training (he has a higher wage). Therefore, the firm will have no incentive to invest in basic skills training, but the

worker himself will have a strong incentive to do so. Workers are often able to invest in their basic skills on the job by taking a wage cut so as to indirectly "pay" for their training costs (that is, to compensate the firm that is incurring these costs but has nothing to gain from this training).

The same is not true for job-specific training, however. Job-specific training results in gains to a worker's employer (in terms of the worker's productivity), but it does not result in gains to the worker in the labor market. Because the worker will have no market gains from job-specific training, he will not pay for this training. But the firm will gladly pay.

This reasoning suggests that under our economic framework, firms should be willing to pay only for job-specific training. The workers themselves should bear the costs of improving their general skills.

---

part time in 2014, compared to only 12.1 percent of men in the labor force. We will also see in the Evidence-Based Economics feature that according to recent research, among a group of MBAs, women were much more likely to take time off work (27 percent versus 10 percent) or leave the labor force than were men. Because of this time spent away, women typically gain less job-specific and industry-specific human capital than men.

### Differences in Compensating Wage Differentials

Just as people achieve different levels of education based on their schooling choices, they also choose different types of work. For example, some work is very high risk—construction work, trucking, mining, and military service are all industries with significant mortality rates. For the labor market to be in equilibrium, it must be true that the marginal worker is paid a wage high enough so that she is indifferent between working in her current job and working in her best lower-risk (but lower-wage) alternative.

**Compensating wage differentials**
are wage premiums paid to attract workers to otherwise undesirable occupations.

The wage differences that are used to attract workers to otherwise undesirable occupations are known as **compensating wage differentials**. Wage differentials based on risk and unpleasantness are important factors to consider when examining wage differences across jobs, but there are also reasons we may see workers in the same job getting paid differently. For instance, the office conditions might be unpleasant, local housing prices and rents might be high, or the local air quality might be low.

We can see some evidence of compensating differentials at work in Exhibit 11.10, which lists average annual salaries taken from the Bureau of Labor Statistics. For example, consider the case of the fast-food cook versus the garbage collector. Both positions have no degree requirements and involve relatively little training, but garbage collectors are paid nearly twice the annual salary of fast-food cooks. Why? Again, it is important to remember that an equilibrium wage makes the marginal person with a particular set of skills indifferent to either job. In this case, it is likely that in order to motivate individuals to wake up early and be willing to handle refuse as their job, they would need more pay than for a life of fast-paced food preparation.

### Discrimination in the Job Market

Will workers with the same productivity always receive the same wage for exactly the same job? Will they even be hired for the same job? Not necessarily. A third major factor in determining wages in the labor market is the nature and extent of discrimination that is present. Economists have pinpointed two major theories for why employers might discriminate: *taste-based discrimination* and *statistical discrimination*.

## Exhibit 11.10 Average Annual Salary in 2015 by Occupation

Here we see occupations with a varying degree of required training and desirability listed with their respective annual salaries.

*Source:* Data from Bureau of Labor Statistics, U.S. Department of Labor, *Occupational Employment Statistics.* Retrieved May, 2016 from http://www.bls.gov/oes/current/oes_nat.htm.

| Occupation | Average Annual Salary |
|------------|----------------------|
| Fast-food cook | $19,610 |
| Retail salesperson | $26,340 |
| Garbage collector | $36,370 |
| Embalmer | $41,490 |
| Firefighter | $49,330 |
| Explosives worker | $52,580 |
| Financial analyst | $95,320 |
| Nuclear engineer | $106,060 |
| Economist | $109,230 |
| Surgeon | $247,520 |

**Taste-based discrimination** occurs when people's preferences cause them to discriminate against a certain group.

The Nobel Prize–winning economist Gary Becker is famous in part for developing the market implications of **taste-based discrimination**, which occurs when people's preferences cause them to discriminate against a certain group.[3] For example, if an employer is a bigot, he might prefer not to work with certain types of people. Some wage statistics are consistent with American employers having a taste for discrimination. For example, among hourly wage workers, non-Hispanic workers make 36 percent more than Hispanic workers in America, on average, as shown in Exhibit 11.11.

It is important to note that wages can be different between groups not only because an employer has a taste for discrimination but also because of other factors, such as human capital—in particular, in the form of education and experience. In fact, Hispanic workers have lower educational attainment, on average, than non-Hispanic workers. This difference in human capital could therefore be the driver of the wage differences observed in Exhibit 11.11.

An interesting additional possibility is that wage differences between workers are driven by hard-to-observe factors. For example, perhaps non-Hispanic workers are better employees because their English skills help them to communicate more effectively with coworkers and customers. Maybe differences in communication abilities alone cause some of the differences observed in Exhibit 11.11. Is it discrimination if employers hire on the basis of that perception (whether true or false)?

**Statistical discrimination** occurs when expectations cause people to discriminate against a certain group.

Economists call this type of discrimination **statistical discrimination**. It occurs when employers use an observable variable (such as race or gender) to help determine whether the person will be a good employee. Thus, it occurs when expectations cause people to discriminate against a certain group.

## Exhibit 11.11 Mean Hourly Wage of Hispanic and Non-Hispanic Workers (2015)

For hourly wage workers, non-Hispanics earn more than Hispanic workers. It is important to note, however, that there are numerous possible explanations for this difference, only one of which is taste-based discrimination. What other factors do you think might be contributing to this large wage gap between Hispanic and non-Hispanic workers?

*Source:* Data from Bureau of Labor Statistics, U.S. Department of Labor, *Current Population Survey*

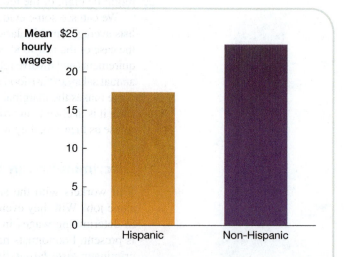

# CHOICE
## &CONSEQUENCE

### Compensating Wage Differentials

What do you want to be when you grow up? As a child, you probably thought about this question from time to time, and now, as a college student, you may have honed your thinking to exclude certain careers. Among the excluded careers may be those of garbage collector, sewage plant worker, or truck driver. Given the choice between becoming a truck driver and, say, a teacher, the majority of students would probably opt for a career path devoted to enriching the minds of youths. The job of teacher is well respected, features reasonable hours, and includes summers off. Driving a truck is monotonous, dangerous, and sedentary (one of the authors of this book has realized this firsthand!).

But what if you learned that the average starting salary for a teacher coming out of college was around $33,000 per year, and the average salary for a truck driver was $51,000? Would you be tempted? What if you learned that being a truck driver in Iraq could get you squarely into the six figures? Now would you reconsider?

The economic principle at work here is a compensating wage differential. If a job is relatively more dangerous,

dirty, or in some other way undesirable, employers must use incentives to lure potential workers away from easier and cleaner jobs. In considering which careers to pursue, people take into account both wages and the amenities of the job—things like convenient hours, prestige, on-the-job risks, and difficulty. When the amenities make a job more appealing, lower wages may be offered because of the number of other incentives. If the amenities are largely negative, however, employers must offer higher wages to attract qualified laborers, which is why teachers and bank tellers make significantly less money than truck drivers.

How much less? How much would you require in extra compensation to be a truck driver rather than a teacher or bank teller?

Statistical discrimination is everywhere around you. When you decide not to eat in a restaurant because its exterior looks run-down or its name sounds tacky, this is a formal statistical discrimination: you are using your expectations about the type of food you are likely to get in a restaurant with a run-down exterior or a tacky name to decide that food in this particular restaurant is not going to be very good either. Statistical discrimination is also commonplace in business. For instance, if you are in your teens or twenties, why do you think your car insurance costs more than your parents' car insurance? It is because the insurance company uses statistical group averages to determine that people your age have more accidents than do people your parents' age. In this way, even though the variable age by itself is not a perfect indicator, it provides some indication of how risky the driver will be. Employers perform similar calculations when deciding on which type of person to hire, and they use gender, race, age, or any other variable they believe is indicative of who will be a good worker.

An important distinction between taste-based and statistical discrimination is that employers are willing to forgo profits when engaging in taste-based discrimination. That is, to cater to their prejudicial preferences, they will not hire or promote a specific type of worker. In contrast, employers engaging in statistical discrimination are trying to *enhance* their profits. We return to how we might measure the impact of discrimination in the labor market in the Evidence-Based Economics feature.

## Changes in Wage Inequality over Time

> **Wage inequality since 1967 has increased dramatically.**

We have just discussed three major reasons for why wages vary across the economy: human capital differences, compensating wage differentials, and discrimination. One outstanding question is how wage differences have changed over time. At first glance, you might think that because discrimination has become less socially acceptable over time—especially since the 1950s and 1960s—wage inequality must have decreased. You might be surprised, however, to see Exhibit 11.12, which plots the wage distribution for the United States from 1967 to 2015. It shows wage trends for people in the bottom decile, in the middle, and in the top decile of the wage distribution.

The exhibit shows that wage inequality since 1967 has increased dramatically. Whereas earners in the top decile have increased their annual earnings by almost $40,000 per year, the earnings of those in the bottom decile remained effectively flat. A similar story plays out for the median wage earner. This dramatic change in wage inequality over time is likely due to several sources, but economists have pinpointed one factor in particular that has driven a large wedge between high- and low-earning workers: technological change.

**Exhibit 11.12** U.S. Annual Earnings—Top 10 Percent, Median, and Bottom 10 Percent of Wage Distribution

By following the three time series, we can see that while workers in the bottom decile (blue line) and at the fiftieth percentile (or the "median," red line) of the wage distribution have experienced little to no growth in their (real) annual earnings since 1967, those in the top decile (green line) have seen a large increase in their annual earnings. One explanation is that skill-biased technological change increased top wage earners' marginal product.

*Source:* Data from Bureau of Labor Statistics, U.S. Department of Labor, *Current Population Survey.*

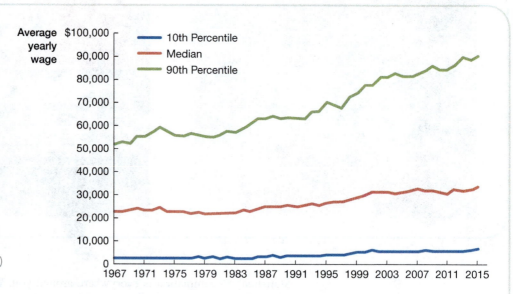

## LETTING THE
# DATA SPEAK

## Broadband and Inequality

A stark illustration of how certain new technologies, especially those related to information communications, have been skill biased comes from the rollout of broadband technology in Norway. Starting in 2000, a large Norwegian program invested in broadband infrastructure to ensure low-cost access to high-speed Internet for all areas of Norway. But because the funding for the program was limited, it was rolled out in certain areas before others.

Exploiting this differential timing of when broadband was introduced in different parts of Norway, economists Anders Akerman, Ingvil Gaarder, and Magne Mogstad investigated how access to broadband technology by households and firms impacts the wages and employment of workers with different levels of schooling.[4] They find more rapid wage growth for workers with a college degree, and less rapid wage growth for workers with a high school degree and especially those without a high school diploma. Employment growth was also more rapid for college workers after the introduction of broadband. Their analysis also indicates that these effects are caused by firms having access to broadband technology and changing their demand for skills.

**Skill-biased technological changes** increase the productivity of skilled workers relative to that of unskilled workers.

As we discussed earlier, technology can be either labor saving or labor complementary. It can also be skill saving or skill complementary, more often referred to as *skill biased*. **Skill-biased technological changes** increase the productivity of skilled workers relative to that of unskilled workers. The primary technological change over this time period has been advances in computing power. This change appears to have been broadly skill biased, improving the marginal productivity of skilled workers and causing the demand for their labor and pay to increase.

On the flip side, enhanced computing power has also replaced many tasks performed by the unskilled, thereby decreasing the labor demand for such workers and lowering their wages. This effect can be observed throughout the economy: many customer service centers are now automated by voice-recognition software. In the past, trouble with a telephone bill would not have been handled by communication with an automaton. Likewise, cars, pizzas, and even the beds we sleep in are now being made by advanced technologies. Technology has advanced so far and so fast over the past few decades that perhaps before you get your first job, robots behind the counter at the local fast-food franchise may smile and ask, "Would you like fries and a Coke with that hamburger?"

## 11.4 The Market for Other Factors of Production: Physical Capital and Land

Despite our focus so far on labor as an input to production, there are other factors equally important to the production process. In this section, we discuss the market for physical capital (such as machines) and the market for land.

Recall that the value to a firm of adding each consecutive unit of labor is given by multiplying the output price and the marginal product of labor. We denoted this marginal value as VMPL (value of marginal product of labor), and derived the optimal action of the firm to hire labor up to the point where the wage rate is equal to VMPL.

A firm's physical capital requires an identical treatment. As we discussed in Chapter 6, physical capital is any good, including machines and buildings, used for production. It may be the belt on an assembly line, the credit card machine at a restaurant, or the forklift at a construction site. Similar to hiring workers, a firm will expand its physical capital until it is not worthwhile to do so. This implies that just as The Wisconsin Cheeseman

The **value of marginal product of physical capital** is the contribution of an additional unit of physical capital to a firm's revenues.

**Land** includes the solid surface of the earth and natural resources.

The **rental price** of a good is the cost of using that good for some specific period of time.

hired labor until VMPL = wage, it will employ physical capital until the *value of the marginal product of physical capital* (VMPK)—economists commonly denote physical capital with a K—equals the price of physical capital. The **value of marginal product of physical capital** is the contribution of an additional unit of physical capital to a firm's revenues.

The same is true for uses of *land*. **Land** includes the solid surface of the earth where structures are built and natural resources. A firm will continue to purchase and use land—say for building space—until the value of the marginal product of land equals the price of land.

Although the economic framework for deciding how much of the three inputs to use is identical, labor has one major difference from physical capital and land: both physical capital and land can be either rented or owned, whereas labor (of others) cannot be owned. When rented, the firm must pay the *rental price* of physical capital, and to use land it must pay the *rental price* of land. By **rental price**, we mean the price of using a good for a specific period of time. For simplicity, we assume that the firm rents physical capital and land rather than owns them; we treat investment more broadly in Chapter 15.

To make this discussion more concrete, let's consider an example of how we can arrive at an equilibrium in the physical capital market. Suppose that a labor-saving technological innovation makes it possible for The Wisconsin Cheeseman to use only one unit of labor—a computer programmer—to produce cheese boxes. Recall that the number of machines on the assembly line determines how many cheese boxes The Cheeseman produces. Exhibit 11.13 represents the production schedule for physical capital, where each unit of physical capital is one machine. Suppose that the equilibrium price of cheese boxes remains at $2. This means that the value of marginal product of physical capital (VMPK) = $2 × marginal product of capital per unit (MPK). This relationship is displayed in column (4) of Exhibit 11.13.

In Exhibit 11.14 we plot this schedule. If the market for machines has a rental price of $80 per machine, then we can see that The Cheeseman will use 10 machines in its assembly line, producing 524 cheese boxes per day. This is optimal, because the firm has set VMPK = market rental rate, thereby maximizing its profits.

**Exhibit 11.13 Production Schedule for The Wisconsin Cheeseman**

As before, The Cheeseman is tasked with choosing how much output to generate per day. The difference now is that The Cheeseman's output is determined by the number of machines it purchases. The table summarizes the number of machines it will need for any given level of output and how much value each additional machine adds. Column (1) shows cheese boxes produced per day, column (2) shows the number of machines used in production, column (3) shows the marginal product of each additional machine, and column (4) shows the dollar value of this additional output (VMPK).

| (1) Output per Day | (2) Number of Machines | (3) Marginal Product of Physical Capital (MPK) | (4) VMPK = MPK × P = Column (3) × $2 |
|---|---|---|---|
| 0 | 0 | | |
| 50 | 1 | 50 | $100 |
| 104 | 2 | 54 | $108 |
| 161 | 3 | 57 | $114 |
| 227 | 4 | 66 | $132 |
| 294 | 5 | 67 | $134 |
| 346 | 6 | 52 | $104 |
| 396 | 7 | 50 | $100 |
| 442 | 8 | 46 | $ 92 |
| 484 | 9 | 42 | $ 84 |
| 524 | 10 | 40 | $ 80 |
| 561 | 11 | 37 | $ 74 |
| 596 | 12 | 35 | $ 70 |
| 628 | 13 | 32 | $ 64 |
| 658 | 14 | 30 | $ 60 |
| 685 | 15 | 27 | $ 54 |
| 710 | 16 | 25 | $ 50 |
| 734 | 17 | 24 | $ 48 |

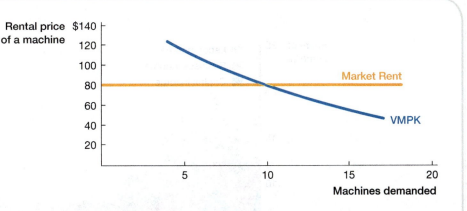

**Exhibit 11.14 Demand for Physical Capital**

As with labor, a derived demand market exists for machines. Here we graph the quantity of machines demanded at each price (rental rate). We assume that the marginal cost of an additional machine is $80 (orange line). This allows us to identify the equilibrium quantity as 10 machines.

We can arrive at equilibrium in the land market using an identical approach. This will determine how much land The Cheeseman demands.

So how does The Cheeseman put all of this together and choose its optimal mix of labor, physical capital, and land? You will not be surprised to learn that The Cheeseman considers marginal benefits and marginal costs when making its choices. In this case, The Cheeseman optimizes by hiring inputs until their marginal cost equals their marginal benefit. In equilibrium, this will lead to the marginal product from the last dollar spent on each input being equalized (this is similar to the "equal bang for your buck" story that we learned about in Chapter 5 and resources being allocated efficiently in Chapter 7).

> The Cheeseman optimizes by hiring inputs until their marginal cost equals their marginal benefit.

# LETTING THE
# DATA SPEAK

## The Top 1 Percent Share and Capital Income

As we have seen in Exhibit 11.12, there has been a notable increase in wage inequality in the U.S. labor market over the last four decades. In many ways, however, this exhibit understates how much the rich have become richer. Economists Thomas Piketty and Emmanuel Saez have highlighted this phenomenon by focusing on the share of the top 1 percent in national income—meaning the share of total income in the United States that goes to the richest 1 percent of households.[5] Exhibit 11.15 shows a striking increase in the top 1 percent share. In the 1970s, the richest 1 percent of households captured about 8 percent of national income. In the 2010s, this number rose to 18 percent.

This staggering rise in inequality has caused great alarm among many commentators and citizens, both because it shows how unequally the gains of economic growth over the past four decades have been shared and because it may signal that we are moving toward a society that is more deeply segregated between the haves (the very rich) and the have-nots (the rest of us). Indeed, this sharp increase in the top 1 percent share was one of the factors fueling the Occupy Wall Street movement, which claimed

to speak for the "99 percent"—all of those who were left out of this top 1 percent.

Some, including Thomas Piketty in his bestseller *Capital in the Twenty-First Century*, also worried that just like in the so-called Gilded Age at the turn of the previous century, it wasn't just labor income but also the unequally distributed capital income that was propelling this wide gulf between the top 1 percent and the remaining 99 percent.[6] As we have just seen, owners of physical capital and land will receive returns for these factors of production, and the ownership of these factors may be highly concentrated. If so, high returns for physical capital or land might be a key driver of the rise in the top 1 percent share.

Exhibit 11.15 shows that the share of the top 1 percent was indeed very high in the early decades of the twentieth century, and the top one-percenters of that era got the majority of their income from capital and business income (meaning income for ownership of businesses and other entrepreneurial activities). In particular, approximately 50 percent of their income came from capital, and another 30 percent from business income. So the very rich of the Gilded Age were mostly "rentiers," earning their huge

*(continued)*

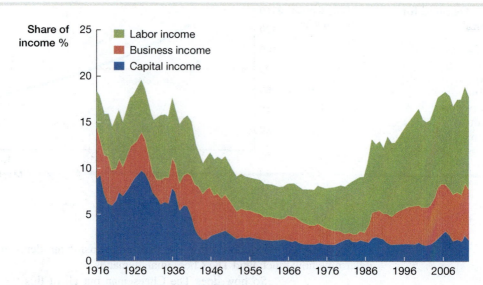

**Exhibit 11.15** Top 1 Percent Income Share, Broken Down by Source

The top 1 percent share, the share of national income going to the richest 1 percent of households, declined from very high levels in the 1910s and 1920s to about 8 percent in the 1960s and 1970s. It then grew very rapidly to reach about 18 percent in the 2010s. We also see, however, that the very rich in the 1910s and 1920s earned most of their income from capital and ownership of businesses, while the mega-rich of today derive the majority of their income from labor.

fortunes from their holdings of capital and sometimes ownership of big, very profitable businesses.

However, we can also see from the same data that today's very rich do not much resemble the top 1 percent of the Gilded Age. About 60 percent of the income of the top 1 percent today comes from labor, and another 30 percent from business income. Capital income has a small role in their fortunes. This is quite consistent with who the very rich are today. They are highly successful entrepreneurs, such as Bill Gates, Steve Jobs, or Mark Zuckerberg, whose incomes derive from their ownership of usually successful companies and from their high labor earnings (as they are also the most highly paid employees of their businesses). Today's top earners also include generously remunerated managers in finance, technology, management consulting and industry, as well as highly paid surgeons, lawyers, sportspeople, and entertainers. We are living in an era of rapidly increasing inequality, but the anatomy of this inequality differs dramatically from what we have seen historically.

## EVIDENCE-BASED ECONOMICS

### Q: Is there discrimination in the labor market?

Have economists found evidence that discrimination might exist in labor markets? The answer is unequivocally yes—studies analyzing several different labor markets have made a case that discrimination against minorities and women exists. The studies are typically split between field experiments and studies that use statistical techniques to analyze existing (naturally occurring) data.

One intriguing example of a field experiment is a study by economists Claudia Goldin and Cecilia Rouse.[7] They use notes from a series of auditions among national orchestras to determine whether blind auditions—those in which musicians audition behind a screen—help women relatively more than men.

The authors considered three rounds of auditions: preliminary, semifinal, and final. They found that for women who made it to the finals, a blind audition increased their likelihood of winning by 33 percentage points. What this means is that women were much more likely to be chosen for national orchestras when the judges were not aware of their gender. As the authors note, without blind judging, discrimination has limited the employment of female musicians.

A related field experiment focusing on hiring practices in sales, administrative support, clerical, and customer services jobs was conducted by economists Marianne Bertrand and Sendhil Mullainathan.[8] Following a long line of research using similar techniques, the authors focused on testing for discrimination against African Americans in the workforce. They sent nearly 5,000 resumes in response to help-wanted ads in Chicago and Boston, randomly assigning Caucasian-sounding names, such as Emily or Greg, and African-American-sounding names, such as Lakisha or Jamal, to the identical resume. The outcome they were interested in was whether a given resume generated a callback or an e-mail for an interview.

We would expect that, without discrimination, callbacks would be distributed evenly between African-American-sounding and Caucasian-sounding names. After all, each group had identical resumes. Yet, Bertrand and Mullainathan found that resumes with Caucasian-sounding names had a 9.65 percent chance of receiving a callback, while resumes with African-American-sounding names had only a 6.45 percent chance. This means that those with Caucasian-sounding names were about 50 percent more likely to receive a callback than those with African-American-sounding names.

These two studies provide evidence of discrimination against two different classes of individuals—women in the case of orchestra hiring and people with African-American-sounding names in the case of the sales and clerical jobs.

One aspect that is left on the sidelines in these two studies is the relative wages of people once they are hired. Economists Kerwin Charles and Jon Guryan tackled this issue by examining a large data set on wages.[9] They used careful statistical techniques in an attempt to account for differences in productivity and human capital as well as differences in compensating wage differentials. Their key result is that taste-based discrimination accounts for as much as one-fourth of the gap in wages between African Americans and Caucasians. This level of discrimination accounts for an average total loss in annual earnings for African Americans of thousands of dollars. As you can see, this is real money that is being redistributed because of discrimination. But the good news is that the researchers found that this type of discrimination has lessened over time.

These three studies have only scratched the surface of empirical work that explores the issue of discrimination. Overall, a fair amount of evidence suggests that there is discrimination in labor markets, and in some cases, it is leading to considerable differences in wages across groups of people. What remains difficult to determine is whether such discrimination is taste-based or statistical. Can you think of research ideas to determine the precise nature of discrimination?[10]

It is also important to recognize that not all labor market differences between men and women or between different ethnic groups are due to discrimination. More recent work by Claudia Goldin, this time with Marianne Bertrand and Lawrence Katz, studied the career dynamics of all MBAs who graduated from a top business school between 1990 and 2006. They found that male and female MBAs have very similar labor market outcomes following completion of their degree, but, over time, men start doing better. After about 16 years, male MBAs earn, on average, 82 percent more than female MBAs earn. Their detailed analysis indicated that three factors accounted for the less rapid rise of women in the business world: women appear to have less job experience before the MBA, tend to work fewer hours every week, and are more likely to have career interruptions than do men. All three of these factors are, in turn, related to childbirth and child-rearing. So women may end up not fulfilling their full potential at work, but discrimination by employers is not the only reason for this.[11]

**Question**

Is there discrimination in the labor market?

**Answer**

Yes.

**Data**

Both survey and field experimental data suggest that discrimination is evident in many labor markets.

**Caveat**

Whether this discrimination is taste-based or statistical is difficult to uncover, and there are also many reasons beyond discrimination for differences in the career dynamics of men and women.

## Summary

- Producers determine the optimal mix of labor, physical capital, and land when making production decisions. Markets for these factors of production operate in much the same way that markets for final goods and services function: firms expand their use until marginal benefits equal marginal costs.

- Determining the demand for labor centers on the concept of the value of marginal product of labor, which is the contribution an additional worker makes to the firm's revenues.

- When making decisions on how to spend our time, we face opportunity cost. There is a trade-off between labor, which comprises activities that earn money, and leisure, which is time spent on activities other than earning money. The opportunity cost for one hour of leisure is the income that we would have earned by working for that hour.

- Large wage differences exist across people and jobs. The differences stem from three main sources: human capital differences, compensating wage differentials, and discrimination.

- As with labor, firms expand their use of physical capital until the value of the marginal product of physical capital equals the price of physical capital, and they likewise use land until the value of the marginal product of land equals the price of land.

## Key Terms

value of marginal product of labor (VMPL) *p. 263*
labor-saving technology *p. 267*
labor-complementary technologies *p. 268*
human capital *p. 270*

compensating wage differentials *p. 271*
taste-based discrimination *p. 272*
statistical discrimination *p. 272*
skill-biased technological changes *p. 275*

value of marginal product of physical capital (VMPK) *p. 276*
land *p. 276*
rental price *p. 276*

# Questions

1. How do firms estimate their demand for labor?

2. How does the labor-leisure trade-off determine the supply of labor?

3. In a competitive labor market, what is the profit-maximizing number of workers that a firm will hire?

4. We showed in this chapter that a profit-maximizing firm will hire the number of workers such that the wage is equal to the value of the marginal product of labor. But, as we saw in Chapter 6, a profit-maximizing firm will produce the quantity of output such that price equals marginal cost. Are these two rules inconsistent?

5. How would the following factors affect equilibrium in the market for labor?

   a. An increase in the demand for the product that a firm is producing

   b. The use of a new technology that halves the time that workers will take to produce a good

   c. An increase in the age when people begin to receive Social Security benefits

6. Suppose wages in the market for plumbers increase. Some plumbers start taking on extra plumbing jobs while others cut back on the number of hours they work. What could explain these two responses?

7. How do labor-saving technologies differ from labor-complementary technologies? Give an example of each.

8. Some people think it's unfair that celebrities like George Clooney earn a lot more than people who add so much more value to society, like teachers. What do you think explains this wage differential?

9. In the United States in 2011, there were 104 fatalities per 100,000 workers in the logging industry. This is the second-highest fatality rate after the fisheries industry. Everything else being equal, would you expect workers in the logging industry to be paid higher wages than workers with similar levels of education in other industries? Explain.

10. What is the difference between statistical and taste-based discrimination? The owner of a company that manufactures automobile parts states that it will not hire gay or lesbian employees. Is this an example of statistical or taste-based discrimination?

11. What factors could explain why wage inequality in the United States has been increasing over the past several decades?

12. How does the market for inputs like labor differ from the market for goods and services?

13. Suppose an identical tax is levied on capital, labor, and land. Would the tax have the same effect in each of these markets? Explain your answer.

# Problems

1. Suppose that, at your firm, the relationship between output produced and the number of workers you hire is as follows:

   | Labor | Total Product Produced |
   |-------|------------------------|
   | 0 | 0 |
   | 1 | 12 |
   | 2 | 23 |
   | 3 | 32 |
   | 4 | 38 |
   | 5 | 42 |
   | 6 | 45 |

   a. Find the marginal product of labor for each worker.

   b. Is the relationship between output and labor consistent with the Law of Diminishing Returns?

   c. Suppose your firm is a perfect competitor in the output market and the labor market. If the price of output is $9 and the wage rate is $27, how many workers should your firm hire?

   d. If the price of output falls to $3 and the wage remains $27, how many workers should your firm hire?

2. Consider the following daily production functions for Pleasanton's three different coffee shops. Each cup of coffee sells for $1.

|  | Arabica Alley | | Barista Bar | | Coffee Cafe | |
| Workers | Total Product | Marginal Product | Total Product | Marginal Product | Total Product | Marginal Product |
| --- | --- | --- | --- | --- | --- | --- |
| 0 | 0 | – | 0 | – | 0 | – |
| 1 | 100 | | 20 | | 40 | |
| 2 | 130 | | 40 | | 70 | |
| 3 | 140 | | 60 | | 100 | |
| 4 | 140 | | 80 | | 110 | |

a. Copy down the table and add the marginal product of labor for each coffee shop. (This is also the value of the marginal product [VMPL] given that the price of coffee is $1.)

b. Suppose you are an influential mayor who likes to plan the economy. There are 8 workers available and your goal is to maximize total coffee production. How many workers should you assign to each coffee shop? Hint: Focus on marginal product.

c. Suppose you are a mayor who believes decentralized labor markets can achieve optimal outcomes. Again, there are 8 eager workers (i.e., supply of labor is fixed at 8). Find the equilibrium wage; how much coffee will be produced? How does this compare to the previous answer?

3. You accept a new job for a wage of $30,000 at a newspaper. You join the sales team, which consists of 10 people who try to sell online subscriptions. Each subscription sells for $200. When you talk to your boss, she says that you are the eleventh worker, and that if you had not joined the team, she would have done okay with just 10 people—but "great to have you, we are more productive with you on board!" If your boss is a smart person who has studied economics, what must she believe about the number of online subscriptions that you will help the team sell?

4. A friend tells you that he thinks that the salespeople who work at Apple stores are paid very low wages, given their productivity. Dividing Apple's revenues by the total number of employees shows that each employee contributed an average of $473,000 in revenues in 2011. But most of Apple's sales staff are paid about $25,000 a year. What is the flaw, if any, in your friend's reasoning?

5. The following table shows the average salary for major league baseball players. As you can see, the average salary of $3,440,000 in 2012 is nearly 20 times larger than the average salary in 1970.

| Year | Average Salary* |
| --- | --- |
| 1970 | $173,397 |
| 1980 | $408,198 |
| 1990 | $1,035,515 |
| 2000 | $2,649,988 |
| 2010 | $3,472,326 |
| 2012 | $3,440,000 |

* In constant 2012 dollars.

a. Explain what economic forces will encourage ball players in 2012 to play an extra year compared to those in 1970.

b. Are there any economic reasons for today's ball players to retire earlier than those in 1970?

6. For a long time, your firm has been paying its workers a wage of $20 per hour, and your employees have been happy to work 40 hours per week at this wage. Business is suddenly booming, and your firm would really like your workers to agree to a 50-hour work week to meet this new demand for your product. You are considering two strategies. Under the first, you would raise the wage for all hours worked from $20 per hour to $22 per hour; under the second, you would leave the wage for the first 40 hours per week at $20 but offer $30 per hour for hours worked above 40 hours (that is, you would offer time-and-a-half for overtime). Both strategies have the same cost of $1,100 if a worker chooses to work 50 hours. Which strategy is more likely to lead your employees to agree to a 50-hour work week?

7. Sketch a typical-looking labor market with a downward sloping aggregate VMPL (labor demand).

a. Label the part of this VMPL curve that maximizes *total* productivity.

b. Label the part of this VMPL curve that maximizes *average* productivity (i.e., output per worker).

c. Add an upward sloping labor supply. Label the intersection with the VMPL curve. Explain why economists believe the wage at the intersection is most efficient.

Add a binding minimum wage (price floor). Has the minimum wage *increased* or *decreased* worker productivity? Briefly explain.

8. The Patient Protection and Affordable Care Act (ACA) requires all employers with at least 50 full-time-equivalent workers to offer health insurance to their full-time employees or pay a fine of up to $2,000 per employee (see http://www.hhs.gov/healthcare/rights/index.html for a description of the ACA). Some people have argued that ACA will lower employment. This problem looks at an important issue in this debate.

a. Suppose the government passes a law that requires firms to offer health insurance to their workers. The cost of the insurance is equal to $1 for each hour an employee works. How will this law affect firms' demand for labor?

**b.** Suppose workers consider a dollar of health insurance paid by firms to be the equivalent of $1 in wages. How will this law affect the supply curve of labor?

**c.** Consider an industry where the equilibrium wage is $15 per hour and 100 workers are employed. How will this law affect the equilibrium quantity of labor in this labor market? How will it affect the equilibrium wage in this industry?

**d.** Now suppose workers consider a dollar of health insurance paid by firms to be worth less than $1 in wages. How will this law affect the equilibrium quantity of labor in this labor market? How will it affect the equilibrium wage in this industry?

9. Joey, Mandy, and Jim have the following labor supply (hours per day, based on hourly pay).

| Wage | Joey | Mandy | Jim |
|------|------|-------|-----|
| $5   | 4    | 0     | 2   |
| $10  | 8    | 4     | 6   |
| $15  | 12   | 8     | 9   |

**a.** Who values their leisure most, Joey, Mandy, or Jim (or is there not enough information to say)?

**b.** What is total labor supply given a wage of $15?

**c.** What if the demand for labor were fixed at 18 (i.e., firms wanted a total of 18 hours per day, regardless of wage). What would be the equilibrium wage?

10. You run a factory that uses pottery wheels to make pots. You can hire anywhere between 1 and 3 skilled artisans (workers), and you can rent 1 or 2 pottery wheels (machines). Pots sell for $100 each. The total product of your factory per day is shown in the following table.

| | | Number of Workers (Labor, L) | | |
|---|---|---|---|---|
| | | 1 | 2 | 3 |
| Number of Machines | 1 | 6 | 9 | 11 |
| (Capital, K) | 2 | 8 | 12 | 15 |

**a.** Given one machine and one worker, how much would you be willing to pay to hire a second worker? (Consider the value of the marginal product of labor.)

**b.** Again starting from one machine and one worker, what rental rate would you be willing to pay to acquire a second machine? (Consider the value of the marginal product of capital.)

**c.** Suppose the wage is $250 per day. How many workers would you hire if you have *one* pottery wheel? How many workers would you hire with *two* pottery wheels?

**d.** Are pottery wheels labor-saving or labor-complementary?

11. For Acme Manufacturing, the marginal product of labor is MPL = 10 − 2L. Acme sells output for $10 per unit.

**a.** Sketch the value of the marginal product of labor (VMPL). How many workers will Acme hire given a wage of $40?

**b.** Repeat, but after the output price increases to $20 per unit. Does this change induce Acme to hire more or fewer workers?

# 12 Monopoly

## Can a monopoly ever be good for society?

Neuroscientists have taught us that the mere mention of the word *monopoly* conjures up negative associations deep in the brain that only such words as *death* and *murder* can match. In this chapter, we explore why that is the case, focusing on the economics of monopolies. Throughout the chapter, we follow Schering-Plough Corporation, a global pharmaceutical company based in the United States, which introduced the allergy drug Claritin in the early 1980s. During the development process, the U.S. government deemed the drug to be truly original and granted Schering-Plough a *patent*, which gave the company the exclusive right to manufacture and sell Claritin for 20 years.

Put yourself into the shoes of the CEO of Schering-Plough at that point in time. If you were CEO, how would you take advantage of this product exclusivity to optimize profits from your new wonder drug?

Your intuition might suggest that delivering enormous profits will be easy. With so many people in need of allergy medicine and no competitors to worry about, you are a *monopolist* and therefore should set very high prices for Claritin, capturing as much consumer surplus from buyers as possible. Knowing that some people might really need Claritin to function from day to day, you might even consider charging as much as $100 or more per tablet!

In this chapter, you will learn about the monopolist's problem—how it is similar to and different from the competitive seller's problem we discussed in Chapter 6. The lesson of this chapter is that a company with market power

## CHAPTER OUTLINE

behaves quite differently from the way that a competitive firm behaves. Compared to competitive firms, monopolists produce less and charge more. They thus make themselves better off, with the potential of earning economic profits in both the short run and the long run. But their gain will come at the cost of making consumers worse off and decreasing social surplus.

All of this has led the public to be quite distrustful of monopolies. For this reason, as we shall see, governments actively monitor and regulate monopolies. However, can a monopoly ever be good for society? We'll attempt to answer that question by the end of the chapter.

## 12.1 Introducing a New Market Structure

Thus far we have assumed that sellers operate in competitive markets: identical goods are produced by many different sellers and sold at the market-determined price. The firm is simply a passive price-taker, and the invisible hand directs the self-interested pursuits of buyers and sellers to yield socially efficient outcomes. Exhibit 12.1 provides an aerial comparison between perfect competition, which we studied in Chapters 6 and 7, and the new market structure that we will be studying in this chapter—monopoly.

Studying perfectly competitive markets provided important insights into how agents interact in markets and how markets equilibrate. But it proves to be a special type of market. A more common market situation is one in which a firm is not simply a price-taker, but a **price-maker**—a seller that sets the price of a good. Such a firm has the ability to set the price of the good because it has **market power**. The rightmost column in Exhibit 12.1 summarizes the most extreme form of market power: a *monopoly*.

A **monopoly** is an industry structure in which only one seller provides a good or service that has no close substitutes. In this way, a monopolist is not concerned with the behavior of other sellers. The price chosen by the monopolist is the one that makes the company the highest profit.

## 12.2 Sources of Market Power

What does it mean to have market power—and what kinds of firms can most easily attain it? Think about the companies that you and your friends interact with daily: an innovative company like Google, for example, or the company that supplies water to your dorm.

**Price-makers** are sellers that set the price of a good.

**Market power** relates to the ability of sellers to affect prices.

A **monopoly** is an industry structure in which only one seller provides a good or service that has no close substitutes.

**Exhibit 12.1** **Two Market Structures**

Many differences exist between perfect competition and monopoly. Each row highlights differences in various characteristics of the two market structures.

| Characteristic | Perfect Competition | Monopoly |
|---|---|---|
| Number of firms/sellers/producers | Many | One |
| Type of product/service sold | Identical (homogeneous) | Good or service with no close substitutes |
| Example of product | Corn grown by various farmers | Patented drugs; tap water |
| Barriers to entry | None: free entry and exit | Yes: high |
| Price-taker or price-maker? | Price-taker; price given by the market | Price-maker—no competitors; no close substitutes |
| Price | $P = MR = MC$ | Set $P > MR = MC$ |
| Demand curve facing the firm | Horizontally sloped; perfectly elastic demand curve | Downward-sloping |
| Social surplus | Maximized | Not maximized, but sometimes society benefits from research and development |
| Equilibrium long-run profits | Zero | Potentially greater than zero |

**Barriers to entry** provide a seller with protection from potential competitors entering the market.

A firm has **legal market power** when it obtains market power through barriers to entry created not by the firm itself but by the government.

A **patent** is the privilege granted to an individual or company by the government, which gives him or her the sole right to produce and sell a good.

A **copyright** is an exclusive right granted by the government to the creator of a literary or artistic work.

*My that sure is a cute and fuzzy copyright infringing puppy.*

Ultimately, the ability of a company to control a market—to gain market power—relies on *barriers to entry.*

**Barriers to entry** are obstacles that prevent potential competitors from entering the market. As such, they provide the seller protection against competition. Barriers to entry range from complete exclusion of market entrants to prevention of a new firm from entering and competing on an equal footing with an incumbent firm.

Two types of market power arise from barriers to entry: **legal market power** and *natural market power.* We now take a look at these two types in more depth.

## Legal Market Power

A firm has legal market power when it obtains market power through barriers to entry created not by the firm itself but by the government. These barriers can take the form of *patents* and *copyrights* that are issued to innovative companies. With a **patent**, the government grants an individual or company the sole right to produce and sell a good or service. For example, when Schering-Plough applied to the government for a patent to produce and sell Claritin, the government granted the company the exclusive right to manufacture and sell the drug for 20 years. With a **copyright**, the government grants an individual or company an exclusive right to intellectual property. For example, when Malcolm Gladwell wrote the best-selling book *Blink*, he copyrighted the work.[1] This meant that he was given a government guarantee that no one else could print and sell the book without his permission. In effect, Gladwell was granted monopoly rights in the sale of his book. Copyright protection is different across countries and in many cases extends long after the author's death. For example, in the United States, it extends decades after the author's death.

Such exclusivity laws represent a significant benefit for the innovator-turned-monopolist. For instance, monopolists Schering-Plough Corporation and Gladwell can charge higher prices than would occur under perfect competition. As consumers, we are all worse off, because we must pay higher prices for these goods, but there are a few silver linings. First, patents and copyrights are only temporary, and eventually the protected goods enter the public domain. At that time, other producers are able to distribute them. Second, blockbuster drugs and best-selling books are difficult and costly to produce, and without the increased incentive for creative activity, the expensive investment to create new prescription drugs or best-selling books might never be made. We return to a discussion of whether patents are indeed helpful in stimulating innovation in the Evidence-Based Economics section at the end of this chapter.

## Natural Market Power

**Natural market power** occurs when a firm obtains market power through barriers to entry created by the firm itself.

A second common source of barriers to entry occurs naturally rather than by design. **Natural market power** occurs when a firm obtains market power through barriers to entry created by the firm itself. In this category, there are two main sources of monopoly power:

1. The monopolist owns or controls a *key resource* necessary for production.
2. There are *economies of scale* in production over the relevant range of output.

## Control of Key Resources

**Key resources** are materials that are essential for the production of a good or service.

**Key resources** are those materials that are essential for the production of a good or service. The most basic way for a firm to develop market power naturally is to control the entire supply of such resources (assuming that no close substitutes exist). For example, if renters

## CHOICE & CONSEQUENCE

### Barriers to Entry Lurk Everywhere

In August 2015, Turing Pharmaceuticals purchased a 62-year-old drug called Daraprim, which is used to treat a life-threatening parasitic infection. Within a month, Turing raised the price from $13.50 to $750 per tablet, increasing the annual cost of treatment for some patients by hundreds of thousands of dollars. The sudden price increase—and former Turing CEO Martin Shkreli's boastful defense of it—attracted widespread media attention and accusations that Turing was price-gouging customers, some of whom were now facing a choice between catastrophic prescription medication bills and, potentially, death.

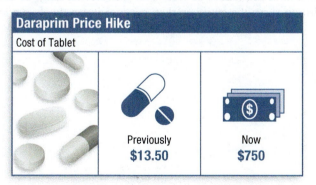

**Daraprim Price Hike**

Cost of Tablet

| Previously | Now |
| --- | --- |
| **$13.50** | **$750** |

Several legislators in Congress saw this episode as part of a broader pattern of pharmaceutical companies acquiring drugs and immediately raising prices. Drug prices even became an important issue during the primaries for the 2016 presidential election, which featured

several proposals to curb costs, including one by Senator Bernie Sanders that would mandate drug companies to pay a rebate to Medicaid if their drug prices rose faster than the rate of inflation.

You might be thinking, wait a minute, the patent has expired—how can they set such a high price? Shouldn't competitors enter the market with generic copies and drive the drug's price down to marginal cost? This intuition is correct—as a 62-year-old drug, Daraprim's patent had expired, meaning the chemical formula could be copied, produced, and sold in the form of a generic drug.

Barriers to entry come in many forms, and their existence can provide important market power. In this case, competitors require time to enter the market—a new manufacturer must first acquire FDA approval to bring a generic to market, and this can take more than 2 years. Indeed, the backlog for permission has climbed in recent years to about 4,000 applications!

These regulatory hurdles, along with other fixed costs, are important barriers to entry which delay would-be competitors from entering the market. Because of these barriers to entry, at the time Turing raised the price of Daraprim, it was the only producer selling the drug in the U.S. market.

Consider Senator Sanders' proposal to tax drug prices mentioned above. Would his idea be better or worse than an alternative proposal that would allow already approved European manufacturers of Daraprim's generic equivalent to enter the U.S. market?

12.1

12.2

12.3

12.4

12.5

12.6

12.7

are willing to pay a premium for an apartment with a lake view and there is only one apartment complex on the lake, the owner of that apartment complex has considerable market power. Likewise, by controlling 80 percent of the production from the world's diamond mines, the South African diamond company De Beers famously exercised significant market power in the diamond market throughout the twentieth century. In a similar fashion, Alcoa controls a key manufacturing resource with its ownership of bauxite (aluminum ore) mines.

Another key resource is individual expertise. For example, Sergey Brin and Larry Page are exceptional at search engine design. Thus, Google's power arose from two of its personnel, whose key economic resource is their creative talents.

In much the same way, Web sites that we use daily, such as eBay, Facebook, and Twitter, control a key resource: they attract the largest numbers of consumers. Their value subsequently increases because of network externalities. **Network externalities** occur when a product's value increases as more consumers begin to use it. Because eBay has the largest number of buyers and sellers, it makes sense for sellers to part with their goods on eBay. Networking of this sort occurs with buyers and sellers on Uber's platform as well: as more riders join the network more drivers will join too. Similarly, Facebook and Twitter today are synonymous with social networking. Because each now has millions of users, each owns a key resource: millions of people log in daily. Accordingly, Facebook is now much more valuable than MySpace, because Facebook has more people using it—a fact that attracts even more customers. In this way, network externalities set off a profitable cycle for Facebook.

**Network externalities** occur when a product's value increases as more consumers begin to use it.

## Economies of Scale

Monopolies also form because it is practical for both producers and consumers. Consider the case of the transmission of electricity. If your town had multiple providers of electricity transmission, there would have to be multiple sets of wires laid throughout town, and extraordinary start-up costs would be borne by multiple providers of electricity (and eventually passed on to you, the consumer).

In this case, it is better to have one provider serve the entire town because of the economies of scale that the single provider enjoys. As we discussed in Chapter 6, economies of scale occur when the average total cost (ATC) per unit of output decreases as total output increases. As your electricity provider increases its transmission, the ATC per unit of output decreases. The intuition is that if your electricity provider wants to hook up and create electricity for a new subdivision, the initial fixed costs will be high, but as more and more houses are added, costs will be spread over more households. Exhibit 12.2 shows just such a relationship between ATC, marginal cost, and output. You will note that in this case we have assumed a constant marginal cost. This means that over the entire production range of interest, the marginal cost is the same. In previous chapters we have dealt with upward-sloping marginal cost curves, but in certain cases a constant marginal cost curve represents a good description of the cost structure of a firm.

For goods and services that have economies of scale over the relevant range of output, it is efficient for a single firm to serve the entire market, because it can do so at a lower

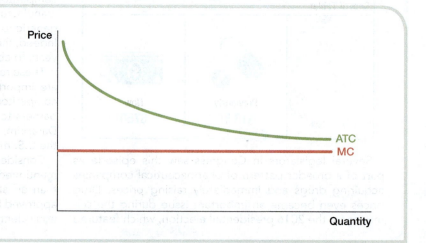

**Exhibit 12.2 Average Total Cost and Marginal Cost for a Natural Monopoly**

Natural monopolies are characterized by substantial fixed costs and economies of scale. To see this, at a low quantity level the ATC is very high, but as quantity increases, the ATC decreases, approaching marginal cost (MC).

12.1

12.2

12.3

12.4

12.5

12.6

12.7

A **natural monopoly** is a market in which one firm can provide a good or service at a lower cost than can two or more firms.

cost than any larger number of firms could. We denote such cases as *natural monopolies*, because they arise naturally. A **natural monopoly** arises because the economies of scale of a single firm make it efficient to have only one provider of a good or service. Often such firms are the first suppliers in a given market, and the cost advantages they achieve through producing a large number of goods preclude would-be competitors from entering the market. Examples of natural monopolies include providers of clean drinking water, natural gas, and electricity.

You may wonder why Facebook, Twitter, and eBay are not considered natural monopolies. All three exhibit network externalities, and such network effects seem to present barriers to entry, don't they? So why aren't these companies considered natural monopolies? Remember that natural monopolies arise because of economies of scale—the firm's ATC curve decreases over the important range of output. But network externalities arise from consumer benefits and have nothing to do with costs and economies of scale. There are some goods that feature both economies of scale and network effects, such as operating system software and telephone networks.

In contrast to monopolies that arise through legal means, natural monopolies emerge when unique cost conditions characterize their industry. Because of these cost conditions, natural monopolists worry less about potential market entrants than do monopolies that arise through legal means. Large economic profits attract entrants like bees to honey in legal monopolies (such as the pharmaceutical, diamond, and Internet industries), but the economic profits in the natural monopoly scenario are not as attractive. This is because potential entrants realize that they cannot achieve the low costs of the natural monopolist, because on entry they likely will "split the market." Such splitting of the market will render much higher costs and lower profits for each seller.

This doesn't mean that industries that are currently monopolized will never evolve to be more competitive. There have been many cases where the market grew sufficiently large that the natural monopoly evolved into a multiseller market. Throughout the 1990s and early 2000s, Microsoft's Internet Explorer was the default browser for just about all Web traffic. Estimates put Internet Explorer's market share at well over 95 percent at its peak. But as the number of households connected to the Internet boomed, new companies entered the market. Even though there are significant economies of scale to developing, coding, testing, and marketing a new browser, the increase in demand has generated opportunities for Mozilla Firefox and Google's Chrome, with Internet Explorer's market-share dropping to below 70 percent.

Regardless of why a firm enjoys market power—whether legally or naturally—it faces exactly the same decision problem when it comes to production and pricing choices. We turn to that discussion now.

## 12.3 The Monopolist's Problem

The monopolist's problem shares two important similarities with the perfectly competitive seller's problem we discussed in Chapter 6. First, the monopolist must understand how inputs combine to make outputs. Second, the monopolist must know the costs of production. Accordingly, all of the production and cost concepts we learned earlier apply directly to the monopolist's problem.

We do, however, find one important difference between the perfectly competitive seller's decision problem and the monopolist's decision problem. Recall from Chapter 6 that to maximize profits, the perfectly competitive firm expands production until marginal cost equals price, where price is determined by the intersection of the market demand and market supply curves.

Chapter 6 also showed that marginal revenue equals price for a perfectly competitive firm because the firm faces a perfectly elastic demand curve (a horizontal demand curve), as shown in panel (a) of Exhibit 12.3. At the market price, the perfectly competitive firm can sell as many units as it wishes. But if it charges a bit more, it will lose all of its business, because consumers can buy an identical good from another seller who is ready to sell at a lower price. Also, if it charges a bit less, it sells the same number of units but does not raise

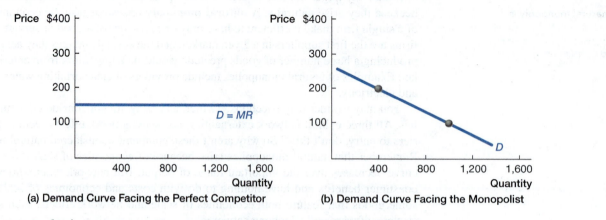

**Exhibit 12.3 Perfectly Competitive Firms and Monopolies Face Different Demand Curves**

Panel (a) shows one of the key results from Chapter 6—that in a perfectly competitive market, the demand curve facing the firm is perfectly elastic. The demand curve faced by the monopolist in panel (b) is the entire market and is therefore downward-sloping. Thus, if the monopolist charges $100, it can sell 1,000 units (yielding revenue of $100 multiplied by 1,000 = $100,000); and if it increases the price to $200, it sells only 400 units (yielding revenue of $80,000).

> Unlike the perfectly competitive firm, the monopoly can increase price and not lose all of its business.

as much revenue, so that would not be profit optimizing. Therefore, a firm facing a perfectly elastic demand curve is a price-taker.

This situation represents the major difference between the perfectly competitive firm's decision problem and the monopolist's decision problem. Because the monopolist is the sole market supplier, it faces the market demand curve, which is downward-sloping, as in panel (b) of Exhibit 12.3. Unlike the perfectly competitive firm, the monopolist can increase price and not lose all of its business. In fact, the market demand curve tells us exactly the trade-off the monopolist faces when it changes its price.

Consider panel (b) of Exhibit 12.3 more carefully. If the monopolist chooses a price of $100, it can sell 1,000 units. If the price is increased to $200, then the monopolist can sell only 400 units. Of course, the monopolist prefers to sell a lot of units for a high price—say, 1,000 units at a price of $200. But the downward-sloping market demand curve that monopolies face makes this outcome impossible. A monopoly is powerful, but it cannot sell at a point above the market demand curve. This raises an important consideration: how does a monopolist's total revenue change when it raises or lowers price?

## Revenue Curves

To illustrate how total revenue changes with price changes, let's consider the task facing you as the CEO of Schering-Plough. Your company is ready to go to the market with Claritin, and you want to figure out how you can make the most money possible from the drug. Even though there might be other medicines for allergies, we will assume that the conceptual model of monopoly applies, because there are no close substitutes for Claritin.

A first step in this process is to understand how much money you will bring in at various price levels—for now, we assume that you have to charge each customer the same price. Recall that the total revenue of a firm is the amount of money it brings in from the sale of its outputs. Marginal revenue is the change in total revenue associated with producing and selling one more unit of output. How do we begin determining total and marginal revenue?

The key is to understand the market demand curve for Claritin. After a thorough market analysis, you determine that a reasonable estimate of the market demand curve is that shown in Exhibit 12.4. The exhibit tells you, for example, that at a price of $5 per pill, you can sell 200 million units of Claritin; and at a price of $3, you can sell 600 million units.

12.1

12.2

12.3

12.4

12.5

12.6

12.7

## Exhibit 12.4 The Market Demand Curve for Claritin

With patent protection from the government, the demand curve that Schering-Plough faces for its sales of Claritin is the entire market. For example, if Schering-Plough chose a price of $4, then it would be able to sell 400 million units, but the demand curve shows that if it chose a price of $6 or higher, it wouldn't sell any Claritin, despite having a monopoly.

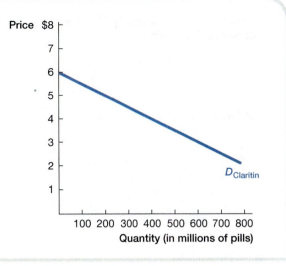

This graphical representation reveals the important trade-off between price and quantity sold that the monopolist faces: a higher price yields more revenue per unit sold, but fewer units sold.

From this demand curve, you can calculate the total revenue and marginal revenue at each price level, as shown in columns 3 and 4 of Exhibit 12.5. The exhibit also includes fixed costs and marginal costs, which you studied in Chapter 6. You might notice that the fixed costs are relatively large and that the marginal cost is constant over the various output levels. High fixed costs are typical for industries that spend large amounts of money on researching and developing products, such as pharmaceutical companies. In such instances, it is not uncommon for marginal cost to be constant over large ranges of output, because mass production of the product leads each additional unit of production to have a constant additional cost per unit.

Another important feature that the numbers in Exhibit 12.5 reveal is the relationship between price and total revenue. Let's consider an example. Assume that you lower the price from $5 to $4. In this case, Exhibit 12.5 reveals that you bring in $600 million more in total revenues. This additional $600 million arises from two effects.

First is a *quantity effect*: the lower price allows you to sell 200 million more units of Claritin. The increase in revenues because of this increased number of sales is shown as

## Exhibit 12.5 Revenues and Costs for Claritin at Different Levels of Output

Revenue and cost data are summarized for Schering-Plough (the data are not actual data). The data show that marginal cost is constant. Although these data are hypothetical, the constant marginal cost of $1 per pill approximates the nature of Schering-Plough's marginal costs (constant everywhere). Marginal revenue is calculated at each point for small changes.

| Quantity (in millions of pills) | Price | Total Revenue (in millions) | Marginal Revenue | Total Cost (in millions) | Fixed Cost (in millions) | Marginal Cost | ATC |
|---|---|---|---|---|---|---|---|
| 100 | $5.50 | $550 | $5 | $110 | $10 | $1.00 | $1.10 |
| 200 | $5.00 | $1,000 | $4 | $210 | $10 | $1.00 | $1.05 |
| 300 | $4.50 | $1,350 | $3 | $310 | $10 | $1.00 | $1.033 |
| 400 | $4.00 | $1,600 | $2 | $410 | $10 | $1.00 | $1.025 |
| 500 | $3.50 | $1,750 | $1 | $510 | $10 | $1.00 | $1.02 |
| 600 | $3.00 | $1,800 | $0 | $610 | $10 | $1.00 | $1.017 |
| 700 | $2.50 | $1,750 | –$1 | $710 | $10 | $1.00 | $1.014 |
| 800 | $2.00 | $1,600 | –$2 | $810 | $10 | $1.00 | $1.013 |
| 900 | $1.50 | $1,350 | –$3 | $910 | $10 | $1.00 | $1.011 |
| 1,000 | $1.00 | $1,000 | –$4 | $1,010 | $10 | $1.00 | $1.01 |
| 1,100 | $0.50 | $550 | –$5 | $1,110 | $10 | $1.00 | $1.009 |

## Exhibit 12.6 The Quantity Effect and the Price Effect on Revenues for Claritin

If Schering-Plough set a price of $5 per pill, then it would sell 200 million Claritin pills annually. If it lowered its price to $4 per pill, there would be two effects on total revenue. First, the lower price would lead to more sales (from 200 million to 400 million) and more revenue; this quantity effect is captured by the green box. Second, the lower price would lead to lost revenues from the original consumers: the 200 million consumers who were buying at $5 per pill are now paying only $4 per pill. This lost revenue from these consumers is called the price effect and is captured by the pink box.

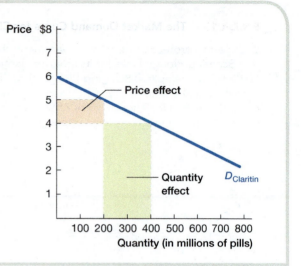

the green-shaded region in Exhibit 12.6. Computing the area of the green-shaded region (base times height) yields an increase in revenues of $800 million (200 million multiplied by $4).

But there is a flip side. Those people who were buying at the old price of $5 now only have to pay $4. This loss in revenues is known as the *price effect*; it is shaded pink in Exhibit 12.6. Calculating the area of the pink rectangle, we find that the price effect is equal to $200 million (200 million multiplied by $1). In sum, therefore, the increase in total revenues from the price change is $800 million − $200 million = $600 million. In this case, the price effect is smaller than the quantity effect. As we learned in Chapter 5, this means that demand is elastic over this range of the demand curve.

These observations reveal a more general pattern at work. With price decreases—moving down the demand curve—when the quantity effect dominates the price effect, then total revenue increases. If the price effect dominates the quantity effect, then total revenue falls. Alternatively, if one considers price increases—moving up the demand curve—the nature of these relationships reverses. That is, with price increases, if the quantity effect dominates the price effect, then total revenue decreases. If the price effect dominates the quantity effect, then total revenue increases. The following table summarizes these effects.

| Event | Quantity Effect Dominates | Price Effect Dominates |
| --- | --- | --- |
| Price decreases | Total revenue increases | Total revenue decreases |
| Price increases | Total revenue decreases | Total revenue increases |

## Price, Marginal Revenue, and Total Revenue

We are now in a position to put this intuition into action. Exhibit 12.7 shows how price, marginal revenue, and total revenue are related. Panel (a) uses the information from Exhibit 12.5 to graph the demand curve and the marginal revenue curve for Claritin. The curves begin at the same point on the price axis, because the price of Claritin is the marginal revenue from selling the first unit of Claritin. Thereafter, marginal revenue lies below the demand curve, and as quantity expands the difference between the demand curve and the marginal revenue curve grows larger. This is because for the monopoly to increase its sales, it must lower the price on all goods sold.

In this example, we find that the marginal revenue curve is twice as steep as the demand curve, causing it to reach the quantity axis at 600 million units, whereas the demand curve reaches it at 1.2 billion units. In fact, this will be the case for every linear demand curve, because the slope of the marginal revenue curve is twice as large (in absolute value) as the slope of the demand curve.

A second important aspect that Exhibit 12.7 reveals is the relationship between marginal revenue and total revenue. Panel (b) shows the total revenue curve for Claritin, which

12.1

12.2

12.3

12.4

12.5

12.6

12.7

**Exhibit 12.7** Relationship Among Price, Marginal Revenue, and Total Revenue

Panel (a) combines the demand curve for Claritin from Exhibit 12.4 with the marginal revenue curve faced by Schering-Plough. The marginal revenue curve shows the additional revenue generated for Schering-Plough at each quantity level. When marginal revenue crosses the quantity axis (at 600 million), total revenue decreases with further sales (see panel (b)). This means that total revenue is maximized when the marginal revenue curve crosses the x-axis.

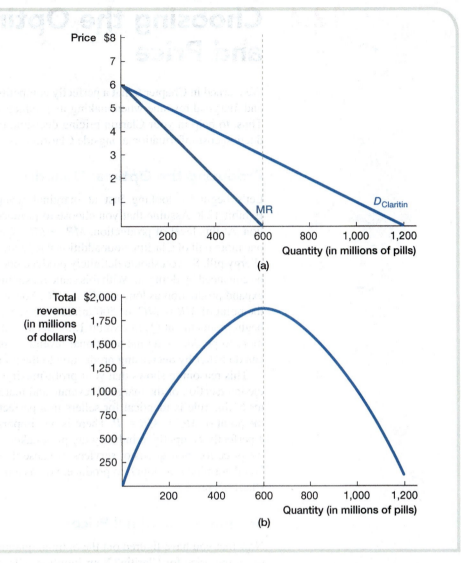

is hill-shaped. Exhibit 12.7 shows that when total revenue is rising, marginal revenue is positive. This makes sense, because if total revenue is increasing, marginal revenue must be positive. Alternatively, when total revenue is falling, marginal revenue is negative. For this reason, total revenue is at its maximum when the marginal revenue curve crosses the x-axis (quantity axis)—that is the point where an additional unit of output causes marginal revenue to equal zero.

A third important insight from the curves is that a price of $3 maximizes total revenue. This price is exactly in the middle of the demand curve. As we learned in Chapter 5, this means that for prices above $3 (the elastic portion of the demand curve), a price increase will lower total revenue. Alternatively, for prices below $3 (the inelastic portion of the demand curve), a price increase will raise total revenue. A general lesson is that if Schering-Plough desires to maximize total revenue, it should set price equal to $3, where the price elasticity of demand equals 1.

To perform your job of choosing the optimal price to maximize profits, you can now begin to see how you can eliminate some price levels from consideration. For example, would you ever choose a price of $1.50? No, because at this price, the marginal revenue from the last unit sold is negative, –$3 (see Exhibit 12.5). In other words, you are decreasing total revenues by selling that last unit! From this reasoning, you can see that you would never price below $3, which is the price at which marginal revenue turns negative. To do so would only lower revenues and increase costs.

12.1

12.2

12.3

12.4

12.5

12.6

12.7

## 12.4 Choosing the Optimal Quantity and Price

We learned in Chapter 6 that a perfectly competitive firm must consider both marginal cost and marginal revenue when making its production decision. A monopolist is no different. Thus, to help in your Claritin pricing decision, columns 5–8 in Exhibit 12.5 include production cost information alongside Claritin revenue information.

### Producing the Optimal Quantity

Let's begin by looking just at marginal revenue and marginal cost, as depicted in Exhibit 12.8. Assume that you choose to produce at quantity level $Q_L$, which is 300 million. At this level of production, $MR > MC$, specifically, $3 > $1. Thus, if you produce one more unit of Claritin, your additional revenue exceeds the additional cost of making the allergy pill. So you should definitely produce one more pill at $Q_L$, because your profits will be enhanced by doing so. With this same reasoning, you can see that you should continue to expand production as long as $MR > MC$. You stop increasing production when you reach the point of $MR = MC$, or 500 million units. Similar logic can be applied if you initially begin producing at $Q_H$ in Exhibit 12.8. Because $MC > MR$ at this point, the last unit costs more to produce than the additional revenue it brought in, resulting in lower profits. You can do better by decreasing production to the point of $MR = MC$.

This reasoning shows that your profit-maximizing level of output produced is given by the intersection of the marginal revenue and marginal cost curves. As we learned in Chapter 6, this rule is identical for sellers in a perfectly competitive industry, who produce at the point of $MC = MR = P$. There is one important difference, though: whereas firms in a perfectly competitive industry are price-takers, monopolists are price-makers—they set the price for their goods or services, because there are no competitors. In this sense, after you determine how much to produce, you as a monopolist need to determine where to set Claritin's price.

### Setting the Optimal Price

Now that you have figured out the optimal quantity, how do you start to think about where to set the price for Claritin? Your intuition tells you that if millions of people desperately want Claritin, you should set a very high price, whereas if only a few thousand people are vaguely interested in Claritin, you should set a low price. This intuition is spot-on: your pricing decision is, in fact, critically linked to the nature of the market demand curve.

**Exhibit 12.8 Marginal Revenue and Marginal Cost for Claritin**

If Schering-Plough produces at $Q_L$, then the 300 millionth pill will earn $3 in additional revenue (marginal revenue) and cost $1 to produce. At this point Schering-Plough should expand production. Why? It will earn more profits! By the same logic, consider $Q_H$, where Schering-Plough is producing so many units that the marginal cost exceeds the marginal revenue. The last unit of production costs more to produce than it generates in revenue.

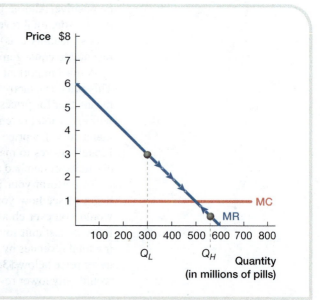

12.1

12.2

12.3

12.4

12.5

12.6

12.7

**Exhibit 12.9 Choosing the Profit-Maximizing Price for Claritin**

Schering-Plough expands production until *MC = MR*. To determine the price that maximizes profits, it goes directly upward to the demand curve and over to the y-axis (the price axis) to determine the profit-maximizing price. In this case, a price of $3.50 is the profit-maximizing price for Schering-Plough.

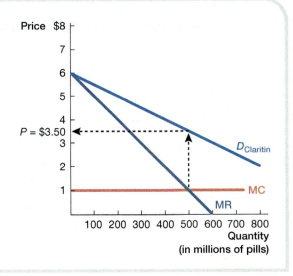

One way for you to ease the pain of allergy season is to purchase allergy drugs, such as Claritin.

Exhibit 12.9 graphs the demand curve, the marginal revenue curve, and the marginal cost curve. Once we have found the quantity level at which $MR = MC$, your job as the monopolist is to choose the highest possible price that permits you to sell the entire quantity that you have produced. Graphically, you can find this price by using the demand curve.

As shown by the vertical arrow in Exhibit 12.9, you determine Claritin's price by looking at the demand curve to see what price consumers are willing to pay for the quantity you put on the market. Following the arrows in Exhibit 12.9, you see that you maximize your firm's profits by setting a price of $3.50, because this is the highest price that you can charge and still sell the 500 million pills that you have produced (if you search the Web, you might find that Internet prices for a Claritin pill are currently around $0.50 per pill; for illustrative purposes, we chose our equilibrium price to be in the range of observed prices over the lifetime of the Claritin patent).

The following simple flow chart shows the steps in the production and pricing decisions facing the monopolist:

You will likely note that this approach is quite similar to the decision making of our perfectly competitive firm in Chapter 6, but with one major difference: price is set at a level higher than marginal cost for a monopolist, whereas price is equal to marginal cost for a perfectly competitive firm.

In sum, the optimal pricing decision rules are as follows:

Monopolist: Set $P > MR = MC$; Perfectly competitive firm: $P = MR = MC$.

Note that the marginal decision making concerning the level of production is identical across these two market structures: expand production until $MC = MR$. The major difference arises from the fact that the firm in a competitive industry does not set its price (the market does), whereas the monopolist sets price based on the market demand curve. By inspection of Exhibit 12.9, we can see that the monopolist sets a price that is on the elastic portion of the demand curve (recall from Chapter 5 that the top half of a linear demand curve is elastic).

> **Price is set at a level higher than marginal costs for a monopolist, whereas price is equal to marginal cost for a perfectly competitive firm.**

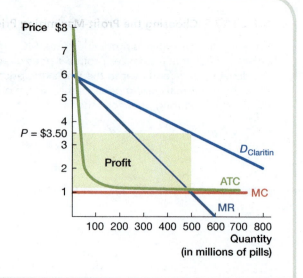

**Exhibit 12.10 Computing Profits for a Monopolist**

Similar to the perfectly competitive firm, Schering-Plough computes profit as quantity times the difference between price and ATC [Profit = Quantity × (P − ATC)]. In this case, the green rectangle shows profit, which equals the difference between the price of each pill ($3.50) and the ATC ($1.02), multiplied by 500 million.

## How a Monopolist Calculates Profits

How much will your company earn in economic profits from Claritin if you follow this optimal decision rule? Computing economic profits for a monopoly works exactly the same as computing economic profits for a perfectly competitive firm:

$$\text{Profits} = \text{Total revenue} - \text{Total cost} = (P \times Q) - (ATC \times Q) = (P - ATC) \times Q.$$

Taking the numbers from Exhibit 12.5, we can compute monopoly profits in equilibrium. The green-shaded area in Exhibit 12.10 graphically depicts the total profits. To summarize how we obtain this green-shaded area, we begin by finding the point where $MC = MR$. This gives us the profit-maximizing output of 500 million units. Moving upward from this point to the demand curve, we find the profit-maximizing price of $3.50. At that quantity, subtracting the ATC of $1.02 from the price of $3.50 gives us $2.48 of profits per unit sold. We then multiply this number by 500 million units to obtain total economic profits of $1.24 billion:

$$\$1,240,000,000 = \text{Total revenue} - \text{Total cost} = (\$3.50 - \$1.02) \times 500,000,000.$$

As we discussed earlier, in perfectly competitive markets, entry causes long-run economic profits to be zero. For a monopoly, economic profits remain. This is because there is no threat of entry from competitors because of barriers to entry. Therefore, no new entrants threaten to increase supply and push the price down to eliminate economic profits.

## Does a Monopoly Have a Supply Curve?

At this point, you may have found it curious that there has been no mention of monopoly supply curves. After all, Exhibit 12.9 shows the price and quantity combination at which a monopolistic firm will produce by using only the marginal revenue, marginal cost, and demand curves. No supply curve! The reason is simple: monopolists, unlike sellers in competitive markets, do not have a supply curve.

To understand why this is the case, first consider what the supply curve of a competitive market represents. To create a supply curve under perfect competition, it is necessary for firms to be price-*takers*, whose production is based on the given market price. Under this assumption, we simply determine the quantity at which the marginal cost of producing the last unit of a good is equal to the market price. Thus, in a competitive market, a supply curve shows all price and quantity combinations at which firms will produce.

Monopolists, as price-*makers*, do not vary their production based on market price because they set the price; it makes no sense to ask how much of a good a monopolist will produce at a given price. Like sellers in competitive markets, monopolists will produce at the point where their marginal revenue is equal to their marginal cost. But as you have just learned, marginal revenue depends on the negatively sloped demand curve that the monopolist faces. Because a monopolist's production decision is based on demand, it cannot be depicted as an independent supply curve.

12.1
12.2
12.3
12.4
12.5
12.6
12.7

# 12.5 The "Broken" Invisible Hand: The Cost of Monopoly

In Chapter 7 we learned that the invisible hand creates harmony between individual and social interests. Such synchronization has the very attractive feature that social surplus is maximized in the competitive equilibrium. The power of the invisible hand is such that even in markets composed of only self-interested people, the overall well-being of society is maximized. One important factor that can break the powerful result of the invisible hand is market power. A firm that exercises market power causes a reallocation of resources toward itself, thereby sacrificing social surplus.

One way to think about this is to consider the market for Claritin before and after Schering-Plough's patent expired. In 1981, Schering-Plough was awarded a monopoly, in the form of a patent, on Claritin. Twenty years later, Schering-Plough's monopoly rights expired, and generic prescription drug companies could suddenly enter the market and sell close substitutes, such as Allegra.[2] This entry process drastically changed the market for Claritin in a number of ways.

> A firm that exercises market power causes a reallocation of resources toward itself, thereby sacrificing social surplus.

Panel (a) of Exhibit 12.11 shows the long-run equilibrium of the market after Claritin's patent expiration prompted entry by competitive firms. Firms have a constant marginal cost curve, so $ATC = MC$. You might wonder about fixed costs. Recall from Chapter 6 that since we are in the long run, there are no fixed costs.

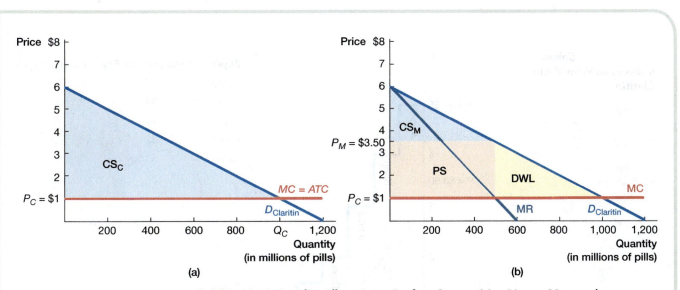

**Exhibit 12.11 Surplus Allocations: Perfect Competition Versus Monopoly**

Panel (a) shows the consumer surplus from a perfectly competitive market ($CS_C$), which is the area under the demand curve and above the market price. Panel (b) shows what happens to consumer surplus ($CS_M$) when the monopolist maximizes profits: consumer surplus is substantially reduced, with some of it going to the monopolist (labeled PS), and another large piece that is a deadweight loss (DWL).

The equilibrium price is now dramatically lower—just $1 per pill. This lower price prompts a boom in quantity demanded, all the way to 1 billion pills. Consumer surplus in this perfectly competitive market is depicted by the blue area below the demand curve and above the marginal cost curve. In equilibrium, consumer surplus is $2.5 billion ($\frac{1}{2} \times 1$ billion $\times$ ($6 − $1)).

To compare outcomes across markets, panel (b) of Exhibit 12.11 presents surplus outcomes before Claritin's patent expired. When Schering-Plough's patent was still in effect, consumer surplus was dramatically smaller: $625 million ($\frac{1}{2} \times 500$ million $\times$ ($3.50 − $1)). Schering-Plough's monopoly power allowed it to capture surplus from consumers. This captured surplus is represented by the pink-shaded box labeled PS.

Schering-Plough's monopolistic pricing didn't just capture surplus from consumers, however. Importantly, social surplus is smaller when Schering-Plough exercises monopoly power. This cost to society is deadweight loss and is represented as the yellow triangle labeled DWL in panel (b). This is surplus that would exist in the competitive equilibrium but is lost when Schering-Plough is a monopolist. The deadweight loss from Claritin's monopolistic pricing is $625 million ($\frac{1}{2} \times 500$ million $\times$ ($3.50 − $1)).

Does this mean that patents are counterproductive? Not necessarily. Remember that because fixed costs were so high to develop Claritin, the government had to create an incentive to induce companies to spend money on research and development. The incentive that is used with pharmaceutical companies is a temporary patent, and the cost to society of this incentive is the deadweight loss from monopoly while the patent is held. Overall, was the bargain worth it? We'll explore that question in more depth below.

## 12.6 Restoring Efficiency

Beyond waiting until the Claritin patent expires, are there any other means by which to restore efficiency in this market? The answer is yes. To illustrate, consider Exhibit 12.12 and its accompanying table, which provides a glimpse of five buyers in the market for Claritin. In this example, Augie is willing to pay $5 per pill, Noah $4, Joyce $3, Dawn $2, and Greta $1.50. At the monopolist's price of $3.50, only Augie and Noah buy Claritin, even though Joyce, Dawn, and Greta are all willing to pay values above marginal cost.

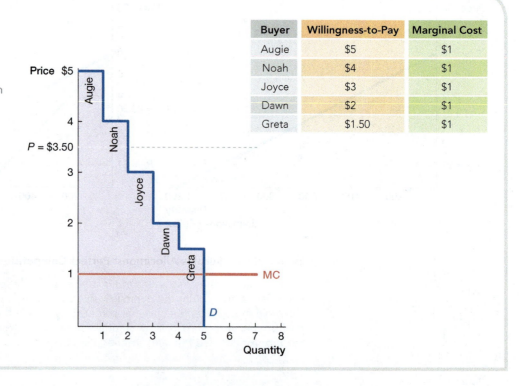

**Exhibit 12.12 Select Individuals Who Value Claritin**

The exhibit and table show the maximum price that each buyer would pay for one Claritin pill. The marginal cost for producing remains $1 per unit.

| Buyer | Willingness-to-Pay | Marginal Cost |
|---|---|---|
| Augie | $5 | $1 |
| Noah | $4 | $1 |
| Joyce | $3 | $1 |
| Dawn | $2 | $1 |
| Greta | $1.50 | $1 |

One way to restore social efficiency (that is, maximize social surplus) is to have a social planner choose the monopolist's quantity and price. This "all-knowing" social planner would need to know both the monopolist's marginal cost and the buyer's willingness to pay for the Claritin pill. The social planner would want consumers like Joyce, Dawn, and Greta to buy Claritin because their willingness-to-pay values are all higher than the marginal cost of producing Claritin. If they buy, social surplus increases by the difference between their willingness-to-pay values and the marginal cost of production: $2 + $1 + $0.50 = $3.50. Indeed, the social planner could choose the same outcome as that which results in the perfectly competitive equilibrium, because that outcome maximizes social surplus.

In analyzing how much Schering-Plough produces in its monopoly equilibrium, the planner would view the quantity produced as too low. This is because Schering-Plough uses its market power to maximize profits by producing too few units and charging too much. In this way, it has "broken" the efficient outcome of the invisible hand that we discussed in Chapter 7. To restore efficiency, the social planner would direct Schering-Plough to produce many more Claritin pills than the firm would prefer to produce and set price equal to marginal cost.

So why doesn't Schering-Plough produce extra Claritin pills and charge a slightly lower price to Joyce, Dawn, and Greta? The reason is that by so doing, it would then have to charge a slightly lower price to *all* buyers, such as Augie and Noah—a move that would lower profits, as we showed earlier in the chapter in our discussion of optimal profits and the price and quantity effects associated with changing price.

Because the all-knowing social planner is merely a mythical construct, we can ask whether there is any practical, realistic way to attempt to reach the maximum level of social surplus achieved in a perfectly competitive market. Is there any recourse beyond having the government step in and mandate Schering-Plough's price? The answer is yes, but we suspect that it is an approach that may make you less than fully comfortable. Let's discuss that now.

## Three Degrees of Price Discrimination

Have you ever wondered why some people seem to get all the deals? Maybe you buy a plane ticket home for $500, only to learn that the frequent flyer in the seat next to you paid $350. Likewise, you might get irked if you're standing in a checkout line at Walmart when the man in front of you pulls out a coupon for a free T-shirt—the same shirt you're about to purchase for $15!

In such situations, consumers are often displeased and struck by the perceived unfairness of the transaction. Producers, however, are ecstatic because of their success at *price discrimination*. **Price discrimination** occurs when firms charge different consumers different prices for the same good or service. Provided that buyers who receive low prices cannot simply turn around and sell to buyers who receive high prices (we call this arbitrage), companies might be able to enhance their profits by engaging in price discrimination.

We typically discuss three types of price discrimination:

1. **First-degree,** or **perfect price discrimination**, in which consumers are charged the maximum price they are willing to pay
2. **Second-degree price discrimination**, in which consumers are charged different prices based on characteristics of their purchase, such as the quantity they purchase
3. **Third-degree price discrimination**, in which different groups of consumers are charged different prices based on their own attributes (such as age, gender, or location)

Let's see how first-degree price discrimination works by continuing with the example from Exhibit 12.12. In this scenario, if Schering-Plough knew each individual's willingness to pay, it would charge each of the five consumers exactly that amount—$5 per pill for Augie, $4 for Noah, $3 for Joyce, $2 for Dawn, and $1.50 for Greta. By so doing, Schering-Plough can extract all consumer surplus from the buyers.

Extending this logic to the entire market reveals some interesting insights. If you, as the monopolist, were able to perfectly price discriminate, then the outcome would be not only to maximize your own profits but also to maximize social surplus. To see why, let's

**Price discrimination** occurs when firms charge different consumers different prices for the same good or service.

**Perfect price discrimination**, also known as **first-degree price discrimination**, occurs when a firm charges each buyer exactly his or her willingness to pay.

**Second-degree price discrimination** occurs when consumers are charged different prices based on characteristics of their purchase.

**Third-degree price discrimination** occurs when price varies based on a customer's attributes.

12.1

12.2

12.3

12.4

12.5

12.6

12.7

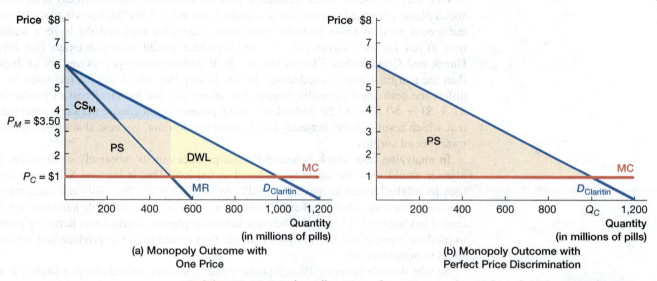

**Exhibit 12.13** Surplus Allocations for a Monopoly: With and Without Perfect Price Discrimination

Panel (a) summarizes the outcome from the monopolist problem. Panel (b) shows that with perfect price discrimination, the monopolist captures consumer surplus and the deadweight loss by charging consumers their willingness to pay.

> **If you as the monopolist were able to perfectly price discriminate, then the outcome would be not only to maximize your own profits but also to maximize social surplus.**

reconsider the monopoly outcome, which is summarized in panel (a) of Exhibit 12.13. Panel (b) of the exhibit shows the monopoly outcome with perfect price discrimination. As panel (b) shows, with perfect price discrimination you expand production until the demand curve intersects the marginal cost curve (point $Q_C$). When doing so, Schering-Plough's producer surplus includes the entire consumer surplus and the deadweight loss because it expands production until $P = MC$, and charges each consumer his or her willingness to pay.

The exhibit shows that you have been able to dramatically increase Schering-Plough's surplus through perfect price discrimination. Yet it also shows that consumers clearly suffer. Because the monopolist is able to extract every penny each consumer would be willing to pay when it practices first-degree price discrimination, consumer surplus equals zero.

We are now in a position to compare social surplus in the Claritin market before and after first-degree price discrimination. The entire story is found in Exhibit 12.13, which shows that with perfect price discrimination, we have completely eliminated the deadweight loss of monopoly. Thus, perfect price discrimination is *socially efficient*: it provides the maximum level of social surplus. This equilibrium is also a Pareto-efficient equilibrium (as we discussed in Chapter 7), because no one can be made better off without making someone else worse off. What might concern you is the extreme inequity in the allocation of surplus—buyers receive no surplus and the seller receives all of it!

In practice, perfect price discrimination is difficult to achieve for two reasons. First, it is hard to charge every consumer a unique price. Second, it is challenging to know every consumer's willingness to pay. Therefore, other forms of price discrimination are more prevalent in practice. In many of these cases, the monopolist does not know the exact willingness to pay of different consumers but can still improve its profits by charging different prices based on perceived differences in willingness to pay.

We focus next on third-degree price discrimination because it affects all of us daily. Third-degree price discrimination occurs when price varies by customer or location attributes. You might wonder why movie theaters, restaurants, golf courses, and the like charge children and senior citizens a lower price. Likewise, economists have found that sometimes car dealerships base their negotiating practices on the gender or race of the car buyer. These are all attempts to price discriminate based on an observable characteristic that the seller believes is correlated to the consumer's willingness to pay. In such cases, the monopolist segments its customers into groups and maximizes profits by effectively acting like a monopolist in each submarket, setting $MR = MC$ in each.

Following up on our Claritin example, if the willingness-to-pay values for Augie, Noah, Joyce, Dawn, and Greta were indicative of the population at large, it would be profitable for the firm to segment by gender and charge men a higher price than it charges women. For example, simply moving from charging one price of $3.50 to charging men $4 per pill and women $2 per pill would increase profits significantly. By paying $4 instead of $3.50, Augie and Noah provide $1 more in total profits. And, whereas at a price of $3.50 the three women do not purchase Claritin and therefore add nothing to Schering-Plough's profits, when they are charged $2, they add $2 to profits because both Joyce and Dawn now purchase Claritin.

Both first- and third-degree price discrimination are examples in which the monopolist charges different prices to different people based on their perceived differences in willingness to pay. There are important cases, however, when sellers are not able to differentiate among types of consumers. Perhaps they do not have good indicators of how much various

# LETTING THE DATA SPEAK

## Third-Degree Price Discrimination in Action

Third-degree price discrimination can often rear its ugly head. Consider a recent field experiment that compared people confined to wheelchairs with a group of non-disabled people. The subjects of interest were in need of car repairs. For the disabled, it's a hassle to even leave the house, much less shop around for a few price quotes. So there are real search differences between those who are disabled and those who are not.

It turns out that the disabled aren't the only ones who know this. Mechanics know it, too, and adjust the prices they charge the disabled accordingly.

We know this because field experiments[3] have been conducted that have randomized whether a disabled or nondisabled person brings a banged-up (but still specially equipped for the disabled) car to an auto repair shop. What do the data say?

If it happens that a disabled person is the one who is asking for a price quote, then the price he is charged is 20 percent higher than the price a non-disabled person is charged. You can see this in the accompanying graph by just comparing the orange and purple bars above the word Baseline: the disabled are quoted an average price of $600, whereas the non-disabled pay around $500.

You might be thinking that this isn't necessarily price discrimination based on search differences. It might just be that mechanics don't like people in wheelchairs. But the same study tested this idea by also having every person in both groups say the following line when they were getting a quote, "I am getting a few price quotes today."

Turns out that just saying this simple line caused the price quotes that the handicapped were getting to drop a lot. To

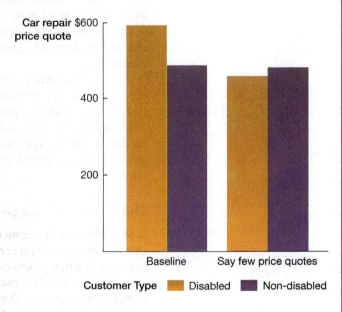

see this, just compare the first orange bar to the one above "Say few price quotes" in the graph.

What about the non-disabled? Their price quotes stayed about the same, suggesting that there was never any doubt in the minds of mechanics that the non-disabled shop around for the best price.

This case represents an example of third-degree price discrimination: body shop mechanics were using the fact that the disabled had a hard time searching, so they tended to charge all disabled people a higher price in an effort to enhance their shops' profits.

consumers are willing to pay. Even in this situation price discrimination can exist. For example, Apple gives discounts if you purchase a large quantity of song downloads from its iTunes music store. Tire salespersons often sell four tires for $200 and one for $75. Bakeries sell a dozen doughnuts for $7, whereas two doughnuts sell for $1.50. Likewise, a standard arrangement between industrial customers and providers is that those who buy in bulk enjoy substantial discounts.

In cases where consumers are charged different prices based on characteristics of their purchase, second-degree price discrimination is said to exist. Beyond the examples above, can you think of situations in which you were a consumer and a firm practiced second-degree price discrimination on you?

## 12.7 Government Policy Toward Monopoly

**Antitrust policy** aims to regulate and prevent anticompetitive pricing.

The U.S. Department of Justice and many similar agencies in other countries actively attempt to keep various industries in check. One of their main purposes, sometimes referred to as **antitrust policy**, is to prevent anticompetitive pricing, low quantities, and deadweight loss from emerging and dominating markets. Some monopolies, such as natural monopolies, are unavoidable. But, as we learned in this chapter, monopoly pricing is potentially detrimental to society and quite costly for consumers. The goal of antitrust policy is to keep markets open and competitive.

In the United States, antitrust policy started in 1890 with the Sherman Act, even though several states had adopted similar statutes prior to this legislation. This was the era of the so-called "robber barons"—men such as John D. Rockefeller, Andrew Carnegie, and Cornelius Vanderbilt, who had dominated certain industries and who were often accused of using questionable methods and unfair practices. The Sherman Act and the policies of Presidents Theodore Roosevelt and Woodrow Wilson were pitched against such monopolies.

The Sherman Act prohibited any agreements or actions that would put restraints on trade—in essence, prohibiting firms from monopolizing markets. Moreover, it made such attempts felonies, punishable not only by large fines but also by prison sentences. These antitrust policies led to the breakup of Standard Oil and introduced greater regulation of other large monopolies, including the dominant banks of the era, which were becoming increasingly powerful. Today, U.S. antitrust policy is still based on the Sherman Act.

### The Microsoft Case

In May 1998, the Department of Justice filed a lawsuit under the Sherman Act against arguably the most successful corporation of the 1990s, Microsoft. It claimed that Microsoft was engaging in unfair practices in order to monopolize the market. The crux of the case concerned the fact that Microsoft was bundling its Windows operating system with its Internet Explorer browser. The Department of Justice argued that Microsoft made it effectively impossible for alternative browsers, such as Netscape, to maintain a large market share. As a result, Microsoft was accused of achieving monopoly power through unfair practices. The suit was filed the day Windows 98 was released with Internet Explorer bundled with the operating system.

After a long trial, the ruling ultimately went against Microsoft—both in this case brought by the U.S. Department of Justice and in similar cases brought against it in Europe by the European Commission. At some point it even seemed possible that Microsoft would be broken into separate companies—one unit for selling the Windows operating system and the other for selling applications software. In the end, Microsoft paid various fines and agreed to change its operating system and marketing practices to make it easier for alternative browsers and other applications to be used with Windows.

Bill Gates spent much of his time defending Microsoft in an antitrust case filed by the U.S. Department of Justice in 1998.

The Microsoft case is interesting, not only because it illustrates the power of antitrust laws in the United States but also because it raises questions about what should be considered monopoly power in today's new and dynamic industries. Could Microsoft really develop a monopoly in the same way as Standard Oil did in the oil business? Some believe that the answer is yes, and this reasoning was the one that prevailed in the courts. In fact, some economists believe that the dangers of such monopolization are even stronger today, because many software products are subject to network externalities. Compatibility issues are the main source of such network effects, and they are undoubtedly present in many products.

A simple example of a network effect is your choice of a DVD player. At some point, both HD DVD and Blu-ray were viable choices for the next generation of DVDs. Network effects are important in consumer choices—when all your friends purchase and use Blu-ray, then HD DVD becomes much less attractive for you, because you won't be able to exchange discs with them. Ultimately, if all stores carry mostly Blu-ray, then it will be difficult for you even to find HD DVD discs. Such network effects were the basis of the claim that in many software-related industries, products that achieve sufficient market share become difficult to compete against and thus develop monopoly power.

Other economists recognize the importance of network effects but nevertheless believe that software and other IT industries are inherently competitive and cannot be monopolized in the same way that the oil business was a century ago. This group thought that the Department of Justice's case against Microsoft was beyond the scope of the original Sherman Act. They argued that if Microsoft's operating system became too expensive, a new operating system, with greater compatibility with other products, would be supplied at a lower price, because software innovations cannot come to an end. There are always potential competitors watching the industry, and they will seize any opportunity to make a profit as soon as it becomes available. The Microsoft case still remains one of the most debated among economists today.

## Price Regulation

In the past, one government solution has been to allow the monopoly to keep its market share but regulate the price it may charge. The idea is that a lower price will expand the purchase opportunities for consumers. This seems like a simple enough solution . . . until it is time to decide on the "fair" price a monopolist may charge. Two pricing options have dominated discussions: setting price equal to marginal cost, and setting price equal to ATC.

It may seem that the proper choice is obvious: set price equal to marginal cost, because, as we know, that is the price at which total surplus is maximized. A price set at marginal cost is called the **efficient** or **socially optimal price**. Unfortunately, the choice is not this simple. As we have learned, in some cases marginal cost is lower than ATC at every level of quantity (this occurred in our Claritin example). This means that setting price equal to marginal cost will cause the firm's total revenue to be less than the total cost, so the firm will experience an economic loss and will eventually exit the industry if this sort of regulation is imposed.

An **efficient** or **socially optimal price** is set at marginal cost.

One solution to this problem is to have the government make up for any losses incurred by the monopolist. Unfortunately, the government must raise this money through taxes, and as we learned in Chapter 10, government taxes lead to a deadweight loss. Another solution is to allow the monopolist to charge a higher price—a price equal to its ATC. This price level is called a **fair-returns price**. Although the fair-returns price does not maximize surplus—we again have a deadweight loss—it does allow the monopolist to make zero economic profits. Then the monopolist can stay in business without the government making up for the losses incurred.

A price set at average total cost is a **fair-returns price**.

Unfortunately, these two forms of regulation have their own efficiency problems. The main one is that the firm now has no incentive to minimize costs, because in either case it is guaranteed to make zero economic profits. There is also a lack of profit motive to innovate and produce new goods and services, because the firm will not reap the economic rewards.

Now that we have considered ways in which government can regulate monopoly, we should consider whether regulating monopoly is the right course of action in the first place. Both cases result in costs to consumers. With an unregulated monopoly, consumers pay a higher price, quantity is lower than is socially optimal, and a deadweight loss is incurred. With a regulated monopoly, consumers pay a lower price but there is a deadweight loss either as a result of "tax and transfer" to the monopolist or as the result of an inefficient price. Many economists have argued that allowing unregulated monopolies to exist is, in practice, more efficient than price regulation. We turn to some of this evidence now.

## Q: Can a monopoly ever be good for society?

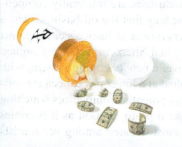

**Research and development (R&D)** is the investment by firms in the creation of products not yet available on the market.

After learning the rather grim details about monopoly pricing and the deadweight loss associated with monopolies, many might wish to turn their backs on monopolies forever. You might think, "What could be worse than greedy monopolists rolling in money at the expense of ripped-off customers?" Indeed, that is what happened when you set the price for Claritin tablets for Schering-Plough.

Perhaps this is why such countries as Canada and India do not permit such extravagant monopoly profits. In Canada, the government controls prices for pharmaceuticals, and India does not provide innovators strong patent protection. Maybe these countries have it right—why not restrict monopolists in some shape or form?

We must keep in mind that it is the ability to make extraordinary profits that serves as an important motivator for many inventors. Firms that are allowed monopoly profits search out every possible avenue for innovative technologies that they can bring to market, whether it is a cure for AIDS or code for a search engine that will make our lives easier. If we lived in a world of perfect competition, firms would have less incentive to invest in the creation of new products—**research and development (R&D)**—because they would not enjoy the same levels of profit from innovation. Through entry, economic profits would be driven to zero in the long run.

This presents us with a conundrum: if we allow a firm to have monopoly power, we are assuredly not maximizing social surplus because of deadweight loss. But if we do not grant innovators protection, society might not benefit from a wide variety of goods and services, because profits may not be available to spur invention. In the case of Claritin, the issue boils down to whether you want to suffer with more sneezing, itchier eyes, and a runnier nose or pay $3.50 per tablet for Claritin.

The question naturally becomes an empirical one. Just how much more innovation do we have because of patent and copyright protection?

When a company obtains a patent, it receives exclusive rights to produce and sell a good or service. This exclusive right allows the firm to act as a monopolist and to set its own price, which, as we have learned in this chapter, is higher than the equilibrium price in a perfectly competitive market. If what we've discussed thus far about monopolies is true, then why would the government encourage and even provide the legal framework for such monopolistic behavior?

The answer is innovation.

There's no perfect data set to address the impact of patent and copyright protection on innovation, but let's discuss several sources to develop an understanding. Our first stop will be the nineteenth-century World's Fairs.

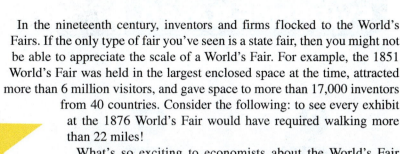

In the nineteenth century, inventors and firms flocked to the World's Fairs. If the only type of fair you've seen is a state fair, then you might not be able to appreciate the scale of a World's Fair. For example, the 1851 World's Fair was held in the largest enclosed space at the time, attracted more than 6 million visitors, and gave space to more than 17,000 inventors from 40 countries. Consider the following: to see every exhibit at the 1876 World's Fair would have required walking more than 22 miles!

What's so exciting to economists about the World's Fair is that at the time, patent laws varied considerably from country to country, and unlike today, it was very difficult to patent an invention outside the country of origin. As a result, data from guides for the nineteenth-century World's Fairs, which had information on the country of the inventor, the industry of the invention, and whether the inventor had patented his or her invention, are a perfect test of the idea that patent laws are necessary for innovation.

An analysis of these data yields a nuanced answer that makes perfect sense: some industries need patent protection more than others.[4] In particular, inventors from countries without strong patent laws focused their attention on hard-to-duplicate inventions like scientific instruments and food processing because they could easily hide the production techniques required to keep their invention a secret. In contrast, inventors from countries with strong patent protection provided the bulk of innovations for manufacturing and other machinery, in part because these innovations are easily reverse engineered.

What does this mean for us today? First, for innovations that aren't easily kept secret, we need patent protection. But not all industries need the same level of protection. For example, pharmaceutical drugs, which are easily copied by competitors that specialize in mass-producing generic drugs, might need a lot more protection than a clothing company that develops a new textile shrouded in secrecy.

However, too much protection isn't a guarantee of more innovation in the long run. In the 1990s, two major efforts were undertaken to decode the human genome. One was an open-source effort, called the Human Genome Project. The other was a private effort by a firm called Celera. As time went on, some pieces of the genome were decoded by the Human Genome Project first and made freely available to everyone. Other pieces were decoded by Celera first, but in those instances Celera used intellectual property law to prevent the Human Genome Project from decoding their sequences.

The difference in subsequent research on parts of the genome sequenced by the Human Genome Project and parts sequenced by Celera is overwhelming. On average, 70 percent more scientific work was conducted on Human Genome Project sequences than on Celera sequences.[5]

The takeaway is that innovation doesn't just respond to incentives—it also requires inventors to be able to stand on the shoulders of those who came before them. In that vein, the monopoly power enjoyed by patent and copyright holders may both spur and hinder innovation. The optimal policy for granting innovators a monopoly over their invention should balance these costs and benefits.

Analysis of more than 20 years of data on competition and innovation seems to support this contention. In particular, the relationship between the level of competition that firms face and the amount of innovation arising from firms shows that innovation isn't driven by (1) firms that face perfect competition or (2) firms that have an iron-clad monopoly. Rather, those firms in market structures in between—firms that enjoy some monopolistic power but are in industries with plenty of brilliant competitors to mimic and spur innovation—are the best at driving technological advancements.[6]

### Question

Can a monopoly ever be good for society?

### Answer

Evidence suggests that market power can be an important factor in innovation.

### Data

Patent laws and World's Fair inventions, human genome sequencing, patent data, and industry competitiveness.

### Caveat

The data paint the strongest picture for firms that enjoy some monopolistic power but are in industries with plenty of brilliant competitors to mimic and spur innovation.

## Summary

- A monopoly is an industry structure in which only one firm provides a good or service that has no close substitutes. Monopolies arise because of barriers to entry, which take two forms: legal and natural. In the legal form, government creates the barrier, as with a patent or copyright. In the natural form, control of key resources or achieving economies of scale (for example, when providing goods such as natural gas and electricity) can result in a natural monopoly.

- Barriers to entry permit the monopolist to exercise market power when making quantity and pricing decisions. The optimal action of the monopolist is to set Price > Marginal revenue = Marginal cost. This differs from a perfectly competitive industry, where Price = Marginal cost = Marginal revenue.

- In equilibrium, monopoly leads to less quantity and higher prices compared to a perfectly competitive market equilibrium. In this way, because consumers are standing by ready to purchase from the monopolist for a price greater than marginal cost, social surplus is not maximized, leading to a deadweight loss.

- Monopolies may sometimes be appropriate, and understanding whether a firm is occupying a monopoly status appropriately is a major concern of U.S. lawmakers. Even though there are costs to allowing firms to have monopoly power, the extra profit incentive might translate into better and more productive research and development for new products, medicines, and technologies.

## Key Terms

price-makers *p. 285*
market power *p. 285*
monopoly *p. 285*
barriers to entry *p. 286*
legal market power *p. 286*
patent *p. 286*
copyright *p. 286*
natural market power *p. 287*

key resources *p. 287*
network externalities *p. 288*
natural monopoly *p. 289*
price discrimination *p. 299*
perfect or first-degree price
  discrimination *p. 299*
second-degree price discrimination
  *p. 299*

third-degree price discrimination
  *p. 299*
antitrust policy *p. 302*
efficient or socially optimal price
  *p. 303*
fair-returns price *p. 303*
research and development (R&D)
  *p. 304*

# Questions

*All questions are available in MyEconLab for practice and instructor assignment.*

1. What is meant by market power? What are the ways in which a monopoly gains market power?

2. Use a graph to explain the difference between a competitive firm's ATC curve and the ATC curve of a natural monopoly.

3. What does it mean to say that a good generates network externalities?

4. Why is national defense better off as a natural monopoly? What other industry or service do you think should be a natural monopoly?

5. How does a natural monopoly differ from a firm that becomes a monopoly due to network effects?

6. People who need life-saving drugs cannot do without them and surely will be willing to pay very high prices for them. So why can't producers of life-saving drugs charge any price that they wish?

7. What is the shape of a monopolist's demand curve and marginal revenue curve?

8. What is the relationship between price, marginal revenue, and total revenue for a monopolist?

9. Both competitive firms and monopolies produce at the level where marginal cost equals marginal revenue. Other things remaining the same, why then is the price lower in a competitive market than in a monopoly?

10. Why does a monopoly firm not have a supply curve?

11. Examine the following statements and identify the type of price discrimination in each case.

    a. A popular club in a city waives its entry fees for women who arrive before 11 p.m.

    b. A combo meal of a burger, a soft drink, and fries at a fast-food outlet costs less than how much it would cost to buy each item separately.

    c. A guy selling counterfeit watches on the street states a different price to each person who wants to buy a watch.

12. To restrict a firm's monopoly power, why can't antitrust authorities just set a price floor or a price ceiling in the market?

13. Are there any cases where a monopoly is beneficial to the economy? Explain.

# Problems

*All problems are available in MyEconLab for practice and instructor assignment.*

1. As this chapter explains, a monopoly is an industry structure in which only one firm provides a good or service that has no close substitutes. This question explores the last part of this definition further.

    a. At one time Sirius Satellite Radio and XM Satellite Radio were the only two satellite radio providers in the United States. The Department of Justice and the Federal Communications Commission approved the merger of the two companies in 2008 even though Sirius-XM would then control 100 percent of the satellite radio market. How do you think the two companies convinced the Department of Justice and the Federal Communications Commission to allow the merger to proceed?

    b. In 1947, the U.S. government charged the DuPont Company with a violation of the Sherman Act. The government argued that DuPont was monopolizing the cellophane market. At trial, the government showed that DuPont produced nearly 75 percent of all cellophane sold in the United States each year. Nonetheless, the U.S. Supreme Court ruled in favor of DuPont and dismissed the case. How do you think DuPont convinced the Supreme Court that it had not violated the Sherman Act?

2. Critically analyze the following scenarios and explain whether you agree or disagree.

    a. Janet knows a lot of people who do not like Marmite, a yeast extract that is used as a spread on toast. She says that Marmite is so unpopular that Unilever, the company that manufactures Marmite, cannot possibly have any monopoly power.

    b. Edgar says that a single firm in the wind power industry is unlikely to have a significant degree of monopoly power for an extended period of time. Since the cost of producing an additional unit of wind energy is so low, a large number of firms can enter the market and compete away economic profits.

3. Textbook publishers hope to maximize profits. Authors, however, face very different incentives. Authors are typically paid royalties, which are a specified percentage of total revenue from the sale of a book. And so, for example, if an author's contract says that she will receive 20 percent of the revenues from the sale of a text and the publisher's total revenues are $100,000, the author's royalties will be $20,000. Who will prefer a higher price for the text, the publisher or the author?

4. You run a company that has a monopoly on a new drug that treats arthritis. The price is $10 per dose, and you sell 10 million doses per day. Market research shows that a reduction of price by $2 will increase sales to 11 million doses per day. On a graph, show the price effect (loss of revenue due to the lower price) and quantity effect

(increase in revenue due to higher quantity). Find the area of each of these rectangles. Based on these calculations, what is the effect of cutting price on total revenue: increase, decrease, or no change?

**5.** You are a monopolist facing the following demand schedule. You produce a good at a constant marginal cost of $4 per unit.

| Quantity | Price |
|----------|-------|
| 1 | $14 |
| 2 | $12 |
| 3 | $10 |
| 4 | $8 |

**a.** Calculate the marginal revenue for each row (assume revenue is zero when quantity is zero).

**b.** What is the profit-maximizing quantity? Try to answer the question without actually calculating profit.

**c.** Assuming a fixed cost of $10 to operate, what is the profit?

**6.** You are a monopolist that sells textbooks to undergraduate students. Currently you sell 100 books at a price of $100 each, for revenue of $10,000. Each book is essentially costless to print, so you ignore fixed costs and focus on maximizing revenue. Based on research by your marketing team, you learn that some students will not buy the book if the price goes up. Also, if you cut the price, more students will buy the book.

**a.** If the elasticity of demand is −0.5, what will be your new revenue if you raise the price by 10 percent?

**b.** If the elasticity of demand is −2, should you raise the price or lower the price? Briefly explain without performing any calculations.

**7.** The following graph shows the demand, marginal revenue, and marginal cost curves in a monopoly market.

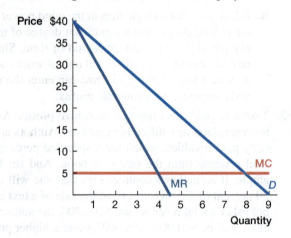

**a.** Identify the profit-maximizing price and quantity for this monopolist.

**b.** What are the values of the consumer surplus, producer surplus, and deadweight loss in the market?

**c.** How would consumer surplus change if this market were competitive?

**8.** Priceline is a Web site that sells flights and hotel bookings based on the price that a consumer states he or she is willing to pay. So consumers who want to book a flight or a hotel room need to tell Priceline the price they are willing to pay, and the seller lets Priceline know whether it is willing to accept that price.

**a.** How do sellers make profits by using this form of pricing?

**b.** In 1999, Priceline attempted to replicate this pricing strategy with groceries and gasoline. Using this pricing strategy with these two goods soon proved unprofitable. What could explain this?

**9.** Suppose you are a monopolist and you have two customers, Joseph and Monique. Each will buy either zero or one unit of the good you produce. Joseph is willing to pay up to $50 for your product; Monique is willing to pay up to $20. You produce this good at a constant average and marginal cost of $5.

**a.** If you could not engage in price discrimination, what price would you charge? How much profit would you earn?

**b.** If you could practice price discrimination, what prices would you charge? How much profit would you earn? For simplicity, assume that if consumers are indifferent between buying and not buying, they will buy.

**10.** For simplicity, consider a monopolist with no costs whatsoever; thus profit is revenue, which is just price multiplied by quantity. Demand consists of two groups. There are 14 adults: 10 are willing to pay $30 and 4 are willing to pay $20. There are also 16 children: 6 are willing to pay $20 and 10 are willing to pay $10.

**a.** What is best single (uniform) price to charge? Hint: Guess and check, and focus on $10, $20, or $30 as the price.

**b.** What if the monopolist could price discriminate by setting a different price for each group? How much should it charge adults and how much should it charge children?

**c.** Explain how, without even doing any calculations, we know that profits given a single price cannot be larger than profits given two different prices.

**11.** Imagine that you arrive at an economics experiment with six other people and are told that you will simulate a market. You will be the only seller. The other five people will be assigned a dollar value that they will receive if they buy the good for any amount of money (so if a person's value is $6, he will buy the good for any price less than $6 and will be happy). You are also given the following demand curve and told that it represents the values that the "buyers" are assigned.

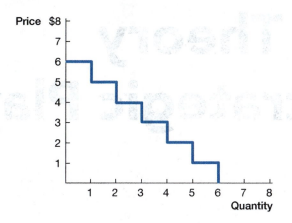

**a.** If you are told that you can produce as many units as you like at a cost of $2 per unit, what would your marginal cost curve look like? Add the marginal cost curve that you face as the monopolist to the graph.

**b.** Draw the marginal revenue curve that you face as the monopolist, based on the demand curve given above.

**c.** What price will you set and what quantity will you produce if you have to post one price at which everyone can purchase the good?

**d.** Based on the price and quantity you selected in part c, what will the consumer surplus be? What will the producer surplus be? Is there a deadweight loss?

**e.** Imagine that you are told that now you can have a discussion with each buyer privately to negotiate a price. Would you still charge everyone the same price? Explain your answer.

**f.** Calculate the surplus and the deadweight loss for the scenario with perfect price discrimination.

**12.** A monopolist with constant marginal cost of $4 faces demand $Q_D = 20 - 2P$. This implies that the inverse demand curve is $P = 10 - (1/2)Q$ and that the marginal revenue is $MR = 10 - Q$.

**a.** Sketch demand, marginal revenue, and marginal cost.

**b.** What quantity and price will the monopolist set?

**c.** What is the producer surplus (profit, ignoring fixed costs) for the firm?

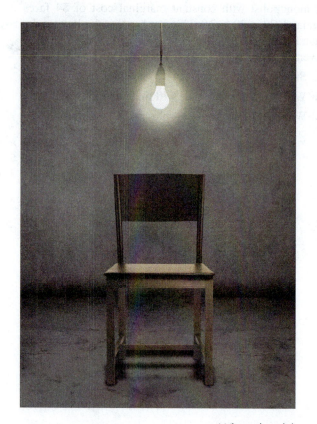

## Is there value in putting yourself in someone else's shoes?

Imagine yourself in the shoes of a person who has just committed armed robbery of a bank. You and your partner in crime, Josie, are caught in the get-away vehicle, but before apprehension you both toss your guns into a storm drain. The police take both of you in to the local precinct and place you in separate interrogation rooms. When the detectives enter your room, they outline a set of three options for you and tell you that they are giving Josie the same three options:

1. If neither of you confesses to having a gun during the crime, you are both looking at jail time of 2 years for the robbery.
2. If one confesses to having a gun, the confessor goes free and the other serves substantial jail time—10 years.
3. If both of you confess to having a gun, then jail terms will be negotiated down to 5 years.

What should you do?

The simple economic framework we have developed thus far is not equipped to handle situations like these where your "payoffs" (satisfaction, profits, etc.) depend on the behavior of others and your behavior affects their payoffs. These situations include, among others, how to allocate scarce resources in partnerships, firms, friendships, and families. You may wonder what economics has to do with friendships and families. Well, as it turns out, a lot.

## CHAPTER OUTLINE

**Game theory** is the study of strategic interactions.

**Game theory** is the study of situations in which the payoffs of one agent depend not only on his or her actions, but also on the actions of others. It emerged as a branch of mathematics that first focused on the analysis of parlor games. For example, when you're playing poker and trying to figure out your opponent's next move, you're using game theory concepts. In 2000, a UCLA grad student named Chris Ferguson applied game theory concepts at the World Series of Poker, helping him secure prize money of $1.5 million and the championship bracelet (his father taught game theory at UCLA!). But its use is considerably broader than in parlor games. Economists, political scientists, and sociologists use game theory to analyze a variety of problems, ranging from competition between firms (as we will see in Chapter 14), negotiations and bargaining (Chapter 17), social cooperation (as we discuss in this chapter and in Chapter 18), voting and other political decisions, and many others.

In this chapter, we present the basic tools of game theory and explain how they are useful for understanding and analyzing many different economic decisions. Such an understanding provides you with an invaluable resource for studying individual interactions that you face daily and for analyzing topics as varied as international trade negotiations, nuclear arms races, and labor arbitration. We will learn that many times it is, indeed, quite valuable to put yourself in another's shoes.

## 13.1 Simultaneous-Move Games

Let's return to the scene of the crime in the opening anecdote and explore how a game theorist would look at your problem. To begin, it is important to recognize the three key elements of any game:

**Strategies** comprise a complete plan describing how a player will act.

1. The players
2. The **strategies**
3. The payoffs

Let's first identify these three key elements in this particular game:

*Players:* You and Josie
*Strategies:* Confess or hold out
*Payoffs:* See Exhibit 13.1

A **payoff matrix** represents the payoffs for each action players can take.

A **payoff matrix** represents the payoffs for each action players can take in a game. In the payoff matrix shown in Exhibit 13.1, one player's actions are read across in rows; the other player's actions are read down in columns. The cells where the actions intersect give the payoffs, which for now are assumed to correspond only to the number of years in

## Exhibit 13.1 Payoffs in the Prisoners' Dilemma

The payoff matrix gives each player's payoff from every possible combination of strategies of all players in the game. For example, in the prisoners' dilemma, which has two players, the payoff matrix shows that if you confess and Josie also confesses, you will each serve 5 years in prison. In contrast, if you both hold out, you will each receive 2-year prison sentences.

|  | | Column Player: Josie | |
|---|---|---|---|
| | | Confess | Hold Out |
| Row Player: You | Confess | • You get 5 years<br>• Josie gets 5 years | • You are released<br>• Josie gets 10 years |
| | Hold Out | • You get 10 years<br>• Josie is released | • You get 2 years<br>• Josie gets 2 years |

prison each player receives. In particular, more years in jail represent lower payoffs. Game theory can easily include things like loyalty and kindness payoffs, but here we remove those considerations.

The convention in writing payoff matrices is that the first number listed is always the payoff to the Row Player, and to make it even clearer, we have also put this number in red. The second number listed, which is in blue, is always the payoff to the Column Player. So, in this game, if you—the first player—confess and Josie also confesses, you each get 5 years in prison.

The scenario depicted in Exhibit 13.1 is a classic one known as the "prisoners' dilemma." Despite its simplicity, the prisoners' dilemma illustrates several important features common to game theory. It involves interactions among a few players (in this case, two). This game is called a **simultaneous-move game**, because players select their actions at the same time. In the prisoners' dilemma, this implies that both you and Josie have to pick your action simultaneously without knowing the other person's choice. But it is assumed that you each do know the entire payoff matrix—that is, you each know the payoffs for both players.

When constructing a payoff matrix, it is important to understand that all relevant benefits and costs of each action are taken into account. In this example, we assume that the payoffs represent all relevant payoffs to this game. Thus, we are assuming that other potentially important features, such as retribution after jail time is served, do not influence the payoffs of this game.

We are now in a position to ask the question game theory equips us to answer: what should you do?

### Best Responses and the Prisoners' Dilemma

A first step in figuring out how to play any game is to put yourself in the shoes of the other player. That is, a good way to reason through which action you should choose—confess or hold out—is to think about what every possible action of the other player might be and then what *your* best choice will be for each of them. For example, suppose that Josie decides to confess. In that case, your payoffs when she chooses to hold out are no longer relevant—you should simply focus on the situation in which she confesses. So, we can strike the column for Hold Out in Exhibit 13.1. We then end up with the single column shown in Exhibit 13.2.

> A first step in figuring out how to play any game is to put yourself in the shoes of the other player.

Exhibit 13.2 makes it clear that in this instance, when you hold out and Josie confesses, you will receive 10 years in prison, whereas if you also confess, you will serve 5 years. Therefore, your *best response* when you expect Josie to confess is to confess yourself. A **best response** is simply one player's optimal strategy, taking the other player's strategy as given.

Suppose, instead, that you expect Josie to hold out. With the same best-response approach as used above, we now strike the column for Confess in Exhibit 13.1. After doing so, we obtain Exhibit 13.3.

Going through the same steps, you see that confessing allows you to walk away with no jail time, whereas holding out puts you in prison for 2 years. Your best response in this case

In **simultaneous-move games** players pick their actions at the same time.

A strategy of a player is a **best response** to the strategies of the others in the game if, taking the other players' strategy as given, it gives her greater payoffs than any other strategy she has available.

**Exhibit 13.2  Prisoners' Dilemma Game with Your Partner Confessing**

To determine your best response to a specific strategy by Josie, you first consider the column corresponding to that strategy. In this case, you take the column for Josie corresponding to Confess. You then compare your payoffs under your two strategies, Confess and Hold Out. You can see that when you confess in this case you will get 5 years, whereas if you hold out, you will get 10 years.

|  | Josie<br>Confess |
|---|---|
| **You** Confess | • You get 5 years<br>• Josie gets 5 years |
| Hold Out | • You get 10 years<br>• Josie is released |

**Exhibit 13.3  Prisoners' Dilemma Game with Your Partner Holding Out**

To determine your best response to Josie's holding out, you consider the column under Josie's strategy of Hold Out and again compare your payoffs under your two possible strategies. In this case, if you confess you will walk free, and if you hold out you will spend 2 years in prison.

|  | Josie<br>Hold Out |
|---|---|
| **You** Confess | • You are released<br>• Josie gets 10 years |
| Hold Out | • You get 2 years<br>• Josie gets 2 years |

is again to confess. You now understand that no matter what you think Josie will do, you should always confess. This means that when you are placed in such a game, you should always choose to confess, regardless of what you think your partner will do.

### Dominant Strategies and Dominant Strategy Equilibrium

A **dominant strategy** is a best response to every possible strategy of the other player(s).

When a player has the same best response to every possible strategy of the other player(s), then we say that the player has a **dominant strategy**. In the game of Exhibit 13.1, confessing is a dominant strategy, because it is your best response to any strategy choice of your partner.

In the prisoners' dilemma game, after doing the same exercise for Josie, you realize that Josie has a dominant strategy of confessing, too. When a dominant strategy exists for both players, the notion of equilibrium for the game is straightforward. A strategy combination for the players is a **dominant strategy equilibrium** if the relevant strategy for each player is a dominant strategy. In the game above, there is a dominant strategy equilibrium: both players should confess because confessing is a dominant strategy for each player—that is, by confessing, they receive a higher payoff than they would buy holding out regardless of what the other player does.

A combination of strategies is a **dominant strategy equilibrium** if the relevant strategy for each player is a dominant strategy.

Interestingly, this equilibrium leads to an outcome that is *not* best for both players. Even though both you and Josie would be better off if you both held out, the dominant strategy equilibrium is for both of you to confess! This situation is the heart of the paradox that we have been studying so far—the prisoners' dilemma. The "dilemma" part arises because by confessing, you and Josie will each spend 5 years in prison. However, if you were both to hold out, you would each spend 2 years in prison. Because less prison time is preferred to more, the (Confess, Confess) strategy combination gives strictly lower payoffs to both players than (Hold Out, Hold Out). Nevertheless, it is not in your (or in Josie's) best interest to hold out, and this leads to the unique dominant strategy equilibrium in which you both confess. Thus the dilemma arises.

### Games without Dominant Strategies

The prisoners' dilemma game has a dominant strategy for each player. Yet, there are many games without a dominant strategy. Consider the case wherein you and your friend Gina, both avid surfers, open up a surf shop—Hang Ten in Da Den. Your main competition is

**Exhibit 13.4** The Advertising Game

In this payoff matrix, the payoffs of the two surf shops depend on whether each decides to advertise or not to advertise. For example, the cell at the top left corner shows that if you both advertise, you will each receive a payoff of $400, while the cell at the bottom right shows that if you both choose not to advertise, you will each receive a payoff of $800.

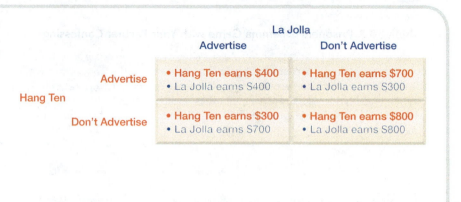

|  |  | La Jolla | |
|  |  | **Advertise** | **Don't Advertise** |
|  | **Advertise** | • Hang Ten earns $400<br>• La Jolla earns $400 | • Hang Ten earns $700<br>• La Jolla earns $300 |
| **Hang Ten** | **Don't Advertise** | • Hang Ten earns $300<br>• La Jolla earns $700 | • Hang Ten earns $800<br>• La Jolla earns $800 |

a surf shop down the street, La Jolla Surf Shop. One key decision that you must make is whether to advertise. In fact, both your shop and La Jolla Surf Shop have similar decisions to make, which we assume are made simultaneously. After doing the necessary market research, you construct Exhibit 13.4, which provides the payoffs for this simple game.

A summary of the three key elements in this game are as follows:

*Players:* Hang Ten in Da Den and the La Jolla Surf Shop
*Strategies:* To advertise or not to advertise
*Payoffs:* See Exhibit 13.4

In the exhibit, the two rows correspond to your strategies, and the two columns correspond to La Jolla Surf Shop's strategies. The top left cell gives both surf shops' daily profits of $400 if both opt to advertise. In contrast, the lower right cell indicates that if both do not advertise, each shop earns a daily profit of $800. The higher profits from each of you not advertising are explained by the high cost of advertising and its lack of effectiveness: in this market, the main effect of advertising is to steal business from the other shop, not to persuade new customers to enter the market.

The other two cells (lower left and upper right) show the scenarios in which one of the shops advertises and the other does not. In these cases, whoever is advertising does considerably better than the other shop, because the surf shop that advertises attracts some consumers from the other shop. For example, if you place ads and La Jolla Surf Shop does not, you earn $700 per day while La Jolla Surf Shop earns only $300 per day.

What should you do? Let's start by considering your best response. Suppose that you expect La Jolla Surf Shop to advertise. How should you best respond? Consider Exhibit 13.5, which excludes the column for Don't Advertise from Exhibit 13.4.

Exhibit 13.5 makes it clear that when La Jolla Surf Shop chooses to advertise, your surf shop will earn $400 if you choose to advertise and will earn $300 if you do not. Therefore, your *best response* is to advertise when you expect that La Jolla Surf Shop will advertise, because $400 > $300.

Suppose, instead, that you expect La Jolla Surf Shop to not place advertisements. We now strike the column for Advertise from Exhibit 13.4, and we are left with Exhibit 13.6. Your best response when La Jolla Surf Shop chooses not to advertise is to not advertise yourself. This is because when advertising your shop earns $700, and when not advertising your shop earns $800, making you prefer not to advertise.

**Exhibit 13.5** When La Jolla Surf Shop Advertises

To determine your best response to La Jolla choosing to advertise, you take the column under Advertise (corresponding to La Jolla's choice of advertising) and compare your payoffs from advertising to not advertising. In this case, advertising gives you $400, whereas not advertising gives you $300. You should advertise.

|  |  | La Jolla |
|  |  | **Advertise** |
|  | **Advertise** | • Hang Ten earns $400<br>• La Jolla earns $400 |
| **Hang Ten** | **Don't Advertise** | • Hang Ten earns $300<br>• La Jolla earns $700 |

**Exhibit 13.6** **When La Jolla Surf Shop Does Not Advertise**

To determine your best response to La Jolla choosing not to advertise, you take the column under Don't Advertise, and compare your payoffs from advertising and not advertising. In this case, advertising gives you $700, whereas not advertising gives you $800. You should not advertise.

|  | La Jolla<br>Don't Advertise |
|---|---|
| **Hang Ten**<br>Advertise | • Hang Ten earns $700<br>• La Jolla earns S300 |
| Don't Advertise | • Hang Ten earns $800<br>• La Jolla earns S800 |

Do you have a dominant strategy in this game? No; this is because your optimal strategy depends on what La Jolla Surf Shop chooses. Does La Jolla Surf Shop have a dominant strategy? By similar reasoning, it also does not have a dominant strategy. Thus there is no dominant strategy for your surf shop or for La Jolla Surf Shop. In this case, you remain unsure as to what to do, because your optimal choice depends on the choice of La Jolla Surf Shop. This particular game illustrates a key concept in game theory: you don't always have a simple best response (a dominant strategy) that works against all strategies of others, as you do in games with a dominant strategy, such as the prisoners' dilemma game.

Life doesn't always present a game that has a dominant strategy. In the advertising example, what is best for your shop depends on what you expect the La Jolla Surf Shop to do. In such cases, where should we expect to end up in the payoff matrix—does your shop advertise? Does La Jolla Surf Shop advertise? Do both of you advertise? What is the equilibrium of this game?

## 13.2 Nash Equilibrium

Recall that the notion of equilibrium we used in markets requires that all individuals are simultaneously optimizing given the prices that they face in the market and their income levels. To put this differently, no individual can (unilaterally) change his strategy and be better off (or improve his payoff). This is intuitive: if a player did have a strategy that made him better off, then he would choose that strategy instead of the one he chose.

### A Beautiful Mind

If you are a movie buff, you have surely seen the film based on the life of John Nash—a Hollywood blockbuster called *A Beautiful Mind*. The film was nominated for eight Academy Awards, winning best picture in 2001. The film focuses on Nash's mathematical genius and his struggle with paranoid schizophrenia.

Nash earned a doctorate in mathematics from Princeton University in 1950 with a twenty-eight-page dissertation on game theory.[1]

Those twenty-eight pages played a central role in developing the foundation of game theory as we know it today. For this reason, the relevant notion of equilibrium in games is referred to as a "Nash equilibrium." Nash was awarded the 1994 Nobel Prize in Economics for this contribution.

A strategy combination is a **Nash equilibrium** if each strategy is a best response to the strategies of others.

This is the essence of the equilibrium concept proposed by John Nash: in equilibrium, no player in a game can change strategy and improve his or her payoff. Therefore, a combination of strategies is a **Nash equilibrium** if each player chooses a strategy that is a best response to the strategies of others—that is, players are choosing strategies that are mutual best responses. What this means is that no one can change her choice and be better off. Accordingly, the dominant strategy equilibrium that we found in the prisoner's dilemma game is a Nash equilibrium.

This notion of equilibrium depends on two critical factors: (1) that all players understand the game and the payoffs associated with each strategy (so that they will choose what is best for themselves) and (2) that all players understand that *other* players understand the game.

In the context of a Nash equilibrium, we expect that an individual forms correct expectations about the intentions of other players in the game. As we will see when we consider experimental evidence on game theory later in this chapter, experience with a game may be necessary before we can safely assume that people act in the way that we think they are going to act.

## Finding a Nash Equilibrium

The key to finding Nash equilibria in simultaneous-move games is to follow the logic of finding best responses. Let's return to the advertising decision. Begin by asking yourself: if La Jolla Surf Shop advertises, what should your shop do? As reasoned through above, your best response is to advertise. You then need to ask: once in this cell of the payoff matrix, does either surf shop have a reason to change its strategy?

The answer is no. La Jolla will not change its strategy because if it did, it would earn $300 rather than $400. Likewise, you will not change your strategy because if you did, you also would earn $300 rather than $400. Therefore, both shops choosing to advertise is a Nash equilibrium. That is, once both of you have opted to advertise, neither of you has an incentive to change your behavior.

Suppose instead that La Jolla Surf Shop chooses not to advertise. In this case, what should your shop do? As reasoned through above, your best response is not to advertise. Once in this cell, does either surf shop have a reason to change its strategy?

The answer is again no. La Jolla Surf Shop will not change its strategy because if it did, it would earn $700 rather than $800. Likewise, you will not want to change your strategy because if you did, you would earn $700 rather than $800. Therefore, not advertising is a Nash equilibrium for both surf shops. Once in that cell, neither of you has an incentive to change your strategy. Accordingly, in this particular game we have *two* Nash equilibria:

1. Your shop: advertise; La Jolla Surf Shop: advertise
2. Your shop: don't advertise; La Jolla Surf Shop: don't advertise

To illustrate how to find these two Nash equilibria in a payoff matrix, Exhibit 13.7 revisits the advertising game.

Let's begin by thinking about what would happen if you choose to advertise and La Jolla does not. You will find yourself in the top right cell. Can you do better? Yes. In this case, you would like to change your choice because $800 > $700—thus the red arrow pointing downward from this box (it is red because it refers to you, the Row Player). Likewise, La Jolla would like to change its choice—thus the blue arrow pointing leftward from this box.

You can then use the same reasoning from the bottom left cell. If you are in this cell, both you and La Jolla will again change your behavior: you will opt to advertise because $400 > $300, and La Jolla will not advertise because $800 > $700. This shows that the Nash equilibria are best-response strategies with two arrows pointing in: (Advertise, Advertise) and (Don't Advertise, Don't Advertise). Once two arrows point inward, you can be certain that you have found a Nash equilibrium.

It might at first seem odd that there are two Nash equilibria in the advertising game. But a moment's reflection reveals that this is quite natural. It's only worthwhile for you to advertise when La Jolla advertises, and vice versa. It is, in fact, a common occurrence in game theory to have more than one Nash equilibrium, and in these cases, other factors, such as those we discuss in the box that follows, may determine which of the two equilibria are played.

**La Jolla**

|  | Advertise | Don't Advertise |
|---|---|---|
| **Advertise** | • Hang Ten earns $400<br>• La Jolla earns S400 | • Hang Ten earns $700<br>• La Jolla earns S300 |
| **Don't Advertise** | • Hang Ten earns $300<br>• La Jolla earns S700 | • Hang Ten earns $800<br>• La Jolla earns S800 |

**Hang Ten**

**Exhibit 13.7 Two Nash Equilibria in the Advertising Game**

The key to finding Nash equilibria is to determine whether either player has an incentive to change his strategy once in a cell. Let's begin in the bottom left cell, where you do not advertise and La Jolla advertises. In this case, you would like to change your strategy (that is, the red arrow points upward denoting that if you are in this cell, you would like to change your strategy). La Jolla would also like to move away from this cell (its blue arrow points rightward from this cell). Once you consider every cell using this approach, the arrows are completed, and Nash equilibria occur when both arrows point to a cell. In this example, both strategy combinations (Advertise, Advertise) and (Don't Advertise, Don't Advertise) have the two arrows pointing to them, and both are thus Nash equilibria.

# CHOICE
## &CONSEQUENCE

### Work or Surf?

Game theory doesn't just apply to your surf shop's competition with La Jolla Surf Shop. You and your partner, Gina, are individually just as affected by each other in the shop.

Consider a simple example of working versus surfing. Suppose that your daily payoffs—with no advertising—are described in the payoff matrix to the right. You and Gina both receive $400 per day in net benefits if you each work at the surf shop. However, if you shirk your responsibilities and go surfing while Gina works, your shop does not sell as much, but you receive both the benefits from the shop staying open and the benefits from surfing, which sum to $500. If you both go surfing, however, the shop is closed and you both earn only surfing benefits of $200. What should you do?

In this situation, there are two Nash equilibria, as the best-response arrows demonstrate. One is for you to go surfing while Gina tends to the shop. The other is for you to tend to the shop while Gina surfs. When there are multiple Nash equilibria (as in this case), which equilibrium will actually be played depends on many factors. For example, if Gina is an assertive character and has

always managed to get what she wants in her prior relations with you, we may expect that your working hard and her surfing might be a natural "focal point" and have a greater likelihood of emerging than the other Nash equilibrium.

**Gina**

|  | Work | Surf |
|---|---|---|
| **Work** | • You earn $400<br>• Gina earns S400 | • You earn $300<br>• Gina earns S500 |
| **Surf** | • You earn $500<br>• Gina earns S300 | • You earn $200<br>• Gina earns S200 |

**You**

The payoff matrix of the work-or-surf game shows your payoffs and Gina's payoffs depending on whether each of you chooses to work or surf. In this game, there are two Nash equilibria: (Surf, Work), indicating that you surf and Gina works, and (Work, Surf), corresponding to your working and Gina surfing.

# 13.3 Applications of Nash Equilibria

With the necessary tools in place, we can now begin to study some of the ways in which we apply game theory to understand real-world problems. We'll consider two quite different scenarios: pollution and soccer.

## Tragedy of the Commons Revisited

Game theory is most often used when a few players make choices that affect each other's payoffs. The same type of reasoning applies even when the number of players is large. The tragedy of the commons—the overuse of common resources resulting in a negative externality—which we studied in Chapter 9, can also be viewed as an application of game theory. In particular, the same reasoning as that in the prisoners' dilemma applies to the tragedy of the commons. When all others pollute the environment, it is a best response for you to do so as well. Unfortunately, it is also the best response to pollute when all others actually go to the trouble of "being green." Therefore, in the tragedy of the commons, just as in the prisoners' dilemma, mutually beneficial behavior may not emerge.

Consider the example of the Gowanus Canal, a canal in the New York City borough of Brooklyn. Pollution has become so bad in the canal that the Environmental Protection Agency placed it on its National Priority List. How could things get this bad in a major city?

Game theory can shed insights into the question. Exhibit 13.8 depicts the weekly profits for two firms on the canal: let's call them Firm 1 and Firm 2. It shows that these profits depend on the firms' pollution choices. Each firm's choices affect each other's profit because if one plant pollutes, it affects the productivity of the other (through both worker productivity as well as processing costs—each firm uses water from the canal for production, and dirty water is costly to clean). Unfortunately for the canal, the payoffs also show that, because it is costly to abate pollution, a firm is better off if it pollutes regardless of the other firm's choice.

A summary of the three key elements in this game are as follows:

*Players:* Firm 1 and Firm 2
*Strategies:* To pollute or not to pollute
*Payoffs:* See Exhibit 13.8

As in the prisoners' dilemma game, the dominant strategy equilibrium in Exhibit 13.8 leads to an outcome that is quite bad for both players together: to pollute—even though each player is choosing what is unilaterally best for himself or herself. Both could have earned $70,000 in weekly profits and been better off if they had both chosen not to pollute. Nevertheless, in the dominant strategy equilibrium, both firms choose to pollute, and both they and society (which suffers from greater pollution) are worse off, creating a tragedy of the commons result.

This simple game structure contains some of the important elements of a crucial situation facing many corporations and individuals today: the pressing issue of not dirtying our planet. And the Nash equilibrium of this game highlights exactly why we end up with dirty water and air, and why government intervention might be necessary.

The Gowanus Canal in Brooklyn, one of the most polluted bodies of water in the United States, shows the tragedy of the commons at work. As game theory would predict, when other firms choose to pollute, it's a best response for your firm to do the same. But everyone is worse off as a result.

**Exhibit 13.8 The Tragedy of the Commons Game for Two Firms**

The payoff matrix of the tragedy of the commons game gives Firm 1's and Firm 2's payoffs, depending on whether each decides to pollute or not to pollute.

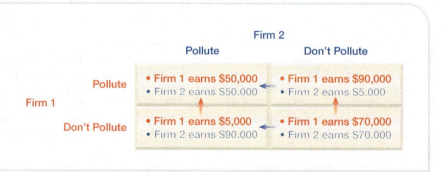

## Zero-Sum Games

Let's move on to something more pleasant—soccer! Suppose that you are the designated penalty kicker for your intramural soccer team. Every time you walk up to the ball, you have an important decision to make: aim for the left of the net or for the right of the net (for simplicity, let's ignore the options of aiming for the middle or shooting high or low). What should you do in such situations?

## Exhibit 13.9 A Zero-Sum Game: Penalty Kicks

The payoff matrix of the penalty kick game gives the payoff of the kicker and the goalie, depending on whether the kicker kicks to the left or right and whether the goalie dives to the left or right (that is, dives to the kicker's left or right). This game is an example of a zero-sum game, because the payoffs of the two players sum to zero, indicating that whatever one wins, the other loses.

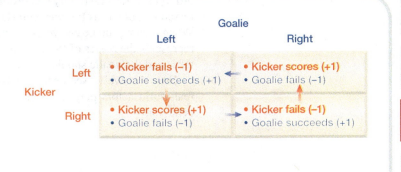

|  | | Goalie | |
|---|---|---|---|
|  | | Left | Right |
| **Kicker** | **Left** | • Kicker fails (–1) <br> • Goalie succeeds (+1) | • Kicker scores (+1) <br> • Goalie fails (–1) |
|  | **Right** | • Kicker scores (+1) <br> • Goalie fails (–1) | • Kicker fails (–1) <br> • Goalie succeeds (+1) |

As in many game-theoretic situations, we can master this question by thinking generally about the incentives of your opponent—the goalie. The goalie will try to anticipate your behavior and will dive to the left or to the right. If he dives to the side where you kick the ball, then he has a pretty good chance of stopping it from going into the net, and if he dives to the opposite side, you are very likely to score.

In this example, the payoff matrix represents a **zero-sum game**, meaning that because one player's loss is another's gain, the sum of the payoffs is zero. Exhibit 13.9 shows that the outcomes for each strategy in the soccer game in fact constitute a zero-sum game. Let's look at this situation in more detail.

In a **zero-sum game** one player's loss is another's gain, so the sum of the payoffs is zero.

A summary of the three key elements in this game are as follows:

*Players:* You and the goalie
*Strategies:* Right or left
*Payoffs:* See Exhibit 13.9

If you both go left, then the goalie is happy and you are not. Thus, the goalie receives 1 unit of net benefits and you receive −1 unit of net benefits. If you kick right and he dives right, then the same payoff results because he saves the shot: +1 for him and −1 for you. However, if the goalie dives to the opposite side of where you kick the ball, then you score, resulting in a payoff of +1 to you and −1 to the goalie. These cells are in the bottom left and top right of the payoff matrix.

Zero-sum games are quite common in the real world. Whenever we sit down to play poker, our gains are another player's losses. Whenever two companies compete to sell to the same consumers, one company's gain is the other one's loss. Redistribution is also often zero-sum: one person's gain is often another's loss.

A **pure strategy** involves always choosing one particular action for a situation.

A **mixed strategy** involves choosing different actions randomly.

Applying our method of finding Nash equilibria, we draw the arrows, as shown in Exhibit 13.9. They show that no Nash equilibrium exists, because no cell in the matrix has two arrows pointing in. Therefore, the notion of Nash equilibrium that we have developed so far doesn't make any predictions about the behavior in the penalty kick game.

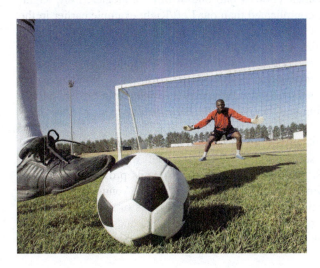

We're not finished yet, however. In games like this, maybe the best strategy is not to choose any one particular action. For example, what happens if you randomly choose between kicking left and kicking right and the goalie chooses randomly too? In that case, you would expect, on average, to be neither the loser with a payoff of −1 nor the winner with a payoff of 1, and thus, on average, you would end up with a payoff of zero.

In fact, choosing randomly has a clear advantage in this game relative to a **pure strategy**, which involves always choosing a single action for a situation. Consider one scenario of a pure strategy for yourself: always kick right. If you always kick right, in time goalies will notice and best respond by always diving right. This will result in a certain negative payoff to you of −1. In fact, reasoning this way, we can see that any kind of predictable behavior by the kicker can be taken advantage of by the goalie, and vice versa. If you are the kicker, you should therefore be as unpredictable as possible. Put differently, you should randomize by playing a **mixed strategy**, which involves choosing between different actions randomly (according to some preassigned probabilities). The essence of a mixed strategy is as follows: you should privately flip a fair coin before each penalty kick. When it comes up heads, you kick right; when it comes up tails, you kick left. This strategy represents the basics of the equilibrium in mixed strategies for this game: both the penalty taker and the goalie should randomize with a probability of 50–50 between left and right.

Now that we've seen some real-world applications of game theory, let's analyze how real-world actors play in similar situations and how well game theory predicts real-life behavior.

# 13.4 How Do People Actually Play Such Games?

Do people really play Nash equilibria in practice? What about dominant strategies—are those frequently played? One might think that the answer to these questions should be a simple yes or no. But these questions are difficult to answer—in both the lab and in the real world—for two main reasons.

The first reason is that we often do not know the exact payoffs of individuals playing the game. In constructing the matrix games in the previous sections, we chose the payoffs and assumed that they were correct. In real-world situations, the payoffs are determined by the attitudes and feelings of individuals as well as by their monetary returns.

A second reason we might not observe what game theory predicts is that it is, in essence, a theory, and models are not literal descriptions of how the world works—they are merely useful abstractions. As such, game theory abstracts from several details. In many situations, one player may be more cunning, wiser, or more experienced than another. For example, of two chess players, the more experienced, more clever player is likely to win. In many matrix games (with two or several players), repetition of the game usually ensures that results come closer to the Nash equilibrium. With these caveats in mind, we turn to an example to illustrate how game theory's predictions fare in real-world situations.

## Game Theory in Penalty Kicks

Consider again the situation faced by penalty kickers and goalies. As you have already learned, the best move for both sides is to employ a mixed strategy—randomly choose left or right for each kick. But is that what actually happens in soccer games?

Three economists decided to analyze all the penalty kicks taken during a 3-year period in the French and Italian elite soccer leagues in order to test game theory.[2] By examining 459 penalty kicks, they were able to test whether the players actually did play mixed-strategy Nash equilibria.

They classified kickers' and goalies' choices into one of three strategies: Left, Right, and Center. This is just a bit more complicated than our Left/Right example earlier in the chapter, but the logic of the game's mixed-strategy Nash equilibrium is the same: penalty kickers and goalies should randomize across the choices.

Amazingly, this is just what the economists found in the data. The kickers and goalies both seemed to be randomizing their direction choices almost perfectly. So chalk up a victory for game theory. It predicted the behavior of these players—who certainly had a lot at stake in the games they were playing and therefore had a lot of incentive to optimize their behavior—very well.

A related study found a similar pattern of randomization in serve choices in professional tennis matches (where predictably serving to the right or to the left would enable the other player to return more effectively).[3] Indeed, this research on tennis provides interesting quotes from two tennis greats when it notes: "After a recent match, Venus Williams said she had shown her opponent, Monica Seles, several different types of serves. 'You have to work on that, because it's very easy to become one-dimensional and just serve to your favorite space and the person is just waiting there.' Seles responded, 'She mixed it up very well.'" Game theory at work!

# EVIDENCE-BASED ECONOMICS

13.1

13.2

13.3

13.4

13.5

## Q: Is there value in putting yourself in someone else's shoes?

The "Beauty Contest" game, introduced by the famous economist John Maynard Keynes, is ideal for illustrating the value of putting yourself in other peoples' shoes. The idea of the game is based on a newspaper contest in which each participant picks the six most attractive people out of one hundred photos. After all selections are tallied, the winner is the contestant who has picked the photos that are most popular across all contestants. Contestants are successful in this game if they select not the person *they* consider most beautiful, but the person they think *others* will find most beautiful. Keynes argued that this is exactly how professional investors in the stock market behave when noting:

> *Professional investments may be likened to those newspaper competitions in which competitors have to pick out the six prettiest faces from one hundred photographs, the prize being awarded to the competitor whose choice most nearly corresponds to the average preference of the competitors as a whole. So each competitor will strive to pick, not those faces which he himself finds prettiest, but those which he thinks likeliest to catch the fancy of the other competitors, all of whom are looking at the problem from the same point of view. It is not a case of choosing those which, to the best of one's judgment, are really the prettiest, nor even those which average opinion genuinely thinks the prettiest. We have reached the third degree where we devote our intelligence to anticipating what average opinion expects the average opinion to be.*[4]

Though this game clearly illustrates the value of putting oneself in other peoples' shoes, it immediately leads to more vexing questions: can people really do this? Can they guess the "average opinion of the average opinion?" How do they actually act in such strategic environments in which forecasting others' actions is key? To answer these questions, let us consider a variant of the game often played in lab experiments. Each contestant submits a number between 0 and 100. The person with the submission closest to $p$ times the *average* guess is the winner. Let us focus on the case where $p = 2/3$, so the winner is the contestant who guesses two-thirds of the average guess. In cases where $p$ times the average guess is between two integers, say 14.2 or 14.7, we always round down to the lower integer—for these two examples that would be 14.

How should you play this game? To answer this question, similar to the notion of a dominant strategy introduced above, we say that a strategy is *dominated* if it yields lower payoffs than some other available strategy. It is a basic tenet of game theory that no player should pick a dominated strategy.

In this game, there are several dominated strategies. The highest average guess possible is clearly 100. This implies that the highest possible winning guess is $(2/3) \times 100$, approximately 67. So picking a number above 67 (between 68 and 100) is a dominated strategy, and you should eliminate all such numbers from consideration. This reasoning doesn't look too difficult. If you can reason like this, surely your intelligent fellow contestants can also do it, and won't pick anything above 67. But if so, they will not submit any number above 67, and the highest average guess possible is 67. If you really believe that your fellow contestants are intelligent enough to avoid dominated strategies, you can be fairly sure that the average guess cannot be above $(2/3) \times 67$, which is approximately 45. So you can apply two rounds of elimination of dominated strategies and conclude that you should not submit anything above 45.

Now you see where we are going. Why stop here? You can repeat the same reasoning again and this time eliminate everything above $(2/3) \times 45$, and so on and so on. Where does this stop? The answer is at 0: if everybody submits 0, then $(2/3) \times 0 = 0$,

*(continued)*

and the winning guess is 0; by submitting a higher bid, you will be sure to lose (rather than being a joint winner with everybody else). This implies that when everybody else is guessing 0, it is a best response to submit 0. Hence, all contestants submitting 0 is a Nash equilibrium. In fact, it is the unique Nash equilibrium, since with the process of elimination we have just seen, all other combinations are ruled out as possible Nash equilibria.

So should you guess 0 when you are playing this game? Is this what game theory is prescribing? Not necessarily. Perhaps your fellow contestants are not so sophisticated as to engage in several rounds of elimination of dominated strategies. Perhaps you are skeptical about their understanding of strategic play. If you do not trust that they will bid 0, you shouldn't either.

This is what Exhibit 13.10, which summarizes the average result from several related experiments, confirms.[5] As you can see, the average guess was 23. If you guessed 0, you would have been very far from the winning submission.

Does this result imply that the unique Nash equilibrium is not relevant in this game? Not really. If the contestants become more familiar with the strategic environment in this game by playing it several times, their guesses start declining toward 0, as Exhibit 13.11 shows.[6] It seems that several contestants submit guesses much higher than 0 at first, because they think that's what other contestants will do. In the next round, they then attempt to more successfully put themselves in the other contestants' shoes and reduce their guesses. This process takes us to an average guess fairly close to 0 in about nine rounds.

Thus not only does success in this game depend on contestants' ability to put themselves in others' shoes, but we also see that people do get better at doing so as they become more familiar with the game.

In the next section, we'll delve into extensive-form games in which players act sequentially, and at the end of the chapter, we'll return to this same question in the context of sequential actions—to understand the value of putting yourself in the shoes of those who will take actions before or after yours.

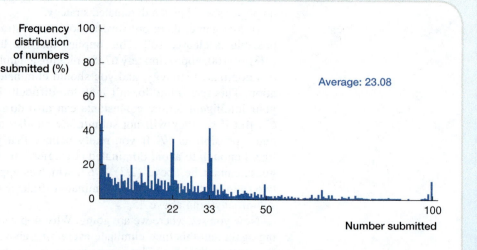

**Exhibit 13.10 Lab Beauty Contests: Distribution of Numbers Submitted**

This exhibit shows the proportion of subjects guessing the numbers between 0 and 100 in lab experiments on the beauty contest with $p = 2/3$.

*Source:* Antoni Bosch-Domènech, Rosemarie Nagel, Albert Satorra, and Jose García-Montalvo, "One, Two, (Three), Infinity: Newspaper and Lab Beauty-Contest Experiments," *American Economic Review* 92(5): 2002, 1687–1701.

Frequency distribution of numbers submitted (%)

Average: 23.08

Number submitted

**Exhibit 13.11** Lab Beauty Contests: Guess Evolution for Multiple Rounds

This exhibit shows how the average guess evolves as contestants play several rounds of the beauty contest in the lab.

*Source:* Werner Guth, Martin Kocher, and Matthias Sutter, "Experimental 'Beauty Contests' with Homogeneous and Heterogeneous Players and with Interior and Boundary Equilibria," *Economic Letters* 74(2): 2002, 219–228.

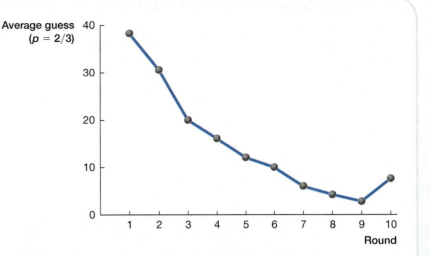

Average guess ($p = 2/3$)

**Question**

Is there value in putting yourself in someone else's shoes?

**Answer**

Yes. But typically, people are able to do so only after they become familiar with the strategic environment.

**Data**

Lab experiments on beauty contest games.

**Caveat**

The extent to which these results generalize is an open question.

## 13.5 Extensive-Form Games

The games that we have discussed so far all revolve around two players choosing an action simultaneously. Suppose that, instead, one player goes first and the other chooses an action only after seeing how the first player chose. This type of situation, which specifies the order of play, is represented by an **extensive-form game**.

An **extensive-form game** is a representation that specifies the order of play in a game.

In extensive-form games, the strategies are a little bit richer than in simultaneous games. For instance, in our work-or-surf game, it might be the case that you can decide to go surfing before Gina has a chance to decide. Accordingly, you decide on whether you are going to work or surf and then Gina, after viewing your choice, decides whether she will work or surf. Or Gina might let you know her strategy before you decide on whether to go surfing: "If you go surfing, I will, too."

Recall that strategies are not only possible actions but are also a description of how a player will act given every possible action of the other player. How do we model games with sequential decisions? As a first step, let's contrast extensive-form and simultaneous-move games. Extensive-form games introduce the sense of timing that is missing in simultaneous-move games. This sense of timing is relevant for negotiations in which different players make offers to one another over time (sequentially). It is also relevant for many more traditional games—in chess, for example, players do not make simultaneous choices. Rather, they "take turns."

A **game tree** is an extensive-form representation of a game.

So we can say that an extensive-form game specifies the order of play and payoffs that will result from different strategies and uses a **game tree** to represent them. To better

**Exhibit 13.12  A Game Tree for the Work-or-Surf Game**

In the extensive form of the work-or-surf game, you first decide whether to work or surf. Then Gina, after observing your choice, decides whether to work or surf. The extensive form is useful in showing the play sequencing. The numbers given at the ends of the branches are the payoffs to you and Gina. For example, if both you and Gina work, you each earn $400.

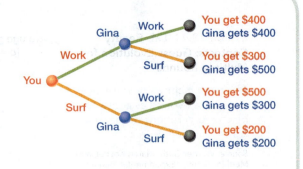

> **Backward induction is the procedure of solving an extensive-form game by first considering the last mover's decision.**

understand the difference between extensive-form and simultaneous-move games, let's discuss more carefully the work-or-surf decision that you and Gina face. Exhibit 13.12 shows the work-or-surf game tree when you are the first mover.

This game tree has three sets of nodes. The first, the red node at the far left, represents the first decision maker, in this case, you. This is the spot where you decide whether you will work or go surfing. In essence, your choice is to travel either the green branch—work—or the orange branch—surf.

Gina's decision comes only after she views your decision, represented by one of the two blue nodes labeled "Gina." Whether you place her at the top node (you decided to work) or at the bottom node (you decided to surf), she has the same decision: work or surf. The payoffs for each of those decisions are at the ends of the branches of the game tree. These payoffs follow our earlier coloring convention. Given this game form, what should you now do?

## Backward Induction

The easiest way of approaching any extensive-form game is to use *backward induction.* **Backward induction** is the procedure of solving an extensive-form game by first considering the last mover's decision. Given the last mover's decision, we then consider the second-to-last mover, and so on. The name derives from the fact that this procedure starts from the end of the game and solves backward.

To use backward induction, you first consider each decision node at the end of the game. If you work (green branch), then Gina finds herself in the top decision node. Now, Gina has the choices depicted in panel (a) of Exhibit 13.13.

Accordingly, Gina chooses between working, which yields payoffs of (you: $400, Gina: $400), and surfing, which yields payoffs of (you: $300, Gina: $500). In this case, Gina should choose to surf, because the net benefits to her are $500, which is $100 higher than

**Backward induction** is the procedure of solving an extensive-form game by first considering the last mover's decision in order to deduce the decisions of all previous movers.

**Exhibit 13.13  Gina's Game Trees If You Decide to Work and If You Decide to Surf**

Backward induction involves starting at the end of the game and solving it backward. In this case, you look at Gina's decision of whether to work or surf after she has observed whether you have chosen to work or to surf. Panel (a) looks at the case following your choice to work; panel (b) looks at the case following your choice to surf.

(a) Gina's Game Tree If You Decide to Work

(b) Gina's Game Tree If You Decide to Surf

the net benefits under the alternative of working ($400). Given that she will choose to surf, your payoff will be $300 if you initially chose to work.

In contrast, if you choose to surf (orange branch), then Gina finds herself at the bottom decision node, as shown in panel (b) of Exhibit 13.13. Here, she again has the choice between working and surfing. If she works, the payoffs are (you: $500, Gina: $300) and if she surfs, the payoffs are (you: $200, Gina: $200). Thus, if you decide to surf, Gina will choose to go to work, because she will earn $100 more in net benefits by working. Given that she will choose to work, your payoff will be $500.

We have now completely described Gina's optimal strategies, which are:

"Choose to work if you surf" and
"Choose to surf if you work."

Why is it important to know Gina's strategies? Because you can now make a decision knowing how Gina will respond to every one of your actions. With this information in hand, you have successfully used backward induction. Such backward induction allows you to make an informed decision as to whether you should work or surf. So, what should you do?

You know that if you choose to go to work, Gina will surf, netting you a payoff of $300. Alternatively, if you choose to surf, she will work, leaving you with a payoff of $500. The decision now seems straightforward: you should go surfing, because you will receive a payoff that is $200 higher than if you go to work.

Recall that when the decisions were made simultaneously, there were two Nash equilibria. Now, with sequential decision making, the backward-induction procedure has delivered a unique equilibrium: you surf and Gina works.

## First-Mover Advantage, Commitment, and Vengeance

The equilibrium described above is much more favorable to you than to Gina: you receive $500, whereas she receives $300. This outcome occurs even though the payoffs to the different actions are the same for you and Gina. We say that the sequential game features a **first-mover advantage** if the first mover earns more benefits than the second mover earns.

A game has a **first-mover advantage** when the first player to act in a sequential game gets a benefit from doing so.

One particularly relevant form of first-mover advantage is the value of *commitment*. To illustrate the main idea, let's consider an extension of the work-or-surf game.

Using backward induction, we obtained a unique equilibrium in this game: you surf and Gina works, even though she would have been better off if you had chosen to work. If only she could threaten you with punishment, using the following strategy: "If you surf, I will go surfing, too!" But such an action is not credible in the sense that when push comes to shove, Gina will choose not to surf when you go surfing, because if she chose not to work, she would forgo $100 in net benefits. So you know that she will choose to work.

Is there any way that Gina can turn the tables on you by taking away the first-mover advantage? In fact, there is. The trick is for her to make a credible commitment. A **commitment** is an action that one cannot turn back on later, even if it is costly. One commitment device would be for her to throw her shop keys into the Pacific Ocean. With no keys, the only way that she can get into the shop is for you to go to work. She has changed the game, making the choice very simple for you. Exhibit 13.14 shows the simple decision tree. Gina has effectively eliminated the possibility that you surf and she works.

**Commitment** refers to the ability to choose and stick with an action that might later be costly.

Now what should you do? It is clear that both outcomes when you work ($400 and $300) are better than when you surf ($200). So, given that Gina has credibly committed to not working without you, the way that you maximize your payoff is to go to work. Gina will then choose to surf, securing a payoff for herself of $500, effectively taking advantage of her credible commitment of tossing her shop keys in the ocean. As demonstrated in Exhibit 13.14, such a credible threat leads to a unique equilibrium that is much more advantageous to Gina.

Several modes of behavior may be understood in light of this example. Suppose, for example, that you can consciously or subconsciously (truthfully, or perhaps just for show) establish a reputation as somebody who bears a grudge and who would seek revenge against misdeeds, even though this behavior is potentially costly for you (because of the conflicts

**Exhibit 13.14** An Extensive-Form Game with a Credible Commitment

A commitment is an action that one cannot take back. Commitments, which come before other actions, can change who has the advantage. If Gina throws her keys into the ocean before you decide whether to work or surf, she will have credibly committed to not working, and this will force you to work instead.

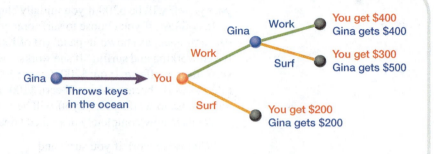

and fights that such revenge will induce). If you can (in the eyes of others) commit to punishing bullies, you likely won't be bullied. This reasoning also suggests that perhaps vengeance or a reputation for revenge-seeking behavior might be supported by game theory.

With this understanding of how sequential games work, let us now turn to the value of putting yourself into someone's shoes—this time, the shoes of another individual who will respond to your actions.

# EVIDENCE-BASED ECONOMICS

## Q: Is there value in putting yourself in someone else's shoes in extensive-form games?

Abraham Lincoln once said, "When I am getting ready to reason with a man, I spend one-third of my time thinking about myself and what I am going to say, and two-thirds about him and what he is going to say." President Lincoln keenly understood that it was necessary to put himself into the other man's shoes before discussions started. Anticipating the demands and strategies of his opponents made Lincoln one of the United States' most celebrated presidents. He thought deeply about the high-stakes sequential games he had to win to steer the United States through the Civil War.

In our first Evidence-Based Economics feature, we saw the value of putting oneself in other players' shoes in a game in which all players act simultaneously. The value of this type of reasoning is related but also in many ways quite different when we turn to extensive-form games, as one now has to forecast how others will play in the future. To understand this point, let us again turn to lab trust game experiments.

One variant of the trust game is shown in Exhibit 13.15. There are two players, you and Bernie. You are the first mover and must decide whether to trust Bernie. The associated payoffs to this game are as follows: (1) If you choose not to trust Bernie, then both you and Bernie receive a payoff of $10. (2) If you choose to trust Bernie, then Bernie must choose to either defect or cooperate. If he defects, then you receive nothing and Bernie receives $30. If Bernie cooperates, then both of you receive $15.

How will you play this game?

Assuming that Exhibit 13.15 contains all relevant payoffs, then you should use backward induction to solve this game. If you put yourself into Bernie's shoes, you would defect if given the chance. This is because by defecting, Bernie earns $30, which is greater than his cooperation earnings of $15. So you should choose not to trust Bernie, because you now know that if you did trust him, he would choose to defect, because $30 is greater than $15. So the equilibrium of this game is for you not to trust Bernie. This is a bad outcome in the sense that it is not socially efficient: instead of earning a total of $30, you and Bernie only earn $20 ($10 each), because

**Exhibit 13.15** A Trust Game Between You and Bernie

This is the extensive-form game representing trust. You move first and decide whether to trust or not to trust Bernie. If you trust Bernie, then he has to decide whether to cooperate or defect.

You

Don't Trust Bernie          Trust Bernie

Your payoff = $10
Bernie's payoff = S10

Bernie

Defect          Cooperate

Your payoff = $0
Bernie's payoff = S30

Your payoff = $15
Bernie's payoff = S15

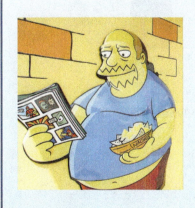

Bernie Madoff, possibly under arrest.

you do not trust Bernie. In this way, the trust game is a sequential prisoners' dilemma game.

You will notice that many situations in the real world look like this game. Every time you trust a stranger, or even a friend, there is a risk that person will disappoint you. When you call a plumber to repair your leaking faucet, there is a risk that he will take your money but do a shoddy job and the faucet will start leaking again in a few weeks. When you enter a car lot hoping to find a good deal on a used sports car, you face the same risk—what if the car is a lemon?

If the equilibrium were as characterized in Exhibit 13.15, the world would be a sad and dysfunctional place. What factors could cause the equilibrium in Exhibit 13.15 to be different? One important factor is reputational concerns: if the game is played several times, the players might attempt to develop a reputation. For example, you visit the same coffee shop, bakery, butcher shop, and dry cleaner, and you often hang out with the same friends. In these cases, you and the other agents you are interacting with can develop a reputation for trustworthiness and not misbehaving, and this reputation can then help you achieve better payoffs.

In Exhibit 13.15, even though it makes sense for you not to trust Bernie in a one-shot game, if you were to play many, many, many times, it might make sense for you to trust Bernie and for Bernie to play nicely, because you would both be better off if you received $15 every round of play rather than $10 each. This long-run strategy might shed light on the kinds of interactions we observe constantly in the real world—for example, why businesspeople trust one another, or friends and families share trust.

How can we shed light on such a game in the real world and compare behavior in one-shot versus repeated games? One approach is to run a field experiment, which is what one of the authors of this book (John List) did at several sports card trading shows.[7] At these shows, dealers—think Comic Book Guy from *The Simpsons*—set up booths to buy and sell sports cards. Just like many goods we purchase, sports cards have uncertain quality. Not every Derek Jeter rookie card is the same, and just as an experienced mechanic can inspect a car and determine its quality, an elaborate grading system understood by licensed experts is used to determine the quality of trading cards. This quality then determines the value of the card.

John List recruited buyers to approach sellers and purchase baseball cards from sellers who promised to deliver a "Mint" card. (In the baseball card market, there are various degrees of "Mint," determined by grading services or authenticators.) The sellers in the experiment were either local dealers, who frequented the card shows often and therefore had a reputation to uphold, or non-local dealers, who lived in another city and therefore rarely frequented the local card shows. Accordingly, they had little reputation at stake. After each transaction, the buyers secretly turned the goods over to List so that he could have the true grade ascertained by a licensed expert.

# EVIDENCE-BASED ECONOMICS *(continued)*

13.1

13.2

13.3

13.4

13.5

It is reasonable to believe that local dealers have more of a reputational concern than non-local dealers do, but there might also be other important differences between them. For example, local dealers might just care more about local customers. To make sure that his findings were not driven by these other differences, List organized a second field experiment in which he had buyers purchase sporting event ticket stubs (stubs of the tickets that permit you entry into a sporting event) at two different points in time. In the first instance, no professional grading service was available to evaluate the quality of the stubs. Directly before the second time period, a grading service had emerged to evaluate ticket stubs. Again, after each transaction, the buyers secretly turned their goods over to List so that he could have the true grade ascertained by a licensed expert. If local dealers were just different or cared about their customers, we should see similar behavior in the two different time instances. However, if they were motivated by reputational concerns, they should be much more likely to sell high-quality ticket stubs after introduction of the grading service.

Exhibit 13.16 summarizes the results of the experiments. In the first experiment, among the set of non-local sellers, fewer than 10 percent of the cards were at the level promised by the dealer (the leftmost bar in Exhibit 13.16). But at the same time, those sellers who *did* have reputational concerns provided nearly 50 percent of cards at the promised quality level. This is evidence consistent with the importance of reputation.

In the second field experiment, List found that before the third-party quality verification service was introduced, the local dealers had no qualms about selling low-quality cards. In fact, they were not much better than the non-local dealers in the first experiment! The second two columns in Exhibit 13.16 show that only 18 percent of the ticket stubs purchased before the introduction of the quality service were at or above the quality level promised by the seller. After the introduction of the service, though, quality levels shot up.

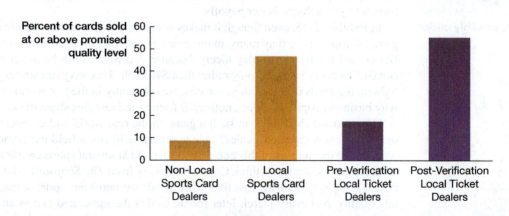

**Exhibit 13.16** Percentage of Sales at or above Promised Quality Level by Dealer Type

This exhibit shows the percent of cards sold at or above the quality level promised at the trading shows. With verification, non-local dealers of cards only deliver at or above the quality they promise in 10 percent of the transactions. The corresponding number is much higher for local dealers, presumably because they have reputational concerns. They deliver at or above the quality they promise in nearly 50 percent of the transactions. The exhibit also shows the importance of quality verification: local dealers deliver on their promises considerably more often when verification is possible.

These experiments thus show that reputational concerns are quite important. In particular, these reputational concerns made local sellers much more likely to deliver cards at the quality level they promised.

In terms of the trust game between you and Bernie, these results show that if Bernie, who is playing after you, does not have reputational concerns, he will often defect rather than cooperate, leaving you with the short end of the stick. In contrast, he is much more likely to cooperate when he does have reputational concerns. So it is rather important for you to be able to put yourself in Bernie's shoes and understand how he will play. This is in fact an illustration of a more general phenomenon: in games when the second mover has little incentive, it is important for the first mover to use backward induction before making his or her move. Such backward induction can save a lot of money. If reputational concerns are important, and you know that to be true, your behavior is much different (and payoffs much higher) than when the second mover is not trustworthy.

|  |  |  |  |
|:---:|:---:|:---:|:---:|
| **Question** | **Answer** | **Data** | **Caveat** |
| Is there value in putting yourself into someone else's shoes? | In many economic situations, there is great value. | Field experiments on trust. | Many features can influence how people behave, and the experiment focuses on only a few of those reasons for cooperation. |

# CHOICE —
## &CONSEQUENCE

### There Is More to Life Than Money

The data from the sports card market show that some sellers deliver high quality even when they have no reputational concerns or there is no financial incentive to do so. Such behavior is in line with people tipping at restaurants to which they never plan to return, anonymous donors giving to private charities, and some firms installing costly pollution abatement equipment voluntarily.

One reason for such deviations from Nash predictions is the presence of *social preferences*, meaning that the individual's benefits are defined not only by his or her own payoffs but also by the payoffs of others. Social preferences play an important role in many economic interactions, and we discuss them in greater detail in Chapter 18.

## Summary

- Game theory provides us with the tools to examine situations when players' payoffs are intertwined. Whether decisions are made simultaneously or sequentially, game theory is about being able to see the world through the eyes of your opponent and understand the opponent's incentives.

- The key concepts of game theory are best responses and Nash equilibria. A best response is one agent's optimal strategy (action) taking the other player's strategy as given. When the same strategy is a best response against any possible strategies of the other players, then it is a dominant strategy. In most games, players do not possess such a dominant strategy, making their best responses depend on the strategy choices of other players.

- A Nash equilibrium arises if each player chooses a strategy that is a best response to the strategies of other players. Put differently, a Nash equilibrium is a combination of strategies that are mutual best responses.

- The concept of Nash equilibrium enables us to make predictions about behavior in a range of situations, including those that can be modeled as the prisoners' dilemma, the tragedy of the commons, and zero-sum games. It also helps us understand why trustworthy behavior is more likely to emerge when players have reputational concerns.

## Key Terms

game theory *p. 311*
strategies *p. 311*
payoff matrix *p. 311*
simultaneous-move games *p. 312*
best response *p. 312*
dominant strategy *p. 313*

dominant strategy equilibrium *p. 313*
Nash equilibrium *p. 316*
zero-sum game *p. 319*
pure strategy *p. 319*
mixed strategy *p. 319*
extensive-form game *p. 323*

game tree *p. 323*
backward induction *p. 324*
first-mover advantage *p. 325*
commitment *p. 325*

## Questions

*All questions are available in* MyEconLab *for practice and instructor assignment.*

1. What is a dominant strategy equilibrium?

2. Is a player's best response in a game the same as his dominant strategy? Explain.

3. What is meant by the "prisoners' dilemma"? Do the players in the prisoners' dilemma game have a dominant strategy?

4. What is a Nash equilibrium? How is a Nash equilibrium different from a dominant strategy equilibrium?

5. How can the tragedy of the commons be modeled as a prisoners' dilemma game?

6. What is a zero-sum game? Can you think of any zero-sum games in real life?

7. What is the difference between a pure strategy and a mixed strategy?

8. Suppose that a player has a dominant strategy. Would she choose to play a mixed strategy (such as playing two strategies, each with probability 50-50)? Why or why not?

9. Although there are many examples of game theory in the real world, how well do you think specifics like payoff matrices, Nash equilibria, and dominant strategies translate to reality?

10. When can backward induction be used to arrive at the equilibrium for a game?

11. What is meant by the first-mover advantage? How does commitment matter in a game with a first-mover advantage?

   a. Some games have a first-mover advantage and other games do not. Suppose you were playing rock-paper-scissors as an extensive-form game. First you choose rock, paper, or scissors, and then your opponent makes a choice. Is there a first-mover advantage in this game?

**b.** Two firms are thinking of entering a new market. If only one of them enters, it will make high profits. If two firms enter, then both will suffer losses. Suppose that the game is played sequentially, with firm 1 deciding first. Does this firm have a first-mover advantage?

**12.** The trust game shown in Exhibit 13.15 is a sequential prisoners' dilemma; as the payoff matrix shows, the outcome of the game is not socially efficient. What factors could cause this equilibrium to be different in real life?

**13.** Economic agents (for example, consumers or firms) often do things that at first glance seem to be inconsistent with their self-interest. People tip at restaurants when they are on vacation, even if they have no intention of returning to the same place. Some firms install costly pollution abatement equipment voluntarily. How can these deviations from Nash predictions be explained?

# Problems

*All problems are available in* MyEconLab *for practice and instructor assignment.*

**1.** Suppose the cable TV companies Astounding Cable and Broadcast Cable are in your city. They both must decide on a high advertising budget, a moderate advertising budget, or a low advertising budget. They will make their decisions simultaneously. Their payoffs are as follows:

| Astounding/ Broadcast | High | Medium | Low |
|---|---|---|---|
| **High** | Astounding earns $2 million | Astounding earns $5 million | Astounding earns $4 million |
| | Broadcast earns $5 million | Broadcast earns $7 million | Broadcast earns $9 million |
| **Medium** | Astounding earns $6 million | Astounding earns $8 million | Astounding earns $5 million |
| | Broadcast earns $4 million | Broadcast earns $6 million | Broadcast earns $2 million |
| **Low** | Astounding earns $1 million | Astounding earns $0 million | Astounding earns $3 million |
| | Broadcast earns $2 million | Broadcast earns $5 million | Broadcast earns $3 million |

**a.** Does Astounding have a dominant strategy? If so, what is it?

**b.** Does Broadcast have a dominant strategy? If so, what is it?

**c.** Is there a dominant strategy equilibrium? If so, what is it?

**d.** Are there any Nash equilibria in this game? If so, what are they?

**2.** Suppose Russia is deciding to Invade or Not Invade its neighbor Ukraine. The United States has to decide to Be Tough or Make Concessions. They will make their decisions simultaneously. Their payoffs are as follows:

| United States/ Russia | Not Invade | Invade |
|---|---|---|
| **Be Tough** | United States gets 5 | United States gets 7 |
| | Russia gets 4 | Russia gets 3 |
| **Make Concessions** | United States gets 3 | United States gets 1 |
| | Russia gets 5 | Russia gets 9 |

**a.** What is the United States' best response when Russia chooses Not Invade?

**b.** What is the United States' best response when Russia chooses Invade?

**c.** What is Russia's best response when the United States chooses Be Tough?

**d.** What is Russia's best response when the United States chooses Make Concessions?

**e.** What is the Nash equilibrium of this game?

**3.** In the movie *The Princess Bride*, the hero disguised as the pirate Westley is engaged in a game of wits with the villain Vizzini. Westley puts poison in either his own glass of wine or in Vizzini's glass. Vizzini will choose to drink from his own glass or from Westley's; Westley drinks from the glass Vizzini does not choose. (You should think of this as a game where players move simultaneously, since Vizzini does not see which glass Westley has chosen).

**a.** Construct the payoff matrix for this game. Assume drinking the poison and dying gives a payoff of –10 and staying alive has a payoff of 10.

**b.** Does Vizzini have a dominant strategy? Does Westley have a dominant strategy?

**c.** Does this game have a Nash equilibrium where players use pure strategies?

**d.** Now suppose that Westley has another strategy, which is not to put poison in either glass, and this will give him a utility of $a$ regardless of Vizzini's choice of strategy. For what values of $a$ does Westley have a dominant strategy?

**4.** It is possible for two-player games to be quite asymmetric: Each player might have a different set of options, and the payoffs may be quite different. Consider the following example between a large firm and a small firm (the first number in each box denotes the large firm's payoff, the second number shows the small firm's payoff):

|  |  | Small Firm (player 2) | |
|  |  | Expand Operation | Stay Small |
| --- | --- | --- | --- |
| Large Firm (player 1) | High Price | 50, 20 | 60, 10 |
|  | Medium Price | 60, 20 | 70, 10 |
|  | Low Price | 40, 0 | 90, 10 |

**a.** Does either firm have a dominant strategy?

**b.** Find all Nash equilibria.

**5.** *A Beautiful Mind*, a movie about John Nash, fails to properly demonstrate a Nash equilibrium. It attempts to do so in a bar scene where men at a bar (Nash and his friends) plan to ask women to dance. There is one beautiful woman that the men consider the most attractive, as well as several other women. Nash assumes the "less attractive" women will only accept an offer to dance if the man extending the offer has not first been rejected by the beautiful woman. In the movie, Nash proposes that all the men agree to not ask the beautiful woman in the first place.

**a.** Nash's proposal may lead to a good outcome for each man, but it is *not* a Nash equilibrium. Why not?

**b.** The movie initially shows all the men asking the beautiful woman to dance. To be fair, this is also *not* a Nash equilibrium. Why not?

Why *is* it a Nash equilibrium if exactly *one* man asks the beautiful woman to dance?

**6.** We might suppose a soccer player has three options when taking a penalty kick: Kick right (KR), kick left (KL), or kick down the center (KC). The goalie can choose to dive right (DR), dive left (DL), or stand in the center (SC). Assume the goalie blocks the kick whenever he guesses correctly (+1), but fails to make the save otherwise (−1). The payoff for the kicker is the opposite. Write this game as a matrix. Are there any pure-strategy Nash equilibria?

**7.** Use a matrix to model a two-player game of rock-paper-scissors with a payoff of 1 if you win, −1 if you lose, and 0 if you tie.

**a.** Draw the payoff matrix for this game.

**b.** Is there an equilibrium in this game where players use pure strategies?

**c.** Why should you use a mixed strategy to play this game?

**8.** Two gas stations, A and B, are locked in a price war. Each player has the option of raising its price (R) or continuing to charge the low price (C). They will choose strategies simultaneously. If both choose C, they will both suffer a loss of $100. If one chooses R and the other chooses C, (i) the one that chooses R loses many of its customers and earns $0, and (ii) the one that chooses C wins many new customers and earns $1,000. If they both choose R, the price war ends and they each earn $500.

**a.** Draw the payoff matrix for this game.

**b.** Does either player have a dominant strategy? Explain.

**c.** How many Nash equilibria does this game have? Defend your answer carefully.

**9.** Consider a game with two players, 1 and 2. They play the extensive-form game summarized in the following game tree:

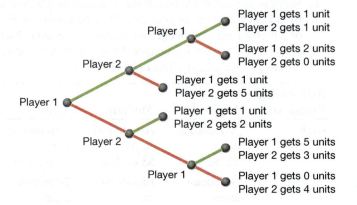

**a.** Suppose Player 1 is choosing between Green and Red for his second move. Which will he choose if:

  **i.** Green, Green has been played.

  **ii.** Red, Red has been played.

**b.** Suppose Player 2 is choosing between Green and Red, knowing the information above. Which will she choose if:

  **i.** Green has been played.

  **ii.** Red has been played.

**c.** Finally, suppose Player 1 is choosing between Green and Red in the first move. Given the information above, which will he choose?

**d.** Now describe the path that gives an equilibrium in this extensive-form game.

**10.** Jones TV and Smith TV are the only two stores in your town that sell flat-panel TV sets. First, Jones will choose whether to charge high prices or low prices. Smith will see Jones's decision and then choose high or low prices. If they both choose High, each earns $10,000. If they both choose Low, each earns $8,000. If one chooses High and the other chooses Low, the one that chose

High earns $6,000 and the one that chose Low earns $14,000.

**a.** Draw the game tree. Use backward induction to solve this game.

**b.** Suppose Smith goes to Jones and promises to choose High if Jones chooses High. Is this a credible promise?

**c.** Now suppose Jones starts a new policy that says it will always match or beat Smith's price. It advertises the new policy heavily and so must choose Low if Smith chooses Low. So the game now has the following structure. First, Jones chooses High or Low. Second, Smith chooses High or Low. Third, if Jones has chosen High and Smith has chosen Low, Jones meets Smith's price and chooses Low. Draw the game tree. Use backward induction to solve this game.

**11.** While at the airport, you hear over the loudspeaker an offer to be bumped off your current flight in exchange for $100 travel credit. After it becomes clear nobody will take this offer, the offer is increased to $200. A few minutes later, the airline offers $300; then $400, and so on. Individually, each passenger wants to take the offer, but collectively it is best for people to hold out. The strategic dynamic can be modeled with a two player "centipede game" (the name is based on the shape of the game tree), shown below. Use backward induction to determine the equilibrium in this game.

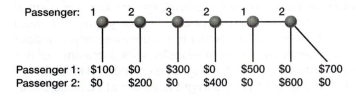

| Passenger: | 1 | 2 | 3 | 2 | 1 | 2 | |
| --- | --- | --- | --- | --- | --- | --- | --- |
| Passenger 1: | $100 | $0 | $300 | $0 | $500 | $0 | $700 |
| Passenger 2: | $0 | $200 | $0 | $400 | $0 | $600 | $0 |

**12.** Pat's and Geno's are two rival cheesesteak restaurants in Philadelphia, Pennsylvania, that are located across the street from each other. Since they serve almost the same food, they are fiercely competitive. With the weather in Philly improving, sales at both firms are expected to increase over the next few months. Suppose both firms are now considering expanding their menu to include cheesecake and other desserts to boost sales further. The payoffs are given in the following table:

| | | Pat's | |
| --- | --- | --- | --- |
| | | Introduce Desserts | Don't Introduce Desserts |
| Geno's | Introduce Desserts | Pat's profits will increase by $60,000 / Geno's profits will increase by $60,000 | Pat's profits will increase by $10,000 / Geno's profits will increase by $80,000 |
| | Don't Introduce Desserts | Pat's profits will increase by $80,000 / Geno's profits will increase by $10,000 | Pat's profits will increase by $20,000 / Geno's profits will increase by $20,000 |

**a.** Suppose Geno's and Pat's make their decisions simultaneously. What is the Nash equilibrium in this game?

**b.** Now suppose that Pat's will decide whether or not to introduce desserts and then Geno's will decide. Draw the game tree for this extensive-form game.

**c.** Use backward induction to determine how the extensive-form version of this game will be played.

**13.** Two competing firms must choose their quantity of production simultaneously. Each firm can choose either a High quantity of 3 or a Low quantity of 2. The price for both firms is $9 - Q$, where $Q$ is the sum of both quantities. Costs are zero; the profit is simply price times quantity. For example, if firm 1 chooses High and firm 2 chooses Low, then price is $9 - (3 + 2) = 4$; payoff for firm 1 is 12 while payoff for firm 2 is 8.

**a.** Draw the complete matrix for this game.

**b.** Find all Nash equilibria.

**c.** If this game were instead played sequentially, would there be a first-mover advantage? Briefly explain.

# Oligopoly and Monopolistic Competition

## How many firms are necessary to make a market competitive?

As an economist working at the Council of Economic Advisers, one of this book's authors worked with the Antitrust Division of the Department of Justice to examine whether the dominance of a few large producers of off-road engines increased market prices. This very question arises for many important industries that touch our lives daily. Consider Apple, and whether its pricing of e-books or its dominance of the digital music market with iTunes might be considered anticompetitive. A first thought that you might have is that because there are only a few competitors to Apple on the digital music front—mainly Google Play and Amazon.com's MP3 store for digital purchases and Spotify for streaming—the industry must not be very competitive.

Does simply counting the number of firms in an industry tell us whether the market is competitive? If so, then how many firms do we need to make a market competitive?

So far, we've studied two extreme market structures: perfect competition, which features many firms, and monopoly, in which a single firm supplies the entire market. As useful as these models are, they do not provide the necessary tools to help you answer the question of how many firms are necessary to make a market competitive. For this task, you need more realistic models of market structure, which lie somewhere between perfect competition and monopoly.

## CHAPTER OUTLINE

# KEY
## IDEAS

- Two market structures that lie between perfect competition and monopoly are oligopoly and monopolistic competition.

- In both of these markets, the seller must recognize actions of competitors.

- In oligopolies, economic profits in the long run can be positive.

- In monopolistically competitive markets, entry and exit drive economic profits to zero in the long run.

- Several important variables—such as the number of firms in the industry, the degree of product differentiation, entry barriers, and the presence or absence of collusion—determine the competitiveness of a market.

In this chapter, we study the two market structures that do, in fact, fall between the two extremes of perfect competition and monopoly: *oligopoly* and *monopolistic competition*. An important point of difference between these two market structures and the two extreme market types studied so far is that we must now consider interaction between firms. In so doing, we learn about the nature of competition and how prices are set in such industries. If you read novels, go to the movies, drink Pepsi or Coke, wear designer clothing, or just like to play around on your Mac that you purchased at Best Buy, you are already familiar with products in oligopolistic and monopolistically competitive industries.

This chapter will help you understand the economics underlying these industries. We will learn that in some instances, even markets with only two firms yield competitive outcomes. In other cases, prices that more closely approximate monopoly prices can result when several firms serve a market. By the end of the chapter, you will have acquired the economic tools to help you understand just how many firms it takes to make a market competitive. And, you'll learn that much more than just the number of firms determines market prices and producer profits.

## 14.1  Two More Market Structures

Every day you buy goods and services, such as books and music, from firms that do not naturally fit within the perfectly competitive or monopoly models. You might be thinking, how do Starbucks and Dunkin' Donuts fit in? First, they are price-makers, so they do not fall into the perfectly competitive category. Second, they do not have a monopoly, since they compete fiercely with other sellers of coffee and food products.

Coffee and tasty foods are typical examples of **differentiated products**, which are goods that are similar but are not perfect substitutes. They contrast with **homogeneous products**, which are those goods that are identical and are therefore perfect substitutes. Soybeans grown by different farmers are perfect substitutes; books produced by different authors are not.

Industries differ not only in whether their products are differentiated or homogeneous but also in the number of sellers present in the industry. Some industries will have a few sellers, like the airline industry or cable TV carriers in your area. Other industries will have

**Differentiated products** refer to goods that are similar but are not perfect substitutes.

**Homogeneous products** refer to goods that are identical and so are perfect substitutes.

**Exhibit 14.1 Characteristics of Four Market Structures**

Between the two extremes of perfect competition and monopoly, there are oligopoly and monopolistic competition. In oligopoly, only a few firms are competing, which could be in the context of either homogeneous or differentiated products. In monopolistic competition, many firms sell differentiated products, and each enjoys some degree of market power.

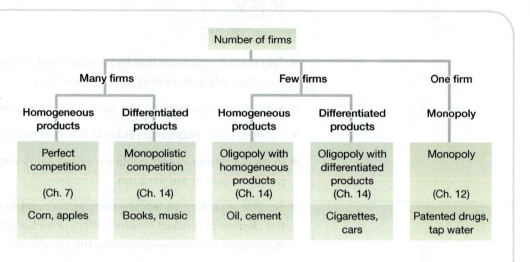

many sellers, like the book or music industries. A useful classification of market structures must therefore distinguish industries along two dimensions:

1. The number of firms supplying a given product
2. The degree of product differentiation

These distinctions lead us to introduce two more market structures, which we present in Exhibit 14.1.

Our first new market structure is **oligopoly**, which applies when there are only a few suppliers of a product. As Exhibit 14.1 shows, oligopolies can feature either homogeneous or differentiated products. Because in an oligopoly only a few firms are operating, each firm's profits and profit-maximizing choices depend on other firms' actions.

Our second new market structure is **monopolistic competition**. That might sound like an oxymoron—how can a monopoly be competitive? The name reflects the basic tension between market power and competitive forces that exists in this market type. All firms in a monopolistically competitive industry face a downward-sloping demand curve, so they have market power and choose their own price, just as monopolists do. These characteristics account for the first part of the name. What's *competitive* about such markets is that there are no restrictions on entry—any number of firms can enter the industry at any time. This means that firms in a monopolistically competitive industry, despite having pricing power, make zero economic profits in the long run. As Exhibit 14.1 shows, similar to a perfectly competitive industry, *monopolistic competition* features many competing firms, but unlike perfect competition, the sellers produce and sell differentiated products.

As we proceed through the chapter, you may want to refer back to Exhibit 14.1, which outlines the similarities and differences between the four types of market structures. We begin with oligopoly.

**Oligopoly** is the market structure that applies when there are few firms competing.

**Monopolistic competition** is the market structure that applies when there are many competing firms and products are differentiated.

## 14.2 Oligopoly

*Oligopoly* is a word that might strike you as rather strange. It stems from Greek origins: *oligoi* meaning "a few" and *polein* meaning "to sell." Put them together and you have a term referring to a market structure in which there are only a few suppliers of a product. You encounter oligopolies everywhere. As you push your cart down the soap aisle at the local supermarket, you may notice several different brands of bar soap—for instance, Ivory, Camay, Irish Spring, Caress, Dove, Lifebuoy, and Lever 2000. But if you look more closely, you will see that there are only a few suppliers—among them, Procter and Gamble, Colgate Palmolive, and Lever Brothers.

Oligopolies are tricky to analyze, because all sorts of market outcomes can happen, depending on the circumstances. For instance, only three companies—Seagate, Western Digital, and Hitachi—control almost three-quarters of the market for computer hard drives, but they ruthlessly cut prices on one another, and their rivalry has driven prices very close to marginal cost. At the same time, luxury goods makers like Louis Vuitton, Chanel, and Gucci seldom get into price wars.

If you refer back to Exhibit 14.1, you will see that oligopolies can be usefully divided into two categories: those that sell homogeneous goods (for example, hard drives or oil) and those that sell differentiated goods (for example, cigarettes or soda). In this chapter, we discuss two models to help us understand oligopoly:

1. Oligopoly model with homogeneous (identical) products
2. Oligopoly model with differentiated products

The first model, oligopoly with identical products, is similar to the monopoly model, but one key difference is that the oligopolist must recognize the behavior of its competitors, whereas the monopolist does not. The second model, oligopoly with differentiated products, is linked to the monopolistic competition market structure with one major exception: entry is impeded in the oligopoly, whereas there is free entry in the monopolistically competitive market.

## The Oligopolist's Problem

The oligopolist's problem shares important similarities with the two market types discussed in previous chapters—perfect competition and monopoly. And several of the concepts we have learned, such as those relating to production and cost, apply directly to the oligopolist's problem. From there, the oligopolist's problem can be described as having two unique features:

1. Due to cost advantages associated with the economies of scale of oligopoly or other barriers to entry, entry and exit will not necessarily push the market to zero economic profits in the long run (as is the case with perfect competition and monopolistic competition).
2. Because of relatively few competitors, the sellers that do occupy the market interact strategically.

## Oligopoly Model with Homogeneous Products

**Duopoly** refers to a two-firm industry.

One of the simplest cases of oligopoly is an industry with only two competing firms—a **duopoly**. Suppose that these two firms compete against one another by setting prices. Consumers observe these prices and then choose from which firm to buy. Such a model is commonly called *Bertrand competition*, after the famous French mathematician Joseph Louis François Bertrand, who first studied the interactions among competing firms that set prices.

To begin, let's suppose that the industry of interest is landscaping and that there are currently two landscaping firms in the city: your company, Dogwood, and a competitor, Rose Petal. You both provide lawn mowing and shrubbery trimming services. In addition, because the local labor market conditions affect you both equally, you have the same marginal cost, which is $30 per landscape job (and you can perform as many jobs as you can get at this marginal cost). We'll make one further assumption: consumers view your services as identical to Rose Petal's services. This means that you and Rose Petal are selling perfect substitutes.

With only two companies, it sounds like a pretty serious oligopoly, right? We would likely expect both firms to have a lot of market power and therefore be able to charge a high price.

To understand how this market works, we first turn to the demand side. Customers in this market have a simple demand rule: they hire landscaping services from the company that sells at the lower price. If both landscapers charge the same price, the consumer flips a coin to determine which firm to choose. The simple demand rule means, in effect, that the landscaper charging the lower price will get all of the demand. If both companies charge the same price, each company will get half of the demand.

**Exhibit 14.2** **Market Demand Curve for an Oligopoly with Homogeneous Products**

The exhibit depicts the market demand curve for landscape jobs, which are assumed to be homogeneous. The market has a total demand of 1,000 land-scaping jobs per week, provided that the price is $50 or below. At any price above $50, the market demand is zero.

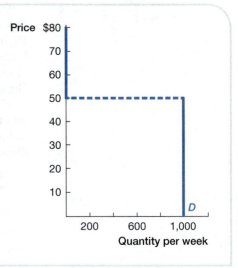

The **residual demand curve** is the demand that is not met by other firms and depends on the prices of all firms in the industry.

The final element you need to know to make your pricing decision is the market demand. For simplicity, let's say that the market has a total demand of 1,000 landscaping jobs per week, provided that the price is $50 or below. At any price above $50, the market demand is zero (because at high prices, people do their own yard work). Exhibit 14.2 presents the market demand curve for this situation.

What is directly relevant for a firm's profit-maximizing decisions is not the market demand curve but its **residual demand curve**, which is the demand that is not met by other firms. This residual demand curve depends on the prices charged by all firms in the market. We can derive your residual demand curve in this case from the market demand curve as a function of your price $P_{DW}$ and Rose Petal's price $P_{RP}$. In particular, in this example it is given as

1,000, if your price is less than Rose Petal's, or $P_{DW} < P_{RP}$;

1,000/2, if your price is equal to Rose Petal's, or $P_{DW} = P_{RP}$;

0, if your price is more than Rose Petal's, or $P_{DW} > P_{RP}$.

Contrasted with the market demand curve, which depends on the "market price"—the minimum of the prices charged in the market—the residual demand curve depends on the prices charged by both you and Rose Petal.

## Doing the Best You Can: How Should You Price to Maximize Profits?

The task facing you is now clear-cut: you should choose the price that maximizes your profits, realizing that you will sell according to the demand structure above. How should you start? A first consideration is determining costs. Recall that the marginal cost is assumed to be $30 per job for both you and Rose Petal.

A second consideration is to understand how your behavior affects Rose Petal's behavior. Let's start with some simple strategies. Say that you begin by charging a price of $50 and Rose Petal charges $45. What happens in this case? Because your price is higher than Rose Petal's price, Rose Petal will reap all of the business and will earn $15 above its marginal cost on each of the 1,000 landscaping jobs ($15 = $45 − $30).

Is this a Nash equilibrium? Remember from Chapter 13 that a Nash equilibrium occurs when each player chooses a strategy that is a best response to the strategies of others. On some reflection, you can see that this is not a Nash equilibrium, because given Rose Petal's price, you can do better.

How? The answer is to charge a price slightly below $45; in that way, you undercut Rose Petal's price. For example, if you charge a price of $44, you effectively steal the entire market from Rose Petal, and now your company earns profits—in fact, you earn $14 more than your marginal cost on every job ($14 = $44 − $30). We depict this situation in Exhibit 14.3.

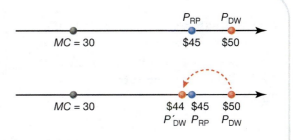

**Exhibit 14.3 Dueling Duopolies and a Pricing Response**

In a duopoly with homogeneous products, the best response of a firm that has a higher price is to undercut its rival, as long as its rival's price is above marginal cost (denoted $MC = \$30$ in the exhibit). So in this exhibit, when your price is $P_{DW} = \$50$ and that of Rose Petal is $P_{RP} = \$45$, you can increase your profits by cutting your price from \$50 to $P'_{DW} = \$44$ (which will increase your sales from 0 to 1,000).

How does Rose Petal now view the situation? Because the price is above marginal cost $MC = \$30$, Rose Petal views this situation in the same manner that you viewed the top portion of Exhibit 14.3. So this is not a Nash equilibrium—given your pricing behavior, Rose Petal can do better. To do so, it can undercut *you*, and charge \$43 per landscaping job. This pricing move permits Rose Petal to capture all of the market back from you. And it is now earning \$13 above its marginal cost for every completed job.

When does all of this price-cutting end? In other words, what is the Nash equilibrium? Seeing this example through to the end, you will realize that the price-cutting goes on until we reach the unique Nash equilibrium: both firms charge a price equal to marginal cost, or \$30 per landscaping job. That is, $P_{DW} = P_{RP} = MC = \$30$ is the unique Nash equilibrium. In this equilibrium, each of the two companies ends up supplying half of the market, and because both are selling at marginal cost, they both earn zero economic profits.

To convince yourself that this is a Nash equilibrium, you should ask: are there any other strategies that these two firms could use to make an economic profit? If not, then both firms are playing their best responses, and we have found a Nash equilibrium. The key observation is that, starting from $P_{DW} = P_{RP} = MC$, neither firm can increase its profits. If you try to charge a bit more, you sell nothing. If you cut the price further, you will not cover your marginal cost ($P_{DW} < MC = \$30$), so this is not a good strategy either, because you will actually lose money on every landscaping job. Both your firm and Rose Petal would obviously like to make an economic profit, but if either of you raises your price above marginal cost by just a penny, the other will receive all of the business. So the outcome isn't the most preferable outcome for you or Rose Petal, but neither of you can do better by unilaterally changing your price. This is the definition of a Nash equilibrium. (That this is the unique Nash equilibrium also follows from the argument in the previous paragraph, showing that no other combination of prices can be a Nash equilibrium.)

So there is a surprising conclusion to the model of an oligopoly with homogeneous products: in this model, firms engage in quite tough competition in trying to gain market share. In fact, the market outcome is the same as it would be in a perfectly competitive industry: price equals marginal cost in equilibrium. This competitiveness comes from the fact that any one firm can steal all of the market from the other by dropping its price slightly. The strong undercutting incentive leads both firms to lower their prices to marginal cost (recall, however, that zero profits here means no additional profits above the payments to all factors of production, including capital and business owners' time and effort, so there is no reason for the firm making zero profits to shut down operations).

This model shares similarities with the prisoners' dilemma game that we discussed in Chapter 13. Even though both you and Rose Petal would be better off if you both chose a high price, the unique equilibrium is for each of you to choose a low price.

## Oligopoly Model with Differentiated Products

So far in our discussion of oligopoly models, we have assumed that sellers are engaged in competition to sell homogeneous products. Often, however, a more realistic description of an industry is a set of firms that make similar but not homogeneous products. A Boeing airliner is not the same as an Airbus; video game consoles from Microsoft, Nintendo, and Sony are not the same; and a flight on American Airlines is not the same as a flight

**When there are a few firms selling products that aren't identical, the key is to explicitly account for consumers' willingness to substitute among the products.**

on Southwest, even though these examples are of products in the same industry. Economists refer to a market in which multiple varieties of a common product type are available as a *differentiated product market*. When there are a few firms selling products that aren't identical, the key is to explicitly account for consumers' willingness to substitute among the products.

Therefore, this is not the "all-or-nothing" demand a firm faces with different prices for homogeneous products. With differentiated products, we assume that consumers view the firms' products as being somewhat distinct. As we'll see, this differentiation helps the seller a lot. As we just learned, when products are homogeneous, the incentive to undercut price is so intense that firms drive the market price down to marginal cost, thereby earning zero economic profits. But that won't happen here, as we'll see in the following example.

To illustrate, let's consider the soft drink industry, where there are two major players: Coca Cola and Pepsi. Because many consumers view the two companies' products as similar, when either firm cuts its prices, it will gain market share from the other. Put differently, if Coke raises its price, Pepsi sells more soda. Likewise, Coke will sell more when Pepsi raises its price.

But in this case, the firms' products aren't exact substitutes (that is, they are not homogeneous goods). In fact, some diehard consumers of Coca Cola would not readily switch to Pepsi, and likewise some consumers would not consider drinking Coca Cola when Pepsi is available. So the price-cutting company won't take the entire market just because it prices a bit lower than the other firm. Some people are still going to prefer its competitor's product, even at a higher price. This reasoning implies that we can never have an equilibrium in which both firms price at marginal cost and make zero profits—as was the case with homogeneous products. Specifically, pricing at marginal cost could never be a best response for either firm, even if the other firm were setting its price equal to marginal cost. This is easy to see. Suppose Pepsi set its price equal to marginal cost. Clearly by setting prices as low as possible, Coca Cola would increase its sales, but if its price were equal to its marginal cost, it would still make zero profits. If it increased the price above this level, it would lose a lot of market share to Pepsi. But because of the diehard Coca Cola customers who would not readily switch to Pepsi, its sales would not go down to zero following such a price increase, and, from the remaining customers, it would earn positive profits. Since it made zero profits when price was equal to marginal cost, this argument shows that in an oligopoly with differentiated products, the equilibrium cannot have price equal to marginal cost and zero profits.

So, how should Pepsi and Coke determine their prices? Let us highlight the main intuition here. Much like any firm that we have studied thus far, the idea is to set marginal revenue equal to marginal cost. In this case, each firm must put itself in the other's shoes to recognize how its prices will affect the prices of its competitor. For example, Pepsi executives must estimate the demand for Pepsi given every possible price for Coke. They can then construct their optimal price for every contingency. They must also estimate what price Coke is likely to set. Coke makes the same calculations to figure out its best response to changes in Pepsi's prices. Note that the equilibrium is determined by the actions of both Pepsi and Coke. The relevant concept that got us to this point is once again Nash equilibrium, which means that both firms set their prices as best responses to each other.

Though we cannot determine these prices without knowing the exact way in which Pepsi's demand affects Coke's price, and vice versa, we can derive some important lessons. The less substitutable the two products are—meaning that there are more diehard consumers committed to each product—the further away we will be from the situation with homogeneous products, and the higher the prices will be. So a key consideration of the executives of both companies is to estimate how much of the market considers the two sodas as close substitutes and how much of it would not easily switch from one product to the other.

In summary, we have seen that with homogeneous products, two firms competing head-to-head are sufficient to bring the price down to marginal cost. This is no longer true with differentiated products. In fact, in an oligopoly with

Coke versus Pepsi—an example of oligopoly with differentiated products.

# LETTING THE
# DATA SPEAK

## Airline Price Wars

Airlines have always been known for their rather cutthroat brand of competition. In this business, competition is fierce. When a new, low-price competitor called Southwest Airlines entered the industry in 1967 and shook it up, economists sat back and watched the price wars begin.

In fact, in their research, economists Austan Goolsbee and Chad Syverson have found that price wars began well before Southwest entered the market.[1] These economists studied the three quarters after Southwest announced that it would create flights but before it actually started selling tickets (so, for example, after Southwest announced it would serve Dallas-to-Chicago flights but before it began to sell Dallas-to-Chicago tickets). They found that prices were 24 percent lower during these three quarters—before actual entry could be suspected as a contributing factor.

Why would airlines respond to a competitor before the competitor is actually competing? One reason may be that airlines attempt to "capture" as many consumers as possible. For example, by selling special frequent-flyer deals and luring new customers into a long-term relationship, airlines may be able to compete with new entrants like Southwest.

Before Southwest entered the market, it was not worthwhile for airlines to offer such deals, but faced with new competition, the airlines might have decided that enticing new customer loyalty was worth it.

Another reason prices might have fallen before Southwest entered the market is because the long-term value of the market had decreased, making collusion less profitable. We discuss the economic elements of collusion next.

differentiated products, firms typically make positive economic profits, and some oligopolies persist in the long run with positive profits because of barriers to entry (for example, established brands often act as barriers to entry).

But what happens if there is a third firm supplying soda to the market? In that case, the market would continue to be an oligopoly, but now with three firms. In oligopoly with differentiated products, price will typically be lower with three firms competing compared to two firms competing (this contrasts with oligopoly with homogeneous products where, as we just saw, price is equal to marginal cost even with two firms). As the number of firms in an oligopolistic market increases further, prices tend to decline toward marginal cost. If enough entry occurs, it could cause the market to turn into a monopolistically competitive structure. In that case, we have to turn to the monopolistically competitive model, which we present later in this chapter, to understand what would happen.

### Collusion: Another Way to Keep Prices High

When the government opened bidding for the Federal Communications Commission's spectrum licenses, which allowed cellular phone companies to compete for a specified frequency band to provide wireless communication services in a particular market, several

> It's not in the interest of one company to collude if the other *is* colluding.

puzzling bids were put forth. US West, for some reason, kept submitting bids that ended in the numbers 378, while other companies chose round figures. What is the logic behind this puzzling behavior?

The fact of the matter is that US West was in tight competition for a frequency band in Rochester, Minnesota, block 378 (a zone of airspace). By submitting bids that ended in 378, US West was signaling its intentions to competitors—in many cases, it was signaling that competitors should stand down and stop bidding on this frequency band.

The standard oligopoly models discussed so far cannot explain such puzzling behavior. To get at the motivations behind the behavior, we must consider a model of *collusion*.

# LETTING THE
# DATA SPEAK

## Apple versus Samsung

Our discussion of oligopoly with differentiated products makes three important points. First, these differentiated products, such as Pepsi and Coke, are *substitutes*, so when one company reduces prices or makes its product more attractive, this will reduce the demand for the product of the other firms in the market. Second, because products are differentiated, no company will be able to capture the entire market. Third, when consumers view the products as less substitutable, prices will be higher.

The competition between Apple and Samsung, the two giants of the smartphone market, illustrates all three points. First, in the recent past, whenever one company has released a new phone—usually with a slew of new, enticing features—it has gained market share at the expense of the other. For example, Exhibit 14.4 shows that Apple's market share jumped from around 15 percent to around 22 percent after the release of the iPhone 4S at the end of 2012, while Samsung's market share fell from around 33 percent to 29 percent. Just a few months later, with the release of the Samsung Galaxy 4, the trend reversed, with Samsung back up to 33 percent and Apple down to 18 percent. (We must be careful about reading too much into this graph, however; because the two companies control so much of the market, one company's loss in market share will tend to, at least in the short term, drive up the other company's market share.)

You've seen evidence of the second point if you've ever passed an Apple store on the day of a new iPhone release.

Every year, huge lines form in front of Apple stores around the world. Some true diehards even camp outside for days before the event. These Apple devotees are attracted to the iPhone as a distinct product—one that runs the Apple operating system or gives them access to apps like FaceTime.

These lines also provide indirect support for the third point. New models are priced significantly higher than older ones. For instance, the newly released iPhone 5 was priced at $650 relative to $450 for the previous model. Apple then charged $750 for the next model, iPhone 6-plus. These price differences do not reflect the higher costs of the new models. The iPhone 6-plus, for example, cost an estimated $231.50 to make, compared to an estimated $187.00 for the iPhone 4. That extra $250 in price increase, then, is largely reflecting the higher markup that Apple is able to charge because the new model is less of a substitute for the available products that Samsung offers.

While Samsung has its own fans, the numbers suggest that it faces a more elastic demand curve than its Silicon Valley opponent. In 2015, despite its smaller market share, Apple gained 91 percent of smartphone profits—Samsung, only 14 percent.[2] Indeed, Samsung had to lower the cost of the Galaxy 6S after poor sales performance. With new, cheap smartphones entering the market every year, the company may have trouble differentiating itself. Later in this chapter, we'll discuss what happens when new firms start to enter a market with differentiated products.

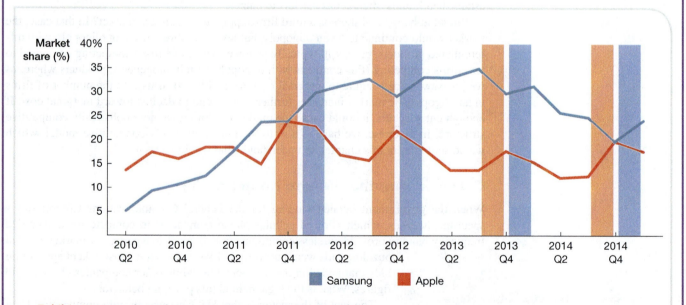

**Exhibit 14.4** Apple and Samsung Smartphone Market Share

The blue and red lines show the market share of Samsung and Apple, respectively, in percent. The shaded bars show the timing of new smartphone releases; the red bars show approximate times of iPhone releases, while the blue bars show approximate times of Samsung Galaxy releases.

**Collusion** occurs when firms conspire to set the quantity they produce or the prices they charge.

**Collusion** occurs when rival firms conspire among themselves to set prices or to control production quantities rather than let the free market determine them.

To see how collusion works, let's return to your firm and Rose Petal—duopolists in the landscaping business. In the Bertrand model discussed above, we found that the Nash equilibrium resulted in zero economic profits. One way around this zero-profits "problem" is to engage in collusion over prices. Imagine that over coffee you and the CEO of Rose Petal decide to collude by setting your prices jointly rather than independently.

How should you set prices jointly? One model of how an oligopoly might behave is for all the firms to coordinate and collectively act as a monopolist and then split the monopoly profits among themselves. This type of oligopoly structure makes sense on one level, with regard to the total profits of the industry as a whole. We know that absent price discrimination, monopoly profits are the highest profits that can be obtained from a given market. Therefore, jointly acting together to earn monopoly profits is the best an industry can do in terms of profit.

That means that both your firm and Rose Petal can collude and set prices at $50 per landscaping job. At this price, the market demand is 1,000 jobs, and if both firms have the same price, half of the consumers will go to each firm; therefore both firms will make considerable economic profits. Accordingly, collusion is much more profitable than competition for both of you.

So, should we expect prices in a duopoly to always reach monopoly levels when the two firms can communicate and set prices jointly? There are two main reasons we might be skeptical. First, even when firms agree on collusion, they have an incentive to disregard their agreements and engage in secret price-cutting to capture more of the profits for themselves. Thus, although collusion is a great deal for oligopolists, it is difficult to sustain. Second, as we discuss later in this section, such price-fixing is illegal. The potential punishment for engaging in such actions has a strong discouraging effect.

**The Breakdown of Collusive Agreements** Although collusion sounds easy in principle—let's both set a high price and make a lot of money—in practice, it has proven difficult. The logic behind its difficulty lies in game theory: each company has the incentive to cheat on the collusive agreement. Even if both sellers have agreed to collude, they would rather cheat on that agreement than keep their word.

Let's reconsider the landscaping game to see this reasoning. Consider the situation in which the oligopolists are considering cheating on a collusive agreement. For example, let us assume that you and Rose Petal have agreed to set a high price—$50 per job. You each must decide whether to stick with $50 per job or cut the price, which defines a simple game. In fact, the situation is similar to the prisoners' dilemma game we studied in Chapter 13. Your dominant strategy is to cheat on that agreement and secretly cut your price a little bit, say to $49.50 per job. Faced with a price of $49.50 from you and $50 from Rose Petal for this homogeneous service, all consumers will be attracted by your lower price. Therefore, you can take over the entire market with a slight price cut, nearly doubling your economic profits.

Much like confessing in the prisoners' dilemma game in Chapter 13, cheating in this game is a dominant strategy for both you and Rose Petal. This means that the only equilibrium is for you and Rose Petal to continue to cheat until you set price at marginal cost.

**When Collusion Can Work** Is it possible to sustain collusion if firms recognize that they will be playing this game over and over rather than just once? The answer is yes. There are two important considerations that determine how successful a collusive arrangement is:

1. Detection and punishment of cheaters
2. The long-term value of the market

If another player can cheat without being detected—such as giving customers a secret price discount—then it is difficult to maintain collusive agreements on keeping prices high. Sellers simply give secret price discounts, because it is their dominant strategy to do so.

# LETTING THE
# DATA SPEAK

## To Cheat or Not to Cheat: That Is the Question

Up to this point, we have discussed models in which sellers set prices. In another type of oligopoly model, sellers compete on quantities rather than prices. This type of model is called *Cournot competition*, after Antoine Augustin Cournot, a French philosopher and mathematician, who modeled duopolies focusing on quantity choices rather than on price competition.

Perhaps the most famous group that chooses to collude by setting quantities is OPEC. OPEC (Organization of the Petroleum Exporting Countries) is an oil **cartel** that coordinates the policies of several major oil-producing countries. Maybe in the past you've grumbled about OPEC as you forked over $80 to fill up the gas tank for your trek home for the summer holiday. Yet even OPEC has a problem keeping the price of its good—oil—high.

This problem arises from the natural instability of collusive arrangements that we have just learned: each country can increase its profits by pumping more oil, but if they all do so, they will depress prices, reducing everybody's profits.

OPEC meets monthly to decide on production quotas for each member. Frequently, however, the members choose not to abide by the agreement and subsequently overpump oil. And by "frequently," we mean "pretty much all the time." Take a look at Exhibit 14.5, which shows OPEC's production quota agreements and its actual production from 2001 to October 2015. The blue line shows OPEC's stated production ceiling. The red line records the actual total production of the cartel. It's obvious that OPEC's member nations can't stick to their agreements. In fact, in only 17 of the 178 months shown is actual production at or below the agreed-on quota. The data say a lot about each member's temptation to cheat on the agreement.

Though OPEC is the world's most famous—and perhaps most successful—cartel, it has not been able to control oil prices over the past decade. This is not only because of the tensions among OPEC members, but also because non-OPEC countries have become very important suppliers. Since the 1990s, countries like the United States, Russia, and Brazil have steadily expanded their oil production; by 2008, seven of the fifteen largest world oil producers were not members of OPEC. Indeed, note that the green world production line in Exhibit 14.5 has risen steadily in recent years, despite flat OPEC production; OPEC's share has dropped from

mid-1990s highs of around 40 percent to around 33 percent in recent years. The United States has exhibited a particularly striking rise, aided by recent advances in fracking, a technique that enables the extraction of oil from tight shale rock formations. In 2000, 23,000 U.S. fracking wells produced 102,000 barrels per day; by 2015, 300,000 fracking wells were producing more than 4.3 million barrels per day.[3]

In 2014, this burgeoning oil supply sent prices into a precipitous downward spiral, from over $100 a barrel in June 2014 to under $50 by the end of 2015. Still, OPEC members, reluctant to cede their global market share, continued to produce above quotas. Some countries, like Saudi Arabia, even expanded oil production. At the end of 2015, Saudi Arabia was producing 10.2 million barrels per day, up from 8 million barrels per day in 2010. Panel (b) of Exhibit 14.5 displays this dual trend: the dotted black line, plotted on the right axis, shows the drop in price, while the colored lines, plotted on the left axis, show the increased production of Iraq, Saudi Arabia, and, for comparison, the United States. With members overproducing and prices still falling, OPEC had lost its ability to function as an effective cartel; in December 2015, it eliminated quotas entirely. As the Iraqi oil minister put it, "Americans don't have any ceiling. Russians don't have any ceiling. Why should OPEC have a ceiling?"[4]

A **cartel** is a formal organization of producers who agree on anticompetitive actions.

Suppose a cheater has been detected. How might he or she be punished? Consider one long-term strategy that you might want to adopt if you are playing the game with Rose Petal: I will keep my price at $50 per job provided that you also keep your price at $50 per job; if you ever cut your price, then I will cut my price to a very low level, say $30, forever. This type of strategy provides incentives for both firms to keep their prices at

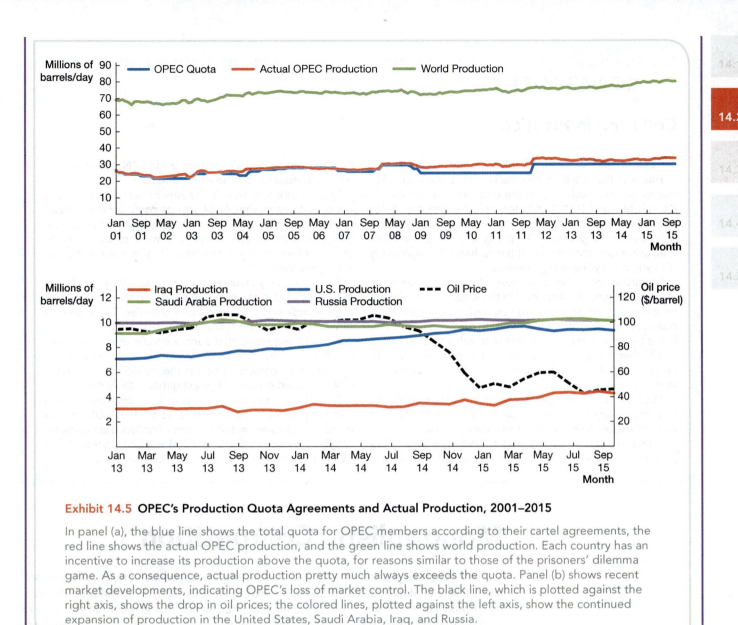

**Exhibit 14.5 OPEC's Production Quota Agreements and Actual Production, 2001–2015**

In panel (a), the blue line shows the total quota for OPEC members according to their cartel agreements, the red line shows the actual OPEC production, and the green line shows world production. Each country has an incentive to increase its production above the quota, for reasons similar to those of the prisoners' dilemma game. As a consequence, actual production pretty much always exceeds the quota. Panel (b) shows recent market developments, indicating OPEC's loss of market control. The black line, which is plotted against the right axis, shows the drop in oil prices; the colored lines, plotted against the left axis, show the continued expansion of production in the United States, Saudi Arabia, Iraq, and Russia.

A **grim strategy** is a plan by one player to price a good at marginal cost forever if the other cheats on their collusive agreement.

$50: if you both keep your price at that level, you will both enjoy extraordinary profits. But should Rose Petal cut its price, as soon as you find out about it, you price at marginal cost, or $30 per job forever, thus denying Rose Petal the high profits that it would have enjoyed with the collusive agreement. This type of punishment strategy is called a **grim strategy**.

A second consideration that is important to whether colluders will cheat is the long-term value of the market. The key is how you both trade off today's profits against tomorrow's profits. A colluder who values future monopoly profits more than current cheating profits will abide by the collusive agreement. In this view, impatient firms, for example those in danger of bankruptcy and therefore in desperate need of profits today, are more likely to cheat on the collusive agreement. In addition, if the government bans a product, then firms selling that product will know that on the last day of legal sales, no individual firm has an incentive to continue playing a cooperative strategy, so all firms cut prices on the last day. This type of incentive might have been at work when airlines began cutting prices long before Southwest entered the market (see the Letting the Data Speak feature on airline price wars earlier in the chapter).

### Collusion in Practice

"The competitor is our friend, the customer is our enemy."

This was the credo in the market for lysine—an additive for animal feed—during the mid-1990s, when Archer Daniels Midland (ADM) colluded with a number of Asian and European agricultural companies to inflate the price of lysine. This might seem like pretty small stuff, but ADM is an enormous corporation. It has its hand in nearly every dish you eat. Lysine is big business.

As hard as collusion is to prove, it might be harder to actually execute. As discussed in this chapter, the biggest problem is being able to trust your co-conspirators. Most economic models of collusion tend to rely on punishment. If one party reneges on its promise to sell a small quantity at a higher price, then presumably that party will have to be punished in order for collusion to stand any chance of working.

ADM and its co-conspirators weren't able to punish one another, mostly because without a proper audit study, it was impossible to know who was cutting prices.

In fact, on one tape capturing a meeting where prices were fixed, an executive suggests that an accounting firm be called in to actually run an audit—"Never mind the legal consequences," the exec states.

No, punishment wasn't the mechanism at work here. Instead, it seems that ADM and its confederates utilized the power of social norms. One tape captures an executive saying to his competitors, "I want to be closer to you than I am to any customers. They're not my friends. You're my friends."

Every company involved tried to establish its credibility in this social manner, often by posturing that competitors were friends and customers were enemies. This mantra is repeatedly caught on secretly recorded tapes. To a certain extent, it's surprising that such a simple mechanism was so effective. The zaniness of the entire arrangement was played up for comedic effect in the movie *The Informant*, which focused on the FBI investigation into ADM.

Even if it makes for humorous fodder now, this zaniness was still profitable. Some estimates are that ADM and its co-conspirators extracted millions of dollars from consumers. But they eventually paid. ADM was hit by a record fine by the Department of Justice in December 2013.[5]

## 14.3 Monopolistic Competition

We now return to the final major market structure, monopolistic competition. You will recall that a monopolistically competitive market features many firms offering differentiated products. Once we give it some thought, we can see that goods from this type of market structure touch our lives daily: our morning coffee, the clothes we put on every morning, the bike we ride to school, our choice of restaurants for lunch, the movie we watch at night, and the novel we take to bed are all examples of goods supplied by monopolistically competitive industries.

### The Monopolistic Competitor's Problem

The monopolistic competitor's problem shares important similarities with the problems of the perfect competitor in Chapters 6 and 7 and the monopolist in Chapter 12. Most importantly, in the short run the mechanics of monopolistic competition are identical to those for the monopolist's problem, whereas in the long run the equilibrium mirrors perfect competition.

To see these insights in action, let's assume that you have just accepted a part-time job at Dairy Queen, where your job responsibilities include providing advice on pricing. Exhibit 14.6 provides the daily residual demand curve for Dairy Queen ice cream cones—this is the residual demand curve, because it gives the demand that is not met by other producers and thus is left to be satisfied by Dairy Queen. Because Dairy Queen sells ice cream that is different from the several other ice cream shops in the city, the demand curve it faces is downward-sloping, as in Exhibit 14.6. Thus, much like a monopolist, a monopolistically competitive firm can increase price and not lose all of its business. In fact, the demand curve it faces tells us exactly the trade-off Dairy Queen faces when it changes its price. The marginal revenue curve, as depicted in Exhibit 14.6, is similar in shape to the monopolist's marginal revenue curve.

**Exhibit 14.6** Dairy Queen's Demand Curve and Marginal Revenue Curve

The (residual) demand curve *D* facing a monopolistically competitive firm is downward-sloping, much like the demand curve facing the monopolist. As a result, the marginal revenue curve *MR* is below the demand curve, again just like the marginal revenue curve facing a monopolist.

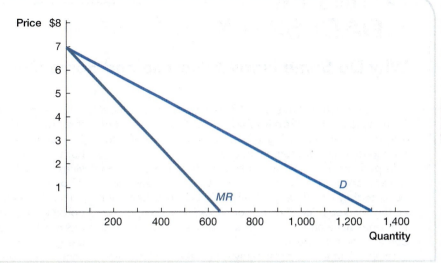

## Doing the Best You Can: How a Monopolistic Competitor Maximizes Profits

How should you advise Dairy Queen to maximize its profits? You may not be surprised to learn that the decision rule to maximize profits is identical to that for the monopolist:

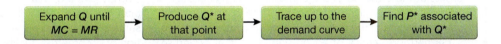

Expand **Q** until **MC = MR** → Produce **Q\*** at that point → Trace up to the demand curve → Find **P\*** associated with **Q\***

Exhibit 14.7 shows how this works in practice. It depicts the demand curve, the marginal revenue curve, and the marginal cost curve for Dairy Queen. As a monopolistic competitor, Dairy Queen must figure out the quantity and price that maximizes its profits. The optimal quantity is found by setting marginal revenue equal to marginal cost, that is, $MC = MR$. To determine the optimal price $P^*$, you trace up to the residual demand curve to see what price consumers are willing to pay for the quantity that you put on the market. Exhibit 14.7 reveals that Dairy Queen can maximize its profits by producing a quantity level of 520 ice cream cones and charging a price of $4.00.

The optimal decision rules are therefore:

Monopolist and monopolistic competitor: Set $P^* > MR = MC$.
Perfect competitor: Set $P^* = MR = MC$.

**Exhibit 14.7** Optimal Pricing Strategy for a Monopolistic Competitor

The solution to the monopolistic competitor's problem is identical to the profit-maximizing choice of a monopolist: find where $MC = MR$; drop straight down to find quantity; go straight up to the demand curve; and go left to the $y$-axis to find the profit-maximizing price $P^*$.

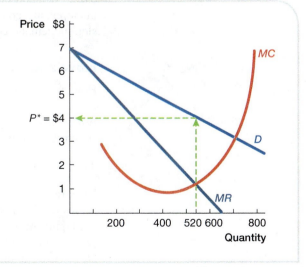

# LETTING THE
## DATA SPEAK

### Why Do Some Firms Advertise and Some Don't?

One way in which firms can differentiate their products from those of other firms is to advertise. The right kind of advertising can lead to higher prices and higher profits for the monopolistically competitive firm.

In perfectly competitive markets, such as the corn and wheat markets, there is no incentive for firms to advertise, because they can already sell all the goods that they want at the market price. But a monopolistically competitive firm does have an incentive to advertise—to increase the demand for its product.

Let's look at an example: many winemakers often advertise the superiority of their wines. One example is Kendall-Jackson. If its advertising is successful, consumers believe that Kendall-Jackson wines are superior to other wines. They are then willing to pay a premium for the Kendall-Jackson wines and are less willing to substitute away from such wines—even if the Kendall-Jackson wines are more expensive but very similar to those of other winemakers. In this instance, Kendall-Jackson increases its economic profits at the expense of the consumer. It is this aspect of advertising—the taking advantage of the consumer—that constitutes one of the major arguments against advertising.

Furthermore, critics of advertising claim that advertisements rarely give the public valuable information about the product. Instead, they present misleading situations that convince people that they need a product when they really don't, or that a product is far superior to that of its competitors when it really isn't.

In the past, the government has barred certain industries from advertising. A 1984 article in the *American Economic Review* by John Kwoka concluded that such bans on advertising in the field of optometric services actually increased the price for the services by 20 percent.[6]

Initially, this finding may seem counterintuitive—wouldn't optometrists, who were banned from advertising and thus did not have to shell out advertising dollars, be able to charge a lower price? Well, the answer is yes, but because consumers found it difficult to obtain information about the optometry market without any ads to look at, optometrists faced lower competition and could get away with charging higher prices.

Furthermore, advertising can give consumers a signal as to the quality of the service. For example, optometry is a business that relies heavily on repeat customers. Accordingly, an optometrist needs repeat patients in order to afford advertising. Because of this, only those optometrists who believe their patients will be satisfied enough to return after the initial visit will pay for advertising, and thus consumers can look to advertisements to give them an indication of optometrist quality.

These reasons, and the empirical evidence that shows a decrease in price when advertising is allowed, has led the government to repeal many of the advertising bans that had been put in place and allow firms to advertise their business as they see fit.

This summary of the optimal decision rule highlights the fact that the decision concerning the relationship between marginal revenue and marginal cost, which determines the level of production, is identical across the three market structures of perfect competition, monopoly, and monopolistic competition: expand production until $MC = MR$. The major difference arises with the firm in a perfectly competitive industry: it faces a perfectly elastic demand curve for its product, which leads to $P = MR$. For the monopolist and monopolistic competitor, however, we have $P > MR$ because they face a downward-sloping demand curve.

### How a Monopolistic Competitor Calculates Profits

How much does Dairy Queen earn per day if it follows the optimal decision rule of setting $P^* > MR = MC$? Computing economic profits for the monopolistically competitive firm works exactly the same way as computing economic profits for the other three market structures, that is,

$$\text{Profits} = \text{Total revenue} - \text{Total cost} = (P \times Q) - (ATC \times Q) = (P - ATC) \times Q.$$

Panel (a) of Exhibit 14.8 reveals the intuition of this calculation by superimposing the cost curves on the demand and marginal revenue curves. The exhibit shows that the level of economic profits is calculated as the area of the green rectangle, which equals 520 cones × ($4 − $2) = $1,040. Because average total cost is below the profit-maximizing price ($P > ATC$) at this quantity level, the firm is making positive economic profits.

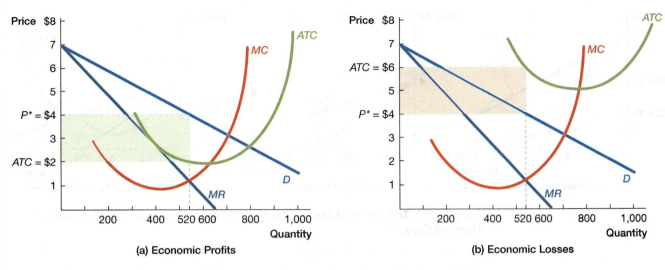

**Exhibit 14.8 Economic Profits and Economic Losses**

In panel (a), the profit-maximizing price-quantity combination gives economic profits, as shown by the green rectangle. The base of this rectangle is equal to quantity, and its height is the distance between average total cost (ATC) and price. In panel (b), even at the profit-maximizing price-quantity combination, the firm incurs a loss, as shown by the pink rectangle. This is because average total cost is very high (due to high fixed costs) in this example.

Similar to sellers in all market structures, economic profits are not *ensured* for the seller in a monopolistically competitive industry. Consider panel (b) of Exhibit 14.8, which is an example of Dairy Queen losing money. That is, because price is less than average total cost, there are losses for Dairy Queen. The level of losses is equal to the pink-shaded rectangle: Total revenue − Total cost = $(P - ATC) \times Q$, which is $520 \times (\$4 - \$6) = -\$1,040$.

Could the situation in panel (b) of Exhibit 14.8 be a short-run equilibrium for Dairy Queen? To answer this question, we consider the decision rule of whether to shut down or continue production in the short run. The decision rule that Dairy Queen should follow, when facing negative economic profits in the short run, is exactly the same as that followed by sellers in the other three market structures that we have studied:

> What's *competitive* about monopolistically competitive industries is that there are no restrictions on entry—firms can freely enter and exit the industry at any time.

1. If total revenues cover variable costs, then continue to produce in the short run.
2. If total revenues do not cover variable costs, then shutdown is optimal, as you will lose less money by shutting down and paying fixed costs than you would by operating.

You might be wondering what happens in the long run. We now turn to a discussion of long-run equilibrium in a monopolistically competitive industry.

## Long-Run Equilibrium in a Monopolistically Competitive Industry

So far, the analysis has been identical to the decision problem facing a monopolist. When we consider what happens in the long run for a monopolistically competitive industry, however, the analysis changes starkly—as noted above, from one that looks like the monopolist's problem to one that looks like the perfect competitor's problem. Recall that what's *competitive* about monopolistically competitive industries is that there are no restrictions on entry and exit—firms can freely enter and exit the industry at any time. What does this mean for the economic profits in the long run for firms in a monopolistically competitive industry?

Let's first discuss the case of positive economic profits in the short run, which is shown in panel (a) of Exhibit 14.8. Is this a long-run equilibrium? No. The reason is that with

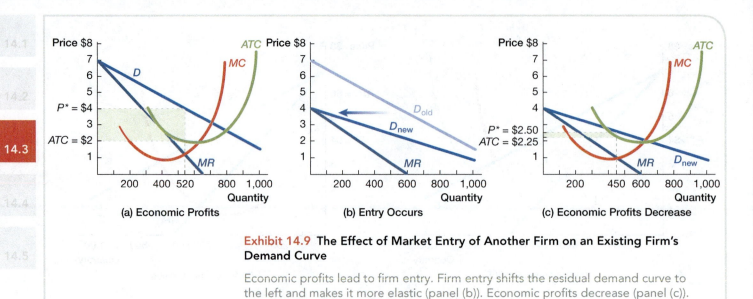

**Exhibit 14.9 The Effect of Market Entry of Another Firm on an Existing Firm's Demand Curve**

Economic profits lead to firm entry. Firm entry shifts the residual demand curve to the left and makes it more elastic (panel (b)). Economic profits decrease (panel (c)). Entry will continue as long as economics profits remain positive.

positive economic profits, sellers will be attracted to this market. *The key to understanding what happens in monopolistically competitive markets is to recognize what happens to the demand curves of the market's existing firm(s) when another firm enters.*

We know that when there are more substitutes for a good, a firm's residual demand curve shifts to the left and becomes more elastic (less steep). The leftward shift implies that at a given price, the quantity demanded will now be less than what it was before the shift. The more elastic demand curve leads to a lower markup over marginal cost (recall the analysis of monopoly pricing in Chapter 12). To illustrate these ideas, consider the case of Baskin-Robbins deciding to open a store down the street from Dairy Queen. Now there are more substitution possibilities for consumers. Entry of another seller means that Dairy Queen has a residual demand curve that is flatter than what it previously faced. And because demand is being split across more firms, not only is the residual demand curve Dairy Queen faces flatter but it has also shifted to the left.

Exhibit 14.9 shows how the residual demand curve for Dairy Queen changes because of this market entry. Panel (a) of the exhibit repeats panel (a) of Exhibit 14.8 and shows Dairy Queen's profit-maximizing quantity and price that we discussed earlier. Panel (b) shows the new demand curve juxtaposed against the old demand curve. Notice how the new demand curve, $D_{new}$, is both flatter than, and to the left of, $D_{old}$. The marginal revenue curve shifts accordingly.

Even after entry, though, Dairy Queen should continue to act as if it is a monopolist over its residual demand curve. Thus, its maximization problem remains the same: choose quantity where $MR = MC$, and set price using the residual demand curve. In this case, panel (c) of Exhibit 14.9 shows that Dairy Queen produces 450 ice cream cones per day. Dairy Queen's profit-maximizing price is now $2.50, and it earns profits equal to the green-shaded area in panel (c).

As the exhibit shows, Dairy Queen is still earning economic profits. We should therefore expect more firms to enter. Each firm that enters will further shift leftward Dairy Queen's residual demand curve as well as make it more elastic.

When does entry stop? Similar to a perfectly competitive industry, entry stops when there are no longer economic profits. This point is shown in Exhibit 14.10. At the long-run equilibrium, Dairy Queen sells 400 cones per day at a price of $2 per cone. Why is Dairy Queen's economic profit zero in equilibrium? Because at this point, price equals average total cost; thus, profits are zero, since profits $= (P - ATC) \times Q = (\$2 - \$2) \times 400 = 0$. Dairy Queen is just covering its costs of operations (variable and fixed) at this point.

Although the end result of entry is identical to the equilibrium in a perfectly competitive industry—zero economic profits—the mechanics are quite different. Recall that in a perfectly competitive industry, market changes operate through *shifts* in the market supply

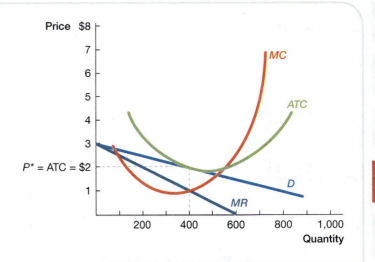

**Exhibit 14.10** Zero Profits in Long-Run Equilibrium

The long-run equilibrium in a monopolistically competitive industry is obtained when entry (or exit) stops at the point where the profit-maximizing price is equal to average total cost, yielding zero economic profits.

curve (see Exhibit 6.16 in Chapter 6). In monopolistic competition, market changes occur because the *residual demand curve becomes flatter and shifts leftward with entry*.

Because entry pushes economic profits to zero in the long run, monopolistically competitive firms have an incentive to continually try to distinguish themselves from rivals—in this way, such markets are perpetually in motion. For example, we are barraged by many different advertisements, commercials, and brand names, as well as a never-ending series of modest product innovations. Just consider how Taco Bell continually produces a "new" product from a different assortment of meats, beans, and cheeses. Or how Microsoft continually develops new features for Word and Excel. These "upgraded," "improved," and "new" products are all in the spirit of the ongoing pursuit of the firm to distance itself and its products from potential entrants. In some cases, these attempts at diversification might increase production costs, which also contributes to why, in long-run equilibrium, these firms earn zero economic profit.

Similar market dynamics would have occurred had we started with economic losses (panel (b) of Exhibit 14.8), where price was less than average total cost. In a market with free entry and exit, this situation would have induced Dairy Queen, or other ice cream shops, to exit the ice cream business. This is because—just as in a monopoly, oligopoly, or perfectly competitive market—losses in an industry cause existing sellers to seek greener pastures in the long run. Firm exit will cause the demand curve facing existing individual sellers to shift rightward and steepen (become less elastic).

## 14.4 The "Broken" Invisible Hand

As we learned in Chapter 12, one important factor that can "break" the powerful result of the invisible hand is market power. Compared to a competitive market, monopolists will be able to charge a price greater than marginal cost, thereby reducing sales and thus total surplus (consumer plus producer surplus). We learned earlier in this chapter that this is also the case for oligopoly with differentiated products. In both market structures, firms have market power and are able to charge prices greater than marginal cost, reducing total surplus.

What about monopolistic competition? With free entry and exit, economic profits in the long-run equilibrium equal zero: in good times sellers enter until all profits are exhausted, and in bad times sellers exit until all losses are extinguished. Such a feature is an important determinant of whether the invisible hand can operate to ensure that selfish agents are maximizing social well-being. So, does that mean that the invisible hand operates effectively in the monopolistically competitive case? In other words, is total surplus maximized under monopolistic competition? The answer is no.

Exhibit 14.11 shows the intuition behind why total surplus is not maximized in a monopolistically competitive market. The key difference between the perfectly competitive industry and monopolistic competition is that the latter restricts quantity to keep price higher.

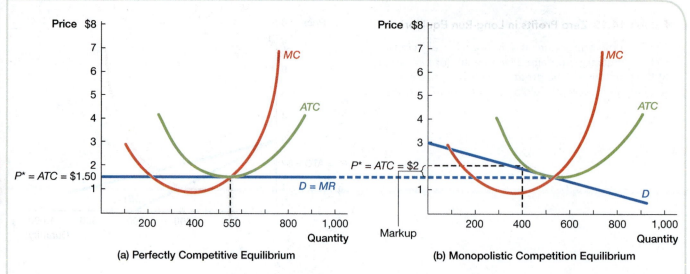

**(a) Perfectly Competitive Equilibrium**

**(b) Monopolistic Competition Equilibrium**

**Exhibit 14.11 Equilibria for a Perfectly Competitive Market and a Monopolistically Competitive Market**

A perfectly competitive industry produces a quantity that minimizes average total cost, which results in a price equaling marginal cost. There is deadweight loss in a monopolistically competitive industry, because production occurs at less than the efficient scale—no firm can grow large enough to reach the minimum of its *ATC* curve, and price is above marginal cost (denoted as "Markup" in the exhibit).

> **The key difference between the perfectly competitive industry and monopolistic competition is that the latter restricts quantity to keep price higher.**

Panel (a) of Exhibit 14.11 depicts the equilibrium for the perfectly competitive industry, in which all firms are producing at the minimum of their average total cost curves. Thus, firms in a perfectly competitive market produce goods using the least amount of resources. This is an important implication of the invisible hand.

But as panel (b) of Exhibit 14.11 shows, the same does not happen under monopolistic competition. The fact that monopolistic competitors each have a downward-sloping demand curve causes them to act differently than a perfectly competitive seller. First, they produce at a level that is below the efficient scale of production (the minimum of the *ATC* curve). Second, they mark up price above its marginal cost. Both of these features are shown in panel (b) of Exhibit 14.11. The markup causes some buyers who are ready, willing, and able to purchase the good at a price at or above marginal cost to be forced out of the market. Because of this fact, there is deadweight loss, as the monopolistic competitor produces too little compared to the socially efficient production level. The monopolistic competitor does not engage in this extra production, because it would then need to cut the price it charges other customers, resulting in lower economic profits.

## Regulating Market Power

So, should the government step in and regulate oligopolistic and monopolistically competitive markets? There is no straightforward answer to this question. In some cases, the answer is definitely yes. But in some others, the costs of regulation may exceed the benefits.

A clear case in which government regulation is warranted is successful collusion. As we have seen, oligopolists may be tempted to enter into collusive agreements to increase their profits at the expense of consumers. One of the main roles of antitrust policy in most countries, particularly in the United States, is to prevent these types of collusive agreements.

Another strategy oligopolists use to increase their market power is to merge with their competitors. Mergers refer to a situation in which two companies form a single company. Starting from an oligopoly with two firms, the merger will lead to a monopoly and thus to greater market power. The cornerstones of U.S. antitrust policy, the Sherman Antitrust

Act of 1890 and the Clayton Act of 1914, are concerned with the regulation of mergers. In particular, the Department of Justice (DOJ) reviews merger cases and decides whether the main objective is to increase market power or whether there are important efficiency gains from such a merger.

One of the main approaches the DOJ adopts in its analysis of mergers is to calculate the industry concentration. An industry is deemed concentrated when a few firms account for a large fraction of total sales in that industry. Crucially, what the DOJ looks at, and what economic theory suggests to be important, isn't the number of active firms in the market, but how *concentrated* the market is (meaning whether the distribution of sales in the market is dominated by only a few firms). When a merger stands to increase concentration significantly, the DOJ is less likely to allow the merger.

One of the tools that the DOJ uses to guide its enforcement of the Sherman Act is the **Herfindahl-Hirschman Index** (HHI). The HHI is a measure of market concentration, which is calculated by squaring the market share of each firm competing in the market and then summing the resulting numbers (squaring is done because it gives larger firms greater weight). For example, if there are two firms in an industry and one firm accounts for 75 percent of the sales and the other 25 percent, the HHI is equal to $75^2 + 25^2 = 6,250$. The higher the HHI, the more concentrated the industry. The HHI approaches zero when a market consists of a large number of firms with relatively equal market shares.

The **Herfindahl-Hirschman Index** is a measure of market concentration to estimate the degree of competition within an industry.

Even though the HHI doesn't tell us everything about an industry, it can inform our understanding of industries. For example, take the following three industries: bottled water, motor vehicles, and computers. Which do you think has the highest HHI? The lowest? Estimates from the Department of Commerce suggest that bottled water is the most concentrated, with an HHI of 2,873. Motor vehicles are next with an HHI of 2,639, and computers are the least concentrated with an HHI of 854. A general rule of thumb is that markets in which the HHI is less than 1,000 are considered not concentrated, those between 1,000 and 1,800 are considered to be moderately concentrated, and those in which the HHI is in excess of 1,800 are considered to be concentrated. One should not just rely on concentration to decide the competitiveness of an industry. Recall, for example, the landscaping oligopoly discussed in Section 14.2. There, the degree of concentration was high, but Bertrand competition ensured that price was equal to marginal cost.

There are also limits to how effectively the government can use regulation to reduce market power, particularly in monopolistically competitive markets with many producers. Imagine if the government had to regulate prices for every product sold in monopolistically competitive industries. And imagine further that it would set the number and type of entrants for each product line. This type of intervention would border on a command economy, and there are many difficulties with that approach, as we discussed in Chapter 7.

All in all, economists favor regulation for monopolies and for highly concentrated oligopolies, but are generally comfortable with permitting the more limited market power of monopolistically competitive firms, even though this still reduces total surplus to the economy. Yet, with this lost surplus comes a market structure that provides a variety of products, which is a good feature of monopolistic competition.

# 14.5 Summing Up: Four Market Structures

We now have studied the four major market types. In Chapters 4–7, we focused on perfect competition. In Chapter 12, we studied monopolists. Between the two extreme market structures—perfect competition and monopoly—are monopolistic competition and oligopoly. Exhibit 14.12 provides a summary of the four market structures across several dimensions.

As we just learned, monopolistic competition and oligopoly share many features with monopolies, including the ability to set prices. The primary difference across these three market structures is the number of competitors, or the number of sellers. A monopoly has only one seller. But monopolistic competition and oligopoly are market structures with more than one seller, and because of this fact, they have to concern themselves with the actions of other firms.

**Exhibit 14.12** Four Market Structures

The four market structures are summarized here. Each row highlights the number of firms in that market, degree of product differentiation, barriers to entry, pricing behavior, residual demand curve, social surplus, and long-run profits of each market structure.

| | Perfect Competition | Monopolistic Competition | Oligopoly | Monopoly |
|---|---|---|---|---|
| Number of Firms/Sellers/Producers | Many | Many | A few | One |
| Type of Product/Service Sold | Identical (homogeneous) | Slightly differentiated | Identical or differentiated | Single, undifferentiated product or service |
| Example of Product | Corn grown by various farmers | Books; CDs | Oil (identical); cars (differentiated) | Patented drugs; tap water |
| Barriers to Entry | None; free entry and exit | None; free entry and exit | Yes | Yes; high |
| Price-Taker or Price-Maker? | Price-taker; price given by the market | Price-maker; with a recognition of other sellers | Price-maker; with a strong recognition of other sellers | Price-maker; no competitors, no perfect substitutes |
| Price | $P = MR = MC$ | Set $P > MR = MC$ | Set $P > MR = MC$, or $P = MR = MC$, depending on type of competition and product differentiation | Set $P > MR = MC$ |
| Residual Demand Curve | Horizontally sloped; perfectly elastic demand curve | Downward-sloping; slightly differentiated products are available | Downward-sloping | Downward-sloping |
| Social Surplus | Maximized | Not maximized, but society might benefit from product diversity | Not maximized | Not maximized, but sometimes society benefits from research and development |
| Long-run Profits | Zero | Zero | Zero or more than zero | More than zero |

# EVIDENCE-BASED ECONOMICS

## Q: How many firms are necessary to make a market competitive?

How can we know whether there are enough firms in a market to make it competitive? In Chapter 6, we learned that the market is perfectly competitive if there are many firms—so many that each can take the market price of the good that it is supplying as given. But we also learned in the present chapter that just two firms can be sufficient for the market price to be equal to the marginal cost. So how do we answer this question?

Two economists, Timothy Bresnahan and Peter Reiss, came up with a unique angle to obtain an answer.[7] They reasoned that if a market is already effectively competitive, the addition of one more firm should not change prices. Take another look at Exhibit 14.9, which shows that when existing firms have market power, the entry of one more firm will make the market "more competitive" and will reduce prices. In contrast, recall that in a perfectly competitive market, both consumers and producers are price-takers, and neither can influence the market price. In a perfectly competitive market, if the size of the market increases, new firms will enter the market to meet the additional demand, but this will not reduce prices (in fact, new firms, just like existing firms, will be operating at the minimum point of their average total cost curve; recall Exhibits 7.5 and 7.6 in Chapter 7). In summary, when firms have significant market power, further entry reduces prices, while in a competitive market, further entry should leave prices unchanged.

### Exhibit 14.13 Tire Prices and Tire Quality in Selected U.S. Towns

When there are four or five dealers, prices are virtually the same. With three dealers, prices are higher, but this mostly reflects the higher tire mileage rating in these markets. Overall, there is relatively little variation in prices in markets with three, four, or five dealers, suggesting that competition between three or four dealers is sufficient for the tire market to be effectively competitive.

| | Number of Tire Dealers in the Market | | | | |
|---|---|---|---|---|---|
| | One | Two | Three | Four | Five |
| Price | 54.9 | 55.7 | 54.4 | 51.6 | 52.0 |
| Tire Mileage Rating | 44.5 | 47.0 | 47.7 | 45.4 | 43.8 |

Bresnahan and Reiss examined the prices of tires to find out when further entry leads to no further price decreases. Their investigation thus answers our question of when the market becomes effectively competitive. They obtained information on prices and the number of tire dealers across different towns in the western United States. To approximate markets, they limited the sample to 157 small towns that had at least an 80-mile round-trip to the nearest large city (if there was a large city nearby, the prices in a particular small town would be less relevant, because the residents of the small town could buy their tires in the nearby city).

Exhibit 14.13 shows the average tire prices in different towns classified according to whether the towns had one, two, three, four, or five tire dealers. One major reason there were different numbers of tire dealers in different towns was because the population varied across towns. As the quality of tires could vary within the sample, the second row of the exhibit shows the average tire mileage rating, which is a measure of average tire quality. It is important to know the quality of a product, because otherwise we might observe distinct prices not due to differences in market power, but simply due to differences in quality.

Exhibit 14.13 shows a remarkable pattern. There is practically no difference in prices between markets with four and five tire dealers. In fact, Bresnahan and Reiss show that the price difference between markets with three and four dealers is mostly due to the differences in the tire mileage ratings; that is, the average quality of tires appears to be higher in towns with three dealers. Once this difference in tire quality is accounted for, there is no evidence that prices are different between markets with three or four dealers. In sum, the evidence from the Bresnahan and Reiss study suggests that three or four firms are sufficient for the tire market to be (effectively) competitive.

At this point, you may be wondering whether towns with different numbers of tire dealers were systematically different along other dimensions. If so, the comparison of prices across towns could be contaminated by such differences. One way of dealing with this problem is to investigate the same question with a laboratory experiment, where such confounding differences will not arise.

Two economists, Martin Dufwenberg and Uri Gneezy, did just that.[8] They designed an experiment in which a number of sellers each chose a bid (selling price) between 2 and 100. Whichever seller made the lowest bid (set the lowest price) kept the dollar amount equal to his or her bid. You may notice the similarity between this experiment and the oligopoly model with homogeneous products. When there are two sellers, this is identical to the duopoly model we studied. Our analysis in that case suggested that each seller should engage in cutthroat competition and bid 2.

You might also reason, though, that in a duopoly, you are playing against just one other seller, and you may try to go for a higher bid and take home more money if you happen to have the lower bid. Dufwenberg and Gneezy, in fact, found that in a duopoly, average bids were just below 50, so the experiment does not mirror the theory. However, when the number of sellers increased to four, the sellers acted much more competitively. In fact, with four sellers, the average winning bid at the end of ten rounds of play was close to 2! Thus, in the lab too, it appears that *four competitors are sufficient to drive the equilibrium toward the competitive outcome*. As economic theory predicts, prices depend on the fierceness of competition, and empirical research suggests that the number of competitors does not have to be very large to bring prices very close to the competitive level. Interestingly, this research shows that even in markets with a large HHI, intense competition can be observed.

Although this empirical evidence suggests that four is an important number, we should take great care not to overgeneralize this point. It might be the case that in other industries or in other cities (or in other experiments), it takes many more or fewer firms to generate a competitive market. In the end, economic theory and empirical insights can inform us of general principles, such as when and where to expect anticompetitive pricing, and when to suspect that such pricing is having an important influence. But statements on the actual existence, or effectiveness, of anticompetitive arrangements are quite difficult to make without actually investigating the industry itself.

**Question**

How many firms are necessary to make a market competitive?

**Answer**

In many industries and in the lab, approximately three or four.

**Data**

Data on tire prices across various cities combined with data from lab experiments.

**Caveat**

Other market specifics beyond the number of sellers also affect the nature of competition. As such, we are unsure how far we can generalize the results.

## Summary

- Oligopoly and monopolistic competition are two market structures that lie between the market extremes of perfect competition and monopoly. Firms in these market structures must consider the behavior of competitors, whereas neither a monopolist nor firms in a perfectly competitive industry need do so.

- No single model of oligopoly is applicable to every situation. The equilibrium outcome will depend on the unique features of the market—whether the goods are homogeneous or differentiated, how many firms are in the industry, and whether collusion is sustainable. Nevertheless, there are some important general lessons from the study of oligopoly. Economic profits of firms will be higher when goods are differentiated, when there are fewer firms in the industry (unless the goods are in fact homogeneous), and when collusion is sustainable.

- In the short run, behavior of the monopolistic competitor and the monopolist are identical: set Price > Marginal revenue = Marginal cost. In the long run, entry and exit cause the equilibrium in a monopolistically competitive industry—zero economic profits—to be identical to equilibrium in perfect competition.

- Economics provides a useful set of tools to begin a discussion of whether a market is competitive, but there is no one factor—such as the number of firms—that wholly dictates the nature of competition in a specific industry.

# Key Terms

differentiated products *p. 335*
homogeneous products *p. 335*
oligopoly *p. 336*
monopolistic competition *p. 336*

duopoly *p. 337*
residual demand curve *p. 338*
collusion *p. 343*
cartel *p. 344*

grim strategy *p. 345*
Herfindahl-Hirschman
 Index *p. 353*

# Questions

*All questions are available in MyEconLab for practice and instructor assignment.*

1. How are the products sold by a monopolistically competitive firm different from the products sold in a perfectly competitive market?

2. How is a monopolistically competitive market similar to a perfectly competitive market? Do monopolistically competitive markets and monopolies share any common features?

3. Both monopolies and monopolistically competitive firms set marginal revenue equal to marginal cost to maximize profit. Given the same cost curves, would you expect prices to be higher in a monopoly or a monopolistically competitive market?

4. Will a monopolistically competitive firm continue to operate in the short run despite earning negative economic profit? Explain your answer.

5. Monopolistically competitive firms earn zero economic profit in the long run as do perfectly competitive firms. Does this mean that total surplus is maximized in a monopolistically competitive market?

6. What happens in a monopolistically competitive market with the entry of new firms?

7. Consider a noncollusive duopoly model with both firms supplying bottled drinking water. The firms choose prices simultaneously. The marginal cost for each firm is $1.50. The market demand is shown by the figure given below.

a. Find the residual demand curves for each of the firms.

b. What pricing strategy by each firm would be a Nash equilibrium in this model?

c. Find the Nash equilibrium when the two firms can collude effectively.

8. In the model of an oligopoly with identical (homogeneous) products, what is the price likely to be?

9. How do oligopolistic firms that sell differentiated products determine their prices?

10. Suppose there are four firms in a market and each of them sells differentiated products. Does it make sense for these firms to engage in a price war? Why or why not?

11. When is a collusive agreement between two firms likely to break down?

12. Suppose the refrigerator industry has an HHI of 2,500 while the aluminum industry's HHI is 6,850. Is this information sufficient to conclude that the aluminum market is more concentrated than the market for refrigerators? Explain your answer.

13. Decide whether each of the following statements is true or false for each of three different types of markets: perfect competition, monopoly, and monopolistic competition.

    a. Firms equate price and marginal cost.

    b. Firms equate marginal revenue and marginal cost.

    c. Firms earn economic profits in the long run.

    d. Firms produce the quantity that minimizes long-run average cost.

    e. New firms are free to enter this industry.

# Problems

*All questions are available in MyEconLab for practice and instructor assignment.*

1. Acme is currently the only grocery store in town. Bi-Rite is thinking of entering this market. They will play the following game. First, Bi-Rite will decide whether or not to enter. If it does not enter, then the game ends, Acme earns a payoff of 50, and Bi-Rite earns a payoff of 0. If Bi-Rite does enter, then Acme has to decide to fight by slashing

its prices or to accommodate. If Acme decides to fight, then Acme and Bi-Rite each earn 10; if Acme accommodates, then each earns 20.

**a.** Draw the game tree for this game.

**b.** Use backward induction to figure out how this game will be played.

2. With the growth of the Internet, there are many online retailers and many buyers who shop online.

**a.** Why, given the growth of the Internet, would you expect to find that different firms would charge very similar prices for the same good?

**b.** Despite the logic of the first part of this question, several recent studies have found that different online retailers often charge quite different prices. How might you explain this result?

3. Consider a duopoly with homogeneous products, where two competing firms pick price (Bertrand duopoly). In this chapter you learned that both firms will choose price equal to the marginal cost (MC). But what happens if the the two firms have *unequal* marginal costs? Suppose that Dogwood has $MC = \$40$ and Rose Petal has $MC = \$25$. Assume firms can set prices such as \$29.99.

**a.** Explain why it is not a Nash equilibrium for both firms to set a high price such as \$60.

**b.** Explain why it is not a Nash equilibrium for both firms to set a price equal to the lower marginal cost of \$25.

**c.** Explain why it is not a Nash equilibrium for each firm to set a price equal to their respective marginal costs.

**d.** What is a Nash equilibrium? Which firm sells? At what price?

4. The diagram below shows the short-run demand curve (*D*), marginal revenue curve (*MR*), average total cost curve (*ATC*), and marginal cost curve (*MC*) for a firm in a monopolistically competitive market.

**a.** What level of output should this firm produce?

**b.** What price should this firm charge?

**c.** Will this firm earn a profit or will it earn a loss?

**d.** Would you expect entry or would you expect exit in this industry?

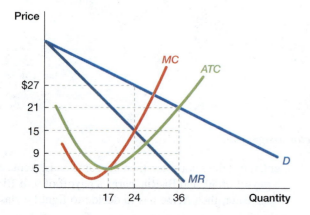

5. Make three copies of the following diagram and label them (i), (ii) and (iii). Add three different residual demand curves faced by a monopolist: (i) very steep (inelastic), (ii) relatively flat (elastic), and (iii) horizontal (perfectly elastic). Draw the residual demand such that a monopolist earns zero economic profit.

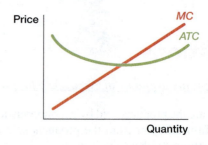

**a.** Which sketch corresponds to a firm that faces perfect competition?

**b.** Which sketch, without actually representing perfect competition, is close to perfect competition in terms of the price and quantity?

**c.** Using your diagrams, explain how "perfect competition" is a special case of "monopolistic competition."

6. Tobacco companies have often argued that they advertise to attract more people who already smoke and not to persuade more people to begin smoking. Suppose there were just two cigarette manufacturers, Jones and Smith. Each can either advertise or not advertise. If neither advertises, they each capture 50 percent of the market and each earns \$10 million. If they both advertise, they again split the market evenly, but each spends \$2 million on ads and so each earns just \$8 million (remember, advertising is not supposed to encourage more people to smoke). If one company advertises but the other does not, then the company that advertises attracts many of its rival's customers. As a result, the company that advertises earns \$12 million and the company that does not earns just \$6 million.

**a.** Show that advertising is a dominant strategy.

**b.** Suppose the government proposes a ban on cigarette ads. Should the two cigarette companies favor the ban or should they oppose the ban if advertising did not persuade some people to become smokers?

7. Coke and Pepsi each choose one of two prices: "Low" ($P = \$2$) or "High" ($P = \$3$). There are 50 buyers who will pick the lowest price option. However, if the prices are the same, 25 will buy from Coke and 25 from Pepsi. For simplicity, assume there are no costs, so profit is just price times quantity.

**a.** Draw the payoff matrix and find all pure-strategy Nash equilibria.

**b.** Now assume that each company has 20 loyal buyers who buy their brand regardless of price. This leaves 10 non-loyal buyers that pick the less expensive option. Again, non-loyal buyers split evenly if the prices are the same. Draw the new payoff matrix and find all pure-strategy Nash equilibria.

8. Major league baseball teams have imposed what is commonly called the "luxury tax" on themselves. A team is subject to the tax if its payroll exceeds a specified level. The annual threshold for the luxury tax is $189 million for 2014–16. A team that exceeds the threshold must pay 17.5 to 50 percent of the amount by which its payroll is above the threshold, where the "tax rate" depends on the number of years the team is over the limit. This question looks at why teams might subject themselves to this tax.

a. Suppose there are two major league baseball teams, Team 1 and Team 2. They will both choose to offer either high salaries to players or low salaries. They will make their decisions simultaneously. If both choose low each will earn $0; if both choose high each will earn $400. If one chooses high and the other chooses low, the team that chooses high will attract the best players and will earn $600, but the team that chooses low will earn just $300. Show that high is a dominant strategy but that both teams would be better off if both chose low.

b. Under a 1922 Supreme Court decision, major league baseball is not subject to many antitrust laws. Suppose these two teams agree to a "luxury tax." Under this luxury tax, a team that chooses high must pay a tax of $250. Find the new equilibrium in this game.

c. Some people might argue that the luxury tax in baseball is not an important determinant of major league salaries. As evidence, they show that team payrolls rarely exceed the threshold level and so teams rarely pay the tax. What does your answer to this question suggest about logic of this claim?

9. Telesource and Belair are two of the largest firms in the wireless carrier market in a certain country. Together, these firms account for more than 80 percent of the market.

a. Given that both firms differentiate their products, how is a Nash equilibrium achieved in this market?

b. Suppose both Telesource and Belair decide to collude and set the same price. Their payoffs from cheating and colluding are given in the matrix below. What is the Nash equilibrium in this game?

|  |  | Telesource | |
|---|---|---|---|
|  |  | Collude | Cheat |
| **Belair** | Collude | Belair earns $12 million / Telesource earns $12 million | Belair earns $2 million / Telesource earns $15 million |
|  | Cheat | Belair earns $15 million / Telesource earns $2 million | Belair earns $10 million / Telesource earns $10 million |

10. Suppose the world demand schedule for oil is as follows:

| Price per Barrel | Quantity Demanded |
|---|---|
| $50 | 40 |
| $75 | 30 |
| $125 | 20 |

There are two oil-producing countries, A and B. Each will produce either 10 or 20 barrels of oil. To keep things simple, assume they can produce this oil at zero cost.

a. There are four possible outcomes: A produces 10 or 20 and B produces 10 or 20. Find each country's profit for each of these four possibilities.

b. Suppose these countries choose the quantity of oil to produce simultaneously and without consulting with one another. Show that each country will produce 20 barrels of oil and each will earn a profit of $1,000.

c. The oil ministers realize they can do better if they collude and agree that each will produce 10. How much profit will each country earn if each produces 10 instead of 20?

d. Will country A have an incentive to cheat and produce 20 instead of 10? Will country B have an incentive to cheat and produce 20 instead of 10?

11. Suppose there are five firms in an industry. Their sales (that is, total revenue) are as follows:

- Firm 1: $90 million
- Firm 2: $50 million
- Firm 3: $36 million
- Firm 4: $14 million
- Firm 5: $10 million

Compute the Herfindahl-Hirschman Index (HHI) for this industry.

12. Suppose all you know about Boeing and Airbus is that Boeing sells about 40 percent of all comercial aircraft, while Airbus sells around 25 percent.

a. Based on this information, what is the largest the Herfindahl-Hirschman Index (HHI) might be? (Hint: Assume there is just one other firm in the market.)

b. What is the *smallest* the HHI might be? Based on this, can we say with confidence that the comercial aircraft industry is "concentrated"?

13. A firm in a monopolistically competitive environment discovers that in the long run it faces inverse demand $P = 10 - (1/2)Q$, which means its marginal revenue is $MR = 10 - Q$. The firm's marginal cost is a constant $MC = \$4$.

a. Sketch these three curves on a graph.

b. Based on the profit-maximizing condition $MC = MR$, what quantity and price should this firm set?

c. What must be the fixed cost for this firm, given it makes zero economic profits?

d. As accurately as possible, add the ATC curve to your graph. Carefully consider the ATC at the profit maximizing price.

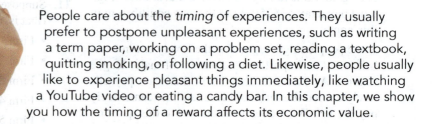

# 15 Trade-offs Involving Time and Risk

## Do people exhibit a preference for immediate gratification?

People care about the *timing* of experiences. They usually prefer to postpone unpleasant experiences, such as writing a term paper, working on a problem set, reading a textbook, quitting smoking, or following a diet. Likewise, people usually like to experience pleasant things immediately, like watching a YouTube video or eating a candy bar. In this chapter, we show you how the timing of a reward affects its economic value.

## CHAPTER OUTLINE

| 15.1 | 15.2 | 15.3 | EBE | 15.4 | 15.5 |
|------|------|------|-----|------|------|
| **Modeling Time and Risk** | **The Time Value of Money** | **Time Preferences** | **Do people exhibit a preference for immediate gratification?** | **Probability and Risk** | **Risk Preferences** |

# 15.1 Modeling Time and Risk

Most decisions have costs and benefits that occur at different times. Consider going to college. Lots of college costs come now—hard work, forgone wages (opportunity cost), and tuition payments. In contrast, many of the economic benefits from a college education come later in life, especially higher wages. If someone is going to make an optimal choice about whether or not to get a college degree, they'll need to somehow put all the costs and benefits into comparable units and add them up.

Other activities are also associated with up-front costs and delayed benefits: for instance, exercising, eating your vegetables, and saving. To analyze choices like these, we need to understand how to predict and value the delayed benefits. Is it optimal to invest a dollar today, so that I can consume the dollar and all the interest I've earned on it when I retire decades later?

This chapter also discusses how risk affects economic value. To an economist, risk is not a four-letter word—risky options are not necessarily bad options. Risk just means that some of the costs and benefits are not fixed in advance. For example, when you marry someone, you recognize that the success of the marriage is not completely predictable. A person's income, health, and even tastes can change. During a wedding ceremony couples acknowledge some of these risks when they vow "to have and to hold from this day forward; for better, for worse, for richer, for poorer, in sickness and in health."

Of course, political events are also somewhat unpredictable. The morning of election day, at the end of the 2016 presidential campaign, the leading prediction site was forecasting a 28 percent chance that Donald Trump (now President Trump) would win the election.[1] In other words, the forecasters thought that President Trump had a bit more than a 1 in 4 chance of winning. Uncertainty about who will win an election is a type of risk. Both Hillary Clinton and Donald Trump had a risk of losing on election night. We'll come back to this probability later in the chapter.

In general, almost all investments have risky returns. How will the stock market perform? How will housing prices change? Will the degree that you are earning in college turn out to be valuable, or will employers look for different skills in the future? In this chapter, we use economic analysis to evaluate such risks.

The tools that economists use to value delayed rewards have much in common with the tools that we use to value risky rewards. In both cases, economists weight rewards. When economists value rewards that will be experienced in the future, we multiply the reward by a positive factor that is *less than 1* to capture the idea that future rewards are worth less than current rewards. That's a mathematical way of capturing the idea that delayed gratification matters less to us than immediate gratification. When a reward might not occur, economists incorporate this risk by multiplying the reward by the positive probability (again, less than 1) that the reward will occur. This chapter explains how these time- and risk-weighting factors are determined and shows you how to use them.

Even good choices involve risk.

# 15.2 The Time Value of Money

Financial markets enable people to transfer money through time. For example, to move money into the future, depositors "lend" money to a bank now and then withdraw it, with interest, at a future date.

Economists call such a change an *intertemporal transformation*. "Inter" means between—for instance, when you travel between countries you are traveling internationally. "Temporal" refers to time. Intertemporal transformations move resources between time periods.

## Future Value and the Compounding of Interest

The key variable that summarizes an intertemporal transformation of money is the interest payment. Let's consider a simple example. Imagine that you deposit $100 in a bank account. The amount of an original investment—in this case $100—is referred to as **principal**. **Interest** is the payment received for temporarily giving up the use of one's money. How much money will you have in the account after 1 year, assuming that the account pays an annual interest rate of $r$? The bank account contains your principal of $100 plus interest of $r \times \$100$. In most cases, the interest rate is positive, but occasionally it can be negative. In this chapter, we'll use examples with zero or positive interest rates.

For example, if the interest rate is 5 percent, then the interest rate can be written in several formats that all have the same meaning:

$$r = 5\% = \frac{5}{100} = 0.05.$$

So an interest rate of 5 percent (in other words, 5%) has the same meaning mathematically as $r = 0.05$. For a 5 percent interest rate and a $100 deposit, the 1-year interest payment would be $0.05 \times \$100 = \$5$. The total value of the account at the end of a year can then be written as

$$\$100 + (r \times \$100) = (1 + r) \times \$100.$$

This is the sum of the principal and the interest, and it is referred to as the **future value** after 1 year of accumulation.

Suppose that you decide to leave all your money—principal plus interest—on deposit at the end of the first year. Your account balance at the beginning of Year 2 is $(1 + r) \times \$100$. Let's call this amount the "Balance." During Year 2 you will receive interest on the balance from the end of Year 1, or interest of $(r) \times (\text{Balance})$. At the end of Year 2 your account will contain the amount that you had in the account at the end of Year 1, which is what we called Balance, plus the interest that you received in Year 2:

$$(\text{Balance}) + (r) \times (\text{Balance}) = (1 + r) \times (\text{Balance}).$$

Since the Balance from the end of Year 1 was $(1 + r) \times \$100$, the amount at the end of Year 2 is

$$(1 + r) \times \text{Balance} = (1 + r) \times (1 + r) \times \$100 = (1 + r)^2 \times \$100.$$

Do you notice a pattern? If you left your money at the bank for 1 year, you would get this much back at the end of Year 1:

$$(1 + r) \times \$100.$$

If you left your money at the bank for 2 years, you would get this much back at the end of Year 2:

$$(1 + r)^2 \times \$100.$$

For each extra year that you leave your money in the bank, you can multiply your final balance by an additional factor of $(1 + r)$. Consequently, if you leave your money with the bank for $T$ years, you would get this much back at the end of year $T$:

$$\text{Future value} = (1 + r)^T \times (\text{Principal}).$$

---

**Principal** is the amount of an original investment.

**Interest** is the payment received for temporarily giving up the use of money.

The sum of principal and interest is referred to as **future value**.

The **compound interest equation** or **future value equation** calculates the future value of an investment with interest rate r that leaves all interest payments in the account until the final withdrawal in year T.

**How to do it:** The compound interest equation includes the expression $(1 + r)^T$. Use the financial calculator available on MyEconLab to evaluate this expression for any interest rate r and any time horizon T. Most hand-held calculators also have an exponent function that multiplies a number by itself T times.

This is called the **compound interest equation** or the **future value equation**. In this equation, r is the interest rate, and T is the number of years that the investment lasts. To derive the compound interest equation, we assume that none of your interest payments are being withdrawn along the way. Accordingly, you earn interest on *past* interest payments, because all earlier interest payments remain in the account until the final withdrawal in year T. To capture the idea of earning interest on interest, economists say that the interest is *compounding*.

The compound interest equation has some remarkable properties. Notice that the equation has an exponential term, $(1 + r)^T$, with exponent T. This implies that the balance of your account grows multiplicatively each year. In other words, each year the account increases by the multiplicative factor $(1 + r)$.

Such compound growth can be very powerful, which is convenient if you are trying to save for college tuition, build up a large nest egg for retirement, or prepare for any number of future financial goals. To see the power of compound growth, it helps to think about a few examples. Suppose you put $1 into an account at age 20, and let the money compound (without touching it) until you retire at age 70. In this example, the duration of the investment is $70 - 20 = 50$ years, so $T = 50$. We want to know how much money you'll have in this account at the end of that 50-year period. Note that this is just the amount of money—for instance, dollars—in the account, which does not adjust for the fact that inflation will erode the buying power of a dollar over time. We discuss how to make inflation adjustments in other chapters.

Let's begin by considering a very special case in which $r = 0.00$. When the interest rate is exactly 0, your final balance will be:

$$(1 + r)^T \times \$1 = (1 + 0.00)^{50} \times \$1 = 1^{50} \times \$1 = \$1.$$

Because $1^{50} = 1$, you emerge with $1 at the end of your 50-year wait. You've earned no interest, and your final withdrawal, $1, is exactly equal to your principal, $1.

Let's now consider some other interest rates. Here's where things get funky. Exhibit 15.1 plots the function $(1 + r)^T$ for a range of interest rates. The figure shows the value of your balance as your age rises from 20 to 70. The five different lines show what happens when the interest rate $(r)$ takes on five different values: 2, 4, 6, 8, or 10 percent.

You can see that something extraordinary happens. If the interest rate is 2 percent, your $1 of principal grows to $2.69. In other words, your money nearly triples over 50 years.

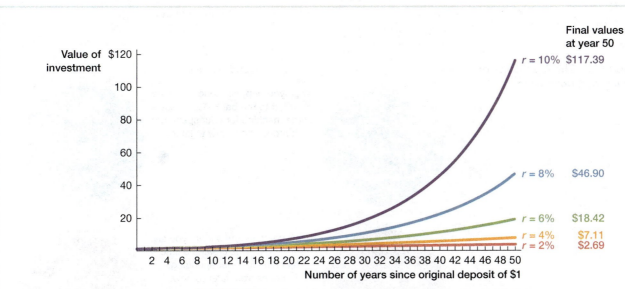

**Exhibit 15.1 Value of a $1 Investment over the Next 50 Years**

Each line plots the value of $1 invested at a constant interest rate r for T years. For example, after 50 years of compound growth, $1 of principal invested at an interest rate of 8 percent has a future value of $1 × (1 + 0.08)$^{50}$ = $46.90. For large interest rates, compound growth generates explosive returns.

That's not bad. But what if the interest rate is 10 percent? Then your deposit grows to $117.39. That's not a typo. Your $1 deposit grows **117** times as large over 50 years.

Because the future value is $(1 + r)^T \times$ (Principal), the growth factor for your principal is the same whether the original principal is $1 or $1,000. So a $1,000 original deposit would grow to about $117,390. Compound growth can be very powerful. Saving when you are young—and letting the interest compound—reaps enormous benefits when you are old.

Let's again consider the case of $1 of principal and split the $117.39 final account value into (1) principal and (2) interest. When the bank pays you at the end of 50 years, $1 is repayment of principal, so the remaining $116.39 is the payment of interest. In this case, the interest payment greatly exceeds the repayment of principal. Recall that the interest payment is what the bank pays you over and above your principal, for the privilege of using your money.

### Borrowing Versus Lending

Interest payments come in two basic categories, depending on whether you are a lender or a borrower. We have already discussed the interest that you *receive* from a bank as a depositor. In contrast, you make interest payments to the bank if you borrow money from the bank—for instance, by carrying debt on your bank-issued credit card or by obtaining a home mortgage from the bank.

Making a deposit effectively transfers spending from the present to the future. You deposit money now, and you withdraw it (with interest) in the future. When you borrow from the bank you generate the opposite direction of time travel. If you anticipate having money in the future, but you want to spend it now, you borrow. Accordingly, borrowing enables you to spend future income today. Exhibit 15.2 summarizes visually how lending and borrowing affect the timing of your spending.

Interest on a deposit and interest on a loan work the same way. With a deposit, you receive

$$(1 + r)^T \times (\text{Principal amount})$$

when you withdraw the money, with interest, in $T$ years. With a loan, you pay

$$(1 + r)^T \times (\text{Loan amount})$$

Saving money when young reaps returns when old. Most working households should save 10 to 20 percent of their pre-tax income.

> **Borrowing enables you to spend future income today.**

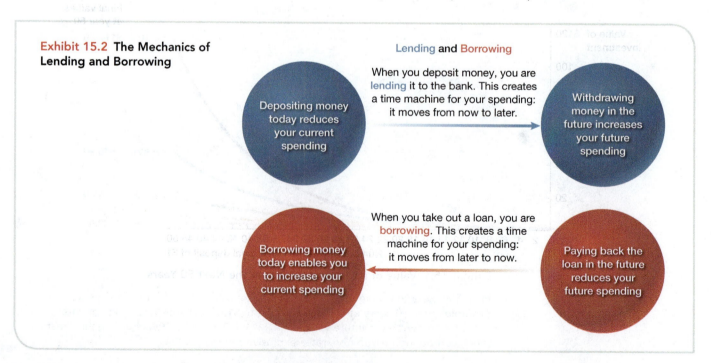

**Exhibit 15.2 The Mechanics of Lending and Borrowing**

Lending and Borrowing

Depositing money today reduces your current spending

When you deposit money, you are lending it to the bank. This creates a time machine for your spending: it moves from now to later.

Withdrawing money in the future increases your future spending

Borrowing money today enables you to increase your current spending

When you take out a loan, you are borrowing. This creates a time machine for your spending: it moves from later to now.

Paying back the loan in the future reduces your future spending when you pay back the loan, with interest, in $T$ years (assuming, in this example, that no periodic interest payments are made along the way). These are just two sides of the same transaction. Note that both expressions have the same multiplicative factor, $(1 + r)^T$. Consequently, we can use the plots in Exhibit 15.1 to calculate the payments associated with compounding deposits *or* compounding loans. The mathematical equations are exactly the same in both cases.

There is one key difference, however, between loans and deposits. Typical interest rates on loans tend to be higher than typical interest rates paid on investments. For example, it is not uncommon to borrow at 15 percent interest or even 20 percent interest on a credit card. Such high interest rates can produce enormous repayments. By way of illustration, consider a 50-year loan of $1,000 at a 15 percent interest rate. Suppose that no payments were made until year 50, so the loan was compounding for 50 years. For this scenario, the amount due after 50 years would be

$$(1 + 0.15)^{50} \times \$1,000 = \$1,083,657.$$

That's over 1 million dollars due after 50 years of compound interest!

In practice, such enormous repayments almost never occur on a $1,000 loan. No bank would let you wait 50 years to repay your credit card debt. The bank anticipates that a borrower with 1 million dollars due is more likely to declare bankruptcy than to repay. So the banks don't wait 50 years to get their money back. They'll require interest payments along the way.

Consequently, when thinking about loans, it is helpful to consider time horizons that are much shorter than 50 years. A 1 year, $1,000 loan at a 15 percent rate of interest will cost the borrower $150 in interest.

## Present Value and Discounting

Suppose someone asked you to lend them money to help fund the construction of a strip mall.

"You lend me $10,000, and I will repay you $20,000 in 20 years."

Assume that you have good reasons to trust this person, and you can rely on him to repay your money with certainty. So you are confident that this is a risk-free loan. Even with that confidence, it's still not clear whether you should take him up on his offer.

In such a situation, an economist would ask what alternative use you could make of your $10,000. (To keep things simple, we'll focus on alternative uses that are also risk free.) In other words, an economist thinks about opportunity cost. What is the next-best investment for your $10,000 of principal?

Suppose that you have another risk-free investment option that will pay 5 percent interest. So you face a choice. Do you participate in the strip mall project, or do you take the alternative project with the 5 percent return?

To compare these projects, you could ask, "If I have access to an investment with a 5 percent return, how much money would I need today to produce $20,000 20 years from now?" We can express this question as a mathematical equation that is similar to the equations that we have already been studying in this chapter:

$$(1 + 0.05)^{20} \times \$x = \$20,000.$$

In this equation, $x$ is the amount of money that you would need right now to generate $20,000 in 20 years, assuming that you have access to an investment that will provide an annual return of 5 percent. To solve for $x$, we just divide both sides by $(1 + 0.05)^{20}$ to find

$$\$x = \frac{\$20,000}{(1.05)^{20}} = \$7,538.$$

In this case, $x = \$7,538$. You could take $7,538 right now, invest it in a project that has a 5 percent return, and it will deliver $20,000 in 20 years. Consequently, $20,000 in 20 years is worth $7,538 to you right now.

The variable $x$ is the *present value* of $20,000 in 20 years, or in this case, the present value of the strip mall project. The **present value** of a future payment is the amount of money that would need to be invested today to produce that future payment. Economists say that the present value is the *discounted* value of the future payment. The present value equation is:

The **present value** of a future payment is the amount of money that would need to be invested today to produce that future payment. In other words, the present value is the discounted value of the future payment.

$$\text{Present value} = \frac{\text{Payment } T \text{ periods from now}}{(1 + r)^T}.$$

Note that $(1 + r)$ is greater than 1, so multiplying $(1 + r)$ by itself $T$ times yields an expression $(1 + r)^T$ that is also greater than 1. Therefore, in the present value equation the future payment—the payment $T$ periods from now—is divided by a denominator that is greater than 1. In other words, the future payment is *discounted* to calculate the present value.

It is useful to remember that discounting brings back money to the present (present value) and involves a reduction in magnitude; compounding takes present money into the future (future value) and involves an increase in magnitude.

> Discounting brings back money to the present (present value) and involves a reduction in magnitude; compounding takes present money into the future (future value) and involves an increase in magnitude.

It is helpful to write the present value equation in a slightly different form:

$$\text{Present value} = \left[\frac{1}{(1 + r)^T}\right] \times (\text{Payment } T \text{ periods from now}).$$

This version of the equation is mathematically identical to the previous one, but the second version emphasizes that we are multiplying the future payment by a factor that is less than 1. That factor is the ratio in the square brackets.

You can see that the strip mall offer is a bad deal the instant you calculate that its present value is only $7,538. You don't need an economist to tell you that you should not pay $10,000—which is the present cost of buying into the strip mall project—for something that is only worth $7,538. Economists say that this offer has a negative *net present value*, because the up-front cost of $10,000 exceeds $7,538, which is the discounted value of the delayed benefits. The **net present value** of an investment is the present value of the benefits minus the present value of the costs.

The **net present value** of a project is the present value of the benefits minus the present value of the costs.

$$(\text{Present value of the benefits}) - (\text{Present value of the costs}) = \text{Net present value}.$$

For our example, the net present value is

$$\$7,538 - \$10,000 = -\$2,462.$$

A positive net present value represents a "go" decision for a project; a negative net present value represents a "no-go."

The present value concepts are useful tools, because many economic opportunities generate complex streams of future payments. We can now collapse all those future payments to a single number—the net present value of the project.

To further illustrate the concept of net present value, consider another investment opportunity. Pay $10,000 today. In return, you'll receive two future payments: $10,000 in 10 years and $10,000 in 15 years. Is this a good deal? We can use the present value equation to answer this question. We'll use a 5 percent rate of interest.

First, let's calculate the present value of $10,000 in 10 years:

$$\text{Present value of } \$10,000 \text{ in } 10 \text{ years} = \frac{\$10,000}{(1.05)^{10}} = \$6,139.$$

Now let's calculate the present value of $10,000 in 15 years:

$$\text{Present value of } \$10,000 \text{ in } 15 \text{ years} = \frac{\$10,000}{(1.05)^{15}} = \$4,810.$$

These two present values sum up to

$$\$6,139 + \$4,810 = \$10,949.$$

So this project is a good deal. You pay $10,000 today for a project with a present value of $10,949. In other words, the net present value of the project is positive:

$$(\text{Present value of the benefits}) - (\text{Present value of the costs}) = \text{Net present value},$$

or

$$\$10,949 - \$10,000 = \$949.$$

Net present value is one of the most important tools in economics and is universally used by businesses and governments to decide which projects to implement. In the problems at the end of this chapter, you'll get more practice applying this concept.

# 15.3 Time Preferences

We just showed you how to discount future monetary payments to calculate a present value. We can also discount other future activities. For example, people discount future pleasures—like massages or donuts—when these goods are compared to other pleasures that are available right now.

To illustrate this idea, suppose you were asked to choose between a 60-minute massage in a year or a 50-minute massage right now. Which one would you take? Most people prefer the shorter, earlier massage. This reflects an important principle: people want pleasurable events to occur sooner rather than later. We now show you how economic models reflect this preference for earlier rewards.

### Time Discounting

Suppose there is some future activity that will generate pleasure or some other form of well-being. Suppose that this benefit is not money—for instance, the pleasure of getting a massage. Economists refer to general well-being as **utility**. To make future utility comparable to current utility, we need to multiply the future utility by a factor that is less than 1. In general, this won't be exactly the same factor that we use for monetary payments. However, both the factors that multiplicatively discount future monetary payments and the factors that multiplicatively discount future utility are less than 1. In most economic circumstances, stuff that comes in the future is worth less than stuff that comes right now.

To make these ideas concrete, suppose that an hour-long massage generates 60 units of utility—one *util* for every minute the massage lasts. A **util** is a single unit of utility. Suppose that people discount utility that will occur 1 year from now by multiplying those future utils by $\frac{1}{2}$. A multiplicative weight (between 0 and 1) is called a *discount weight*— a **discount weight** multiplies delayed utils to translate them into current utils. Using a discount weight of $\frac{1}{2}$, we can determine whether a person prefers 50 current utils (from a 50-minute massage) or 60 utils in a year (from a 60-minute massage). In this example, the 60 future utils have a discounted value of

$$\tfrac{1}{2}(60 \text{ utils in a year}) = 30 \text{ current utils}.$$

We now have the answer. If a person discounts delayed utils with a weight of $\frac{1}{2}$, then she prefers 50 utils right now to 60 utils in a year's time. In present value, the 60 delayed utils are worth only 30 utils now. Discount weights enable us to compare delayed utils and immediate utils, helping us identify the preferred option. Once we know your discount weight for a particular time horizon—the psychological value that you place on a delayed util—we can predict the intertemporal trade-offs that you will make.

Here's another example that illustrates these ideas. Suppose you are considering whether to eat a hot fudge sundae. Assume that the sundae offers immediate pleasures of 6 utils and delayed costs of 8 utils. The delayed costs would include things like reduced health and fitness.

First, let's imagine that you did not discount the future, so that your discount weight on future utils is 1. Then you would skip the hot fudge sundae, since the costs exceed the benefits.

$$\text{Benefit} - \text{Cost} = \text{Net benefits},$$

**Utility** in economics is a measure of satisfaction or happiness that comes from consuming a good or service.

A **util** is an individual unit of utility.

A **discount weight** multiplies delayed utils to translate them into current utils.

or

$$6 - 8 = -2.$$

Since the net benefit is negative, you decide not to eat the sundae.

Suppose instead that you do discount the future. Then, it's not obvious what you would do. For example, if your discount weight were $1/2$, then

$$(\text{Immediate benefit}) - (\text{Discounted value of delayed cost}) = 6 - (\tfrac{1}{2})8 = +2.$$

This calculation implies that you would eat the sundae, since the net benefit is positive.

Now suppose that you care a bit more about the future. Suppose that you discount the future with a weight of $7/8$. In other words, we are now assuming that a util in the future is worth $7/8$ as much as a util today. Then we have

$$(\text{Immediate benefit}) - (\text{Discounted value of delayed cost}) = 6 - (\tfrac{7}{8})8 = -1.$$

With a discount weight of $7/8$, the delayed discounted cost is $(7/8)8 = 7$. This is high enough to exceed the immediate benefit of eating the sundae, which is 6. Since $7 > 6$, you decide to forgo the sundae.

These examples illustrate an important general principle. The greater your discount weight—in other words, the more highly you weight things that happen in the future—the more your current decisions are driven by the future consequences of those decisions.

## Preference Reversals

Let's now enrich our sundae example by thinking about the way that you discount over several days. Suppose that you discount in the following special way. You place full weight on the present and half weight on all future days.

| | Today | Tomorrow | Day After Tomorrow |
|---|---|---|---|
| Weight | 1 | $1/2$ | $1/2$ |

This is a slightly odd pattern of weights. It implies that you psychologically draw a sharp distinction between now and all later periods. To you, what really matters is whether a reward comes now (today) or later. Note that the weight you put on tomorrow is the same as the weight you put on the day after tomorrow. For you, all future days are roughly alike. It is today that is special. We call this type of preference pattern *present bias*.

Let's again think about your preferences for eating ice cream. Today, you are happy to eat the ice cream, because the immediate benefit exceeds the discounted value of the delayed cost:

$$(\text{Immediate benefit}) - (\text{Discounted value of delayed cost}) = 6 - (\tfrac{1}{2})8 = 2.$$

Suppose however, that the ice cream parlor is unexpectedly closed today. Your friend asks you if you'd like to come back tomorrow. What is your answer?

From today's perspective, both tomorrow and the day after tomorrow have the same weight of 1/2. From today's perspective, the value of eating ice cream tomorrow is

$$(\text{Discounted value of delayed benefit}) - (\text{Discounted value of delayed cost})$$
$$= (\tfrac{1}{2})6 - (\tfrac{1}{2})8 = -1.$$

Because the discounted net benefit is negative, you decide not to eat ice cream tomorrow.

This preference pattern is an example of a *preference reversal*. You decided that you wanted to eat ice cream today. But you also decided that you do not want to eat ice cream tomorrow. Of course, this is not entirely consistent. Once the sun rises tomorrow morning, it will once again be like today and you'll once again want to eat ice cream. If you are always planning to stop eating ice cream tomorrow, when will your diet actually begin?

Preference reversals arise from discount weights like the ones described above. Specifically, those discount weights imply that today gets much more weight than tomorrow does, but tomorrow and the day after tomorrow receive the same (or nearly the same) weight. There are also discount weights that do not generate preference reversals.

Most economists do not have a view on what discount weights you should have. Instead, we believe that discount weights reflect your tastes. If you sharply devalue things that occur in the future, you have low future discount weights. If you care about the future as much as the present, you have future discount weights that are close to 1. Economists are interested in measuring people's discount weights. Knowing how consumers discount the future helps economists predict people's choices and design public policies that suit people's preferences for intertemporal trade-offs.

## CHOICE & CONSEQUENCE

### Failing to Anticipate Preference Reversals

There is nothing necessarily irrational about a preference reversal, such as those that we have discussed. However, it is not rational to mispredict those preference changes. For example, if you join an expensive gym expecting to exercise twice a week for the next year but you never actually exercise, that's a forecasting error. Your forecast is irrational if you keep mistakenly believing that you are going to start exercising in the near future. At some point, you need to admit to yourself that you are not going to use the gym, so you can then cancel your membership.

Rational people will correctly anticipate their own future behavior. For example, if you are never going to exercise, then you should not pay for a gym membership in the first place. Or maybe you should find a way to force yourself to exercise—perhaps by making a commitment to meet a friend at the gym. To make optimal choices, we need to correctly anticipate our own future behavior. Basing your forecast on your current preference for future behavior is not necessarily rational. You need to base your forecast on the preferences that you will hold when the moment to act actually arrives.

It's easy to *intend* to write your term paper tomorrow. It's easy to *intend* to exercise tomorrow. It's easy to *intend* to get out of bed at 7 A.M. tomorrow. Do your good intentions match your actions?

If you are looking for a way to force yourself to live up to your good intentions, you could explore an option like using an outside "enforcer." For example, there is a Web site called stickk.com, where you can make a monetary commitment to exercise, quit smoking, wake up on time, or anything else that you are trying to do. On this Web site you can pledge, for instance, that if you fail to go to the gym, you will donate $100 to an organization that you dislike—such as the campaign of a candidate that you don't support. After making this irrevocable pledge, you choose a "referee" who can easily monitor your activities (and be relied on to report truthfully). If you go to the gym, this referee tells stickk.com that you succeeded, and you keep your $100. If you don't go to the gym, the referee reports that you failed, and your credit card is automatically charged $100 to pay the anti-campaign. Would this motivate you to exercise?

## EVIDENCE-BASED ECONOMICS

### Q: Do people exhibit a preference for immediate gratification?

This looks like your lucky day. You have just been approached by a market tester taking orders for *free* snacks. Here is the list of options: apple, banana, potato chips, Mars bar, Snickers bar, or *borrelnoten*. (You happen to be Dutch, so you know that borrelnoten is a popular salty snack in the Netherlands.)

Order the snack you want, and the market tester will return in a week to bring you whatever you chose. Which free snack would you select now to eat next week? Pause for a moment and think about it before continuing.

One week later, the market tester returns and tells you that what you chose a week ago does not matter after all. Instead, you can choose whatever you want from the original list of snacks, regardless of what you previously ordered. Do you think you would pick the same snack that you chose a week ago? Or would you switch? If you switched, how do you think your choice might change now that you are going to immediately eat whatever you choose?

When Dutch workers were asked to order a snack 1 week in advance, 74 percent asked for a healthy snack: bananas or apples.[2] However, when the researchers came back a week later and offered the same subjects the choice of a snack for immediate consumption, only 30 percent of the workers chose fruit. On average, subjects exhibited a preference reversal. Asked ahead of time, they ordered something healthy. But when the moment of truth arrived, many subjects switched their priorities and went for the salty snack or the candy.

People exhibit many kinds of preference reversals. On Sunday night, students decide to get to the library early on Monday morning. On Monday morning, students sleep in. Would-be exercisers pay for gym memberships with good intentions. But it turns out that it's never the right time to exercise, and visits fall short of expectations. Dieters have good intentions about what they will eat later in the day. But when the dessert cart arrives, the diet is postponed until the next day. People choose hard work, exercise, and healthy snacks for their *future* selves. But they want immediate gratification for the present. This leads to a pattern of preference reversals, as patient plans for the future are often overturned when the future arrives.

Why do we resolve to eat healthfully before we go to dinner and then change our minds when the dessert cart arrives?

**Question**

Do people exhibit a preference for immediate gratification?

**Answer**

When picking a snack a week in advance, people choose relatively healthy foods, like an apple. When picking a snack for immediate consumption, people choose relatively unhealthy foods, like a chocolate bar.

**Data**

A field experiment involving 200 Dutch workers between the ages of 20 and 40. The experiment was conducted by Daniel Read and Barbara van Leeuwen.

**Caveat**

Did people learn something meaningful during the intervening week that made them change their minds? Or did they really experience a conflict between good intentions (eat fruit next week) and less healthy actions (take the chocolate when it's snack time)?

## 15.4 Probability and Risk

We've completed our discussion of how time affects the value of economic goods and services. We now turn to our other major topic in this chapter: *risk*.

**Risk** exists when an outcome is not known with certainty in advance.

To an economist, **risk** exists when outcomes are not known with certainty in advance. Risk can even exist if all possible outcomes are "good" outcomes. For example, if you are a contestant on a game show and you will win either $500 or $5,000 (and have no chance of going home empty handed), it is still the case that your outcome is risky. If something is risky, then it is said to have a component that is **random**.

If something is risky, then it is said to have a component that is **random**.

### Roulette Wheels and Probabilities

To understand risk, it is useful to start by thinking about a roulette wheel. In an American casino, a roulette wheel has thirty-eight equal-sized pockets, or "slots." The person in charge of a roulette wheel is called the croupier. The croupier spins a small white ball around the outer ring of the roulette wheel. The ball starts to slow down and falls into the center of the wheel. The ball bounces around the center of the wheel, eventually coming to rest in one of the thirty-eight pockets.

An American roulette wheel has thirty-eight pockets. The croupier spins the ball along the outer ring of the roulette wheel.

If a roulette wheel is not rigged by the casino—there are laws against that—there is a 1-in-38 chance that the ball will land in any particular pocket. Without getting too philosophical, let's analyze what this statement means and how we can use roulette wheels to understand most of what you need to know about risk.

To make our discussion easier, imagine a different, hypothetical roulette wheel with 100 pockets, labeled from 1 to 100. We're going to work with this 100-pocket roulette wheel for the rest of the chapter. Suppose we spin our new 100-pocket wheel once. What is the chance that you will win if you bet on the number 79 (and no other number)? The answer is 1 in 100:

$$\text{Likelihood of winning if you bet on a single number} = \frac{1}{100} = 0.01 = 1\%.$$

Suppose instead that you bet on both the numbers 79 and 16. What is the chance you will win in this scenario? There are now two ways to win—either by spinning 79 or by spinning 16. So the likelihood of winning is 2 in 100:

$$\text{Likelihood of winning if you bet on two numbers} = \frac{2}{100} = 0.02 = 2\%.$$

You can see the pattern here. Now suppose that you have bets on the following ten different numbers: 11, 22, 33, 44, 55, 66, 77, 88, 99, and 100. What is the chance of winning? You have ten ways to win, and there are 100 possible outcomes. So the likelihood of winning is 10 in 100:

$$\text{Likelihood of winning if you bet on ten numbers} = \frac{10}{100} = 0.1 = 10\%.$$

A **probability** is the frequency with which something occurs.

A **probability** is the frequency with which something occurs. In the world of our imaginary roulette wheel, the probability of a specific number coming up is 1 in 100, which we can write as a ratio: 1/100, or 1 percent. Think of the ratio as the frequency of the event occurring.

The probability that one of $N$ particular numbers comes up is just $N/100$. Here are two examples. First, because there are 50 even numbers from 1 to 100 ($N = 50$), the probability of spinning an even number is 50/100, which is 0.5, or 50 percent. Second, the probability of spinning a number less than or equal to 60 is 60/100, which is 0.6, or 60 percent.

### Independence and the Gambler's Fallacy

When two random outcomes are **independent**, knowing about one outcome does not help you predict the other outcome.

Fair roulette wheels have a special property. The outcome of one spin of the wheel will not help you predict the outcome of the next spin. This lack of connection between spins is called *independence*. When two random outcomes are **independent**, knowing about one outcome does not help you predict the other outcome.

## LETTING THE
# DATA SPEAK

## Roulette Wheels and Elections

We can also use roulette wheels to think about political events. As voting for the 2016 U.S. presidential election got under way, the leading political forecaster (Nate Silver)[3] was predicting a 28 percent chance of a victory for the Republican candidate, Donald Trump, and a 72 percent chance of a victory for the Democratic candidate, Hillary Clinton. These are the chances of a Trump or Clinton victory (*not* a prediction about the share of voters who would choose Trump or Clinton). Using our roulette wheel, you can picture this as 28 pockets marked "Trump presidency" and 72 pockets marked "Clinton presidency."

As the polls came in, many political commentators (and Clinton voters) expressed complete shock that Trump had won. However, the people reading Nate Silver's forecasts probably weren't very surprised (if they understood probability, as you now do). On our hypothetical roulette wheel, there were more pockets marked Clinton, but that didn't mean that a Trump presidency was impossible or even very unlikely. Of the 100 pockets on the wheel, 28 were for Trump. Accordingly, the chance of a Trump victory was about equal to the chance that you would find an undergraduate sleeping if you picked a random time during a weekday to call her: 7/24 = 29 percent.[4] Once we put it that way, it's easy to see why Nate Silver's readers should not have been shocked when Trump won.

At first glance, this independence property seems like a natural feature of roulette wheels. After all, if the outcome of the next spin were partly predictable, that might give gamblers an advantage over the house. But the idea that one spin does not predict the next pushes you to accept some interesting consequences.

Suppose you are playing at our imaginary wheel and that you have been betting on the number 64 every time. Suppose that 64 comes up three times in a row. Wow. That was good luck! You might be tempted to say that the table is "hot." Or that the number 64 is "hot." Maybe you are on a streak? Alternatively, you might decide to reach the *opposite* conclusion. Maybe you should bet on a different number now that 64 has come up three times in a row. It would be shocking if 64 came up again!

These are all tempting conclusions, but they are all wrong. If you are betting on 64 with each spin, the *likelihood of winning on the next spin is always 1 in 100*. This is true whether or not 64 came up on the last spin. This is true even if 64 came up ten times in a row on the last ten spins. Whatever the past history of spins, the likelihood that 64 will come up on the next spin is always 1 in 100.

Many gamblers don't understand the independence property. Some gamblers believe in streaks: if they got lucky on the last spin, they mistakenly believe that they have a higher chance of winning on the next spin. This mistake is called the *hot hand fallacy*. Other gamblers believe that the roulette wheel somehow evens out from one spin to the next: "if the ball landed on the number 64 in the last spin, the chance of 64 coming up on the next spin is less than 1 in 100." This last mistake—believing the wheel somehow tends to avoid repeats—is called the *gambler's fallacy*.

You simply need to remember that roulette wheels don't have memory. What happened on the last spin has no bearing on the next spin. In the language of statistics, the spins are independent of one another. Failing to appreciate independence is a good way to get drawn into gambling. If you mistakenly believe that the last spin somehow helps you predict the next one, then you might mistakenly believe that you know how to "beat" the casino. Of course, you'll have it backwards, because the more you play roulette, the more money you should expect to lose. We'll calculate how much you'll lose a little bit later in this chapter.

## Expected Value

Now that you've had an introduction to probabilities, we can put these ideas to work. We are going to calculate an **expected value**, which is the sum of all possible outcomes or values, each weighted by its probability of occurring. To explain what this means, it is easiest to work through an example.

**Expected value** is the sum of all possible outcomes or values, each weighted by its probability of occurring.

Let's return to the imaginary roulette wheel. Suppose that you have the following agreement with the house. "If the ball ends up on the number 64, you win $100. If the ball ends up on 15, you lose $200. If the ball ends up on any other number, nothing happens." How much will you win on average? In other words, how much would you win on average if you played this bet many times?

We can calculate this average payoff by multiplying the probability of each possible outcome by the dollars associated with each outcome. Here's how:

$$(\text{Probability of "64"}) \times (\$100) + (\text{Probability of "15"}) \times (-\$200)$$
$$+ (\text{Probability of all other numbers}) \times (\$0)$$

$$= \frac{1}{100}(\$100) + \frac{1}{100}(-\$200) + \frac{98}{100}(\$0)$$
$$= \$1 - \$2 + \$0$$
$$= -\$1.$$

The probabilities are 1/100 for the outcome of winning $100 (spinning a "64"), 1/100 for the outcome of losing $200 (spinning a "15"), and 98/100 for the outcome that "nothing happens" (spinning any number other than "64" and "15"). The dollar outcomes are weighted by their associated probabilities. The average payoff, which is the expected value of this bet, is −$1.

Now consider a different bet. "If the ball ends up on 50 or a number less than 50, you win $200. If the ball ends up on 51 or a number greater than 51, you lose $100." What is the expected value of this bet?

Since there are 50 numbers on the imaginary roulette wheel less than or equal to 50, the probability of winning $200 is 50/100, or 50 percent. Because there are 50 numbers on the imaginary roulette wheel greater than or equal to 51, the probability of losing $100 is 50/100, or 50 percent. Therefore, the expected value of this gamble is $50:

$$(\text{Probability of winning } \$200) \times (\$200) + (\text{Probability of losing } \$100) \times (-\$100)$$

$$= \frac{50}{100}(\$200) + \frac{50}{100}(-\$100)$$

$$= \$100 - \$50$$

$$= \$50.$$

### Extended Warranties

Almost all risk that we face is outside casinos. We can use the imaginary roulette wheel to study these kinds of "gambles" too. We'll illustrate the general applicability of these tools by using them to study the economic costs and benefits of an extended warranty.

Assume that you are buying a $300 TV from BestBuy. The TV automatically comes with a 1-year warranty. Suppose that you can extend that warranty so that it covers years two and three. Suppose further that the extended warranty costs $75. This is the typical cost of an extended warranty on a $300 TV. Is the extended warranty a good deal?

## CHOICE & CONSEQUENCE

### Is Gambling Worthwhile?

We've explained that roulette tables don't have memory. They don't have patterns; they don't have streaks; they don't avoid repeats. Because there are no patterns that gamblers can exploit, gamblers can't beat the casino in a game of roulette. Let's calculate how much gamblers lose when they play roulette.

We'll keep our imaginary 100-pocket roulette wheel, but we'll set things up to roughly mimic the odds that gamblers have at a real American roulette table. Assume that the rules work the following way. If the wheel spins any number from 1 through 47, you win x dollars. If the wheel spins any number from 48 through 100, you lose x dollars. What is your expected winning from playing this game (with "bet" x)?

$$\text{Expected winning} = \frac{47}{100}(\$x) + \frac{53}{100}(-\$x)$$

$$= \$x\left[\frac{47}{100} - \frac{53}{100}\right]$$

$$= \$x \times \frac{-6}{100}$$

$$= -6\% \text{ of } \$x.$$

On average, you will lose 6 percent of the amount you bet. Of course, this doesn't mean that you will actually lose this exact amount on each outing to the roulette table. Some nights you'll lose more and some nights you'll lose less, depending on your luck on that visit to the casino. But on average, you'll lose 6 percent of the money you bet.

You now know the expected cost of playing roulette.[5] If you bet $100 per spin of the wheel, then you should expect to lose $6 on average per spin. If the wheel spins forty times in an hour, and you bet on each spin, you should expect to lose 40 × $6 = $240 per hour.

Economists are not interested in scolding people about gambling. If gambling is fun for you, economists won't try to talk you out of the casino. But we do want you to understand the costs of gambling, so you can make an informed decision. Economists and statisticians can't help rolling their eyes when people say that they have a system that enables them to break even at the roulette table. The actual expected financial cost is about 6 percent of each bet that you make. It's up to you to decide whether gambling is entertaining enough to justify this implied price.

Let's calculate the net present value of the extended warranty. To do this, we'll need to estimate the frequency with which TVs break down. Suppose that each year, the probability of a breakdown is about $\frac{10}{100} = 10$ percent. In other words, each year the chance of a breakdown is equivalent to the chance of spinning a number from 1 through 10 on our imaginary 100-pocket roulette wheel. (This is the actual frequency of breakdowns for the least reliable brands.)

If you have an extended warranty, what do you get in the event of a breakdown? Your out-of-date TV is repaired or replaced. But an out-of-date TV is not as valuable as it was when you originally bought it. During its second year of use, you can replace the original $300 TV with an equally good TV by spending only $250. During its third year of use, you can replace the original TV with an equally good TV by spending only $200. As technology improves, you can replace your old TV with less expensive, more recently built models. To sum up, your TV is worth only $250 in year two and only $200 in year three.

The cost of the extended warranty is paid now. But the benefit of getting a potential replacement TV is realized in year two or year three. We need to discount those delayed benefits. Let's assume that you are buying the TV and the extended warranty on credit, and your interest rate on your credit card is 10 percent.

Now we have all the information that we need to calculate the net present value of buying the extended warranty:

$$\frac{10}{100} \times \frac{\$250}{(1 + 0.10)^2} + \frac{10}{100} \times \frac{\$200}{(1 + 0.10)^3} - \$75 = \$20.66 + \$15.03 - \$75$$

$$= -\$39.31.$$

Let's interpret the individual terms in the equation above. The first term, $\frac{10}{100} \times \frac{\$250}{(1 + 0.10)^2}$, is the value of having the extended warranty during the second year of ownership. The TV breaks with a probability of $\frac{10}{100} = 10$ percent. If it breaks, the extended warranty gives you the right to demand a replacement, which is worth $250. To calculate the present value of this replacement, we divide by $(1 + r)^2 = (1 + 0.10)^2$, where the exponent of 2 reflects the assumption that the payment is received 2 years from today.

The second term, $\frac{10}{100} \times \frac{\$200}{(1 + 0.10)^3}$, is the value of having the extended warranty during the third year of ownership. Once again, the TV breaks in the third year with a probability of $\frac{10}{100} = 10$ percent. If it breaks, the extended warranty gives you the right to demand a replacement, which is worth $200. To calculate the present value of this replacement, we divide by $(1 + r)^3 = (1 + 0.10)^3$, where the exponent of 3 reflects the assumption that the payment is received three years from today.

The third term, $-\$75$, is the cost of the extended warranty, which is paid at the moment that you purchase the TV. Because it is a cash outflow from you to BestBuy, it is negative.

The net present value is negative and large. As you can see above, the extended warranty provides expected benefits—in other words, the probability-weighted and discounted replacement TVs—with the present value of

$$\$20.66 + \$15.03 = \$35.69,$$

but the extended warranty costs $75. So the net present value of the extended warranty is $35.69 − $75 = −$39.31. Extended warranties are a bad deal for most consumers, unless you are psychologically highly averse to the prospect of a broken TV and the financial cost of replacing it.

Moreover, our analysis ignored some additional reasons to avoid extended warranties, including the potential to misplace the warranty and time-consuming logistics: "Please call again later. Call volume to our warranty center is heavier than anticipated."

## 15.5 Risk Preferences

Empirical evidence reveals that many people actually are extremely averse to the chance of a small financial loss and are therefore willing to buy expensive insurance to reduce the risk of such losses (like the extended warranty that we just discussed). Consequently, stores like BestBuy aggressively market extended warranties, and these extended warranties are the source of most of BestBuy's accounting profits. BestBuy doesn't make an accounting profit when it sells a television set without an extended warranty.

**Loss aversion** is the idea that people psychologically weight a loss much more heavily than they psychologically weight a gain.

A high level of aversion to small financial losses is referred to as *loss aversion*. **Loss aversion** is the idea that people psychologically weight a loss much more heavily than they psychologically weight a gain. When researchers empirically study this difference in weights, the researchers usually find that losses are psychologically weighted twice as heavily as gains. This degree of loss aversion implies that a person would be indifferent between $0 for sure or a coin toss with the following two outcomes: heads is a gain of $200 and tails is a loss of $100. With loss aversion, the psychological value of this coin toss is

$$\frac{50}{100} \times (\$200) + \frac{50}{100} \times 2 \times (-\$100) = \$0.$$

Note that only the loss is weighted by the special factor of 2, which reflects the impact of loss aversion.

Economists are of two minds about loss aversion. Some believe that loss aversion is a bias that students should be taught to overcome. Other economists believe that loss aversion is a legitimate preference that should be respected. Daniel Kahneman and Amos Tversky first showed that loss aversion is a common behavior, though they didn't take a position on whether loss aversion is a bias or a legitimate preference.[6] Their work led to a Nobel Prize that was awarded to Kahneman. (Tversky died at a young age, and the Nobel is not given posthumously.)

Loss aversion is one important example of a risk preference. In general, economists distinguish three categories of risk preferences: *risk aversion*, *risk seeking*, and *risk neutrality*. To understand these concepts, consider a person choosing between two investments with the *same* expected rate of return but one investment has a fixed return and the other investment has a risky return. For example, imagine that the safe investment has a guaranteed rate of return of 3 percent, whereas the risky investment has a 50 percent chance of returning 6 percent and a 50 percent chance of a returning 0 percent. Both investments have an expected return of 3 percent, but they achieve that expected return with different amounts of risk. Which investment would you choose if you were putting $1,000 into the investment?

When people are **risk averse**, they prefer the investment with the fixed return. When people are **risk seeking**, they prefer the investment with the risky return. When people are **risk neutral**, they don't care about the level of risk and are therefore indifferent between the two investments. Thousands of empirical studies have shown that people are risk averse in most situations.

Consider a person choosing between two investments with the same expected rate of return but one investment has a fixed return and the other investment has a risky return. When people are **risk averse**, they prefer the investment with the fixed return. When people are **risk seeking**, they prefer the investment with the risky return. When people are **risk neutral**, they don't care about the level of risk and are therefore indifferent between the two investments.

# Summary

- Most decisions have benefits and costs that occur at different times. To optimize, economic agents need to translate all benefits and costs into a single time period, so they can be compared.

- Interest is the payment received for temporarily giving up the use of money.

- The present value of a future payment is the amount of money that would need to be invested today to produce that future payment. The net present value of a project is the present value of the benefits minus the present value of the costs.

- Utility is a measure of satisfaction or well-being. Utils are individual units of utility. A discount weight multiplies delayed utils to translate them into current utils.

- Risk means that some of the costs and benefits are not fixed in advance.

- A probability is the frequency with which something occurs. For example, a probability of 0.12 means that the event will happen 12 percent of the time on average, or 12 times (on average) out of every 100 attempts. An expected value is a probability-weighted value.

- Loss aversion is the property that people psychologically weight a loss much more heavily than they psychologically weight a gain.

- If two investments have the same expected return, but one investment has a fixed return and the other investment has a risky return, people with risk aversion prefer the investment with the fixed return.

# Key Terms

principal *p. 362*
interest *p. 362*
future value *p. 362*
compound interest equation or future
  value equation *p. 363*
present value *p. 366*
net present value *p. 366*

utility *p. 367*
util *p. 367*
discount weight *p. 367*
risk *p. 370*
random *p. 370*
probability *p. 371*
independent *p. 371*

expected value *p. 372*
loss aversion *p. 375*
risk averse *p. 375*
risk seeking *p. 375*
risk neutral *p. 375*

# Questions

*All questions are available in MyEconLab for practice and instructor assignment.*

1. Is $1,000 received today worth as much as $1,000 received 1 year from now? Explain your answer.

2. How is the present value of a future payment calculated?

3. How is net present value used to decide whether a project should be undertaken?

4. The greater your discount weight, the more your current decisions are driven by the future consequences of those decisions. Do you agree? Explain.

5. What is meant by present bias?

6. What is meant by a preference reversal?

7. When is an outcome risky?

8. How is the probability of an event defined?

9. When are outcomes said to be independent? What is meant by the gambler's fallacy?

10. What is meant by expected value? How is it calculated?

11. Why might it make sense to avoid paying for extended warranties on TVs and small home appliances?

# Problems

*All problems are available in MyEconLab for practice and instructor assignment.*

1. The "Rule of 70" is a simple way to estimate how long it will take something to double in value: divide 70 by the annual percentage growth rate; the number you calculate is the doubling time, in years. For example, $70/4 = 17.5$; thus it takes about 17.5 years for a bank account to double in value, assuming 4 percent interest. Based on this method, what is the doubling time given an interest rate of 2 percent, 5 percent, and 10 percent?

2. When you were born, your parents deposited $10,000 in the bank. The bank offered a fixed interest rate of 4 percent. On your eighteenth birthday, your parents decide to withdraw the money that they deposited to pay for your college tuition. How much money can they expect to withdraw? Assume that interest is compounded annually.

3. Suppose you won the Powerball lottery on January 1, 2017. You can choose to receive the entire amount of $400 million either as a lump sum on January 1, 2017, or you can receive four equal annual payments of $102 million paid on January 1 in 2017, 2018, 2019, and 2020. Assume that your lottery winnings are not taxed.

   a. Which option has a higher present value? Assume the interest rate is 2 percent.

   b. Instead suppose that the interest rate is 1 percent. Would your answer to part (a) change?

4. You are considering purchasing a new piece of equipment for your factory. The equipment will cost $3,000 right now and can be used for 3 years. If you purchase it, the machine will generate earnings of $1,100 at the end of its first year of operation, $1,210 at the end of its second year of operation; and $1,331 at the end of its third year of operation. After that, the machine will generate no more earnings and have no resale value.

   a. What is the net present value of this investment if the interest rate is 8 percent? 10 percent? 12 percent?

   b. What is the highest interest rate at which you would be willing to buy this equipment?

5. Stafford loans are student loans that the federal government provides to graduate and undergraduate students to fund their education. Since Stafford loans can be extended up to 30 years, the Congressional Budget Office calculates the cost of these loans by discounting the future cash flows from the loan using the interest rate on the 30-year Treasury bond. The risk of default on the 30-year Treasury bond is extremely low. In contrast, over the life of a Stafford loan, on average about 20 percent of the amount due is never repaid. What do you think are the implications of using the yield on the 30-year bond to calculate the cost of student loans?

6. You observe a banker give $75 for a bond that pays out $100 in one year. Based on this observation, what do you conclude about the interest rate? Suppose that the price of this bond today suddenly increases to $80. Now what do you conclude about the interest rate? (Remember even though the price changes, the bond itself still pays $100 a year from now.) Does an increase in the price of bonds today imply market interests rates have gone up or gone down?

7. This chapter talked about the idea of independent events.

   a. Suppose you draw a card from a standard deck of cards, you put that card back in the deck, and draw a second card. Are the events "Draw a diamond the first time" and "Draw a diamond the second time" independent events?

   b. Suppose you draw a card from a standard deck of cards, you do *not* put that card back in the deck, and draw a second card. Are the events "Draw a diamond the first time" and "Draw a diamond the second time" independent events?

8. Say whether or not each of the following statements assumes *independence* between events:

   a. "There is no such thing as a 'hot hand': A basketball player is just as likely to make her next shot regardless of whether she made her last shot."

   b. "I notice that when one student scores above average, there is a higher probability that other students in the same classroom will also score above average."

   c. "We are totally safe since we own many mortgage-backed securities, and the probability of default for one security does not depend on the probability of default of our other securities."

9. You are considering playing a card game. The rules of the game are such that you pick a card from a standard deck of fifty-two cards and if the card is a diamond, you win $30. The catch is, you have to pay the dealer a fee of $10 to play this game. What is the expected value of this gamble? [Hint: In a standard deck of cards, $1/4$ of the cards are diamonds.]

10. Your house is worth $400,000, and you have $300,000 in a savings account. There is a 1 percent chance of a fire in your house during the next year. If the fire occurs, there will be $300,000 in damage.

    a. Suppose you do not have fire insurance. If the fire occurs, you will have to pay $300,000 to repair your house. What is the expected value of your wealth (including both the value of your home and your savings account) at the end of the year?

    b. We will say that an insurance policy is fair insurance if the premium for the policy equals the expected value of the claims the insurance company will have to pay. An insurance company offers you a fire insurance policy. If a fire occurs, it will pay to repair your home. The annual premium for the policy is $3,000. Has the insurance company offered you fair insurance?

    c. If you are risk averse, would you buy this insurance policy? Defend your answer.

11. You are a venture capitalist who has just purchased a stake in a small company. You believe that a year from now this company may no longer exist, in which case your stake is worthless; there is an 80 percent chance of this happening. However, there is a 10 percent chance your stake will be worth $1 million dollars, and a 10 percent chance your stake will be worth $20 million dollars. What is the expected value of your stake in this young company?

12. Assume the interest rate is 50 percent. What is the present value of a payment of $60 paid 1 year from now? How about the present value of $60 paid today *and* $60 paid a year from now? *Challenge question*: What about $60 paid today, plus $60 paid a year from now, plus $60 paid the year after that, and so on, *forever*? [Hint: If $x < 1$, then $1 + x + x^2 + \ldots = 1/(1 - x)$.]

# 16 The Economics of Information

## Why do new cars lose considerable value the minute they are driven off the lot?

You're ready to drive your shiny new Kia Optima off the dealer's lot. You've saved carefully for the down payment, and now it's yours. Your older, shoot-from-the-hip brother—your consultant in all things car related—is with you as you take the turn out of the lot.

"Well," he observes, "your car just went down in value."

"What do you mean?" you ask, a bit indignantly.

"If you sold this car tomorrow to someone, it would go for far less than you just paid."

"No way."

"Any future buyer is going to worry about lemons."

"But this isn't a lemon!"

"The buyer won't know that. So the price will have to adjust."

Leave it to your brother to look at the glass-half-empty situation, and make your car out to be a lemon—a low-value, defective car. But he has actually touched on an important economic concept called *asymmetric information*, which means that one party has superior information to another party. How does such a situation fit into the models that we have presented thus far? The answer is not very well, because so far, we have only considered cases where information is symmetric—that is, buyers and sellers have exactly the same information about the goods and services up for sale. In this chapter, we'll learn about situations in which an agent on one side of the market has an informational advantage over an agent on the other side. For example, used car

## CHAPTER OUTLINE

- In many markets, buyers and sellers have different information, which can lead to market inefficiencies.

- Asymmetry in information is due to either hidden characteristics or hidden actions.

- In cases with hidden characteristics, agents can use their private information to decide whether to participate in a transaction or a market, causing adverse selection.

- In cases with hidden actions, an agent can take an action that adversely affects another agent, causing moral hazard.

- There are both private and government solutions to reduce the effects of adverse selection and moral hazard.

salespersons know more about their cars than buyers do, you know more about your health than health insurance companies do, and investment banks know more about their financial risk than regulators do. Such asymmetry has important implications for economic decision making. We also discuss the interesting market and government solutions that have arisen to solve the negative effects of asymmetric information and see how thinking about information asymmetries can help us answer our opening question.

## 16.1 Asymmetric Information

Upon some reflection, you will find that life presents many interactions in which one party to a transaction has different information from the other—information that the other party cares about. We refer to such discrepancies in knowledge between buyers and sellers as **asymmetric information**. We also say that the party with information that the other party to the transaction does not possess has *private information*.

We can distinguish two kinds of asymmetric information: first, **hidden characteristics**, in which one party in a transaction observes some characteristics of the good or service that the other doesn't observe; second, **hidden actions**, in which one party in a transaction takes actions that are relevant for, but not observed by, the other party. For instance, rust patches on a secondhand car can be hidden characteristics—although the car salesperson knows all too well about their existence, potential customers might not. You can probably think of even more examples of hidden actions; consider, for example, factory workers who try to hide from their employer the fact that they are taking an extra 10 minutes on their lunch break.

Both types of asymmetric information can have profound impacts on markets—impacts that are, from a social standpoint, quite negative. If the information gaps are large enough, it is possible in theory for a market to completely shut down, even if everyone could benefit from trade! Interestingly, the people who suffer from such market failure include not only those with an informational disadvantage but also those with the extra information. We'll explain why shortly. Given the large gains from exchange that asymmetric information can destroy, it's not

In a market with **asymmetric information**, the information available to sellers and buyers differs.

**Hidden characteristics** exist when one party in a transaction observes characteristics of the good or service that the other doesn't observe.

**Hidden actions** occur when one side takes actions that are relevant for, but not observed by, the other party.

> If information gaps are large enough, it is possible in theory for a market to completely shut down, even if everyone could benefit from trade.

surprising that many institutions have arisen to mitigate its effects. Before we get to those institutions, though, let's first look in more depth at transactions with hidden characteristics and then at transactions with hidden actions.

## Hidden Characteristics: Adverse Selection in the Used Car Market

Suppose that instead of buying a brand-new car, as in our chapter-opening scenario, you decide to buy a used car. You begin your search by going online and scanning the local newspaper ads. You find a few nice-sounding vehicles in your price range, including a Ford Fusion and a Toyota Prius. But you end up focusing on a Dodge Smart Car, advertised for $5,000. As you think about buying the car, though, a few doubts begin to creep into your mind: why is this person selling such a neat car for only $5,000? Does he expect it to break down? Did it already have problems? Does it look clean because it was just fished out of the local pond? You can't answer these questions; only the owner has information on the extent of his own car's problems, so you're justifiably afraid you might be stuck with a product of low quality—in this case, a lemon.

Suspicious of such private sellers, you decide to try a used car lot. There you find slightly higher prices for similar cars than you found online. You see a car you like, but, once again, uncertainty enters your mind: where did the dealer get this car? Was it repossessed from an owner who never had the oil changed? Maybe the fresh coat of paint is hiding fire damage. Will the dealer honor his warranty claim? As with the private sellers, the dealer knows much of this information. But such private information is valuable, so there is an incentive for the dealer to withhold important facts about the car. Have you ever heard of a seller admitting that the odometer has been rolled back? Well, the National Highway Traffic Safety Administration determined that more than 450,000 vehicles sold each year have odometers that have been rolled back.

How does such information asymmetry affect the market? To illustrate, let's say that you decide to purchase the Dodge Smart Car offered by a private seller. To understand how information asymmetry plays out, we first need to make some simplifying assumptions. Let's assume that there are two kinds of cars available: high-quality cars ("peaches") and low-quality cars ("lemons"). Let's further suppose that to you, these cars look exactly the same, but you know that half of them are lemons and half are peaches. Only the seller actually knows whether he has a lemon or a peach. Because lemons constantly break down and need repairs often, they are worth zero to you and to the seller. In contrast, the peaches are sturdy, reliable vehicles that both you and the seller value. Suppose, for example, that the value of such a peach to you is $5,000 and to the seller is $4,000. What if this market is the same as those standard markets we've studied so far? In that case, we would have a separate price for lemons and a separate price for peaches. Lemons would be priced at $0, and peaches would sell somewhere between $4,000 and $5,000, depending on the number of sellers and buyers in the market. Thus, only peaches would be traded, and there would be gains to trade because buyers would value the cars more than sellers would (in fact, the gains from a trade would be $1,000: $5,000 − $4,000). In this way, at least one of you would be better off because of the trade, and if the price was between $4,000 and $5,000, then both of you would be better off. For example, if you bought the car at $4,500, both you and the dealer would be $500 better off.

So, the outcome when quality is fully observable to everyone is that people in the market are at least as well off after the transaction as before. This is how well-functioning markets work—they raise the welfare of their participants.

But now let's think about what would happen under asymmetric information, where the seller knows if his car is a peach or a lemon but you do not. All that you know is that half of the used cars you are looking at are peaches and half are lemons. You thus recognize that the probability of any particular car being a peach is 50 percent. Suppose also that you are *risk neutral*. You will recall from Chapter 15 that this means you will evaluate risky choices using expected values. For example, suppose a coin is flipped, and if it ends up heads you win $10, and if it ends up tails you lose $10. If you are risk neutral, then this gamble is worth zero to you (or writing it mathematically, $1/2 \times (10) + 1/2 \times (-10) = 0$).

Knowing this, what is the most that you would now be willing to pay for the car? Because you value peaches at $5,000 and lemons at $0, and a car has a 50 percent chance of being either, as a risk-neutral buyer you will evaluate the expected value of buying a car of unknown quality as $1/2 \times (5,000) + 1/2 \times (0) = \$2,500$. This means that if you pay more than $2,500, you will be making a bad choice, since your expected value is $2,500.

Now let's think about the seller, who values peaches at $4,000 and lemons at $0. Would the seller give you a peach for $2,500? No, because he values peaches at $4,000. Instead, at $2,500, only owners of lemons will be offering their cars. Thus, if you are willing to pay $2,500 for a used car, the only car you will ever get from a private seller in this market is a lemon. Because sellers have private information on the car, you can now see what happens in this market: *the best you can do is to buy a lemon!* Knowing this, you are not willing to buy any used car that is actually offered for sale. In this case, asymmetric information causes the entire market to shut down, even when there are substantial gains to trade!

The phenomenon illustrated here is a specific type of asymmetric information problem known as *adverse selection*. **Adverse selection** occurs when one agent in a transaction knows about a hidden characteristic of a good and decides whether to participate in the transaction on the basis of this (private) information. In our example, sellers of lemons gain from entering the market. But the limiting case discussed above shows that it is in theory possible for the market to completely shut down even if everyone could benefit from trade. Ironically, in this case, even the people who have superior information may be harmed.

> In a market with **adverse selection**, one agent in a transaction knows about a hidden characteristic of a good and decides whether to participate in the transaction on the basis of this information.

## Hidden Characteristics: Adverse Selection in the Health Insurance Market

Adverse selection in the used car market arises because sellers have private information. But there are also prominent adverse selection examples in which buyers have private information. One such instance occurs in health insurance markets, where the term "adverse selection" was originally introduced.

As we learned in Chapter 15, risk-averse individuals benefit from having insurance against major risks. Without health insurance, even a routine hospital visit in the United States might cost an individual several thousand dollars, and major surgeries and hospital stays can bankrupt all but the wealthiest of families. It is therefore natural that individuals and families should seek insurance against such risks. Since the passage of the Affordable Care Act (or so-called Obamacare) in 2010, they are in fact mandated to do so, and we will see why such mandates may actually make sense from an economic perspective.

In theory, the health insurance market works just like other insurance markets. Individuals sign up for a health plan and pay monthly premiums. In return, the health insurance company covers a large fraction of the costs for most doctor visits, hospital stays, and procedures.

The problem of adverse selection again complicates things. In the used car market, adverse selection results from the fact that sellers know the quality of their car, while buyers do not. In health insurance markets, there is a similar asymmetry; now, though, *buyers* of insurance have superior information, because they have a better idea about their health than insurance companies do.

Once this asymmetry is in place, the wheels of adverse selection are in motion. To illustrate its effects in health insurance markets, let's assume that there are two types of individuals: high-risk and low-risk. High-risk individuals are less healthy and are more likely to need expensive treatment in the near future. Clearly, health insurance programs will attract a disproportionate number of high-risk individuals. But these are exactly the individuals that health insurance companies do not want to attract, because they are more often in need of expensive care.

Similar to the market for used cars, the adverse selection problem in the health insurance market can create major inefficiencies. One possibility is similar to the extreme outcome that we witnessed in the used car market: in the same way that bad cars drove out good ones, high-risk individuals can drive out low-risk individuals in the health insurance market.

How does this work? Health insurance companies might start charging higher premiums, because they expect to attract many high-risk individuals, but then these higher premiums might discourage low-risk individuals from seeking health insurance. This causes even higher premiums. The cycle, sometimes called the "death spiral," continues, and, in theory, can unravel all the way to its logical conclusion: insurance companies charging such high premiums that no one ends up insured!

## Market Solutions to Adverse Selection: Signaling

Are markets helpless against adverse selection? Not entirely. In practice, there are ways of dealing with it. One prominent solution for used cars is third-party certification markets, such as CARFAX, to ensure that the used car is not a lemon. More generally, we observe Educational Testing Services (ETS) offering SAT tests for college applicants, *U.S. News & World Report* ranking universities, Underwriters Laboratories certifying consumer and industrial products, Moody's reporting corporate bond ratings, and accounting companies auditing financial reports for public corporations.

Such market-based solutions can help move markets plagued by adverse selection toward efficient operation. Another mechanism that has arisen to combat the adverse selection problem is that of warranties. *Warranties*, which we first encountered in Chapter 15, are guarantees of quality issued directly by either the manufacturer or the seller. For example, when you buy a big-screen television, the manufacturer often provides a 1-year warranty on parts and services. For cars, manufacturers typically provide a 3-year, or 36,000-mile, warranty on the major parts, such as the engine and transmission.

**Signaling** refers to an action that an individual with private information takes in order to convince others about his information.

A warranty is an example of **signaling**, in which an individual with private information takes action—sends a signal—to convince someone without the information that his services or his products are high quality. How can a warranty be effective in signaling a high-quality good? The idea is that warranties are particularly expensive for low-quality products, because these tend to break down more often. But then, because low-quality producers will shy away from offering warranties, the very fact that a seller offers a warranty suggests that he or she is likely to be selling a high-quality product. If it were costless for sellers to provide warranties, then the signal would not be informative. But because warranties are potentially very expensive, low-quality goods are less likely to have warranties. In the next Evidence-Based Economics section, we discuss the value of automobile certification in the used car market.

Signaling does not just take place on the seller side of the market. Buyers, too, engage in signaling. For example, how can you, as a buyer of health insurance, send a signal of your quality (health)? One way is to show proof of annual physicals and overall good health prospects in the long run—exercising, not smoking, and not taking a lot of risks. Similarly, in the car insurance market, you signal that you are a safe driver by getting good grades in school and passing your driver competency tests.

| Aaa | smallest degree of risk |
| Aa | very low credit risk |
| A | low credit risk |
| Baa | moderate credit risk |
| Ba | questionable credit quality |
| B | generally poor credit quality |
| Caa | extremely poor credit quality |
| Ca | highly speculative |
| C | potential recovery values are low |

Market-based solutions can help limit adverse selection. Third-party certification mechanisms such as Moody's ratings for corporate bonds, warranties for various products, and SAT tests for college applicants help—to a degree—to balance information asymmetries.

# CHOICE

# &CONSEQUENCE

## Are You Sending a Signal Right Now?

Why do more-educated workers earn more than less-educated workers? We learned in Chapter 11 that workers are paid the value of their marginal product. Thus one reason people are paid differently is because they have different productivities. However, in many jobs, it is difficult to determine individual productivity. For example, in a consulting firm, no two people manage the same client, so it's difficult to say that any one individual did well handling a given case—there isn't a proper comparison available. This is different from the scenario we considered in Chapters 6 and 11, where each Cheeseman worker packaged a definite number of cheese boxes and the production of one worker could be directly compared to that of another worker.

Nobel Prize–winning economist Michael Spence suggested an alternative explanation for why more-educated workers earn more than less-educated ones.[1] Spence developed the theory of signaling, whereby in markets with asymmetric information and adverse selection, individuals could choose costly signals to reveal their private information. Education might be such a signal. With a college degree, you might be telling the world—and in particular, potential employers—that you have been successfully admitted to a selective college program and that you have the capacity to perform well in a variety of courses.

Such signaling is similar to Toshiba providing a warranty for its plasma TVs, or Ford guaranteeing its car engines for 3 years or 36,000 miles. The key to why signaling can work in the case of obtaining a college degree is that the signal is sufficiently scarce (not everybody has such a degree) and it is more costly to obtain for lower-ability students than for higher-ability students—because, for example, lower-ability students have to spend more time and effort to succeed in their studies. These features imply that by acquiring your degree, you are sending a strong signal to your employers that you are a high-ability candidate.

# EVIDENCE-BASED ECONOMICS

## Q: Why do new cars lose considerable value the minute they are driven off the lot?

So is the popular wisdom true that the value of a new car will plunge the instant it is driven off the lot? Are there any data to back up that claim?

Exhibit 16.1 provides several illustrative examples showing that this claim is indeed true. The numbers in the exhibit show the price gap in 2010 between 2009 unused year-old cars and 2009 used year-old cars (both certified used cars and noncertified used cars).

What the numbers show is a 20 to 40 percent price difference between new and used cars. Could these percentage differences be due entirely to a year of wear and tear? Perhaps it's because people don't like driving a car that someone else drove before them? Nobel Prize–winning economist George Akerlof's classic article on the economics of information, published in 1970, starts with the observation that the low price of used cars does not seem entirely justified by wear and tear or by the fact that people don't like driving cars that others have previously owned.[2]

Akerlof proposed an explanation based on asymmetric information. You will recall that this explanation rests on the observation that cars sold by their owners might have low prices because people are worried about getting a lemon. This explanation is supported

**Exhibit 16.1** Price Ranges of New and Used Cars

Used cars sell for about 20 to 40 percent less than new cars of the same model year, particularly when they are not certified by dealers.

| Vehicle | Price Range in 2010 |
| --- | --- |
| 2009 Toyota Prius (new) | $22,000–24,000 |
| 2009 Toyota Prius (dealer certified) | $19,000–22,000 |
| 2009 Toyota Prius (used) | $16,000–20,000 |
| 2009 Honda Civic (new) | $20,000–24,000 |
| 2009 Honda Civic (dealer certified) | $16,000–21,000 |
| 2009 Honda Civic (used) | $12,000–16,000 |
| 2009 Ford Fusion (new) | $19,000–26,000 |
| 2009 Ford Fusion (dealer certified) | $16,000–20,000 |
| 2009 Ford Fusion (used) | $14,000–18,000 |
| 2009 Ford Edge (new) | $25,000–33,000 |
| 2009 Ford Edge (dealer certified) | $24,000–31,000 |
| 2009 Ford Edge (used) | $21,000–24,000 |

by the data in Exhibit 16.1, which show that consumers pay a premium for transacting with dealers instead of with private parties. Even though you probably shouldn't fully trust used car salespersons either, dealer-certified cars come with warranties, and dealers have a reputation to protect, thus reducing the extent of the adverse selection problem and convincing buyers to pay higher prices for such dealer-certified vehicles.

Such evidence suggests the presence of a lemons market, because dealer certification is one way in which customers ensure they aren't getting a lemon. If buyers want to go to private sellers, they take on an increased risk of getting a lemon. However, there are lots of other differences between private sellers and dealers. To find a market for lemons, we would need proof that the used cars sold actually *were* lemons. One way of getting such proof is to study the maintenance records of cars sold and those not sold in the private used car market.

The U.S. Census Bureau Truck Inventory and Use Survey of 1977 allowed economists Michael Pratt and George Hoffer[3] to look at the maintenance records of a random sampling of pickup trucks purchased new and used. They found considerable differences between those cars kept by their original owners and those cars that people bought used. They concluded that there is evidence of lemons actually reaching the market.

Similar evidence has emerged suggesting that lemons might be clogging the used car market in the Basel City region of Switzerland. Economists Winand Emons and George Sheldon[4] analyzed the vehicle-safety inspection records of all cars in that region. They found that the probability of having a major defect was higher among those cars sold privately, supporting the idea of adverse selection in the used car market. Notably, they found exactly the opposite trend in cars sold by dealers who provided certification for used cars, thus supporting the hypothesis that market mechanisms emerge to combat a lemons problem.

**Question**

Why do new cars lose considerable value the minute they are driven off the lot?

**Answer**

Adverse selection considerably influences the private car market.

**Data**

U.S. Census Bureau Truck Inventory and Use Survey, 1977.

**Caveat**

There is some evidence of a lemons market, but the question remains controversial.

## CHOICE
## &CONSEQUENCE

### A Tale of a Tail

Although the exact importance of signaling in the labor market is controversial, an interesting example of signaling comes from a very unusual corner: the tail of the peacock.[5] Peacocks have famously ornate plumage, often referred to as their tail, which has yard-long feathers and brilliant, iridescent blue-green colors. This tail puzzled evolutionary biologists for a long time. The tail is costly to grow and what's more, it makes the peacock less mobile and an easier prey for predators. Natural selection should have eliminated it.

The reason it has not been eliminated is that peahens seem to have a preference for mating with peacocks with such ostentatious tails. This fact by itself could explain the evolution of the tail. But is it just an accident that peahens prefer to mate with peacocks with such showy tails? Some biologists argue that it is not an accident at all: the tail is a signal. Only healthy peacocks with good genes can develop such brightly colored plumage. Thus, the plumage is a costly way of signaling good genes. It is a valuable signal, precisely because it is costly and it

cannot be easily copied by weak or sickly peacocks with lower quality genes. The debate about the exact origins of the peacock's tail in biology is by no means settled. But it shows the possibility of signaling in nature and animal behavior.

## 16.2 Hidden Actions: Markets with Moral Hazard

We have explored the first type of asymmetric information in which there are hidden characteristics observable by one party in a transaction and not the other. We now look at a second type of asymmetric information: hidden actions. Hidden actions occur when an agent does not observe relevant actions taken by another agent with whom she's transacting. When hidden actions on the part of one agent influence another agent's payoffs, we say that there is **moral hazard**. An example would be an employee's level of due diligence in his job while being unobserved by his employer.

The notion of moral hazard is usually associated with risk and insurance markets, but it reaches far beyond. The basic idea is that people tend to take more risks if they don't have to bear the costs of their behavior. So, for example, an insured driver doesn't bear the full marginal cost he imposes on the insurance company when driving more miles or more aggressively. In particular, he does not receive an insurance penalty for aggressive driving, such as fishtailing on snow-covered roads or tailgating another car on the highway. Both actions are associated with an increased probability of being in an accident, in which case the insurance company will usually have to pay. If drivers had to pay for damages, they would drive more safely; with insurance, however, they have less of an incentive to avoid actions that raise the likelihood of being in an accident.

Likewise, once insured, home owners near water do not have full incentives to protect themselves from the adverse effects of floods. Some have argued that the National Flood Insurance Program administered by the U.S. government encourages home owners to build—and sometimes *rebuild*—too close to water. As you might guess, knowing that one's beach house will be fully covered

**Moral hazard** is another term for actions that are taken by one party but are relevant for and not observed by the other party in the transaction.

> People tend to take more risks if they don't have to bear the costs of their behavior.

# LETTING THE
# DATA SPEAK

## Moral Hazard on Your Bike

Moral hazard arises, for example, when people who have insurance behave more recklessly. But, do they really? Think of something close to home: wearing a helmet when you're pedaling away on your bike. This is a form of insurance. In case of an accident, you don't have to suffer the full consequences, so you are "insured" against major head damage.

Interestingly, the evidence shows that bicyclists wearing helmets have significantly fewer head injuries but significantly more non-head injuries than bicyclists not wearing helmets.[6] This result suggests that they were, in fact, taking extra risks that they would have avoided without helmets. Of course, even with such riskier behavior, helmets protect you against severe injuries, and we definitely recommend that you wear them!

Also of note is the possibility that bicycle helmets change not only risk-taking by bicyclists but also the behavior of automobile drivers. At least, that's the evidence from an enterprising psychologist from England who rode his bike around fitted with sensors that could tell how close he was to the road's edge and how close a car was when it passed

him.[7] He found that when he wore a helmet, drivers left him much less room.

This evidence definitely does not suggest that you should leave your helmet at home. Just as football players are constantly told to hit only with their shoulder pads, bicyclists should be warned of the risks they might unwittingly take when they strap on a helmet.

by insurance in case of a storm surge doesn't do much to discourage building in a vulnerable location. In effect, the insurance subsidizes risky behavior.

Moral hazard extends well beyond insurance markets. Employee theft represents perhaps the clearest example of moral hazard in the workplace. Experts estimate that employee theft costs American businesses hundreds of billions of dollars annually and is increasing at alarming rates—some say by 15 percent per year. This is an example of a hidden action, because if the employees are good at stealing, they do so in a way that the employer cannot detect.

Under moral hazard, the uninformed party can sometimes design a contract to incentivize the party with private information. Economists refer to such relationships as a **principal–agent relationship**. The party with the hidden action (thus with the private information) is the *agent*. The uninformed party, who can design a contract before the agent chooses his action, is the *principal*. This contract determines the agent's payoff (for example, wage or salary when the principal is an employer and the agent a worker) as a function of his success or failure or other indicators of his performance. The principal tries to structure the contract so as to provide appropriate incentives to the agent (for example, so as to incentivize the worker to work hard).

> The party with the hidden action (thus with the private information) is the *agent*. The uninformed party, who can design a contract before the agent chooses his action, is the *principal*.

In a **principal–agent relationship**, the principal designs a contract specifying the payments to the agent as a function of his or her performance, and the agent takes an action that influences performance and thus the payoff of the principal.

### Market Solutions to Moral Hazard in the Labor Market: Efficiency Wages

In a principal–agent relationship, the principal's problem is to create clever plans to mitigate moral hazard. Whether it is a car insurance company trying to induce safer driving habits or an employer trying to stop employee theft, such incentive schemes are everywhere. For their part, economists have spent decades studying such incentive schemes.

An early example of one such clever innovation in the labor market can be found at Ford Motor Company. Led by Henry Ford, it was one of the most important corporations

Was Henry Ford kindhearted or simply a shrewd businessman?

**Efficiency wages** are wages above the lowest pay that workers would accept; employers use them to increase motivation and productivity.

in the United States in the early twentieth century.[8] In 1914, Henry Ford did something that at first appeared strange, even paradoxical, in the context of our competitive labor market models. He increased the daily minimum wage of Ford employees from $2.34 to $5.00.

Why would a profit-maximizing employer increase his employees' pay above competitive levels? One possibility is that Ford might have been acting altruistically, out of some type of social responsibility. However, Ford's own account puts the motivation for the five-dollar day as follows: "There was no charity in any way involved. . . . We wanted to pay these wages so that the business would be on a lasting foundation. We were building for the future."[9]

Ford's strategy is consistent with profit maximization in a world of asymmetric information. In fact, what Ford did was an example of paying what economists call *efficiency wages*. **Efficiency wages** refer to wages above the lowest pay workers will accept; employers use the higher wage to increase productivity (people work harder to avoid losing their high-paying jobs). Ford appears to have had such an objective, as he later noted: "The payment of five dollars a day for an eight-hour day was one of the finest cost-cutting moves we ever made."[10]

How could moral hazard be a problem in a Ford factory? Imagine yourself on the assembly line 100 years ago. Your chore is to check for defective parts. Such work is quite monotonous, as is evident by the high turnover and absenteeism rates that Ford was facing before 1914. But there is only a small chance that if you exert low effort, you will be detected by your line manager, thus making your effort choice a hidden action. With a limited scope for being held accountable for mistakes and careless work, many would be tempted not to work hard.

Here is where the problem of asymmetric information arises. The manager at Ford can't tell exactly how many parts an employee checks, just as the manager at a movie theater can't tell whether his employee has swept under all of the seats or only a few between showings. Shirking from one's responsibilities would be an example of moral hazard on the job.

The basic idea behind Ford's solution to the moral hazard problem is that a worker's effort rises when her wages increase. There are several potential reasons for this relationship.

1. Higher-paid workers might wish to work harder because a higher-paying job is more valuable to them, and the risk of not succeeding in this job—and thus having to quit or be fired—becomes potentially more costly.

2. Higher wages might encourage workers to stay longer with the company, reducing turnover and thus the costs the employers will incur for recruiting and training new employees. Moreover, the longer employment relationships that result with low turnover might increase worker productivity through experience effects. Higher wages might thus increase profits via both channels.

3. Higher pay might motivate the worker psychologically. For example, workers who perceive generosity from their employers might perceive this as a "gift" and reciprocate by working harder at their jobs—a phenomenon sometimes dubbed "gift exchange" in the economics literature.

### Market Solutions to Moral Hazard in the Insurance Market: "Putting Your Skin in the Game"

Just as with adverse selection, many market mechanisms have arisen to reduce moral hazard. One of the key approaches is to align the principal's and agent's incentives. Within insurance markets, that means aligning policyholders' incentives with those of the insurer. A typical technique to achieve this goal is to make certain that the insured individuals have some "skin in the game" and will have to share the costs that their actions impose on their insurer. There are several ways to accomplish such an alignment of payoffs between policyholders and insurers.

1. *Deductibles* form the portion of claims that policyholders must pay for out of their own pockets. A person with a $500 deductible on his auto insurance, for example, who causes an accident leading to $5,000 of damage, will obtain only $4,500 from

# LETTING THE
## DATA SPEAK

### Designing Incentives for Teachers

Suppose that you are the school superintendent in your school district and you want to improve K–12 education. You are told that a major problem is that the teachers do not work hard enough to invest in the children. They should be given stronger incentives. Your deputy, who has completed the first part of a course on the economics of information, suggests that this can be achieved by making teachers' pay a function of the test score improvements of pupils. The higher the test score improvement of the students, the greater the compensation of the teachers. Would you go ahead with such a plan?

As part of a field experiment in the Chicago Heights school district, Roland Fryer, Steve Levitt, John List, and Sally Sadoff implemented precisely such a plan.[11] At the beginning of the school year, certain teachers were informed that they could participate in a pay-for-performance bonus program based on how their students improved on standardized tests. The program used an end-of-year test to measure the students' improvement relative to the beginning of the year and then awarded the bonus based on those scores. Teachers could earn as much as $8,000—more than 15 percent of their annual salary—if their students improved. Other teachers were assigned to the control group to make sure that any differences in test score improvement were due to the incentive program.

On the face of it, providing incentives to teachers sounds like a good idea. Moral hazard is endemic in all service occupations, and teaching is no exception. In the study, the researchers did find that the merit pay worked: students in classrooms with an incentive teacher did much better than those students who had teachers with no financial incentive. Importantly, the researchers were careful to proctor the tests and have them graded independently, just in case the incentives in this program caused unscrupulous behavior among teachers.

But there is also a dark side to incentivizing teachers. A different study by economists Steve Levitt and Brian Jacob used data from actual standardized tests administered to third through eighth graders in the Chicago Public Schools system.[12] These test scores were being used to identify

schools for closures and repurposing. Jacob and Levitt uncovered an intriguing yet disturbing trend: endemic teacher cheating in response to these incentives. By identifying hard-to-believe strings of answers in a student's test and similarities between certain answer strings across students in a particular classroom or school (all telltale signs of teachers giving the answers to students), they found that teacher cheating increased significantly in response to incentives. The lesson is that hidden actions in many real-world situations, such as teaching, are multifaceted. Incentives should be designed carefully, taking all dimensions of hidden actions into account, or else they might lead to improvements in some dimensions but also significant deterioration in others.

the insurer. By imposing some of the costs of claims directly on policyholders, the insurer gives them an incentive to take actions that reduce the likelihood of claims.

2. *Co-payments* work similarly. These are payments (most commonly applied in health insurance markets) that the policyholder makes whenever filing a claim. The $5 or $10 fee you pay for each prescription you obtain through a prescription drug plan, for example, is a common type of co-payment.

3. In *coinsurance,* the responsibility for paying claims is split between the insurer and the policyholder on a set schedule. Many health insurance policies, for instance, pay 80 percent of costs. The policyholder remains responsible for the other 20 percent.

The purpose of each of these three devices is to give policyholders some incentive to reduce the size or likelihood of their claims. These and other practices reduce the impact of

# EVIDENCE-BASED ECONOMICS

## Q: Why is private health insurance so expensive?

Health insurance is a first-order issue for society but a difficult one for economists. Competition can spur innovation, lower prices, and in general, increase efficiency. Yet when it comes to health insurance, the case for competition is murky. As described earlier in the chapter, if insurance companies have no way of figuring out the health status of each person interested in an insurance policy, then there is no guarantee that competition will lead to a vibrant health insurance industry. This leads to potential gains from government intervention, such as the Obamacare program we discussed earlier.

In the mid-1990s, a small-scale test of this problem occurred at Harvard University. For ages, Harvard had offered its employees many different insurance plans and had subsidized all of the plans at high levels. For example, the change in premium from the cheapest healthcare option to the most expensive was over $600, but employees only had to pay an extra $300 to get all of that extra coverage, because Harvard was subsidizing their health premiums. Then in 1995, as healthcare prices were skyrocketing, Harvard decided to have employees actually pay the extra cost of their expensive healthcare plans. It instituted a program whereby all plans were subsidized at the same base level, and consumers had to pay all the extra costs for their more expensive plans. What resulted was that prices went up for every plan, but they went up the most for the most expensive plans.

For some employees, this new plan went into effect in 1995. For others, it went into effect in 1996. Using this difference, economists David Cutler and Sarah Reber were able to test the influence of asymmetric information on the introduction of increased price competition and how beneficial competition would be for the provision of healthcare.[13]

They found that there was a significant increase in adverse selection with the introduction of increased price competition: healthy people decided it wasn't worth it to pay the extra price for the fancy healthcare plans, which increased the percentage of unhealthy people in the most expensive plans. This adverse selection increased the price of the most expensive plans. The authors estimated that the cost of this adverse selection was quite substantial, equivalent to about 2–4 percent of baseline healthcare spending at Harvard—meaning that the cost of greater adverse selection to Harvard staff, on average, was as if the baseline care plans were 2–4 percent more expensive.

So asymmetric information can cause private insurance to have a steeper price tag than it would have otherwise. Can government intervention help? We turn to this topic next.

**Question**

Why is private health insurance so expensive?

**Answer**

The Harvard experiment shows evidence of adverse selection—healthier patients opt out of expensive healthcare coverage.

**Data**

Harvard University employee healthcare choices.

**Caveat**

The results are from a single change in the prices of health insurance plans affecting employees at a single university.

moral hazard on insurance markets. But it's important to remember that even when its effects are dampened by these devices, moral hazard can still create inefficiencies and affect the structure of the markets in which it is a factor.

# 16.3 Government Policy in a World of Asymmetric Information

Even when private solutions to adverse selection and moral hazard are effective, there might remain gains to government intervention. To see why, let's consider the case of healthcare. We know that unhealthy people are more likely to require medical care and are therefore more likely to purchase insurance. This adverse selection problem drives up insurance companies' costs, leading to higher prices. If prices increase so much that the marginal consumer decides to opt out of health insurance, the problem is exacerbated until only the sickest consumers are insured at high prices or the market collapses.

The data are broadly consistent with such death spirals, leading to the unraveling of insurance coverage in the United States before the implementation of the Patient Protection and Affordable Care Act (commonly referred to as the Affordable Care Act (ACA), or Obamacare). For example, in the spring of 2010, more than 8 million of the 46 million uninsured were between the ages of 18 and 24, and approximately 16.5 million were between the ages of 18 and 34. These younger workers presumably have better health than the average American (who is 36.7 years old) and can be considered as relatively low risk. As they decide not to get health insurance, the average risk of those seeking insurance increases, which necessitates higher premiums and encourages yet more low-risk individuals to drop out of the market. This sort of death spiral in the health insurance market due to adverse selection was in fact one of the motivations for Obamacare, which, by making health insurance mandatory, was intended to prevent such unraveling.

The underlying problem is one of hidden characteristics: people who purchase health insurance have more information about their likely medical costs than insurers do. An important implication of these hidden characteristics is that even when everyone wants insurance, and will pay more for insurance than the health costs they expect to incur, the market will not necessarily provide insurance to everyone. Accordingly, there is a role for government to step in and potentially improve market outcomes.

The ACA made health insurance mandatory, potentially preventing the market from completely unraveling. The mandate works as a tax: beginning in 2016, individuals who do not have health insurance would pay about $60 per month. The act was signed into law by President Obama in March of 2010.

The goal of the ACA was to increase health insurance coverage for Americans by increasing quality and decreasing the price. Price could potentially decrease because the ACA forces healthier people to buy insurance, lessening the adverse selection problem.

Did this actually work in practice?

Although it is too early to tell whether the ACA worked as anticipated, there is a blueprint that economists have empirically examined to explore a similar question. The ACA is very similar to the Massachusetts universal healthcare reform of 2006, in that the Massachusetts plan also included an *individual mandate*. Three economists, Amitabh Chandra, Jonathan Gruber, and Robin McKnight, tested whether the mandate alleviated the adverse selection problem in the Massachusetts health insurance market.[14] By comparing the numbers of healthy and unhealthy enrollees just before and after the mandate, they found that the rate of healthy enrollees nearly tripled, while the rate of unhealthy enrollees only doubled. The finding that the rate of enrollment rose among healthier people suggests that the Massachusetts mandate helped reduce the adverse selection problem.

In March 2010, President Obama signed into law the Affordable Care Act.

The next step is to explore how health insurance prices were influenced. This research is ongoing, but consistent with economic theory, the empirical work has shown that there has been a decrease in the average price of premiums statewide due to the Massachusetts reform.

## Government Intervention and Moral Hazard

Can government intervention alleviate problems of moral hazard? The answer is yes, and such interventions are all around us. Let's continue with our healthcare example. With the introduction of the ACA or the Massachusetts reform, a number of potential problems might arise. For example, moral hazard could lead to citizens taking less care of their health than when they did not have insurance. With excellent insurance coverage in place, individuals might be more likely to engage in risky activities such as smoking or might engage in fewer preventative activities such as health checkups and screenings.

How can the government intervene to mitigate such moral hazard? One option is to introduce taxes to curb risky behaviors or introduce subsidies to promote healthy choices. As we have already seen, another option is to introduce deductibles and co-payments, similar to what private providers do today.

Of course, government intervention because of asymmetric information goes well beyond healthcare. For example, states mandate car insurance and design incentives to encourage safe driving habits.

> The government can improve equity, but often at the cost of reduced efficiency.

While in theory these solutions make a lot of sense, in practice, as we learned in Chapter 10, the government faces real challenges. First, the market solutions we have discussed prevent the wholesale collapse of the market (which we saw is a possibility in the case of lemons), and may even achieve a greater level of efficiency than government regulation might secure. Second, even in those cases where there are improvements to be made, similar problems of asymmetric information that limit private trade can prevent effective government action. After all, the government cannot observe hidden characteristics or hidden actions either.

In many cases, the problems are the costs created by government policies intended to create a more equitable distribution of income and resources in the presence of asymmetric information. These problems are at the root of the famous trade-off between equity and efficiency, which we discussed in Chapter 10: the government can improve equity, but often at the cost of reduced efficiency.

## The Equity-Efficiency Trade-off

Economists understand that some amount of unemployment has always existed in market economies and is largely unavoidable. It takes time for workers to find jobs suited to their skills and interests. But when workers are unemployed, they receive no labor income and their families suffer. Most advanced market economies strive to achieve greater equity by providing unemployment benefits in order to reduce such fluctuations in worker incomes. But unemployment benefits also create costs because of moral hazard.

Moral hazard is present in the problem facing unemployed workers because an individual's efforts to find a job and decision whether to take an offer are private information. It would be difficult to design an unemployment benefit system that stipulates that generous unemployment benefits will be available to workers who are "trying hard to get jobs." Generous unemployment benefits imply weaker incentives to look for work and the possibility of a longer duration of unemployment.

The presence of moral hazard in the behavior of unemployed workers introduces an unavoidable trade-off in the design of unemployment benefits: greater equity and insurance for unemployed workers and their families come at the cost of reducing worker effort to find new jobs. Naturally, this trade-off does not mean that unemployment benefits are unnecessary or undesirable, but it might imply that unemployment benefits should not be so generous as to remove all incentives to search for new jobs. For example, providing workers with unemployment benefits that are equal to the wage that they would earn if working would definitely be a bad idea.

# LETTING THE
## DATA SPEAK

### Moral Hazard Among Job Seekers

The role of moral hazard in the job-seeking behavior of unemployed workers is illustrated by several studies. In the United States, unemployed workers spend an average of just 41 minutes per weekday looking for a job. This number increases to more than 60 minutes per weekday in the week before their unemployment benefits expire (in most states, unemployment benefits expire after 6 months of unemployment).

This evidence suggests that in the presence of unemployment insurance, unemployed workers do not exert as much effort seeking a new job as they would have done without the insurance.[15] Consistent with this perspective, European workers, who typically receive more generous unemployment benefits than workers in the United States, appear to spend less time looking for a new job.

The job-seeking behavior of unemployed workers also confirms that they are more eager to find jobs right before their benefits expire. In Austria, for example, a typical unemployed worker is estimated to be 2.4 times more likely to exit unemployment in the week right before benefits expire than in other weeks.[16]

According to studies, unemployed workers don't exert as much effort in finding a job as they would without insurance.

### Crime and Punishment as a Principal–Agent Problem

Problems of asymmetric information are relevant not only when governments engage in redistribution, as in the unemployment benefit case, but also when they try to enforce law and order. Nobel Prize–winning economists Gary Becker and George Stigler suggested that the problem of how to monitor and punish crime should be thought of as a principal–agent problem, with society acting as the principal and a citizen subject to regulations as the agent.

Government rules are everywhere. All states enforce laws, uphold property rights, and prevent crimes. If they didn't, society would have to suffer through the detrimental actions of quite a few bad apples. At the other extreme, if a state wanted to prevent all crime, it would need to have an unmanageably large police force. Somewhere in between, each type of government finds its optimal level of crime and punishment.

Gary Becker and George Stigler suggested that crime could be thought of as a principal–agent relationship under moral hazard because the actions of the agent, whether he or she has broken the law or committed a crime, are not perfectly observable by the principal, in this case the state (or the government).[17] Viewed through this perspective, crime prevention is a problem in the design of incentives. Becker and Stigler then suggested that, to a first approximation, incentives will be shaped by expected punishment, defined as the product of two terms:

Expected punishment = Probability of detection × Punishment if detected.

Thus, either the probability of detection needs to be sufficiently high or punishment if detected has to be severe enough to achieve the level of expected punishment necessary to prevent a crime.

Becker noted that although ensuring a high probability of detection is costly for society, increasing the punishment if detected is not so costly. The optimal "penal code" should have a relatively small probability of detection and thus a small police force, but it should impose a heavy punishment against those who are detected. This is a powerful framework for thinking about the design of laws and their enforcement. It potentially explains why many small crimes go unpunished but how society might still successfully create sufficient deterrence against other, more serious crimes.

## Summary

- Many real-world markets are characterized by asymmetric information because of important informational disparities between buyers and sellers.

- One type of asymmetric information is driven by hidden characteristics, meaning that certain characteristics are hidden from either sellers or buyers. Hidden characteristics lead to adverse selection when agents can use their private information to decide whether to participate in a transaction.

- Another type of asymmetric information is due to hidden actions, which arise when one party to a transaction can take actions not observed by the other party that affect everyone's payoffs. Hidden actions lead to moral hazard problems.

- Although the market has developed means to deal with information asymmetries—such as warranties, deductibles, certification, and efficiency wages—in many situations, these may be insufficient, and government intervention may be useful to limit the inefficiencies that asymmetric information creates.

## Key Terms

asymmetric information *p. 379*
hidden characteristics *p. 379*
hidden actions *p. 379*

adverse selection *p. 381*
signaling *p. 382*
moral hazard *p. 385*

principal–agent relationship *p. 386*
efficiency wages *p. 387*

## Questions

*All questions are available in MyEconLab for practice and instructor assignment.*

1. What is asymmetric information? What are the two kinds of asymmetric information?

2. Explain why "bad cars drive out the good ones" in the market for used cars.

3. Why does adverse selection occur in the health insurance market?

4. How do third-party certifications and warranties solve the adverse selection problem in the used car market? Explain your answer.

5. Explain the following terms:
   a. Principal–agent relationship
   b. Moral hazard

6. When do firms pay efficiency wages? What is the relationship between moral hazard and efficiency wages?

7. Does the presence of asymmetric information necessarily imply that governments should intervene in a market?

8. How might unemployment benefits create a moral hazard problem?

9. Explain the potential costs of high-powered incentives by considering the case of providing incentives to police officers. Would it be a good idea to pay higher wages to police officers if they make more arrests?

10. How can crime and punishment be modeled as a principal–agent problem? What does the model suggest about crime prevention?

## Problems

*All problems are available in MyEconLab for practice and instructor assignment.*

1. Your new car is stolen just days after you buy it. You purchased it for $20,000 but the insurance company believes it is worth only $16,000.
   a. Why would the insurance company believe it is only worth $16,000?
   b. Is it worth more than $16,000 to you given your private information on the car?

2. There are fifty low-risk people in a town and fifty high-risk people. A low-risk person has an average of $1,000 in medical expenses each year and is willing to pay $1,200

for medical insurance (because his expenses could be much greater than $1,000 and he is risk averse). A high-risk person has an average of $2,000 in medical expenses each year and is willing to pay $2,400 for medical insurance. Insurance companies are unable to tell who is high-risk and who is low-risk.

    **a.** Show that an insurance company would lose money if it offered medical insurance at a price of $1,600.

    **b.** Show that if the insurance company offered medical insurance at a price of $2,200, low-risk people would not be insured. Calculate total surplus if the price is $2,200.

    **c.** Now suppose the government in this town passes a law that requires everyone to purchase medical insurance and sets the price of insurance at $1,600. Calculate total surplus under this law.

    **d.** The 2010 Patient Protection and Affordable Care Act (commonly called the Affordable Care Act, or "Obamacare") includes an individual mandate that requires everyone to have health insurance. Does this question suggest that there is an efficiency argument to be made in favor of the individual mandate? Defend your answer carefully.

3. Consider used mattresses. There are three types: "like-new" (value of $600), "lightly-used" (value of $300), and "bed-bug-infested" (value of $0). Only the seller knows the type.

    **a.** Suppose the price of used mattresses is $400. Which sellers would attempt to sell? Based on this premise, what is the expected value for the buyers? Why does $400 *not* work as an equilibrium price?

    **b.** Explain why $150 would not work as an equilibrium price.

    **c.** Is there any way for an owner of a mattress that has no bed bugs to sell?

4. All used cars are lemons or peaches. Owners know whether or not their car is a lemon, but buyers do not—that is, the quality of a car is private information. There are many more buyers than sellers. Buyers value a peach at $4,000 and a lemon at $200; owners value a peach at $3,000 and a lemon at $100. Owners can have their cars inspected for $100. If they do have their cars inspected, they will receive a certificate that shows whether the car is a lemon or a peach. Show that owners of peaches will have their cars inspected and will sell those cars for $4,000. Show also that the owners of lemons will not obtain a certificate and will sell their cars for $200.

5. Suppose some workers are capable and others are extraordinary. Firms are willing to pay capable workers a salary of $12,000 and extraordinary workers a salary of $15,000. Workers know if they are capable or extraordinary but firms do not—that is, ability is private information. It would cost capable persons $6,000 to earn a college degree, but it would cost extraordinary persons just $2,000 to earn a college degree since they can finish their education much faster. Show that in equilibrium in this labor market (i) extraordinary people go to college but capable people do not, and (ii) firms pay college graduates $15,000 and high school graduates $12,000.

6. The U.S. government, like many governments throughout the world, bailed out large financial institutions that were thought to be "too big to fail" during the 2008 financial crisis. Some critics of the bailouts argued that these policies created a moral hazard problem: banks would undertake too many risky projects if they knew that the government would bail them out if the project failed. This question explores this moral hazard problem.

    **a.** Suppose a bank has the opportunity to invest in a risky project. If the project is successful, the bank will earn $80; if it is unsuccessful, the bank will lose $100. The probability that the project will be successful is 0.5. What is the expected value of investing in this project? If the bank is risk neutral, will the bank make this investment?

    **b.** Now suppose the government has a policy that helps banks that are suffering losses. Under this policy, the government will give a bank 30 percent of the bank's losses if a project is unsuccessful. Thus, if the project in this problem is unsuccessful, the government will give the bank $0.30 \times \$100$, or $30. What is the expected value of investing in this project? If the bank is risk neutral, will the bank make this investment?

7. Steven Levitt and Chad Syverson compared instances of home sales in which real estate agents were hired by others to sell a home to instances in which an agent sold his or her own home. They found that homes owned by real estate agents sold for 3.7 percent more than other houses and stayed on the market 9.5 days longer, everything else being equal. How could moral hazard explain these results?

8. The problem of public goods provision (discussed earlier in the textbook) can also be thought of as a problem of asymmetric information. Suppose there is a house with five roommates. Each roommate places the following value on having a communal fridge, which costs $500. Given that the total value is $540, it is economically efficient for the roommates to purchase the fridge.

| | Value (Willingness to Pay) |
| --- | --- |
| Roommate A | $150 |
| Roommate B | $150 |
| Roommate C | $80 |
| Roommate D | $80 |
| Roommate E | $80 |

    **a.** Suppose each roommate is asked to pay $100 if the fridge is purchased. What would happen if the purchase decision was put to a vote?

    **b.** What if, instead, each roommate could decide on her contribution? Why might this plan not work? Why is there asymmetric information in this situation? And why might this plan work if there were no asymmetric information?

9. Janet Yellen, the Chair of the Federal Reserve, is married to the Nobel Prize-winning economist George A. Akerlof. When they hired babysitters in the 1980s, they decided to pay wages that were higher than the going wage for babysitters. If they could get a babysitter at a lower wage, what could explain why they decided to pay more?

10. The government wants to reduce white-collar crime.

   a. Suppose for the moment that innocent people are never wrongly convicted of a crime. Explain why the Becker model of crime and punishment suggests that we increase the fines people pay if they are convicted instead of hiring more people to investigate white-collar crime.

   b. Now suppose that mistakes happen and innocent people are sometimes convicted of white-collar crime. Why in this case might we want to hire more investigators instead of raising fines? What role does equity or fairness play in this case?

11. Suppose there are 1,001 sellers with used cars that they value at (i.e., their willingness to accept is) $0, $100, $200, $300, . . . , $9,900, $10,000. There are many buyers who place a higher value on each car than the current owners: $1,000 higher, to be exact. For example, a car worth $3,700 to a seller would be worth $4,700 to a buyer. Find an equilibrium price. In other words, find a price at which it makes sense for buyers to buy, given what they know about the sellers.

## How should you bid in an eBay auction?

As you strain to understand Kepler's First Law for your astronomy test tomorrow, you can't resist peeking at your most recent eBay struggle. Some guy named "MrBigTime" repeatedly tops your bids for a second-generation Apple iPad.

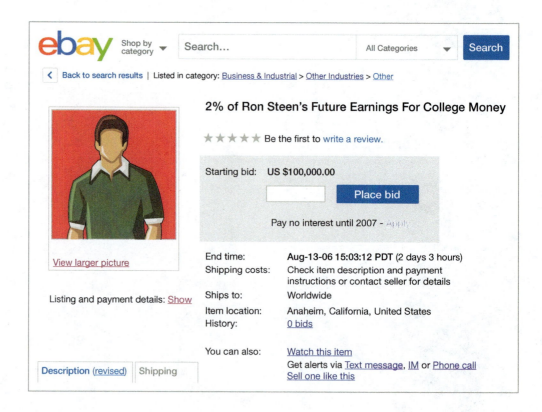

eBay Shop by category ▾ | Search... | All Categories ▾ | Search

‹ Back to search results | Listed in category: Business & Industrial > Other Industries > Other

**2% of Ron Steen's Future Earnings For College Money**

★ ★ ★ ★ ★ Be the first to write a review.

Starting bid:  US $100,000.00

[            ]  **Place bid**

Pay no interest until 2007 - Apply

End time:           Aug-13-06 15:03:12 PDT (2 days 3 hours)
Shipping costs:     Check item description and payment
                    instructions or contact seller for details
Ships to:           Worldwide
Item location:      Anaheim, California, United States
History:            0 bids

You can also:       Watch this item
                    Get alerts via Text message, IM or Phone call
                    Sell one like this

View larger picture

Listing and payment details: Show

Description (revised) | Shipping

## CHAPTER OUTLINE

- Auctions are increasingly used to sell goods and services.

- There are four major types of auctions: English, Dutch, first-price, and second-price auctions. Economic theory predicts that under certain assumptions they yield identical revenues for the seller.

- Bargaining is another frequent way that goods and services are exchanged.

- Bargaining power importantly determines the terms of exchange.

The auction ends at midnight tonight, and you contemplate your best strategy going forward—bid aggressively now or place a winning bid at the last possible moment (a ploy known as "sniping")? You just cannot get your mind back to astronomy. This auction is much too exciting—there's no time to worry about heavenly bodies now.

Anyone who has bid in an auction can relate. Auctions seem to bring out the animal spirits—heart thumping, palms sweating. Perhaps this is why they have become a normal way of life for millions of people around the globe who wish to buy, sell, or trade. In the United States alone, more than 20 percent of adults participate in online auctions. And they buy and sell all sorts of things. In 2006, a college student posted 2 percent of his future earnings for sale on eBay in exchange for the highest investment in his college education.

Up to this point, we have treated you, the consumer, as a price-taker who purchases what best suits your preferences at the market price (assuming you can afford the item). In no way are you able to affect the price you pay—you are just one of many consumers. In reality, there are many situations where you do have some influence over the price that you pay for goods. On eBay, for example, the highest bidder wins the item and pays an amount equal to her bid. In markets where buyers and sellers engage in active bargaining over prices, such as for cars, houses, and many home appliances, you are an active participant in setting prices by negotiating directly with the seller.

In this chapter, we explore the economics behind situations where you, the consumer, can affect the price you pay. Once again, optimization will be a key component: you will do the best you can in these new economic settings. We discuss how you should optimize in such settings—whether you should adopt a bid-sniping strategy on eBay, for example, or whether you should walk away from a car deal. We also examine how these same bargaining principles affect your everyday life, perhaps in ways that you never would have imagined. This pursuit will take us into marriage markets and will help us answer a second question: who determines how the household spends its money?

*Can you at least wait until your aunt leaves before you auction her gift?*

# 17.1 Auctions

An **auction** is a market process in which potential buyers bid on a good and the highest bidder receives the good.

An **auction** is a market process in which potential buyers bid on a good and the highest bidder receives the good. Auctions have a long and storied past. From the slave auctions in ancient Egypt to the marriage auctions for brides in Asia Minor to the Praetorian Guard auctioning off the Roman Empire in AD 193, auctions have been used to allocate goods and services for centuries. While auctions have served an important purpose throughout history and are now used to sell almost anything one can imagine—vintage wines, foreclosed homes, pollution permits, baseball cards, and even future streams of people's incomes, as shown in the photograph at the beginning of this chapter—economists have only recently come to understand the various auction formats we find in markets today.

Why are some goods auctioned at the highest bid price instead of being sold at posted prices like products at Walmart or Home Depot? Put simply, some goods don't have well-established prices, making auctions a particularly useful method of selling that encourages *price discovery*. For example, when you are thinking of selling a painting given to you by your grandparents that might be of interest to only a handful of buyers, auctioning it off might be a good way of discovering what the appropriate price will be and finding the right sort of buyers. In general, it is common for goods that are unique, with relatively few buyers, to be auctioned. For other goods that are interchangeable and have both many sellers and many buyers, price discovery isn't so much of an issue. Accordingly, goods such as cans of tuna and peaches typically sell at grocery stores with posted prices.

> Some goods don't have well-established prices, making auctions a particularly useful method of selling that encourages *price discovery*.

However, with the advent of the Internet, auctions have moved beyond the selling of exotic goods with a small number of buyers. It is now easy to find ordinary goods, such as books, golf balls, iPads, and notebooks—goods for which price discovery isn't the main consideration—for sale in auctions every day. For sellers, Internet auctions represent a quick way to sell items. No one has quite been able to come up with any single reason as to why auctions have become so popular for consumers (although their popularity may have reached its peak[1]). One factor is that auctions can be fun. Many buyers might get a thrill from competing for the Apple iPad on eBay, with the possibility of getting a really good deal, rather than walking into the Apple store and paying the posted price.

These attractive features have led to tremendous growth in participation in online auctions. As an indication of this growth, Exhibit 17.1 provides data from eBay's quarterly financial statements on their real sales volume from 2005 through the third quarter of 2016. Just over the past decade, eBay's sales volume has increased from roughly $14 billion to nearly $20 billion, showing the vibrancy of online markets.

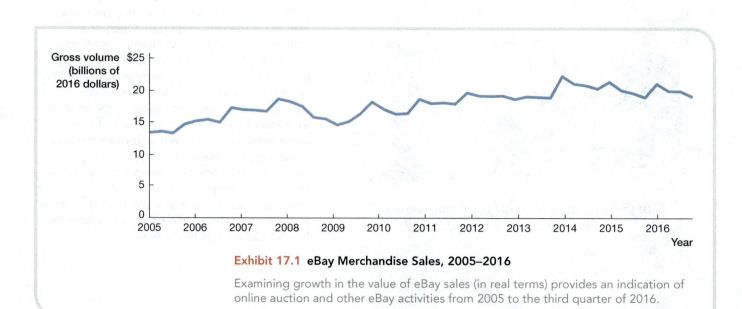

**Exhibit 17.1** **eBay Merchandise Sales, 2005–2016**

Examining growth in the value of eBay sales (in real terms) provides an indication of online auction and other eBay activities from 2005 to the third quarter of 2016.

## Exhibit 17.2 Bidder Valuations for Raiders Tickets

The five bidders to the right all have their own independent and private values for the Oakland Raiders tickets. These values represent the maximum amount they would be willing to pay for a pair of tickets.

| Bidder | Value |
| --- | --- |
| Ashley | $250 |
| Billy | $200 |
| Carol | $150 |
| Dalton | $100 |
| Eli | $50 |

In this section, we focus on several common auction formats. Across these formats, we will keep an eye on how people bid, what prices they pay, and what revenues sellers receive. You will find that auction analysis helps us understand the formation of markets and is an excellent application of game theory, which we presented in Chapter 13.

Let's begin with some simplifying assumptions. We'll assume that bidders each have their own *private* valuation of a good—in other words, their own willingness to pay—that is unknown to other bidders and to the seller. Let's also assume, for simplicity, that an auction has five bidders who are interested in bidding on a pair of Oakland Raiders National Football League (NFL) football tickets.

The bidders have willingness-to-pay values as given in Exhibit 17.2. Of the five bidders, Ashley has the highest willingness to pay for the Raiders tickets: $250. This means that the maximum that Ashley will pay for the tickets is $250. The person with the lowest valuation is Eli. He is willing to pay $50 for the tickets. Billy, Carol, and Dalton all have values in between those of Ashley and Eli. Given these values, we'll now see how our bidders fare in different types of auctions. But before doing so you might ask: why doesn't the seller just charge Ashley $250 for the Raiders tickets? The answer is that the seller doesn't know Ashley's willingness to pay (her private valuation), and the auction is useful partly because the seller doesn't need to know this information (and this is, of course, related to the role of price discovery in auctions).

You can even get Raiders tickets in an auction.

## Types of Auctions

There are many kinds of auctions. For our purposes, auctions can be usefully split along two features:

1. How people place their bids
2. How price is determined

People typically place their bids by either *open outcry* or *sealed bid*.

An **open-outcry auction** is an auction where bids are public, and bidders compete actively against one another. A **sealed bid auction** is one in which bidders place their bids privately, so that no other bidder knows the bid of another participant. The second feature that distinguishes auctions is how price is determined. In some cases, people pay what they actually bid. In others, another bidder's bid—usually the next highest bid—determines the price. These two distinctions—how bids are made and the way in which price is determined—lead to four major auction types:

1. Open outcry: English auctions
2. Open outcry: Dutch auctions
3. Sealed bid: first-price auctions
4. Sealed bid: second-price auctions

In all four cases, we will develop some economic intuition to guide optimal bidding strategies—intuition that will involve a bit of game theory.

An **open-outcry auction** is an auction in which bids are public.

A **sealed bid auction** is an auction in which bids are private, so that no bidder knows the bid of any other participant.

The chance of getting a really good deal makes auctions attractive to buyers and fun!

An **English auction** is an open-outcry auction in which the price increases until there is only one standing bid. That bidder wins the item and pays his bid.

*I don't have a soul anymore but I do have some nice collectable mugs.*

Today you never know what you will find at auction!

All in all, this empirical evidence suggests that it's probably best to spend your time studying astronomy, not sniping!

# Open Outcry: English Auctions

The *English auction* is probably the auction most familiar to you. This is the "going, going, gone" kind of auction used at establishments like Sotheby's when it sells expensive paintings and antiques, and what you may have witnessed first-hand at estate auctions. An English auction consists of an auctioneer and several bidders. The auctioneer begins the bidding process by announcing a low starting bid. From this point on, bidders bid directly against one another, and each bid must improve upon the previous one. When no bidder is willing to bid any higher, the bidder with the highest bid pays her bid and wins the good. In sum, an **English auction** is an open-outcry auction in which the price increases until there is only one standing bid. That bidder wins the item and pays the bid.

You might recognize this format as having features similar to many online auctions, such as eBay: bids are shown publicly, and price increases until the end of the auction (an "ascending" price determination), when the high bidder wins and pays his bid. English auctions are commonly used to sell real estate, foreclosed homes, cars, and antiques and are popular for raising money for charity.

**Optimizing in an English Auction** What should your optimal strategy be in an English auction? To answer this question, put yourself in Ashley's shoes as we auction off the pair of Raiders tickets. Say that the auctioneer begins at a price of $25 and asks who would like to bid. Looking at the values in Exhibit 17.2, we see that Ashley, as well as the other four bidders, will bid at this price, because each of them has a value for the tickets exceeding $25. Therefore, Ashley should bid at this price. She does so because as a bidder in this type of auction, she is willing to bid *up to* her value for the object, but no more, because she will have to pay her bid if she wins.

Next consider Eli. With the same reasoning as above, he should *not* be willing to bid more than $50 for the Raiders tickets. Therefore, when bidding reaches $50, Eli will no longer bid. This is because if he bids above $50 and wins, he will lose consumer surplus, because he values the tickets at only $50. It just doesn't make sense for Eli to bid any amount greater than $50, and he should drop out at $50.

Let's continue with the bidding process. What happens when the price reaches $100? Dalton, who should not bid more than $100, now drops out. What about when the bids reach $150? Now Carol stops bidding. This process continues until we reach $200. Let's say that Ashley bids $200 for the Raiders tickets. Does Billy bid? No, because he would have to bid higher than $200. He values the tickets *at* $200, so he will not bid any higher. Ashley therefore wins the Raiders tickets and pays $200, netting herself $50 in consumer surplus ($250 − $200).

What we just observed is a general result in an English auction: it is a dominant strategy to bid until the price is above your value for the item. In Chapter 13, we noted that a dominant strategy is a strategy that gives you the highest payoffs, regardless of the other players' actions. Thus, the dominant strategy equilibrium—and also therefore the Nash equilibrium in the English auction—is for everyone to bid in this manner.

In equilibrium, the winner will be the highest-value bidder, and she will pay a price equal to the second-highest value (or slightly more if the second-highest bidder bids his value exactly—for this example, if Billy had bid $200, then Ashley would have won with a bid of $200.01). So in auctioning off the Raiders tickets at an English auction, the seller should receive approximately $200 in revenues for the tickets.

# LETTING THE
# DATA SPEAK

## To Snipe or Not to Snipe?

If you've participated in auctions on eBay and Amazon.com, you may have noticed that their rules differ slightly: eBay auctions end at a prespecified time, but Amazon.com auctions end when 10 minutes have gone by without a bid. This small difference leads to bidders placing lots of last-minute bids on eBay auctions—a practice known as *sniping*. Both Web sites offer the option of entering a maximum bid and letting a proxy bidding service automatically place bids in minimum increments until the maximum bid is reached, but many eBayers still snipe at the last minute.

So just how many more snipe bids do bidders on eBay make? Nobel Prize–winning economist Alvin Roth and Axel Ockenfels found that 20 percent of individuals place their final bids in the last 60 minutes of an eBay auction compared to 7 percent of Amazon users.[2] They also discovered that in their sample, at least 40 percent of eBay auctions had last bids placed in the 5 minutes prior to close, with 12 percent in the last 10 seconds!

Do you think that it makes sense to wait until the last minute or second to bid?

Research by economists Sean Gray and David Reiley provides some insights.[3] They explored the benefits of eBay sniping with a field experiment. The two economists ran an experiment in which they themselves placed bids on pairs of identical items (such as DVD movies and die-cast Hot Wheels cars), placing their maximum bid on one item of the pair days before the auction's end and placing the same bid on the other item just 10 seconds before the auction's end time. Results from 70 pairs of objects show no statistically significant benefit to sniping, as final prices for the items were approximately the same.

All in all, this empirical evidence suggests that it's probably best to spend your time studying astronomy, not sniping! This evidence provides some insight into how you should bid in eBay auctions, the topic of our chapter-opening question.

How much would you pay?

A **Dutch auction** is an open-outcry auction in which the price decreases until a bidder stops the auction. The bidder who stops the auction wins the item and pays her bid.

## Open Outcry: Dutch Auctions

In the seventeenth century, tulip mania hit the Netherlands. In what many consider to be the first documented economic bubble, it was widely noted that *single* tulip bulbs were selling for more than 10 times the annual income of day laborers. At the height of the mania, 12 acres of land traded for a single bulb. As we might expect, the speculative bubble fostered many creative ways in which tulips were exchanged. Perhaps the most interesting was the *Dutch auction*.

The **Dutch auction** is also an outcry auction. But one big difference from the English auction is that in a Dutch auction, the auctioneer begins the bidding at an offer price far *above* any bidder's value and lowers price in increments until one of the bidders accepts the offer. That is, the auction continues in a descending order of values until someone announces that he is willing to buy at a given price. The first person who accepts at a given price wins the auction and pays that price. In this way, the Dutch auction is an open-outcry *descending* price auction, whereas the English auction is an open-outcry *ascending* price auction.

The Dutch auction is probably not very familiar to you, but it continues to be used in modern economies. Beyond the tulip auctions in Amsterdam (which still thrive today), Dutch auctions are used by the U.S. Department of the Treasury to sell securities. Even private firms use Dutch auctions: when Google first offered its stock to the public, it made use of a variation on the Dutch auction: OpenIPO. Likewise, many other firms have also used Dutch auctions to repurchase stock shares in their companies.

**Optimizing in a Dutch Auction**   To consider your optimal strategy in a Dutch auction, let's return to our ticket auction. Let's say that the auctioneer begins the bidding at a price of $500. Would anyone accept that price? Scanning the individual values in Exhibit 17.2, we see that none of the five bidders will purchase at this price. The closest is Ashley, but because she is willing to pay only $250, she will not bid at a price of $500. If she did, she would lose $250 in surplus ($500 – $250). So, because no one buys at $500, after a certain period of time the auctioneer lowers his price to $490 . . . then to $480 . . . then to $470, and so on.

When will the auction end? Who will win, and what will he or she pay?

Deciding how to bid in a Dutch auction is a bit more difficult than in the English auction, where you simply bid until the price reaches your maximum willingness to pay. To see this, let's consider Ashley's decision when the price in the Dutch auction reaches $250.

Should she announce that she would like to purchase at this price? If she does, then she will win the tickets but will pay $250. This price will yield zero consumer surplus for her ($0 = $250 − $250). Alternatively, she could "let it ride" and not buy at this price. In this case, she runs the risk of not winning. Crucially, she does not know the values of the other four bidders or how they will bid, so the trade-off facing her is a purchase with zero consumer surplus now versus a *chance* of a higher surplus later. Let's assume she lets the auction continue.

When no one buys at $250, the auctioneer lowers the price to $240. Now Ashley has another decision. She can accept the $240 price and gain $10 in consumer surplus ($250 − $240) with certainty, or she can wait until a lower price is announced with the downside risk of someone else buying before her, which will lead to zero consumer surplus for her. What should she do now?

At this point, we need further assumptions to provide guidance to Ashley on her optimal bidding strategy. As you might have guessed, one crucial assumption concerns risk preferences. Recall from Chapter 15 that we refer to people who are neither risk averse nor risk seeking as *risk neutral*. Consider the following bet: a coin is flipped, and if it ends up heads you win $10, and if it ends up tails you lose $10. A risk seeker gladly accepts this bet, a risk averter declines, and a risk-neutral person is indifferent. Risk neutrality is a convenient benchmark for small and moderate stakes, and here we will assume that bidders are risk neutral.

So given risk neutrality, when should Ashley jump in with her bid? The higher her bid, the lower her surplus will be, but also the higher the likelihood will be that she'll be the first bidder and win the Raiders tickets. Given that underlying all of Ashley's decision making is her private value, we can see that in such an auction, the higher her valuation, the more she should bid. Another factor should also influence her bidding: the number of bidders competing against her in the auction. If she's only one of two people in the auction, she can take more chances and let the price decrease substantially. But if she is competing with several others, then the chances are that somebody else will jump in before her unless she bids aggressively.

A simple strategy for Ashley to optimize in this case is to multiply her willingness to pay ($250) by the number of competitors (4) divided by the total number of bidders in the auction (5). (Under some assumptions, this strategy can be derived as a Nash equilibrium, but we do not need to get into these derivations).

Since her willingness to pay is $250, and there are four other bidders (five bidders in total), this rule implies that Ashley's optimal action is to announce "buy" when the price reaches $250 × 4/5 = $200. It turns out that this type of strategy is a Nash equilibrium for all bidders, meaning that it is a best response for Ashley to do this when others are also using the same strategy (bid 4/5 times their own valuation). As a result, in this Nash equilibrium we expect Eli, for example, to announce "buy" when the price reaches $40($50 × 4/5).

In general, as the number of bidders gets really low—say, just two bidders—you bid much less aggressively, which of course makes sense. According to the rule in the previous paragraph, Ashley should bid $250 × 1/2 = $125 when there are two bidders.

In contrast, when the competition intensifies—say, the number of bidders goes to 100—you bid much closer to your individual value. With the above rule, for example, Ashley will bid at $250 × 99/100 = $247.50 with 100 bidders.

If everyone follows this optimizing rule, then in the Dutch auction the bidder with the highest value will win the auction and will pay $200. This is because Ashley is the first to announce "buy," and she will do so at $200. She will therefore receive $50 in consumer surplus. And the seller of the Raiders tickets receives $200 in revenues.

Interestingly, this is identical to what the seller received in the English auction. Note, however, that there is no general rule that the actual payments will be identical between the two auctions. For example, if we changed Billy's valuation in Exhibit 17.2 to $210, then in the Dutch auction Ashley would win again and pay $200 (Billy's strategy would now be to bid $210 × 4/5 = $168, but again Ashley will clinch the good at $200 before this happens). However, in the English auction, Billy would raise his bid until the price reached $210, and thus Ashley would now end up paying more, $210 instead of $200.

But, what *is* remarkable is that two features are identical in the English and the Dutch auction: first, Ashley, who has the highest valuation, wins in both auction types. Second, although the actual revenues generated by the two auctions can be different depending on the exact valuations of the bidders, it turns out that the *expected revenues* are the same. Think of it this way: if we ran several auctions with many different goods and many different bidders with varying valuations in each auction, on average the revenues that we should expect to raise using each auction type are identical. That is, in theory, the English and Dutch auctions should raise the same amount of money. We will see next that this is actually a much more general phenomenon.

### Sealed Bid: First-Price Auctions

The two types of auctions we've discussed thus far—English and Dutch auctions—are known as open-outcry auctions in that they are public in nature. Auctions have also arisen in which bidders are allowed to make bids privately. These are known as *sealed bid auctions*. In sealed bid auctions, all bids are made privately, so that each bidder knows only her own bid. That is, bidders in this type of auction submit their bids simultaneously without knowing the bids of the other auction participants. One example of a popular type of sealed bid auction is called a **first-price auction**. In a first-price auction, all bidders write down their bids privately on cards and hand them to the auctioneer. The winner is the person who has submitted the highest bid; this person wins the item and pays a price equal to her bid.

A **first-price auction** is an auction in which bidders privately submit bids at the same time. The highest bidder wins the item and pays an amount equal to her bid.

**Optimizing in a First-Price Auction**   Let's now return to the auction for the Raiders tickets (again with the values given in Exhibit 17.2). How should Ashley bid in this type of auction? She will not bid more than $250, because she would lose consumer surplus if she were to win with a bid above $250—for example, if she bids $275 and wins, she will realize a $25 loss because the price she pays ($275) is $25 higher than her value for the tickets. So is $250 her optimal bid? That will certainly give her the best chance of winning. But even if she does win, she'll receive zero consumer surplus, because she is paying her maximum willingness to pay. So should she perhaps think about bidding a bit lower? If so, how much lower?

Notice that the trade-off here is exactly the same one Ashley faced in the Dutch auction: a lower bid is less likely to win, but she receives more consumer surplus if she does win. So you may not be surprised to learn that the optimal bidding strategy in a first-price auction is the same as that for the Dutch auction.

Therefore, Ashley's optimizing strategy is to submit a bid of $200, or 4/5 of her willingness to pay ($250). The other bidders should use similar strategies when submitting their bids. For example, Eli should submit a bid of $40 ($40 = $50 × 4/5). The equilibrium in the first-price auction is for everyone to bid in this manner. Provided everyone does so, no one benefits from changing his or her bid.

Thus, the seller of the Raiders tickets again receives $200 in revenues, and Ashley receives $50 in consumer surplus.

### Sealed Bid: Second-Price Auctions

Collectibles markets represent one of the most vibrant venues where auctions flourish. Whether antiques, baseball cards, comic books, pins, or Star Wars memorabilia, avid collectors around the globe have hundreds of opportunities daily to bid in auctions to bolster their collections. The market for stamps represents perhaps the oldest and most robust collectors' market. Today, at any given time, eBay has thousands of active stamp auctions. But the number of auctions was not always so large. The hobby of stamp collecting began in earnest in the 1850s. The first 100 stamp auctions took place from 1870 to 1882, most of them in New York City. In the 1890s, such auctions became common, with more than 2,000 auctions held worldwide by 1900.

These auctions were typically run using English auction rules. However, many individuals from out of town wished to bid in the auctions. Accommodations were soon made to such individuals who wished to bid without having to travel to the auction in person. For example, an 1878 stamp auction catalogue reads that "out-of-town collectors may have equal facilities for purchasing with city collectors, bids may be sent to the auctioneers . . .

A **second-price auction** is an auction in which bidders privately submit bids at the same time. The highest bidder wins the item and pays an amount equal to the second-highest bid.

who will . . . represent their bids the same as though they were personally present, and without charge." In those cases where all city bid offerings were lower than the highest mailed-in bid, the highest mail bidder won and paid the *second-highest bid*. The **second-price auction** was born!

Modern second-price auctions share many similarities to the 1878 stamp auction. For instance, much like first-price auctions, all bidders write down their bids privately and hand them to the auctioneer. The winner is the person who has submitted the highest bid. The major difference between the first- and second-price auctions arises when it comes time to pay for the good. In second-price auctions, the highest bidder pays a price equal to the *second*-highest bid. Why this seemingly arbitrary rule?

**Optimizing in a Second-Price Auction**   To discover the logic behind this type of auction, we consider our optimal bidding strategy in a second-price auction for the Raiders tickets. A key consideration is that if you win in this type of auction, you do not pay your bid but rather pay the second-highest bid. This situation is much different from the other three auction formats discussed above, in which you always pay your bid. In particular, the main reason Ashley did not bid $250 in the first-price auction was because to do so guaranteed her zero consumer surplus.

Should Ashley now bid more than $250 because that will increase her chances of winning? This might make sense, because she will only have to pay the second-highest bid. Or maybe she should bid less than $250.

You might be surprised to learn that in this auction, it is a *dominant strategy* to bid exactly your willingness to pay for the item. Let's see why bidding $250 is a dominant strategy for Ashley in this case. We'll do this in two steps: first, we'll see why Ashley should not overbid (that is, why she shouldn't bid more than $250), and then we'll see why she should not bid lower than $250.

*Why shouldn't Ashley bid more than $250?*

Suppose that, between Billy, Carol, Dalton, and Eli, Billy has the highest bid at $200. Suppose also that Ashley bids $100 more than her value, that is, $350 instead of her true value of $250. In this case, Ashley wins and pays $200 (the second-highest bid). But you will also recognize that in this case, Ashley would have done just as well by bidding her true value of $250: she would have won and once again paid $200. In fact, this will be the case whenever the second-highest bid in the auction is below $250: a $250 bid from Ashley does just as well as a bid above $250.

But next consider the case in which Billy bids $300. Now, bidding $350, Ashley again wins the auction, but she will have to pay the second-highest bid, which is Billy's $300. Uh oh! Ashley now has won the tickets but has to pay $300 for them, which is $50 more than her valuation of $250. Not a good deal. If, instead, she had just bid her true valuation, $250, she would have let Billy win, which is preferable from Ashley's viewpoint given Billy's bid.

This reasoning shows that both Ashley and Billy are better off bidding their valuations, because by overbidding, they risk ending up with the tickets at a price that leads to negative consumer surplus.

This is a general result: *any time you bid above your value in a second-price auction, you expose yourself to losses at no gain.* There is no gain, because if you win when you do not want to win, you will pay too much. Alternatively, if when bidding your value you win the auction, bidding above your true value has no gain.

What about bidding below your value? We turn to this next.

*Why shouldn't Ashley bid less than $250?*

Let's start by assuming that Ashley bids $100 below her value—a bid of $150 instead of her valuation of $250—but that the highest bid comes from Billy, who bids $200. In this case, Billy wins the auction and pays the second-highest bid ($150). Ashley should have won the auction, because she has the highest value. In fact, if she had bid her value of $250, she would have won and paid the second-highest bid, $200, and secured a surplus of $50 for herself. So by underbidding, she has just lost out on $50 in surplus. It is clear that bidding below her value hurt her in this case.

What if all the other bids were much lower? For example, suppose that the highest bid from the others is $100. Is Ashley then better off bidding lower than her value in this case? No. Now, Ashley wins and pays the second-highest bid ($100). Note that Ashley would have done just as well by bidding her value of $250: she would have won and paid $100 either way. So in this case, bidding below her value would have had no benefit for Ashley. This, too, is a general result: *any time you bid below your value in a second-price auction, you gain nothing and you risk not getting the good, even though it is selling below your valuation.*

These two examples highlight a general economic principle: in a second-price auction, a person should bid his value. This is a dominant strategy—you cannot do better by using any other strategy. Since bidding their values is a dominant strategy for all players in the second-price auction, this also means that bidding their values is a Nash equilibrium (and also a dominant strategy equilibrium).

This leads to a somewhat surprising set of insights. In all four auctions, the winner is the bidder with the highest valuation. Moreover, all four auctions have the same expected revenue. So, in all of these cases, Ashley wins the tickets and pays $200, the seller receives $200 in revenues, and Ashley receives $50 in consumer surplus.

## The Revenue Equivalence Theorem

Exhibit 17.3 summarizes the four major auction formats from the perspectives of bidders and sellers (for the valuations given in Exhibit 17.2). It highlights that in all four cases, the bidder with the highest value (Ashley) wins, and also, given the valuations in Exhibit 17.2, she pays $200 for the tickets. Though, as already noted, it is not necessarily the case that each auction format will always generate exactly the same revenue, the result is that they will generate the same *expected revenue*. This is in fact the essence of a general result known as the **revenue equivalence theorem**: the four major auction types will, in expectation, raise the same amount of money for the auctioneer.

> The four major auction types will, in expectation, raise the same amount of money for the auctioneer.

The **revenue equivalence theorem** states that under certain assumptions, the four auction types are expected to raise the same revenues.

William Vickrey, a Nobel Prize–winning economist, was the first to point out that different auction formats yield identical expected revenue outcomes under certain assumptions.[4] Applying game theory to the study of auctions, Vickrey went even further to develop the following insights, which our discussion so far illustrates:

1. Bidders should view Dutch auctions and first-price auctions in the same way: that is, a bidder in a Dutch auction should wait until the price falls to the exact amount she would have bid if she had been participating in a first-price auction. In this sense, your strategy is the same whether you are bidding in a Dutch or a first-price auction.

2. In both the English auction and the second-price auction, dominant strategies are at work. For the English auction, it is a dominant strategy to bid up until the price reaches your maximum willingness to pay for the good. As a result, the highest-value bidder wins the auction and pays a price equal to the second-highest bid (which is the second-highest bidder's value). Your strategy as a bidder in a second-price auction is similar: you have a dominant strategy to bid your value. If everyone

**Exhibit 17.3** Summary of Revenue Determination in the Four Auction Types

Here, we summarize the results of the four major types of auction. Note that all four auctions generate a $200 revenue. Though the exact revenue generated by these auction types could differ, the revenue equivalence theorem guarantees that all four auctions lead to the same expected revenue.

| Agent | English Auction | Dutch Auction | First-Price Auction | Second-Price Auction |
|---|---|---|---|---|
| Bidder | Bidder with highest value wins (Ashley at $200) | Bidder with highest value wins (Ashley at $200) | Bidder with highest value wins (Ashley at $200) | Bidder with highest value wins (Ashley at $250) |
| Seller | Seller receives $200 | Seller receives $200 | Seller receives $200 | Seller receives $200 |

follows his dominant strategy, the highest bidder will pay a price equal to the second-highest bid (which is the second-highest bidder's value).

You might be thinking: this is all well and good in theory, but what actually happens in practice, when the assumptions of the theory are not guaranteed to hold? We turn to that question next.

## EVIDENCE-BASED ECONOMICS

### Q: How should you bid in an eBay auction?

Empirical tests of auction theory have been conducted primarily through the use of laboratory experiments. These experiments mainly test for the revenue equivalence we described above of the four auction formats—that is, they are conducted to answer the question: do all four auction forms yield the same revenue for the auctioneer? These experiments also test whether individual bidders follow the strategies that we have just discussed.

In a creative study, economist David Reiley ran auctions on the Internet to test whether real-world bidding behavior follows the predictions of auction theory.[5] To do so, Reiley purchased more than $2,000 of Magic cards—a collectible card game—and resold them via the four auction formats on the Internet. His basic procedure was to auction two copies of the same card in two different auction formats in order to make direct comparisons of the revenue earned in each one.

For example, he purchased two Chandra (one of the two chief wizards) playing cards, and auctioned one in a Dutch auction and the other in a first-price auction. Likewise, he purchased two Jace (the other chief wizard) cards, and auctioned one in an English auction and one in a second-price auction. This approach ensured that when he compared revenues and bids across the two auction formats—say, the Dutch auction and the first-price auction—his goods were identical, thus permitting a clean test of auction theory.

A first test of consistency with the revenue equivalence theorem is that, for a given playing card (Chandra), the average revenue raised in a Dutch auction (which proxies for expected revenue to which the revenue equivalence theorem applies) should be the same as the average revenue raised in a first-price auction. Recall that in our discussion, these two auction types encouraged the same bidding strategy (depending on the number of competing bidders) and led to the same expected revenue. In other words, the *difference* between the amount of revenue that a Chandra earns in a Dutch auction and the revenue that same card earns in a first-price auction should be zero. Reiley tested the above equivalence with matched pairs of identical cards.

In Reiley's experiment, it turns out that on average across all of his auctions, the difference in revenue is greater than zero. He found that he could expect to earn $0.32 more selling the card through a Dutch auction than through a first-price auction. Given that the cards sold for roughly $4.50 on average, this difference is noteworthy.

Similarly, Reiley used matched pairs of identical Magic cards to see whether revenue from an English auction was equivalent to revenue from a second-price auction. Here, he found no significant differences between bidding in an English auction and a second-price auction, consistent with the revenue equivalence theorem.

Thus, in the case of these Magic card auction experiments, our bidding theory holds up pretty well in the outcomes for the English and second-price auctions, but it is a little off on the comparison between the Dutch and first-price auctions. Before advancing a win or loss for auction theory, much more work is necessary. Even as you read this passage, the debate rages on concerning how well auction theory predicts behavior in the field.

Why do you think the Dutch auction raises more money than the first-price auction? Can you think of clever ways to test auction theory using Internet auctions?

### Question

How should you bid in an eBay auction? Do bidders behave this way?

### Answer

Our theory detailed above provides insights on how to bid; the evidence is mixed on whether bidders behave this way.

### Data

Field experiment on eBay using Magic trading cards.

### Caveat

The field is evolving, with both experimental data and naturally occurring data lending insights into how well auction theory explains real behavior.

## 17.2 Bargaining

So far in this chapter, we have focused on markets where buyers compete with one another to buy a good. Sellers are passive in the sense that once they choose the auction format, they sit back and watch people fight it out. A different form of exchange is bilateral bargaining (or bilateral negotiation, as we discussed in Chapter 7). Bilateral bargaining is a form of exchange that has one seller actively negotiating with one buyer over the terms of trade. If you have ever used the "best offer" option on eBay, you are experienced at bilateral bargaining. Or if you have visited a flea market, you know something about bilateral bargaining—the exhilaration of a bustling marketplace where merchants offer their goods and services to shoppers looking for the thrill of the "deal." If you are a skilled bargainer, you know this thrill very well—the feeling of haggling and winding up with a great price.

Bilateral bargaining has constituted the foundation of markets for centuries—from Athen's Agora to Rome's Forum to the medieval fairs and markets in England to the 1,000-year-old *souk* in Morocco. Today there are substantial bazaars and flea markets that dot the landscape of developed and developing countries alike. Although it is difficult to provide an economic estimate of the importance of such markets, the National Flea Market Association reports that the number of flea markets in the United States and the recorded gross sales have grown substantially over the past several years, with more than 2 million licensed vendors and more than $30 billion in sales annually. This is surely a vast underestimate, however, because a nontrivial portion of the transactions are carried out by nonlicensed vendors via nontaxed sales. More broadly, such markets are of great importance, especially in developing countries, where the institution represents an integral part of the allocation of goods and services in the formal market.

### What Determines Bargaining Outcomes?

You might wonder in bargaining situations who has the upper hand—why, for example, do some sellers always seem to get great prices, while in other cases, buyers seem to get the better deals?

As you might have guessed, much of it comes down to the benefits and costs inherent in the potential exchange. In bargaining terms, the most important element that determines final outcomes is called **bargaining power**. Two principles—the cost of failing to come to an agreement and the influence of one partner on the other—are generally used to describe the bargaining power of each partner engaged in bargaining. For instance, if your influence

**Bargaining power** describes the relative power an individual has in negotiations with another individual.

over the other agent increases, then your bargaining power increases. But if your cost of not coming to an agreement increases, then your bargaining power goes down.

Let's put this intuition to work with an example. Say that for months you have been desperately trying to find a part-time job. The local economy continues to sputter, so no one near campus is hiring. Suddenly a job is posted that fits your desires perfectly. The firm—Caribou Coffee—advertises that it needs just one person. But when you arrive to apply, you find yourself in a line of 500 people who are also interested in the position.

After the initial screening, you find yourself in a final pool of ten applicants. Management interviews you again and finds you to be an attractive candidate, but you know that chances are the other nine are equally qualified. Near the end of the interview, you are asked what wage would be needed for you to accept the job. How should you respond?

You should begin by asking yourself who has the bargaining power in this situation. First, you realize that you have little influence over Caribou Coffee—it can hire any of the other nine applicants, who seemingly are equally qualified and are thus perfect substitutes for you. Second, the cost to you of not coming to an agreement is quite high—you have been trying to find a job for months, and finally the perfect fit is here. But Caribou has a very low cost of not coming to an agreement with you, because there are several other qualified applicants seeking this job.

You have now decided that you have little bargaining power in this case. This means that Caribou Coffee can offer the minimum wage and little in the way of employee benefits should it be so inclined. So, because it seems that you are at Caribou's mercy, you conclude that you should let them know that your compensation demands are minimal.

What could change in this example that would give you more bargaining power? Let's assume that a new Walmart locates in your town, bringing hundreds of jobs to the local community. Now bargaining power has changed, since your outside options have improved. Thanks to the presence of a new potential employer, you are less inclined to settle for a low wage package from Caribou, and when asked what wage you will need, you are thus likely to be bolder, because it is no longer as costly for you to fail to come to an agreement with Caribou: there's a real possibility that you can obtain a similar job at Walmart. You also have more influence over Caribou, because now the number of other workers competing for that job decreases, as Walmart will employ many people in the local community.

> Bargaining power relates to "who holds the chips." . . . The person who has . . . a lower cost of not coming to an agreement and . . . a greater influence over the other person . . . "holds the chips."

As you can see, bargaining power relates to "who holds the chips" or who has the power in the negotiations. The person who has, first, a lower cost of not coming to an agreement and, second, a greater influence over the other person, has the bargaining power and "holds the chips." In turn, bargaining power helps to determine whether, and at what terms, the parties transact.

## Bargaining in Action: The Ultimatum Game

How can we go about testing whether economic models can predict what will happen in bargaining situations? If a person with no bargaining power meets someone with much greater bargaining power, will the result be as predicted: the person with no bargaining power gets nothing? One way to test this conjecture is to use a laboratory experiment.

As a college student, you may already have been recruited by a mass e-mail from your school's economics or psychology department, asking you to participate in a laboratory experiment. It might even have been for the game that we now examine—the ultimatum game.

In this game, half of the subjects (Proposers) are given some amount of money—say, $10—and they are paired with a person (Responder) who receives nothing. The game consists of two decisions, one to be made by those playing the role of Proposers and the other by those playing the role of Responders. Each Proposer chooses how much of her $10 to offer the Responder. Each Responder then decides whether to accept or reject the offer. An acceptance leads to the proposed allocation taking place, and a rejection leads to both players walking away with zero. Exhibit 17.4 displays the game.

If you were a Proposer, how much would you choose to offer?

We can make use of game theory to find an answer. As explained in Chapter 13, this is an extensive-form game, and you can use backward induction to determine how you should

## Exhibit 17.4 The Ultimatum Game

The game begins with the Proposer's decision. The Proposer can offer any amount from $0 to $10, which we represent as a smooth curve between $0 and $10 in the exhibit. Once the Proposer makes a decision ($x in the exhibit), that decision is conveyed to the Responder as the Proposer's offer. Now, the Responder decides whether to accept the offer (pocketing $x and leaving the Proposer with $10 − x) or to reject the offer (leaving both players with $0).

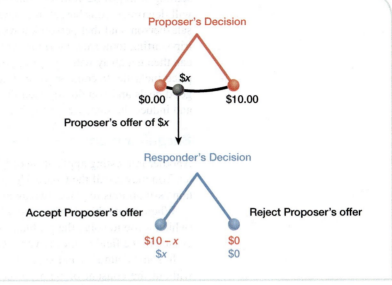

play. That is, you can work backward from the Responder's optimal actions to find out how you should play.

So let's start at the last nodes of the game tree in Exhibit 17.4 and consider the second mover (the Responder). Suppose she receives an offer of 10 cents. If she says no, she'll get 0; if she says yes, she'll receive the 10 cents. Assuming that she prefers more money to less, it will be in her best interest to accept the offer. You'll see that this reasoning applies to any positive offer, so any amount the Proposer chooses to offer, the Responder is likely to accept. By backward induction, you understand that the Responder will accept any positive offer and arrive at the conclusion that your optimal offer is the lowest possible amount— say, one penny. Thus the equilibrium in the ultimatum game takes a simple form: the Proposer offers the lowest amount possible to the Responder, and the Responder accepts that offer. As we discussed in Chapter 13, this game has therefore a first-mover advantage.

This equilibrium might strike you as a bad deal for the Responder. As the Responder, you have no bargaining power; the Proposer holds all of the chips. But the arrangement still doesn't seem quite right to you—if it costs you only a penny to reject the offer of the Proposer, why not reject it because the proposed split is not fair?

In fact, experimental evidence suggests that such low offers are often rejected. Indeed, Proposers seem to sense that their low offers won't fly, so they rarely offer the paltry figure of just one penny. Instead, their optimal offer is determined by how much they fear a rejection (and ultimately winding up with nothing).

So is this outcome a rejection of the bargaining model? No. It just tells us that something else beyond money—such as fairness—is also important to people. We return to a discussion of fairness and other social preferences in Chapter 18.

More important to the bargaining model are two observations from the vast experimental data. First, Proposers, who have more bargaining power than Responders in the ultimatum game (because they hold a first-mover advantage), usually end up with more than half ($5) of the $10 when bargains are struck (when Responders accept their offer). In games executed all over the world, Proposers in general end up with $6 or so, providing evidence that the person with the greater bargaining power does walk away with more of the spoils.

Second, information can importantly determine which player "holds the chips" in bargaining. For example, there is a variant of the ultimatum game in which the Proposer knows exactly how much money there is to split, and the Responder does not know this. What do experiments show in these cases where the Proposer has more information and thus "holds the chips?" The Proposer's gains are much closer to the entire $10.

In practice, many other factors other than being the first mover determine bargaining power. Some agents will have a reputation for being a tough bargainer, and this will naturally increase their bargaining power. For example, if you know that the Responder has a reputation for never accepting anything less than $8, you may just give up and offer her $8, settling with just $2 yourself. In other situations, how badly you need the good in question will determine your bargaining power. For instance, if you are bargaining with a used-car salesperson, and that person knows that you need the car immediately for a cross-country trip starting tomorrow morning, you won't have much bargaining power. The salesperson can then get away with charging you a high price, because she knows that your demand is price-inelastic. In contrast, if she knows that you have already searched for and found other good deals and you do not need the car urgently, this will increase your bargaining power and induce the salesperson to give you a good deal, because you are price-elastic.

## Bargaining and the Coase Theorem

Another interesting application of bargaining ties us back to lessons from a previous chapter. You may recall the Coase Theorem from Chapter 9. This theorem states that with certain assumptions in place, two agents can always bargain to reach the efficient outcome.

Where might this theorem apply? In addition to the situations we considered in Chapter 9 (which arose to solve the problem of externalities), the Coase Theorem has particular relevance in the field of law. Divorce law is one such area.

In some countries and such U.S. states as Mississippi and Tennessee, divorce is illegal without the consent of both partners in a marriage (unless there are grounds for "fault divorces"); in others, such as California and Virginia, people have the right to get a divorce whether their partner likes it or not. We'll term the first case "need two to divorce" and the second case "need only one to divorce." Now consider the question: within a state, should a change from "need two to divorce" to "need one to divorce"—in effect, making getting a divorce easier—increase divorce rates?

The Coase Theorem implies that the answer should be no. To see why, imagine a marriage in which one partner (Adam) wants a divorce, and the other (Barb) does not. Of course, happiness in marriage cannot just be measured in money. But we can attach a monetary value to the strength of Adam and Barb's feelings, and the happiness they will get from marriage, by considering how much they would sacrifice to obtain a divorce (Adam's case) and avoid a divorce (Barb's case). Suppose this is $5,000 for Adam and $10,000 for Barb.

Let's first consider the case where Adam and Barb reside in a state with the less stringent "need one to divorce" laws. Here, only one person is required to initiate the divorce, and hence the one partner wanting the divorce (Adam) is legally decisive and holds the marriage rights. Therefore, the distribution of bargaining power under these laws favors Adam. But recall that Barb values the marriage more than Adam values the divorce. So according to the Coase Theorem, we should expect that Barb will pay Adam to prevent a divorce from taking place. More specifically, Barb will prevent Adam from initiating a divorce by paying some amount between $5,000 (Adam's value of getting a divorce) and $10,000 (Barb's maximum value for staying married). Of course, in reality, this payment may not take the form of actual money changing hands. It may be that Adam does fewer household chores or dictates how the money the couple has in the bank is spent. The important thing is that the marriage can be saved by certain transfers from Barb to Adam. And notably, with such a deal, both Adam and Barb are better off—Adam receives a transfer that is above the $5,000 value of divorce, and Barb keeps the marriage alive for less than $10,000.

What about in a "need two to divorce" state? The answer is no divorce once again. In this case, Barb is legally decisive and holds the marriage rights and thus has more bargaining power. As it stands, Adam's value from divorce is low relative to Barb's value from marriage. To arrange a divorce, Adam would need to compensate Barb (to get Barb to agree) with more than $10,000 (for example, offering alimony). Given that Adam only values the divorce at $5,000, the divorce will never take place in this case either. Thus, we see that no matter whose side the law falls on, the decision to get a divorce does not change. Importantly, note that while the identity of the legally decisive partner changes depending on the law, it is always the economically advantaged partner—meaning the partner who values marriage or divorce more—who determines the final outcome, giving a deeper

Economics extends everywhere, even to divorce.

**Exhibit 17.5 The Coase Theorem in Action**

Provided the assumptions of the Coase Theorem hold and Barb values marriage more than Adam values divorce, no divorce will take place under either set of divorce laws.

| Case | Outcome |
| --- | --- |
| Divorce requires consent of both partners | The partner who values divorce at $5,000 (Adam) is not willing to pay the partner who values marriage at $10,000 (Barb) enough to buy the divorce.<br><br>Result: No divorce. |
| Divorce requires consent of one partner | The partner who values marriage at $10,000 (Barb) pays the partner who does not (Adam) an amount above $5,000 and below $10,000.<br><br>Result: No divorce. |

insight behind what it means, in bargaining, to "hold the chips." Note also that at no point does it matter how much larger Barb's value is than Adam's—this example works just the same if we replace $10,000 with $5,001.

But there is an important implication of the divorce laws: because they determine the distribution of bargaining power, they have an impact on how the gains from the efficient outcome are divided. In one case Adam receives transfers from Barb to keep the marriage alive, in the other case he doesn't. So the Coase Theorem in general implies that whether a particular relationship remains active and agreement is reached doesn't depend on who has the rights to make the decision in the first place, but the distribution of the gains from this relationship depends very much on the initial allocation of rights.

Exhibit 17.5 summarizes our discussion and shows that an efficient outcome arises no matter how lawyers and judges decide to construct divorce rights.

Try the opposite case for yourself, imagining that the happy partner values the marriage only at $5,000, while the unhappy partner values divorce at $10,000. You will again find that the divorce rate is identical—in this case, the divorce will take place under both laws! Do you think that the data conform to these predictions?

*A **unitary model** of the household assumes that a family maximizes its happiness under a budget constraint that pools all of its income, wealth, and time.*

## EVIDENCE-BASED ECONOMICS

## Q: Who determines how the household spends its money?

Do you ever wonder how your life will unfold after college? Perhaps you will find a high-paying job, marry, and have three kids. Maybe, instead, you will have three kids with a spouse who has a high-paying job. Perhaps these two cases seem identical—you might be saying to yourself, "Who cares about who makes the money, as long as we have it?" Such thinking implicitly assumes what economists call a **unitary model**: a dollar in the pocket of one spouse is the same as a dollar in the pocket of the other. In consumption terms, this means that the family maximizes its happiness under a budget constraint that pools all of its income, wealth, and time.

Is this model a correct depiction of reality? For example, in a unitary model, if the husband in a household won $500 playing the lottery, the household would buy the same goods and services as it would if the wife had instead won the lottery.

If we instead think of the household decisions as determined by a bargaining game, how will things change? Recall the two important features underlying bargaining

# EVIDENCE-BASED ECONOMICS

*(continued)*

power—the cost of failing to come to an agreement and the influence of one partner on another. In terms of the first feature, a low-income husband may have a great deal to lose if his high-income wife decides to divorce him—an outcome that may occur if the couple fails to agree on how to spend their earnings. However, if the husband receives an unexpected windfall of income, he may suddenly find his bargaining power increase significantly. Consequently, we would expect that after the windfall gain of the husband, spending in this household would be more aligned with the husband's preferences.

Economists have studied the bargaining power hypothesis by examining data from a unique natural experiment in the United Kingdom.[6] In the late 1970s, the United Kingdom changed the form of its universal child benefit program. Before the change, men in the household received the child benefit dollars. After the change, receipt of the benefit income shifted from fathers to mothers in two-parent families.

What do you think the economists found happened after the change? The authors compared household spending before and after the tax law change. They found that after the change, there was a dramatic shift toward increased expenditures on women's and children's clothing relative to men's clothing. These expenditure items are commonly known to be driven by women's preferences. So when bargaining power shifted, so did the consumption patterns of the household.

A related study finds similar but much more consequential patterns. Economist Nancy Qian studied how mortality and education patterns changed when prices for tea and orchards changed in China.[7] The changes in the rigid central planning institutions that started being reformed after the death of Chairman Mao brought a significant increase in the price of tea, which is generally produced by women in China. These changes also altered the price of orchard products, which generally rely on male labor. These changes provided Qian with information that she could use to test the role of bargaining power.

Interestingly, depending on which commodity had a significant price change in the local area, children in the households under study had quite different outcomes. For example, Qian found that an increase in the value of tea improved female survival rates—meaning that female children were much more likely to live longer after the price of tea increased. Moreover, price increases in tea influenced educational attainment of both boys and girls by about 0.2 years (in many countries, women value their kids' education more highly than men value their kids' education). Alternatively, increasing male income (through increases in the value of orchard products) by the same amount actually *decreased* educational attainment of girls and had no effect on the educational attainment of boys. The likely explanation is that women care much more about the health and education of their children than their husbands do, and when women earn more, they are able to spend more to improve these outcomes.

Both these studies provide empirical evidence of the power of the bargaining model. The lesson here is that you should always be aware of bargaining power, even in situations where you least expect it to matter—as in the household buying decision!

|  **Question** |  **Answer** |  **Data** |  **Caveat** |
|---|---|---|---|
| Who determines how the household spends its money? | The person who has the greatest bargaining power; one important determinant of bargaining power is who earns the most money. | Natural experiments in the United Kingdom and China that make use of changes in the relative incomes of husbands and wives. | Other factors are important, and the relative weighting of each is an open empirical question. |

# DATA SPEAK

## Sex Ratios Change Bargaining Power Too

Above we discussed how female bargaining power can arise from additional income and favorable price changes. Another potential channel for increasing female bargaining power is the sex ratio—the ratio of men to women in a population. The intuition is that as the sex ratio rises, women become relatively more scarce and therefore will have greater bargaining power.

To establish this relationship empirically, John List and two colleagues surveyed households in China with high and low shares of ethnic minorities.[8]

Sex ratios vary across ethnicities in China because the one-child policy, which restricted families to a single child, did not apply as strictly to China's ethnic minorities. The one-child policy, when it applies, creates a more distorted sex ratio. For this reason, holding all else equal, it is likely that the sex ratio in areas with low shares of ethnic minorities is higher than in areas with high shares of ethnic minorities.

Upon identifying these areas, List and colleagues randomly surveyed households with a three-part survey.

First, all members were asked to record their subjective opinion of their importance in the household. The second component asked about who handles household finances (an objective measure of bargaining power). Third, they had each person participate in an experiment wherein they split money between the household and a charity in China. For this third component, each person received 100 yuan to make a decision (in private). Then the exercise was repeated, but as a collective decision of the household.

Their results suggest that in areas where sex ratios are higher, female bargaining power is stronger in that women report more decision-making power, are more likely to handle household finances, and are more likely to have the collective allocation choice match their private choice. This evidence complements the data from the labor markets we have discussed and shows the importance of using economics to understand what happens in the household.

## Summary

- In many cases the interaction of buyers and sellers has a role in determining the price of the item being traded. For this reason, studying auctions and bilateral bargaining expands our understanding of how resources are allocated.

- There are four common auctions: English, Dutch, and first- and second-price auctions. Though these auctions work very differently and optimizing behaviors vary considerably across them, under certain assumptions the outcomes they yield have some remarkable similarities. In particular, with all of these auction formats, the buyer with the highest valuation wins the item being auctioned, and the expected revenue of the seller is the same.

- Bargaining power of an individual—who "holds the chips" in bargaining—is critical in determining whether, and at what price, the trade will take place.

- In situations where the Coase Theorem applies, the distribution of bargaining power will not affect whether the efficient outcome is reached, but it will determine how the gains from this outcome are divided.

# Key Terms

auction *p. 398*
open-outcry auction *p. 399*
sealed bid auction *p. 399*
English auction *p. 400*

Dutch auction *p. 401*
first-price auction *p. 403*
second-price auction *p. 404*

revenue equivalence theorem *p. 405*
bargaining power *p. 407*
unitary model *p. 411*

# Questions

*All questions are available in* MyEconLab *for practice and instructor assignment.*

1. How do auctions help in price discovery?

2. What is the difference between an open-outcry auction and a sealed bid auction?

3. What is an English auction?

4. What is the dominant strategy for a bidder in an English auction?

5. What is meant by sniping in an auction? Does it make sense to snipe to win an auction?

6. What is a Dutch auction?

7. What is meant by risk neutrality?

8. Suppose a bet is placed on the outcome of the flip of a coin—if the coin comes up heads, you get $25 and if it comes up tails, you lose $25. If you accepted this bet, does it imply that you are risk averse, risk neutral, or risk loving?

9. What are the similarities between an English auction and a Dutch auction?

10. What does the revenue equivalence theorem state?

11. What is meant by bargaining power? What are the two factors that determine an individual's bargaining power?

12. How does the ultimatum game work? What does experimental evidence show about the outcome of the ultimatum game?

13. Explain why in situations where the Coase Theorem applies, bargaining power does not influence whether the efficient outcome is reached, but it does affect the distribution of gains.

# Problems

*All problems are available in MyEconLab for practice and instructor assignment.*

1. An escalation clause in a real estate contract specifies what a prospective buyer will offer for a home if the seller receives multiple offers. An escalation clause typically includes three elements:

   - The buyer's initial offer

   - How much that offer will rise above any other competitive bid

   - The maximum amount the buyer will offer in case of multiple offers

   So, for example, an escalation clause might state that a buyer is offering $200,000 for a home and that the buyer will bid $1,000 more than other offers up to a maximum of $250,000.

   Suppose you are willing to pay up to $300,000 for a house that is for sale. You decide to include an escalation clause in the contract. What is the maximum amount you should specify in the contract that you will pay if the seller receives multiple offers?

2. According to this chapter, in a first-price sealed bid auction (or a Dutch auction), a bidder should multiply her willingness to pay by the number of *other* bidders, then divide by the *total* number of bidders. Suppose you are willing to pay $60 for a pair of shoes that are being auctioned on eBay with a first-price sealed bid auction.

   a. If you believe there are five other bidders, what should you bid?

   b. If you believe there are ten other bidders, what should you bid?

   c. When does it make sense to bid very close to $60?

3. The original Filene's Basement in Boston had a unique pricing system. Every article in the store was marked with a tag showing the price and the date the article was first put on sale. Twelve days later, if it had not been sold, the price was reduced by 25 percent. Six selling days later, it was cut by 50 percent, and after an additional 6 days, it was offered at 75 percent off the original price. After 6 more days, it was given to charity if it had not been sold.

   a. Was the Filene's plan similar to any of the auctions we studied in this chapter?

   b. Suppose you are interested in a coat you have seen in a store that uses the same pricing system as Filene's Basement. ("The Basement" closed its doors in 2011.) The initial price is $200. You are willing to pay as much as $150. Could it be optimal to buy the coat when the price is reduced to $150? Could it be optimal to wait 6 days and try to buy the coat when the price is reduced to $100? Could it be optimal to wait 12 days and try to buy the coat when the price is reduced to $50?

4. A town wants to build a new bridge. Construction firms are asked to submit sealed bids. The town will award the contract to the firm that submits the lowest bid and will pay the firm the amount of the second-lowest bid, that is, the town will conduct a second-price procurement auction. So, for example, if Firm A bids $8 million, Firm B bids $9 million, and Firm C bids $10 million, then the city will award the contract to Firm A (it submitted the lowest bid) and pay Firm A $9 million (the amount of the second-lowest bid). Suppose your firm is willing to build the bridge for a minimum of $9 million.

   a. Show that bidding $9 million is a better strategy than bidding some amount below $9 million—say, $7 million.

   b. Show that bidding $9 million is a better strategy than bidding some amount above $9 million—say, $11 million.

5. U.S. Treasury notes are sold at a discount. For example, a buyer might offer $950 for a $1,000 note that will become due in 2 years because (as Chapter 15 explains) money received in the future is not as valuable as money received now. In September 1992, the U.S. Treasury began selling 2-year and 5-year Treasury notes using a uniform-price auction, in which all winning bidders pay the same price. Before September 1992, the Treasury used a discriminatory-price auction to sell securities. The following simple example illustrates the difference between the two types of auctions. Bidders A and B each submit a sealed bid for 2-year Treasury notes of $1,000. Bidder A bids $950; Bidder B bids $925.

Suppose the Treasury accepts both bids. In a uniform-price auction, A and B both pay $925; in a discriminatory-price auction A would pay $950 and B would pay $925. Suppose you are willing to pay up to $950 for 2-year Treasury bills.

a. Show that a uniform-price auction is similar to a second-price auction.

b. Should you bid $950 if the Treasury is using a discriminatory-price auction?

c. Should you bid $950 if the Treasury is using a uniform-price auction?

6. You have learned that in a second-price auction you should always bid your actual willingness to pay; not a penny more and not a penny less. Proving why this is *always* best, no matter what others bid, is somewhat subtle. However, it is relatively easy to argue that at least some of the time, not bidding your value is a bad idea. Suppose you are willing to pay $150 for an item being sold via a second-price auction.

a. You decide to "overbid": $160. Describe the full situation (i.e., bids that others might place) in which you will regret bidding $160 rather than $150.

b. You decide to "underbid": $130. Describe the full situation (i.e., bids that others might place) in which you will regret bidding $130 rather than $150.

7. The owners and the players' union are negotiating over a contract for the upcoming hockey season. In October, the owners will make an offer to the union. If they reach an agreement, they will share $50 of revenues. So, for example, if the owners offer the players $10 in October and the players accept, then the players receive $10 and the owners keep the remaining $40. If the players reject the offer, then they go on strike and negotiations resume in November. In November, the players will make an offer to the owners. If they reach an agreement, they will share just $20 of revenues (revenues have fallen because of the strike). So, for example, if the players offer the owners $10 in November and the owners accept, then the owners receive $10 and the players keep the remaining $10. If the owners reject the November offer, then the strike continues for the rest of the season and the players and the owners both receive zero.

a. What would you expect to happen in November if there is a strike in October? (Hint: Think about the ultimatum game.)

b. Use backward induction to find what would happen in October. For simplicity, assume that if someone is indifferent between accepting or rejecting an offer, they will accept the offer.

8. Consider what would happen in the ultimatum game (with offers between $0 and $10) if the Responder were able to fully commit in advance. It would be as if the Responder had moved first; he would declare which offers he plans to accept, and which he plans to reject. This means that the so-called "Responder" is now the player who gets to declare an ultimatum. Describe the equilibrium in this game.

9. The Johnson Steel Company generates water pollution when it makes steel. It could eliminate this pollution at a cost of $700. The Smith family lives downstream. It suffers $1,000 of damages from the water pollution Johnson creates. Assume that transaction costs are zero.

a. Suppose first that the law states that Johnson has the right to pollute. Show that if Johnson and the Smith family negotiate, Johnson will eliminate the pollution.

b. Now suppose the law is changed so that the Smith family has the right to enjoy clean water. Show that Johnson will eliminate the pollution even if Johnson and the Smith family can negotiate. Is the Smith family better off now than in part (a)?

10. Ronald Coase used the example of a farmer and railroad tracks to explain bargaining. Sparks from trains running on tracks near farmland would set off fires in the fields. To avoid this, railroad companies would either have to stop running trains on tracks along fields or incur a cost in fixing a spark arrester along these tracks. Farmers could avoid the cost of fires by leaving land near railroads empty. Suppose that the cost of preventing a fire was equal to $20,000 for a railroad company and that not having a fire in the field was worth $10,000 to a farmer. Consider the case where the law stipulated that railroads could not throw sparks along fields. What would be the outcome?

11. Space heaters are dangerous. The U.S. Consumer Product Safety Commission estimates that more than 25,000 residential fires every year are associated with the use of space heaters, resulting in more than 300 deaths. This question asks you to think about the Coase Theorem and the assignment of liability from these accidents. Suppose a company could produce a space heater that is perfectly safe for $225 or a standard space heater for $200. Suppose further that a consumer who buys a space heater will receive $275 of benefits. If she buys a traditional space heater, she will incur (on average) $60 of damages, but she will not incur damages if she purchases a safe model.

a. Show that efficiency requires the firm to produce safe space heaters.

b. Suppose the law states that firms are not liable for the damages associated with space heater accidents. Show that the firm will sell only safe space heaters.

c. Now suppose Congress passes a law that says firms are liable for the damages from space heaters, and so on average a firm that sells a standard space heater will have to pay $60 in damages. Show that the firm will produce safe space heaters.

12. This chapter illustrates how the Coase Theorem can be applied to explain the outcome of a divorce in two different systems. In both cases, where the unhappy partner values the divorce at $5,000 and the happy partner values the marriage at $10,000, the equilibrium is "no divorce." Now assume that the situation is reversed: the happy partner, who does not want a divorce, places a lower value on the marriage ($5,000); the unhappy partner, who wants a divorce, values the divorce at a higher value ($10,000). Applying the same concept, analyze the outcome of the marriage under two scenarios: "right not to divorce" and "right to divorce."

# 18 Social Economics

## Do people care about fairness?

If you have made it this far in the book, you might be feeling a bit uneasy. You might have come to the grave conclusion that the mythical *Homo economicus*—the economic man serving as the backbone of the discipline of economics—is essentially an unsavory species with which you are unfamiliar. He is self-absorbed in the pursuit of material wealth and unswerving in his drive to satisfy his own needs before the needs of others. As an employer, he hires at the lowest wage possible; as a seller, he charges whatever the market will bear; and as a producer, he pursues profits even at the cost of imposing negative externalities (for example, pollution) on other citizens.

In spite of its obvious simplicities, this economic paradigm has served us well in providing a coherent framework within which to model human behavior. But in the past few decades, some economists have considered an alternative—an economic agent who does not always make decisions solely to promote her own wealth. Instead, this more "human" economic agent cares about others and the fairness of her actions.

As we have stressed throughout this book, economics does not tell us what people *should* value. Rather, it provides us with tools to help us understand how they should behave once we know what they value. In this chapter, we focus on a variant of *Homo economicus* who acts more selflessly and who is influenced by his surroundings. In doing so, we discuss the economics of charity, fairness, trust, and revenge. This allows us to answer the chapter-opening question of whether people care about fairness. We also consider the importance of peers in

> Some economists have considered . . . an economic agent who does not always make decisions solely to promote her own wealth. This more "human" economic agent cares about others and the fairness of her actions.

## CHAPTER OUTLINE

| 18.1 | EBE | 18.2 | 18.3 |
|------|-----|------|------|
| The Economics of Charity and Fairness | Do people care about fairness? | The Economics of Trust and Revenge | How Others Influence Our Decisions |

## KEY IDEAS

- Many people have preferences that go beyond material wealth.

- Charity, fairness, trust, revenge, and conforming to those around us represent a few examples.

- Economic tools can be used to understand when such factors will play an important role.

- Economists have found that such behaviors are important when their opportunity cost is low.

shaping the decisions that we make daily. We will find that peer effects are all around us, affecting our waistlines, our finances, and how hard we work at our jobs. In all these cases, economic tools provide us with a deeper understanding of when we should expect such considerations to have importance—the key is the opportunity cost of such actions.

# 18.1 The Economics of Charity and Fairness

In Chapter 5, we learned about three necessary ingredients for the buyer's problem:

1. What you want
2. Prices of goods and services
3. How much money you have to spend

Together, these elements provide the foundations for demand curves. Even though we have exclusively focused on tangible goods in our discussions thus far—sweaters, jeans, DVDs, iPads, and the like—the economic model is flexible enough to describe your demand for intangibles, such as charity and fairness. Just as your preferences, budget constraint and market price determine whether you purchase an iPad, they also determine your charitable contributions and how much "fairness" you demand in resource allocations. We turn now to a consideration of each.

## The Economics of Charity

As a child, you were most likely taught to help those in need. If your brother falls down, help him up. If a friend is in trouble, lend her a hand. If a stranger needs directions, do the best you can to help. As an adult, you are now better able to help others. For example, you can serve soup at the local food pantry or you can donate money to help save the rain forests. As we discussed in Chapter 9, such activities have become very important in modern economies.

Exhibit 18.1 provides a summary of self-reported volunteerism around the globe. What we observe overall is a tremendous amount of volunteering in these forty-two sampled countries. For example, almost 50 percent of the adult population of Myanmar volunteered some time to at least one charitable cause in the month prior to the survey. Citizens in many other countries give their time, too: in the United Kingdom, 32 percent of people give their time. In Australia, Kenya, and the United States, more than one in three people volunteer their time to charitable causes every year. Beyond helping others, one motivation for volunteerism is because it makes us feel good (think of that warm, fuzzy feeling you get when helping those in need). Thus, even though the opportunity cost of our time might be quite high, we give our time to help others.

Another important way in which people help charitable causes is to give money. As we have already learned in Chapter 9, although governments are major providers of public goods, they are not the sole providers. Indeed, many public goods are routinely supplied through other channels. For example, National Public Radio all around the United States relies on private donations to broadcast. Even rainforests can be saved, thanks to private cash donations to the World Wildlife Fund. And cures for ailments ranging from carpal tunnel syndrome to heart disease have resulted in part from charitable gifts.

So what is the scope of private donations of money? As we learned in Chapter 9, individual contributions to charitable causes have increased to more than 2 percent of U.S. GDP. To put this number into perspective, consider that Greece's most recent GDP—the value of

Volunteers contribute their time to charities, such as the Salvation Army, while others contribute by giving money to charitable causes.

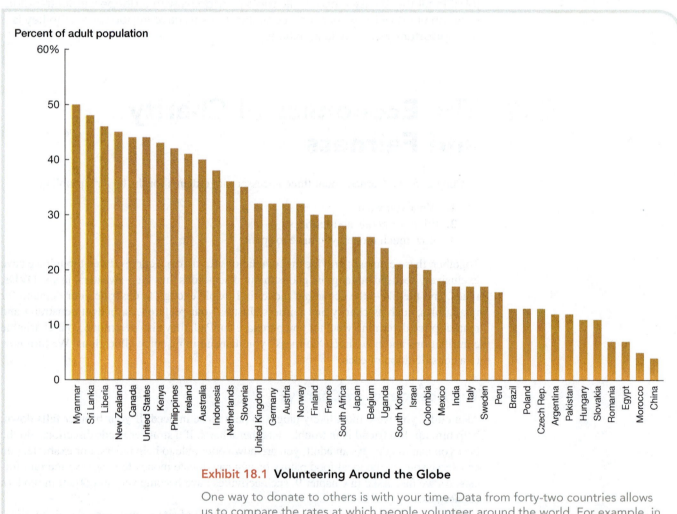

**Exhibit 18.1  Volunteering Around the Globe**

One way to donate to others is with your time. Data from forty-two countries allows us to compare the rates at which people volunteer around the world. For example, in Myanmar, around 50 percent of the adult population volunteers some amount of time during the year. But the United States is no slouch either, coming in sixth with more than 40 percent of its adult population volunteering time.

*Source:* Data from Charities Aid Foundation's World Giving Index report, November 2015.

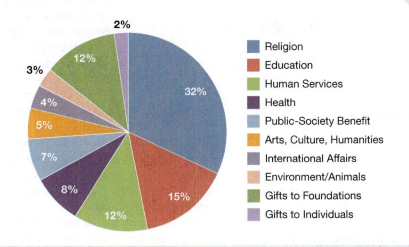

**Exhibit 18.2** U.S. Household Giving in 2014 by Recipient Status

As is typical in the United States, in 2014 the majority of charitable contributions were to religious causes. Education and environmental causes are also a high priority for U.S. donors.

*Source:* Data from Giving USA 2014.

all of the goods and services produced by the Greek economy—is less than this amount, about $286 billion!

You might wonder where all this money goes. Exhibit 18.2 provides a glimpse from 2014, which represents a typical year. The majority of contributions—32 percent—by U.S. households went to religious causes. But most people who contribute do so to more than one cause. These remaining gifts are commonly directed to educational purposes, health-care/medical research, the poor, and combined purposes, as can be seen in Exhibit 18.2. Every so often, major events happen that lead to an outpouring of gifts above and beyond the typical flows documented in Exhibit 18.2. For example, when Hurricane Katrina struck the United States in 2005, monetary donations broke records that were previously set by the 9/11 relief efforts.

# LETTING THE
# DATA SPEAK

## Do People Donate Less When It's Costlier to Give?

The act of giving, just like apples and shoes, can be viewed as an economic good. And, as with other economic goods, we economists like to ask the question: if the price increases, does the quantity demanded decrease? And, if so, by how much? This gives us a price elasticity of demand (as we discussed in Chapter 5).

But how do you increase the price of charitable giving?

One way is by reducing its current tax-advantaged status. In the United States, individuals as well as corporations pay taxes on their incomes. However, any of this income that is donated to charities is tax deductible. For example, imagine that you face a tax rate of 30 percent. Now let's say that you decide to send your favorite charity $100. How much does your donation really cost? Since you can account for charitable contributions when you pay taxes, your gift of $100 is equal to $70 in after-tax income (that is, if you had decided not to give the $100 to charity, you would have pocketed $70: $100 (earnings) − $30 (taxes)).

Now let's assume that your tax rate drops to 15 percent; what do you think happens?

Note that the opportunity cost of that charitable gift has changed: your gift of $100 is now equivalent to $85 in after-tax income (that is, if you decided not to give the $100 to charity, you would have pocketed $85: $100 (earnings) − $15 (taxes)). So, the price of giving the $100 has just increased from $70 to $85. How do you think such a change affects individuals?

Economist Charles Clotfelter asked this very question in his analysis of the effect of the Tax Reform Act of 1986 on the amount of charitable contributions from U.S. taxpayers.[1] The Tax Act of 1986 reduced the highest tax rate faced by individuals in the United States, producing the very situation that we describe above for the highest earners.

And the result?

Clotfelter found that one group was quite sensitive to this tax change: individuals in the highest income brackets reduced their contributions to charity considerably. In essence, they responded as our model of an optimizer predicts they should: as the price of charity increases, quantity demanded (amount given to charity) decreases.

**Only after we know why people give can we provide the proper incentives to promote giving.**

**Pure altruism** is a behavior whose primary motivation is to help others.

**Impure altruism** is a behavior whose primary motivation is to help oneself feel good.

**Why Do People Give to Charity?**   An active area of research in economics has developed to explore possible explanations for why people give to charity. Only after we know why people give can we provide the proper incentives to promote giving, should we wish to do so. Economists view the reasons for giving as falling into two broad categories: to help others and to help oneself.

We denote the first category as **pure altruism**, whose primary motivation is to help others. This is not unlike the conventional notion of altruism, which typically entails a concern for the well-being of others. It is "pure" in the sense that when people give time or money to a charity, they do so solely to help someone or some cause. For example, if you or your parents gave money or time to Hurricane Sandy victims, it might have been because you were simply trying to help people in need. Likewise, if you march for cancer awareness, it might be because you want to help others who could be stricken with the disease.

An alternative reason people might give to charity is to help *themselves* in an indirect way. Economists refer to this type of giving as **impure altruism**, to indicate the selfish motives underlying the gift. Impure altruism involves giving in order to capture some private return, like "feeling good" (or, similarly, to avoid a private cost to not giving, which may result, for example, from others thinking that you are uncaring toward the plight of the needy or are stingy). So impure altruism is primarily motivated by selfish considerations—not just to help another person ("out of the goodness of our hearts"). Indeed, people can be influenced to make charitable gifts by many factors, such as social pressure, guilt, or a desire to earn prestige, friendship, or respect. This doesn't mean that impure altruism

## LETTING THE DATA SPEAK

### Why Do People Give to Charity?

Imagine you come home to find a flyer on your door that says, "Fundraisers from a children's hospital will be visiting this address between 10 and 11 a.m. tomorrow morning to ask for contributions." Would you change your schedule to make sure to be home between 10 and 11 a.m.? Would you change your schedule to make sure *not* to be at home? What factors would play into your decision?

One aspect of impure altruism is social pressure: you give to a charity not because you want to help others, but because of the social pressure applied to you by others. By asking themselves, "Do people give because they *like to give*, or do people give because they *dislike not giving*?," John List, together with Stefano DellaVigna and Ulrike Malmendier, set out to test the power of pure altruism and social pressure in a door-to-door field experiment.[2]

Their goal was to determine how much money was given because of pure altruism and how much because of social pressure. Their hypothesis was that some people give to charities not because they care about the charity, but because they are asked to do so by a person, and they care about what others think of them.

Solicitors were dispatched to the suburbs of Chicago to ask for money for a children's hospital. Sometimes, however, the experimenters put flyers on doors to warn households that solicitors would be coming at a specific time the next day.

In theory, if people dislike being asked for money, then they will try to avoid answering the door during the time specified for charitable solicitations. The result?

Although fewer people answered the door when they knew a solicitor was coming, those who did gave more to the charity, on average, than their counterparts who answered the door without knowing that there would be a solicitation. This finding suggests that some people give to charity because of social pressure and avoid interaction with a solicitor when possible. It also raises the intriguing possibility that people who do answer the door knowing that there will be a solicitation are more altruistic than their counterparts.

In terms of the split between social pressure and pure altruism, the authors found that nearly 75 percent of the giving was due to social pressure. Can you think of other ways to test what drives giving to charity?

is a bad thing; if the deed gets done, then so be it. But as with anything in life, it is good to understand the true motivations behind the action. For charities, this understanding is particularly important, because policymakers interested in engineering greater gifts of time and money need to know the exact motivations driving such behavior.

## The Economics of Fairness

Throughout this text we have studied the behavior of economic agents. Whether dealing with individuals, households, or firms, there was no scope for fairness, or any other social preference, to play a role. A good's price was determined by the intersection of the market supply and market demand curves. Similarly, wages of workers were given by the intersection of labor demand and labor supply.

Even though we know intuitively that social preferences, such as fairness, altruism, and revenge, can play roles in our decision making, for simplicity we ignored them to focus on other important issues. We turn now to a consideration of how such preferences might lead us to revise our economic model.

**Fairness on Television?**   You may have heard of the TV game show *Friend or Foe?*. The show, which was hosted by MTV diva Kennedy, premiered on June 3, 2002, and lasted two seasons. The game show worked as follows. After two-person teams were formed, each team was separated into "isolation chambers," where trivia rounds were played. The two-person teams worked together to answer the questions in order to build a "trust fund." A team's "trust fund" could range from $200 to $22,200.

After the trivia portion of the show was complete, the winnings were to be divided beween the players. The division depended on both players' choices. There were three possible outcomes:

1. "Friend-Friend"—If both players chose "Friend," the total trivia winnings were divided equally between them.
2. "Friend-Foe"—If only one player chose "Friend" and the other chose "Foe," the person who chose Foe received the entire amount, leaving the player who chose Friend with nothing.
3. "Foe-Foe"—If both players chose "Foe," then they each walked away with nothing.

Exhibit 18.3 provides the payoff outcomes for one of the games, where we assume that you are playing with another player named Joe for $16,400.

A summary of the three key elements in this game is as follows:

*Players*: You and Joe
*Strategies*: Friend or Foe
*Payoffs*: See Exhibit 18.3

What should you do? If you are only interested in money, your best strategy is to always play "Foe." This is because this choice never leads to lower payoffs than playing "Friend."

How do you think people actually played this game on TV?[3] (For some excellent footage of people in action playing this prisoners' dilemma, we invite you to visit https://www.youtube.com/watch?v=035_OxEw9Io.) Overall, the choices were exactly split—of the 234 players examined, 50 percent chose "Friend" and 50 percent chose "Foe." Thus, even

**Exhibit 18.3** *Friend or Foe?* TV Game Show: A Variant of the Prisoners' Dilemma

By representing the *Friend or Foe?* game in matrix form, we can easily compare your and Joe's payoffs and strategies to figure out the predicted outcome. If you and Joe both choose "Friend," you each earn $8,200. But the incentive to play "Foe" is high — potentially doubling your earnings unless you both play "Foe."

|  |  | Joe | |
|---|---|---|---|
|  |  | **Friend** | **Foe** |
| **You** | **Friend** | • You get $8,200<br>• Joe gets $8,200 | • You get $0<br>• Joe gets $16,400 |
|  | **Foe** | • You get $16,400<br>• Joe gets $0 | • You get $0<br>• Joe gets $0 |

**Exhibit 18.4** *Friend or Foe?* TV Game Show with
Fairness Preferences

Unlike in Exhibit 18.3, an additional penalty is now
imposed on whoever chooses to play "Foe." Depending on the size of this fairness penalty,
the unsatisfying prediction of ("Foe, Foe") from
Exhibit 18.3 might change to a more socially efficient
outcome.

though choosing "Foe" is the best action if you want to make as much money as possible,
only half of the participants did so.

Although there are several reasons why this might be the case, one of them is that people
have preferences for fairness. That is, they think it's unfair to take all the money that they
have just earned in a partnership. Specifically, we can define **fairness** as the willingness of
individuals to sacrifice their own well-being to either improve on the well-being of others
or to punish those whom they perceive as behaving unkindly.

How would we revise the payoffs in Exhibit 18.3 to account for such preferences? When
players have fairness preferences, the total payoffs need to reflect both the monetary payoff
and considerations of fairness. For example, maybe you believe that Joe has fairness preferences, too, and when playing this game you view the payoffs in Exhibit 18.4 as applicable.

Now, when making your choice, you consider not only the monetary payoff but also the
"fairness penalty" contained in the payoff matrix, which you incur when you play "Foe"
(that is, you incur the fairness penalty when you play in an "unfair" manner, choosing
"Foe" and reducing the payoff of the other player). Suppose that this "fairness penalty" is
$5,000. Note that as a player, you are simply guessing the magnitude of this number. If you
make these assumptions, then you simply insert a $5,000 fairness penalty in the matrix and
optimize with the new numbers. Inserting $5,000 as the penalty for choosing "Foe" in Ex-
hibit 18.4 yields Exhibit 18.5, which shows the new payoffs when such penalties are used.

**Fairness in the Lab?**   Although fairness preferences might certainly be at work driving
the *Friend or Foe?* decisions, there are other factors at work as well. For example, it is
possible that contestants recognize that they are playing in front of millions of people who
are scrutinizing their every move—employers, spouses, parents, and even their own kids.
For these sorts of reasons, economists have turned to laboratory experiments to measure
fairness preferences. One such game that is commonly employed is the Ultimatum Game,
which is a one-shot bargaining situation between two players. Exhibit 18.6 displays the
game, which was previously discussed in Chapter 17.

> **Fairness** is the willingness of
> individuals to sacrifice their own
> well-being to either improve on the
> well-being of others or punish those
> whom they perceive as behaving
> unkindly.

**Exhibit 18.5** *Friend or Foe?* TV Game Show with a
$5,000 Fairness Penalty

Here, the fairness penalty is set at $5,000 and
included in the payoff matrix. Once this has been
done, we are back to our standard game theory
analysis—all of the new fairness concerns are
already reflected in the payoffs. With such a fairness
penalty, if you and Joe find yourselves playing
("Friend, Foe"), neither of you has any reason to
change your action, and the same is true if you play
("Foe, Friend").

## Exhibit 18.6  The Ultimatum Game

The Ultimatum Game begins with the Proposer's decision. The Proposer can offer anywhere between $0 and $10, which we represent as a smooth curve between $0 and $10 in the exhibit. Once the Proposer makes a decision ($x in the exhibit), that decision is conveyed to the Responder as the Proposer's offer. Now, the Responder decides whether to accept the offer (pocketing $x and leaving the Proposer with $10 − x) or to reject the offer (leaving both play-ers with $0). The red numbers at the bottom give the Proposer's payoff, and blue numbers are for the Responder.

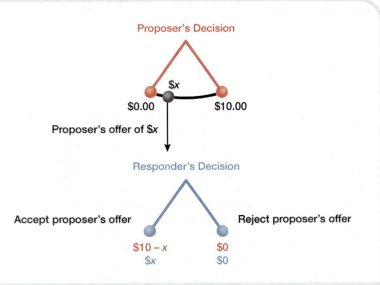

In the Ultimatum Game, a Proposer is given an amount of money to split between him-self and a Responder. Say that this amount is $10. The Responder is told how the pot has been split and then decides whether or not to accept the Proposer's decision. Say that the proposed split is $9 for the Proposer and $1 for the Responder. If the Responder accepts this allocation, the Proposer and Responder are paid their proposed shares—in this ex-ample, $9 to the Proposer, $1 to the Responder. But if the Responder rejects the proposal, both the Proposer and the Responder receive nothing.

As a quick refresher, let's revisit what game theory tells us about the predicted outcome of the Ultimatum Game. If both players are only concerned with their own well-being, we can use the payoffs in Exhibit 18.6 and backward induction to determine how they will play the game. Assuming that the Responder prefers more money to less, we have already shown in Chapter 17 that the Responder accepts any positive offer, meaning that the Pro-poser will offer the lowest positive amount—in this case, 1 cent.

Even though game theory has stark predictions in this case, we typi-cally do not find this result in laboratory experiments. In fact, a majority of Proposers offer amounts between 25 percent and 50 percent of the original pot, with few offers below 5 percent. Furthermore, Responders frequently reject offers below 20 percent. Why does this happen?

One prominent explanation is based on the players' sense of fair-ness. Recall that people can view selfish behavior as unfair and may wish to punish it; in this game, Responders are willing to reject unfair offers, giving up some of their own share in order to punish those they perceive as acting selfishly or unfairly. Note, however, that this behav-ior is not at odds with economics per se: recall that economics does not tell us what people should value. For example, economics does not prescribe that people should or should not value fairness any more than it says that people should or should not value fast cars, a clean environment, or freckles on coworkers' faces. What economics *does* predict is that, just as people should give more to charity when the op-portunity cost of doing so is lower, a person valuing fairness should demand more of it at lower prices and less of it at higher prices, hold-ing all else equal—something we discuss in greater detail next.

Is that an ultimatum?

As such, Responders shouldn't always be willing to punish unfair-ness. Sacrificing one's well-being to punish an offer of a 90–10 split when the pot is only $10 is understandably easier to do than when the pot is $5,000 (the difference between a punish-ment price of $1 and $500). Thus, we may expect that as the opportunity cost of exercising fairness concerns increases, the likelihood that an individual will exercise them decreases. Even in the context of fairness preferences, reasoning through the problem with economics can take us quite far. We return to this idea in the Evidence-Based Economics section.

## LETTING THE
# DATA SPEAK

### Dictators in the Lab

Say you have volunteered for an economics experiment. On entering the lab, you are told that you have been paired with an anonymous partner who is in another room and that the two of you will be splitting a pot of cash. The person assigned the role of Allocator decides how the money is to be divided, and the other, called the Recipient, must accept whatever choice the Allocator makes.

You have been randomly assigned the role of Allocator and must choose how much of $10 to give to the Recipient and how much of it to keep for yourself. In effect, you are the Dictator. The lab assistants assure you that your identity will remain anonymous to the person you're paired with, so you can be as selfish or as generous as you want. How would you, as the Dictator, split the $10?

Typically, in the Dictator Game, a little more than half of Allocators send the Recipient some of the money, with the average share being about 20 percent of the original pie.

Odds are that you won't decide to split the $10 evenly with the Recipient.

But how would your choice change if, instead of being in separate rooms, you and the Recipient were sitting face to face? What if, instead of allocating shares to an anonymous person, the two of you knew one another?

Lab experiments such as these have shown us that the degree of social distance not only between the participants, but also between the participants and the experimenter, has an effect on the Allocators' choices. One such experiment found that when no one (including even the experimenters) would ever know the Allocators' choices, more than 60 percent of people kept the entire pot.[4] However, when the Allocator and Recipient were instructed simply to look at each other in silence for a few seconds before the Allocator made his or her choice, approximately 70 percent divided the money evenly.

## EVIDENCE-BASED ECONOMICS

### Q: Do people care about fairness?

The Ultimatum Game provides a direct interaction in which the Proposer sets a "take-it-or-leave-it" price and the Responder must make a decision on accepting or rejecting. There are many economic decisions that we have discussed that share this quality: a monopolist setting a price; an oligopolist proposing a collusive agreement; or more generally, any bargaining situation that has a take-it-or-leave-it element.

One of the most robust findings in experimental economics is that many Responders in ultimatum games reject unfair offers, leaving themselves and their bargaining partner with a zero payoff. However, in and of itself, this outcome is not at odds with economic theory—as we have just noted, nothing in economic theory says that people should not care about others' utility. Rather, economics predicts that people will demand greater fairness when the "price" of fairness is lower, meaning that they can punish unfair behavior at a lower opportunity cost. Is this prediction borne out?

To answer this question, let's trace how economists have investigated fairness. Since the early 1980s, the Ultimatum Game has been one of the most popular experiments in laboratory economics. It has been played hundreds of times by your typical college student and even by natives of the Peruvian Amazon. Dozens of people have had their brains scanned while playing this game. By and large, what the research has found is that Proposers in the game typically offer about 40 percent of the money they are endowed with and Responders reject about 16 percent of the offers. Small offers are much more likely to be rejected than large offers.

Rejecting a positive offer in the Ultimatum Game involves a monetary cost, and whether behavior changes when this cost increases is a question of economic import. The main economic prediction in this setting is this: Responders will be willing to reject unequal offers when the cost of doing so is low but will find it hard to reject such offers when the stakes are large. Many of us might be willing to reject an offer of 1 percent of $10, yet how many of us would reject 1 percent of $10 million?

Some economists have recently tested this prediction. They traveled to poor villages in northeastern India to run the Ultimatum Game.[5] By using subjects from poor villages, the researchers could afford to offer what were considered by the villagers to be large stakes. In these villages, they executed ultimatum games that varied the stakes by a factor of 1,000, permitting them to explore the game over different pot sizes of 20, 200, 2,000 and 20,000 rupees. These amounts corresponded, at the time, to $0.41, $4.10, $41, and $410, respectively. What this means to the people taking part in the experiment becomes clearer when we put it into context: the average daily income in these villages at the time was 100 rupees ($2.05).

The results from the game are summarized in Exhibit 18.7. Panel (a) of Exhibit 18.7 shows the offer proportions across the four stakes levels, in other words, the different percentages offered for various pies. What we find is that for lower stakes, the offer proportions are higher than for the larger stakes. It seems that Proposers recognize that Responders will have a difficult time rejecting an unfair offer in the high-stakes (20,000-rupee) treatment, as the average offer is only a little more than 10 percent of the pie. So what do you think happens to these low proposals in the high-stakes treatment? Do they get rejected?

Panel (b) of Exhibit 18.7, which shows rejection rates for offers less than or equal to 20 percent of the pie, provides the answer. In short, even though people rejected small offers when the stakes were small, very few people rejected them when the stakes were large. Panel (b) of Exhibit 18.7 shows that even when Proposers made very low offers, once the stakes became large, almost no one rejected the offer. In the 20,000-rupee treatment, for example, only one of the twenty-four offers at or below 20 percent was rejected. That's a very small rejection rate, considering that the average offer in that treatment group was just a little bit more than 10 percent of the pot. And this is much

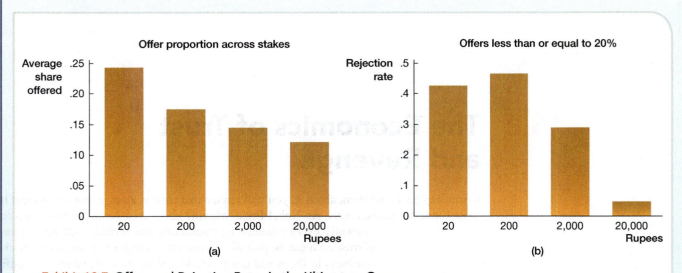

**Exhibit 18.7 Offers and Rejection Rates in the Ultimatum Game**

The first pattern of data that emerges is that as the size of the pie increases (from 20 rupees to 20,000 rupees), the share of the pie that the Proposer offers to the Responder decreases. This finding alone suggests that stakes matter, but without the data on rejection rates, we have only part of the story. Panel (a) shows the average proportion of the stakes offered to the Responder. Bars represent our four stake treatments of 20, 200, 2,000, and 20,000 rupees to be shared in the Ultimatum Game. Panel (b) focuses on those offers that are 20 percent of the total pie or less. We see conclusive evidence for the importance of the stakes of the game. Whereas over 40 percent of low offers are rejected at the lower stakes, less than 5 percent of such offers are rejected when the total pie is 20,000 rupees. This also explains why Proposers thought they could make lower offers with higher stakes. This evidence shows that fairness, just like any other economic good, responds to price.

smaller than the 40 percent to 50 percent rejection rate observed in the lower-stakes treatments.

This experiment highlights the power of economics by showing that people do value fairness—but will go only so far when enforcing it. When the cost is low, people vigorously punish unfair offers. But they aren't as willing to punish if it is really expensive to do so. If it costs them too much, they will let their fairness preferences take a backseat. This result is comforting for economists in that it shows that even issues such as fairness have a place in our economic framework: the power of economic reasoning extends well beyond production and consumption of goods and services, such as cars, bicycles, iPhones, and haircuts.

> People do value fairness—but will go only so far when enforcing it.

**Question**

Do people care about fairness?

**Answer**

Yes, many people will pay a small price to punish others who are not being fair. But fairness considerations become less important as the cost of being fair increases.

**Data**

Experimental data from the field in India.

**Caveat**

This is one study performed in a remote part of the world, and the stakes must be increased sufficiently to find that fairness considerations become less important as the cost of being fair increases.

# 18.2 The Economics of Trust and Revenge

If you step back and think about it, you will realize that trust is an essential component in most economic transactions. As Nobel Prize–winning economist Kenneth Arrow wrote, "virtually every commercial transaction has within itself an element of trust … it can be plausibly argued that much of the economic backwardness in the world can be explained by the lack of mutual confidence."[6] Of course, if someone takes advantage of your trust, you might consider exacting one of humankind's oldest acts: revenge. In this section, we discuss the economics of trust and revenge.

> Trust is an essential component in most economic transactions.

### The Economics of Trust

Trust and trustworthiness are everywhere in life. You trust that the meal that you ate the last time you dined out was processed, stored, and prepared in the safest manner possible. Likewise, when confiding in a friend, you rely on her trustworthiness to hold your deepest secrets. Economists have come to recognize that most economic transactions require trust and trustworthiness, because it is rarely the case that all dimensions of a transaction can be contractually specified and enforced. For instance, it is difficult for Ford Motor Company

## Exhibit 18.8  A Trust Game Between Jen and Gary

In the Trust Game, Jen is the first mover and has to decide whether to trust Gary and let Gary have the final say, or not to trust Gary and settle the game in the first move. Given that Gary, if selfish, will defect, Jen would maximize her earnings by settling the game in her move and never giving Gary a chance. Unfortunately, both players are worse off in this case relative to the case where Jen trusts Gary and he cooperates with her.

Jen

Don't trust Gary      Trust Gary

Jen's payoff = $10
Gary's payoff = $10

Gary

Defect      Cooperate

Jen's payoff = $0
Gary's payoff = $30

Jen's payoff = $15
Gary's payoff = $15

to monitor the every move of line workers in a factory; workers need to be trusted not to commit sabotage or steal from the plant. Likewise, parties to a commercial transaction must have some degree of trust that each will fulfill the agreed-on contract. Otherwise, all of their time would be spent in court. You might recall from Chapter 16 that these are moral hazard considerations.

Economists have recently begun to study the nature and extent of trust and trustworthiness of people. One popular approach is to use laboratory experiments and observe people in "trust games." One variant of the trust game is shown in Exhibit 18.8. In this game, there are two players, Jen and Gary, who have never met and make their decisions anonymously. Jen is the first mover and thus, at the outset, must choose whether to trust Gary or not trust him. If she does not trust Gary, then both she and Gary receive a payoff of $10. If she chooses to trust Gary, then Gary chooses either to defect or cooperate. If he defects, then Jen receives nothing and Gary receives $30. If Gary cooperates, then both he and Jen receive $15.

If you were in Jen's shoes, how would you decide? Likewise, if you were in Gary's shoes, and Jen trusted you, how would you respond?

Assuming that Exhibit 18.8 contains all relevant payoffs, then you should use backward induction, as we learned in Chapter 13, to solve this game. Put in Gary's shoes, you would defect if given the chance, because by so doing you earn $30, which is greater than your cooperation earnings of $15. Put in Jen's shoes, you should recognize that Gary's defection will probably occur because of the larger payoff ($30 is greater than $15) coming his way. Thus, you should choose not to trust Gary.

The equilibrium of this game is therefore for Jen not to trust Gary. But this is a bad outcome in the sense that it is not socially efficient: instead of earning a total of $30 between them, they earn only $20 ($10 each), because Jen does not trust Gary. You will notice that many situations in the real world look like this game. Every time you trust a stranger, or even a friend, there is a risk that he or she will disappoint you. When you call a plumber to repair your leaking faucet, there is a risk that he will take your money but do a shoddy job and the faucet will start leaking again the next day. If the equilibrium of the trust game in Exhibit 18.8, and the equilibria of many related games we play during our daily lives, always involved the second player (Gary) defecting and the first player (Jen) not trusting her partner, the world would be a sad and quite dysfunctional place.

What factors could cause the equilibrium to be different? One important factor is that Gary might have a preference for being trustworthy. In the same way that there could be a penalty for not being fair, as in *Friend or Foe?*, there could be a penalty for Gary if he were to be untrustworthy. Let's say that the penalty is that he would feel terrible when he acts in such a manner.

Exhibit 18.9 shows what the game between Jen and Gary would look like when Gary has a penalty equivalent to $20 for choosing defection. Because of this penalty, his benefits from defection are now $10 rather than $30. Studying Exhibit 18.9, we see that Gary will now prefer to cooperate rather than defect. Recognizing such an outcome, Jen will now prefer to trust Gary rather than not

Is this an economic calculation?

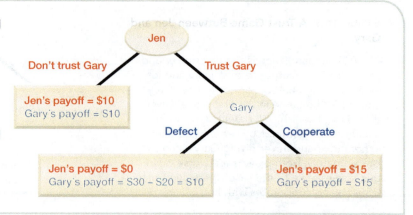

**Exhibit 18.9 A Trust Game Between Jen and Gary with a $20 Guilt Penalty**

As with Exhibit 18.5, even when we include social preferences in the payoffs, the game can be analyzed using our standard toolkit. In this case, Gary experiences a guilt penalty of $20 for betraying Jen's trust in the first move. This guilt penalty is high enough that Gary will instead cooperate to maximize his earnings. Knowing this, Jen will trust Gary, leading to the outcome (Trust Gary, Cooperate).

Jen

Don't trust Gary — Trust Gary

Jen's payoff = $10
Gary's payoff = S10

Gary

Defect — Cooperate

Jen's payoff = $0
Gary's payoff = S30 – S20 = S10

Jen's payoff = $15
Gary's payoff = S15

trust him. Thus, simply allowing trustworthiness to be part of the equation could considerably change the incentives facing the agents and move them to a more socially efficient equilibrium.

Another factor that can move the players from the original "bad" equilibrium is if the game stretches out to a long run—that is, if the game is played several times over. Even though in a one-shot game with the original payoffs it makes sense for Jen to not trust Gary, if they were to play many times, it might make sense for Jen to trust him, because they can both be better off if they each receive $15 every time they play rather than $10. This is exactly the same reasoning that we saw in Chapter 14, supporting collusion as a long-run arrangement between oligopolists.

Let's be a little more explicit about why this is the case. Exhibit 18.8 shows that in such a repeated relationship, if Jen and Gary cooperate, each will get $15 every time they play the game. Now let's say that Gary defects. In this case, he receives $30 once, but, from then on, Jen will choose not to trust Gary, leaving each player with $10 every time they play. Thus, defecting will increase Gary's current payoff at the cost of reducing his future payoffs. Taking this trade-off into account, both players might find it in their interest to cooperate as a long-run strategy. In this way, the incentive of future cooperation can effectively discourage defection.

This long-run strategy might shed light on the kinds of interactions we constantly observe in the real world—for example, why friends and families share trust. Similar ideas can apply to society at large if we think of people as playing a "game of life." If you behave badly by stealing a classmate's lecture notes, then your friends might develop a negative opinion of you and will be less willing to cooperate with you in the future. By casting yourself as dishonest, you can be hurt significantly in the future. You might lose future job opportunities and the trust of friends, and might even find that people seek to punish your past actions in their private dealings with you.

## The Economics of Revenge

So far, we have focused our discussion primarily on "nice" features of human behavior: charity, fairness, and trust. However, there are preferences that can be distinctly "not nice," such as revenge. Still, we will find that the ability to exact revenge can actually serve a useful purpose. Consider an example from medieval Europe. To promote social order, the communes in the tenth century kept the peace through the threat of revenge: in other words, an "eye for an eye" policy was in place. Even though exacting revenge by punishing people for antisocial behavior was costly, it was theorized to be efficient, because it reduced misbehavior by townspeople.

It is not difficult to find examples of the economics of revenge in modern economies: corporal punishment, public lashings, and other severe means to address misbehavior are to be found around the globe. But is this to promote social order? And do individuals punish this antisocial behavior of others even when it is costly to them? For example, say you witness a hit-and-run accident: do you take the time to call in the license plate number to the police and go to the precinct and carefully fill out a police report? On a much different

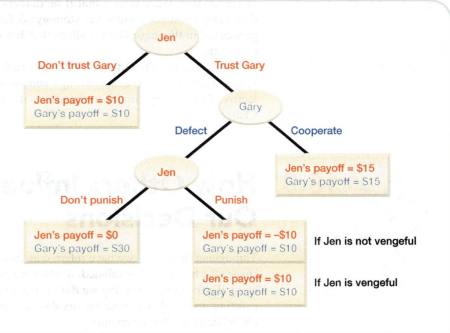

**Exhibit 18.10** A Trust Game Between Jen and Gary with a Punishment Option

In many real-world settings, rather than being helpless against Gary's defection as in Exhibit 18.9, Jen would be able to punish this sort of behavior from Gary. Here, we model this by modifying the trust game and giving Jen the first and final say on the outcome of the game. If Jen isn't vengeful, the game ends just as in Exhibit 18.9—knowing that Gary will defect, Jen ends the game in the first move and doesn't trust Gary. However, if Jen is vengeful, then Gary will cooperate when it's time to decide, preferring $15 to the inevitable $10 he gets if he defects against a vengeful Jen.

**Jen**

Don't trust Gary / Trust Gary

Jen's payoff = $10
Gary's payoff = S10

**Gary**

Defect / Cooperate

Jen's payoff = $15
Gary's payoff = S15

**Jen**

Don't punish / Punish

Jen's payoff = $0
Gary's payoff = S30

Jen's payoff = −$10
Gary's payoff = S10    **If Jen is not vengeful**

Jen's payoff = $10
Gary's payoff = S10    **If Jen is vengeful**

level, do you yell at someone for cutting in line, knowing that you run the risk of being labeled "aggressive" or "tacky" by others?

We can study the economics of revenge more formally by extending the Trust Game example. Imagine that after Gary decides whether to cooperate or defect, Jen can impose a fine of $20 on Gary. But imposing the fine will cost Jen $10. How does adding such a revenge option change the equilibrium of the Trust Game?

Exhibit 18.10 shows the effect. At the end of the game tree, we have allowed different payoffs for Jen. In the first case, she's not vengeful, so she suffers when she imposes a fine on Gary (she's lost $10 and thus receives a payoff of −$10). In the second case, she is vengeful and she actually derives satisfaction from imposing the fine on Gary (because she's getting revenge on him for not returning her trust). Assuming that this satisfaction is worth $20 to her, her total payoff is $20 + (−$10) = $10.

If Jen is not vengeful and Gary knows this fact, then Gary knows that she will not impose the penalty. So he continues to defect if given the option. But, if Jen *is*

# CHOICE
## &CONSEQUENCE

### Does Revenge Have an Evolutionary Logic?

The rule that supported long-run trust in the repeated trust game between Jen and Gary was "cooperate until your partner turns on you, and then turn on him." If both players use this strategy, they likely will not have to face the pain of betrayal—the threat of retaliation is too high to make defection worthwhile. Many people, businesses, and even countries have built trusting relationships from the expectation that uncooperative behavior would lead to revenge. In fact, such thinking may have an evolutionary root.

Biologists and anthropologists currently are locked in a heated debate over the power of *group selection*. Several

scholars, such as Robert Boyd, Peter Richerson, Elliott Sober, and David Sloan Wilson, are working to show that, although selection may favor selfish individuals, groups that have built trusting, cooperative relationships should outlast groups composed entirely of selfish individuals.[7] Individual selection implies that the strongest *person* will survive to pass on his or her genes, while group selection implies that the strongest *groups* will survive to pass on their genes. A general rule of thumb in this research is that "selfishness beats altruism within groups, but altruistic groups beat selfish groups."[8] How could we test whether this concept is at work in markets?

vengeful, then Gary knows that if he defects, Jen will happily punish him. Knowing this, Gary must reconsider his strategy: defection doesn't look so good anymore. In particular, in this case Gary realizes that Jen will impose the fine and now chooses to cooperate.

Therefore, we have identified another path to a good equilibrium: the threat of revenge. Jen's ability to exact revenge convinces Gary to act in the interests of the collective. This is very similar to the effect of credible commitments that we discussed in Chapter 13.

# 18.3 How Others Influence Our Decisions

Throughout this book, we have referred at various times to our preferences. What factors shape whether we're fair-minded, whether we give in to social pressure, whether we really enjoy the feeling of knowing we did the right thing, or whether we take satisfaction from exacting revenge? Are these factors different from those determining whether we prefer chocolate or vanilla ice cream?

## Where Do Our Preferences Come From?

Our preferences are partially determined by biological and chemical processes (for example, children prefer sweet flavors). In many applications, we can take them as "given" in our economic model. Other dimensions of our preferences, however, are shaped by socialization, access to information, and indoctrination.

We are not born with a preference for watching TV or playing video games. These are preferences that we acquire. Such preferences are a function of the society in which we live. We learn to pattern our behavior in ways considered appropriate to that of society. And the influence of society, especially through friends and family, is an important part of socialization.

Our preferences are also shaped by a more unsavory force: **indoctrination**. Indoctrination is the process by which agents imbue society with their ideology or opinion. Part of this indoctrination is benign—it's just the process of providing information. For example, antismoking campaigns pay to advertise widely because they believe these ads cause people not to smoke. These groups successfully cultivate a cultural norm against smoking. Most of us prefer not to smoke partly because we have been provided with information about the negative health effects of smoking and partly because we know that our society frowns on smoking.

Far different from the potentially helpful spread of information is the power of organizations to change people's preferences through indoctrination. The dangerous temptation of governments and powerful individuals to influence citizens with ideologies or opinions has plagued many countries. For instance, today many North Korean citizens believe that an economy that is centrally planned is preferred to one guided by market forces. As we learned in Chapter 7, this is clearly not the case in theory or practice.

**Indoctrination** is the process by which agents imbue society with their ideology or opinion.

## The Economics of Peer Effects

In Chapter 12, we discussed how others influence our lives through *network externalities*. For example, because many of your friends use Twitter, you might feel compelled to get a Twitter account as well. If all your friends have seen the new X-Men movie and keep talking about it, then you might feel obliged to go and watch it so as not to be left out in the dark, even if this movie doesn't look like it will appeal to you. Equally as important is the influence of others beyond these network externalities. Every day we see people, listen to them, and converse about the correct course of action. What jeans should I wear when I go out tonight? What is the next hot stock? What kind of shoes should I buy?

Our friends and acquaintances are a major force in shaping both our preferences and the choices we make in life.

## LETTING THE — DATA SPEAK

### Is Economics Bad for You?

Perhaps you will not be surprised to learn that at least three separate laboratory experiments have shown that economics majors cooperate less than students from other disciplines.[9] Whether in a prisoners' dilemma experiment or a dictator game, a student of economics tends to exhibit behavior more in line with the selfish *Homo economicus* than with a more cooperative economic human.

Is this a form of indoctrination? Could it be that economics makes people less social and more selfish?

There are at least two other explanations for these results. First, it might be the case that the economics discipline attracts students who are more "selfish" than the average student. That is, the selection of students who enter the economics major is different from those who enter other majors—those who enter economics are more attracted to dollars. This makes sense, because economics majors tend to do quite well in terms of earnings after graduation.

Equally as plausible might be the case that economics majors have misunderstood economic science as prescribing the "correct" behavior in such games. As you now know, as far as economists are concerned, as long as you are making the best choice for yourself given the information you have, you're acting rationally. This doesn't necessarily mean that you maximize your income or that you act selfishly.

But a common misconception is that economics tells us that we *should be* completely selfish—promoting our own earnings at the expense of others. In this way of thinking, economics students are always figuring out the equilibrium in monetary payoffs, to the exclusion of other social preferences.

Perhaps you know the ultimate answer to this question through your interactions with economics majors. We, as economics professors, would like to learn the truth!

---

**Peer effects** are the influence of the decisions of others on our own choices.

For better or worse, our social surroundings affect the decisions that we make daily. No one person or group decided that flare-leg jeans would be cool in the 1960s, acid-wash would be cool in the 1980s, and Kim Kardashian's frayed hemline jeans would be "in" right now. But the trends are there.

Our friends and acquaintances are a major force in shaping both our preferences and the choices we make in life. Economists call the influence of the decisions of others on our own choices **peer effects**. People tend to gather information from those around them and use this information to decide on their own behavior. Both the characteristics of our peers—their talents and skills—and their choices affect our lives.

A few examples will help illustrate the power of peers and also reveal why it is challenging to identify peer effects convincingly in the data. The first is a study by economists Oriana Bandiera and Imran Rasul, who noticed interesting peer effects when studying farmers and their adoption of sunflower seed farming in Mozambique.[10] They examined how social ties in the community influenced the adoption of new technology to raise sunflower seeds. They found that those who adopted the sunflower seeds knew a significantly greater number of other people who had switched to farming sunflower seeds than those who chose not to adopt. Intuitively, this outcome makes sense.

Imagine that you are a farmer presented with the option of farming a new crop. You'd be more likely to adopt it if you knew that several people had already done so rather than just one or two people. Why does such a relationship exist between the adoption decision of peers and an individual's decision? One possibility is that each farmer is learning from his or her peers whether sunflower seeds have high productivity: the more your peers adopt, the more likely you are to be convinced that this is a good idea. Another possibility is that the adoption decisions of peers create social pressure: you might not want to be the only one who hasn't adopted. Yet another possibility is that neighboring farmers' lands are of similar quality and type, and if you are in an area where sunflower seeds are likely to increase yields significantly, then both you and your peers will be more likely to adopt.

*Peer effects are everywhere.*

In a study that is closer to home, economist Bruce Sacerdote sought to study peer effects in college dorms.[11] He uncovered what he called the "freshman roommate effect." Exploring a natural experiment in which nearly 1,600 Dartmouth college freshmen were randomly assigned a roommate, Sacerdote examined the effects that roommates had on one another. Among other results, he reported that roommates had a significant effect on each other's GPA! It seems that having a roommate who studies all the time helps you to study more yourself. If you are unhappy about your GPA, however, don't go hunting down your roommate just yet, as Sacerdote and other scholars have found that many other important factors influence your GPA, too.

Though clever, Sacerdote's study is also open to alternative interpretations. Imagine that your roommate has no effect on you, but your room happens to be next to a busy train station with frequent service in the middle of the night. Both you and your roommate will get no sleep as trains whiz around you. At semester's end, both you and your roommate may have low GPAs, but this is not because one of you has influenced the other, but because both of you have been subject to a "common shock"—in this case, train noise keeping you awake all night.

## Following the Crowd: Herding

Crowds tend together for a purpose: whether at school, a concert, or a roadside accident, people tend to flock to one another. In these cases, there is usually something specific that attracts attention. However, people can flock together without good reason. In economics, **herding** occurs when individuals conform to the decisions of others.

In general, there are two reasons individuals might decide to herd. The first might simply be that they are afraid of being wrong—for this reason, they might not value their own instincts highly. Another is the assumption that if many people are making the same decision, they must be doing so for a reason. You might have heard the adage at amusement parks: if there is a long line, jump in it, because something good is at the end. Herding creates an informational equilibrium in which people trust the wisdom of others and ignore their own information.

For example, imagine that you are walking down a street and decide that you will stop to eat lunch. You look around for a diner and see two across the street from each another. Both diners are empty. Knowing nothing about them, you randomly choose Big Al's Diner over Kelly's Diner. In so doing, you might have cost Kelly's more than just your own patronage. Let's see why.

Five minutes later, another hungry person walks by looking for somewhere to eat. He, too, sees Kelly's and Big Al's. Perhaps he has heard from some of his friends that Kelly's has good food. But he also sees that Big Al's has a customer (you) and that Kelly's is empty. He takes this information as a signal of quality—Big Al's must be better because it has more customers than Kelly's, and perhaps that customer, you, went to Big Al's because of some valuable information. So he ignores his private information (what he has heard from his friends) and follows you to Big Al's. As more and more people come looking for a diner, they, too, apply this reasoning and follow the herd. So Kelly's sits empty, while Big Al's is full.

This phenomenon is known as an **information cascade**, which occurs when people make choices based on the decisions of others rather than on their own private information—for example, the second customer ignoring the information from friends to follow you to Big Al's. It might seem reasonable to do this, because other people often make decisions based on some relevant information. The results of an information cascade, however, can be significant. For example, some economists view information cascades as an important reason behind significant asset price increases and subsequent corrections. For instance, people rush to buy the next big thing in the stock market, and the share price rises abnormally high. The subsequent correction lowers the share price, leading to considerable losses for those who got in late.

**Herding** is a behavior of individuals who conform to the decisions of others.

An **information cascade** occurs when people make the same decisions as others, ignoring their own private information.

*Excuse me. Can you direct us to the nearest sea cliff?*

# LETTING THE
# DATA SPEAK

## Your Peers Affect Your Waistline

The most commonly studied example of peer effects is in the classroom—how peers in your classroom affect you in economically important ways. One group of economists has taken the study of peer effects into a quite different direction. Scott Carrell, Mark Hoekstra, and James West used the random assignment of peer groups in the U.S. Air Force Academy (USAFA) to consider how peer effects impact fitness. Do you think poor fitness or obesity is linked to peer effects? The answer may surprise you.

Carrell, Hoekstra, and West studied the impact of peers on physical ability by using high school and college physical fitness results for students in the USAFA.[12] The USAFA is somewhat unique in that college students are randomly assigned to groups (squadrons) with approximately thirty other students, and these groups spend the majority of their time together. Further, the physical fitness of students at the USAFA is motivated through common training monitored relatively closely through a Physical Education Average score. The score combines a number of different physical activities and certain physical fitness requirements.

We show one of the main results from the research in Exhibit 18.11. The x-axis of the figure shows the proportion of students in the thirty-student USAFA groups who were in the lowest quintile (20 percent of least physically fit freshmen) for a high school measure of fitness involving various activities, such as pull-ups and push-ups. The y-axis records the probability of failing the USAFA fitness requirement. The curves on the graph represent high school fitness. These curves show a stark result: the probability of a student failing the fitness exam increases as the number of unfit students around him increases. Similar to our discussion of the Dartmouth roommate study, this result could be explained by several factors, including some "common shocks" that influence all members of a squadron. Nevertheless, it strongly suggests that the physical fitness of people around you is correlated with your own health!

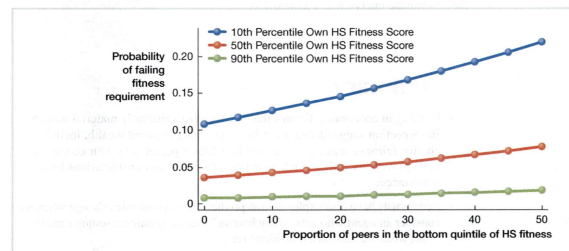

**Exhibit 18.11** The Effects of Peers on Health

Starting with the green curve, we can see that individuals who were in the 90th percentile of high school fitness seem to be unaffected by their peers in terms of probability of failing the USAFA fitness test. However, as we move toward individuals closer to average (red line) and below average (blue line) fitness in high school, the pattern emerges that the probability of failing the USAFA fitness test increases as the average fitness of your peer group drops (moving left to right along the x-axis).

Another place where information cascades potentially play an important role is in job interviews. An employer might look at a candidate's resume and see that he has been unemployed for some time. Even if the interview goes well and the candidate seems well suited for the job, the employer might interpret the information that the candidate has so far been unsuccessful in finding work as a signal that everyone else thinks this worker is

### Are You an Internet Explorer?

Of all the complaints about the Internet, one you will never hear is that there is a shortage of people expressing their opinions. Between the blogosphere, Twitter, and Facebook, if you have an opinion, you can get it onto the Internet (whether anyone reads it is an entirely different question).

With all of these opinions floating around, most people have little trouble finding the blogs and comments of like-minded individuals; psychologists call this phenomenon *confirmation bias*. Confirmation bias predicts that people only read articles that reaffirm their own beliefs, thus entrenching them further in their own prejudices.

Not all agree, however. A study of the 2004 election concludes that Internet users may be some of the most balanced media consumers.[13] Internet articles, especially blogs, are often formatted to present critiques of others' arguments and then provide the link to the original commentary. This fingertip access to both sides of an argument makes reading contradictory opinions much easier, not to mention cheaper, than subscribing to both the *New York Times* and *The Wall Street Journal*.

unqualified. The employer could then think that she is missing something important in her evaluation of the worker and might ignore her own positive signals in favor of the information contained in the candidate's unemployment history. She won't offer the interviewee a job, and neither will the next employer, or the next . . . this information cascade prolongs the unfortunate interviewee's joblessness.

## Summary

- Nothing in economics dictates that agents must value only material wealth. Introspection suggests that we value many things beyond wealth, including charity, fairness, trust, revenge, and how others perceive us. Our economic tools provide us with an understanding of when such considerations have importance.

- Economists have also explored how predictions in economics change when we consider an agent who acts "more human." Our economic reasoning remains intact when we add such considerations.

- In this way, predictions from the standard economic model are quite robust and help us study features of our economy—fairness, revenge, charity, trust, peer effects—that were not previously well understood.

- Taken together, these factors help us understand the world around us and how economics can be extended to every corner of our economy.

## Key Terms

pure altruism *p. 420*
impure altruism *p. 420*
fairness *p. 422*

indoctrination *p. 430*
peer effects *p. 431*

herding *p. 432*
information cascade *p. 432*

# Questions

*All questions are available in MyEconLab for practice and instructor assignment.*

1. How does the standard model of *Homo economicus* differ from the *Homo economicus* that is studied in behavioral and social economics?

2. Suppose the act of giving is viewed as an economic good. How can the price of charitable donations be measured? Does the quantity demanded decrease as the price of giving increases?

3. Is it correct to say that people give to charity only out of selflessness and concern for the well-being of others? Explain your answer.

4. Refer to the experiment in the chapter on soliciting donations for a children's hospital. Experimenters put flyers on doors saying that solicitors would be stopping by at a particular time. Fewer people opened the door when they knew that a solicitor would be coming, but those who did gave more money, on average, than others who did not know. What can you infer about pure and impure altruism from the results of this experiment?

5. In the context of this chapter, what is meant by having a preference for fairness?

6. In the *Friend or Foe?* game, Foe is a (weakly) dominant strategy for both players. What can explain why, in roughly 50 percent of decisions, players chose Friend and split the sum of money with the other player?

7. Why do lab experiments show a different outcome for the Ultimatum Game compared to the outcome predicted by game theory?

8. In the Dictator Game, the Allocator decides how a certain sum of money is to be divided, and the Recipient must accept whatever choice the Allocator makes. How does the outcome of the game differ when the Allocator remains anonymous to the Recipient versus when the Allocator faces the Recipient?

9. Consider a trust game between two players. Suppose the players care only about their own payoffs. The payoffs are such that, in equilibrium, the players do not trust each other, leading to a socially inefficient equilibrium. How could the game be changed so that in equilibrium, the players do trust each other?

10. How does indoctrination affect our preferences? Explain with an example.

11. What does it mean to say that a good exhibits network externalities? Can you think of a good that you use because it has network externalities?

12. What does herding mean? Why do individuals decide to herd?

13. What is an information cascade? Explain with examples.

# Problems

*All problems are available in MyEconLab for practice and instructor assignment.*

1. Under the tax law in 2012, you could claim all of your charitable contributions as a deduction on your federal income tax (if you decided to itemize your deductions), and the top marginal tax rate was 35 percent.

    a. What is the cost of a $100 charitable contribution under 2012 tax law for someone who itemizes and who is in the top tax bracket?

    b. The top marginal tax rate was raised to 39.6 percent in 2013. How would this change affect the cost of a $100 charitable contribution for someone who is in the top tax bracket?

    c. One proposed change to the 2012 law would have left the top tax rate at 35 percent but would have placed a cap on itemized deductions of $25,000. Mr. Smith is in the top tax bracket and has $25,000 of deductions for property taxes and interest on a mortgage. How would this change affect Mr. Smith's cost of a $100 charitable contribution?

2. Consider a three-person version of the Ultimatum Game: The Responder does not receive any money but instead decides whether to accept on behalf of a third-party bystander. Otherwise the structure is like that of the Ultimatum game in which the Proposer first decides how to split $10.00. Suppose that in this version you observe the Responder typically only accepts equal splits of $5.00 each (or splits that give a bigger share?), and typically rejects all other offers. How would you interpret this sort of result?

3. There are five people in a village. Each has $10. The village is prone to flooding. Flooding is reduced if people contribute to flood-control efforts. In particular, *each* person in the village receives $0.50 of benefits when someone contributes $1 to flood control (flood control is a public good). So suppose, for example, that each person contributes $4 to flood control. Total contributions will equal $5 \times \$4 = \$20$, each person will be left with $\$10 - \$4 = \$6$ to purchase

goods such as food and clothing, and each person will receive 0.5 × $20 = $10 in benefits from flood control. Everyone in the village makes their decision about contributions without talking to anyone else in the village.

**a.** Suppose people care only about their consumption of goods and their benefits from flood control. Show that contributing $0 is a dominant strategy.

**b.** Now suppose that each person cares about the total welfare in the village, including their benefits from flood control. Show that everyone in the village will contribute their entire $10 to flood control.

4. Let's add a twist to the Ultimatum Game: there is $10.00 to be split, but if the Responder rejects the offer, then he gets $2.00 and the Proposer gets $4.00. Use backward induction to determine the equilibrium. Assume that $0.01 is the smallest increment of money possible.

5. Assume that a charity hired you to improve its results on donations. You decide to mail letters asking for donations. You use three different types of letters:

Letter A: Control—standard letter asking for money.

Letter B: "Once and Done"—standard letter but with a statement at the front noting that: "Make one gift now and we'll never ask for another donation again!"

Letter C: Soft "Once and Done"—an upfront statement of: "It takes only one gift to save a child's life forever."

The results are as follows:

Letter B ("Once and Done") raises much more money than Letter A (Control): In most cases, at least double.

Letter C (Soft "Once and Done") raises more money than Letter A.

Letter B raises about 50 percent more money than Letter C.

Of the concepts we have discussed in the chapter—social pressure, altruism, and herding—which do you think is most responsible for the success of treatment B?

6. In Mario Puzo's *The Godfather*, Michael Corleone (played by Al Pacino in the movie version of the book) would like to meet with Virgil "The Turk" Sollozzo. Michael is concerned that if he meets with Sollozzo, Sollozzo will kill him. We can think of their problem as a game. First, Michael decides whether to meet. If they do not meet, suppose Sollozzo and the Corleones each get a payoff of zero. If they do agree to meet, then Sollozzo will decide whether to kill Michael. If he decides to kill him, then Sollozzo gets a payoff of 20 and the Corleones get a payoff of −10; if he does not kill him, then each gets a payoff of 10.

**a.** Draw the game tree.

**b.** Use backward induction to show that Michael will not agree to meet.

**c.** The Bocchicchio family had a well-deserved reputation for ruthlessness. They had a simple code of vengeance; if you were responsible for the death of a member of their family, they would kill a member of yours, regardless of the cost to them. Suppose that when Michael meets with Sollozzo, he also hires a member of the Bocchicchio family to go to Michael's house. There, the "hostage" will be guarded by Michael's men. If Michael does not return safely, Michael's men will kill the hostage. The Bocchicchio family, seeking revenge, will blame Sollozzo for the death, since Sollozzo made the promise that Michael would not be harmed, and will eventually kill Sollozzo. If Michael and Sollozzo are both killed, the Corleone family and Sollozzo each gets a payoff of −10. Use backward induction to determine how this game will be played.

7. Consider the Ultimatum Game played in reverse: The Responder moves first and decides preemptively whether to accept or reject whatever split the Proposer eventually determines. If the Responder chooses to reject, both players get nothing; but if the Responder accepts, then the Proposer decides how to split $10.00 between the two players. Describe the equilibrium predicted by standard economic theory. To the extent this outcome is not what happens in practice, speculate as to why not.

8. What if the Trust Game were played in reverse? Gary first decides whether to cooperate (Gary gets $15, Jen gets $15) or defect (Gary gets $30, Jen gets $0). Jen then decides whether to accept this outcome or give $10 to both players. What is the equilibrium? How does this compare to the outcome when the game is played in the typical order?

9. Maya and Paul want to watch a movie. There are two movies available: a comedy and an action film. Maya loves comedies, whereas Paul enjoys action films.

**a.** As separate individuals, which movie will Maya choose? Which one will Paul choose? Why?

**b.** If Maya and Paul are on a date, what factors (other than the movie genre) would affect their choices? If Maya decides to watch the comedy, which movie should Paul choose to get the highest payoff?

**c.** Suppose a group of people just came out of the movie theater gushing about how great the comedy was and another group complaining that the action film was really bad. What movie should Maya and Paul choose? How is this herd behavior? How can it lead to an information cascade?

10. A field experiment was conducted to see how others' opinions affect a user's ratings online. Whenever a comment was added on a certain social news site, researchers randomly assigned an up vote, a down vote, or no vote. The researchers conducting the experiment noted that comments that were given an up vote were more likely to get another up vote compared to the comments that were given other ratings. What do you think could explain this?

**11.** There was a sharp increase in the number of the long-term unemployed following the recession that began in December 2007. Rand Ghayad did the following study to better understand long-term unemployment. He sent out 3,600 fake resumes in response to 600 job openings. He varied the length of time his fake applicants had been out of work, how often they had switched jobs, and their work experience. He found that the longer the "applicants" were out of work, the less likely they were to be offered an interview. How could you use the idea of an information cascade to explain the results of this study?

**12.** You must decide whether to eat at Burger Hut or Pizza King, two local restaurants that are right next to each other. You have heard a few good things about Burger Hut, so your prior is that there is a 60% chance it is better; thus there is a 40% chance Pizza King is better. However, when you arrive to eat, you see one customer at Pizza King but nobody at Burger Hut. You believe that any person off the street, when given two options, will pick the better restaurant 75% of the time. Based on what you believe and what you have seen, what is the probability that Pizza King is the better restaurant?

# Endnotes

## Chapter 1

1. Earnings estimate is from the 2014 census data: http://www. census.gov/content/dam/Census/library/publications/2015/demo/ p60-252.pdf.

2. See Facebook's own website: http://newsroom.fb.com/company-info/ and http://www.businessinsider.com/how-much-time-people-spend-on-facebook-per-day-2015-7.

3. Adam Nagourney, "California Imposes First Mandatory Water Restrictions to Deal with Drought," *New York Times,* April 1, 2015, http://www.nytimes.com/2015/04/02/us/california-imposes-first-ever-water-restrictions-to-deal-with-drought.html?_r=0.

4. Ian Lovett, "In California, Stingy Water Users Are Fined, While the Rich Soak," *New York Times*, November 21, 2015, http:// www.nytimes.com/2015/11/22/us/stingy-water-users-in-fined-in-drough t-while-the-rich-soak.html.

## Chapter 2

1. These data for 2015–2016 are from the College Board: https:// trends.collegeboard.org/sites/default/files/2016-trends-college-pricing-web_1.pdf.

2. S. A. Mehr, A. Schachner, R. C. Katz, and E. S. Spelke, "Two Randomized Trials Provide No Consistent Evidence for Nonmusical Cognitive Benefits of Brief Preschool Music Enrichment," *PLoS ONE* 8(12): 2013, e82007. doi:10.1371/ journal.pone.0082007.

3. Andrew M. Francis and Hugo M. Mialon, " 'A Diamond Is Forever' and Other Fairy Tales: The Relationship Between Wedding Expenses and Marriage Duration," September 15, 2014. Available at the Social Science Research Network: http:// ssrn.com/abstract=2501480 or http://dx.doi.org/10.2139/ ssrn.2501480.

4. Philip Oreopoulos, "Estimating Average and Local Treatment Effects of Education When Compulsory Schooling Laws Really Matter," *American Economic Review* 96(1): 2006, 152–175.

## Chapter 2 Appendix

1. Steven D. Levitt, John A. List, and Sally Sadoff, "The Effect of Performance-Based Incentives on Educational Achievement: Evidence from a Randomized Experiment," NBER Working Paper 22107, Cambridge, MA: National Bureau of Economic Research, 2016.

## Chapter 3

1. John Y. Campbell, Tarun Ramadorai, and Benjamin Ranish, "Getting Better or Feeling Better? How Equity Investors Respond to Investment Experience," NBER Working Paper 20000, Cambridge, MA: National Bureau of Economic Research, 2014, http://www. nber.org/papers/w20000.

2. James Frew and Beth Wilson, "Apartment Rents and Locations in Portland, Oregon: 1992–2002," *Journal of Real Estate Research* 29(2): 2007, 201–217.

## Chapter 4

1. Chico Harlan, "The Hummer Is Back. Thank Falling Oil Prices," *Washington Post*, November 10, 2014. https://www. washingtonpost.com/news/wonk/wp/2014/11/10/the-hummer-is-back-thank-falling-oil-prices/.

2. Source: International Energy Agency.

3. Source: International Energy Agency.

4. Fred Ferretti, "The Way We Were: A Look Back at the Late Great Gas Shortage," *New York Times,* April 15, 1974, p. 386. Subsequent quotes are from the same article.

5. Stephanie McCrummen and Aymar Jean, "17 Hurt as Computer Sale Turns into Stampede," *Washington Post*, August 17, 2005. http://www.washingtonpost.com/wp-dyn/content/article/2005/ 08/16/AR2005081600738.htm.

## Chapter 5

1. Kevin G. Volpp, Andrea G. Levy, David A. Asch, Jesse A. Berlin, John J. Murphy, Angela Gomez, Harold Sox, Jingsan Zhu, and Caryn Lerman, "A Randomized Controlled Trial of Financial Incentives for Smoking Cessation," *Cancer Epidemiology Biomarkers Prevention* 15(1): 2006, 8–12.

2. Kate Cahill and Rafael Perera, "Competitions and Incentives for Smoking Cessation," *Cochrane Database of Systematic Reviews* 3: 2008, 1–36.

3. George Baltas, "Modelling Category Demand in Retail Chains," *Journal of the Operational Research Society* 56(11): 2005, 1258–1264; Frank J. Chaloupka, Michael Grossman, and Henry Saffer, "The Effects of Price on Alcohol Consumption and Alcohol-Related Problems," *Alcohol Research and Health* 26(1): 2002, 22–34; Craig A. Gallet and John A. List, "Cigarette Demand: A Meta-Analysis of Elasticities," *Health Economics* 12(10): 2003, 821–835; Thomas F. Hogarty and Kenneth G. Elzinga, "The Demand for Beer," *Review of Economics and Statistics* 54(2): 1972, 195–198; Fred Kuchler, Abebayehu Tegene, and J. Michael Harris, "Taxing Snack Foods: Manipulating Diet Quality or Financing Information Programs?" *Applied Economic Perspectives and Policy* 27(1): 2005, 4–20; and USDA Economic Research Service Commodity and Food Elasticities Database, July 5, 2012, http://www.ers.usda.gov/data-products/commodity-and-food-elasticities.aspx#.UsYKP_RDvW1.

4. Angus Deaton, "Estimation of Own- and Cross-Price Elasticities from Household Survey Data," *Journal of Econometrics* 36(1): 1987, 7–30; Edwin T. Fujii, Mohammed Khaled, and James Mak, "An Almost Ideal Demand System for Visitor Expenditures," *Journal of Transport Economics and Policy* 19(2): 1985, 161–171; and Tatiana Andreyeva, Michael W. Long, and Kelly D. Brownell, "The Impact of Food Prices on Consumption: A Systematic Review of Research on the Price Elasticity of Demand for Food," *American Journal of Public Health* 100(2): 2010, 216–222.

5. Oskar R. Harmon, "The Income Elasticity of Demand for Single-Family Owner-Occupied Housing: An Empirical Reconciliation," *Journal of Urban Economics* 24(2): 1988, 173–185; Livio

Di Matteo, "The Income Elasticity of Health Care Spending," *European Journal of Health Economics* 4(1): 2003, 20–29; Bengt Kristrom and Pere Riera, "Is the Income Elasticity of Environmental Improvements Less Than One?" *Environmental and Resource Economics* 7(1): 1996, 45–55; E. Raphael Branch, "Short Run Income Elasticity of Demand for Residential Electricity Using Consumer Expenditure Survey Data," *Energy Journal* 4: 1993, 111–122; Jonathan E. Hughes, Christopher R. Knittel, and Daniel Sperling, "Evidence of a Shift in the Short-Run Price Elasticity of Gasoline Demand," NBER Working Paper 12530, Cambridge, MA: National Bureau of Economic Research, 2006; Laura Blanciforti and Richard Green, "An Almost Ideal Demand System Incorporating Habits: An Analysis of Expenditures on Food and Aggregate Commodity Groups," *Review of Economics and Statistics* 65(3): 1983, 511–515; Howarth E. Bouis, "The Effect of Income on Demand for Food in Poor Countries: Are Our Food Consumption Databases Giving Us Reliable Estimates?" *Journal of Development Economics* 44(1): 1994, 199–226; Neil Paulley, Richard Balcombe, Roger Mackett, Helena Titheridge, John Preston, Mark Wardman, Jeremy Shires, and Peter White, "The Demand for Public Transport: The Effects of Fares, Quality of Service, Income and Car Ownership," *Transport Policy* 13(4): 2006, 295–306; Arthur Van Soest and Peter Kooreman, "A Micro-Econometric Analysis of Vacation Behaviour," *Journal of Applied Econometrics* 2(3): 1987, 215–226; Bertrand Melenberg and Arthur Van Soest, "Parametric and Semi-Parametric Modelling of Vacation Expenditures," *Journal of Applied Econometrics* 11(1): 1996, 59–76; and Eric S. Belsky, Xiao Di Zhu, and Dan McCue, "Multiple-Home Ownership and the Income Elasticity of Housing Demand," Cambridge, MA: Joint Center for Housing Studies, Graduate School of Design, and John F. Kennedy School of Government, Harvard University, 2006.

6. Tatiana Andreyeva, Michael W. Long, and Kelly D. Brownell, "The Impact of Food Prices on Consumption: A Systematic Review of Research on the Price Elasticity of Demand for Food," *American Journal of Public Health* 100(2): 2010, 216–222.

## Chapter 6

1. This actually happened to one of the authors.

2. Based on Adam Malecek, "Wisconsin Cheeseman Closing," Sun Prairie Channel 3000.com, January 20, 2011.

3. Alec Brandon, John List, and Michael Price, "The Effects of Ethanol Subsidies on Producers," working paper, Chicago: University of Chicago.

## Chapter 7

1. Adam Smith, *The Wealth of Nations* (London: William Strahan and Thomas Cadell, 1776).

2. Vernon Smith, "Microeconomic Systems as an Experimental Science," *American Economic Review* 72(5): 1982, 923–955. American Economic Association.

3. Portland, Oregon, Bureau of Transportation, "Report on Uber and Lyft," 2015. Online at http://www.portlandoregon.gov/novick/article/537131.

4. Uber, "4 Septembers of UberX in NYC," *Uber Newsroom*, October 6, 2015.

5. Jonathan Hall and Chris Nosko, "Dynamic Labor Supply in the Sharing Economy," working paper, 2015. http://www.sole-jole.org/16433.pdf.

6. Steven Horwitz, "Wal-Mart to the Rescue: Private Enterprise's Response to Hurricane Katrina," *Independent Review* 13(4): 2009, 511–528.

7. Friedrich A. Hayek, "The Use of Knowledge in Society," *American Economic Review* 35(4): 1945, 519–530.

8. This box is based on Mark Albright, "Kmart's Blue Light Back On," *Tampa Bay Times,* May 16, 2007, http://www.sptimes.com/2007/05/16/Business/Kmart_s_blue_light_ba.shtml.

## Chapter 8

1. Fair Trade Labelling Organizations International, *Annual Report 2009–10*.

2. Hal Weitzman, "The Bitter Cost of 'Fair Trade' Coffee," *Financial Times*, September 8, 2006.

3. Lorenzo Caliendo and Fernando Parro, "Estimates of the Trade and Welfare Effects of NAFTA," *Review of Economic Studies* 82(1): 2014, 1–44.

4. Paul Krugman, "Growing World Trade: Causes and Consequences," *Brookings Papers on Economic Activity*, Economic Studies Program 26: 1995, 327–377; and Robert Z. Lawrence, Matthew J. Slaughter, Robert E. Hall, Steven J. Davis, and Robert H. Topel, "International Trade and American Wages in the 1980s: Giant Sucking Sound or Small Hiccup?" *Brookings Papers on Economic Activity*, Microeconomics 2: 1993, 161–226.

5. Robert Z. Lawrence, "Slow Real Wage Growth and U.S. Income Inequality: Is Trade to Blame?" Conference paper prepared for "Is Free Trade Still Optimal in the 21st Century?" International Business School at Brandeis University, 2007.

6. Justin R. Pierce and Peter K. Schott, "The Surprisingly Swift Decline of U.S. Manufacturing Employment," *American Economic Review* 106(7): 2016, 1632–1662.

7. Paul Krugman, "Trade and Wages, Reconsidered," *Brookings Papers on Economic Activity* Spring, 2008, 103–154.

## Chapter 9

1. This is a true story; we withhold identities to protect the professor.

2. Bryan L. Boulier, Tejwant S. Datta, and Robert S. Goldfarb, "Vaccination Externalities," *B.E. Journal of Economic Analysis & Policy* 7(1): 2007, article 23.

3. See, for example, F. Rall Walsh, III, and Mark D. Zoback, "Oklahoma's Recent Earthquakes and Saltwater Disposal," *Science Advances*, June 18, 2015. http://advances.sciencemag.org/content/1/5/e1500195.full.

4. Kenneth Y. Chay and Michael Greenstone, "Does Air Quality Matter? Evidence from the Housing Market," *Journal of Political Economy* 113(2): 2005, 376-424.

5. David H. Folz and Jacqueline N. Giles, "Municipal Experience with 'Pay-as-You-Throw' Policies: Findings from a National Survey," *State and Local Government Review* 34(2): 2002, 105–115.

6. Joseph M. Sulock, "The Free Rider and Voting Paradox 'Games'," *Journal of Economic Education* 21(1): 1990, 65–69.

7. Garrett Hardin, "The Tragedy of the Commons," *Science* 162(3859): 1968, 1243–1248; William Forster Lloyd, *Two Lectures on the Checks to Population* (1833).

8. Elinor Ostrom, *Governing the Commons: The Evolution of Institutions for Collective Action* (Cambridge: Cambridge University Press, 1990). See also Peter J. Deadman, Edella Schlager, and Randy Gimblett, "Simulating Common Pool Resource Management Experiments with Adaptive Agents Employing Alternate Communication Routines," *Journal of Artificial Societies and Social Simulation* 3(2): 2000, 22.

### Chapter 10

9. Jonathan Leape, "The London Congestion Charge," *Journal of Economic Perspectives* 20(4): 2006, 157–176.

10. Hybrid vehicles emit less pollution, and this was the reason for the tax break. This is an excellent example of the trade-off inherent in using a tax policy to reduce congestion and pollution.

### Chapter 10

1. *America's Fiscal Insolvency and Its Generational Consequences: Testimony to the Senate Budget Committee* (2015) (Statement of Laurence J. Kotlikoff, Professor of Economics, Boston University).

2. See William Niskanen, "The Peculiar Economics of Bureaucracy," *American Economic Review* 58(2): 1968, 293–305.

3. Arthur M. Okun, *Equality and Efficiency, the Big Tradeoff*, Washington, D.C.: Brookings Institution Press, 1975.

4. Ritva Reinikka and Jakob Svensson, "Local Capture: Evidence from a Central Government Transfer Program in Uganda," *Quarterly Journal of Economics* 119(2): 2004, 679–705.

5. The data come from a 1987 U.S. Department of Justice report.

6. Barry Bosworth and Gary Burtless, "Effects of Tax Reform on Labor Supply, Investment, and Saving," *Journal of Economic Perspectives* 6(1): 1992, 3–25.

7. There are, of course, exceptions to this. For a summary of elasticities in the literature, see Blundell and MaCurdy (1999). Blundell and MaCurdy (1999), Saez, Slemrod, and Giertz (2012), and Goolsbee (2000) conclude that the elasticity on hours supplied is close to zero for men. Richard Blundell and Thomas MaCurdy, "Labor Supply: A Review of Alternative Approaches," in *Handbook of Labor Economics* (Vol. 3C), eds. O. Ashenfelter and D. Card, Amsterdam: Elsevier North Holland, 1999; Emmanuel Saez, Joel Slemrod, and Seth H. Giertz, "The Elasticity of Taxable Income with Respect to Marginal Tax Rates: A Critical Review," *Journal of Economic Literature* 50(1): 2012, 3–50; Austan Goolsbee, "What Happens When You Tax the Rich? Evidence from Executive Compensation," *Journal of Political Economy* 108(2): 2000, 352–378.

8. Martin Feldstein, "The Effect of Marginal Tax Rates on Taxable Income: A Panel Study of the 1986 Tax Reform Act," *Journal of Political Economy* 103(3): 1995, 551–572; Gerald E. Auten and Robert Carroll, "Behavior of the Affluent and the 1986 Tax Reform Act," in *Proceedings of the 87th Annual Conference on Taxation of the National Tax Association* (1995): 7–12.

9. Jonathan M. Karpoff, "Public Versus Private Initiative in Arctic Exploration: The Effects of Incentives and Organizational Structure," *Journal of Political Economy* 109(1): 2001, 38–78.

10. Ufuk Akcigit, Salomé Baslandze, and Stefanie Stantcheva, "Taxation and the International Mobility of Inventors," *American Economic Review* 106(10): 2016, 2930-81.

### Chapter 11

1. Gerald S. Oettinger, "An Empirical Analysis of the Daily Labor Supply of Stadium Vendors," *Journal of Political Economy* 107(2): 1999, 360–392.

2. Joshua Angrist, "The Economic Returns to Schooling in the West Bank and Gaza Strip," *American Economic Review* 85(5): 1995, 1065–1087.

3. Gary S. Becker, *The Economics of Discrimination*, Chicago: University of Chicago Press, 1957.

4. Anders Akerman, Ingvil Gaarder, and Magne Mogstad, "The Skill Complementarity of Broadband Internet," *Quarterly Journal of Economics* 130(4): 2015, 1781–1824.

5. Thomas Piketty and Emmanuel Saez, "Income Inequality in the United States, 1913–1998," *Quarterly Journal of Economics* 118(1): 2003, 1–39.

6. Thomas Piketty, *Capital in the Twenty-First Century*, Cambridge, MA: Belknap Press of Harvard University, 2014.

7. Claudia Goldin and Cecilia Rouse, "Orchestrating Impartiality: The Impact of 'Blind' Auditions on Female Musicians," *American Economic Review* 90(4): 2000, 715–741.

8. Marianne Bertrand and Sendhil Mullainathan, "Are Emily and Greg More Employable Than Lakisha and Jamal? A Field Experiment on Labor Market Discrimination," *American Economic Review* 94(4): 2004, 991–1013.

9. Kerwin Charles and Jonathan Guryan, "Prejudice and Wages: An Empirical Assessment of Becker's *The Economics of Discrimination*," *Journal of Political Economy* 116(5): 2008, 773–809.

10. For one attempt at doing so using a field experiment, see John A. List, "The Nature and Extent of Discrimination in the Marketplace: Evidence from the Field," *Quarterly Journal of Economics* 119(1): 2004, 49–89. This study uses a series of field experiments to show that women, the elderly, and African Americans receive higher price quotes in the sportscar market due to statistical discrimination.

11. Marianna Bertrand, Claudia Goldin, and Lawrence F. Katz, "Dynamics of the Gender Gap for Young Professionals in the Financial and Corporate Sectors," *American Economic Journal: Applied Economics* 2(3): 2010, 228–255.

### Chapter 12

1. Malcolm Gladwell, *Blink: The Power of Thinking without Thinking* (New York: Hachette Book Group USA, 2007).

2. The expiration of the Claritin patent was to occur on June 19, 2000. However, Schering-Plough requested, and was awarded, a 2-year extension. This extended the patent until June 19, 2002, when it expired.

3. Uri Gneezy, John A. List, and Michael K. Price, "Toward an Understanding of Why People Discriminate: Evidence from a Series of Natural Field Experiments," NBER Working Paper 17855, Cambridge, MA: National Bureau of Economic Research, 2012.

4. Petra Moser, "How Do Patent Laws Influence Innovation? Evidence from Nineteenth-Century World's Fairs," *American Economic Review* 95(4): 2005, 1214–1236.

5. Heidi Williams, "Intellectual Project Rights and Innovation: Evidence from the Human Genome Project," *Journal of Political Economy* 121(1): 2013, 1–27.

6. Philippe Aghion, Nick Bloom, Richard Blundell, Rachel Griffith, and Peter Howitt, "Competition and Innovation: An Inverted-U Relationship," *Quarterly Journal of Economics* 120(2): 2005, 701–728.

### Chapter 13

1. John F. Nash, Jr., "Non-Cooperative Games," PhD thesis, Mathematics Department, Princeton University, 1950.

2. Pierre-Andre Chiappori, Steven D. Levitt, and Timothy Groseclose, "Testing Mixed-Strategy Equilibria When Players Are Heterogeneous: The Case of Penalty Kicks in Soccer," *American Economic Review* 92(4): 2002, 1138–1151.

3. Mark Walker and John Wooders, "Minimax Play at Wimbledon," *American Economic Review* 91(5): 2001, 1521–1538.

4. John Maynard Keynes, *The General Theory of Employment, Interest, and Money*, London: Macmillan, 1936.

5. Antoni Bosch-Domènech, Rosemarie Nagel, Albert Satorra, and Jose García-Montalvo, "One, Two, (Three), Infinity: Newspaper and Lab Beauty-Contest Experiments," *American Economic Review* 92(5): 2002, 1687–1701.

6. Werner Guth, Martin Kocher, and Matthias Sutter, "Experimental 'Beauty Contests' with Homogeneous and Heterogeneous Players and with Interior and Boundary Equilibria," *Economic Letters* 74(2): 2002, 219–228.

7. John A. List, "The Behavioralist Meets the Market: Measuring Social Preferences and Reputation Effects in Actual Transactions," *Journal of Political Economy* 114(1): 2006, 1–37.

## Chapter 14

1. Austan Goolsbee and Chad Syverson, "How Do Incumbents Respond to the Threat of Entry? Evidence from the Major Airlines," *Quarterly Journal of Economics* 123(4): 2008, 1611–1633.

2. http://www.forbes.com/sites/chuckjones/2016/02/21/apples-iphone-market-share-vs-profits/#35921ee146f8.

3. http://www.eia.gov/todayinenergy/detail.cfm?id=25372.

4. Laura Hurst, Nayla Razzouk, and Julian Lee, "OPEC Unity Shattered as Saudi-Led Policy Leads to No Limits," *Bloomberg News,* December 4, 2015.

5. https://www.justice.gov/opa/pr/adm-subsidiary-pleads-guilty-conspiracy-violate-foreign-corrupt-practices-act.

6. John E. Kwoka, Jr., "Advertising and the Price and Quality of Optometric Services," *American Economic Review* 74(1): 1984, 211–216.

7. Timothy F. Bresnahan and Peter C. Reiss, "Entry and Competition in Concentrated Markets," *Journal of Political Economy* 99(5): 1991, 977–1009.

8. Martin Dufwenberg and Uri Gneezy, "Price Competition and Market Concentration: An Experimental Study," *International Journal of Industrial Organization* 18(1): 2000, 7–22.

## Chapter 15

1. Nate Silver's site, FiveThirtyEight.com.

2. Daniel Read and Barbara van Leeuwen, "Predicting Hunger: The Effects of Appetite and Delay on Choice," *Organizational Behavior and Human Decision Processes* 76(2): 1998, 189–205.

3. See Nate Silver's site, FiveThirtyEight.com.

4. See the Jawbone survey: https://jawbone.com/blog/university-students-sleep/.

5. On an actual roulette wheel in the United States, the expected loss per spin is 5.3 percent of the bet you make.

6. Daniel Kahneman and Amos Tversky, "Prospect Theory: An Analysis of Decision under Risk," *Econometrica* 47(2): 1979, 263–292.

## Chapter 16

1. Michael A. Spence, "Job Market Signaling," *Quarterly Journal of Economics* 87(3): 1973, 355–374.

2. George A. Akerlof, "The Market for 'Lemons': Quality Uncertainty and the Market Mechanism," *Quarterly Journal of Economics* 84(3): 1970, 488–500.

3. Michael D. Pratt and George E. Hoffer, "Test of the Lemons Model: Comment," *American Economic Review* 74(4): 1984, 798–800.

4. Winand Emons and George Sheldon, "The Market for Used Cars: A New Test of the Lemons Model," Discussion Paper Series 26353, Hamburg Institute of International Economics, 2002.

5. Sean B. Carroll, *Making of the Fittest*, New York: W. W. Norton & Company, 2007.

6. Frank T. McDermott, John C. Lane, G. A. Brazenor, and Elizabeth A. Debney, "The Effectiveness of Bicyclist Helmets: A Study of 1710 Casualties," *Journal of Trauma and Acute Care Surgery* 34(6): 1993, 834–845.

7. Ian Walker, "Drivers Overtaking Bicyclists: Objective Data on the Effects of Riding Position, Helmet Use, Vehicle Type and Apparent Gender," *Accident Analysis and Prevention* 39(2): 2007, 417–425.

8. This discussion draws on Daniel M. G. Raff and Lawrence H. Summers, "Did Henry Ford Pay Efficiency Wages?" *Journal of Labor Economics* 5(4): 1987, S57–S86.

9. Henry Ford, *My Life and Work,* Garden City, NY: Double Day, 1922, pp. 126, 127, 167.

10. Henry Ford, *My Life and Work,* Garden City, NY: Double Day, 1922, pp. 126, 127, 167.

11. Roland G. Fryer, Jr., Steven D. Levitt, John A. List, and Sally Sadoff, "Enhancing the Efficacy of Teacher Incentives Through Loss Aversion: A Field Experiment," NBER Working Paper 18237, Cambridge, MA: National Bureau of Economic Research, 2012.

12. Brian A. Jacob and Steven D. Levitt, "Rotten Apples: An Investigation of the Prevalence and Predictors of Teacher Cheating," *Quarterly Journal of Economics* 118(3): 2003, 843–877.

13. David M. Cutler and Sarah J. Reber, "Paying for Health Insurance: The Trade-off Between Competition and Adverse Selection," *Quarterly Journal of Economics* 113(2): 1998, 433–466.

14. Amitabh Chandra, Jonathan Gruber, and Robin McKnight, "The Importance of the Individual Mandate—Evidence from Massachusetts," *New England Journal of Medicine* 364(4): 2011, 293–295.

15. Alan B. Krueger and Andreas Mueller, "Job Search and Unemployment Insurance: New Evidence from Time Use Data," *Journal of Public Economics* 94(3): 2010, 298–307.

16. David Card, Raj Chetty, and Andrea Weber, "The Spike at Benefit Exhaustion: Leaving the Unemployment System or Starting a New Job?" *American Economic Review* 97(2): 2007, 113–118.

17. Gary S. Becker, "Crime and Punishment: An Economic Approach," *Journal of Political Economy* 76(2): 1968, 169–217; Gary S. Becker and George J. Stigler, "Law Enforcement, Malfeasance, and Compensation of Enforcers," *Journal of Legal Studies* 3(1): 1974, 1–18.

## Chapter 17

1. Recent research by Einav, Farronato, Levin, and Sundaresan shows that on eBay, the fraction of items sold in auctions fell from about 80 percent at the beginning of 2008 to less than 30 percent in 2011, with a corresponding increase in the fraction of items sold with posted prices; Liran Einav, Chiara Farronato, Jonathan D. Levin, and Neel Sundaresan, "Sales Mechanisms in Online

Markets: What Happened to Internet Auctions?" NBER Working Paper 19021, Cambridge, MA: National Bureau of Economic Research, 2013.

2. Alvin E. Roth and Axel Ockenfels, "Last-Minute Bidding and the Rules for Ending Second-Price Auctions: Evidence from eBay and Amazon Auctions on the Internet," *American Economic Review* 92(4): 2002, 1093–1103.

3. Sean Gray and David H. Reiley, "Measuring the Benefits to Sniping on eBay: Evidence from a Field Experiment," *Journal of Economics and Management* 9(2): 2013, 137–152.

4. William Vickrey, "Counterspeculation, Auctions, and Competitive Sealed Tenders," *Journal of Finance* 16(1): 1961, 8–37.

5. David Lucking-Reiley, "Using Field Experiments to Test Equivalence Between Auction Formats: Magic on the Internet," *American Economic Review* 89(5): 1999, 1063–1080.

6. Shelly J. Lundberg, Robert A. Pollak, and Terence J. Wales, "Do Husbands and Wives Pool Their Resources? Evidence from the United Kingdom Child Benefit," *Journal of Human Resources* 32(3): 1996, 463–480.

7. Nancy Qian, "Missing Women and the Price of Tea in China: The Effect of Sex-Specific Earnings on Sex Imbalance," *Quarterly Journal of Economics* 123(3): 2008, 1251–1285.

8. Erwin Bulte, Qin Tu, and John A. List, "Battle of the Sexes: How Sex Ratios Affect Female Bargaining Power," *Economic Development and Cultural Change* 64(1): 2015, 143–161.

## Chapter 18

1. Charles T. Clotfelter, "The Impact of Tax Reform on Charitable Giving: A 1989 Perspective," NBER Working Paper 3273, Cambridge, MA: National Bureau of Economic Research, 1990.

2. Stefano DellaVigna, John A. List, and Ulrike Malmendier, "Testing for Altruism and Social Pressure in Charitable Giving," *Quarterly Journal of Economics* 127(1): 2012, 1–56.

3. These results are reported in John A. List, "Friend or Foe? A Natural Experiment of the Prisoner's Dilemma," *Review of Economics and Statistics* 88(3): 2006, 463–471.

4. Iris Bohnet and Bruno S. Frey, "Social Distance and Other-Regarding Behavior in Dictator Games: Comment," *American Economic Review* 89(1): 1999, 335–339.

5. Steffen Andersen, Seda Ertac, Uri Gneezy, Moshe Hoffman, and John A. List, "Stakes Matter in Ultimatum Games," *American Economic Review* 101(7): 2011, 3427–3439.

6. Kenneth J. Arrow, "Gifts and Exchanges," *Philosophy & Public Affairs* 1(4): 1972, 343–362.

7. Peter J. Richerson and Robert Boyd, *Not by Genes Alone: How Culture Transformed Human Evolution*, Chicago: University of Chicago Press, 2008; and Elliott Sober and David Sloan Wilson, eds., *Unto Others: The Evolution and Psychology of Unselfish Behavior*, Cambridge, MA: Harvard University Press, 1999.

8. David Sloan Wilson and Edward O. Wilson, "Rethinking the Theoretical Foundation of Sociobiology," *Quarterly Review of Biology* 82(4): 2007, 327–348.

9. Gerald Marwell and Ruth E. Ames, "Economists Free Ride, Does Anyone Else? Experiments on the Provision of Public Goods, IV," *Journal of Public Economics* 15(3): 1981, 295–310; John R. Carter and Michael D. Irons, "Are Economists Different, and If So, Why?" *Journal of Economic Perspectives* 5(2): 1991, 171–177; and Robert H. Frank, Thomas Gilovich, and Dennis T. Regan, "Does Studying Economics Inhibit Cooperation?" *Journal of Economic Perspectives* 7(2): 1993, 159–171.

10. Oriana Bandiera and Imran Rasul, "Social Networks and Technology Adoption in Northern Mozambique," *Economic Journal* 116(514): 2006, 869–902.

11. Bruce Sacerdote, "Peer Effects with Random Assignment: Results for Dartmouth Roommates," *Quarterly Journal of Economics* 116(2): 2001, 681–704.

12. Scott E. Carrell, Mark Hoekstra, and James E. West, "Is Poor Fitness Contagious? Evidence from Randomly Assigned Friends," *Journal of Public Economics* 95(7–8): 2011, 657–663.

13. John B. Horrigan, Kelly Garrett, and Paul Resnick, *The Internet and Democratic Debate*, Washington, D.C.: Pew Internet and American Life Project, 2004.

# Glossary

**Absolute advantage** Absolute advantage is the ability of an individual, firm, or country to produce more of a certain good than other competing producers, given the same amount of resources.

**Accounting profits** Accounting profits are equal to total revenue minus explicit costs.

**Adverse selection** In a market with adverse selection, one agent in a transaction knows about a hidden characteristic of a good and decides whether to participate in the transaction on the basis of this information.

**Aggregation** The process of adding up individual behaviors is referred to as aggregation.

**Antitrust policy** Antitrust policy aims to regulate and prevent anticompetitive pricing.

**Arc elasticity** The arc elasticity is a method of calculating elasticities that measures at the midpoint of the demand range.

**Asymmetric information** In a market with asymmetric information, the information available to sellers and buyers differs.

**Auction** An auction is a market process in which potential buyers bid on a good and the highest bidder receives the good.

**Average fixed cost (AFC)** Average fixed cost is the total fixed cost divided by the total output.

**Average tax rate** The average tax rate for a household is given by total taxes paid divided by total income.

**Average total cost (ATC)** Average total cost is the total cost divided by the total output.

**Average variable cost (AVC)** Average variable cost is the total variable cost divided by the total output.

**Average** The mean, or average, is the sum of all the different values divided by the number of values.

**Backward induction** Backward induction is the procedure of solving an extensive-form game by first considering the last mover's decision in order to deduce the decisions of all previous movers.

**Bar chart** A bar chart uses bars of different heights or lengths to indicate the properties of different groups.

**Bargaining power** Bargaining power describes the relative power an individual has in negotiations with another individual.

**Barriers to entry** Barriers to entry provide a seller with protection from potential competitors entering the market.

**Behavioral economics** Behavioral economics jointly analyzes the economic and psychological factors that explain human behavior.

**Best response** A strategy of a player is a best response to the strategies of the others in the game if, taking the other players' strategies as given, it gives her greater payoffs than any other strategy she has available.

**Bilateral negotiation** A bilateral negotiation is a market mechanism in which a single seller and a single buyer privately negotiate with bids and asks.

**Budget constraint** A budget constraint shows the bundles of goods or services that a consumer can choose given her limited budget.

**Budget deficit** A budget deficit occurs when tax revenues do not cover government spending.

**Budget set** A budget set is the set of all possible bundles of goods and services that can be purchased with a consumer's income.

**Budget surplus** A budget surplus occurs when tax revenues exceed government spending.

**Cartel** A cartel is a formal organization of producers who agree on anticompetitive actions.

**Causation** Causation occurs when one thing directly affects another through a cause-and-effect relationship.

**Club good** A club good is non-rival but excludable.

**Coase Theorem** The Coase Theorem states that private bargaining will result in an efficient allocation of resources.

**Collusion** Collusion occurs when firms conspire to set the quantity they produce or the prices they charge.

**Command-and-control regulation** Command-and-control regulation either directly restricts the level of production or mandates the use of certain technologies.

**Commitment** Commitment refers to the ability to choose and stick with an action that might later be costly.

**Common pool resource goods** Common pool resource goods are a class of goods that are rival and non-excludable.

**Comparative advantage** Comparative advantage is the ability of an individual, firm, or country to produce a certain good at a lower opportunity cost than other producers.

**Compensating wage differentials** Compensating wage differentials are wage premiums paid to attract workers to otherwise undesirable occupations.

**Competitive equilibrium** The competitive equilibrium is the crossing point of the supply curve and the demand curve.

**Competitive equilibrium price** The competitive equilibrium price equates quantity supplied and quantity demanded.

**Competitive equilibrium quantity** The competitive equilibrium quantity is the quantity that corresponds to the competitive equilibrium price.

**Complements** Two goods are complements when a fall in the price of one leads to a right shift in the demand curve for the other.

**Compound interest equation** The compound interest equation or future value equation calculates the future value of an investment with interest rate $r$ that leaves all interest payments in the account until the final withdrawal in year $T$.

**Constant returns to scale** Constant returns to scale occur when average total cost does not change as the quantity produced changes.

**Consumer sovereignty** Consumer sovereignty is the view that choices made by a consumer reflect his or her true preferences, and outsiders, including the government, should not interfere with these choices.

**Consumer surplus** Consumer surplus is the difference between the willingness to pay and the price paid for the good.

**Coordination problem** When the interests of economic agents coincide, a coordination problem of bringing the agents together to trade arises.

**Copyright** A copyright is an exclusive right granted by the government to the creator of a literary or artistic work.

**Corporate income taxes** Corporate income taxes are taxes paid by firms to the government from their profits.

**Corrective subsidies** Corrective subsidies, or Pigouvian subsidies, are designed to induce agents who produce positive externalities to increase quantity toward the socially optimal level.

**Correlation** A correlation means that two variables tend to change at the same time.

**Corruption** Corruption refers to the misuse of public funds or the distortion of the allocation of resources for personal gain.

**Cost of production** The cost of production is what a firm must pay for its inputs.

**Cost-benefit analysis** Cost-benefit analysis is a calculation that adds up costs and benefits using a common unit of measurement, like dollars.

**Cross-price elasticity of demand** Cross-price elasticity of demand measures the percentage change in quantity demanded of a good due to a percentage change in another good's price.

**Data** Data are facts, measurements, or statistics that describe the world.

**Deadweight loss** Deadweight loss is the decrease in social surplus from a market distortion.

**Demand curve** The demand curve plots the quantity demanded at different prices. A demand curve plots the demand schedule.

**Demand curve shifts** The demand curve shifts when the quantity demanded changes at a given price.

**Demand schedule** A demand schedule is a table that reports the quantity demanded at different prices, holding all else equal.

**Dependent variable** A dependent variable is a variable whose value depends on another variable.

**Differentiated products** Differentiated products refer to goods that are similar but are not perfect substitutes.

**Diminishing marginal benefit** As you consume more of a good, your willingness to pay for an additional unit declines.

**Direct regulation** Direct regulation, or command-and-control regulation, refers to direct actions by the government to control the amount of a certain activity.

**Discount weight** A discount weight multiplies delayed utils to translate them into current utils.

**Diseconomies of scale** Diseconomies of scale occur when average total cost rises as the quantity produced increases.

**Dominant strategy** A dominant strategy is one best response to every possible strategy of the other player(s).

**Dominant strategy equilibrium** A combination of strategies is a dominant strategy equilibrium if each strategy is a dominant strategy.

**Double oral auction** A double oral auction is a market where sellers orally state asks and buyers orally state offers.

**Duopoly** Duopoly refers to a two-firm industry.

**Dutch auction** A Dutch auction is an open-outcry auction in which the price decreases until a bidder stops the auction. The bidder who stops the auction wins the item and pays his bid.

**Economic agent** An economic agent is an individual or a group that makes choices.

**Economic profits** Economic profits are equal to total revenue minus both explicit and implicit costs.

**Economics** Economics is the study of how agents choose to allocate scarce resources and how those choices affect society.

**Economies of scale** Economies of scale occur when average total cost falls as the quantity produced increases.

**Efficiency wages** Efficiency wages are wages above the lowest pay that workers would accept; employers use them to increase motivation and productivity.

**Efficient price** An efficient price, or socially optimal price, is a price set at marginal cost.

**Elastic demand** Goods that have elastic demand have a price elasticity of demand greater than 1.

**Elasticity** Elasticity is the measure of sensitivity of one variable to a change in another.

**Empirical evidence** Empirical evidence is a set of facts established by observation and measurement.

**Empiricism** Empiricism is analysis that uses data. Economists use data to test theories and to determine what is causing things to happen in the world.

**English auction** An English auction is an open-outcry auction in which the price increases until there is only one standing bid. That bidder wins the item and pays his bid.

**Equilibrium** Equilibrium is the situation in which everyone is simultaneously optimizing, so nobody would benefit personally by changing his or her own behavior.

**Equity** Equity is concerned with the distribution of resources across society.

**Equity-efficiency trade-off** The equity-efficiency trade-off refers to the trade-off between ensuring an equitable allocation of resources (equity) and increasing social surplus or total output (efficiency).

**Excess demand** When the market price is below the competitive equilibrium price, quantity demanded exceeds quantity supplied, creating excess demand.

**Excess supply** When the market price is above the competitive equilibrium price, quantity supplied exceeds quantity demanded, creating excess supply.

**Excise taxes** Excise taxes are taxes paid when purchasing a specific good.

**Exit** Exit is a long-run decision to leave the market.

**Expected value** Expected value is the sum of all possible outcomes or values, each weighted by its probability of occurring.

**Experiment** An experiment is a controlled method of investigating causal relationships among variables.

**Export** An export is any good that is produced domestically but sold abroad.

**Extensive-form game** An extensive-form game is a representation of games that specifies the order of play.

**Externality** An externality occurs when an economic activity has either a spillover cost or a spillover benefit on a bystander.

**Fairness** Fairness is the willingness of individuals to sacrifice their own well-being to either improve upon the well-being of others or to punish those who they perceive as behaving unkindly.

**Fair-returns price** A fair-returns price is a price set at average total cost.

**Firm** A firm is any business entity that produces and sells goods or services.

**First-degree price discrimination** Perfect price discrimination, also known as first-degree price discrimination, occurs when a firm charges each buyer exactly his or her willingness to pay.

**First-mover advantage** A game has a first-mover advantage when the first player to act in a sequential game gets a benefit from doing so.

**First-price auction** A first-price auction is an auction in which bidders privately submit bids at the same time. The highest bidder wins the item and pays an amount equal to her bid.

**Fixed cost** A fixed cost is the cost of fixed factors of production, which a firm must pay even if it produces zero output.

**Fixed factor of production** A fixed factor of production is an input that cannot be changed in the short run.

**Free trade** Free trade is the ability to trade without hindrance or encouragement from the government.

**Free-rider problem** A free-rider problem occurs when an individual who has no incentive to pay for a good does not pay for that good because nonpayment does not prevent consumption.

**Future value** The sum of principal and interest is referred to as future value.

**Future value equation** The compound interest equation or future value equation calculates the future value of an investment with interest rate $r$ that leaves all interest payments in the account until the final withdrawal in year $T$.

**Game theory** Game theory is the study of strategic interactions.

**Game tree** A game tree is an extensive-form representation of a game.

**Globalization** Globalization is the shift toward more open, integrated economies that participate in foreign trade and investment.

**Government failures** Government failures refer to inefficiencies caused by a government's interventions.

**Grim strategy** A grim strategy is a plan by one player to price a good at marginal cost forever if the other cheats on his agreement.

**Gross domestic product (GDP)** Gross domestic product (GDP) is the market value of final goods and services produced in a country in a given period of time.

**Herding** Herding is a behavior of individuals who conform to the decisions of others.

**Herfindahl-Hirschman Index** The Herfindahl-Hirschman Index is a measure of market concentration to estimate the degree of competition within an industry.

**Hidden actions** Hidden actions occur when one side takes actions that are relevant for, but not observed by, the other party.

**Hidden characteristics** Hidden characteristics occur when one side observes something about the good being transacted that is both relevant for and not observed by the other party.

**Holding all else equal** "Holding all else equal" implies that everything else in the economy is held constant. The Latin phrase *ceteris paribus* means "with other things the same" and is sometimes used in economic writing to mean the same thing as "holding all else equal."

**Homogeneous products** Homogeneous products refer to goods that are identical, and so are perfect substitutes.

**Human capital** Human capital is each person's stock of skills for producing output or economic value.

**Hypotheses** Hypotheses are predictions (typically generated by a model) that can be tested with data.

**Import** An import is any good that is produced abroad but sold domestically.

**Impure altruism** Impure altruism is a motivation solely to help oneself feel good.

**Incentive problem** When the optimizing actions of two economic agents are not aligned, these agents face an incentive problem.

**Income effect** An income effect is a consumption change that results when a price change moves the consumer to a lower or higher indifference curve.

**Income elasticity of demand** The income elasticity of demand measures the percentage change in quantity demanded due to a percentage change in income.

**Independent** When two random outcomes are independent, knowing about one outcome does not help you predict the other outcome.

**Independent variable** An independent variable is a variable whose value does not depend on that of another variable; in an experiment it is manipulated by the experimenter.

**Indifference curve** An indifference curve is the set of bundles that provide an equal level of satisfaction for the consumer.

**Indoctrination** Indoctrination is the process by which agents imbue society with their ideology or opinion.

**Inelastic demand** Goods that have inelastic demand have a price elasticity of demand less than 1.

**Inferior good** For an inferior good, an increase in income causes the demand curve to shift to the left (holding the good's price fixed), or in other words, causes consumers to buy less of the good.

**Information cascade** An information cascade occurs when people make the same decisions as others, ignoring their own private information.

**Input** An input is a good or service used to produce another good or service.

**Interest** Interest is the payment received for temporarily giving up the use of money.

**Internalizing the externality** When an agent accounts for the full costs and benefits of his actions, he is internalizing the externality.

**Key resources** Key resources are materials that are essential for the production of a good or service.

**Labor-complementary technology** Labor-complementary technology is a type of technology that complements existing labor inputs, increasing the marginal product of labor.

**Labor-saving technology** Labor-saving technology is a type of technology that substitutes for existing labor inputs, reducing the marginal product of labor.

**Land** Land includes the solid surface of the earth and natural resources.

**Law of demand** In almost all cases, the quantity demanded rises when the price falls (holding all else equal).

**Law of Diminishing Returns** The Law of Diminishing Returns states that successive increases in inputs eventually lead to less additional output.

**Law of Supply** In almost all cases, the quantity supplied rises when the price rises (holding all else equal).

**Legal market power** Legal market power occurs when a firm obtains market power through barriers to entry created not by the firm itself, but by the government.

**Long run** The long run is a period of time when all of a firm's inputs can be varied.

**Loss aversion** Loss aversion is the idea that people psychologically weight a loss more heavily than they psychologically weight a gain.

**Macroeconomics** Macroeconomics is the study of the economy as a whole. Macroeconomists study economy-wide phenomena, like the growth rate of a country's total economic output, the inflation rate, or the unemployment rate.

**Marginal analysis** Marginal analysis is a cost-benefit calculation that studies the difference between a feasible alternative and the next feasible alternative.

**Marginal cost** Marginal cost is the change in total cost associated with producing one more unit of output or moving from one feasible alternative to the next feasible alternative.

**Marginal product** Marginal product is the change in total output associated with using one more unit of input.

**Marginal revenue** Marginal revenue is the change in total revenue associated with producing one more unit of output.

**Marginal tax rate** The marginal tax rate refers to how much of the last dollar earned is paid out in tax.

**Market** A market is a group of economic agents who are trading a good or service, and the rules and arrangements for trading.

**Market demand curve** The market demand curve is the sum of the individual demand curves of all the potential buyers. It plots the relationship between the total quantity demanded and the market price, holding all else equal.

**Market power** Market power relates to the ability of sellers to affect prices.

**Market price** If all sellers and all buyers face the same price, it is referred to as the market price.

**Market supply curve** The market supply curve is the sum of the individual supply curves of all the potential sellers. It plots the relationship between the total quantity supplied and the market price, holding all else equal.

**Market-based regulatory approach** A market-based regulatory approach internalizes externalities by harnessing the power of market forces.

**Mean** The mean, or average, is the sum of all the different values divided by the number of values.

**Median** The median value is calculated by ordering the numbers from least to greatest and then finding the value halfway through the list.

**Microeconomics** Microeconomics is the study of how individuals, households, firms, and governments make choices, and how those choices affect prices, the allocation of resources, and the well-being of other agents.

**Mixed strategy** A mixed strategy involves choosing different actions randomly.

**Model** A model is a simplified description, or representation, of the world. Sometimes, economists will refer to a model as a *theory*. These terms are often used interchangeably.

**Monopolistic competition** Monopolistic competition is the market structure that applies when there are many competing firms and products are differentiated.

**Monopoly** Monopoly is an industry structure in which only one seller provides a good or service that has no close substitutes.

**Moral hazard** Moral hazard is another term for actions that are taken by one party but are relevant for and not observed by the other party in the transaction.

**Movement along the demand curve** If a good's own price changes and its demand curve hasn't shifted, the own price change produces a movement along the demand curve.

**Movement along the supply curve** If a good's own price changes and its supply curve hasn't shifted, the own price change produces a movement along the supply curve.

**Nash equilibrium** A strategy combination is a Nash equilibrium if each strategy is a best response to the strategies of others.

**Natural experiment** A natural experiment is an empirical study in which some process—out of the control of the experimenter—has assigned subjects to control and treatment groups in a random or nearly random way.

**Natural market power** Natural market power occurs when a firm obtains market power through barriers to entry created by the firm itself.

**Natural monopoly** A natural monopoly is a market in which one firm can provide a good or service at a lower cost than two or more firms.

**Negative correlation** Negative correlation implies that two variables tend to move in opposite directions.

**Negatively related** Two variables are negatively related if the variables move in opposite directions.

**Net benefit** The net benefit is the sum of the benefits of choosing an alternative minus the sum of the costs of choosing that alternative.

**Net importer** A net importer refers to a country in which imports are worth more than exports over a given time period.

**Net present value** The net present value of a project is the present value of the benefits minus the present value of the costs.

**Network externalities** Network externalities occur when a product's value increases as more consumers begin to use it.

**Non-excludable good** Once a non-excludable good is produced, it is not possible to exclude people from using the good.

**Non-rival good** A non-rival good is a good whose consumption by one person does not prevent consumption by others.

**Normal good** For a normal good, an increase in income causes the demand curve to shift to the right (holding the good's price fixed), or in other words, causes consumers to buy more of the good.

**Normative economics** Normative economics is an analysis that recommends what an individual or society ought to do.

**North American Free Trade Agreement** The North American Free Trade Agreement (NAFTA) is an agreement signed by Canada, Mexico, and the United States to create a trilateral trade bloc and reduce trade barriers among the three countries.

**Oligopoly** Oligopoly is the market structure that applies when there are few firms competing.

**Omitted variable** An omitted variable is something that has been left out of a study that, if included, would explain why two variables that are in the study are correlated.

**Open outcry auction** An open outcry auction is an auction in which bids are public.

**Opportunity cost** Opportunity cost is the best alternative use of a resource.

**Optimization** Optimization means choosing the best feasible option, given whatever (limited) information the economic agent has.

**Optimum** The optimum is the best feasible choice. In other words, the optimum is the optimal choice.

**Pareto efficient** An outcome is Pareto efficient if no individual can be made better off without making one else worse off.

**Patent** A patent is the privilege granted to an individual or company by the government, which gives him or her the sole right to produce and sell a good.

**Paternalism** Paternalism is the view that consumers do not always know what is best for them, and the government should encourage or induce them to change their actions.

**Payoff matrix** A payoff matrix represents the payoffs for each action players can take.

**Payroll tax** A payroll tax (also known as social insurance tax) is a tax on the wages of workers.

**Pecuniary externality** A pecuniary externality occurs when a market transaction affects other people only through market prices.

**Peer effects** Peer effects are the influence of the decisions of others on our own choices.

**Perfect price discrimination** Perfect price discrimination, also known as first-degree price discrimination, occurs when a firm charges each buyer exactly his or her willingness to pay.

**Perfectly competitive market** In a perfectly competitive market, (1) sellers all sell an identical good or service, and (2) any individual buyer or any individual seller isn't powerful enough on his or her own to affect the market price of that good or service.

**Perfectly elastic demand** A very small increase in price causes consumers to stop using goods that have perfectly elastic demand.

**Perfectly inelastic demand** Quantity demanded is unaffected by prices of goods with perfectly inelastic demand.

**Physical capital** Physical capital is any good, including machines and buildings, used for production.

**Pie chart** A pie chart is a circular chart split into segments, with each showing the percentages of parts relative to the whole.

**Pigouvian subsidies** Corrective subsidies, or Pigouvian subsidies, are designed to induce agents who produce positive externalities to increase quantity toward the socially optimal level.

**Pigouvian tax** A Pigouvian tax, or a corrective tax, is a tax designed to induce agents who produce negative externalities to reduce quantity toward the socially optimal level.

**Positive correlation** A positive correlation implies that two variables tend to move in the same direction.

**Positive economics** Positive economics is analysis that generates objective descriptions or predictions, which can be verified with data.

**Positively related** Two variables are positively related if the variables move in the same direction.

**Present value** The present value of a future payment is the amount of money that would need to be invested today to produce that future payment. In other words, the present value is the discounted value of the future payment.

**Price ceiling** A price ceiling is a cap or maximum price of a market good.

**Price control** A price control is a government restriction on the price of a good or service.

**Price discrimination** Price discrimination occurs when firms charge different consumers different prices for the same good or service.

**Price elasticity of demand** The price elasticity of demand measures the percentage change in quantity demanded of a good due to a percentage change in its price.

**Price elasticity of supply** Price elasticity of supply is the measure of how responsive quantity supplied is to price changes.

**Price floor** A price floor is a lower limit on the price of a market good.

**Price-maker** A price-maker is a seller that sets the price of a good.

**Price-taker** A price-taker is a buyer or seller who accepts the market price—buyers can't bargain for a lower price and sellers can't bargain for a higher price.

**Principal** Principal is the amount of an original investment.

**Principal-agent relationship** In a principal-agent relationship, the principal designs a contract specifying the payments to the agent as a function of his or her performance, and the agent takes an action that influences performance and thus the payoff of the principal.

**Principle of optimization at the margin** The principle of optimization at the margin states that an optimal feasible alternative has the property that moving to it makes you better off and moving away from it makes you worse off.

**Private provision of public goods** Private provision of public goods takes place when private citizens make contributions to the production or maintenance of a public good.

**Probability** A probability is the frequency with which something occurs.

**Producer surplus** Producer surplus is the difference between the market price and the marginal cost curve.

**Production** Production is the process by which the transformation of inputs to outputs occurs.

**Production possibilities curve** A production possibilities curve shows the relationship between the maximum production of one good for a given level of production of another good.

**Profits** The profits of a firm are equal to its revenues minus its costs.

**Progressive tax system** A progressive tax system involves higher tax rates on those earning higher incomes.

**Property right** A property right gives someone ownership of a property or resources.

**Proportional tax system** In a proportional tax system, households pay the same percentage of their incomes in taxes regardless of their income level.

**Protectionism** Protectionism is the idea that free trade can be harmful, and government intervention is necessary to control trade.

**Public good** A public good is both non-rival and non-excludable.

**Pure altruism** Pure altruism is a motivation solely to help others.

**Pure strategy** A pure strategy involves always choosing one particular action for a situation.

**Quantity demanded** Quantity demanded is the amount of a good that buyers are willing to purchase at a given price.

**Quantity supplied** Quantity supplied is the amount of a good or service that sellers are willing to sell at a given price.

**Random** If something is risky, then it is said to have a component that is random.

**Randomization** Randomization is the assignment of subjects by chance, rather than by choice, to a treatment group or control group.

**Receipts** Tax revenues, or receipts, are the money a government collects through a tax.

**Regressive tax system** A regressive tax system involves lower tax rates on those earning higher incomes.

**Regulation** Regulation refers to actions by the federal or local government directed at influencing market outcomes, such as the quantity traded of a good or service, its price, or its quality and safety.

**Rental price** The rental price of a good is the cost of using the good for some specific period of time.

**Research and development (R&D)** Research and development (R&D) refers to the activities directed at improving scientific knowledge, generating new innovations, or implementing existing knowledge in production in order to improve the technology of a firm or an economy.

**Reservation value** Reservation value is the price at which a trading partner is indifferent between making the trade and not doing so.

**Residual demand curve** The residual demand curve is the demand that is not met by other firms and depends on the prices of all firms in the industry.

**Revenue** Revenue is the amount of money the firm brings in from the sale of its outputs.

**Revenue equivalence theorem** The revenue equivalence theorem states that under certain assumptions, the four auction types are expected to raise the same revenues.

**Reverse causality** Reverse causality occurs when we mix up the direction of cause and effect.

**Risk** Risk exists when an outcome is not known with certainty in advance.

**Risk averse** Consider a person choosing between two investments with the same expected rate of return but one investment has a fixed return and the other investment has a risky return. When people are risk averse, they prefer the investment with the fixed return.

**Risk neutral** Consider a person choosing between two investments with the same expected rate of return but one investment has a fixed return and the other investment has a risky return. When people are risk neutral, they don't care about the level of risk and are therefore indifferent between the two investments.

**Risk seeking** Consider a person choosing between two investments with the same expected rate of return but one investment has a fixed return and the other investment has a risky return. When people are risk seeking, they prefer the investment with the risky return.

**Sales taxes** Sales taxes are paid by a buyer, as a percentage of the sale price of an item.

**Scarce resources** Scarce resources are things that people want, where the quantity that people want exceeds the quantity that is available.

**Scarcity** Scarcity is the situation of having unlimited wants in a world of limited resources.

**Scientific method** The scientific method is the name for the ongoing process that economists and other scientists use to (1) develop models of the world and (2) test those models with data.

**Sealed bid auction** A sealed bid auction is an auction in which bids are private so that no bidder knows the bid of any other participant.

**Second-degree price discrimination** Second-degree price discrimination occurs when consumers are charged different prices based on characteristics of their purchase.

**Second-price auction** A second-price auction is an auction in which bidders privately submit bids at the same time. The highest bidder wins the item and pays an amount equal to the second-highest bid.

**Short run** The short run is a period of time when only some of a firm's inputs can be varied.

**Shutdown** Shutdown is a short-run decision to not produce anything during a specific period.

**Signaling** Signaling refers to an action that an individual with private information takes in order to convince others about his information.

**Simultaneous move games** In simultaneous move games, players pick their actions at the same time.

**Skill-biased technological changes** Skill-biased technological changes increase the productivity of skilled workers relative to that of unskilled workers.

**Slope** The slope is the change in the value of the variable plotted on the vertical axis divided by the change in the value of the variable plotted on the horizontal axis.

**Social surplus** Social surplus is the sum of consumer surplus and producer surplus.

**Specialization** Specialization is the result of workers developing a certain skill set in order to increase total productivity.

**Statistical discrimination** Statistical discrimination occurs when expectations cause people to discriminate against a certain group.

**Strategies** Strategies comprise a complete plan describing how a player will act.

**Substitutes** Two goods are substitutes when a fall in the price of one leads to a left shift in the demand curve for the other.

**Substitution effect** A substitution effect is a consumption change that results when a price change moves the *consumer along a given indifference curve.*

**Sunk costs** Sunk costs are costs that, once committed, can never be recovered and should not affect current and future production decisions.

**Supply curve** The supply curve plots the quantity supplied at different prices. A supply curve plots the supply schedule.

**Supply curve shifts** The supply curve shifts when the quantity supplied changes at a given price.

**Supply schedule** A supply schedule is a table that reports the quantity supplied at different prices, holding all else equal.

**Tariffs** Tariffs are taxes levied on goods and services transported across political boundaries.

**Taste-based discrimination** Taste-based discrimination occurs when people's preferences cause them to discriminate against a certain group.

**Tax incidence** Tax incidence refers to how the burden of taxation is distributed.

**Tax revenues** Tax revenues, or receipts, are the money a government collects through a tax.

**Terms of trade** The terms of trade is the negotiated exchange rate of goods for goods.

**Third-degree price discrimination** Third-degree price discrimination occurs when price varies based on a customer's attributes.

**Time series graph** A time series graph displays data at different points in time.

**Total cost** Total cost is the sum of variable and fixed costs.

**Trade-off** An economic agent faces a trade-off when the agent needs to give up one thing to get something else.

**Tragedy of the commons** The tragedy of the commons results when common pool resources are dramatically overused.

**Transaction costs** Transaction costs are the costs of making an economic exchange.

**Transfer payments** Transfer payments occur when the government gives part of its tax revenue to some individual or group.

**Unit elastic demand** Goods that have unit elastic demand have a price elasticity of demand equal to 1.

**Util** A util is an individual unit of utility.

**Utility** In economics, utility is a measure of satisfaction or happiness that comes from consuming a good or service.

**Value of marginal product of labor** The value of marginal product of labor is the contribution of an additional worker to a firm's revenues.

**Value of marginal product of physical capital** The value of marginal product of physical capital is the contribution of an additional unit of physical capital to a firm's revenues.

**Variable** A variable is a factor that is likely to change or vary.

**Variable cost** A variable cost is the cost of variable factors of production, which change along with a firm's output.

**Variable factor of production** A variable factor of production is an input that can be changed in the short run.

**Welfare state** The welfare state refers to the set of insurance, regulation, and transfer programs operated by the government, including unemployment benefits, pensions, and government-run and financed healthcare.

**Willingness to accept** Willingness to accept is the lowest price that a seller is willing to get paid to sell an extra unit of a good. Willingness to accept is the same as the marginal cost of production.

**Willingness to pay** Willingness to pay is the highest price that a buyer is willing to pay for an extra unit of a good.

**World price** A world price is the prevailing price of a good on the world market.

**Zero correlation** Zero correlation implies that two variables have movements that are not related.

**Zero-sum game** In a zero-sum game, one player's loss is another's gain, so the sum of the payoffs is zero.

# Credits

Chapter 1: p. 2: blue Porsche, F1online digitale Bildagentur GmbH/Alamy Stock Photo; p. 5: roller skater, Chase Jarvis/Getty Images; p. 6: whooping crane, Critterbiz/Shutterstock; p. 12 top: cappuccino, By-studio/Fotolia; p. 12 middle left: iPhone, D. Hurst/Alamy Stock Photo; p. 12 middle right: Eiffel Tower, Samott/Fotolia; p. 12 bottom: beach, Wirepec/Fotolia; p. 15: man jumping turnstile, Mauro Speziale/Getty Images.

Chapter 2: p. 20: graduation cap and money, Zimmytws/Shutterstock; p. 22: New York subway map, Martin Shields/Alamy Stock Photo; p. 27: runners, Photos by Sharon/Alamy Stock Photo; p. 28: Christmas package, DK Images/Alamy Stock Photo; p. 28: Macy's ad, Amy Sinns/Alamy Stock Photo; p. 28: red bar chart, Robert Kneschke/Shutterstock; p. 29: bride and groom, nataliakabliuk/Fotolia.

Chapter 3: p. 42: globe concept for commute, Pablo Scapinachis/Shutterstock; p. 45: park bench, Vladimirs Koskins/Shutterstock; p. 53: map of Portland, Oregon, Pearson Education; p. 54: Mount Hood, Portland, Oregon, Vincentlouis/Fotolia; p. 55: Boston-area subway map, based on Ryan Nickum, Estately, Inc.

Chapter 4: p. 58: gas price sign, Eric Glenn/Alamy Stock Photo; p. 60: flowers, DutchScenery/Fotolia; p. 60: two gas signs, Lynne Sladky/AP Images; p. 62: Hummer and smart car, Gudellaphoto/Fotolia; p. 63: stadium crowd, Monjiro/Fotolia; p. 66: Spam, Helen Sessions/Alamy Stock Photo; p. 69: oil rig, Paul Andrew Lawrence/Alamy Stock Photo; p. 73: oil refinery burning, John Moore/Getty Images; p. 79: Hess gas station, ClassicStock/Alamy Stock Photo; p. 79: sorry no gas sign, Everett Collection/Newsco.

Chapter 5: p. 86: cigarette butt, Milos Luzanin/Shutterstock; p. 97: re-use, cigarette butt, Milos Luzanin/Shutterstock; p. 99: man smoking, ArtFamily/Fotolia, p. 99: money, Figura13/Fotolia; p. 104: b&w cartoon, www.CartoonStock.com.

Chapter 6: p. 114: corn on the cob with gas nozzle, James Steidl/Shutterstock; p. 127: red phone, Karen Roach/Fotolia; p. 130: woman in antique car, Sueddeutsche Zeitung Photo/Alamy Stock Photo; p. 132: Serious Competition cartoon, Pearson Education, Inc.

Chapter 7: p. 144: hand holding world, Andrey Armyagov/Fotolia; p. 146: iPhone, Richard Sharrocks/Alamy Stock Photo; p. 151: Adam Smith cartoon, Pearson Education, Inc.; p. 156: hurricane off Florida coast, NASA; p. 157: Uber app, Evelyn Hockstein/Polaris/Newscom; p. 161: Walmart trucks, Nicholas Kamm/Getty Images; p. 163: satellite of North and South Korea, Universal Images Group North America LLC/Alamy Stock Photo; p. 165: cartoon, cartoonresource/Fotolia.

Chapter 8: p. 172: WTO, Dang Ngo/ZUMAPress/Newscom; p. 174: Bill Gates, ES Imagery/Alamy Stock Photo; p. 181: Lebron James, Cal Sport Media/Alamy Stock Photo; p. 186: world cartoon, Pearson Education, Inc.; p. 187: Fair Trade label, Joerg Boethling/Alamy Stock Photo; p. 188: man repairing shoes, Francis Dean/Dean Pictures/Newscom; p. 190: cartoon, Pearson Education, Inc.; p. 191: hard drive, Huguette Roe/Shutterstock; p. 193: badges, Fredex/Shutterstock; p. 194: WTO sign, Dang Ngo/ZUMAPress/Newscom.

Chapter 9: p. 200: congestion charging sign, Stephen Finn/Shutterstock; p. 202: Fiddlers Ferry Power Station, Alan Novelli/Alamy Stock Photo; p. 206: nurse giving injection, Dmitry Lobanov/Shutterstock; p.209: Energy Star logo, EnergyStar.gov; p. 211: house broken in two, Panther Media GmbH/Alamy Stock Photo; p. 215: cartoon, Pearson Education, Inc.; p. 216: three garbage bags, Antonio Gravante/Fotolia; p. 222: tidal pool, Blueeyes/Shutterstock; p. 222: panda, Silver-John/Fotolia; p. 224: fish, Dewitt/Shutterstock; p. 225: congestion charging sign, Stephen Finn/Shutterstock.

Chapter 10: p. 230: George Washington, MJ007/Shutterstock; p. 243: Margaret Thatcher and Ronald Regan, Tribune Content Agency LLC/Alamy Stock Photo; p. 250: cartoon, Pearson Education, Inc.

Chapter 11: p. 260: glass ceiling, Bobkeenan Photography/Shutterstock; p. 261: female construction worker, DJTaylor/Shutterstock; p. 270: football players, Elsa/Getty Images; p. 270: boys with basketball coach, kali9/Getty Images; p. 273: teacher helping boy, ESB Professional/Shutterstock; p. 273: woman and truck, Blend Images/Shutterstock; p. 278: glass ceiling, Bobkeenan Photography/Shutterstock.

Chapter 12: p. 284: pill bottle, Eric Strand/Shutterstock; p. 286: cartoon, Pearson Education; p. 295: woman sneezing, Zea Lenanet/Fotolia; p. 303: Bill Gates, Richard Ellis/Alamy Stock Photo; p. 305: lightbulb, Sergey Furtaev/Shutterstock.

Chapter 13: p. 310: empty chair, Phase4Studios/Shutterstock; p. 315: circuit board brain, VLADGRIN/Shutterstock; p. 318: Gowanus Canal, James Burger/Alamy Stock Photo; p. 319: soccer ball and players, Gallo Images/Alamy Stock Photo; p. 327: Bernie Madoff, Everett Collection Inc/Alamy Stock Photo; p. 327: comic book guy, Everett Collection Inc/Alamy Stock Photo.

Chapter 14: p. 329: cartoon scales of justice, Imagezoo/Superstock; p. 340: Pepsi and Coke machines, Alpha and Omega Collection/Alamy Stock Photo; p. 341: dollar sign clouds and plane, Eteimaging/Shutterstock; p. 344: OPEC, JEGAS RA/Fotolia.

Chapter 15: p. 360: chocolate bar, Givaga/Shutterstock; p. 361: bride and groom, stock_colors/E+/Getty Images; p. 364: piggy bank, Archideaphoto/Shutterstock; p. 370: dessert cart, SuperStock/Alamy Stock Photo; p. 371: roulette wheel, Vojtech Vlk/Fotolia; p. 373: people gambling, Benoit Daoust/123RF.

Chapter 16: p. 378: cartoon lemon car, Cory Thoman/ Shutterstock; p. 382, left: credit ranking, Tomasz Bidermann/Shutterstock; p. 382, middle: warranty, Newart-Graphics/Shutterstock; p. 382, right: pencil and test, Anaken2012/Shutterstock; p. 383, top: mortar and degree, Pixelrobot/Fotolia; p. 385: peacock, Qayyum125/Fotolia; p. 386: bicycle and car, Dan Race/Fotolia; p. 387: The Detroit Journal image, The Detroit Journal; p. 388: protester, ZUMA Press, Inc./Alamy Stock Photo; p. 389: pen to paper, Tomek Pa/Shutterstock; p. 390: Obama and child, Pete Marovich/ZUMA Press/Newscom; p. 392: man sleeping on laptop, Milles Studio/Shutterstock.

Chapter 17: p. 397: cartoon, Pearson Education, Inc.; p. 399: Raiders fans, ZUMA Press, Inc.; p. 400, top: fine art auction, Fuse/Corbis/Getty Images; p. 400, bottom: cartoon, Pearson Education, Inc.; p. 401: red flame tulip, Derek Harris; p. 406: Magic cards, Phil Velasquez/KRT; p. 410: divorce decree and gavel, zimmytws/Shutterstock; p. 411: couple arm wrestling, Monika Wisniewska/Shutterstock.

Chapter 18: p. 416: scales of justice with money and heart, Sebastian Kaulitzki/Shutterstock; p. 418: Salvation Army, Ann E Parry/Alamy Stock Photo; p. 420: elderly woman, Edbockstock/Fotolia; p. 423: two men, Lipik/Shutterstock; p. 427: woman standing on chair, Blend Images/Alamy Stock Photo; p. 431: cartoon, Pearson Education, Inc.; p. 432: cartoon, Pearson Education, Inc.

# Index

Note: Key terms and the page on which they are defined appear in **boldface.**

electricity market, externalities and,
    201–203
Emons, Winand, 384
**empirical evidence, 22**
**empiricism, 7**
    overview, 15
    scientific method, 21–26
employee theft, 386
energy-efficient products, 209–210
energy markets
    demand curve shifts, 65–67
    electricity market, externalities and,
        201–203
    Evidence-Based Economics, 67–68
    government intervention and, 78–79
    imports and exports, 185
    market demand curve, 64–65
    market equilibrium, 73–78
    OPEC cartel and collusion, 344–345
    overview, 59–61
    quantity demanded, 61
    seller, behavior of, 69–73
ENERGY STAR program, 209–210
**English auction, 399, 400–401, 406**
    optimizing in, 400
entry
    competitive markets, 354–356
    cost structures, firm differences, 142–143
    free entry, **132**
    invisible hand, industries, 152–154
    monopolistic competition, 349–351
environmental concerns
    ENERGY STAR program, 209–210
    externalities, overview, 201–202
    fair trade products, 187
    free trade, opposition to, 190, 191
    private provision of public goods, 221
    U.S. Environmental Protection Agency
        (EPA), 209, 215, 318
equal bang for your buck rule, 91
equation, cost of doing business, 118–120
**equilibrium, 7**
    bilateral negotiation, 167–168
    corrective taxes and subsidies, 213–215
    cost structures, effects of, 142–143
    dominant strategy equilibrium, 313
    double oral auction, 166–167
    extensive-form games, 323–326
    externalities, overview, 201–207
    firm market exit, 133–134
    government intervention and, 78–79
    invisible hand, industries, 152–154
    in labor markets, 266–269
    monopolies, patent expiration effects,
        297–298

monopolistic competition, 349–351
Nash equilibrium, finding, 315–317
oligopolies, 338–339, 340
overview of, 13–14
Pareto efficiency, 147–148
physical capital, 275–277
price discrimination, degrees of, 299–302
price fixing and, 80
producer surplus, 127–128
profits, 123–124
public goods and, 220
revenue curves, 120–121
social surplus, 146–147
subsidies, effects of, 137–138
tariffs, effects of, 191–193
taxation, deadweight loss and, 240–245
tragedy of the commons, 223–224, 318
Ultimatum Game, 408–410
world price and, 186–190
zero-sum games, 319–320
**equity,** 164–**165**
**equity-efficiency trade-off, 250–252**
ethanol subsidies, 114, 135–138
ethics, public policy decisions, 5–6
evidence-based analysis. *See* empiricism
Evidence-Based Economics
    cars, value of, 383–384
    eBay, bidding, 406–407
    education and earnings, 24, 30–31
    ethanol subsidy affect on producers,
        135–138
    externalities, congestion charges,
        225–226
    externalities and earthquakes, 211–213
    Facebook, cost of, 11–13
    fairness, 424–426
    firm number for competitive markets,
        354–356
    free trade and jobs, 194–195
    game theory, 321–323, 326–329
    gasoline prices, 67–68
    government, optimal size of, 253–254
    health insurance, costs of, 389
    household spending, 411–412
    housing costs and location, 52–55
    immediate gratification, 369–370
    invisible hand, 165–168
    labor market, discrimination in, 278–280
    monopoly, benefits of, 304–306
    smoking, incentives to stop, 97–99
    Uber and the invisible hand, 157–160
Excel, 351
**excess demand, 75**
**excess supply, 74**
**excise taxes, 233**

exit, **130**–131
    cost structures, firm differences, 142–143
    invisible hand, industries, 152–154
    monopolistic competition, 349–351
expected revenues, auction bidders, 403
**expected value, 372**–373
**experiment, 29**–30
    results from ethanol subsidy study, 138
experimental design, 35–36
explicit costs, profit and, 123
**exports, 181**
    tariffs, effects of, 191–193
    trade between countries, 184–190
    trade between states, 180–184
extended warranties, 373–374
**extensive-form games, 323**–326
**externalities, 202**
    bargaining, 208
    Choice & Consequence, 218, 224
    common pool resource goods, 222–224
    congestion charges, 225–226
    Evidence-Based Economics, 211–213
    government solutions, 210–215,
        245–246
    imposing taxes to correct, 238
    internalizing the, 207–208
    network externalities, 288
    overview of, 200–207
    pecuniary externalities, 206–**207**
    positive, flu vaccinations as, 206
    private solutions, 207–210
    property right, 208–209
    public goods, 216–222
    value calculations, 215
ExxonMobil, 69–72

**F**

Facebook, 2, 11–13, 288, 289
**fairness,** economics of, 416–426, **422**
**fair-returns price, 303**
fair trade products, 187
feasibility
    concept of, 7–8
    optimization and, 43
Federal Communications Commission
    (FCC), 307, 341
Federal Emergency Management Agency
    (FEMA), 161
Federal Insurance Contribution Act (FICA)
    taxes, 233
Federal Reserve, 395
Ferguson, Chris, 310
FICA. *See* Federal Insurance Contribution
    Act taxes
Finland, 239